F/C

748

**Norfolk Record Society**
**Volume LXXVI for 2012**

The Right honourable Robert Earl & Vicount Yarmouth Baron of Paston Lord Lieutenant Vice Admirall of the County of Norfolke

DE MIEVX IE PENSE EN MIEVLX

B. Reading Sculp.

Robert Paston, first earl of Yarmouth, *c.*1676
(© National Portrait Gallery, London)

# THE WHIRLPOOL OF MISADVENTURES

## Letters of Robert Paston, First Earl of Yarmouth 1663–1679

Edited by

JEAN AGNEW

Norfolk Record Society

Volume LXXVI for 2012

© The Norfolk Record Society, 2012

First Published in 2012
by The Norfolk Record Society

ISBN 978-0-9556357-5-5

Produced by John Saunders Design & Production, Eastbourne
Printed and bound in Great Britain by
T J International Ltd, Padstow, Cornwall

# Contents

Illustrations                                          ix

Acknowledgements                                       xi

Introduction                                            1

Editorial notes
   1. The letters                       29
   2. The transcriptions                31
   3. The ciphers                       32
   4. The index                         32
   5. Editorial conventions             33

Abbreviations                                          34

Bibliography                                           35

LETTERS OF ROBERT PASTON,
FIRST EARL OF YARMOUTH                                 39

Appendix 1: Decoding the ciphers                      387

Appendix 2: Notes on the first earl of Yarmouth
   and his family                      390

Index                                                 393

# Illustrations

Robert Paston, first earl of Yarmouth, *c.*1676          *Frontispiece*
  (© National Portrait Gallery, London, NPG D21454)

Key to the Paston cipher used in 1677–1678          386
  (© The British Library Board, Add. MSS 27447, f.304)

# Acknowledgements

This volume is the result of a conversation in 2009 with Dr John Alban, the Norfolk county archivist: seldom can a chance remark have become a firm proposal at such lightning speed. The majority of the letters transcribed here are held by the Norfolk Record Office as part of the Bradfer-Lawrence collection and are the only major collection of Paston Letters outside the British Library. I am indebted to Dr Alban and the staff of the Norfolk Record Office for their help, support and friendship.

Thanks are due to the British Library for making their letters of Robert Paston, earl of Yarmouth, available to me, for supplying me with disks, and for permitting me to use their key to the Paston cipher for 1677–1678 as an illustration in this book. I am also grateful to the National Portrait Gallery for permission to reproduce their print of Lord Yarmouth as the frontispiece. Publication has been assisted by a grant from the Scouloudi Foundation in association with the Institute of Historical Research.

Finally, although I have received help and advice from many people, I owe special thanks to Professor Carole Rawcliffe, Mrs Elizabeth Rutledge and Mr Paul Rutledge, both for their expertise and for their practical help.

JEAN AGNEW

# INTRODUCTION

The Paston family rose to prosperity in the fifteenth century and by the seventeenth century they were the richest gentry family in Norfolk. They achieved an earldom and the lord lieutenancy of the county in the 1670s but sixty years later had disappeared without trace. The decline of the family began under the Commonwealth but accelerated in the lifetime of Robert Paston (1631–1683), first earl of Yarmouth, descending into what he described as a whirlpool of misadventures. A large body of his correspondence has survived, but it seems almost to have been selected at random. The letters start in 1663, the first letter from Robert himself dating from November 1664 when he was thirty three. Nothing survives from his youth, there is no correspondence with his father, nothing relates to either of their grand tours, and there is virtually nothing about his two younger brothers who died in their twenties.[1] There are no letters to his wife during their first thirteen years of marriage, and none for the years 1667–1674; there are only two letters from his wife, and very few from his children. Moreover hardly any records exist relating to the Paston estates or their household. The only steward's accounts to have survived run from 1654–1656,[2] and there is a list of some debts outstanding in the 1670s,[3] but in general their expenditure cannot be tracked, and their cash flow is invisible. All that can be ascertained is that they lived wildly beyond their means. So although the surviving source material reveals some of the truth about the family's decline, it certainly does not contain the whole truth.

Information about Robert Paston's early life is sparse. He was born on 29 May 1631, and his mother died when he was five. His father Sir William Paston was a learned man, a lover of art and a collector, an antiquary and a natural philosopher. After the death of his wife, Lady Katherine Bertie, he embarked on an extended grand tour in 1638, returning in 1640. In July of that year he married again: his second wife was Margaret Hewitt, daughter of Sir William Hewitt, a wealthy London merchant.[4] There were no children of this marriage. Robert attended Westminster School and was admitted as a fellow commoner at Trinity College Cambridge in March 1646. He left without a degree but had certainly not wasted his time as in later life he could still read and speak Latin and Greek. His grand tour was more limited than that of his father, who had visited the Near East, but he returned speaking fluent French, and matured into a man of culture and scholarship with, like his father, a keen interest in natural philosophy.

On 15 June 1651 Robert married Rebecca Clayton, daughter of Sir Jasper Clayton, a London merchant; she was then about sixteen. Their marriage settlement has not survived but what purports to be a copy, dated 1 May 1652, is to be found in several eighteenth-century abstracts of title.[5] The Pastons' eldest son William was born in 1654, which fits this date; however further research has shown that their

[1] British Library: Add. MSS 36988, ff 82–86    [2] NRO: AYL 712    [3] Below pp 138–9
[4] R.W. Ketton-Cremer, 'Sir William Paston', *Norfolk Assembly* (London, 1957), pp 17–40
[5] NRO: AYL 59, 91–2

eldest child was Margaret who came of age on 20 January 1673 and was thus born in 1652.[6] Since the date of this settlement is suspect[7] then the information it contains must also be treated with caution. Rebecca's dowry is stated to be £8,000. Although this is not impossible it seems suspiciously high in a family where six children survived to adulthood; Sir Jasper Clayton's will[8] leaves bequests in hundreds rather than thousands of pounds, and he left only £5 to his eldest daughter Mary Nourse, who married a London brewer from a gentry family, 'in regard I have advanced her in marriage and given her a considerable portion'.[9] There is no information about Rebecca's early life. Her later letters suggest that she had little formal education, but she did own books,[10] and she had some knowledge of arithmetic and book-keeping as it was she who checked the Oxnead steward's accounts.[11] Paston clearly adored her: 'When I take the penn in my hand to you I can never leave of [ʃ], meethinkes I am conversing with you which to mee is the pleasantest conversation in the world & the greatest joy I have in itt and the expectation of your letters are the best expectations I have and the reading of them the pleasantest moments ...'.[12] The marriage appears to have been very happy and the couple were affectionate parents and fond – even doting – grandparents.

In the 1650s Robert became a friend of Thomas Henshaw, the alchemist and writer.[13] It was presumably through him that he met John Evelyn, the diarist, who records dining with Henshaw, Paston and Paston's brother-in-law John Clayton in December 1656.[14] Paston was then able to put Thomas Browne, the Norwich physician and author of *Religio Medici*, in touch with Evelyn.[15] Browne was a great friend of Paston's cousin Thomas Le Gros to whom he dedicated *Hydrotaphia*, and Paston corresponded with him about Greek and Roman coins, archaeology, and alchemy.[16] Henshaw instructed Paston and Clayton in alchemy from the early 1650s and Paston's interest in alchemy deepened as his health declined in the 1660s. Even in his early thirties he was greatly overweight and endured frequent attacks of gout, which prevented him from enjoying the active sports of a country gentleman. He had

[6] Vallance v. Welldon (TNA: C111/119–120).

[7] In one of the abstracts the clerk actually states that he has only seen a copy of this deed. There are three references in the transcriptions to pies baked for wedding anniversaries, one for each year of marriage, and these all place the marriage in 1651.

[8] Will of Sir Jasper Clayton, 31 July 1660 (TNA: PROB11/300).

[9] By contrast, Sir William Paston's father-in-law, Sir William Hewitt, another London merchant, mentions three sons and two unmarried daughters in his will dated 3 May 1636 and leaves those daughters, who included Paston's stepmother Margaret, £4000 apiece as a marriage portion (TNA: PROB11/175).

[10] Below p. 52. Her mother Lady Clayton owned a number of history books and sermons at the time of her death (TNA: PROB32/35/206).

[11] Below p. 328                                                                    [12] Below p. 227

[13] Thomas Henshaw (1618–1700), FRS, alchemist and writer, a lifelong friend and mentor of Robert Paston. He was sometimes known as 'Halophilus' (salt lover); for his career and his work on saltpetre *see* Stephen Pasmore, 'Thomas Henshaw, FRS (1618–1700)' (*Notes and Records of the Royal Society of London*, Vol. 36, No. 2 (Feb. 1982), pp 177–188).

[14] Donald R. Dickson, 'Thomas Henshaw and Sir Robert Paston's Pursuit of the Red Elixir: an early collaboration between fellows of the Royal Society' (*Notes and Records of the Royal Society of London*, vol. 51, no. 1 (Jan. 1997), p.73, n.15).

[15] Thomas Browne to John Evelyn, 21 Jan 1658 (Simon Wilkin (ed.), *The Works of Sir Thomas Browne*, (Norwich, 1836) I, pp 373–379).

[16] *ibid.*, pp 7, 411–413

also begun to suffer from depression which recurred at intervals throughout his life.

There is no further information about Robert Paston until 13 June 1657, the date of a settlement whereby Sir William Paston paid debts incurred by Robert amounting to £10,000.[17] Since the usual reasons for gentry overspending – building, gambling, and cutting a dash at court – cannot explain such indebtedness in a young royalist living in Cromwellian England who had not yet come into his inheritance, this settlement gives substance to the claim of John Hildeyard in his funeral sermon preached at Robert Paston's death, that Paston had sent money to the King in exile and had even borrowed 'fearing his sovereign might want'.[18] Sir William's price for settling Robert's debts was that most of his estates should be entailed on Robert's sons, leaving him as merely tenant for life and thus unable to sell any of the land in the settlement until his eldest son came of age and could join with him to bar the entail. The deed also made provision for a larger jointure for Rebecca which may have been an inducement to secure Robert's agreement to the entail.

Sir William Paston wrote a new will[19] on 3 November 1662 after the deaths of both of his younger sons. The will had three purposes. The first was to assign money for the payment of his debts. The second was to ensure a generous income for his widow: a deed of 1659 is quoted which augmented Lady Paston's jointure – and the will states that she was to receive an immediate gift of £500; a detailed list is given of her jewellery, horses, coach, furniture, cabinets, plate, and the contents of various luxurious rooms at Oxnead and Sir William's London house in Queen Street, all of which were to be hers. The third was to provide for his grand-daughter Margaret who was to have an annuity of £100 and a dowry of £4,000 at the age of twenty-one or upon her marriage if sooner. The only reason for making a ten-year-old child financially independent of her parents could have been that she was not expected to live with them. Moreover her annuity was stated to be for the lifetime of her step-grandmother Margaret, Lady Paston. The only two sources which refer to the child during the 1650s suggest that in both 1655 and 1658 she was part of her grand-parents' household[20] and it seems clear that Sir William expected her to continue to live with Lady Paston. The only individual bequest to Robert was one half of Sir William's cabinets of stone and ebony, and Robert's four sons are not mentioned by name. Sir William appointed trustees to manage the settlement of his debts and to act as his executors, but Robert was to be allowed to take on the executorship if he entered into a bond to the trustees for the penal sum of £20,000. Sir William died on 22 February 1663 and Robert proved the will on 25 May following (with no further recorded mention of the bond) and so came into his inheritance.

The Pastons had long been an extremely wealthy family. Sir William's estate was valued by the Committee for Compounding at £5,594 8s 0½d. This was the most valuable royalist estate in Norfolk and outstanding for a gentry family – many

---

[17] NRO: AYL 91/5, 92

[18] John Hildeyard, *A Sermon Preached at the Funeral of ... Robert Earl and Viscount Yarmouth* (London, 1683), p.24, hereafter Hildeyard, *Sermon*

[19] Will of Sir William Paston (TNA: PROB11/311)

[20] The Oxnead household accounts include 'a baby [i.e. a doll] for young Miss' in 1655 when only Sir William and Lady Paston were resident (NRO: AYL 712); Sir William Persall to Sir William Paston, 24 Sep 1658, 'I kisse the fayre hands of pritty Misse' (British Library: Add. MSS 36988, f.80).

aristocratic families had less. Sir William compounded for his estates in 1644 paying £1,376 8s 4d, three times as much as any other family in Norfolk, and the earl of Manchester subsequently relieved him of plate worth £1,100 for the support of the army of the Eastern Association.[21] These expenses and Robert's debts forced Sir William to sell his estates at Caister and Winterton, and elsewhere.[22] However Robert still inherited a large estate, with right of presentation to eight livings, and a beautiful house at Oxnead with fine gardens running down to the river Bure. The house had been built by Admiral Sir Clement Paston in about 1580 and bequeathed by him to his nephew Sir William Paston (1528–1610) who was Robert's great-great-grandfather. Thereafter the family had lived at Oxnead rather than in the older and less comfortable manor house at Paston. The house was extensively modernised by Robert's father who employed the architect and sculptor Nicholas Stone (1586/7–1647) who embellished the original house and gardens and added a wing in the Palladian style.[23] No contemporary picture of Oxnead has survived although one was painted for Robert in the 1660s.[24] When the estates were sold to Lord Anson in the mid-eighteenth century the house was in a ruinous condition and the greater part was shortly afterwards demolished. A conjectural drawing was made in 1807 by the architect John Adey Repton whose uncle had been tenant at Oxnead:[25] the style of Stone's wing was so advanced for Norfolk in the 1630s that Repton concluded that it must have been built as a banqueting house for Charles II's visit in 1671. It cannot have had much use by Sir William as a banqueting house in the Commonwealth period but it contained other rooms: for example, Sir William speaks in his will of his wife's closet 'in the new building at Oxnead'.

When the house was inherited by Sir Robert it was assessed at forty-five hearths and was looked upon as one of the showpieces of Norfolk for its luxurious furnishings, extensive library, and collection of pictures and objets d'art.[26] It is likely that Sir William was responsible for the purchase of the bulk of the latter; Nicholas Stone's son was buying for him in Italy in the late 1630s,[27] and Sir William himself bought many treasures on his extensive grand tour which he showed to his friends on his return.[28] No accounts or letters have survived showing further purchases by Sir Robert, but it is certain that he continued to embellish his house.[29] His love for

---

[21] Ketton-Cremer, 'Sir William Paston', pp 32–34; R.W. Ketton-Cremer, 'The End of the Pastons', *Norfolk Portraits* (1944), p.25; Hildeyard, *Sermon*, p.25.

[22] NRO: AYL 59, 91, Y/C 31/7/19, 21, MC 233/1–2; West Sussex R.O., Shillinglee MSS, 16/11; TNA: PROB11/311, will of Sir William Paston.

[23] Ketton-Cremer, 'Sir William Paston', pp 20–22       [24] Below p.73

[25] W.H. Bartlett & John Britten, *Architectural Antiquities of Great Britain* (London, 1809), ii, following p.98; *The Gentleman's Magazine*, January 1844, pp 21–24.

[26] The Yarmouth collection is the subject of a painting known as 'The Paston Treasure' dating from the 1670s in Norwich Castle Museum *see* Robert Wenley, 'Robert Paston and the Yarmouth Collection' (*Norfolk Archaeology*, XLI pt II (1991), pp 113–144), and R.W. Ketton-Cremer, 'The Treasure of Oxnead', *Norfolk Assembly* (London, 1957), pp 212–222.

[27] Colin Platt, *The Great Rebuildings of Tudor and Stuart England* (London 1994), pp 87-89

[28] Paston's cousin Thomas Knyvett wrote on 8 Feb 1640: 'heer is a world full of curiosityes & some very rich ones, as cabinets & juells', *see* Bertram Schofield (ed.), *The Knyvett Letters, 1620–1644* (NRS (1949), XX, p.94).

[29] For example, a Florentine inlaid side table commissioned by Robert Paston was sold at Christie's in 1992 for £137,500 (Lot 119/Sale 4721).

Oxnead ('the sweetest place in the world') is frequently expressed in his letters but is generally followed by the wish that he had a little more money to make it still finer. Paston was never happier than when he was at Oxnead but this seems to have been the one topic on which he and his wife did not agree. Rebecca was a Londoner, her father had a house in Lombard Street in the city, and while Sir William was alive the young Pastons lived at Parson's Green,[30] a little way out of London. There are hints in Robert's letters that Rebecca found Oxnead uncomfortable, that she suffered from frequent colds, and was lonely and sometimes depressed. The contrast in their attitudes is revealed by Robert's appalled answer to a letter of 1665 in which she suggested that since it was already the end of February and she was coming up to London in early April for her lying in, he might just as well stay in London and not bother to return to Oxnead at all.[31] Part of the problem may have been that she was not related to any of the leading Norfolk gentry families and seems to have had no close friends there. Robert on the other hand was related to everyone. Centuries of intermarriage meant that he was a cousin of, among others, the Coke, Windham, Le Gros, Heveningham, Berney, Potts and Bedingfeld families, and more recently through his grandmother Katherine Knyvett he was a cousin of the Hollands, Bacons, Rouses, Pettuses, Burwells, and Aydes: indeed there were few families of any standing in the county to whom he was not related.

Although he had inherited a very substantial estate, Sir Robert had also inherited a load of debt, and the income from the estate had declined steeply over the previous twenty years. One of the few surviving rentals from Oxnead shows a total income of only £2,670 12s 2d in 1662,[32] although in 1664 the valuation as let was £3,166 5s 8d.[33] This was still wealthy for a gentry family but they may no longer have been the wealthiest family in Norfolk.[34] Moreover Sir Robert had heavy outgoings: he was paying his stepmother a jointure of about £600 p.a.,[35] and a further £100 p.a. to his aunt Frances, widow of his uncle Thomas.[36] His stepmother's jointure was for her life, regardless of whether she remarried, and she was still in her mid-forties. Sir Robert's relations with his father can only be guessed at, but the correspondence makes it clear that he was on very bad terms with his stepmother.[37] His daughter Margaret had been removed from her care to Oxnead, and she was allowed only very limited access to his second child William.

To avoid selling the unentailed part of his estates to pay his father's and his own debts Sir Robert entered into mortgages for £6,000 in 1663 and 1664,[38] but he needed to find a way to improve his income. There were two immediate possibilities. The part of his estate with the most potential for improvement was Southtown opposite the town

[30] Parson's Green at Fulham, Middlesex, then a village on the outskirts of London

[31] Below p. 56                                              [32] Rental 1660–1662 (NRO: AYL 92).

[33] Vallance v Welldon (TNA: C111/120).

[34] James M. Rosenheim, *The Townshends of Raynham* (Middletown, CT, 1989), p.65, hereafter Rosenheim, *Townshends*

[35] As a rough guide, a jointure was about one tenth of a woman's dowry; Margaret, Lady Paston's dowry was £4,000, and her jointure had been augmented by £200 p.a. in a deed of 1659 quoted in Sir William's will.                           [36] Receipts, etc. (NRO: NRS 4004, 4013).

[37] He actually omitted her from the family history drawn up in 1674 (Cambridge University Library: MS Add. 6968).

[38] NRO: AYL 59, 91/6, HARE 5949, 5969; Corrance v. Paston, 1669 (TNA: C5/465/83).

of Great Yarmouth on the west side of the river Yare, then in Suffolk. If the merchants of Yarmouth could be persuaded to expand their businesses into Southtown, Paston's rent roll would also expand and the increased trade of the town would benefit all parties. The second possibility was to obtain some kind of grant from the King. Although the royalists had greeted the Restoration with rapture, it soon became clear that there was never going to be enough money to satisfy their expectations, particularly as moderate supporters of the Commonwealth had to be conciliated. For example, Paston's contemporary Sir Horatio Townsend of Raynham served in two protectorate parliaments but was a moderate who worked for the Restoration and was one of the twelve representatives from the Commons who escorted Charles II from Breda. In 1661 he was raised to the peerage and appointed lord lieutenant of Norfolk. There were hundreds of royalist families who had been impoverished by their support for the King but most of the rewards went to those with the strongest claims – those who had fought for the royalist cause or shared the King's exile. Robert's maternal grandfather had been killed at the battle of Edgehill, but in spite of the money sent to support the court in exile, the Pastons themselves had been quite moderate royalists and had held local office under the Commonwealth. Robert was too young to have fought in the civil wars and there is no evidence to confirm suggestions that he spent some time at the Stuart court in exile although he may have done so while on his grand tour which was probably took place between 1649 and 1651. He had been one of the party which had ridden out to welcome Charles II on his restoration and had been knighted, but if he was to hope for any significant reward from the King, he needed to do something further to win his gratitude.

Paston had been in parliament since 1660 when he was returned for Thetford, and from 1661 he was member for Castle Rising. The parliamentary session of November 1664 to March 1665 was to be momentous for him. Since the Yarmouth merchants showed no inclination to take advantage of his offers he introduced a Bill in parliament to give equal rights of lading and unlading to Southtown.[39] At the same time he was asked to propose the sum of £2,500,000 for the King's supply. Paston had apparently been chosen for this task by the Clarendon administration because he was a rich and independent country member without court affiliations.[40] Paston jumped at this opportunity; his speech was short and to the point;[41] the Commons appear to have been stunned by the size of the sum which he insisted was needed for the Dutch War, and the Bill was passed. The King's delight was so great that Paston was, as he wrote to Rebecca, 'looked on in a capacity of not being denied anything in his Majesty's power'.[42] Paston's Yarmouth Bill immediately received court backing; however its passage through the Lords was not entirely due to pressure from the King – Paston himself had a considerable connection among the peers.

An anonymous memorandum written in 1682,[43] supporting a possible political come-

[39] Perry Gauci, *Politics and Society in Great Yarmouth 1660–1722* (Oxford, 1996), pp 112–7) [hereafter Gauci, *Great Yarmouth*]

[40] *The Life of Edward Earl of Clarendon ... written by himself* (Oxford, 1827), II, pp 309–15.

[41] Paston 'was no great speaker, but delivered what he had a mind to say very clearly' *(ibid.,* p.309).

[42] Below p.46

[43] *Calendar of State Papers, Domestic* [hereafter *CSPD*], *1682*, pp 54–6; R.W. Ketton-Cremer argues convincingly *(Norfolk Archaeology* XXVIII (1842) pp 76–7) that the memorandum was written by Humphrey

back by Lord Townshend, describes Townshend's feelings at being 'supplanted by one he looked on as a creature of his own, he having brought him first to court and there helped to advance him from a mean fortune to his present share in the King's favour'. This accusation is nonsense (although it is surprising how often it has been repeated[44]): Paston was a baronet and head of a rich and ancient gentry family described by Henry Howard, the future duke of Norfolk, as 'for many descents the most antient of all the gentry heere without competition'[45] and he was also cousin to many members of the House of Lords. His mother Lady Katherine Bertie was a sister of the second earl of Lindsey. Her mother was a Montagu which meant that Paston was a cousin of the earls of Manchester and Sandwich, and of Ralph Montagu the future duke of Montagu. Lady Katherine's grandmother was Lady Mary de Vere, daughter of the sixteenth earl of Oxford, through whom Paston had an enormous aristocratic connection. Finally, the descendants of Eleanor Paston who married the first earl of Rutland (died 1543) included the earls of Rutland, Exeter, Shrewsbury, Westmorland, and the dukes of Norfolk and Buckingham.[46] The fact that Paston was barely acquainted (if at all) with many of these people was unimportant: his place in society was assured from birth.

Nevertheless, it is possible that Lord Townshend did help Paston early in his career as a member of parliament. When Paston was elected a member of the Convention Parliament in 1660, it is likely that Townshend, who had been a member of parliament since 1656, was pleased to show him the ropes; and when Paston was in the happy position of looking for something to ask from the King, it may have been Townshend (whom Paston described as 'the best friend I have in the world' in 1665) who suggested that he ask the King for a grant of the farm of one of the petty customs as he himself was granted the farm of exported coal in April 1665,[47] although Paston may also have had advice from his friend John, Lord Mordaunt, who had been one of the farmers of the customs of coals from Newcastle since 1660.[48]

Paston asked for, and was granted, the farm of the customs on wood and wooden ware, earth and earthen ware, glass and glass ware, stone and stone ware, oranges, lemons, citrons, and pomegranates; these miscellaneous commodities were still included in the great farm of the customs so Paston's farm for twenty-one years did not begin until Michaelmas 1667 when the previous lease of the great farm expired. He had originally offered an annual rent of £2,700; however the situation was altered by the Fire of London in 1666 which caused a surge in the demand for timber for rebuilding, and he was obliged to renegotiate for a rent of £6,500.[49] He was originally expecting to make a profit of about £3,000 a year from the customs and assured his

Prideaux (1648–1724), dean of Norwich; Prideaux, who was born in Cornwall and educated at Oxford, was only installed as a prebendary of Norwich in August 1681 and had had very little time to absorb the history of the Norfolk gentry families.

[44] J.R. Jones, 'The First Whig Party in Norfolk' (*Durham University Journal*, 46 (1953–4), p.14); J.T. Evans, *Seventeenth-century Norwich: politics, religion and government, 1620–1690* (Oxford, 1979), p.268; V.L. Stater, 'Continuity and Change in English Provincial Politics: Robert Paston in Norfolk, 1675–1683' (*Albion*, 25 (1993), p.197). [45] Below p.136

[46] Paston's aristocratic connections are detailed in Francis Sandford's history of the Paston family, 1674 (Cambridge University Library: MS Add. 6968); for a partial transcript *see* Francis Worship, 'Account of a MS Genealogy of the Paston Family in the Possession of His Grace the Duke of Newcastle' (*Norfolk Archaeology*, IV (1855), pp 1–55). [47] *CSPD, 1664–5*, 24 Apr 1665

[48] *Calendar of Treasury Books* [hereafter *CTB*], *1, 1660–1667*, pp 109, 399 [49] Below p.76.

wife 'I know soe much what the want of money is and what the streightness of a fortune is that if itt pleaseth God Ile make use of God's providence to provide for the one' and 'if I once gett money I thinke I shall knowe the way how to live to myself and keep the maine'.[50] Moreover, the King had been extremely gracious to Paston and had promised him a peerage, although not immediately as it would look like 'a contract', and in January 1667 he made Paston a gentleman of the privy chamber. The future of the Pastons seemed assured.

By 1669 however, they were in serious financial difficulties and were facing legal proceedings for the re-payment of their mortgages with interest, and other actions for debt. As a member of parliament Paston was safe from arrest, but there was a real fear of a sheriff proceeding with an execution against his property at Oxnead, as Henshaw advised him to 'disfurnish your closet and a few rooms of your richest furniture'.[51] There are few details in the letters but it is clear that Paston's mother-in-law Lady Clayton had lent the couple money on the security of their jewels, and that they owed money to most of the Clayton family, and to many of their friends and acquaintances. The only two letters to have survived from Rebecca to Robert show her in London in 1669 attempting to stave off some legal action. In the absence of accounts or other financial papers it is impossible to work out exactly how they had arrived at this state of affairs, but the correspondence makes two things clear. First, before the warrant for the wood farm had even been issued the couple had started spending money. There were new buildings to house the servants at Oxnead, a former dairy was converted into a private chapel, part of the house was refurbished, some new plate and furniture was purchased, and London servants were hired. A large sum of money had had to be borrowed to pay the first instalment of the wood farm rent, but Paston was already behind with this rent in January 1669,[52] and there was interest unpaid on his various mortgages. Second, the wood farm was not producing as much as expected, and was very slow in producing anything at all.

However bad Paston's financial situation, he could usually comfort himself with the existence of one or more money-making schemes which might one day make his family's fortune. In 1669 he still had the enthusiastic support of his brother-in-law Sir John Clayton. Clayton was about the same age as Paston and shared many of his interests and, as Paston's brother-in-law, now moved in circles which he was unlikely to have reached on his own. Returning from a day spent in the company of the duke of Buckingham, Edmund Waller the poet, and Christopher Wren – 'nothing but the quintessence of wit & most excellent discourse' – he acknowledged his debt: 'for which I must thank you as being the creator of this, & of all other good fortune I have hitherto had in this world'.[53] Both young men became fellows of the Royal Society in 1661 and shared the growing interest of the aristocracy and gentry in science and technology, partly from intellectual curiosity, and partly from the realisation that they could be profitable. It was an age when landowners eagerly invested in mining, canals, and land drainage. Paston and Clayton devised a scheme for the erection of a number of lighthouses[54] and in 1669 won the support of Sir Thomas Osborne, one

---

[50] Below p.53.    [51] Below p.84.    [52] *CTB, 3, 1669–1672*, pp 5, 179.    [53] Below p.86.
[54] St. Nicholas Gatt, Great Yarmouth, Cromer, the mouth of the Humber, Flamborough Head, and Ferne Island; below pp 89–90, 93, 261.

of the commissioners for the navy and the husband of Paston's cousin Bridget Bertie. The scheme eventually failed because of the difficulty of setting up a system for the collection of fees from ships' masters without the support of Trinity House.

Clayton also shared Paston's enthusiasm for alchemy, both young men having their own laboratories. The search for the philosopher's stone, believed to turn base metals into gold, had long been considered fit only for the lunatic fringe of alchemists, and those who became involved were popularly represented as fraudsters or fools.[55] Neither description fits Henshaw, Paston and Clayton, but they appear to have devoted their leisure hours to this search for a number of years. Prompted by Paston, Henshaw obtained and studied numerous ancient texts by alchemists who claimed to have discovered the stone but who were studiously vague about the methods used. While not questioning their underlying theories Henshaw used the kind of empirical methods which, by the next century, would gradually transform the mystery of alchemy into the science of chemistry.[56] Under his guidance Paston and Clayton repeated many of the processes described, using quantities of mercury, sulphur, salt-petre and ammonia, and he urged them to keep careful notes of their experiments. In 1669 Paston's financial crisis did not stop him from re-equipping his laboratory with every kind of glass vial.[57] Progress was slow and results were ambiguous. Paston appears to have complained of this to Henshaw in 1671, who pointed out that he had done his best to dissuade him and Clayton from a project with so little chance of success, that he had given up much of his own time ('which else I should have other-wise employed') working through the source material for him, that he had never pretended to revelations, secret demonstrations or recipes found in abbey walls, and that he would be well pleased if Paston would abandon 'this sooty imployment unsuit-able to the calling of a gentleman', but he 'could not live without a castle in the ayre'.[58] On the other hand Henshaw didn't have Paston's debts: if ever a man needed to discover the philosopher's stone, it was Robert Paston. A few weeks later he was taking their findings sufficiently seriously to warn Paston to speak in French or Latin when he and Clayton discussed the experiments in front of his laboratory assistant, and he suggested that the three of them should come to some kind of agreement about secrecy.[59] His hopes were short lived although the experiments continued[60] but most of Henshaw's later correspondence with Paston has not survived.

Although there is unfortunately no correspondence between Robert and Rebecca in the years 1670–1674, there is a useful group of letters beginning in 1671 to Sir Robert Clayton of the firm of London scriveners Clayton & Morris who were financiers specialising in the arrangement of loans and mortgages and the management of gentry debt.[61] They had been handling the Pastons' affairs at least since the previous

[55] See for example, Ben Johnson, *The Alchemist*, a play which was performed in the 1660s and with which all three men must have been familiar.

[56] Dickson, 'Thomas Henshaw and Robert Paston's Pursuit of the Red Elixir', pp 57–76

[57] Below p.85.          [58] Below p.125.          [59] Below p.133.

[60] See letter from Paston to Sir Thomas Browne, 10 Sep 1674 (Wilkin (ed.), *The Works of Sir Thomas Browne*, I, pp 411–13).

[61] Clayton financial letters and papers (NRO: NRS 4004–4029, MS 3317–18, 3327, 3346, 3349a-b, 3350–51); F.T Melton, *Sir Robert Clayton and the Origins of English Deposit Banking, 1658–1685* (Cambridge, 1986); both Pastons address Sir Robert as cousin, but any relationship was very distant. Clayton & Morris also managed some of Townshend's mortgage debts (Rosenheim, *Townshends*, p.89), and were involved in the affairs of other Norfolk gentry (NRO: MS 3210–3437).

year. The financial crisis of 1669 culminated in a bailout in March 1671 by Sir John Clayton and his mother who lent the Pastons £13,000 on the security of their estates to pay off their mortgages.[62] This was probably arranged by Sir Robert Clayton and his partner.

Unfortunately 1671 was a very expensive year for the Pastons. Their eldest son William embarked on his grand tour and most of his letters lament how expensive everything was and how in spite of his and his companion's utmost endeavours to live cheaply their money simply crumbled away. Their eldest daughter Margaret, now costing her parents a small fortune in clothes,[63] fell in love with a young ensign called Henry Rumbold who had been serving in Tangier. His family were known to the Pastons and Claytons, having lived at Parson's Green, but apart from that he had nothing to recommend him, being penniless, half Spanish and a Roman Catholic.[64] Margaret, who was still under age, had been left a dowry of £4,000 with no strings attached by her grandfather Sir William Paston, which according to Henshaw had given her a false opinion that she was 'at her own disposall, and the confidence to choose for herself'. Accordingly she obtained an authenticated copy of the will to show to the young man, who then not surprisingly proved very difficult to dislodge.[65] Unfortunately the end of the story is not contained in the letters but the young couple were separated. Apart from his dislike of the match, there could hardly have been a more inconvenient time for Paston to raise Margaret's dowry, which was secured on the Southtown estate, as the whole episode took place only a few weeks before the King's visit to Norfolk.

The King and Queen visited Norfolk with a great retinue at the end of September 1671, where they were entertained by the Earl Marshal (later duke of Norfolk) at Norwich, Lord Townsend at Raynham, Sir John Hobart at Blickling, and Paston at Oxnead.[66] No trouble or expense was spared by Paston to make the King's visit to Oxnead the highlight of the tour, vast accounts were run up with suppliers and trades people and his friends' orchards as far away as London were ransacked for fruit, but when the King on arrival remarked that he was now 'safe in the house of his friend'[67] it must have seemed to Paston that life could afford no greater happiness and that whatever the cost the King's visit was worth it. Only a few miscellaneous accounts of expenditure for the visit have survived, still unpaid several years later,[68] so it is impossible to calculate the total: Paston himself later said that he had spent three times the dowry of an earl's daughter.[69] This conspicuous expenditure no doubt enraged his creditors. On 10 October one of them, Charles Cornwallis, wrote 'His Majesty hath beene highly treated by the Norfolke gentlemen, among others by Sir Robert Paston, I admire his way of paying debts' and complained that Paston's mortgages, in which

---

[62] NRO: AYL 59, 91, Y/D 41–87      [63] Below pp 138–9.

[64] Horace Rumbold, 'Notes on the History of the Family of Rumbold in the Seventeenth Century' (*Transactions of the Royal Historical Society (new series)* (1892), 6, pp 145–165); it is not clear on what evidence Rumbold stated that Henry was escorting Margaret Paston home from Tangier, together with Lady Middleton, when they fell in love, when the letters state that he was being asked to escort Lady Middleton out to join her husband, and few things are less likely than that the Pastons would have allowed their unmarried and richly-dowered daughter to travel to Tangier.

[65] Below p.131.      [66] Below p.136.      [67] Hildeyard, *Sermon*, p.25.      [68] Below pp 138–9.

[69] Hildeyard, *Sermon*, p.25

he was concerned, had not been paid off.[70] On the previous day Paston had written to Sir Joseph Williamson, secretary of state, stating that the income from the wood farm had been anticipated for the next four or five years, that he had a mortgage of £10,000, and was 'hated and oppressed on every side', and he offered to sell the Southtown estate to the King.[71] Paston was accustomed to living in debt, haphazardly paying some interest and paying off creditors by taking out new mortgages or borrowing against the profits of the wood farm. He never sold land. His offering to sell Southtown (which was unentailed) to the King was a new departure and, coupled with the language in this letter, suggests that he had become seriously upset, perhaps by a direct confrontation with a creditor. Although there is no proof, this may have been the point at which Sir John Clayton, who was at Oxnead for the King's visit, discovered (possibly through Cornwallis) that the loan he and his mother had made to Paston in March had not been used to pay off the mortgages – in all probability most of it had been spent on the royal visit. Whenever Clayton discovered this betrayal he is certain to have quarrelled with Paston. Although Paston remained on good terms with his mother-in-law, his relationship with Clayton grew progressively worse. By 1676 the two men were barely on speaking terms and by 1678 Paston believed that Clayton was working to undermine his various financial projects.

Since the King was not interested in purchasing the Southtown estate the Pastons' next move was to find an heiress for their eldest son. In April 1671 Paston had written to Sir Edwin Rich of Lincoln's Inn who had lent him money 'pray be mindful of a wife ... for my son: who is very well in France but shall waite on any lady you recommend.'[72] It is not known whether Rich put forward any names but early in 1672 the Pastons were hoping to arrange a marriage for William with Susanna Bonfois, heiress of a London merchant.[73] When this fell through Rebecca asked Sir Robert Clayton's help in arranging a marriage with Sir Robert Vyner's step-daughter,[74] the greatest merchant heiress of the decade, but within a few weeks she was proudly telling Clayton the terms of her son's imminent marriage with the King's eldest illegitimate daughter. Unfortunately there is no information at all about the making of this match. Charlotte Jemima Howard, born circa 1650, was the daughter of Elizabeth, viscountess Shannon; in 1672 she was a widow with a young daughter, her husband, the heir presumptive to the earldom of Suffolk, having died of smallpox in 1669. She married William Paston on 17 July 1672 and it appears to have been a happy marriage.[75] Very little information has survived about Charlotte but from remarks in family letters it seems that although the young couple lived in London she enjoyed her visits to Norfolk. Her mother was one of the Killigrew family, courtiers and playwrights, and a descendant of Sir Nicholas Bacon (1510–1579), the lord keeper.[76] Charlotte's

---

[70] Charles Cornwallis to Lady Mary Heveningham, 10 Oct 1671 (NRO: MC 107/4); Cornwallis was one of the brothers of Frances Paston, widow of Sir Robert's uncle Thomas Paston.

[71] *CSPD, 1671*, p.516

[72] Paston to Rich, 25 Apr 1671 (Folger Shakespeare Library: X.d.451 (15))      [73] Below p.138.

[74] Rebecca, Lady Paston to Sir Robert Clayton, 23 May 1672 (NRO: NRS 4008)

[75] Mary Killigrew to Rebecca, countess of Yarmouth [1684] (British Library: Add. MSS 36988, ff 229–230)

[76] Lady Shannon's parents were Sir Robert Killigrew and Sir Nicholas's granddaughter Mary Wodehouse.

Norfolk ancestry is not referred to in any of the letters, but her relationship to many Norfolk gentry families must have been well known. Rebecca reported to Sir Robert Clayton that her son was to have £1,000 per annum, that no jointure would be asked for until the estates were freed from debt, and that the King was to give him a lodging in the court and a coach and horses.[77] The bride also had a grant of £500 p.a., made in 1667 on her first marriage, which was now continued.[78] The expenses of the wedding were steep – the King himself gave the bride away – and in August Paston asked Rich for a further loan, hinting that the King intended to 'fix eminently his favours' in the Paston family.[79] In September Paston reported to Sir Robert Clayton that the King had again promised to make him a peer, adding 'and therefore doe suppose will give mee all just opportunites to make mee sutable to itt'.[80] Paston did not receive his long-awaited peerage until the next year, being created viscount Yarmouth in August 1673,[81] but in the previous January a grant was made of £2,000 p.a. to be paid to Messrs Clayton & Morris out of Paston's rents for the wood farm for the remainder of the term of 21 years for the settlement of his debts, which would amount to £30,000 in total.[82]

Shortly before Paston received his peerage Sir Thomas Osborne had been appointed lord treasurer, and he no doubt used his influence on Paston's behalf: as Charles Hatton wrote to his brother 'My Lord Treasurer is created Viscount Latimer, and recovered of his late sickness. Sr Robert Paston, Ld Viscount Yarmouth, his son maryed ye Lady Chanon's daughter, wch, together wth my Ld Treasurer's interest, who is his great friend, advanced him to this dignity.'[83] These same events were reported by Girolamo Alberti di Conti, Venetian resident in England: 'On the other hand the treasurer ... had scarcely recovered from his dangerous illness ere he obtained the honour of being created viscount Latimer. On the same occasion the king generously acknowledged the merit of Sir Robert Paston by making him viscount Yarmouth. He is not only allied by blood with the noblest families of England but his own is most ancient, dating from William the Conqueror.'[84] This fulsome tribute to Paston was no doubt inspired by the fact that Alberti had just married or was about to marry Paston's eldest daughter.

Margaret may have met Alberti first just after the Rumbold affair, when he accompanied the court on the King's progress to Norfolk in September 1671.[85] He had become the Venetian resident at the end of 1670 having been previously secretary to

[77] Rebecca, Lady Paston to Sir Robert Clayton, 16 July 1672 (NRO: NRS 4008); Vyner's stepdaughter Bridget Hyde (1662–1733) later married Peregrine Osborne, viscount Dunblane, second son of Lord Danby; the King eventually settled £3,000 p.a. on William Paston (British Library: Add. MSS 27448, ff 251–2).       [78] *CTB, 4, 1672–1675*, pp 479, 483

[79] Paston to Rich, 8 Aug 1672 (Folger Shakespeare Library: X.d.451 (16))

[80] Sir Robert Paston to Sir Robert Clayton, 2 Sep 1672 (NRO: NRS 4018)

[81] Paston's peerage was expected a year earlier, as Samuel Pepys wrote to Lord Henry Howard in August 1672 asking to succeed him as member for Castle Rising (Guy le la Bédoyère, *The Letters of Samuel Pepys* (Woodbridge, 2006), pp 91–92). Initially the delay may have been so that he did not outrank Howard who was created earl of Norwich in October 1672.

[82] *CTB, 4, 1672–1675*, p 46. The fact that the money was taken from the rent and paid direct to Clayton & Morris suggests that someone had taken Paston's measure.

[83] Edward Maunde Thompson (ed.), *Correspondence of the Family of Hatton* (Camden Society, 1878–1879, I, p.115)       [84] *Calendar of State Papers Venetian* [hereafter *CSPV*], *1673–1675*, p.91

[85] *CSPV, 1671–1672*, p.110

the embassy: as Paston's grant included the customs of glass and glassware, and the best quality glass came from Venice, it is likely that he had long been acquainted with Alberti. There is no information about the couple's courtship: between September and December 1672, the Pastons were in hopes of arranging a marriage for Margaret with Sir John Godolphin.[86] Six months later however in June 1673, Margaret was clearly on the brink of marrying Alberti, as Paston was discussing with Sir Robert Clayton the need to raise her dowry which was secured on the Southtown estate.[87] The Pastons could not have been happy about the marriage of their daughter with a foreigner and a Roman Catholic, but Margaret was now of age and her dowry had been left to her with no strings attached. Moreover Alberti was not an adventurer: he was a man of intelligence and sophistication who had been a diplomat for the previous twelve years, and he came of a distinguished and wealthy Venetian family. There was nothing to do but to make the best of it. Margaret had nominally inherited the estate of Southtown when she came of age in January 1673 and had lost it on her marriage with an 'alien'. A series of grants and mortgages enabled Paston to raise £4,000 against the estate to give to the Albertis but the legal processes were slow and the Albertis were still in London in 1675 long after Alberti had been replaced as resident, which caused them considerable financial loss.[88] Paston was determined to keep the ownership of Southtown for himself as he was still optimistic that the estate could be developed for trade although the Great Yarmouth merchants thus far showed no inclination to invest in it.

There are no letters from Paston, now Lord Yarmouth, to his wife between 1667 and September 1675, and in that period the political scene had changed completely. After the fall of Clarendon in 1667 rival politicians struggled for power. The Cavalier Parliament continued to sit intermittently (it was not dissolved until 1679) but the euphoria of the Restoration had long since evaporated and had been replaced by a more critical spirit. The King's policy of alliance with the French was much disliked. The country had fought a series of unpopular, inconclusive, and expensive wars against the Dutch, and parliament was becoming increasingly reluctant to vote the necessary supply; moreover the difficulties of levying and collecting taxes meant that the full amounts voted were never realised. The King could hardly be blamed for the fact that he had no legitimate children, but he was certainly blamed for squandering huge sums on his mistresses and their offspring, and with the example of a dissolute and expensive court before their eyes, it was natural for MPs to accuse the administration of inefficiency and corruption. It was now widely suspected that the duke of York, the heir to the throne, was a Roman Catholic, and dislike and fear of Roman Catholics was almost universal. Although the King himself had backed legislation ensuring toleration for Catholics and dissenters, Lord Danby's administration was moving firmly towards Anglicanism. To be sure of getting legislation through, Danby was building up a 'court party' in parliament. An opposition in parliament began to form around Lord Shaftesbury and became known as the 'country party'.

[86] Sir Robert Paston to Sir Robert Clayton, 4 Sep, 5 Dec 1672 (NRO: NNAS 4018).
[87] Sir Robert Paston to Sir Robert Clayton, 30 June 1673 (NRO: NNAS 4018).
[88] TNA, C111/119–20, C205/1/15, C5/536/15; *CSPV, 1673–1675*, pp 91n, 420, 442; *CSPD, 1673–1675*, p.330. It is not clear however why matters dragged on until 1675.

By 1675, Lord Townsend was a disappointed man: he felt that his efforts and expenditure as lord lieutenant had been insufficiently appreciated. He had received no further marks of royal favour and was over £30,000 in debt.[89] In 1673 he had supported the election of Sir John Hobart of Blickling as one of the knights of the shire for Norfolk. Hobart had been a member Cromwell's 'upper house', and he was married to one of the daughters of John Hampden, the parliamentarian, so his election was deeply unpopular with the Norfolk royalists, even though it had been uncontested. Townshend, who had once pursued dissenters, was now prepared to tolerate them, and became increasingly overbearing and aggressive towards those who did not share his views. However he still retained the support of Sir John Holland, MP for Aldeburgh, a popular moderate who was vocal in parliament against excessive taxation and the extravagance of the court.[90]

The first indication of the existence of party in Norfolk came in two parliamentary by-elections in 1675, the first to be contested since the Restoration. In April Lord Danby's son-in-law Robert Coke of Holkham stood for King's Lynn and his opponent was backed by Lord Townshend; Coke won but his election expenses came to £10,000. And in May Sir Robert Kemp stood for the county, again supported by Townshend, but was opposed by Sir Neville Catelyn who was put up, apparently against his will, by the high Anglican party. Paston had already promised his vote and that of his tenants for Kemp,[91] but it was hinted to him in letters from several writers that if he were to back Catelyn, Kemp could be defeated, and his chaplain John Gough wrote about the heavy-handed electioneering of Townshend and his supporters 'there are wise men that think they have extreamly lost themselves by this buisnesse in the affections of the country & now that there is room to receive another, who will stand by them, into their hearts'.[92] Kemp was elected on 10 May and although there was no appeal against his election, the threats and sharp practice used to achieve it created rifts in the county which were widely deplored and which were to deepen over the years.[93]

On 9 August 1675 Paston was shot by highwaymen who fired into his carriage as he drove from Kensington. It was a flesh wound (and as one unsympathetic commentator remarked 'he hath flesh enough to spare'[94]) but one which caused great anxiety as the risk of infection was high. When he eventually returned to Norfolk on 16 September he was met by a cavalcade, a procession of friends and well-wishers in their coaches and on horseback who escorted him home in a triumphal procession passing through Norwich, with bells ringing and crowds cheering. Cavalcades were usually reserved for lords lieutenant and visiting dignitaries and this underlined Paston's personal popularity which owed much to his honesty, politeness and sweet

[89]  Rosenheim, *Townshends*, p.83

[90]  Holland made a speech in the House of Commons on 18 October 1675 which was highly critical of the financial mismanagement of the government and the extravagance of the court; he also attacked the frequent prorogations of parliament, the stop of the exchequer in 1672, and the burden of taxation on the people *see* John Miller, 'A Moderate in the First Age of Party: the Dilemmas of Sir John Holland, 1675–1685' (*English Historical Review*, CXIV, 1999, pp pp 861–62) [hereafter Miller, 'Sir John Holland'].

[91]  Yarmouth to Townshend, 2 July 1674 (HMC 19: 11th R.IV. *Townshend*), quoted in Miller, 'Sir John Holland', pp 859–60                                         [92]  Below p.157.

[93]  Hobart to Windham, 28 Jan 1679 (NRO: WKC7/6)

[94]  John Verney to Sir Ralph Verney (HMC 6: 7th R.I., p.465)

temper. He himself was surprised but highly gratified. A fortnight later he visited Great Yarmouth to be inaugurated as their new high steward to which position he had been appointed in January on the death of Lord Clarendon. The reception he received there surpassed all expectation: he was greeted with flags flying, bells ringing, and a salute from all the guns in the harbour, he was entertained nobly, and his retinue was not charged a penny in the inns, even their horses' fodder was provided free. However Paston was well aware that the county was dividing into two camps, and wrote 'I doe nott thinke these favors don mee soe extraordinarily will relish with som of this country ...'.[95] In November Townshend's follower John Pell was appointed to the costly and troublesome office of high sheriff although Townshend had explicitly asked for him to be excused. Townshend's response was to organise an agreement between a number of his supporters to subscribe towards the expenses of Pell and future sheriffs, and where possible to cut costs.[96] This agreement, dated 12 January 1676, was Townshend's parting shot. Not only was it an act of defiance, it was highly divisive: party politics which had previously only been seen at elections were now becoming the norm.

Paston had never been on more than civil terms with Sir John Hobart and his earlier friendship with Lord Townshend appears to have worn out,[97] probably as a result of Townshend's alliance with Hobart. Townshend was about to pay the penalty for his opposition to Lord Danby's son-in-law at King's Lynn and his support of Lord Shaftesbury's opposition party:[98] he lost his lord lieutenancy in the following February and Paston succeeded him. The questions arise: how far was Paston personally ambitious to win the lord lieutenancy for himself, and how far did he initiate the campaign against Townshend?

The Paston letters in the Norfolk Record Office and the British Library contain three copies of an anonymous letter, dated 10 May 1675, to an unnamed member of the House of Commons describing the proceedings at the election of Sir Robert Kemp, and detailing the underhand tricks played by Sir John Hobart, with the support of Lord Townshend, to prevent the votes of Sir Neville Catelyn's supporters from being counted.[99] There is also a copy memorandum in the same hand as one of these letters listing the evil consequences which could arise from continuing a person in the office of lord lieutenant for a number of years. On the same sheet is a copy of a letter from a gentleman in Norfolk to his son in London,[100] dated 29 November 1675, suggesting that he confer with Rebecca, now Lady Yarmouth, and tell her that they can carry on 'what seemes here designed' by subscriptions of many gentleman and clergy, and that she will then tell the Earl Marshal and others.

---

[95] Below p.176.

[96] James M. Rosenheim, 'Party Organisation at the Local Level: the Norfolk Sheriff's Subscription of 1676' (*The Historical Journal*, 29, 3 (1986), pp 713–722).

[97] The Pastons were on sufficiently friendly terms to visit the Townshends at Raynham in November 1671 (Rosenheim, *Townshends*, p.39n).

[98] He gave his proxy vote in the House of Lords to Shaftesbury (NRO: MC1601/22).

[99] Below pp 159–62; British Library: Add. MSS 27447, f.344, 350–3

[100] British Library: Add. MSS 27447, f.353. This was probably written by Sir Henry Bedingfeld to his son (Miller, 'Sir John Holland', p.863n); a case, but not such a good one, could be made for the author being Sir William Doyly: both men were supporters of Paston and both had adult sons who were politically active.

Thus a campaign to promote Paston in Townshend's place had already been put in motion. A letter from Margaret Lady Bedingfeld to Rebecca written in October 1676[101] makes it clear that she and her husband were part of this campaign, and it seems likely that Paston's cavalcades had been to some extent orchestrated by the opposition to Lord Townshend, but there is no information anywhere as to who initiated the campaign.

Paston was later to deny that he had sought to be lord lieutenant[102] and on a personal level there seems no reason to doubt this. His health had deteriorated since the 1660s, and although not a complete invalid (he was still capable of occasionally getting up at four in the morning to go sea fishing)[103] his obesity, gout, scurvy,[104] and recurrent depression would have made him reluctant to be obliged to lead a more active life. Although he had been a deputy lieutenant since 1660 he had attended very few meetings, probably because these were primarily concerned with militia affairs and his health had prevented him from playing any role in the militia. His scientific and other intellectual interests, coupled with his inability to take part in the field sports which were normal for country gentlemen, seem to have led him to lead a rather private life mixing only with his close friends and relatives: his cousin Margaret Bedingfeld, in the letter mentioned above, states that she and her husband are telling everyone of Paston's wit, candour, and sweetness of temper, and laments that 'My lord hath not had the fortune to be knowne enough ...'. Moreover, although his pride in the antiquity and achievements of his family had led him to canvass the King for a peerage and to commission a beautiful and expensive history of his family from the herald Francis Sandford,[105] it would not necessarily have prompted him to aspire to the lieutenancy. He was a realist and would have been well aware that the honour could ruin him: only men of fortune could be lords lieutenant as they were obliged to live and to entertain on a lavish scale. But in the 1670s there were only three noblemen in Norfolk with sufficient wealth and status to be lord lieutenant: they were Townshend, Paston (now viscount Yarmouth), and the Earl Marshal (the future duke of Norfolk); and the Earl Marshal, in most ways the obvious candidate, was ruled out because he was a Roman Catholic.

Paston's financial position remained extremely shaky. In 1671 he had claimed that his estates were worth £3,920 2s 2d p.a. as let.[106] In theory at least he had an additional income of over £3,000 p.a. from his farms of wood, glass, and oranges etc. In practice some part of this went to his brother-in-law Sir John Clayton with whom he was in partnership and he had borrowed against his own share. In the early 1670s before he received his title his debts stood at about £22,000.[107] From 1673 money from the rent he paid for his wood farm went to the firm of Clayton & Morris to settle

---

[101] Below pp 183–4

[102] British Library: Add. MSS 41656, f.54, quoted in Stater, 'Continuity and Change', p.206.

[103] Below p.225.

[104] The term scurvy was sometimes used quite loosely for an illness characterized by pains in the limbs, subcutaneous eruptions, and general debility. Paston does not mention tenderness of gums or loosened teeth which would confirm that he had what is called scurvy in the present day.

[105] It is illustrated with 260 superbly painted coats of arms (Cambridge University Library, MS Add. 6968).

[106] Vallance v. Welldon (TNA: C111/120)                    [107] NRO: NRS 4013

his debts, and on his petition this rent had been reduced early in 1674.[108] Nevertheless many of the mortgages had not been paid off, accruing interest that can only be guessed at, and involving him in expensive lawsuits. He still had three younger sons and two daughters to settle, and was now maintaining a permanent establishment for his wife in London. The lighthouse project and the search for the philosopher's stone continued, and his appointment as high steward of Great Yarmouth had given him fresh hopes of persuading the Yarmouth merchants to invest in Southtown, particularly if he was granted permission to build a new custom house on his side.

Any personal reluctance which Paston may have felt, however, would not have been strong enough to make him refuse to serve his King,[109] and he would also have been extremely reluctant to disoblige Lord Danby without whose influence most of the King's promises would have failed to materialise.[110] Lord Danby knew Paston's financial circumstances: he held out to him the possibility that Paston would benefit from his plans to re-lease the excise to bring more profit to the Crown and to reward the cavaliers,[111] and other financial inducements may have been offered as bait. In February 1676 Paston was so uncharacteristically buoyant that he wrote to Sir Robert Clayton 'I am now neare making my fortune'.[112] Danby had already helped Paston's second son Robert, as it was presumably he who earlier in 1675 had arranged for him to accompany the young earl of Plymouth on his grand tour, thus giving him the opportunity to make a lifelong friend and patron.[113] Plymouth was second of the King's illegitimate sons and was then about seventeen; the oldest, and favourite, was the duke of Monmouth who had been taken up by the country party as a possible protestant heir to the throne. Plymouth, although an outsider, was Danby's entry in the 'heir to the throne stakes', to be brought into his family first through friendship with Robert Paston and later through marriage with one of Danby's daughters.[114] Moreover Lady Danby was soon promising some great although unspecified advantage for Paston's second daughter Mary.[115] Therefore, although it is unlikely that Paston initiated the attack on Lord Townshend, there was never any doubt that he would agree to take on the office of lord lieutenant, and he served from 1676 until his death in 1683.

This volume covers his period in office up to March 1679; the letters for these years comprise almost two thirds of the total printed here, the largest group being written by Paston to his wife in London. The Pastons had rented a house in Suffolk

---

[108] *CTB, 4, 1672–1675*, pp 209–10, 214

[109] He wrote to Sir John Holland that nothing but the fear of losing the King's favour would have made him accept, see n.102 above.

[110] However he was sufficiently independent to vote for a dissolution in November 1675 against Lord Danby's wishes.

[111] Andrew Browning, *Thomas Osborne, Earl of Danby and Duke of Leeds, 1632–1712* (Glasgow, 1944–1951) I, pp 209–11, III, pp 4–6 [hereafter Browning, *Leeds*].

[112] Lord Yarmouth to Sir Robert Clayton, 5 Feb 1676 (NRO: NRS 4018)

[113] This grand tour was not an unmixed pleasure as Plymouth was a very spoilt young man but Robert Paston wrote in Feb 1675 that he was 'altered in every thing for the better' and worked hard to gain his favour; below pp 148–9, 153.

[114] Robert accompanied Plymouth to the Low Countries in 1677, see below p. 279 and NRO: NRS 4008; Plymouth married Lady Bridget Osborne on 19 Sept 1678. [115] Below p. 218.

Street[116] since at least 1671 and now Rebecca spent much of her time there. By the 1670s her years of childbearing were safely over[117] and she had matured into a forceful and ambitious woman. There can be no doubt that she urged her husband to accept the lord lieutenancy. The marriage was one of equals, she advised and encouraged her husband, and he trusted her judgement, and wrote to her 'you are the hinge our affaires hangs upon'. If he was too busy to write, his secretary or his chaplain reported to her, knowing that she had a complete grasp of politics and personalities in Norfolk, Norwich and Great Yarmouth. In London she appeared at court, made friendships and alliances, traded gossip, flattered, intrigued, and watched out for any advantage which could be seized for her family. The Pastons used a simple cipher when writing to each other; the earliest example dates from 1675.[118] Rebecca instructed her husband to destroy all her letters: she no doubt thought that it would be impossible for him to keep her correspondence safe in such a large house with constant visitors. Consequently there is only one half of this coded correspondence extant. The cipher enabled the Pastons to write freely about their prospects, whether the King could be persuaded to keep his promises, and how far they could rely on help from Lord and Lady Danby to whom Rebecca paid court assiduously.

This was no easy task, and one for which Rebecca was not temperamentally suited. The Danbys appear to have been a most unlikeable couple,[119] and like Lady Danby, Rebecca was an ambitious and strong-willed woman. Her dislike of Lady Danby led to exaggeration and Paston wrote to her 'You tell me allwayes stories of [*Lady Danby*] which I dare sweare she never thinkes of'.[120] Few of Rebecca's own letters have survived. Those to Paston are lively and affectionate and those to Lady Danby are defensive and obsequious,[121] but the replies written by William Aglionby to those she addressed to him when he was accompanying William Paston through France in 1671 show that she could be both rude and aggressive to her social inferiors. This could hardly have failed to arouse hostility, and she may have been additionally disliked in Norfolk because she made it obvious that she preferred London. Sir John Hobart wrote of her 'a great lady layes aboute her with her flaming sword, which if it were well edged would wound as well as defend, but its know[n] to be soe ill sett that it will doe neyther',[122] and the author of the memorandum of 1682 wrote 'The inactiveness of the lord lieutenant is a great discouragement to the party, for, though he is respected for his other good qualities, yet the gentry of his party equally mislike his little love of business and his lady's too much meddling in it.'[123] Paston then had only a year to live and the accusations were substantially true. But since he was so well liked one suspects that his opponents were reduced to attacking him through his

[116] A street of fashionable new houses built by the earl of Suffolk in the 1660s (G.H. Gater & F.R. Hiorns (ed.), *Survey of London*: volume 20 (1940), pp 89–94).

[117] She had borne ten children and lost three.

[118] For details of the Paston ciphers see Appendix 1.

[119] John Evelyn described Danby as 'a man of excellent natural parts, but nothing generous or grateful' (Guy de la Bedoyere (ed.), *The Diary of John Evelyn* (Woodbridge, 1995), p.199), and Lady Danby was famous for her unpleasantness.

[120] Below p.314.                          [121] *see* British Library: Egerton MS 3338, ff 122–127

[122] Hobart to Windham, 1 Mar 1679 (NRO: WKC7/6)

[123] Above pp 6–7, and *see* British Library: Add. MSS 36988, f.233 for a vituperous anonymous letter written after Lord Yarmouth's death to his son William attacking Lady Yarmouth's character.

less popular wife. Nevertheless, Paston adored her and his letters are signed 'your most passionate friend & servant till death', 'with all the facultys of sowle & body I am yours', 'he who loves you above the world', and 'yours to the last'. He constantly lamented their separation and lived for her letters, reading them a dozen times before destroying them because, sadly, he appears to have been the one member of his family in three centuries of letter-writing to obey the command 'burn this'.

On 6 March 1676 Paston was created lord lieutenant of Norfolk, and on 30 March he returned to Oxnead to take up office. He has been seen as the champion of high-flying Anglicans, and this is certainly what Lord Danby expected him to be, but the reality was not so simple. Norfolk had accepted the Commonwealth without much enthusiasm but with very little armed resistance from the royalists; loyalist clergy were ejected but the Norfolk clergy were on the whole broad church, most of them having studied at Cambridge (as did Paston himself), which bred fewer highflyers than Oxford. Edward Reynolds who was appointed bishop of Norwich after the Restoration was a noted moderate, having been a Presbyterian under the protectorate (even though he was an Oxford man), and many moderate nonconformists attended their parish church as well as their meeting house. Paston himself was certainly a high church Anglican for historical, political, doctrinal, and aesthetic reasons,[124] and when Reynolds died he welcomed his replacement by Anthony Sparrow, formerly bishop of Exeter, a notable high church Anglican. Paston's lifelong melancholy did not manifest itself in any form of religious excess. He was devout but his letters do not contain any overt religiosity until the winter of 1678 when he survived a serious illness and was persuaded to give up swearing,[125] and he showed no inclination to impose his views on anyone else: he was tolerant towards both dissenters and Roman Catholics provided they were loyal, and took no part in persecuting Quakers.[126] Rebecca's religion was rather more extreme: for example in 1675 she gave directions to John Gough, rector of Oxnead, for a service of thanksgiving on the recovery of her husband from his wounds which Gough felt obliged to tone down, and thus 'defeated them of an opportunity of mirth who perhaps lay at catch for one'.[127] (Unfortunately Rebecca's directions to Gough have not survived.) She was also seen as the protector and supporter of such highflyers as Dr Owen Hughes, commissary of the archdeaconries of Norfolk and Norwich, whose support of Catelyn against Kemp had aroused the hostility of Lord Townshend and led to his facing a charge of *scandalum magnatum*,[128] and Dr John Hildeyard, rector of Cawston, whose appointment as a JP through her patronage was to add greatly to her unpopularity. Both men wrote her letters full of florid and obsequious hyperbole, extreme even by seventeenth-century standards. Paston was of course their patron, but remarked dispassionately about Hildeyard that parsons were 'silly animals' in the management of their own affairs.[129]

The high Anglican gentry supporting the Norfolk version of the court or 'loyal' party included families like the Astleys and Wodehouses, but they are seldom

[124] For an inventory of the sumptuous furnishings of the chapel at Oxnead *see* British Library: Add. MSS 36988, f.255v, printed in Wenley, 'Robert Paston and the Yarmouth Collection', p.138.

[125] Hildeyard, *Sermon*, pp 28, 31

[126] John Miller, 'Containing Division in Restoration Norwich' (*English Historical Review*, CXXI, 2006, pp 1034, 1039)

[127] Below p.168.     [128] Below p.188.     [129] Below p.231.

mentioned in Paston's letters, and his proceedings at the start of his lieutenancy can be better understood by identifying the most active of his supporters. There were few Roman Catholic gentry in Norfolk and they supported Paston rather than Townshend. The Earl Marshal, the greatest magnate in the county, was a personal friend and patron: Castle Rising, the borough which Paston represented from 1661 to 1673, was in his gift. Although debarred by his religion from playing an active role in politics, the earl had very wide influence in the county and also in Norwich where he lived. Another Roman Catholic, Sir Henry Bedingfeld the elder, who had married Paston's cousin Margaret Paston of Appleton, was a close friend and supporter, as was his son Sir Henry Bedingfeld the younger, and Paston was also on friendly terms with Jack Tasburgh of Bodney. Although there was almost universal fear and mistrust of papists throughout England, like most country gentlemen Paston did not extend this to those Roman Catholics whom he actually knew; indeed one branch of his own family, the Pastons of Appleton, had remained Catholic. At the other end of the spectrum there was Sir William Doyly of Shotesham who had been a friend of Paston's father and a trustee in his will, and who had lent money to Paston.[130] He had been active in the county during the Interregnum but like Townshend was a strong supporter of the Restoration. He was MP for Great Yarmouth where many of the electors were dissenters; and though 'not an active of the nonconformist cause' his own religion can best be described as low church.[131] Doyly, who might have been expected to support Lord Townshend and the emerging country party, was nevertheless one of Paston's most active supporters, and helped to arrange a magnificent cavalcade when he first entered the county as lord lieutenant.

Major Robert Doughty was also an unlikely supporter: he had been a major in a Norfolk regiment of foot under Sir John Hobart in 1650, served as an excise commissioner in the late 1650s, and had married a cousin of Lord Townshend.[132] Doughty lived a few miles from Oxnead at Aylsham, but much of the time he was part of Paston's 'family' at Oxnead with his son John who became Paston's secretary: when Paston closed his letters to his wife he generally presented the services of Mrs Cooper, his housekeeper, John Gough, his chaplain, and Major Doughty. Doughty seems to have been an intelligent man and an efficient organiser and he rapidly emerged as Paston's right-hand man. Although he held no commission in the militia he was involved in its organisation and he became a justice of the peace; even when his son John was suspected of, at best, an indiscretion in revealing information to the opposition party in Norwich, John Gough advised that nothing should be done against him because Major Doughty was too useful to Paston to risk losing him.[133]

[130]  Sir William Doyly (c.1614–1677), of Shotesham, Norfolk, MP for Great Yarmouth.

[131]  Gauci, *Great Yarmouth*, p.105.

[132]  *CSPD, 1650*, p.504; *CSPD, 1658–9*, p.107; marriage of Robert Doughty and Katherine Townshend, 13 Aug 1639 at St Michael at Plea, Norwich; Katherine was the daughter of Roger Townshend of Horstead, see *The Visitation of Norfolk, 1664* (NRS, IV (1933), p.69).

[133]  John Doughty continued in his post at least until 1679 when his father died, and probably longer. In January 1681 Lord Yarmouth wrote to Edward L'estrange that he was without a secretary as he had recommended Doughty for a position in Barbados; he went out there with Sir Richard Dutton, the new governor, and apparently became solicitor general in 1683. (British Library: Add. MSS 27448, f.1; *CSP Colonial, America and West Indies, vol.11, 1681–1685*). It is worth noting that Paston was always extremely averse to hearing anything ill of a friend (Hildeyard, *Sermon*, pp 17–18).

He even won favour with the high Anglicans. Owen Hughes recommended him for the commission of the peace in glowing terms: 'Major Doughty is a person whose worth and integrity render him beloved of all, whose activeness and sagacity have contributed much to our recovery, whose judgement and experience equalls if not exceeds the best is beyond comparison the fittest man to be upon the bench of all mentioned.'[134] Nevertheless there may have been doubt at some stage as to Doughty's religion as he made a point of stating in his will that he was a true son of the protestant church 'as now established by law'.[135] Both Doyly and Doughty are examples of former Commonwealth supporters who had thrived after the Restoration. They were also men whom Paston had known since childhood and knew to be loyal to the King, and at the beginning of his lieutenancy at least he valued loyalty above religious conformity.

Having agreed to serve, Paston acted decisively, indeed 'his unexpected zeal in public affairs begat wonder and admiration'.[136] Almost his first act was to invite all previous deputy lieutenants to continue in office. In this he was acting contrary to the expectations of Lord and Lady Danby, and contrary to the advice given him by both Robert Doughty and Sir Henry Bedingfeld the younger,[137] but he told his wife 'a man in my post must act with decency and soe I will and my owne method in that will bee my best guide'.[138] He could hardly have expected, or wanted, Sir John Hobart to continue to serve, but it is likely that by issuing this general invitation, he hoped to make it easier for Sir John Holland to accept. Holland, a moderate married to a Roman Catholic, was his father's first cousin and his own youngest daughter's godfather.[139] Even when Holland refused Paston continued to try to win him over for the loyal party. In the event, only three others declined to serve: Hobart, Kemp, and Sir Peter Gleane, all with civil expressions of regret and the latter claiming that he would have served under Paston had it not been for his friendship with Townshend. Friendship and kinship were still more important than party: although most of Paston's correspondents referred to Hobart and Holland together as 'the two Sir Johns', Paston himself distinguished sharply between them although both supported the country party, for he detested Hobart but was clearly very fond of Holland.

The new lord lieutenant's most important duty was to settle the militia with competent officers and by this means to reward loyalty and to dispense offices among his supporters. Great Yarmouth posed problems as it was largely nonconformist. Paston had fully intended to promote the royalist and Anglican Sir Thomas Medowe, but found that in spite of this the latter used him 'peremptorily standing upon terms' insisting that the nonconformist militia officers be turned out. Paston quickly realised that Medowe was going to be more trouble than he was worth and proceeded to organise the Great Yarmouth militia without him, adding even more dissenting officers, concluding that though he had 'designed all the kindness in the world' to Medowe, 'itts impossible to please all'.[140] His proceedings certainly did not please Richard Bower, a coffeehouse keeper and government informer in Great Yarmouth,

[134] Hughes to Lady Yarmouth, 1 Mar 1676 (British Library: Add. MSS 36988, f.109v).
[135] NRO: NCC, original will, 1679, no. 8.    [136] Hildeyard, *Sermon*, p.26
[137] Below pp 192, 194–5.    [138] Below p.234.    [139] Below p.223.    [140] Below p.238.

who promptly reported the situation to Sir Joseph Williamson, secretary of state, claiming that the magistrates of Yarmouth were not putting down nonconformist meetings because they were nonconformists themselves, and that the lord lieutenant was too much influenced by Sir William Doyly and Major Doughty.[141] Even the highflyers among the clergy had had sufficient common sense not to attack the lord lieutenant's closest associates: Paston was not putting up with presumption and joined with the dissenting magistrates in closing down Bower's coffeehouse. Once again Paston chose to act as he judged best from his knowledge of local conditions; he set more store by the loyalty of the Great Yarmouth merchants than by their religion.

Life had changed at Oxnead which was now the hub of Norfolk affairs. As the King's representative in the county Paston was obliged to keep court and to entertain on an heroic scale: this was his duty and his obligation. His gentry supporters from around the county now streamed into his house for congratulations, consultations, and dinner. Within three weeks Paston had decided to limit his public dinners to two a week but this proved impossible to keep to as most people rolled up unannounced. His expenses soared: even within a week of Paston's arrival in Norfolk his steward John Hurton was warning Rebecca, who audited his accounts, that 'while expenses run at this very high rate, all the money that can be raised upon Lady rent will never answer them'.[142] The new lease of the excise was now crucial and was discussed in code in virtually every letter, and in July Paston felt sufficiently confident to start recruiting excise officers; but by the autumn his hopes were at an end and the excise was later leased to the previous farmer with a new group of partners.

Paston returned to London in August 1676 and remained there for the best part of a year. He and Rebecca suffered a devastating blow when their much-loved middle daughter died of smallpox in November 1676. Parliament sat from February to May 1677, being adjourned until July; Paston attended regularly and was present on 16 July when there was a further adjournment and he was able to return to Oxnead. When his letters to Rebecca resume in August 1677 it is clear that the family's financial position had worsened, that there was no immediate prospect of any improvement, and he wrote 'all the hopes of my enemies is now to see mee fall for lack of the ingredient which makes all thinges moove cheerefully', his debts being common knowledge in Norfolk.[143] He had already petitioned the King for a grant of £1,900 payable out of the wood farm for the next five years claiming that he was forced by the numbers of people resorting daily to Oxnead 'to live in greater port and expense than his revenue will well maintain', and the grant had been made, though payable to William Goulston of the firm of Clayton & Morris, and a further £1,000 out of the wood farm had been granted to his son William for ten years.[144] Rebecca, ever resourceful, was now in hot pursuit of another opportunity presented by a scheme of Percival Brunskell, a clerk of the Rolls Chapel, to oust the current receiver and surveyor of the greenwax (an office for the collection of various fines and fees from the

[141] *CSPD, 1676–7*, pp 155–7          [142] Below p.197.          [143] Below p.282.
[144] *CTB, 5, 1676–1679*, pp 721, 852, 1117, 1347; William immediately assigned his annuity to William Lightfoot of London (NRO: NRS, 4010, 5019); he also obtained a printing patent (*CSPD, 1678*, pp 156–7); he is said to have still been in receipt of a pension of £2000 p.a. at the time of his death (*The London Magazine*, December 1732)

exchequer courts) and to replace him by a consortium of nobles with himself as the active member.[145] Paston was to be one of the group and it was hoped the office might produce £40,000 p.a. to be shared between them.[146] Here at last was a triumph for Rebecca: after months of negotiations and persuasion the grant was finally made in May 1678. Long before then however Paston had urgent need of money, as one of the MPs for Norwich had died and he was determined to secure the seat for his eldest son. Norwich was the second city in England; all freemen, totalling over 2,800 in 1678, had the vote, including numbers of dissenters.[147] There was some opposition to William Paston's election, but even though the nonconformist mayor created 362 new freemen in a single month, Paston's popularity was such that he was able to secure an overwhelming victory for his son on 10 February 1678.[148] As the day of the election approached he wrote 'I never was soe weary of any business in my life, and shall not embark in the licke kind againe', but in fact his period as an election manager had only just started.

Paston had now been two years in office and had little enthusiasm for it. Apart from the expense and the loss of privacy, there were other pressures which he attempted to cope with by becoming harder and less scrupulous. On 25 March 1678 he wrote 'I now perceive that every mann's business that I cannott compose as I would if I must lay itt to hart will suddainely breake mine and in my troublesom office, where various applications of diverse concernes are made, I must learne to doe as other men in more troublesom places doe lett thinges in their mind runn indifferently', and he resolved not 'to draw an old howse on my head which had better stand rotten then directly tumble ... and pray doe you observe the same methods, winke att thinges you cannot help'. A month later he was working to influence the aldermanic elections in Norwich and separating the sheep from the goats on the bench, and although he wrote to Rebecca 'I resolve after this push to withdraw my self from all thinges that doe nott immediately concerne my place for att this rate a man shall never have a quiett hower', the changing political situation was propelling him into extreme actions.[149]

The country party in parliament around Lord Shaftesbury (soon to be known as the Whig party) was now providing stiff opposition to the court party and beginning to agitate for the exclusion of the Catholic duke of York from the succession to the throne. Most royalists were also unhappy about the prospect of a Catholic King, but their loyalty was to the Crown rather than to individuals, and they were not prepared to let parliament dictate the succession. As the country party was widely known as the 'godly party' memories of the Commonwealth came flooding back and the loyalty of the dissenters became once more suspect. Paston's initially tolerant attitude hardened; politics in Norfolk now became polarised and matters became worse as the year progressed: the discovery of the Popish Plot brought anti-Catholic feeling to new

---

[145] For a hostile account of Brunskell's proceedings *see* Roger North, *Lives of the Norths* (London, 1890), I, pp 138–140); Danby helped to put the current receiver, Thomas Aram, out of place because he was a protégé of his arch-enemy in the treasury, Sir Robert Howard (Stephen B. Baxter, *The Development of the Treasury, 1660–1702* (Cambridge, Mass., 1957), but it is clear from Paston's letters that he could not count on Danby's support.            [146] Below p.317.

[147] John Miller, 'Containing Division in Restoration Norwich', *passim*

[148] For an account of the election see NRO: MS 453            [149] Below p.333.

heights, Danby fell from office and faced impeachment, and parliament was dissolved in January 1679. It is unlikely that the Pastons felt any real regret at Danby's fall. As Henry Savile wrote, 'in the midst of his friendship now and then [were] such mortifications that, although some men may out of point of honour lament him, few besides his own family will do it out of any other reason'.[150] However they appear to have underestimated the political changes that were to follow.

Paston's duty as lord lieutenant was to keep Norfolk loyal to the Crown, and he saw it as part of that duty to ensure that supporters of the court party were elected to the new parliament in 1679. Although he had little difficulty in controlling Norwich where his son and Augustine Briggs were re-elected in spite of opposition from some of the nonconformists, in the election for the knights of the shire he faced opposition from Sir John Hobart and resorted to heavy-handed tactics to ensure the election of the loyalist candidates by writing letters backing Sir Christopher Calthorpe and Sir Nevill Catelyn and questioning the right of anyone else to stand without informing him.[151] These letters were construed as threats, although Paston wrote to his wife 'As for the noyse of the election, & mine & the bishop's letters, trouble nott your head, wee have defeated a strong contrivance against the right interest, and could their harts bee looked into they are ashamed & confounded att itt', and insisted 'for my letters I care nott if they were on the parlament howse dore'.[152] No lord lieutenant was expected to be impartial, and Paston's electioneering in 1679 was no more partisan than that of Townshend in 1675, but in spite of his reassuring words to his wife, he was clearly aware that he had sailed a little too close to the wind. On 7 February 1679 he wrote to Sir Joseph Williamson 'I morally secure myself I shall send up Sir Christopher Calthorpe and Sir Neville Catelyn, men that will not meddle with ministers of state. I am afraid we shall not have a poll for it, for I have been a little bold in my declaration.'[153] As promised, Calthorpe and Catelyn were elected, but the composition of the new House of Commons must have filled him with dismay. Sir John Hobart petitioned against their return and Paston's defence had no chance of success in an overwhelmingly Whig parliament, which promptly overturned the result.[154] In fact Paston had been outstandingly successful in holding both the county and the boroughs for the 'loyal party' and it was in recognition of that that the King, after prompting, gave Paston his coveted earldom in the following July.

The last years of Paston's life are not covered by this volume. His health deteriorated – he had had serious illnesses in the winters of 1677 and 1678 – and although he could afford constant medical attention and the most expensive and esoteric medicines they almost certainly did more harm than good. Latterly he spent less time at Oxnead – his sons had grown up and departed and his youngest daughter was now of an age to appear at court. He and Rebecca never ceased to pursue possible financial advantages although he was losing hope: in 1679 he wrote 'I confess I cannott bee in love with histories without effects, I am old ... and menn's lives are nott long enough to embarke in affaires whose course is soe tedious, and perhapps frivolous, I

[150] William Durrant Cooper (ed.), *Savile Correspondence* (Camden Society, LXII (1858), p.78)
[151] Below p.370.                    [152] Below pp 368–70                    [153] *CSPD, 1679–80*, p.75.
[154] *Journal of the House of Commons*: volume 9: 1667–1687 (1802), March-April 1679. John Hildeyard later claimed that Paston was threatened with impeachment (Hildeyard, *Sermon*, p.22).

wish itt may proove otherwise, for I pray to God every day to crowne your industry with such success as may makes us experience the continuation of his miraculous preservations in many brinkes of approaching ruine & contempt' and he described their mounting debts and the impending lawsuits as a 'whirlepoole of misadventures'.[155]

Most of the letters from the autumn of 1679 until his death relate to his battle to make the city of Norwich surrender their old charter and accept a new one, and he worked tirelessly for the King's interest purging dissenters from the bench and the corporations and organising loyal addresses. Although scarcely able to walk, he attended the House of Lords and opposed attempts to exclude the Catholic duke of York from the succession. He died in London on 8 March 1683 at the age of 51, and was buried at Oxnead. John Hildeyard preached his funeral sermon in Norwich Cathedral.[156] It is impossible to say exactly what he died of, but his daughter Margaret Alberti, who seems to have inherited something of her mother's abrasive manner, wrote to Rebecca 'perhaps if my dear father had contented him self with the holesum aire of pore Oxned without troubleing him with state afairs & folowing the court that your ladyship would not now be a widoe'.[157] But in spite of his constant ill-health (and the hours he had spent in vaporising mercury) he had lived what was considered a normal span for a man of his class – Townshend, Hobart, the duke of Norfolk, and the King were all to die in their fifties – however he died heavily in debt and was unable to make any provision for his four younger children.[158]

William Paston succeeded him as second earl. There was by then probably no chance that the family's financial situation could have been turned round, but the second earl did not make the attempt. Long before his father's death he was himself deeply in debt.[159] Hardly any of his correspondence or financial papers have survived but those that have document an ominous interest in alchemy and mining rather than estate management.[160] He and his mother retained the income from the wood farm and were able to pay some of the first earl's debts, but the independence of the petty farms was coming to an end and the lease expired in 1688.[161] He retained some influence in Norfolk politics, based on his father's personal popularity, but lost much of this by making himself recorder of Norwich against fierce opposition. He was briefly lord chamberlain of the household to James II and converted to Roman Catholicism. After the revolution of 1688 he refused to take the oath of allegiance to William and Mary and was twice imprisoned in the Tower.[162] In 1696 he took the oaths and resumed his seat in the House of Lords. The last personal glimpse of him is in 1708: 'The Earle of Yarmouth is as low as you can imagin; he hath vast debts,

[155] Below pp 377, 378          [156] Hildeyard, *Sermon*

[157] Margaret Alberti to Lady Yarmouth, 28 July 1683 (British Library: Add. MSS 36988, f.220)

[158] TNA: PROB11/373          [159] NRO: NRS 4009–4011, 4019–4029

[160] British Library: Add. MSS 27448, 36988

[161] Baxter, *The Development of the Treasury*, pp 27–8; see *CTB, 8, 1685–1689*, pp 446–7 for the history of the farm and the grants made from the rent, 1685; petition from Lady Yarmouth to James II, [1687], stating they have improved the wood farm from £4000 to £19,000 p.a. and giving details of the family's financial situation (British Library: Add. MSS 27448, ff 251–2).

[162] The best account of the second earl's career is to be found in Ketton-Cremer, 'The End of the Pastons', pp 49–56.

and suffers every thing to run to extremity; soe his goods have been all seised in execution and his lands extended, soe that he hath scarce a servant to attend him or an
horse to ride abroad upon, and yett cannot be perswaded to take any method of put-
teing his affairs into a better posture, wch they are still capable of, if he would set
about it.'[163] Nevertheless he remained active in the House of Lords into the 1720s,
and became a fellow of the Royal Society in 1722. On his death in 1732 the title
became extinct.[164] He died massively in debt and the estates were sold ultimately
fetching £92,700 in 1764, his creditors receiving 11s 3d in the pound.[165]

The Pastons went from being the wealthiest gentry family in Norfolk to total ruin,
and the most rapid and serious decline was in the lifetime of Robert Paston, first earl
of Yarmouth. Without estate accounts and records of expenditure it is impossible to
tell whether there was any point at which things might have been turned around.
There is no information in the letters about Paston's management of his estates or
even whether he took much interest. The 1670s were an unfavourable period for agri-
culture[166] but other Norfolk landowners at this time, such as William Windham of
Felbrigg and Lord Townshend of Raynham, were active in improving their estates.[167]
Paston's agent John Hurton is generally referred to as morose or sullen; he was an
elderly man and may have been resistant to change. On the other hand he may have
been permanently depressed at Paston's unwillingness to invest in his estates. There

[163]  Edward Maunde Thompson (ed.), *Letters of Humphrey Prideaux ... to John Ellis* (Camden Soc. XV, 1875,
p.200)
[164]  The second earl had had four sons, two of whom lived to manhood but predeceased him. The fact
that not one male descendant of the first earl was alive in 1732 was said by some to be the (belated) result
of a curse by a mediaeval prior of Bromholm who prophesied that each generation would produce a Paston
of 'feeble intellect' until the family died poor (Ketton-Cremer, 'The End of the Pastons', pp 55–6; C.J.
Palmer, *The Perlustration of Great Yarmouth*, (Great Yarmouth, 1872) I, pp 130–131). The complex network
of kinship among the Norfolk gentry, the result of interbreeding for generations, would have increased the
risk of physical and mental defects in some of these families. This may have been true of the Pastons, certainly the first earl's grandfather and his uncle had been found incapable of managing their own affairs,
but the first earl's mother Lady Katherine Bertie was not related to his father, Sir William Paston, and
there seems to be no evidence to support suggestions that the first earl's brothers were feeble minded. The
fact that they are poorly documented seems to have been taken as proof that they were obliged to live
secluded lives, whereas the little evidence that exists suggests the opposite. For example the first earl's
youngest brother took his MA at St Catharine's, Cambridge, and died of smallpox in Paris. The first earl
himself also married a woman to whom he was not related and there is no suggestion in the letters that
their sons were anything other than normal: the three younger sons all pursued careers in the army or
navy which resulted in the deaths of the two youngest in their twenties. Their failure to produce heirs for
the earldom should probably be attributed not only to these early deaths but also to the fact that their
impecuniousness had led them all to marry widows, some of advanced years. The three brothers produced
one son each, only one of whom reached maturity, and he, a naval captain, was lost in the wreck of HMS
*Feversham* in 1711. Although there were no male heirs, the first earl had four granddaughters living in 1732,
three of whom married and had children. Finally, although the first earl suffered from lifelong depression,
there is no hint in any of his letters that he had any fear of hereditary insanity.
[165]  Palmer, *Perlustration*, I, p.130: based on these figures, and the National Archives' currency converter
for 2005, plus a conservative 3% p.a. inflation for each year from 2006–2012, the earl's debts in current
money totalled at least £15,000,000.
[166]  John Spurr, *England in the 1670s* (Oxford, 2000), pp 120–123
[167]  *see* Elizabeth Griffiths (ed.), *William Windham's Green Book, 1673–1688* (NRS LXVI, 2002). I am grateful to Dr Griffiths for pointing out to me that Sir Joseph Ashe, the father-in-law of both Windham and
Townshend, had greatly improved his own estate at Downton manor, Wilts, and presumably encouraged
his sons-in-law to do the same.

is simply no evidence. All that is clear is that a great deal of money flowed into the Pastons' hands and flowed out again. There was the income from their estates and from the wood farm.[168] They probably never derived any benefit from the greenwax grant because it was rescinded in 1679 after the fall of Danby left them without a powerful protector, and long before they could have recouped their outlay, and in spite of strenuous efforts by Rebecca and by Percival Brunskell it was never renewed.[169] The King was extremely generous to Paston, even before Danby was in a position to use his influence. Paston has been described as a personal friend of the King's: this is unlikely, most of Charles's inner circle were younger, wittier, and racier, but he may well have liked him – most people did.[170] By the end of Paston's life virtually all the rent he paid to the treasury for the wood farm had been assigned to settle either his debts or his son's debts, but apparently without any real effect. The Pastons did their utmost to get other money-making projects off the ground. There were the lighthouses, the development of Southtown, the projected custom house, the lease of the excise, and the greenwax, and latterly they invested in a papermaking process,[171] and in lead mines in Cheshire and Derbyshire:[172] other projects are hinted at but not documented,[173] and there was the philosopher's stone – for the Pastons there was always a crock of gold at the end of the rainbow.

A number of causes can be identified for the family's financial debacle in the seventeenth century: there was Sir William Paston's building and alterations to Oxnead and his extensive grand tour, the accumulation of the Paston treasure, the fines under the Commonwealth, and the debts incurred by Robert Paston in raising money for the King in exile. Then after the Restoration and the grant of the wood farm, two events put paid to their recovery which might have been achieved, or at least attempted, by serious retrenchment. The first was the King's visit in 1671 which prevented the mortgages from being paid off, and the second was Paston's agreeing to serve as lord lieutenant. There was never any way in which he could have supported the expense which the position demanded of him without a major new source of income. It was not even a position which he enjoyed and it brought long periods of separation from his wife. Rebecca's expenses in London must also be factored into the equation: there was the rent of their London house (first in Suffolk Street, then

---

[168] Estimates of the annual income from the wood farm are so varied as to be almost useless, and there is no information at all as to the expenses and remuneration of the sub-farmers. Roger North in *Lives of the Norths* (quoted in Ketton-Cremer, 'The End of the Pastons', p.52) suggests that the wood farm yielded a total of £100,000 to the Pastons, but on the first earl's death it was valued at only £10,000 for the whole five years it still had to run (TNA: PROB32/33/39).

[169] British Library: Add. MSS 27447, ff 447, 449, 468, 472, 476–479, 484, 486, 490, 27448, ff 11, 162, 193, 205, 217–32. In spite of his poor health (he suffered from asthma), Brunskell proved so tenacious in petitioning about the greenwax and other matters that on 13 April 1700 the lords of the treasury offered him £50 not to trouble the office any more, and to go to New York (*CTB, 6, 1679–1680*, pp 169, 660, 662, *CTB, 7, 1681–1685*, pp 125, 365, 370, 455, *CTB, 9, 1689–1692*, pp 101–115, 416–7, 583; *Journal of the House of Commons, 11*, 9 Apr 1695, 30 Dec 1696; *Calendar of Treasury Papers, 2, 1697–1702*, pp 359–60; *CSPD, 1699*, pp 318, 395; *CTB, 17, 1702*, p.878.

[170] Hildeyard said that he had 'free access ... unto his Majesty upon most occasions' and that the King publicly embraced him in the House of Lords more than once (Hildeyard, *Sermon*, p.26).

[171] Below p.378n.

[172] British Library: Add. MSS 27747, ff 451, 452, 457, 460, 461, 463, 465, 27448, f.40, 53, 143.

[173] Yarmouth to duke of York, 7 Aug 1682 (British Library: Add. MSS 27448, f.111).

in Pall Mall),[174] her chaise, her clothes and her servants. Her efforts brought no permanent success, but without her presence at court, negotiating and intriguing, they would have got nothing at all.

It is interesting to compare Paston's finances with those of Lord Townshend. They are like two lines on a graph, rising and falling in turn, but in 1676 the two lines diverged for ever. Townshend was heavily in debt when he was ousted as lord lieutenant. His first marriage was childless, but in 1673 he had married for a second time and soon had a nursery full of small sons. Consequently he turned his energies to safeguarding their inheritance by improving the management of his estates. But as Townshend's line on the graph rose that of Paston sank. The status of the Paston family was never higher than in 1679 when Robert Paston was made earl of Yarmouth in recognition of his services to the King as lord lieutenant of Norfolk, but financially he was in a state of headlong and irreversible decline. Although the lord lieutenancy was the highest office achieved by a member of the family it ruined them. Paston was unable to escape from his whirlpool of misadventures and the rising tide of debt closed over the heads of his posterity.

[174] Lord Townshend paid £300 p.a. for a house in Soho in the 1680s (Rosenheim, *Townshends*, p.76).

# EDITORIAL NOTES

## The Letters

When Francis Blomefield, the Norfolk county historian, was recovering from an illness in 1735, he was granted access to the muniment room at Oxnead, where his father-in-law was rector, in return for his help in putting the manuscripts there into some kind of order. He reported to Major Thomas Weldon, the son-in-law of the second earl of Yarmouth, that among the thirty or forty chests of archives he had found 'innumerable letters, of good consequence in history'. The earliest of these letters, dating from the fifteenth-century, would have been recognized by Blomefield as unique as there was, and still is, no comparable collection of family correspondence from such an early date. The first selection was published simply as *Original letters, Written during the Reigns of Henry VI, Edward IV and Richard III by Various Persons of Rank or Consequence* (edited by John Fenn) in 1787, and they have been known to successive generations simply as the Paston Letters. More comprehensive editions followed and their full publication was finally completed in 2005.

These and many later documents were removed from the muniment room in circumstances which remain obscure: the second earl of Yarmouth had died in 1732, heavily in debt and without a male heir, the contents of his library, his pictures and furnishings were sold in 1734, and Oxnead rapidly fell into disrepair. Soon after Blomefield's visit it was abandoned and largely demolished. There seems to have been an element of randomness, perhaps reflecting the physical accessibility of the documents, in what was taken. Apart from the fifteenth-century letters, a scattering of papers from the early sixteenth century to the end of the seventeenth century has survived but it contains only two major groups of correspondence: the first is a group of letters of Katherine, Lady Paston (c.1578–1629),[1] the second is a far larger collection of correspondence of her grandson Robert Paston, first earl of Yarmouth (1631–1683).

There seems no doubt that the whole collection passed into Blomefield's possession, and after his death was purchased in 1755 from his widow by his friend and fellow antiquary 'Honest Tom' Martin (1697–1771), a compulsive collector of books and manuscripts. When Martin died his collection was disposed of in a series of auctions and sales. The emergence of such important material from the Oxnead muniment room seems to have given rise to something resembling a feeding frenzy among the Norfolk antiquaries. Bundles were broken up and the letters were dispersed in a number of sales, becoming widely scattered through many collections. David Stoker[2] gives a complete history of the ownership of the fifteenth-century Paston letters, their dispersal, and their gradual acquisition by the British Library. However his article does not trace the ownership of the later material, most of which was also acquired

---

[1] R. Hughey (ed.), *The Correspondence of Lady Katherine Paston, 1603–1627* (NRS, XIV (1941)).

[2] *See* David Stoker, 'Innumerable letters of good consequence in history: the discovery and first publication of the Paston Letters' (*The Library: Transactions of the Bibliographical Society*, XVII, (1995), 107–155).

by the British Library with the exception of two volumes of letters of the first earl of Yarmouth now in the Norfolk Record Office.

In 1773, the Norfolk Record Office letters were in the possession of John Ives (1751–1776), antiquary, herald, and historian of Great Yarmouth, who had helped Martin's widow in the administration of his estate and who bought large numbers of the manuscripts. He presumably chose these letters of the first earl of Yarmouth because they contain interesting material relating to Great Yarmouth. His ownership is documented because in that year he printed *Select Papers* from his collection and included part of Thomas Henshaw's letter to Sir Robert Paston of 13 October 1670.[3] While the letters were in his possession, Ives sorted them into date order and had them bound into two volumes with the bookplate of Francis Blomefield dated 1736.[4] After Ives's death his collections were auctioned in London in 1777 and the volumes were listed as 'Lord Yarmouth's original State Letters, 2 vol'.[5] The volumes next appear in the *Appendix to the Sixth Report of the Historical Manuscripts Commission* (1877, pp 353, 363–390) where most of the letters are printed in part or summarised. At that date they were among the manuscripts of Sir Henry Ingilby of Ripley Castle, Yorks. When part of the Ingilby collection was sold in 1920,[6] they were purchased by Harry Lawrence Bradfer-Lawrence (1887–1965), antiquary and collector, and in 1967, Bradfer-Lawrence's executors deposited the part of his collection relating to Norfolk in the Norfolk Record Office. This included the two volumes of Paston letters which have been transcribed here.

The whereabouts of the volumes is unknown for the hundred years between 1777 and 1877 but in *The Perlustration of Great Yarmouth* the author, C.J. Palmer, states 'Many curious and interesting letters written by the earl, chiefly to his wife, from 1677 to 1680, were in the collection of the late Dawson Turner, Esq.'[7] This description does not exactly fit the Norfolk Record Office volumes which end in 1679, but neither does it fit any of the volumes of letters of the first earl of Yarmouth among the Paston papers at the British Library.[8] Dawson Turner (1775–1858) of Yarmouth, banker, botanist and antiquary, had a massive library and a collection of 34,000 manuscripts and letters, the purchase of which eventually ruined him.[9] Like Ives, Turner collected many documents relating to the history of Great Yarmouth, and the Norfolk Record Office volumes are particularly rich in such material. Turner's collections were sold both before and after his death in a number of auctions and private sales. It has not been possible to identify any letters of the earl of Yarmouth in the Turner sale catalogues, so it cannot be proved that he owned the Norfolk Record Office volumes.

[3] *Select Papers chiefly relating to English Antiquities published from the Originals in the Possession of J. Ives* (1773) pp 39–40.

[4] Inside one of the back boards is an MS note 'Perfect. 30 Octbr 1772' (NRO: BL/Y/2/121). The bindings were damaged by water at the time of the Norwich Library fire in 1994 so the volumes were disbound.

[5] *A Catalogue of the Entire and Valuable Library of John Ives, Jun. which will be sold by Auction, by S. Baker and G. Leigh, beginning Monday, March the 3d, 1777*, p.17, no.449.

[6] Yorkshire Archaeological Society: Bradfer Lawrence MD335/4/11; this is the Ingilby sale catalogue and the entry for the Paston volumes has been annotated '£39 withdrawn'.

[7] C.J. Palmer, *The Perlustration of Great Yarmouth*, (Great Yarmouth, 1872), p.129n.

[8] British Library: Add. MSS 27447–8, 27959, 28621, 36540, 36988.

[9] Nigel Goodman (ed.), *Dawson Turner, a Norfolk Antiquary and his Remarkable Family* (Chichester, 2007).

The contents of these two volumes, comprising about 300 letters up to March 1679, have now been transcribed in full with a few exceptions.[10] The British Library holds 300 to 400 more letters of the earl of Yarmouth in six of their volumes of Paston letters.[11] About 250 of these letters are from the period after March 1679 and most relate to Lord Yarmouth's efforts to persuade the corporation of Norwich to surrender their charter and to accept a new one. It was decided not to include any of these letters as March 1679 presents a natural break, coming just after the election of the knights of the shire, following which Lord Yarmouth returned to London. His petition to the King, dated June 1679, has been added to round off the volume. There are approximately 100 letters in the British Library volumes from the period 1660 to March 1679. Reasons of length made it impossible to include all these letters in the present volume. With some difficulty, just 36 letters from Add. MSS 27447, 28621, and 36988 were selected for insertion into the series transcribed from the Norfolk Record Office volumes. They were chosen as follows: all letters from the first earl of Yarmouth to his wife pre-March 1679 have been included, as have the only two surviving letters from Lady Yarmouth to her husband. All letters from Thomas Henshaw are included because they fill gaps in the run of Henshaw's letters in the Norfolk Record Office volumes, and because they illustrate Lord Yarmouth's intellectual life and leisure pursuits, and a few miscellaneous letters have been added which throw light on Lord Yarmouth's relationships with members of the Norfolk gentry, or which simply improve the narrative.

## The Transcriptions

Unless otherwise stated text is transcribed in full with the original spelling. The modern use of i and j as separate letters has been adopted. The word 'maior' has been transcribed as 'major' or 'mayor' according to the sense. $Y^e$ and $y^t$ have been transcribed as 'the' and 'that'. Suspensions, contractions and abbreviations have normally been expanded to the full modern spelling, unless the contraction makes it clear that a different spelling would have been used, i.e. la$^{pp}$ has been transcribed as ladyshipp. The past tense of verbs has been extended, i.e. lookd and look'd become looked, but look't has been left as written. Doctor has been contracted to Dr where followed by a surname, i.e. the doctor but Dr Browne. K, D, and C have been expanded to King, Duke and Countess. Christian names within the text have been expanded where the abbreviation is unambiguous, but signatures have been left as written. Capitalisation has been modernised. Offices have capitals if used as a form of address, i.e. my Lord Treasurer but the lord treasurer, my Lord Lieutenant but the lord lieutenant. God, the King, and Majesty have been given capital letters throughout the text but otherwise capitals have been used sparingly. Place-names have been transcribed as written but indexed under their modern form. Latin quotations and foreign words are in italics.

Punctuation has been slightly modernised where it helps the sense of the text. The rarest form of punctuation in seventeenth-century letters is the full stop, the most common the semi-colon which is used where a modern writer would use commas,

---

[10] There are a few strays, some letters are damaged, and some are of a purely formal nature.
[11] British Library: Add. MSS 27447–8, 27959, 28621, 36540, 36988

brackets and full stops. The most misleading of these semi-colons have been removed or replaced with something more appropriate. Apostrophes have introduced to indicate possession except where the writer has already done this by adding an 'e': i.e. 'the kings answer' has been changed to 'the king's answer', but 'the kinges answer' has been left as it is. Some full stops have been introduced to make better sense of long passages, and some misplaced or inappropriate commas have been removed, but generally as few changes have been made as possible. Sir Robert Paston's own letters have needed the most editing in this way to make the sense clear.

Many of the letters are endorsed with the date and the name of the sender. Endorsements have only been transcribed where additional information is supplied. Some of the letters from the British Library have endorsements added in a later hand about the subject matter or people mentioned; since many of these are inaccurate, all have been omitted.

Sums of money have been modernised as £ s d. Low numbers in the text have been written in full, i.e. two days not 2 days. Where the letters are dated, these dates are given in a standard form with months and years in full. The new year began on 25 March. Letters dated from 1 January to 24 March show both years, i.e. 1676/7; if the writer of the letter has not used this form of dating it has been added as 1676[/7]. When the year is given in italics and square brackets it has been deduced from internal evidence explained in a footnote. In the seventeenth century England still used the Julian calendar which was ten days behind the Gregorian calendar which was used in much of Europe. Diplomats and merchants always 'double dated' their letters; English travellers generally did so on arrival abroad[12] but stopped when the novelty wore off. It may be assumed that all letters in this volume written from abroad use New Style Gregorian dating, i.e. ten days ahead of the date in England, unless otherwise stated.

**The Ciphers**

Four different ciphers were used in the letters between Lord and Lady Yarmouth between 1675 and 1683, but only Lord Yarmouth's half of the correspondence has survived. Each party used a key, but only two of these are extant. The first is for 1677–78, and the second is for 1682: neither is complete.[13] The ciphers make use of symbols, numbers, and capital letters. The names of individuals or topics identified have been printed in square brackets using a different font, i.e. [*Lady Shannon*]. Where these names are preceded by a symbol, number or letter, they have been deduced from internal evidence, i.e. *37* [*Sir John Clayton*]. If no symbol, letter or number is shown, the name has been taken from a key to the cipher. For details of the deciphering process see Appendix 1.

**The Index**

Individuals have been identified in the index, in some cases more fully than in footnotes. The main sources used have been the *Oxford Dictionary of National Biography*, and B.D. Henning, *The House of Commons, 1660–1690*. These have only been cited when

---

[12] Below pp 109–11      [13] British Library: Add. MSS 27447, ff 303–304.

the footnote refers to their account of some relevant aspect of an individual's career. Peers and baronets have been identified in *The Complete Peerage of England, Scotland, Ireland, Great Britain and the United Kingdom* and *The Complete Baronetage*, edited by G.E.C[okayne]; various copies of Burke's *Peerage* and *Landed Gentry* have also been used, and a number of websites with databases of clergy, office holders, etc., which are included in the bibliography.

## Editorial conventions

| | |
|---|---|
| *  * | Words inserted |
| <   > | Words deleted |
| <  *  *  > | Words deleted including an insertion |
| [*f.*2] | The writer has started a second side |
| [*italics*] | Editorial addition within the text |
| [*word illegible*] | Indicates word that cannot be read |
| [*?*]seeing | Indicates doubt about transcription of word |
| <*word illegible*> | Indicates deleted word which cannot be read |
| <*?*> | Indicates deleted letter/s which cannot be read |
| [*Lady Danby*] | Indicates name decoded from cipher |

# ABBREVIATIONS

| | |
|---|---|
| Add. MSS | Additional Manuscripts (British Library) |
| CSPD | Calendars of State Papers, Domestic |
| CSPV | Calendars of State Papers, Venetian |
| CTB | Calendars of Treasury Books |
| NRO | Norfolk Record Office |
| NRO: BL/Y | Bradfer-Lawrence (Yarmouth Letters) |
| NRS | Norfolk Record Society |
| TNA | The National Archives |

# SELECT BIBLIOGRAPHY

A. MANUSCRIPT SOURCES

**British Library, London**

Add. MSS 27447–8, 27959, 28621, 36540, 36988 (Paston letters)
Sloane MSS 1009, 1928, 2222
Egerton MSS 3329, f.94, 3338

**Cambridge University Library**

Paston genealogical history (MS Add. 6968)

**Folger Shakespeare Library, Washington**

Rich papers (X.d.451)

**The National Archives, London**

Chancery records (C5/465/83; C10/166/86; C111/119–120)
Prerogative wills (PROB 11)
Yarmouth probate inventory (PROB 32/33/39)

**Norfolk Record Office**

Aylsham (AYL)
Bradfer-Lawrence: Yarmouth (BL/Y)
Cornwallis (MC 107/4)
L'Estrange (LEST)
Account of Norwich elections (MS 453)
Norfolk & Norwich Archaeological Society (NNAS C3)
Paston financial papers (MS 3210–3437, NRS 4004–4029)
Townshend (MS 1601)
Wills (NCC)
Windham Ketton Cremer (WKC)


B. PRINTED PRIMARY SOURCES AND COMPILATIONS

*Calendars of State Papers, Domestic, 1660–1685* (1860–1939)
*Calendars of State Papers, Venice, 1669–1675* (1937–1947)
*Calendars of Treasury Books, 1–7, 1660–1685* (1904–1916)
John Hildeyard, *A Sermon preached at the Funeral of ... Robert Earl and Viscount Yarmouth* (London, 1683)
HMC 5: 6th R. (Ingilby) (1877)
HMC 6: 7th R.I. (Frere and Verney) (1879)
HMC 19: 11th R.IV. (Townshend)
HMC 24: 12th R.V. (Rutland II)
HMC 62: Lothian (1905)

Edward Maunde Thompson (ed.), *Correspondence of the Family of Hatton* (Camden
    Society, 1878–1879, I).
    *Letters of Humphrey Prideaux ... to John Ellis*, Camden Society, 1875)
Simon Wilkin (ed.), *The Works of Sir Thomas Browne* (Norwich, 1836)

## C. SECONDARY SOURCES

Stephen B. Baxter, *The Development of the Treasury, 1660–1702* (Cambridge, Mass., 1957)
Francis Blomefield, *An Essay towards a Topographical History of the County of Norfolk*
    (1805–1810)
Andrew Browning, *Thomas Osborne, Earl of Danby and Duke of Leeds, 1632–1712*
    (Glasgow, 1944–1951, 3 vols.)
C.K. Chandaman, *The English Public Revenue, 1660–1688* (Oxford, 1975)
Donald R. Dickson, 'Thomas Henshaw and Sir Robert Paston's Pursuit of the Red
    Elixir: an early collaboration between Fellows of the Royal Society' (*Notes and
    Records of the Royal Society of London*, vol. 51, no. 1 (Jan. 1997), pp 57–76)
J.T. Evans, *Seventeenth-Century Norwich: Politics, Religion and Government, 1620–1690*
    (Oxford, 1979)
P. Gauci, *Politics and Society in Great Yarmouth, 1660–1722* (Oxford, 1996)
B.D. Henning, *The House of Commons, 1660–1690* (London, 1983)
J.R. Jones, 'The First Whig Party in Norfolk' (*Durham University Journal* 46 (1953–4),
    pp 13–21)
R.W. Ketton Cremer, 'Sir William Paston', *Norfolk Assembly* (London, 1957), pp 17–40
    'The End of the Pastons', *Norfolk Portraits* (London, 1944), pp 22–57
    'The Treasure of Oxnead', *Norfolk Assembly* (London, 1957), pp 212–222
A. Marshall, *Intelligence and Espionage in the Reign of Charles II, 1660–1685* (Cambridge,
    1994)
F.T. Melton, *Sir Robert Clayton and the Origins of English Deposit Banking, 1658–1685*
    (Cambridge, 1986)
John Miller, 'A Moderate in the First Age of Party: the Dilemmas of Sir John
    Holland, 1675–1685' (*English Historical Review*, CXIV, 1999, pp 844–874)
    'Containing Division in Restoration Norwich' (*English Historical Review*, CXXI,
    2006, pp 1019–1047)
C.J. Palmer, *The Perlustration of Great Yarmouth*, (Great Yarmouth, 1872)
Stephen Pasmore, 'Thomas Henshaw, F.R.S. (1618–1700)' (*Notes and Records of the
    Royal Society of London*, Vol. 36, No. 2 (Feb., 1982), pp 177–188)
James M. Rosenheim, *The Townshends of Raynham* (Middletown, CT, 1989)
    'Party Organisation at the Local Level: the Norfolk Sheriff's Subscription of
    1676' (*The Historical Journal*, 29, 3 (1986), pp 713–722)
Horace Rumbold, 'Notes on the History of the Family of Rumbold in the Seventeenth
    Century' (*Transactions of the Royal Historical Society (New Series)* (1892), 6: 145–165)
V.L. Stater, 'Continuity and Change in English Provincial Politics: Robert Paston in
    Norfolk, 1675–1683' (*Albion*, 25 (1993), pp 193–216)
Margaret Toynbee, 'Some Friends of Sir Thomas Browne' (*Norfolk Archaeology*, XXXI
    (1957), pp 377–394)

Robert Wenley, 'Robert Paston and the Yarmouth Collection' (*Norfolk Archaeology*, XLI (1991), pp 113–144)

Francis Worship, 'Account of a MS Genealogy of the Paston Family in the possession of His Grace the Duke of Newcastle' (*Norfolk Archaeology*, IV (1855), pp 1–55)

## D. WEBSITES

british-history.ac.uk/

theclergydatabase.org.uk/  (Clergy of the Church of England)

london-gazette.co.uk/  (*The London Gazette*)

luc.edu/history/fac_resources/bucholz/DCO/  (Database of Court Officers 1660–1837)

oxforddnb.com/  (*Oxford Dictionary of National Biography*)

royalsociety.org/catalogue  (Royal Society archives)

venn.csi.cam.ac.uk/ACAD/  (Cambridge alumni)

# THE LETTERS

## John Clayton[1] to Sir Robert Paston

**1663, April 8, Florence.**[2] Deare brother, sorrow comes over night but joy comes in the mourning,[3] this good news assaulted me: but never so pleasing could ever have arrived, this will make me come and give you joy sooner then I designed, now all places are tedious to me, till I see England againe; as soon as the snow is dessolved on the Alpes I intend to cros them for France, & so directly to Paris where I will spend my time till next winter and then for England, there I hope to serve you with gusto. Letters I expect none till you hear that I am at Paris, but as I remove I will write continually to you. My course I think to steer by Vienna, for wee hear that the French army is so far advance[d] towards the confines of Ittaly that there will be no returning that way, I am sorry that I cannot stay so long as to have your comands here, however I shall bring some few knacks[4] with me, that will please you very well. I am so shut up [*sic*] with joy for your great hapynes that I am not able to expres myselfe as I desire, by this time you will certainly find two or three letters which were very large so I can say but little more of my travels than what I have told you, only the entertainement of the Holy Week at Rome where Nox[5] cursed us sufficiently, if you know any frind of yours what has carruncles[6] I have some of the wax of the candle which Nox threw at us on Holy Thursday with these words *extinguantur sicut lumen.*[7]

[*f.*2] I have some thing befallen me hear that will keep up the chores of alchimy, and as strange as ever you heard – the person I have it from is a monck of the right order, a Benedictine, the whole story is miraculous, the stone he tells me he has made, and the proces I have at length fished of him, so as I think I cannot erre in the practise. Just as your letters came, wee were giving fire to the worke but now I shall not stay much longer here, the whole buissines is grounded upon the purrifieing of common [*mercury*][8] which he does in forty dayes and after makes the *sal naturae* or *sulp. philosophorum,*[9] which reduced to a water radically dissolves [*gold and silver*]. This great secret he found in a book hidden in the bottome of a wel[l], inclosed in soadred[10] lead and after that a marble cover, the title of the book *Phoenix Hermetica* with a clavis & six wedges, three of gold, three of silver made by the same proces: This I am master of: and so are you: if all faile, by Eugenius,[11] this will serve to pas[s] away the time five months longer, that is the uttmost of this proces. I had designed to have rambled

---

[1] John Clayton (c.1630–c.1710), knighted 1664, brother of Rebecca, Lady Paston, and original member of the Royal Society.

[2] This is probably dated continental style, i.e. ten days later than in England, *see* p.32 above.

[3] A paraphrase of *Psalm* 30 v.5.    [4] i.e. trifles, knick-knacks.    [5] Night or Death.

[6] i.e. warts    [7] May they be extinguished like light.

[8] Clayton uses alchemical symbols which have not been reproduced here.

[9] i.e the salt of nature or sulphur of philosophers    [10] i.e. soldered

[11] Possibly a reference to Thomas Vaughan (1621–1666), alchemist, who wrote as 'Eugenius Philalethes'; he was a friend of Thomas Henshaw (*see* above p.2), so was presumably known to both Clayton and Paston.

long, but now you are in hapynes[12] my jurny ends: long and tedious shall I think the
minutes till I arrive at Paris, then I hope you will be large in your commands, for I
am, dearest brother,

*Signed*: your most affectionate & overjoyed frind, J Clayton
*Postscript:* Your morning I shall wear with thankes & gusto.
*Addressed:* These for the honourable Sir Robert Paston knight and barronet at Parsons
Green[13]
*NRO: BL/Y/1/3*

## Inventory of jewellery

### 1663, July 30

|  | £ | s | d |
|---|---|---|---|
| An onix stone ring set round with diamonds & rubyes | 20 | 00 | 00 |
| A blackmoore in a sardonix set round with diamonds | 10 | 00 | 00 |
| A ring with a blackmoores head & turbett[14] sett with eight diamonds | 15 | 00 | 00 |
| A sardonix ring with 6 diamonds, a white head | 15 | 00 | 00 |
| A sardonix ring with a torteese on it, at | 04 | 00 | 00 |
| An onix with an anticke face on it haire colour[15] | 05 | 00 | 00 |
| An onix ring with 2 faces | 05 | 00 | 00 |
| A sardonix black & white set round with diamonds | 15 | 00 | 00 |
| A sad onix ring with a George[16] on it | 05 | 00 | 00 |
| An onix ring with a woman & child in it | 01 | 10 | 00 |
| An onix ring with an asse & ox in it | 02 | 10 | 00 |
| An onix ring with 3 colours & 2 diamonds | 07 | 00 | 00 |
| An onix ring with a crest being a lyon | 03 | 00 | 00 |
| An onix at | 01 | 00 | 00 |
| A plaine gold ring with a white & black agate | 01 | 00 | 00 |
| A plaine gold ring with a black agate | 01 | 00 | 00 |
| A slight ring with a darke emerard[17] | 01 | 00 | 00 |
| A munkey face with opall at | 01 | 10 | 00 |
| A soft topaz with a dragon in it | 02 | 10 | 00 |
| An emerald ring with a face in it | 05 | 00 | 00 |
| A free stone with diamonds round at | 10 | 00 | 00 |
| An emerauld ring with 6 rubyes at | 10 | 00 | 00 |
| A free stone at | 01 | 10 | 00 |
| An agate of 3 colours & 2 diamonds | 07 | 00 | 00 |
| 28 rings about 15s a peice | 21 | 00 | 00 |
| A jacinth[18] ring at | 01 | 05 | 00 |

---

[12] It is hard to avoid the suspicion that Clayton was referring to the news of the death of Sir Robert
Paston's father on 22 February 1663.

[13] Parsons Green at Fulham, Middlesex, then a village on the outskirts of London

[14] ? turban          [15] i.e. brown          [16] i.e. a depiction of St George          [17] i.e. emerald

[18] i.e. red or orange zircon

|                                                                        | £ s d |
|------------------------------------------------------------------------|-----------|
| A doublett[19] ring at                                                 | 00–10–00 |
| An opall ring <at> 4 clawes                                            | 01–00–00 |
| A cats eye ring at                                                     | 00–10–00 |
| [f.2] July 30 1663                                                     |           |
| Prized[20]                                                             |           |
| A cornelian ring                                                       | 00–10–00 |
| An agate ring at                                                       | 00–05–00 |
| Eight gold rings at                                                    | 07–15–00 |
| A lockett with a white agate set round with emeralds                   | 07–00–00 |
| An agate lockett transparent                                           | 01–00–00 |
| An agate head enamiled round with flowers                              | 05–00–00 |
| A plaine gold lockett with an agate                                    | 00–10–00 |
| A white agate head lockett sett with emeralds & vermillions            | 05–00–00 |
| A lockett with 6 opalls & a white stone                                | 05–00–00 |
| 3 peices for a hatband with rubyes                                     | 08–00–00 |
| 3 peices for a hatband with small diamonds                             | 10–00–00 |
| 3 pieces for a hatband enamiled turkeen                                | 01–00–00 |
| One white saphyr seale with the coate of armes of the family           | 30–00–00 |
| A blue saphyr ring with the families armes in it                       | 20–00–00 |
| A diamond hatband                                                      | 50–00–00 |
| A diamond ring with 3 great stones and fower or more small stones      | 52–00–00 |
| A ring with a very good jacinth                                        | 25–00–00 |
| A broad saphyr ring with 2 table diamonds                              | 10–00–00 |
| A globe opall at                                                       | 20–00–00 |
| A saphyr                                                               | 15–00–00 |
| A white saphyr ring at                                                 | 06–00–00 |
| A Turkey stone[21] with 2 diamonds                                     | 10–00–00 |
| An egmereen[22]                                                        | 20–00–00 |
| A ruby ring set round with rubyes & 2 diamonds                         | 16–00–00 |
| A Turkey <ring> stone ring at                                          | 02–10–00 |
| A long ruby & 2 table diamonds                                         | 10–00–00 |
| An egmereene ring                                                      | 04–00–00 |
| A grisolett[23] ring at                                                | 05–00–00 |
| [f.3] July 30 1663                                                     |           |
| Prized                                                                 |           |
| An egmereene ring at                                                   | 02–10–00 |
| An opall with the sun set round with diamonds                          | 10–00–00 |
| A foule emerauld at                                                    | 04–00–00 |

[19] i.e. an assembled gem in two contrasting sections

[20] i.e. valued. Sir William had instructed his executors to sell all his personal estate and household stuff apart from some items of jewellery and furniture bequeathed to his widow (TNA: PROB 11/311); the items on page one down to the eight gold rings on the second page were sold to [Francis] Avery for £141 5s, rather less then the valuation; the paper relating to the sale is undated but was before Paston was ennobled in 1673 (NRO: NRS 4013).          [21] i.e. turquoise

[22] i.e. aquamarine          [23] Probably chrysolite, i.e. peridot

| | £ | s | d |
|---|---|---|---|
| A spinnell ruby ring in forme of a heart | 03 | 00 | 00 |
| A table white saphyr ring | 10 | 00 | 00 |
| A garnett ring at | 01 | 05 | 00 |
| A white saphir set round with small diamonds | 07 | 00 | 00 |
| A little *ruby* ring at | 00 | 10 | 00 |
| A grisolett ring att | 05 | 00 | 00 |
| Another grisolett ring at | 01 | 00 | 00 |
| Eight white stone rings at 25s a peice | 10 | 00 | 00 |
| A garnett ring with 12 small dyamonds | 04 | 00 | 00 |
| A ring with 5 diamonds | 07 | 00 | 00 |
| A jacinth ring 8 square | 03 | 00 | 00 |
| A jacinth ring 4 square | 01 | 00 | 00 |
| An ametist ring | 01 | 05 | 00 |
| A cats eye ring with 2 rubyes | 01 | 00 | 00 |
| | **587** | **15** | **00** |

*NRO: BL/Y/1/4*

## Thomas Henshaw[24] to Sir Robert Paston

**1663, November 5.** My honoured patrone, I doe from my heart congratulate your safe arrivall at your owne Oxnet which must now bee the center of your content and the theater of your happines, and well may you rest satisfied with your lot, if you please to compute, to how <how> few of mankinde God hath given so faire a groundworke of earthly happines; and doe not doubt but when you have seriously relished the advantages of that felicity which yet seems to you but a dull quiet, above the troubles, turmoiles, disquiets, and subjections of the *grande monde*, you will dayly give God thankes on your knees for his accumulating so extraordinary favours uppon you; for you are yet but one of the *felices nimium bona si sua norint*.[25] That wee enjoyed our selves in our returne homewards as much as the trouble for parting with such freinds would give us leave, you will I know receive from other pens: therfore I will only tell you that since I came to towne I have been extreamly delighted with reading a chimicall manuscript poeme of one Edward Noell one of those I brought from Swallowfield,[26] who to my judgement understood the whole busines of chymistry as well as any that ever writ, who though hee sayes you must gaine the knowledge of the first matter somewhere else, yet in above a dousen places describes it so plainly that you will easily finde hee meanes no other but what wee have been so long uppon unlesse perhaps hee rather make choyce of some clay or loame.

[24] Above p.2.

[25] Originally '*O fortunatos nimium, sua si bona norint, agricolas*' (O more than happy husbandmen, did they but know their blessings) from Virgil, *Georgics II*, 458–459; Henshaw's version is from the poet Richard Crashaw (1613–1648), which was used by John Dryden in his dedication of *All for Love* to Lord Danby in 1678.

[26] Swallowfield, Berks, home of Sir William Backhouse, who had married his cousin Flower, the daughter and heiress of William Backhouse (1593–1662), alchemist and antiquary; Flower, who subsequently married viscount Cornbury, was named for her aunt, Henshaw's cousin Flower Henshaw, who had married William Backhouse the alchemist's brother Sir John Backhouse (Constance Russell, *Swallowfield and its Owners* (London, 1901), pp 116–123).

There are in him three processes which though perhaps are not so plaine as a litterall lineall processe being written in verse, yet I am confident you will thinke them the most perspicuous of any of that kind you have met with. If I have so much leisure before this day senight I will transcribe them and send them you though they bee something long. That which yet occurres to mee on the reading of them, is somewhat like what wee have indeavoured but failed in. You are first by a strong graduated fire to draw out all the humid part of your subject: in the rectifiying of which you will have first a strong armoniacke spirit which by his discription is just ours, then change your receivour and take the middle part of this humidity by it self and likewise the phlegme by it selfe. Then take the feces remaining in your retort, grinde them very small in a marble, put them into a body with a blind head, powre on them of your middle parts till it swim two fingers over, set them on warme ashes for 24 or 48 houres till you see your liquour tinged, then decant neatly and powre on fresh till you see the liquour no more tinged. When you have good store of this tinged liquour, digest it *in balneo*[27] for four dayes, then distille *per-gradus*[28] in sand and you will bring over the sulphur, which must bee seven times rectified a part, next take the feces again and calcine them till they bee whitish or gray, then with your flegm dissolve and filter till you have made a christalline salt which will bee very fixed, uppon this put in a blind body of your first cleare rectified spirit till it swim a finger over, digest *in balneo* three or four dayes then put on distilling head and draw of the humidity which will bee insipid, repeat this till your fixed salt be increased three times the weight, then in a sand furnace [*f.*2] by degrees force your fire and you will find the greatest part of your salt ascended in the head of your limbecke[29] in a volatile pearly *terra foliata*,[30] which being used *ut scis*[31] will all turn into a liquour. Then on your remaining fixed salt by degrees poure on your rectified sulphur or *anima* which is *medium conjugendi corpus et spiritum*,[32] and digest between till they are incorporated, and in the same manner lastly of the spirit, then digest for eight days then distille [*mercury*][33] *philosoph*[*orum*][34] which radically dissolves all mettle, though the authour goes on from thence to the great worke without adding any mettall at all as many others beside him teach to doe. I suppose the reason why wee missed both the sulphur and fixed salt was that excessive Ghehennall[35] fire at the doctor's[36] for upon my fayth when I wrote[37] it in my furnace at home I had always some fixed salt and have had of it by mee 4 [*ounces*] of it at a time, and it was a sandy gritty salt just as this author describes it. You need not bee curious of great quantities of it for hee says on com[*mon*] [*mercury*] it will multiply *in infinitum* and that there is a sulphur in it. I am the more confirmed since Jacke Clayton told mee last night at the Colledge[38] that our doctor tells him that bye grinding sall armoniacke with the *cap*[*ut*] *mort*[*uum*][39] of our subject hee can sublime a sulphure as red as rubies. The squire[40] came but yesterday from Windsor and the doctor tells him now you are gone it will bee impossible to communicate the

---

[27] In a bath or dish        [28] By degrees        [29] i.e. alembic, used for distillation
[30] Mercurial water        [31] As you know        [32] The means of joining body and spirit
[33] Symbols used in this letter have not been reproduced here.        [34] The mercury of philosophers
[35] i.e. hellish        [36] Possibly Dr Jonathan Goddard (d.1675), FRS, chemist        [37] i.e. wrought
[38] The Royal Society met at Gresham's College; Clayton became a fellow on 9 Oct 1661 and Paston on 18 Dec 1661.
[39] Dead head – used by alchemists to describe a residue left over from a chemical process
[40] John Clayton

dispensation to you, and indeavours to draw in the squire who will not smell of the chouse.[41] Hee sais it has cost the doctor already £1,500.

The squire last night made mee very solemne protestations how much he had loved *you* beyond all men living and is much troubled after those kinde promises of freindship *you made him at Oxnet last* whence this extraordinary dislike should arise; I tould him I did find you had received some dissatisfaction from him, but that it was never my custome to inquire into the particulars of disgusto's between so neare relations.[42] I was yesterday with Mr Love and gave him your letter; hee shewed mee that you promised I should speake to the lord chamberlaines[43] brother for him. I wondered at it you having never spoken one word to mee of it nor I doe I knowe his brother so well as to dare to move him to a courtesy for my self. I tould him I thought it was a mistake in putting my name for Mr Cheeke's[44] who was both willing and able to doe it for him, and so to him I sent him. The King shall bee shewed your inventory of red deare at the first opportunity if Bowles[45] have not yet shewed it to him. *Lege perlege combure.*[46]

*Signed: Je suis sans aucune reserve*, dear Sir Robert, your faythfull old servant, Halophilus *Postscript*: [f.3] I shall not faile by the fit time to provide som scions[47] for you against the time which is February: only let me know your number. There is shortly a curious discourse of Mr Evelyn's[48] by order of the Colledge to com *out* concerning timber trees; sider trees and Sir Paul Neale's and other wayes of making of sider presented to them are to bee added at the end. As soon as it comes out I will take care you shall have one of them. I am just now going to Whitehall to meet Mr Clayton to shew the King the shining diamond.[49]

*Addressed:* For my most honoured freind Sir Robert Paston knight and baronet at Oxnet Halle neare Norwich, this
*NRO BL/Y/1/5*

## John, 1st viscount Mordaunt[50] and others to Sir Robert Paston

**1663, November 14, Sunday night, Villa Cary.** *Epistre generale de Villa Cary a nos tres chers amis a Oxnet*, Monsieur et Madame, else the feminine gender were more worthy then the masculine.

[41] i.e. the deceit

[42] Paston was frequently at odds with Clayton, culminating in a complete breach by 1678 *see* above p.11.

[43] Edward Montagu, 2nd earl of Manchester, was lord chamberlain; he had several brothers.

[44] Thomas Cheeke of Pirgo, Essex, esquire of the body, was an old friend of Paston's, and sometime brother-in-law of the 2nd earl of Manchester, who married five times. He became lieutenant of the Tower of London in 1679 and died in 1688; see introduction to the Archer of Tanworth papers (DR 37) at the Shakespeare Centre Library and Archive, on Access to Archives website.

[45] Sir William Bowles was master of the tents and toils, which were nets for catching deer and other game.

[46] Read through and burn.                                    [47] Stem cuttings for use in grafting.

[48] John Evelyn, *Sylva or a Discourse of Forest Trees* (1664), which included Sir Paul Neile's discourse on cider.

[49] See 'Observations of Mr Clayton's diamond' by Robert Boyle, 28 Oct 1663: that the diamond shines in the dark when struck (Royal Society, RBC/2/34, RBO/2i/77).

[50] John Mordaunt (1626–1675), 1st viscount Mordaunt of Avalon, former royalist conspirator. Mordaunt and his wife Elizabeth lived at Parson's Green at the Villa Cary, which had belonged to Elizabeth's father, Thomas Cary, son of the 1st earl of Monmouth. The Pastons also lived at Parson's Green before inheriting Oxnead and Sir John Clayton lived there after his marriage in 1665.

Retired persons converse most with the Gods, and those [*that*] doe soe may bee justly called saints. These rejoyce at the conversion of a sinner, of which classis I take Mr Clayton to bee. Lett you[*r*] joy bee full, the aforenamed has not only been at church, but this stormy evening has most attentively heard my Lady Mordaunt read one part of the *Duty of Man*.[51]

I doe not remmember it concerned matrimony. I wish it had, for hee has been in Italy, a place as I have heard gives noe good instructions for yoake fellows.

Aretin[*o*][52] was called *il divino*, but the moderne gownemen[53] say hee was carnall, how these two will consist[54] I leave you to determine. I am chiden for being to[*o*] tedious, yet to conclude without entering upon what I only intended, the reall acknolidgement of my respects and obligations to you both were to doe, as I have write I know not what. That past, you have goodnesse to merge the other from your forsaken neighbour of Parsons Green.

[*f*.2][55] What to tell you I canot emadgin,[56] being forbed to rede wats rite allredy; to say any thing of the cont\*r\*y were foly, Oxnet being the mistris of all contry satisfactions, and to trete of the corte were a yet greter foly, we pour contry pepell being totaly ignorant of thayr injoyments. What shall I say then; Bety Mordaunt loves Rebeca Paston, a dule truthe, you might have tould your selfe as much, but if I tell you I love Sir Robert Pasten that's newes, and may poses[57] divert you, at lest with jelosy, if not with merthe, and that's a victory, I thinke a great one, to turne your thoughts to Persons Gren upon any account, and now I have ganed this ground, I would give over but that thay say I must fill my side, with what, lete me think, and now your brouther[58] singes and I canot think, and therfor would send you the remaning paper enosent,[59] but that I fear the knight will not like that presant enosency being a thing he desirs to kepe at a vast distance from him, and to disples[60] hime, now I have begun an adres[*s*] to him were not discret at all, and therfor I will begin a discors of the elements, fire ayre water and earth, and how wise this discorse would be if I hade co[*n*]cerne to right it, I leve you to g[*u*]es[*s*].

[*f*.3][61] *Je n'espere pas de \*dire\* rien que vous puis divertir apres que vous avies leu les deux premier feuliet. Je ne laise pas que de vous ecrire pour vous asurer de mon tres humble service.*

The first's a neigbours worthy & kind[62]
Such another you'l ne'er find
The next's a lady's of the same name
Only excelling more in fame
The last's a virgin's, who has skill
To write as well as kill

---

[51] Presumably *The Whole Duty of Man*, published anonymously in 1657
[52] Pietro Aretino (1492–1556), author, playwright and satirist
[53] Gownmen are usually lawyers or university men but here clergymen may be meant.
[54] i.e. co-exist                    [55] This page is written by Elizabeth, Lady Mordaunt.
[56] i.e. imagine. Most women spelt badly because in the absence of dictionaries they were obliged to resort to phonetics, and because they were seldom taught Latin which would have given them some idea of the roots of many words. This letter and those of Rebecca Paston are easily understood if read aloud.
[57] ? purposes or perhaps – the 'p' has a horizontal contraction mark but so does the 'p' in Paston.
[58] John Clayton              [59] i.e. innocent or blank                    [60] i.e. displease
[61] In an unidentified hand                              [62] In John Clayton's hand

Thus your obligations grow
How you'l returne them? I do not know.
But wonder not to see my hand
Here, tis by command,
For so have I seen an artist paint
This way divell, that way saint.

*Unsigned, written in four hands*
*Addressed*: For Sir Robert Paston, deputy lieutenant of our county of Norfolk, hast
*NRO: BL/Y/1/6*

## Sir Robert Paston to Rebecca, Lady Paston

**[1664], November 29**. My deare hart, since my last I have beene [*at*] Worcester Howse and sufficientlie caressed by the chancelor,[63] but the service I have don the King I must <*word illegible*> repeate is soe greate that I am looked on in a capacitie of nott beeing denied anie thing in his Majesties power. The King intends me personall thanks and great promises I heare, but in modestie I forbeare the court for a while. Itt was the happiest opportunitie for a foundation of somwhat considerable that ever God Allmighty putt into my hands.[64]

My act of parlament[65] was read the second time yesterday and committed to such a committee as I could nott have named a better. I write now from the committee chamber, Mr Crouch[66] is chaireman, I desired itt for he did me soe signall a favor in the Howse in dispatching the second reading that everie bodie thought itt just. Sir John Holland[67] spoke nobly for me, soe did divers others. The regular proceedings is to give summons to the towne of Yermouth to appeare to which purpose the inclosed order is sent to Witton to serve the bayliffs withall, Saterday com sevennight is the day given them. Feare nott the success with all [*f.2*] the advantage imaginable. I hope the plum pies att Christmas will relish with the most gratefull tast, and that we shall have the merriest meeting we ever had, in this world I never had soe much satisfaction as to have served my master soe eminently.

The nog[68] is arrived. Ile send John Leaman downe this weeke.

The day I hope to com downe on will be the twentie second of December if nott the next day after Christmas Day as the necessities of my affaires require then Ile send Billie[69] before, but I must be up againe in ten or twelve dayes for I must nott bee out of the King's eie this parlament. When I come which I long for Ile tell you all. For my Bill I make itt noe request to the King, I keep that for somwhat els.

---

[63] Worcester House in the Strand was the London residence of the earl of Clarendon, lord chancellor.

[64] Paston had introduced a Bill proposing the unprecedented sum of £2,500,000 for the King's supply; for a reprinted copy of his speech *see* British Library: Add. MSS 36988, f.88.

[65] An Act intended to extend the trading privileges of Great Yarmouth to the west bank of the Yare to benefit Paston's proposed development at Southtown, *see* Perry Gauci, *Great Yarmouth*, pp 112–7.

[66] Thomas Crouch, MP for Cambridge University.

[67] Sir John Holland (1603–1701) of Quidenham, MP for Aldeburgh; through his mother, Mary Knyvett, Holland was a first cousin of Sir William Paston, and his friendship with Sir Robert survived their differences in politics in the 1670s; see also p.21 above.

[68] A strong variety of beer, brewed in Norfolk

[69] i.e. their eldest son William (1654–1732), later 2nd earl of Yarmouth

My deare, I long to see thee, if what I write cannott cheere you nothing will. This day an accident fell out to one of our members Sir Richard Everard as he was gooing home his brother in law drew uppon him & cutt him over the pate, how this will be resented we knowe nott.[70] I beeleeve the dowager familie[71] bleed to heare my name in everie one's mouth & that the King is soe kind. Heere inclosed I send you the orders of my bill I have writt to Witton to com up & bring his lease, lett Hurton[72] send mee the counterpart if I have itt nott heare allreadie. My humble service to your mother,[73] my love to the small frie, I charge you be merrie & give God thankes for our good fortune.

*Signed:* Thine for ever, Robt Paston
*Postscript:* Direct your letters to the Howse of Commons
*Addressed:* These present to my honored friend the Ladie Paston att Oxnett in Norfolk [*franked Robert Paston, with postmark*]
*British Library: Add. MSS 27447, ff 324–325*

## Sir Robert Paston to Rebecca, Lady Paston

[*1664*], **December 6**. My deare hart, I am faine to write in a little volume beeing much in hast and a vast deale of business lyng uppon me. I have this day beene retaining my counsell for Saterday, for that is the bloudie day, I have vast friends butt must suffer all the opposition Yermouth can make. I have nott beene att court yett, pray thinke nott butt that I menage my affaires with as much prudence and policy as my pore witt can designe and when I bring anie thing to perfection Ile acquaint you with itt, butt you'l find me struggle hard for somwhat. Colthorpe[74] has nott Witton's lease I was with him [*sic*], I beleeve Mr Earle has itt [*f.2*] though Prattant sent me word this day he delivered *itt* himself to Colthorpe who shewed me everie writing he had of mine. This is a materiall misfortune to me if Earle whome yett I have nott spoken with produceth itt nott, Ile write to Hurton by the next. The Duke[75] is com from sea with all his gallants. My deare I am plyng my affaires for the good of you and my posteritie of which on Christmas Eve he hopes to give you a faire accompt who for ever remaines

*Signed:* your most passionate servant, Robert Paston
*Postscript:* Never lett a writing of mine be parted with without a note under the receiver's hand.
*Addressed*: These present to my honoured friend the Ladie Paston att Oxnett in Norfolk [*franked Robert Paston, and postmark*]
*British Library: Add. MSS 27447, f. 326*

---

[70] Everard was MP for Westminster; on 1 December he complained he had been assaulted by John Elwes (his step-brother) and Peter Killigrew, who were both also MPs.

[71] The family of the dowager Lady Paston, his stepmother, with whom they were on bad terms; she was the sister of Sir Thomas Hewitt of Pishobury, Herts, and Sir William Hewitt of Breckles, Norfolk.

[72] John Hurton, steward at Oxnead

[73] Mary, Lady Clayton (d.1693), widow of Sir Jasper Clayton

[74] Presumably a London lawyer and probably a member of the Calthorpe familn of Norfolk; John Earle of Lincoln's Inn was a lawyer, the son of Erasmus Earle, serjeant at law; Humphrey Prattant was a gentleman servant of Sir William Paston.

[75] James (1633–1701), duke of York and lord high admiral

## Sir Robert Paston to Rebecca, Lady Paston

**[1664], December 8**. My deare hart, this day from the Howse[76] I *went* to Whitehall to my Lord of Bathe's to dinner who with his ladie and manie civill inquiries after you received mee most kindlie. I stayd there till the King came from Sommersett Howse[77] and then went up into the presence where the King was in a verie great croud; as soone as he saw me he came to me from the companie and tooke me into a corner of the roome and told me, Sir Robert Paston your kindnesses to me and more especiallie att this time Ile never forgett and if my favor and respect may ever manifest itt *self to* you *you* are sure of a friend, of me. I humbly thanked his Majestie for his grace, and out of modestie retired into the croud from thence my Lord Bathe went with *me* to the Queene from whome after having kissed her hand I had a complement, the treasurer[78] having told her I was the man. Saterday I am preparing for might & maine and that night you may expect somthing of novells from me, though I hope to tell you itt my self, for I desire you will forthwith issue out orders for the too grey mares to be taken up into the stable [f.2] and Robin's[79] little black horse for the boy, the sorell mare for Rawlins[80] and Billie's little horse led by. By my next Ile tell you when they shall com. I shall endeavor to gett this business through first and then Ile be bold to trie his Majestie for somwhat els which weil discourse in Norfolke. Pray lett Hurton send me up what Ling's last fine was, which as I take itt was £45 for one parcell & £40 for another, I striking of[f] £5 remained [£]80; they would face me downe itt was nott soe much. Sir John if your mother approves has gotten Bellinda's[81] consent to marrie.

Madam Sanderson att court[82] made me large professions of her devotion to you & me and I thinke the woman meanes well.

The court ladies are verie indifferent as to beautie methinkes.

I have this night sent you by the post, if he will carrie itt, a point[83] of my Aunt Bertie's choise and severall ladies' that I mett att Eaton's approbation, he ask £26, she sayth itt is too deare, I hope itt will please. Lett the multiplicitie of my owne busines, in which for want of Mr Bulwer[84] I am faine to be my owne sollicitor, excuse the hast that makes me conclude my selfe for ever to be

---

[76] i.e. the House of Commons

[77] The home of Charles II's mother, the Queen Dowager Henrietta Maria; she settled in France in the following year and died there in 1669.

[78] Thomas Wriothesley, 4th earl of Southampton, lord treasurer

[79] i.e. Paston's second son Robert (1656–1705)

[80] Francis Rawlins, one of Paston's gentleman servants, and the only one of Paston's household to receive an annuity on his death; he was also paid £100 in 1674 for his attendance on William Paston when he had smallpox.

[81] Presumably a poetical name for Alice, daughter of Sir William Bowyer, and widow of William Buggin of North Cray, Kent, whom Clayton married early in the new year.

[82] Bridget Tyrell, wife of Sir William Sanderson, historian; she served as 'mother of the maids' of Queen Catherine of Braganza. Her nephew, Peter Nourse, a London brewer, son of John Nourse of Chilling Place and Wood Eaton (*see* TNA: PROB 11/163) and Philippa Tyrell, was the husband of Rebecca's older sister Mary Clayton (*ODNB*; Mary D. Lobel (ed.), *A History of the County of Oxford*: Volume 5: Bullingdon hundred (1957), pp 309–317).

[83] A roll of lace; Eaton was a fashionable cloth merchant and haberdasher and Aunt Bertie was the wife of one of Paston's uncles.          [84] Thomas Bulwer (c.1612–1694) of Buxton, Paston's attorney

*Signed:* your most humble servant, Robert Paston
*Postscript:* My service to your mother, my love to the young ones
*Addressed:* These present to my honored friend the Ladie Paston att Oxnett in Norfolke
[*franked Robert Paston, and postmark*]
*British Library: Add. MSS 36988, ff 100–101*

## Sir Robert Paston to Rebecca, Lady Paston

[*1664*], **December 13.**[85] My deare hart, yesterday my committee satt and I had a verie full one, my Lord Cornburie[86] and all the chancelor's friends were there and my counsell, the towne of Yermouth had verie little to alleadge for themselves but time which they earnestly implored but the deniall of that is a thing which though I could have carried against them, I was advised to graunt in order to the cleerer passing of my Bill, which is in greater forwardness then the King's owne Bill for the too millions and an halfe, soe after all my friends had named a short time I myself <ha> stood up and desired they might have till the Thursday after twelfe day, which <if> all my friends tells me is the greatest expedition I could have putt to itt and now that is the last day of asking and barrs them of anie plea of retardment in the Lords' Howse. Witton is gon this day out of this towne full of joy and assurance, and by agreement is to mette me att Oxnett too days before twelfe day for I must com away on the Munday to be heare on the Wedensday for my committee sitts on Thursday and before the Thursday after I dare assure you my Act will pass, yett there are enough would oppose itt if they durst. [*f.*2] Therefore looke uppon that as don, itt beeing forwarder then the King's owne Bill, and will assuredly pass att the same time.

I have in prospect somthing els which I beeleeve may be feasible that perhapps may save mee the sale of Mautby.[87] The Yermouth counsell was overheard by to say [*sic*] well you have gotten time for your towne but I feare you will gett nothing els, they dispaire totallie and their journey served for nothing but to lett them see itt is in vaine to contend. When I com downe I shall have severall stories to entertaine you with, and I hope to passe the twelve dayes with as much satisfaction as I ever did on my life, I have heard the same newse in towne you write me from Norfolke but I am wholy bent uppon profitt for my children's sake and I am verie confident the King will nott denie me anie reasonable thing.

Pray send away the horses betimes on Saterday morning, for I intend to com out on Wedensday morning and to be with you if I can on Friday, therefore send me in answer to this letter your last commands for this time I intend to bring downe for Bob a suite & cote somwhat though nott quite licke his brother's, therefore make him noe clothes.[88]

Sir William Killegrew[89] kicks[90] soe damnably for £19 owing for wine that I was this morning constrained to give one Mr Hooker who undertakes to pay him heere

---

[85] The day and month are from the postmark; the year has been deduced from internal evidence.
[86] Henry, viscount Cornbury, was the lord chancellor's eldest son.
[87] Sir William Paston had left his estate at Mautby in trust to his executors to be sold to pay his debts.
[88] Bob or Robin, Paston's second son Robert
[89] Probably Sir William Killigrew (c.1606–1695), the courtier and playwright, rather than his cousin the colonel who died in 1665.    [90] i.e. requests or demands money

a bill uppon Hurton to be sent to Mr Briggs[91] for that sum. My deare I will nott tell you how much I long to see you till I have the happiness of itt for which above all earthly things he longs that is, my deare,

*Signed*: your most passionate servant, Robt Paston
*Postscript:* My service to your mother, my love to my children
*Addressed:* These present to my honored friend the Ladie Paston att Oxnett in Norfolk
[*franked Robert Paston, and postmark*]
*British Library: Add. MSS 27447, ff 327–328*

## Sir Robert Paston to Rebecca, Lady Paston

**1664[/5], January 14, Speaker's Chamber.** My dearest hart, just now I can write thee som good newse. My committee satt all this afternoone where by the opposition of som persons angrie with me for the King's cause there was a long debate to lay aside my Bill but my friends, allthough itt happened soe unluckilie that manie were absent uppon occasions nott to be prevented, att last carried itt cleerelie for me, soe that they seeing how itt would goe sneaked of [*f*] and left butt too[92] to vote against *mee* soe the question att the committee passed cleerelie for the gooing on with my Bill which on Munday I hope to have finished att the committee, for now they are past hurting mee there, but they threaten itt when itt comes to be reported to the Howse butt itt is onelie the malice of a few which I thinke will nott be able to prevaile, I hope to gett my Bill passed the Howse of Commons this next weeke. I was faine to send to Mr Ruttie[93] for £20 for the payment of the Queenes rent[94] which I desire may be payd my Ladie Clayton att Oxnett if she accepts itt, if nott to him, but for all I see I must make use [*f*.2] of itt my self, and make that stay a longer day, I thought I would write you the first victorie and tell you the maine difficultie is past. Ile struggle and doe soundlie for my pore infants, God give me his blessing in all my endeavors.

The historie of Bill's gooing to my Ladie Paston's[95] is this, she sent to me the child might com and dine with her, I sent him in my owne coach with Rawlins to attend him, she made mightie much of him and after dinner carried him to a play, then brought him home, and att parting gave him a twentie shilling peece desiring him she might see him som times though she could see none of us, I told Lewis[96] I should send her thankes which I intend to doe, for the law of civilitie.

He is still att my Lord of Lindsey's[97] till the frost breakes up which the young gallants pray hartilie for.

Your brother and his mistress are come to towne, he dined with me today and I beeleeve writes himself this night, till Munday be over, I stir nott further from home

---

[91] Augustine Briggs (c.1618–1684), alderman and merchant of Norwich    [92] i.e. two
[93] Thomas Rutty (d.1699), London merchant
[94] Thomas Corie to Paston, letter listing some of the Queen's property in Norfolk, 19 June 1665 (British Library: Add. MSS 27447, f.306)
[95] Margaret, Lady Paston, Sir Robert's stepmother with whom he was on bad terms
[96] Lewis Mico or Micqueau, a confidential servant of Sir Robert Paston, and previously of his father (NRO: AYL 712, NNS 4005, 4008)
[97] Montague Bertie (1608–1666), 2nd earl of Lindsey, Paston's uncle

then my Lord Lindsey's from my business, I charge you write him a letter to thanke him for your son besides that he takes as much paines in my business as an horse, soe doth my Lord Townshend.[98] The difficultie of a parlament affaire is nott to be thought without amasement, I can write noe newse till my business is over. Mr Hide's[99] funerall I attended the last night, pray send me up a paire of the little chamber silver candlesticks by the first opportunitie, I hope itt will nott be manie weekes before wee meet in joy soe for this night in hast I take my leave commending you & mine to the protection of that God which I hope will never forsake us heere nor heereafter.

*Signed*: I am, deare hart, yours for ever, Robert Paston
*Addressed:* These present to my Ladie Paston att Oxnett in Norfolke [*franked by Robert Paston*]
*NRO: BL/Y/1/7*

## Sir Robert Paston to Rebecca, Lady Paston

**1664[/5] January 28.** My deare hart, I knowe you are as full of expectation as I am of patience for this post can bring you noe more of newse then the last, the King's Bill beeing the worke of the House which I suppose may this night be finished, and soe engrossed or written faire to be carried up to the Lords' Howse the middle of the next week, and I doe expect to be the man that shall have that honor. On Munday is the King's fast day for the anniversarie of his father,[100] on Tuesday a second order is made for the hearing of my business, soe by the next post I hope to putt you past feare one way or other. My deare, I have my engines att worke to enquire me out somthing to ask. I thought itt fitt to lett you knowe I am nott idle and as soone as I can give you anie accompt I will be sure to doe itt.

The Dutch have made a picture of the House of Commons and out of their mouthes these words issuing (live & die | live & die), att the last the picture of a burly fellowe out of whose mouth coms too millions and an halfe.[101]

This day I have taken som of Don's[102] pills for I had a verie great cold which is nott yett of[*f*] me. My deare as soone as my Yermouth business [*f*.2] [?]is over I shall

---

[98] Horatio, baron Townshend (1630–1687), lord lieutenant of Norfolk and, at this stage, a friend of Paston's

[99] Edward Hyde (1645–1665), third son of the earl of Clarendon; he was buried in Westminster Abbey (*Collectanea Topographica et Genealogica*, VII (London, 1841), p.372).

[100] Charles I was executed on 30 January 1649 and Charles II kept it as a day of prayer and fasting.

[101] Paston was already losing his struggle with obesity. Sir John Denham wrote of him and Clarendon in '*Directions to a Painter concerning the Dutch war*' (1667):
> 'First let our Navy scour through Silver Froth,
> The Oceans burthen, and the Kingdoms both;
> Whose very bulk may represent its Birth,
> From *Hyde* and *Paston*, burthens of the Earth; ...
> *Paston* whose Belly bears more Millions,
> Than *Indian Carracks*, and contains more Tuns.'
However it should be noted that later in the same year he could still ride home from London to Norwich.

[102] i.e. Thomas Henshaw's; Don was probably an abbreviation of '*dominus*' acknowledging Paston's debt to Henshaw for his instruction in alchemy; both Henshaw and Paston also dabbled in pharmacy.

have both time to studie to improove that, and to consider the rest. I long to be with you to discourse your lying in which unless somwhat of certaine advantage happen, I resolve to have in such a lodging as I can convenientlie *procure* with an hired furniture for your owne chamber though if anie thing doe happen I resolve to have an howse in towne to be a refuge uppon occasion.

Tempest[103] is just now with me & has brought me the plate which is verie fine. Ile send you itt downe by the next carts but I desire you will send up the too plaine tankards for a paire much handsomer which you will find in the box. Itt has all past Goldsmiths' Hall and the marke uppon itt, the porringers will please you extreamelie. I have bespoke a case for that chamber plate of Henshaw but itt will be a forthnight before itt is don. I am just now gooing about your bookes which shall be to your content.

The faire ladie you once longed to see is licke to be out of favor for having som inclinations els where as I heare. [104]

My deare, pray God, pray God send us a merrie meeting and that all thinges may goe well which is the desire of

*Signed*: your most affectionate husband & servant, Robt Paston
*Postscript*: For God sake gett som companie to you & wright me word
*Address torn off but postmarked*
*NRO: BL/Y/1/8*

## Sir Robert Paston to Rebecca, Lady Paston

**[1665], February 4**. My dearest hart, I can now tell thee most comfortable newse which is that this day my business was reported in parlament, and the debate lasted manie howres extreame hott on both sides, att last as <att> *to* the decision of both itt came to a question and I carried itt butt by one voyce which was the speaker's casting voyce for though I had my owne besides eightie of a side yett I relinquished that knowing the speaker[105] to be my friend who decided the quarrell for mee; now <if> I have hard luck if they hurt me though the ingrossment comes on Wednesday morning againe into the Howse in order to itts passage to the Lords. I have beene with the speaker since with my Lord Townshend (who is the best friend I have in the world) & Sir John Holland who is a verie kind one to prevent the danger of future risks, soe I hope you need nott doubt to have a finall accompt of this once in a forthnight, butt that which is a reall joy to mee is to find the King soe much concerned for me as to be much offended that for his sake I should run such an hazzard; when itt was over my noble Lord Fitzharding[106] came to mee, Sir says he, I have somwhat to assure you from the King which is that he is studyng a way to gratifie you, therefore lett your friends and your self consider Ile serve you to my utmost power. My Lord Townshend has told mee the [f.2] same againe today and presseth me to be

---

[103] Possibly Robert Tempest, a London goldsmith

[104] Presumably Barbara, Lady Castlemaine, who was several times out of favour with the King for her inclinations elsewhere.          [105] Sir Edward Turnor (1617–1676)

[106] Charles Berkeley (c.1630–1665), 1st viscount Fitzhardinge and later earl of Falmouth, friend of the King

speedie in declaring now I am resolved to ask somwhat that as I told you shall sett me free in the world and putt some money in my purse if the King affords me that first and will give me a title too I will cheerfullie accept itt, but I know soe much what the want of money is and what the streightness of a fortune is that if itt pleaseth God Ile make use of God's providence to provide for the one, and doe hope in som measure to fix itt before I see thee, which shall be time enough to bring you upp presentlie after our Ladie Day which I accompt the beginning of Aprill or there-abouts, that wee may take the pleasure of the [?]faire May June & July and have a touch of the countrie and venison, August & September. My deare feare me nott for menaging my affaire to the best interests, and if I once gett money I thinke I shall knowe the way how to live to myself and keep the maine.

As anie certaine progress goes forward you shall heare from mee and I shall pro-pound to your advice before I ask.

Your brother is married butt to cousin[107] the world marries againe tomorrowe, I write now from his lodging, they all present their service. My deare this will prove a chargable business to mee, butt Ile conquer itt now if I can, the bayliffs of Yermouth looke licke tallowe candles for this day att [f.3] twelve of the clock they thought they had carried all cocksure.

Tomorrowe Ile to Blanges and search the towne for lodgings or an howse to please you.

My deare I hope your prayers will make him prosper who is soe full of business att this houre beeing to goe speake with my Lord Lindsey that I have but time to say

*Signed:* I am your most affectionate servant, Robert Paston
*Addressed:* These present to my honored friend the Ladie Paston att Oxnett in Norfolke
[*franked by Robert Paston, and postmark*]
*British Library: Add. MSS 27447, ff 329–330*

## Sir Robert Paston to Rebecca, Lady Paston

**1664[/5], February 6.** My deare hart, I have made a vowe to God that lett my affaires heere succeed as they will, I will this verie summer build a brick wall of a con-venient heitgh and handsomness about the churchyard, to which purpose I desire you to comply with that promise soe far as immediatelie to send for Franck, lett him give you an accompt how much brick will doe itt & take order with Speering for the burning itt and for other materialls for the worke. My last informed you of the narrowe dispute wee had in the Howse upon the report of my Bill, Thursday itt runns the same risk and truelie by the sett malice of the Presbitereans against itt I doe much doubt the issue, butt when that is don I have my old remedie law, of which I am confident I shall nott fayle and the King I beeleeve would recompence mee soe, as my friends doe som of them wish I may loose itt, butt I will struggle the best I can and God's will be don, I write this to prepare you for the worst that you may nott be surprised if the voices carrie itt on their side.

---

[107] i.e. cozen: to cheat or deceive. Sir John Clayton and Alice Buggins had already married on 16 January 1665 in the church of St Mary Somerset, London, but apparently there was a second service.

The King good man is extreamelie concerned for itt and will nott suffer anie par-lament man to be on the gard butt to attend itt.

I am just now writing a letter of thankes to my Lord Fitzharding for his great kind-ness to mee, what I writt you word about the sitting of the parlament will be true and I hope I may order my business soe as to com downe earlie in March and to bring you up the latter end of the same month. On Sunday last your brother married to owne itt your mother sent his wife by me a present of a bracelett of emraulds & dia-monds worth about fourscore & ten pounds. [f.2] The Duke of Richmond & Sir Charles Sydly came in aboutt ten att night with the duke's fidlers, butt your sister was verie sick and was faine to goe to bed.

Old Mrs Hamden[108] is dead but what legacies she has bestowed on such as had expectations I knowe not yett.

Your plate I hope you will have received before this comes and for your glass case Ile keep itt for your comming to towne.

My Lord of Sunderland has written manie letters to desire he may marrie my Ladie Ann Digby and offers to beg her pardon on his knees.[109]

Itt is most bitter weather heere, as ever was suffered butt I beelieve winter is att the last point.

I have not yett beene att Blakes butt will make itt my business speedilie to give you an accompt that I have found out a place which may be to the accomodation you writt about.

I am sorrie to heare of my fawnes dying, itt is an hard winter butt if experience teacheth you or a just inquiry informes you that the keeper is nott a person that is faithfull I can *have* the old keeper John Woodden againe, att the same wages I have this.

This night your brother has invited me and som companie to supper att the Sun behind the Old Exchange where they intend to dance and be merrie.

I am much concerned for your beeing alone. My Ladie Paston has beene latelie verie ill of a cold, their are some that thinke mee a little inhumane I doe nott give her a visitt butt I re[s]pite that till my uncle Montague[110] assures me to bee well received, for I stand on my punctilios too much to have anie more neglects putt on mee. My deare for this time adieu, for the nott neglecting <feare> pretious opportu-nities feare mee nott butt I would faine give you an accompt of something when itt has som progress in the meane time I hope God will direct me.

*Signed*: My deare, I am your most affectionate husband & servant, Robert Paston
*Addressed*: These present to my honored friend the Ladie Paston att Oxnett in Norfolke
[*franked by Robert Paston*]
*NRO: BL/Y/1/9*

[108] Elizabeth, mother of John Hampden (1595–1643), and grandmother of Lady Trevor and Lady Hobart.

[109] Robert Spencer, 2nd earl of Sunderland, was betrothed to Lady Anne Digby but appears to have got cold feet and fled abroad; he subsequently changed his mind and the couple were married on 9 June 1665.          [110] Montague Bertie, 2nd earl of Lindsey

## Sir Robert Paston to Rebecca, Lady Paston

[*1665*,][111] **February 9**. Victoria: My deare hart, if ever flesh was tired out itt is I that have taken more paines this day then an horse, soe that you must now expect a verie short epistle. This day my friends stuck to me and all the young gallants, my Lord Arran & youthes that never take the paines to com to the Howse, were sent by the King & had the patience to loose their dinner for the Yermouth men's confidence was soe great, as their sollicitor promised noe less then his neck if they failed to carrie itt, and itt was the hardest driven battaile that ever I observed betwixt the kindness of my friends, & the malice of my enemies, in short att foure in the afternoone wee came to the question whether the Bill should pass or noe and by the sound I and all my friends thought wee <att> had lost itt butt uppon the devision of the Howse I found I carried itt by thirtie voyces, soe I am past the malice of the Howse of Commons and must run the risk of the Howse of Lords where wee thinke there is noe danger, God be praysed for this dayes success.

[*f*.2] My deare, my aunt Bertie is the best woman in the world and beeleeve me when you com to be acquainted with her will be as great a comfort to you as anie of your acquaintance, this good ladie has beene all over the towne to looke you a convenient howse and has found a verie exelent brave furnished howse in Lincolnes End Fields in Portugall Rowe, three good roomes of a flowre, now if you would write her a letter what linnen & pewter you desire she will agree for all she is a shrewd woman; Blanges lodgins are £8 a weeke, I have seene them and licke the others better and my aunt has beaten them downe to £3 10s, and sayth she will gett the ten shillings abated, pray my deare take notice of her great kindness and of anie thing to her you would have her to doe and she will take a pride in itt; you may remember you and I were once to see Sir Thomas Osburne & my ladie,[112] this is the next dore to that place but much a better furnished & finished howse, of which by the next you shall have a perticular description, itt will accomodate what you writt for full well, tis quiett good ayre, Blanges a most publiq & a durtie place and vastlie deare.

The plate <came> was sent to the carts but this day, you will receive them next week. They stayed for the tankards, send up your plaine ones, they shall be weighed and allowed for. My deare, when I gett pen in hand I knowe nott where to end, Sir John had a great supper for us att the Sun and there were seven hundred people [*sic*] att itt I thinke but my feares of Yermouth made me melancholie, I hope to see thee shortlie which will be the greatest joy that he *can* undergoe that is

*Signed:* yours for ever, Robert Paston
*Endorsed:* This day I was brought to bed[113]
*Addressed:* These present to my honored friend the Ladie Paston att Oxnett in Norfolke
[*franked Robert Paston, and postmark*]
*British Library: Add. MSS 27447, ff 336–337*

[111] Dated from internal evidence
[112] Sir Thomas Osborne (1632–1712) was married to Paston's first cousin, Lady Bridget Bertie. He became lord treasurer in 1673 and earl of Danby in 1674.
[113] Lady Paston's child was not born until the following June; this letter is not dated with a year so the endorsement must have been added (inaccurately) some time later and must refer to the birth of a child in another year.

## Sir Robert Paston to Rebecca, Lady Paston

[*1665,*][114] **February 21**. My deare hart, yesterday at the Quaker's[115] I had thirteene
lords and earles dined with mee in order to my committee in the afternoone, my Lord
of Lindsey tooke a great manie home with him, soe in the afternoone I had att the committee above thirtie lords and earles, three dukes, counsell on both sides were heard,
butt the King hath beene soe passionate for me as you never heard, sent for my Lord
of Dorsett who was chaireman & my noble friend, and bad him from him tell those
lords that were against mee that he would never breake up the parlament till mine *Act*
were past. Att last after too houres the Lords bad us withdrawe and sent for mee in, my
Lord Lucas asked mee if there were anie thing in my Act prejudiciall to the King's interest, whether I would be contented to referr it to the King, I told him nott onlie soe butt
I would give the King att his choise a peece of land to build a fort on to *keep* mee
and them in awe, my Lord Lindsey stood up & sayd he would be bound I should performe whatever I sayd, then they bad me withdrawe & within a quarter of an howre
whilst the Yermouth men & I were scolding in the lobbey, I was called in againe and
my Lord Dorsett told me from the rest that they thought itt nott soe fitt to impose <&>
anie engagement uppon mee, the King having expressed such a readiness to trust mee,
and bad me give the Lords thankes first that there was a fuller committee then was ever
observed, next that they passed my Bill without amendment, and thirdlie that there was
nott one that gave a [*f.*2] negative voyce, soe I went and gave everie lord perticular
thankes amongst which the Duke[s] of Buckingham & Manchester, Dorsett, Lucas, dis-
erved itt perticularlie. Itt was God's mercie that I could gett out that day for I had kept
my bed three dayes before of a cold and was verie ill though I would nott write soe to
you. The Yermouth men grumbled licke doggs & sweare they have yett £3,000 to
spend att <lawe> lawe butt I doubt they will lett mee alone for acts of parlament are
prettie sure cards. There lacks nothing nowe butt the report to the Howse which will
be tomorrowe or next day, and then the King's passing itt which will be on the last day
of the sessions which wee expect to be Tuesday next. My deare I can by noe meanes
comply with your motion of my nott comming downe, I would nott loose the pleasure
of beeing att home one three weekes for anie thing I can foresee, I approve your time
of the tenth of Aprill against which time Ile accomodate you with a cleane and convenient place of abode though wheresoever you are your own chamber must be of your
owne furnishing, I see others' lodgings, my Lord Townsend att £4 10s a weeke accomodated with furniture would make one sick. Therefore if you can pick up soe much
furniture that may be spared as will goe a good way in a bed & hangings you may doe
yourself a courtesie heere and Oxnett heere after.

I hope to bee att home the middle of March, I must see my wife & children, my
horses & mares, cattle & grounds, for the objection of my friends comming to see mee
itt is a pore one, he that expects to gett anie thing in this world must nott stand on
such thinges, besides the most convincing argument is that I beleeve a journey to
Yermouth will be most necessarie for mee butt I shall have a further prospect into

[114] Dated from internal evidence
[115] The Quaker was a tavern in Great Sanctuary, Westminster (Walter Thornbury, *Old and New London*,
3 (1878), pp 483–91).

my affaires everie day and give you an accompt. Mr Henshawe is out of towne gon to waite on Sir William Backhowse att the assizes att Reading and I am gooing to my cutt of boyld mutton att home all alone and [*two words illegible*] for I have kept to that diett this weeke all but yesterday at the Quaker's, as soone as this is digested I am by promise to wayte on your sister Sir John's ladie and Dr Floyd's wife to a play and the husbands by consent are to goe somwhere els. Pray lett mee see your closett up in itts prime and entertaine mee kindlie. For the keeper Ile send you word by the next, I am affraid if I should give him much warning he might play som rouge's trick with mee therefore I would send one downe first that might oversee him whilst he doth goe then when he is gon I feare he will still sharke[116] uppon me, pray sent me som of your considerations on this point.

For Pegg's[117] valentine [*s*]he shall have a present sent downe by the coach this week. To morrowe I begin my circuit to visitt all the lords in perticular,

*Signed*: my deare I am your most affectionate servant, Robert Paston
*Postscript*: I forgott to tell you that I have a gallon of the best orange flower water in the world for you to drinke given you by Mr Henshaw's brother,[118] say if I shall send itt downe or keep itt heere for you, till you com.
*Addressed*: These present to my honored friend the Ladie Paston att Oxnead in Norfolk
[*franked by Robert Paston, and postmark*]
*British Library: Add. MSS 27447, ff 338–339*

## Sir Robert Paston to Rebecca, Lady Paston

[*1665,*] **February 23**. My dearest deare, I can now tell you my Act is passed the Lords' Howse as well as the Commons yesterday morneing and the parlament will breake up on Tuesday, and then the King will pass itt. The towne and myself are treating to gett yett somthing putt into the Bill which may be for both our advantages butt whether wee shall agree itt or the thing bee don is yett a question. My Lord Townshend is fallen desperatelie ill of an impostume[119] in his head which causeth frequent fainting fitts, and I am in som feare itt may prove dangerous. I am soe verie busie about finishing my owne affaire that I cannott yett give you anie accompt of the wayes I designe to turne itt to my advantage, but a back friend of mine that loves nott the chancelor, my Lord Ashley[120] by name, told the King this morning he would give me £4,000 a yeare for my Bill, the King replied he diserves itt were itt ten times as much butt I have those will tell the King another tale, and in a day or too I shall be able to goe to court my self butt Ile make all sure att home first. I sent for Dickinson[121] this morning to speake to him about what you acquainted me with [*f.2*] butt he sayth his wife & himself are gooing into Yorkeshire this spring soe I did nott

---

[116] i.e. sponge upon or swindle
[117] The Pastons' eldest child Margaret, born 1652
[118] Henshaw had two brothers, Nathaniel and Benjamin.          [119] i.e. a cyst or abscess
[120] Anthony Ashley Cooper, baron Ashley of Wimborne St Giles, later 1st earl of Shaftesbury, leader of the 'country' party from the mid-1670s, and anathema to the royalists. A 'back friend' was an enemy pretending to be a friend.
[121] William Dickinson of Watton Abbey, Yorkshire, later a sub farmer of Paston's wood farm, and surveyor general of the customs.

thinke fitt to press that any farther, you may gett either your cousin Hoggan[122] or som other which will be as good if nott better, pray write me word if yett you have found Mrs Rock her bond, if nott write a line or too your self to Dickinson to gett you such a release under her hand as may secure us from the debt to which for all ought I knowe wee stand verie liable. I beleeve I shall write the next weeke for too or three horses to com up in order to my journey downe.

Nurs[e] Port shewes her fickle humor to leave you now, butt were I as you I would shew my self constant never to admitt her againe.[123]

I shall bespeake the ringles[124] for dishes & the other thing and you may please to change what you will away though I know of none you have unless the tankards that are nott of the newest fashion.

I had a verie kind letter from Will this morning, I am gooing to see him shortlie, I could find in my hart to bring him downe with mee beeing he must com noe more till Christmas nor would I [f.3] have him much att London this[125] hott weather, I am glad to heare you are all well att home. Sir William Doyly presents his service to you and gives you thankes for sending to Shottham,[126] he sweares he is your servant.

This day I dined with my Lord Manchester where there were an hundred & fiftie people. The Dutch have taken six of our shipps about Guinny[127] and throwne above 600 people overbord, man woman & child. The post calls me in hast abruptly to say I am

*Signed:* your most affectionate servant, Robt Paston
*Endorsed:* <have him much att London in the hott weather, I am glad to heare you are all soe well att home>[128]
*Addressed:* These present to my honored friend the Lady Paston att Oxnett in Norfolk [*franked Robert Paston, and postmark*]
*British Library: Add. MSS 27447, ff 334–335*

## Sir Robert Paston to Rebecca, Lady Paston

**1664[/5], February 25.** My dearest hart, thy deare letters are the pleasantest thinges in the world, my last told you of my Act beeing past the Lords' Howse, soe now the Yarmouth men are out of their witts, and wee are uppon a treatie wherein they offer me such large termes[129] for my self provided I will exclude others that I thinke my counsell will agree and by consent wee shall petition the King for his letters pattents to incorporate *us* uppon the indentures sealed and soe stop the Bill in which their is clauses that takes in more then my lands and soe may doe me a mischeif as well as

---

[122] Rebecca's cousins called Hoggan or Hogan have not been traced although they were probably related to the Hogans of North Walsham; *see* below p. 225.

[123] Rebecca clearly relented because Nurse Port was still at Oxnead in 1679.

[124] Probably circular bands

[125] Probably a slip of the pen for 'the', *see* endorsement which was clearly a continuation started on the wrong side by accident.

[126] Shotesham, Norfolk, home of the Doylys     [127] The Gold Coast, East Africa

[128] Paston continued his letter on the back of this sheet by mistake and crossed it out.

[129] The Yarmouth assembly offered to incorporate Paston's lands within the jurisdiction of the town as the best means to limit the impact of the Bill upon the town, *see* Gauci, *Great Yarmouth*, pp 115–6.

them, butt in this I will not be overeached having Sir Charles Harbord,[130] my uncle Montague, Ayliff & Crouch to supervise & draw up my termes which must needes in my prospect render the thing much more advantagious then anie way butt of this wee are uncertaine, if itt goes on Ile send you a coppie of the agreement. I am now gooing to counsell about itt, and therefore must be short butt onelie to tell you I am verie well. My Lord Fitzharding came to visitt mee when I was ill, yester night att your brother's lodging supped the Breames family and som of the Boyers,[131] wee had the Duke of Richmond there & his fiddles and stayd up till three in the morne, nott one word true of the Dutch newse I writt last.

By my next you shall heare newse of a keeper, itt was a sad loss of deere though the winter were verie hard. Pray tell Franck[132] my hopes is in him for planting, remember me to him, lett him knowe I am much concerned for his ilness, if he dies be sure to administer in my name, lock up the howse and lett none enter but by your permission. Soe much for this time from

*Signed*: your affectionate husband & servant, Robert Paston
*Postscript*: Lett Dick prepare foure horses to be readie when I send & one to carrie my luggage, the bay stallion may be one.
*Addressed*: These present to my honored friend the Ladie Paston att Oxnett in Norfolke [*franked, Robert Paston*]
*NRO: BL/Y/1/10*

## Sir Robert Paston to Rebecca, Lady Paston

**1664[/5], March 2.** My deare hart, I find by yours you have received mine. Just now I com from the Lords' Howse where I gott verrie neare the King who this day came in robes & crowne to proroage the parlament which he did till the one & twentieth of June and in case their be noe occasion for us then by proclamation wee shall have further leave to play; after he had made a speech to us and received that of our speakers he gave us to understand how manie wicked spiritts were now att worke contriving & hoping for som issue in the Dutch war that might promote their interests, these he termed publicanes, then the Acts were offered to be passed which were manie in number, amongst the rest my pore one of Yermouth had in my owne hearing the royall assent in these words, *soit fait comme il est desiré*, lett itt be don as is desired: which was nott att all to my greif. My Lord Lindsey came to mee & told me if his vote were now to give itt should be against me for crouding soe hard, for having knocked long att a by dore before wee could gett in; the press drive mee up to the King's verie elbowe & I had licke to have carried my Lady Castlemaine along in the croud who was pleased verie civillie to take notice of mee, after the King went out I waited on him when he went to pull of [*f*] his robes, and as soone as he spied [*me*] he came through all the lords to talke & be merrie with mee, insoemuch [*f.2*] as itt was

---

[130] Sir Charles Harbord (1596–1679) of Stanninghall, Norfolk
[131] i.e. the families of Sir Arnold Braems and Sir William Bowyer, John Clayton's father-in-law. Sir Arnold Braems was married to Margaret, daughter of Sir Thomas Palmer of Wingham, and her sister Hester Palmer married Rebecca's brother, George Clayton.
[132] Presumably an employee at Oxnead

much taken notice of in that place but he is the gratiousest person in the world & I have & [*sic*] strange mind you should kiss his hands before your lyng in.

My Lord Carrington, a peere of this realme, a Roman Catholick, was the last weeke most barbarouslie murthered att Pontoise neare Paris by his man who gave him twentie seven wounds in his bed, lockt the dore, perswades the landladie his lord had sent him to Paris and bad her that none of the footmen should offer to enter whilst he knocked, having rested ill the night before & desirous to take out his sleepes, so he takes horse with all the money som £400 and leaves the rest of the servants to find their lord in this pickle, he was a Dutchman.

My Lord Wentworth died yesterday, Old Cleaveland his father is still alive, the Earle of Suffolke has his bedchamber place and the Duke of Monmouth[133] his regiment of gards.

Coles are heere att that excessive rate for want of trading that this day they are sold for £3 10s a chalder[134] and will be £5 in a day or too butt I hope before wee com to towne they will bee easier. Ile say nothing of an howse till I have fixt on one which as yett I have nott, by my next I may.

My Lord Townshend mends, I hope to com out of towne with him Munday sevenight I would have my horses to bee heere on Saterday sevenight. Ile wright by my next <what> I have bought sumpters[135] *alamode* of leather onelie, [*f.*3] by the carts tomorrowe I shall send [?]readstreakes and seedes for the gardiner.

I am now thinking of Yarmouth business and shall before I com have a draught drawne of itt heere though Fisher[136] tells me Hunt[137] must be sent over to the place to draw a more neat & exact peece, som people thinke itt will be worth £2,000 per annum but without question itt will be considerable, God be thanked for anie thing, I have som other irons in the fire but tis hard to find anie thing, I have learnt this rule refuse nothing, therefore if the King gives mee honor itt shall make mee the harder beggar for somwhat to support itt, butt I beeleeve itt will take up my summer's busines in towne to find out somwhat to beg.

This day I sent my man for a tankard of £10 which to morrowe if itt be anie weather Ile carrie myself, for now itt snowes licke the de'el.

If you have a mind Billie should com with me send up his horse you know itt is neare Easter & no more stirring till Christmas, butt I leave itt to you. Farewell my deare till he sees thee who is

*Signed*: thy most humble servant, Robert Paston
*Postscript*: You must now direct your letters to Mr Smith's at the [?]Peare in the Broad Sanctuarie, Westminster. Mrs Pennant is dead, Mrs Tidy is taken for you & Mrs Fletcher.[138]

---

[133] James Scott (1649–1685), duke of Monmouth, the King's oldest, and favourite, illegitimate son.

[134] A chalder or chaldron was approximately 36 bushels or around 28 cwt of coal.

[135] i.e. packs or saddle bags for a packhorse

[136] John Fisher, auditor, deputy to Sir Charles Harbord, surveyor of the duchy of Cornwall, later deputy surveyor general of Crown lands, died c.1688 (TNA: PROB 11/391). Fisher was employed by the Pastons to audit their estate accounts from the 1650s (NRO: AYL 712), and the accounts of the wood farm (NRO: NRS 4008), but he was also a personal friend and correspondent of Sir Robert.

[137] Probably James Hunt, surveyor (Peter Eden, 'Land surveyors in Norfolk *1550–1850*', *Norfolk Archaeology*, p.35).          [138] These ladies were presumably midwives and nursemaids.

*Addressed*: These present to my honored friend the Ladie Paston att Oxnett in Norfolke
[*franked by Robert Paston*]
*NRO: BL/Y/1/11*

## Sir Robert Paston to Rebecca, Lady Paston

**[*1665*] March 24**. My deare hart, I can say nothing by this post but that I cannott com away on Munday, Wedensday I am confident I shall, I am now running to Parson's Greene where your son is to be my bedfellowe. My business goes well, the broad seale will be on this night. I am faine to borrowe pen & ink in my Lord Arlington's[139] lodging to lett you know I am

*Signed:* your humble servant, Rbt Paston
*Postscript:* Lett my coach meet me on Friday att Norwich and for anie weomen to entertaine me I care for none but yourself and desire to meet you alone att home.
*Addressed:* These present to my honored friend the Ladie Paston att Oxnead in Norfolk
*British Library: Add. MSS 27447, f. 331*

## Sir Robert Paston to Rebecca, Lady Paston

**1665, March 25**. My deare hart, I shall leave all discourse till wee meet and positivelie tell you, on Munday morning I sett forth and hope to bee at Norwich by dinner on Wedensday.

This morning I tooke my leave of the King who above twentie times the day before repeated itt to my friends that none was nearer his hart then my self, that he intended to mend my honor & fortune, the which I had this day from his owne mouth in his bedchamber *viz*: that he will speedilie make mee a nobleman of England, & besides will grant mee what I can find to make a suit for, som politick considerations reprived[140] the honor now, for the King thinkes itt would looke too neare a contract to have just don itt att this time, butt the words and wayes of a Prince are nott to be disputed, I hope I shall make the best advantage of both, in the meane time I shall content my self with the happiness of seeing you,

*Signed:* who am your most affectionate servant, Robert Paston
*Postscript:* I am resolved to save Mautby
*Addressed*: These present to my honored friend the Ladie Paston at Oxnett in Norfolke
*NRO: BL/Y/1/12*

---

[139] Henry Bennett (1618–1685), earl of Arlington, secretary of state for the south
[140] i.e. postponed

## Thomas Townshend[141] to Sir Robert Paston

**1665, June 19, Norwich**. Honoured sir, I must humbly begg the acceptance of that service & humble thanks by my pen, which my abrupt departure from London denyed mee to doe personally as I ought. The truth is the feare of the still increaseing sicknes prevayling with the spleene made me rather run then goe out of towne, and here though wee bee free, yet wee are not so from feare by reason of Yarmouth where the plague is so increased, that from sixteen dying last week tis this week come to thirty.[142] Sir, I am so gladd to hear of my Lady Paston's safe delivery & thereby of hopes of your speedy comeing downe that I could not forbeare this humble & hearty congratulation, though except your usuall great goodnes pardon, it must appear very troublesome bringing no newes but badd. I was this last week att Raynham, where I found my Lord Townshend very ill & newly come out of a more dangerous fitt then any former (as himselfe & family say). His fainting was about three houres & so cold in his hands & feet as nothing could bee liker death but death it selfe insomuch as many strong cordialls together with rubbing his hands & breast & feet with palsie water could very hardly att last bring *him* to heat. Every day since hee has had some touches of it. They much feare it will end in a palsie, hee complaynes his stomack is badd & hee growes weake. What the event may bee is dubious, however it much taks him off his busines, yet hee has appointed a meeting with the deputy lieutenants att Dereham next Thursday, but is uncertayne (in regard of the frequent returne of his fitts) whither hee can goe himself or no. I heard him make a very honorable mention of you dureing that short tyme of my stay there, which was no new thing to mee. I beleeve I shall putt it *to* tryall whither you can alwayes forgive, for I am like ever to bee needing your pardons by these so often repeated bouldnesses. I can say nothing to excuse my self but that you are noble & good & will still indulge,

*Signed:* sir, your most humble & faithful servant, Tho: Tounshend
*Addressed*: Present these to the honorable Sir Robert Paston knight & baronett att Mr Clayton's[143] att the Crowne in Lumbard Street, London [*postmark*]
*NRO: BL/Y/1/13*

## Sir Robert Paston to Rebecca, Lady Paston

**[*1665/6*] March 10, London**. My dearest hart, I hope my last gave you som satisfaction concerning my affaire, this must acquaint you with the second part of the historie, as soone as I had received my warrant,[144] my business was to gett the monie

[141] Presumably Thomas Townshend of Horstead and Norwich, will dated 13 July 1705 (NRO: PRDC 1/2/7, f.235), a distant cousin of Lord Townshend. He was the widower of Paston's cousin Bridget Le Gros (d.1663) and married, second, Sir Thomas Browne's niece Anne Cradock (Blomefield, *Norfolk*, X, pp 443–4).          [142] About 1,800 died of the plague at Yarmouth (Gauci, *Great Yarmouth*, p.117).

[143] Rebecca's younger brother George Clayton (b.1639) lived in the Clayton family's house in Lombard Street in the city of London. The house and the nearby church of St Edmund the King and Martyr, where Sir Jasper Clayton was buried, were destroyed in the Great Fire of London in September 1666.

[144] March 1666, warrant for a grant to Sir Robert Paston of the subsidies on wood and wooden wares, &c ... specifying the rent as £2,000 and inserting a proviso of revocation if found inconvenient (*CSPD, 1665–6*)

for my L[ady] C[astlemaine][145] which Mr Porter[146] brought me in a bag the next day and I beeing belowe in Mrs Bettie Frayser's chamber, Sir Alexander[147] carried them up when she was in bed and licke Jupiter presented Danae with a golden showre, my ladie received them with all complements of my well breeding and severall other good words of mee, Sir Alexander told her that I had a request that since I could nott see her soe often as I would that I begged she would give me her picture for my wife and I to contemplate at home where her memorie was fixed; she replied she had a great honor for my ladie & had the other day hearing she was att Parson's Greene made a perticular visitt <hearing she was then> and intending to have waighted on her, for her picture she sayd she was sorrie she had nott soe good an one as shee wished butt would verrie shortlie give mee the best she had, and be readie to serve me on all occasions. Sir Alexander begged I might kiss her hands before [f.2] I went out of towne to which she sayd I should doe her an honor in't. Pore Bettie Frayser is under a sad mortification for the King having promised her a bedchamber place,[148] her mother in law soe misrepresented her to the Queene that the Queene told the King unless he imposed itt she had rather receeive a poysened dagger, this made the King say he would have nothing further to doe with her servants, has putt the doctor & his wife att variance, and Bettie is forbid her mother's howse & the doctor has never layne with his wife since, the King offered to pay her wages which is £500 a yeare, but att present all's lost.

The storie of Marlingford I licke well, pray send me further word of itt that while I am among the lawyers I may have their opinion of itt, you will doe well to make Hurton produce the evidence & the lease and then they must prove the release which fatall stroke I feare though knowe nothing was strucken by my father, butt perhapps he could nott doe itt. Ile push all the interest to recover itt if you speake with Buller,[149] pray lett me heare by the next. This night I am for Parson's Greene being first to dine with Mr Porter to whose governement you committed me where I feare wee shall be foxed.[150] My love to all and to your selfe the true affections of, my deare,

*Signed:* yours eternallie, Robert Paston

*On same sheet:* Charles Porter to Rebecca, Lady Paston
Madam, att last though through many sad changes Sir Robert hath surmounted all difficultyes and gotten the King's sweet hand, accompanied with many favorable

---

[145] Lady Castlemaine derived a considerable income by using her interest with the King to facilitate all kinds of appointments and grants, but her services did not come cheap and Paston was still paying her in October 1667 (British Library: Add. MSS 27447, f.310).

[146] Charles, later Sir Charles, Porter (1631–1696), a lawyer and future lord chancellor of Ireland. His father Edmund Porter was rector of Heveningham, Norfolk, and prebendary of Norwich.

[147] Paston's intermediary with Lady Castlemaine was Sir Alexander Fraizer, the fashionable doctor who, according to Samuel Pepys, helped court ladies 'to slip their calfes when there is occasion' (quoted in *ODNB*).

[148] Bettie was Sir Alexander Fraizer's daughter by his first marriage. Her stepmother Mary, Lady Fraizer, was a bedchamber woman to the Queen. Bettie's half-sister Carey Fraizer became a maid of honour to the Queen in 1674 and married her cousin Charles, 2nd viscount Mordaunt and 3rd earl of Peterborough. The *Calendars of Treasury Books* show no payments to Bettie to compensate her for her loss.

[149] Thomas Bulwer

[150] i.e. intoxicated. Porter had a reputation for heavy drinking (*ODNB*).

expressions [*f.*3] which intitle him to any further boon he shall ask, I wish your lady-ship much joy and long life to enjoy the advantage of the graunt; I pray madam, doe not beleive I will forfeit your good opinion of my skill in government, what ever Sir Robert sayth there is no danger of a fox, tis true here is a gent that now & then does take a doze, but this day he shall not. I shall make all possible hast to pass the great seale that I may return my charge to your own government where he (I am sure) most passionately longs to be. I am not without hope of wayteing upon him or coming soon after him to have the honour to kiss your hands, I am, madam,
*Signed:* your most humble servant, Ch Porter

*Addressed:* These present to my honored friend the Ladie Paston att Oxnead in Norfolke [*in Paston's hand*]
*British Library: Add. MSS 36988, ff 102–103*

## Sir Robert Paston to Rebecca, Lady Paston

[*1665/6*],[151] **March 17**. My deare hart, yours makes mention of my daughter's ilnes[*s*] for which I am sorrie butt I hope itt will prove but a spring distemper, pray remember mee to her & lett her knowe Ile bring her home a Valentine's gift. I am verie glad my son came nott for though att Radford's[152] their is a most convenient chamber, hung & private to himself, reserved for him, yett wee can by no means agree about a servant, and they have given mee soe manie convincing reasons, which I shall tell you att home, of the hindrance itt's licke to be to his booke that I am cleere-lie of the opinion that for the year & halfe he is to be there to lay the foundation of scolership for his life time, itt's absolutelie nott onelie unecessarie butt inconvenient. I shall now be with you verie shortlie & I would nott have him stir till I com perhaps itt may be before you thinke ont, butt my business is past the aturney generall[153] and will be readie for the broad seale by Tuesday next.

This day I was with my Lord Chancellor to acquaint him I had the warrant, he told me he thought me worthy of this or anie favor the King could doe me, wee parted kindlie with som cherielickums[154] butt all the assurances of friendship that might be, soe that now I knowe nott where the rub will be, if I meet anie more. Sir Nicolas Crisp & one Sir Edmond Turner, a custome howse man, were the men that opposed mee butt I thinke wee are now past all pikes or shall be past the broad seale in three or foure dayes time more.

[*f.*2] Be sure you send betimes to Norwich for the letter by the next post which will

---

[151] The date of this letter poses problems as it is quite clearly written as 1667. Paston normally dated all his letters Old Style, with the year beginning on 25 March, but this letter cannot date from 1667/8 because by then Clarendon was in exile and there was no lord chancellor. In content it appears to follow the previous letter of 10 March, and refers to Paston's warrant (issued in March 1666) and the opposition of Sir Nicholas Crisp, customs official and farmer, who died on 26 February 1666. The letter must there-fore date from 1666 and the year was written as 1667 by a slip of the pen, perhaps because Paston just written a '7' in the day of the month. Turner was one of the new customs farmers and became one of the sub-farmers of Paston's wood farm (NRO: NRS 4018, 10 July 1673).

[152] William Radford (1623–1673), friend of John Aubrey, 'taught school' at Richmond where he died (John Aubrey, *Brief Lives* (ed. Richard W. Barber) (Woodbridge, 1982), p.260).

[153] Sir Geoffrey Palmer (1598–1670)          [154] Probably an exchange of compliments

be on Thursday morning. I am this night againe for Parson's Greene. Sir Alexander Frayser has shewne himself most kind to mee in this business. Jack Carie[155] cutt his owne throat the other night but was kept from going through stick with his worke and remaines yett alive.

Mr Porter is soe carefull of my affaire 'twere nott amiss if in a word you acknowledged itt & remembred your service to his ladie.

Sir William Doyly my old & constant friend is your servant, my love to all the children, pray if my Lord Townshend intends you a visitt putt me of noe putts [*sic*] without the danger be emminent. Adieu till wee meet.

*Signed:* Yours, Robt Paston
*Postscript:* Pray lett the chappell be made readie for paving for the marble will com down in a forthnight – I heare nothing of the nog.
*NRO: BL/Y/1/26*

## Sir Robert Paston to Rebecca, Lady Paston

**1666, May 29**. My deare hart, in order to what I told you, in my last, Mr Earle is now drawing up a coppie of the articles given in by them and approoved by me soe as to morrowe wee shall goe forward amaine with the settlement of our affaire and trulie those few persons I have acquainted with the way doe thinke I have made an exelent bargaine butt you shall knowe further of our proceeds in a day or too.

This day the bells proclaime the King's birth and great preparation for jollitie everie where, I am gooing to court to visitt their Majestyes and therefore take the opportunitie of the morne to write to you nott knowing if I shall gett home by the post howre.

Yesterday I was with my mason for the pavement of the chappell which will be verie noble. I have bespoke a verie handsom chimney peece for the little parlor & harth for £15 and an harth for the little roome, Dutch tyles are verie deare att this time, send me word in your next what quantitie you would have.

You write mee noe word concerning the gooing on of my building, of the too roomes for the servants' hall and the preserving roome.

I doe suppose the time prefixed in my last letter will be the time about which I shall soonest be able to gett out of towne butt if before I shall be glad. [*f.2*] Your mother & sister[156] had best goe downe before mee for I com in the single charriott.

The mixing adrop[157] with calcined earth is a way I would nott have William[158] meddle withall. But I would have onlie *him* gett what quantitie of *caput mort[uum]* he can from adrop in a naked fire. Then would I have him rectifie that verie spiritt drawne of[*f*] by force of fire and keep what itt leaves att the bottome if itt leaves anie thing. The other orders in the paper I would have him persue and give me some accompt, I know nott if Howse's mare foled a mare or an horse fole.

---

[155] However he is identified in the Verney letters as Monmouth Cary (HMC 6: 7th R.I., p.485).
[156] Probably Rebecca's younger sister Prudence Clayton
[157] Adrop was a term used by alchemists to mean the matter out of which mercury is to be extracted for the philosopher's stone, or the philosopher's stone itself.
[158] Paston's laboratory assistant

Just now coms in the squire of the bodie[159] who presents his service and sayth he saw your son verie well, engaged in a game att cricquett on Richmond Greene.

Mr Frayser has brought me the song butt itt's soe simple I would nott send them.

I have beene att court and seene all the world, manie people ask for you, som call mee Lord butt on what grounds I knowe nott, perhapps itt may be but I heare nothing of itt yett.

I must desire you to present my love to my children and for this time bid you fare well. I have returned a bill of £30 uppon Hurton.

*Signed:* Yours eternallie, Robt Paston
*Addressed*: These present to my honored friend the Ladie Paston at Oxnead in Norfolke
*NRO: BL/Y/1/14*

## Sir Robert Paston to Rebecca, Lady Paston

**1666, June 7**. My deare hart, the bells and bonefires the last night proclaimed our signall victorie over the Dutch of which yesterday morning I heard the King make the narrative: wee have destroyed above halfe their navie having sunke and fired above fiftie sayle. Sir Daniel Harvey came yesterday and damped the newse a little in telling how dearelie wee had bought itt. The Generall[160] is hurt in his arme and his leg butt soe little that itt's nothing, Sir William Clarke slaine, so is Bacon, Terne & Whittie,[161] Sir George Askue taken prisoner, Captaine Berckley taken or lost, the Duke & Prince[162] both com into the Gunfleet which is a bay neare Harwich.

My £1,500 subscription[163] makes me mad, my Lord Richardson[164] will fayle me I fear and is uncertaine for himself and my Lord Townshend. My other business is in Sergeant Earle's[165] hands and if wee are soe happie as to agree itt according to his instructions itt will be well for mee, and I hope wee shall nott much varie as to the maine and then I cannott butt hope to make itt worthe neare £3,000 per annum to mine owne self; tomorrowe wee are to meet about itt and if matters can be dispatched in ten dayes time twill be exelent, soe you must keep up your wedding day all <home> *alone*, butt Ile send you downe the best cooke to dress your dinner that ever you had. Yesterday uppon the victorie I had three or foure friends with mee and he dressed dinner noe disparagement to our neighbors cooke much beyound him. I had a letter from my Lord Townshend who congratulates my being a lord, I beleeve itt will be soe: butt I protest to God there's no such thing yett in designe att the court that I can heare of.

[159] Thomas Cheeke    [160] George Monck (1608–1670), 1st duke of Albemarle

[161] Philemon Bacon, Henry Terne and John Whittie, naval officers

[162] i.e. the duke of York and Prince Rupert

[163] From later references it appears that Paston's subscription money was money he had to put down in advance for the wood farm. Farmers of customs and excise always paid rent in advance enabling the treasury to borrow against these sums (C.K. Chandaman, *The English Public Revenue, 1660–1688* (Oxford, 1975), p.21)

[164] Thomas Richardson (c.1627–1674), 2nd baron Cramond, MP for Norfolk; he was a nephew of Paston's step-mother.

[165] Erasmus Earle (c.1590–1667), of Heydon Hall, Norfolk, serjeant at law; he was handling Paston's negotiations with the merchants who would farm the wood customs for him.

[*f.*2] Ile menage all as wiselie as I can.

I am glad you intend to mend the chappell if itt be nott better then my designe Ile promise you Ile alter itt againe. I have sent the paper to the stone cutter what shall be don with the arch in the hall; huswife looke well after itt or els as soone as you are brought to bed Ile pay your coate[166] to som purpose.

Pray wright me word in your next when the stone cutter may bring the pavement downe and when your alteration will be don I shall take order about the Dutch tyle, I pray God we have a good peace for Yermouth's sake.

I can have Robin Jegon's[167] howse in Queenstreet for threescore and ten pounds a yeare which I think a monstrous penniworth[168] and I beleeve in the wardrobe you may find out manie things that will furnish all butt the first flore which must be handsom itt is an howse will largelie serve my familie and there's noe thoughts butt I must be heere somtimes and the charge of lodgings and uncertainetie of the rates of howses is saved in a constant place, stables may be had too convenientlie neare.

Pray write mee word what you thinke to doe with your great bellie for I must provide you quarters, September calls me up and I intend nott to live in anie place long without you, Jegon's howse well cleansed and whited and they out of itt (his wife cannott live a week to an end) and he quitts itt would be another manner of place then you thinke on and itt is a howse of as much conveniencie as I knowe, and beleeve itt London is nott dearer then the cuntrie butt to those that will make itt soe, butt I speake of this butt for the winter time, however such an howse att that rent cannott lie on one's hands.

My Ladie Castlemaine is com back to court <with> and in as good graces as ever, my Lord Abergavennie is dead the last week; the Dutchess of Yorke is a little out of humor as som take notice. I have now noe more to say butt that I do most hartilie wish my self att home. Pray remember me to *my* deare <Billie> children. I am to dine at Richmond on Sunday next att Captaine Cheeke's to see deare Billie.[169] I am glad the building goes on soe well. Pray aske William if this last [*f.*3] salt sublimed[170] soe high as our former salt. Tell *Will* he must coate a coupple of greene bollksheads[171] to sublime itt in a naked fire, when the spiritt coms of noe more insipid. Bid him grind som halfe a dram of the salt he last sublimed with as much running mercurie, att the same time when he putts the [?]casce of the salt of the *caput mort[uum]* to running mercurie and tell me if either (toucheth uppon itt) that is to say disolves itt or which doth best on itt.

My deare I have now noe more to say butt that I am for ever, my deare,

*Signed:* thy most humble servant, Robert Paston
*Addressed*: These present to my honored friend the Ladie Paston att Oxnead in Norfolke
*NRO: BL/Y/1/15*

---

166   To pay someone's coat, i.e. to beat them
167   Probably Robert Jegon of Buxton near Oxnead, who was presumably the son or grandson of John Jegon (1550–1618), bishop of Norwich.
168   i.e. a very good price, a bargain       169   His eldest son, William
170   To sublime is to heat a substance in a vessel so as to convert it into vapour, which is carried off and on cooling is deposited in a solid form.
171   Probably a bolthead or boltshead: a globular flask with a long cylindrical neck used in distillation.

## Sir Robert Paston to Rebecca, Lady Paston

**1666, June 9**. My dearest harte, since my last I have beene in the greatest palk[172] of troubles that ever man was in about my subscription money butt this day my hart is somwhat alleviated & I hope to doe itt the way I thought least of but itt will cost mee above an £100 which is cheape to the rates people give heere, Mr Dee[173] is the man that is licke to accomodate mee and I shall accomodate my self too in the settling my other affaire through my Cousin \<Burales\> Burrell's[174] means and gett my ringbox I think & jewells or order itt soe as nott to loose anie thing as all other people that Everard[175] owes money to are like to doe.

I hope too the next week to finish my *grand affaire* to content, I hope you will licke the way of itt when itt's don I am sure I and my friends approove itt highlie.

Our great victorie coms to less then wee would have had itt butt there has beene shrewd banging of all sides, my cousin Bertie[176] is com on shore, the Generall tis sayd will have the other brush & Prince Rupert refuseth to com resolving to bring another victorie or to die for it. Som shipps of ours that were sayd to be lost are found againe as the *Essex* & the *Swiftsure*.

On Munday if I can gett places the cooke & the gardiner coms downe, the cooke is a most ingenious person to furnish a kitchin as well as to dress the meat, I have provided him heere with netts to take all manner of birds to store the volleries.[177] Pray send mee up word the next in turne when your chappell will be readie for the comming downe of the pavement and trulie I thinke, beeing I bestowe a new marble chimney and harth on our eating parlor, a new sute of guilt leather hangins. Thom Cheek bought a verie handsom sute that will hang more then that roome for £20 but if you would have them strained [*sic*] or otherwise send mee word and tis don.

[*f.*2] I have bought of Mrs Wiseman[178] too quarts of cordiall water of my Ladie

[172] i.e. pack

[173] Rowland Dee, merchant of London, *see* TNA: C10/166/86, Paston v. Cornwallis, and NRO: AYL 91.

[174] Nicholas Burwell (1620–1670) of Grays Inn had recently married Paston's cousin Frances Le Gros of Crostwick (London marriage licence, 7 May 1666). The Burwells had Norfolk connections: Nicholas' sister Mary had married Sir Thomas Rant of Thorpe in 1630, his daughter Mary, by his first marriage, married Sir John Pettus, another Paston cousin, in 1670. Nicholas' brother Sir Jeffrey Burwell (1606–1684) of Rougham Place, Suffolk, had a daughter Mary who married Robert Walpole of Houghton. (*The Visitation of the County of Suffolk, 1664–1668, ODNB,* Margaret Toynbee, 'Some Friends of Sir Thomas Browne' (*Norfolk Archaeology,* XXXI (1957), pp 377–394.).

[175] Charles Everard, who held one of Paston's mortgages, had died of the plague on 28 October 1665. (J.R. Woodhead, *The Rulers of London 1660–1689: A Biographical Record of the Aldermen and Common Councilmen of the City of London* (1966), pp 64–67).

[176] Possibly Charles Bertie (1641–1711), son of the earl of Lindsey, who had a naval commission as a second lieutenant and an army commission as a captain in the Coldstream Guards in 1668.

[177] i.e. bird cages or aviaries

[178] Sir William Paston left £50 to his 'very good friend' Mrs Margaret Wiseman if she should be unmarried at the time of his death (TNA: PROB 11/311); she was presumably a cousin of Margaret, Lady Paston, whose mother was a sister of Sir Richard Wiseman of Lincoln's Inn, and she appears to have been living with the older Pastons in London in 1658 (British Library: Add. MSS 36988, f.80). There are further references to a Mrs Wiseman as a friend of the younger Pastons, and even as resident at Oxnead in 1671 – on this latter instance she is referred to as 'Cousin Wiseman' by Thomas Henshaw. Henshaw's cousin Major Thomas Henshaw, the royalist plotter, had a half-brother John Wiseman (*A Collection of the State Papers of John Thurloe,* volume 2: 1654 (1742), pp 356–369), whose daughter she may have been. It has not

Hewytt's[179] and may have too more if you send mee word in time and a pottle of snayle water,[180] I knowe nott what stock you have butt lett me alone if ever setled for making these waters to content [*sic*].

The letters from the west make Robin Hewytt[181] nott soe blith as he was, the paines have returned they say through the misfortune of the asses beeing killed by doggs which gave her milke, the doctors say she is in a verie weake condition but may with time recover which I think nott for above a yeare.

I doe give leave for once to the keeper's wife to ly in in the park.

As soone as ever I can Ile com, I hope one forthnight more will dispatch mee to you, on Wedensday you had att a venture best send too horses to Norwich for the cooke & gardiner. I thinke Harrie Oliver ought in justice to show this gardiner what's don, I have nott seene the gardiner this week but have sent to find him out and to take places in the coach for Munday.

To morrowe I am for the squire of the bodies[182] at Richmond att dinner with your son Will, to night for Sergeant Earle and remember I tell you neare if nott £3,000 *per annum*.

Remember mee to all my children, I am sorrie you were soe sick butt if itt were quickning you'l be the better for it. My deare pray hasten on the chappell that som way or other itt may be don; I have noe more to say now but that I am, my deare,

*Signed:* your most humble servant, Robt Paston
*Postscript:* Since I writt the cooke cannott goe till Friday next and I beeleeve the gardiner att the same time soe send noe horses till you heare further.
*Addressed:* These present to my honored friend the Ladie Paston att Oxnead in Norfolke
*NRO: BL/Y/1/16*


## Thomas Henshaw to Sir Robert Paston

**1666, June 11, Kensington**. [*Pa*]*tron colendissimo,*[183] I shall never faile in my obedience, though I find by experience I shall faile too often in my ability to serve you: for proof of both I have sent you the draught[184] you commanded me to make; which

been possible to distinguish between these various Mrs Wisemans (if the references are indeed to more than one person) and they have been indexed together.

[179] There is a recipe for 'Lady Hewet's water', a decoction of herbs and spices in sherry-sack, in *The Compleat Housewife* (1727), of which it was claimed 'two or three spoonfuls almost revive from death'. This recipe appears to have been current from the 1660s. However since Mrs Wiseman was a cousin of the Hewitts this batch may have actually been made by Ursula, wife of Sir William Hewitt of Breckles, brother of Lady Paston, or made from a family recipe.

[180] Snail water was for treating diseases of the lungs.

[181] These letters related to the health of Paston's stepmother, Margaret, Lady Paston: it is not clear what she was doing in the West Country, but in 1668 she married Sir George Strode of Leweston, Dorset, a cousin of the Windhams of Felbrigg; Robin Hewytt or Hewitt was one of her brothers.

[182] Thomas Cheeke                                                    [183] i.e. most worshipful

[184] See draft in Henshaw's hand of a letter from Sir Robert Paston to unnamed: the King is known to have promised to ennoble Paston and because this has not happened he fears he will be thought to be out of favour; asks addressee to intercede with the noble lady to once more use her powerful oratory on his behalf (British Library: Add. MSS 36988, f. 99). This draft has been dated both 1672 and 1673 in a later

though it cost me more paines then ever any of that bignes, yet it has not the lucke to please me and I feare will have worse success with you, especially since it is not only to represent your owne thoughts to your own self, but such as you had framed into a garbe and mode fit to have shewed themselves at court, but you know that a curled and painted style was ever as disagreeable to my nature as it is now to my age, which makes me <*word deleted*> so severe that I have no patience with either a swolne, bumbast, affected, forced, or pedanticke peice of rhethoricke, nor can any please me that is not sober, perspicuous, close, nervous, free, *and* the words proper discreet well chosen, not savouring either of the English schoolmaster or French dancing-master. If you ask me why I have not done this suitable to the character I affect, I answer it was either because I could not put my self into wright humour, or else because it was above my genius, so seriously recommending you to make use of the letter you drew up your self, I desire you to dedicate mine rather to the close stoole then Vulcan that you may mend the letter by guilding the paper.

*Signed:* I am sir, your devoted servant, TH
*Addressed:* For Sir Robert Paston, this
*NRO: BL/Y/1/17*

## Sir Robert Paston to Rebecca, Lady Paston

**1666, 12 June**. My dearest hart, thy letters are cordialls and serve to revive me even in the middst of my affaires, which I doe assure are of such a nature as require a greater patience then mine, and a greater prudence to settle, yett when I see the honor and interest of my family concerned in itt, I resolve nott to give itt over, till I have don itt the best I may. My sergeant, though he picks my pocketts, yett is resolved not to leave *mee* in this my great affaire, to write you particulars, till som event, were unnessessarie, but the sergeant's advice to me is to take up my £4,000 in another place, and nott of those that are to have the farme, to which purpose I pray send this enclosed to Mr Earle immediatelie uppon the receipt of itt, to com to Oxnett to take such writings as may be necessarie, and caress him hugelie and give him a peece or too, to engage his love and forthwith pray him to com away to London, for nothing can be don without him, the sooner he comms the sooner the sooner [*sic*] my business will be don, the sergeant and I have allreadie modeled all for his con-trivance and execution, beeleeve itt my deare this thing of mine will pay our debts and make us live comfortably together which you'l presentlie feele the sweet of after the settlement of our affairs; all which I tell you againe depends on Mr Earle's speedie posting away for which you shall engage yourself he shall be noe looser.

Our Dutch victorie has beene dearelie bought and the newse heere is that the French are on our co[a]sts with thirtie thousand mounsieurs yett wee feare them nott, but the Generall will not com ashore nor the Prince till they give a better accompt of the Dutch and itt's sayd wee shall bee readie in three weekes for the other brush.

hand, probably because Paston finally received his peerage in 1673. However it appears to have been orig-inally enclosed with this letter of 11 June 1666 and was presumably addressed to Sir Alexander Fraizer, Paston's intermediary with Lady Castlemaine, see p. 63.

[f.2] Sir Christopher Minns[185] is dead of the wound received, Sir George Ascue is taken prisoner, the leggs and armes that are lost are innumerable.

On Friday next after my cooke has dressed me three or foure dishes in commemoration of the day, I send him downe by the waggon and the gardiner allsoe their beeing birds and other thinges for him to looke after, by the way, he chuseth that passage, there must be too horses for them att Norwich on Wedensday which I think is the day the carts com in.

The painter who will doe all thinges to your hart's desire shall com on Thursday sevenight, he desires to doe the chappell before the pavement is layd as he did itt att Sir Robert Geare's.[186] I am to lett him have £10 in hand, he is a rare civill & industrious fellowe and paints all sorts of wayes to your hart's content therefore take out your penniworths of him *in what shape you approve best*,[187] hee'l shew you in little patterns of the great before he begins soe you may take your choise. I suppose by that time Tyndall will have don, if nott you may imploy him in anie thing els about stairecase or hall.

Never was anie man more solitarie then I amongst soe manie people. I am hartilie wearie of this place if my urgent necessities prevailed nott over my inclinations.

Yesterday I dined att Richmond with your deare son who is soe loth to change his gold that I was faine to supply him with twentie shillings for bird cages and other necessarie implyments. Dick[188] behaves himself soe well that I heare no desires they have to part with him. I found him receving the communion which I approved verie well in one of his ranke that has nobodie to mind him but his owne devotion.

I have nothing now more to say butt that you speed Mr Earle to mee and take a note of what writings he shall thinke most necessarie for the making out my title to such lands as are free for me to engage by alteration of the securities nott forgetting Southtowne wee'l handle them gently.

[f.3] I am more then confident when my business is setled in less then one yeare I shall have a lusty bidder that will give a cleering sum if wee find the sequestration of itt will nott doe the cure in eight or ten yeares and free us of all incumberances of use money whatsoever.

My dearest hart I have soe much of business this day that I can say now more. Mr Dee and my Cousin Burwell & I am treating, I think Dee will prove a better friend then Everard was and I hope wee shall accomodate all there to content. My £1,500 I hope to gett layd downe for nothing by my farmers since I wa[i]ve the £4,000 there.

My deare make much of thyself and remember me on Friday and Ile remember thee; remember mee to my deare children & God send me home to thee by the end of this month.

I thanke thee for the newse of my salt and mercurie – I wish you could send mee word they run both into a water thickish and whitish, pray lett me have a further accompt and how the salt which sublimed in the bollshead agrees with mercurie. My deare adieu.

*Signed:* Thine for ever, Robert Paston

---

[185] Sir Christopher Myngs (c.1625–1666)      [186] Sir Robert Gayer of Stoke, Bucks
[187] This addition is in the margin.      [188] A servant

*Postscript:* Heere is a foolish report of the Duke of Buckingham's killing my Lord Ros[189] butt itt's butt a fable supposed. I forgott to lett you knowe that I *saw* a letter out of the west, my mother continues a very weake woman and Mrs Wiseman never expects to see her more. I thinke she may linger a long while but nott recover – if she be prettie well one day sayth the letter she is verie ill another, soe though she is better then she [*was at*] first wee cannot thinke [*her*] past danger. In the sergeant's letter is mine to himself inclosed, you may seale up the sergeant's and send mine in itt unsealed.

*Addressed*: These present to my honored friend the Ladie Paston att Oxnett in Norfolke
*NRO: BL/Y/1/18*

## Sir Robert Paston to Rebecca, Lady Paston

**1666, June 14**. My deare hart, I received thy deare letter for the which I give thee manee thankes. I am as impatient and eager of beeing att home as you can wish me butt now to com before I have made som settlement is impossible and itt is harder to doe, then you can imagine; if you knew the debates, the discourses, the meetings, the breaches we have, you would pittie me; yesterday all the day wee were debating our articles, and are now att a stand, what to morrowe may produce I cannott tell; I am verie loth to lett itt att £2,300 a year certaine, when as this bargaine runns thus, they are to menage the farme and nott to discompt one pennie proffitt to themselves untill £2,500 per annum be made good too mee, if the farme coms nott to soe much in proffitt I am to have unto a pennie what itt makes, besides the King's *rent* and the sallaries; and when £2,500 is payd to mee, then are wee to com to an accompt of what riseth in proffitt, above that sum which if itt happen to be £1,000, £500 of itt is mine and the other £500 theirs. Now judge you if foure persons of that qualitie are licke to trouble themselves under the hopes of getting £500 amongst them, I know they hope for more and whatsoever they can gett itt's the better for mee, for I am to have as much for my owne share besides the £2,500 per annum as they are to have amongst them all foure. Mr Earle wee heare is gon into Northamptonshire, butt will be att London the next week, butt I have one here, my Cousin Burwell, who is the most zealous man alive for mee and the ablest.

[*f.*2] £2,300 certaine is all is bid by Mr Porter's men which when £230 for the tenth part is payd to the discoverer their remaines for me but £2,070. I hope to gett my subscription money layd downe by the persons that shall deale with mee butt my deare feare itt nott Ile act with the best advice and prudence imaginable and doe hope yett to give a good accompt [*of*] itt in three or four dayes.

Heere is Sir John Holland my next neighbor from whome I have much advice and good companie, hee presents his service to you. I hope by Mr Fisher's help to doe our business without Jack Earle therefore the time of his intended comming which is next week will serve, after this bout Ile promise you Ile never be from you againe.

Heere is a black velvett bed lined through with aurora[190] sattin and embroydered

---

[189] John Manners, Lord Roos, later 1st duke of Rutland; Buckingham claimed the title of baron de Ros through his mother, however he did not kill Manners.

[190] A rich orange colour like the sky at sun-rise

with [?]tintstick on the outside with a sute of hangings of my Ladie Monmouth's to be sold. Mr Burwell can gett them a penniworth.[191] Ile speake to Mrs Frayser about them.

The cooke & gardiner com away by the waggon tomorrowe. You must send horses for them to Norwich on Wedensday. He brings with him som singing birds and som turtles and some tackling to store the volleries, a little dog, the puppie of your sister's little bitch.

I have invited som friends tomorrowe to dinner though Sir John and my ladie cannot be heere nor Don who goes with them to Denham[192] yett their shall be those that loves us verie well.

The painter comms away on Thursday next, I have given him £6 to b[u]y himself tooles and whatsoever he doth agree with him by the great, butt if the chappell be nott readie you may employ him about somwhat els, I would faine have the landskip of my howse drawne from towards Marsham somwhere in that field butt heel find the best view to grace a great picture.

I leave the considerations of your lying in wholy to yourself. [f.3] If anie other thoughts happen lett me knowe, Ile cheapen Jeggon's howse however howses are licke to be cheaper then formerlie.[193] Remember mee to the children, my deare I am

*Signed*: yours for ever, Robt Paston
*Postscript:* I thinke in my last I forgott to tell you that I received your bill for £50 which came when I had nott a souse.[194] Pray God send us fifteene more yeares[195] of matrimonie.
*Addressed*: These present to my honored friend the Ladie Paston att Oxnead in Norfolke
*NRO: BL/Y/1/19*

## Sir Robert Paston to Rebecca, Lady Paston

**1666, June 16**. My deare, if I should tell you the difficulties and disappointments I lie under you would pittie mee butt I hope to surmou[n]t them all and give a good account of my journey att last and hope in a forthnight's time more to be soe happie as to kiss your hands with a sereene browe.

The painter coms away in the Thursday's coach, on Saterday you must send an horse to Norwich for him.

Yesterday I solemnelie kept my wedding day with Sir John Holland and diverse of my friends, I had fifteen pies in a dish.[196]

My deare I onelie sett pen to paper to keep my word everie post and for hast beg your excuse till the next post who am for ever,

*Signed:* your passionate lover & servant, Robt Paston
*British Library: Add. MSS 27447, f. 307*

[191] i.e. at a good price
[192] Alice, wife of Sir John Clayton was a daughter of Sir William Bowyer of Denham, Middlesex.
[193] i.e. following the plague. However the situation was soon reversed after the Great Fire of London, which started on 2 September 1666.
[194] From the French sou; used for any small coin or amount, generally with a negative connotation.
[195] This places the Pastons' marriage in 1651.
[196] i.e. one for each year of marriage

## Sir Robert Paston to Rebecca, Lady Paston

**1666, June 19.** My deare hart, I must take the opportunitie of ill paper to tell you yesterday was the first time I ever missed intelligence from you since I left you, which I impute to the neglect of the post or som other accident. Tomorrowe Mr Earle is expected and then wee shall doe somwhat I hope for my matters will of[*f*] but the raising of the £4,000 is that which sticks in this conjuncture of time. I hope I shall gett these things over butt they are rubbs that mortalls are subject too, and money now scarcer then ever. Ile make what hast I can out of towne & feare nott yett butt all thinges in time will goe well.

The sickness is decreased, eighteen in the whole and eight of the plauge.

The French have cutt all the English throates att St Christopher's[197] and possessed themselves of the iland.

The £1,500 nott yett to bee had butt my Lord Richardson endeavors to save his reputation, manie are in our condition, for till the other brush is over with the Dutch everie man locks up his money.

My deare, I long to heare you are all well and shall never truly joy till I am with you,

*Signed:* who am your humble servant and eternall lover, Robt Paston
*Addressed*: These present to my honored friend the Ladie Paston att Oxnett in Norfolke
*NRO: BL/Y/1/20*

## William Doughty[198] to Sir Robert Paston

**1666, October 8, Aylsham.** *Has discussed with Mr Bulwer the right of presentation to Skeyton living claimed by Mr Spendlove; Dr Browne[199] gives them some comfort as to his brother's health.*

*Signed:* I rest your humble servant to my power, Will Doughty
*Addressed*: These present to the honourable Sir Robert Paston at Mr Hodges house in Lincolns Inn Faields neer Queen Street
*NRO: BL/Y/1/21*

## Inhabitants of Skeyton to Sir Robert Paston

**1666[/7], January 29, Skeyton.** *Thanks from inhabitants of Skeyton for sending and settling amongst them Mr Birton,[200] a very orthodox divine, & conformable to the rites and ceremonies of the Church of England; and a person very sober, able, & ingenious.*

*Signed*: Thomas Deane, Giles Smyth, Robt Smyth, Tho: Bigilsey, Hen: Empson, Thomas Loughrie, Edward Umphrye, [*by mark:*] John Allin, [*by mark:*] John Cou[*??*], Henery Church, Christophar Pank, Raphe Umphrie, Thomas Umphrie, John

---

[197] i.e. St Kitt's in the West Indies     [198] William Doughty (d.1678), of Aylsham
[199] Dr (later Sir) Thomas Browne (1605–1682), physician, antiquary and author. Doughty's brother was Major Robert Doughty (d.1679) of Aylsham. For the latter's career see above pp 20–21.
[200] Daniel Burton, minister at Skeyton till his death in 1704

Sharinge, Willyam Sparow, John Spendlove, Richard Metcalfe, John Martill, [*by mark:*] William Sperin, Nicolas Webster

*Addressed*: To the honorable Sir Robert Paston knight & barronett at his lodgings in Lincolne Inne Filds on the suthsid next doore but one to Queen Stret, London

*Endorsed*: Letter from the parish of Skeyton, Jan the 29: 1666

*NRO: BL/Y/1/22*

## Horatio, Lord Townshend, to Sir Robert Paston

**1667, May 25**. Sir, yours of the 23 instant was very wellcome to mee as all you writ is, for the which I give you most hearty thanks as looking upon it not only as an act of kindniss but of charrity it not being in my power or statione to returne you the like satisfactorie accounts.

I beleeve your entertainment at the meeting of the vertuosi in Arundel House[201] hath bene pleasent.

I confesse I did mistake you in your last in refference to your owne affaire upon the hill of the which I shall give a touch upon the next opportunity upon an English account but whether my loadstone may be effectuall I much feare, yet I know you will accept the good will of him that is capable of so little.

Pray give me leave to begg that you give not waye to mallincolly thoughts, or at least when you come downe leave them behind you, for let us not dispaire if things be nott done at our time as long as there is a possibillity they may bee. I shall be glad to waite on you att Oxnett but not upon [?]seeing up your rest for the finishing your days, I doe not live, as contemptable & insignificant as I am, out of hope of being serviceable to you before you finish your time, as sir,

*Signed:* your most faithfull & humble servant, Townshend

*Addressed*: These for the honorable Sir Robert Paston baronett at his house in Lincolnes Inn Feilds near the path at Duke Street end, London

*NRO: BL/Y/1/23*

## Draft petition from Sir Robert Paston to Charles II[202]

**1667, September 22**. May it please Your Majesty, although I have as legall a graunt as can be passed under your Majesty's great seale of England for my farme of the customs of wood &c grounded upon as true representations and as much cleernesse of debate as anything that ever passed your Majesty's hand, yet since there hath happened some accidents through which the covetousnes or unkindnes of some persons puts a necessity either upon your Majesty or myselfe to be loosers, and to

---

[201] After the fire, Gresham College was used as a temporary Exchange by the London merchants, so the Royal Society met at Arundel House, the London home of Henry Howard (later 6th duke of Norfolk) in Arundel Street just off the Strand, until 1673 when they returned to Gresham College.

[202] This draft in Paston's hand has been extensively amended in his own and another hand. Although deletions and insertions are shown in all other transcripts in this volume, here it would have produced a virtually unintelligible text, so in this instance the transcription shows, as far as is possible, the final version of the petition.

make it appear to the world that your Majesty's losse was never my ayme I have offered the utmost expedient to the lords commissioners to prevent it which is to pay your Majesty during the time of foure yeares that the farmers of the customes have gotten of your Majesty £5,000 a yeare defalcation for my graunt, the same sum that their pretence of the advantages rising by the accident of fire may be nott become lost to your Majesty that soe I may enjoy the rest of my fearme in quiet and they have noe further pretence to a greater defalcation for the future then the rent I pay, if they have anie att all. This I hope will apeare to be a full satisfaction to your Majestie for if this graunt had not bene passed to me it had bene involved in the generall farme of the customes without any other advances of rent.

The £500 a yeare abatement of the old rent your Majesty was gratiouslie pleased to graunt was that I might have a better bargaine of the whole farme, my deserts beeing to small for the one and your Majesty's bounty being to great as not to con-taine the hopes of benefit uppon those narrowe limmits of a full stretcht value beyond which no man at that tyme would advance more. If £7,000 is bid it is by those whose malice tends onely to the destruction of my graunt and not to any true performance with your Majesty and is no argument to destroy a graunt allreadie passed for the farmers themselves since the fire who as well knew the value thereof as anie bodie tooke onely the advantage of the defalcation of £5,000 which I now offer more by £1,700 then they ever set to my owne prejudice. [f.2] But I am now neccessitated to labor under the difficulties as well to cleare myselfe from false informations and pre-tended coppies of letter of too phanatick informers have beene sugested against mee butt that the confidence I had of your Majesty's royall word has as to preserve my intangled estate to which I am butt tenant for life having a great debt upon mee, besides difficulties and expence the compassing of this has added to me, that the day in which your Majesty takes itt out of my hands is the utter ruine & overthrowe of a familie ever loyallie firme to your Majesty's interest.[203]

Butt if in the acquiring of this graunt the whole process whereof lies before the lords commissioners there be found anie fals or indirect dealing I am contented to suffer death & ignominie.

I therefore implore your Majesty that having offered the utmost expedient between me & mine that your Majesty's gratious mercie may be my refuge betwixt the two rocks of my destruction, the abandoning my graunt or beeing broken by the least screw higher if my offer finds no remission from your Majesty's doome which if con-trarie to what I humbly & with all dutyfull submission beg of your Majesty must render me the most miserable person living and though my pretences have nothing of merritt yett I hope the devotion I ever had to my King will protect mee from sinking under the extreamitie that is driven soe hard uppon mee whom noe calamitie

[203] Paston's original lease of the wood farm in April 1666 was for 21 years at a rent of £2,000 p.a. to run from Michaelmas 1667. Following the Great Fire of London there was an increased demand for wood and other bids were put in. Paston finally offered £6,500 p.a. and agreed to a revocation clause in October 1667. Since these negotiations ran past Michaelmas, payment to Paston was suspended. As he and his wife had been spending their profits in advance they were in a desperate situation and appealed to Lady Castlemaine who managed to get the 'stop' lifted. (British Library: Add. MSS 27447, f.310; *CTB, 1, 1660–1667*, p.697, *2, 1667–1668*, pp 72, 74, 79, 81, 82, 84, 86, 88, 97, 104, 106, 108, 142, 195, 196, 198, 221–9, 287, 466, 515; *CSPD, 1665–1666, passim*). For Paston's tenure as 'tenant for life' see introduction p. 3.

nor prosperitie shall ever alter from devoutlie serving your Majesty in all the contrivance [or] execution that coms within the imagination or practise of

*Signed*: your Majesty's most dutyfull & loyall subject, Robt Paston
*Endorsed*: Coppie of my petition sent to the King the 22 of September 1667
*NRO: BL/Y/1/24*

## Edmund Thaxter and Richard Huntington to Sir Robert Paston

**1667, September 25, Yarmouth**. *They had hoped by what was reported by Mr Johnson[204] to have waited upon him at Oxnead. The corporation is unanimous in wishing to unite with him and two or three members will wait on him in London fully authorised not only to confer but to conclude in all things that shall relate to the completing of the union.[205]*

*Signed:* your most humble and fa[ithfull] servant[s], Edm Thaxter, Richd: Huntington, B[ailiffs][206]
*Addressed*: These to the honorable Sir Robert Paston knight and barronett at his lodgings in Lincolnes Inn Fields, present, London
*NRO: BL/Y/1/25*

## Rebecca, Lady Paston to Sir Robert Paston

**[*1668[/9], March*].**[207] ... be in the goverment that cane be out: my Lord Kepper[208] is a good mane and a just, and thought[209] he will not in this thing be kind to us, we must not forgitt what he hath done. I told him I hoped since I had by Mr Burton[210] aquanted him with the [w]hole stait of your afairs he would be so generous as not to lett you sufer for that, but all I cane say was to noe purpos, he is resolved not to medell <with> *for* your conserns, so I shall troubll him noe *mor* for I beleve he will doe you noe good; the King would have given him some crowne lands and an honer, but he hath refused bothe; pray my deare be not discoraged but trust still in God thought[211] all for sak us; he hath promised he will never leave us nor forsake us; I have bine much troubled but now I bless God I am recovered againe, and I will if God bless me goe on briskly againe, the Duk[e] of Bukingham will be your frind,[212] and I hope God will direct us <to> such way as yett if it pleas him he may bless. My Lady Castellmaine had £10,000 the other day; I am glad to hear the King hath mony to give away: she is with child again. Sir William Coventry[213] is in the Tower, and Hary

---

[204] James Johnson, military contractor in Yarmouth, knighted in 1671
[205] The incorporation passed the royal seal in January 1668, see p.58n above; the right hand side of this letter is missing.
[206] Great Yarmouth was governed by 2 bailiffs chosen annually, 24 aldermen, and 48 common councilmen. Following the issue of a new charter the bailiffs were replaced by a mayor in 1684.
[207] Date added in brackets in a later hand, the first sheet is missing.
[208] Sir Orlando Bridgeman (1609–1674), lord keeper of the great seal      [209] i.e. though
[210] Hezekiah Burton (c.1632–1681), chaplain to Sir Orlando Bridgeman and a prebendary of Norwich
[211] i.e. though
[212] Sir Robert Paston is listed among the MPs who voted with the duke of Buckingham in 1669–1671 (Browning, *Leeds*, III, p.39).
[213] Sir William Coventry (1627–1686), MP for Great Yarmouth, lord of the treasury, etc.

Savill with him, hou should have gon to the Gat[e]hous by orders from the Counsill and many frind[s] waire maid to prevaill with the King to send him to the Tower.[214] My Lord and Lady Mordaunt are coming over, my Lord of Peterburogh[215] hath cut of[f] the intaill of his estait and intends to mary his daughter to my Lord Tolington[216] the General's sone, my Lord Mordaunt hath sent over a great ma[n]y oring[e] tre[e]s, and the King heard of it and asked if my [f.2] lord would mak a cakhous[217] of Vila Cary: thay have both lost them self in the world, I hear nobody spak on[e] good word of them, my Lady Harbut[218] is <much> *now* att thear hous, I have sene her twis or this, she doth so lik[e] them and none declairs thair folys more then she doth: I hope Done[219] doth wright to you, he and his wif and Mrs Wisman waire hear last week, and I told him you desired the favor from him he uss to doe you in leting you hear every week; he begs your pardon for what is past and doth promis he will mend for the time to come: all your sons are well, Will dined with me a Sunday hear: I sent to know how Robine doth, <?> Jasper and Tome[220] are now att Musports att Fulham for the small pox is att Mr Crumblum's[221] againe, I will send you cloth for John Woodine this week, I hope you have received all your cloths and lik them, what soe ever is amis pray pardon for truly I am so much consarned for your greater afairs as I cane doe nothing as I should. Pray my deare oblidge me so much as to dispatch my mother's wrightings, and when you have sealed them securily I wish you would doe so generosly as to seall my brother Georg on[e]; for his debt you know he is ingaged for you beside, it would be a great aflixsion to me to have him lous by us, and in doeing this hansomly of your o[w]n acord, will thus oblidg him all way to be sarvisabl to you: doe in this what you pleas, I have not sayd any thing to him, nor doth he aske it of me, but I know he doth rely upon your worthy dealings with him: [f.3] and you know our relasions in the world which will mak a great talk if any thing should fall of inconveniance upon him by our means: truly my deare I think if you would to Mr Charlton and Mr Eaton and Goding[222] doe the saime it would be much for your honer and the more you cloge [sic] it the beter, I wish every body waire secured this way, for that would make you so many shure intrusts in the world, and it may prevent the taking of it away, for nobody will venter upon that when thay know so many peple are to be payd out of it; but doe in this what you will, I ondly hint this things to you; my mother and brother and sister how[223] are very kind to me present you with thear humble sarvis; I wish you would wright a kind leter to my brother[224] for I am very much

---

214 Henry Savile (c.1642–1687) was imprisoned for carrying Coventry's challenge to the duke of Buckingham who had ridiculed him as Sir Cautious Trouble-All in his play *The Country Gentlemen*; he petitioned to be transferred from the Gatehouse prison, Westminster, to the Tower.

215 Henry Mordaunt, 2nd earl of Peterborough, elder brother of John, viscount Mordaunt

216 *recte* Torrington: Christopher Monck, later 2nd earl of Albemarle

217 i.e. shithouse: the connection with oranges is unclear. The Mordaunts were out of favour because of their support for Lord Clarendon.

218 Margaret, Lady Herbert, Elizabeth Mordaunt's mother                    219 i.e. Henshaw

220 Jasper was born before July 1660 as he is mentioned in the will of his grandfather, Sir Jasper Clayton (TNA: PROB11/300); Thomas was born in January 1663.

221 Probably Samuel Cromleholme (1618–1672) who kept a school at Wandsworth at this date while St Paul's school was being rebuilt after the Fire of London.

222 Probably all tradesmen or shopkeepers: Eaton was a fashionable dressmaker and haberdasher, *see* below p.139.                    223 i.e. who                    224 Sir John Clayton

oblidged to him for his company and his co[a]ch every whear; Mr Burton is very much
our frind to his power and is very sorry he can doe noe mor, Mr Cheek I have sene
som four or five tims he asketh very kindly after you, he knoweth nothing of your bisnis
more then what I formerly gave you a compt of, I have not told Mr Henshaw nor any
creatur but Mr Burton, and he told his lord, and now Sir Thomas,[225] <word illegible>
how[226] must if he doth any thing for you know how thing stand with you. My blesing
to my daughter, I must not forgitt to tell you a romanc[e] story which conserneth her;
on Saterday when I came from my [f.4] [?]jorny, and sick, I went to bed, and thear
came on[e] to spak with me hows naim was Mr Wayed, and he sent and I did not
know him so I gatt my brother to goe downe to him, and his bisnis to me was, he
heard I had a daughter and he did now know a gentelman that had £5,000 a year
and mony in his purs[e], which was much in love with her and if I would give him
£1,500 he would make the mach; and he should not medell with on[e] farding of her
porsian, but give it all to her self to doe what she would with it; so my brother told
him he should have the mony if he did doe as he had sayd; he pray my b[r]other to
come to him a Munday and he would consult with his counsell how he might have it
secured; my brother went to him on Munday and he found him in a good lodgine and
all thing very hansom about him, and the landlady in hows hows[227] he was told my
brother he was a hamsher[228] gentellman and had lay thear fouer years, so my brother
told him he came as he promised and the gentellman told him he had bine with his
counsell and was told nothing could secure him but in Chancery you might be releved
and so when he had done this bisnes you might chus whether you would pay him but
if £500 in redy mony might be put in som frind's hands that when he did this thing
he might be shur of it; then he would tell the gentellman's naim, how was a hansom
man, of a good family, and too good houses well furnished, on[e] in London the other
in the contry, and a person well <word deleted> knowne in the world, my brother told
him if he would exsept of your bond he might, els he would trouble him self noe mor
a bout it, I hope this will be a good omen to Peg though nothing more come of this;
my deare I hope you will pardon this long episel, but you say you are alone and mala-
choly and I hope this will devart you. I pray God kep you and send us a happy meting,
to the joy [two words illegible] wif

*Signed:* your R. Paston
*British Library: Add. MSS 36988, ff 89–90*

## Thomas Henshaw to Sir Robert Paston

**1669, March 25**. Deare patrone, in the first place I must thanke you for my stopper
which was *magnifique*, your boy James brought it me on Sunday morning, I will not
loose it in seven houres, but keep it seven yeares if God lend me so long life, and leave
it to my daughter's husband for a legacy, and so it may come to some of yours againe.
Your adventure about Garret's grove is admirable, which I hope you will improve to
the utmost, which I doe augurate may not only give an advantage of great erudition

---

225  Sir Thomas Osborne            226  i.e. who
227  i.e. in whose house           228  ? Hampshire

to your frends' curiosity but also of some valuable treasure to your self, therfore dear sir pursue it, and command your workmen to use all possible caution and tendernesse in theyr prosecution; there is scarse in three ages such noble discoverys dispensed to any man, and therfore pray let not this nor Brampton field[229] want those indeavours are justly due to them. I doe hope these revolutions may bee the vantcurriers[230] of some extraordinary fortune will betide you. When you have the happines to see your Sendivogius,[231] you will easily *find* by my annotations and references to the parallel places that wee have been hitherto under a great mistake, not distinguishing between his magnet and his *agua pontica*,[232] which is drawn out of his *mare nostrum*, that is the great expansion of <the> ayre and ether which is the sea of the *sol caelestris*,[233] by vertue of his chalybs of magnesia, what the meaning of his chalybs which is beyond all others that is found *in ventre Aristis*[234] will bee very plainly discovered to you by the reference to the 16th page. I doe not much wonder you find adrop or peter so hard to run *per deliquint[ur]*[235] after a strong fire given them, I have often found it to my confusion, and you find de Paris[236] could never discover the waye of making a magnet of peter which [*word illegible*] much desired and therfore made use of tartar. Any salt that will draw ayre I suppose is well enough, but you did not take the right course with adrop, for if you had only drawn of the water he had attracted, and not forced him to an *aqua fort*,[237] he would have been attractive againe, which is worth your trying.

You may find by this scrible that the gout hath put my hand out of order, therfore I will for this time conclude with what news wee have, and send you a better epetomy[238] of de Paris when I have better leisure. The Earl of Rochester uppon more sober advise is gone into France, but tis reported did first solemnly aske pardon of Harry Killigrew (who it seemes had an ascendant of [?]terour on him) for the affront he offered his father.[239] Sir J. Denham[240] is gone to see the great secret of the infernall shades, and was buried last night, Le Febre[241] is suddenly dead of an apoplexy, into the office of the King's surveyour Dr Wren[242] is already admitted, and tis beleeved Dr Williams will bee successour to the other. Wee have again a fresh alarum of the King of Spain's[243] death by a letter from Jack Vowell[244] grounded on a report

---

[229] Urns and other Roman relics had been found in Brampton field, between Buxton and Brampton, and in an adjoining field in Oxnead park in the previous year (Wilkin (ed.), *The Works of Sir Thomas Browne*, III, pp 504–5).                                                    [230] i.e. precursors

[231] Michel Sendivogius, Polish alchemist, author of *A New Light of Alchemy* (1605)

[232] Briny water                                                              [233] Heavenly sun

[234] Henshaw quotes extensively from Sendivogius. Seventeenth-century alchemical texts use a very specialised Latin vocabulary so it has been decided not to translate these quotations. The full text of *A New Light of Alchemy* and other works by Sendivogius can be found (in English) on the internet.

[235] ? until soft or melting

[236] Christopher Parisiensis, a Benedictine monk, who wrote a treatise on alchemy

[237] Aqua fortis is a solution of nitric acid which dissolves most metals apart from gold.

[238] i.e. epitome

[239] Rochester had struck Thomas Killigrew in the King's presence, which was technically treason.

[240] Sir John Denham, FRS and surveyor of the works, is buried in Westminster Abbey.

[241] Nicaise Le Febre, professor of chemistry to the King; he was succeeded by Dr Thomas Williams.

[242] Christopher Wren (1632–1723), architect

[243] Charles II of Spain (1661–1700) suffered from congenital maladies due to generations of inbreeding. His death without heirs in 1700 was followed by the War of the Spanish Succession.

[244] John Fowell, governor of Dartmouth

brought into Dartmouth by a ship from Bilboa, who brought news Don John was crowned king, but tis thought wee have had fresher news from Madrid then they and that the King is not dead yet, but not likely to live many monthes. The King of France gave order to his embassadour the Marquis de Villars to see the Spanish King, but he could not be admitted, then his instructions were to to [*sic*] get the best intelligence he could of his health and to send his advertisement by [*f.2*] severall expresses that they might not bee intercepted by the Spanish ministers, his Most Christian Majesty has also commanded all officers and governours in south France to repayre to theyr severall posts that they may bee in a readines to receive his orders, and tis beeleeved as soon as the King of Spaine is dead his army will bee ready to march into that country, not on his pretense who has both solemly abjured, and under his hand and seale renounced that inheritance, but the Daulphin his son is to clayme his right who was not then borne and the King will only serve as a volunteer under him.

The Duke's[245] closet at Whithall was broke open last weeke, and because a rich George[246] which lay on the table, two gold watches, a paire of silver candle stickes were untouched it was thought it was only a designe to rifle his papers which gave a great alarme here, but uppon the Duke's returne he found no papers missing but 700 guinnys besid many gold medals of great value taken out of an iron chest they had wrenched open, the actours not yet discovered. Sir William Coventry and his nephew on theyr submission are released out of the Tower but discharged of being privy counsellor and commissioner of the treasury. The lord keeper grows so infirme that he desires to resigne his office, tis said Bishop Wilkins[247] shall succeed him but I think on no other ground but that he is a great favorite: this day John Crook the bookseller after four monthes sicknes of the dropsy was buried, a caveat for all good fellows. Garnet has to admiration payd me my £100 but I did not nor doe not you take it to reflect on the trifle [*which*] is betweene you and I. I would to God it were as much in my power as I have often wished it to free you from all incumbrances, I should doe it with joy and cheerfulnes. Hodge Vaughan and Godolphin the paige[248] are gone from the King and Duke to bring word how the Queen Mother[249] does who they say is very ill, and has been let bloud three times.

*Unsigned*
*Addressed:* For the honourable Sir Robert Paston at Oxnead neare Norwich, this
*British Library: Add. MSS 36988, ff 91–92*

## Rebecca, Lady Paston to Sir Robert Paston

**[1669], April 29.** My dearest hart, this day my brother's sone was chrisned, Mr Bowyer and Mr Cheek and my self ware gosops,[250] his naime is William, hear dined a great deall of company, my Lady Bowyer and her too daughters, my <brot>

---

[245] i.e. of York          [246] The premier order of knighthood in England

[247] John Wilkins (1614–1672), FRS and natural philosopher, bishop of Chester. In spite of having been Oliver Cromwell's brother-in-law, he became a royal chaplain and his tolerant approach to dissenters made him popular with both the King and Buckingham (*ODNB*).

[248] Roger Vaughan and Sidney Godolphin, page of honour to Charles II

[249] Queen Henrietta Maria who died in September 1669          [250] i.e. godparents

brother Georg and his wif and Mr Palmer,[251] Mr Henchaw, and all our four sons, and I am so tyred with a great diner and all this company as I must beg your pardon if I now wright but a short leter. Mr Cheek tells me he hath wright to you last post, and he hath the promis of my Lord Chamberline that you shall not upon his honor be tuched, and what he hath done is but a thing of forme, and he will <*word illegible*> not give any leave to prosede furder, Mr Cheek hath promised my lord's secritary £5 if he will kep of troubl from you. My Lady Paston is very ill and it tis the towne nus that she cannot recover, she had a fitt of the stone and the docters [*f.2*] gave her a purge which was proper for that and it hath meet with sharpe paines in her bowels and with all this together she hath had a flux and makes blud, and is in extreame paine and complains of a great heat in her bowells, I sent today to know how she did and thay sent me word she had an ill night and is extream ill, I hope God will despos of all things for our good,[252] and then his will be done. I hear Sir George Hambelton is kild in France in a duell, thear was a fire in Durham Yard on[*e*] hows is burnt and a nother blowne up, pray my dear send me money to pay for our sons' bord before I come home, I hope now with in a short time to be with you, in my next I will send you the day, my brother and sister sends you there sarvis, all your sons thear duty, my blesing to my daughters, my love to my cousins Burtons[253] from my dearest hart,

*Signed:* thy most afexsinat wif, R Paston
*Postscript*: I hear Mr Windham's ma[*t*]ch is of[*f*] <againe> with Sir Joseph Ashe's daughter.[254]
*British Library: Add. MSS 28621, f. 28*

## Thomas Henshaw to Sir Robert Paston

**1669, May 5**. Deare patrone, it being now neer eleven at night when my boy came home with your letter, and I being to goe early tomorrow to London where I shall have no convenience to write, I feare I shall not have so much time to converse with you as I desire. I am very sorry to find by your last, that your passion is so much raised and your mind so disturbed by what you have lately received from Parson's Green; I am wholly a stranger to what was transacted between Sir W. Doyly and the Lady Clayton,[255] nor durst I adventure to have any discourse with any of them about it, because I did not find that I [*had*] the permission from you to doe it. But I must

---

[251] George Clayton had married Esther Palmer, sister of Sir Henry Palmer of Wingham, so Mr Palmer was presumably one of her brothers (Henry F. Hepburn, *The Clayton Family* (Wilmington, 1904), p.13).

[252] In 1668 Margaret, Lady Paston had married George Strode (1626–1701) of Lincoln's Inn, MP for Lyme in 1679, but had, as was customary, retained her title. Apart from being on bad terms with her, the Pastons were paying her a substantial jointure, *see* above p.5.

[253] These cousins are never mentioned again. The name of Hezekiah Burton's wife is unknown, but it is possible that she was related in some way to Rebecca and that this kind message was intended to keep Burton active on their behalf.

[254] William Windham (1647–1689) of Felbrigg married Katherine Ashe later in 1669, and her sister Mary married Lord Townshend in 1673. Their father was Sir Joseph Ashe (1617–1686) of Twickenham, MP for Downton.

[255] Mary, Lady Clayton, Paston's mother-in-law; she and her son Sir John were gradually becoming embroiled in the Pastons' financial affairs. It is not clear what precipitated this financial crisis but Paston was behind with his rent for the wood farm in January 1669 (*CTB, 3, 1669–72*, pp 5, 179).

not conceale from you what information I have by accident received from a stranger concerning theyr affaire. He tould me that they uppon some occasion consulting a great lawyer (I think he said it was the attorney general) he tould them that by law (though the jewells were lost) the Lady Clayton might recover the whole £1,500 of you and the interest if she could take her oath that she was not privy to the loosing of them and that she kept them with the same care as if they had been her owne. This I verily beleeve to bee absolutely true according [to] the common law, and doe remember that that [sic] about fifteen or sixteen yeares since I had a diamond ring pawned to me for £15, I had the misfortune to have it stolne from me, which when the mortgager knew he then offered to redeem his ring, which he was pleased to value at £35. A suite was begun against me, but at last it being a meer law case, wee both agreed to refer it to two lawyers, who both decided it in my favour, producing my Lord Cooke's[256] and several other judges' determination of that very case, and so instead of my making good the surplussage of the value they tould the mortgager that if I would sue him he would bee obliged to pay me the £15 and interest notwith-standing his ring was lost. I was tould by another that whatsoever Sir W says to you, he had acknowledged before your lady and sevrall others, that the Lady Clayton might recover the £1,500 of you and interest and that you were bound to acknowl-edge it her kindnes that she did not pretend to it. The same party farther said that the Lady Clayton having with a rash oath of yours complyed to abate £300 of the former debt which was most of it mony lent or disbursed to supply severall pressing occasions of yours, that all the advantage she did designe to make uppon this new light given her of the præeminence of her title was only to hedge in that £300 uppon account of interest which she conceives you had too rigorously cut her of from, whether this bee true or no you best know, I protest before God I had it from none of them but I thought it my duty to tell you what I heard, and the rather because [f.2] if these circumstances bee true, in my small judgement you have no reason to resent it so ill as you seeme to doe. However deare sir, whether I mistake or am mis-informed pray doe no [sic] not you mistake my freedome with you for partiality, for I doe assure you both you and your interests are much dearer to me then any of theyrs can bee, all I aime at is the salving your honour and justice which I know you cannot faile in where you are rightly informed. I had some discourse this day [with] Sir W[illiam] Doyly[257] about securing the goods who tould me he had proposed a way to you by making them over and letting them remaine in the house, I tould him that was but what wee had thought on long since, but on farther conference with lawyers, wee found that if they remained still in the house that could not secure them from being swept away by an execution, and though there might bee some ground for those that had the pretended interest to sue, yet if they should have the good fortune <several words deleted> to overcome the others, it was but to put things to the hazard of an aftergame, and they could recover no more then what the things were apprized at by such as they should imploy before the things were carried away, and then says Sir William what cost his father and him at least £4,000 will hardly bee

---

[256] Sir Edward Coke (1552–1634), lord chief justice

[257] The rest of the paragraph makes it clear that Henshaw was talking to Sir William Doyly the younger, eldest son of Sir William Doyly (d.1677) of Shotesham.

apprized at £400, but says he Sir Robert being so pertinaciously resolved not to have any removed, what other way was left to serve him with but this? But if this bee the hazard you are to run as certainly it is, though you may doe with your owne what you please, yet your owne prudence can best informe you that it were better to disfurnish your closet and a few roomes of your richest furniture and to have them secure against the worst of chanches, then by leaving them there in parade tempt the insolence of those, which when they were removed would perchance not venture to disturbe your quiet with the rest, for his ingaging the sheriffe he made no mention of it to me, if it should bee endeavoured I know the bribe must be very greate; and when things come to an issue the sheriffe will not dare to deferre execution but while perhaps he may give you notice to doe that which may bee don with more security and a great deale lesse charge before that time. If I can possibly I will speake with Sir W tomorrow about the Lady Clayton's busines and give you an impartiall account of what I find. For the Lady Paston though the symptomes of her distemper were just as I writ them, yet you have very rightly prognosticated the successe, for by taking of Barnet waters she is now freed from them all and was this day in a hopefull way of recovery only under a great <a great> weaknes which will cost her a long time to recover, for certainly she is of a very infirme habit of [f.3] body which age is not very likely to improve.

After all these melancholy dispensations let us see if chymystry will afford us any better consolation. I doe clearly agree with you that the operation on *leo viridis*[258] by fire is the most probable and hopefull of all ways, yet I would not have de Paris (whom you will this week receive) neglected now you have proceeded so fairly, the only thing can assure us of any truth in it will the[259] the coagulation of the water aerial of which you have now a sufficient quantitie for all trialls. I thanke you for the account you give me of your late experiments in which you have taken a great deale of care and paines, and though things doe not succeed yet according to expectation I hope wee cannot long misse on so good a subject, though as I writ you I doe suspect by Rumelius's[260] indications of his proceedings he did worke on some kind of loame or marle, yet I beleeve our Saturne is every jot as good, the only thing wee have hitherto failed in is the union of the fixt and volatile which can never bee don till both principles bee made very pure, and especially the fixed [*part*] by very strong fire bee *free* from all volatile parts and impure sulphur for till then he is not thirsty enough to imbibe the female part, if you can meet with any of this fixed part it will bee well worthy your care and attention.

Here is little news saving the hopes of the Queen's be[ing] with child she having missed these two monthes together. It is begun [to be] beleeved that the chancellor[261] may have leave to returne next parliament [*torn*] the Lady Mordant does much interest her selfe in his concernes and does hold caballs with no small ones about *it*, I wish her active humour may doe Lord John no prejudice, I have not yet seen him,

[258] Probably vitriol although it can sometimes mean gold.                    [259] *recte* 'be'

[260] Johann Conrad Rhumel (Rumelius); Henshaw is probably referring to Lancelot Colson's *Philosophia maturata: an Exact Piece of Philosophy, containing the Practick and Operative part thereof in gaining the Philosophers Stone; ... Whereunto is added, a work compiled by St. Dunstan concerning the Philosophers Stone, and the experiments of Rumelius and preparations of Angelo Sala, etc.* (1668).                    [261] Lord Clarendon

and therefor will deferre my French realations till I can doe it more authentically.[262]
*Mon chere [sic] monsieur faisez moy l'honneur de croire que je suis sans reserve*

*Signed*: *Le tout a vous*
*Addressed*: For the honourable Sir Robert Paston at Oxnead neare Norwich, this
*British Library: Add. MSS 36988, ff 93–95*

## Sir John Clayton to Sir Robert Paston

**1669, June 8**. Dear Sir Robert, you shall now no more complane for want of glasses,
for Mr Henshaw & I went togather late Thirsday to choose for you of all sorts to the
value of £5 – to be paid at Michaelmas next, there are bodys & heads all of a piece
& heads with stoples ground to them to fit to large boles heads of green glas which
are the most convenient things in the world, for cohobations[263] of our sr[??] upon its
fixed salt, the rest I can not so well remember, but I will inclose the note of them in
the next letter, these cannot be sent till next Thirsday – besids these I have laid out
£1 10s with Kuffler in two dozen & halfe of glasses with glass stoples which will come
togather at the same time with the other glasses: pray improve & prosecute the experiment you gave me late an account of, for I like it beyond anything that I ever heard
of: I hope by this time you have received news of your wine & oranges, & for Venice
drinking glasses I will indeavor what I can possibly that they may come togather with
these other things by the Thirsday's carrs:[264] the remaining part of your mourning[265]
I sent by the hackny coach late Munday as two cravats, two handkerchers, three paire
of shoes: as to your coach I have taken order for it for £35, you to find inside,[266] &
I think that not deare, this now inclosed will satisfie you further of it according to
your desire: wee have considerd that before this coach can be finished & sent downe
to Oxnett that you may by that time goe into halfe mourning & according to this cal-
culation I have dessigned this coach, the body all of wood handsomely & modestly
carved, & painted black, the outside all leather nailed with black nailes, & this I doubt
not but will please you, for I shall ever now & then give & [sic] eye to it, to see the
bargane handsomely performed: as to the tother thing, which you hinted for your
chapel, there shall be no delay on our parts. I have all ready consulted Don,[267] who
resolved over a glas of clarett, that the history should be the woman of Samaria giving
Our Saviour drink out of her well, he swares there is hyrogliphicke as well as history,
for nothing can be more proper for a buttery transmuted into a chapel: but ralliery
apart, I think it will not do amisse: if you dislike it, choose a better & wee will take
all the care wee can to get it donne, only this by the way, I never saw nor heard of
any such paintings in green, therfore, it must be black & white: in a little while I question not but to provide you some lamp oyle for your purpose. I have a modest request
to make to you from your son Will: but you are not to take notice of it as from him,

---

[262] The Mordaunts had recently returned from Montpellier where Lord Clarendon was living in exile.
[263] To cohobate is to repeat the distillation pouring the liquor back upon the matter remaining in the
vessel.                                                                          [264] i.e. carts or conveyances
[265] Paston was in mourning for his stepmother Margaret, Lady Paston, who had died on 23 May
(NRO: NNAS C3/2/1/3).
[266] i.e. you to fit out the inside                                              [267] Henshaw

that is that he may be discharged from Littleton's Algiers,[268] at the time [f.2] when wee designe to come to Oxnett, that so wee may come all togather, he promises farely how he will slave it away in his studys, & says how that your chaplane can teach him three times more then his master, & that if you please he is content to tarry at home three months before he goes to Cambridge, pray gratifie me in this, for I have partly engaged to perswade you to it, & seriously I think it will be for his good: therfore in your next let me have the joyfull tideings of it to impart to him: my daughter Mis[269] is exceedingly delighted at her letters, & will waite upon you & her cousin Betty,[270] if you will promise not to teach her paw[271] songs, & to pull up he[r] coats, I assure you she takes herselfe to be somebody now & lockes up her letters in her cabinet with great care. As for your stuf suit I will send it as soon as Circeau[272] will give me leave: I think you would doe well to remember your love to your frinds at the customehouse in a cup of nog, not forgeting Mr Burges, who does dayly advance your interest, really I think such a man could not be litt on in the world agane so faithfull & generous: Saterday last I went with the Duke of Buckingham to Denham,[273] with a disigne to buy it, & I hope to effect it for them for he seems to be very fond of it: in our returne home wee dined at Uxbridge, but never in all my life did I pas my day away with such gusto, our company being his grace, Mr Waller,[274] Mr Surveyor Wren & myself, nothing but quintessence of wit & most excellent discourse, of which I wished you a partaker from my hart: I hope I am fixed in his favour, for he continues very kind to me: for which I must ever thank *you* as being the creator of this, & of all other good fortune I have hitherto had in this world: I supose the news of the Queen's miscarige is now stale with you, for it was last Friday, being affryted by an unfortunate accident with one of the King's tame foxes, which stealing after the K[ing] unknowen *into the bed chamber lay there all night &* in the morning very early leaped up upon the bed, & run over the Queen's face & into the bed. Saturday died my Lady Newport of Newport howse: there is a strange letter came to the K[ing] from Catania[275] from my Lord Winchelsea conserning the new eruption of Mount Aetna in so horrible a manner as cannot be expressed, which has consumed sixteen towns & the habitations of 27,000 persons, but it being yesterday morning printed,[276] I shall not trouble you with a farther relation intending to send you the book by Thirsday's hackny coach, so farewell deare Sir Robert

*Signed:* I am ever yours, J Clayton

*Addressed:* These for the honourable Sir Robert Paston baronett at Oxnead neer Norwich in Norfolke

*NRO: BL/Y/1/28*

---

[268] Possibly Adam Littleton, schoolmaster at Westminster and elsewhere; Algiers may be a facetious term for school, i.e. a place of slavery. [269] His eldest daughter Alice

[270] Sir Robert Paston's youngest daughter Elizabeth (c.1667–1686) [271] i.e. improper

[272] Presumably Claude Sourceau of St Paul's Covent Garden, court tailor

[273] Clayton's father-in-law Sir William Bowyer of Denham Court also owned Denham Place which he sold to Sir Roger Hill in 1670. Presumably Buckingham was interested in Denham Place and Clayton was included in the party because of his relationship with the Bowyers.

[274] Edmund Waller (1606–1687), poet [275] On the east coast of Sicily

[276] *A True and Exact Relation of the Late Prodigious Earthquake and Eruption of Mount Aetna* (1669).

# Thomas Henshaw to Sir Robert Paston

**1669, June 19**. Deare patrone, much joy may you have of your seventeen pies! God grant you may both live together till you make them up fifty six (and then t'will bee time to have mercy on the young folkes) and may they bee all pies and never a tart among them. Uppon recollection I find that on the 15th of June I came into this world, and on the same day you enterd into the other world of matrimonie. My almanack tells me it is St Vitus day, may it therfor prove vitall to me and All Vit to you and may you abound in no pies so much as that pie the Frenchman preferd before all others, the *paste à l'Angloise*, the good old English Occa[277] Pie.

You need not doubt but that I keep all your letters by me, but if like a man of busines you would date your letters on the top of the page they would bee the more readie to turne to. I doe hope that though some of mine have *been* guilded in Cl*o*acina's laboratory,[278] and some of them have made wedding sheets for the marriage pies, yet <word deleted> you have made an extract of Rumelius' processe I sent you, which I composed when I had newly read him, and was I think fully inspired by the same spirit he writ by and if it should bee lost I feare I should hardly bee able to doe so well againe.

The next thing I would recommend to you (is what I have often don before) that you would make a paper booke to set down what trialls you make in your ergasterium,[279] adding the dayes and monthes of the yeare, which will bee very usefull & delightfull to you in the review, for memorie is fraile and subject to mistakes.

For the heavenly distillation *of rains* you had on Tuesday was senight much good it you [*sic*], though wee had no such thing here, but some few heat drops that helped only to burne us up the more, which fell a day or two after. Munday, Tuesday and Friday last were excessive hot dayes here.

Your fixed salt though but [? *ounces*][280] in quantity, I like very well the quality of, though your first indeavour must bee to get greater quantities of all the principles. My fixed salt of Saturne that I made twenty years since was very gritty and earthy but not so quite deprived of his sublime ponticity as yours seemes to bee, but the reason was it had never beene so well calcined as yours has, and will no doubt with out any further purification bee a very good basis to fixe all sort of spirits on whether armoniack or acid: but which of these is to bee preferred is the great question which experience can resolve the best, though I am aptest to give my vote for the first, but however Milius'[281] processe ought to have the honour of a triall afforded him though it bee but with an AF[282] from adrop, for the sending it up I think there is no need, the way of it being so plaine and lineary as I remember that there wants no consultation uppon it.

If the middle salt which comes over the [?]helme with violence of fire, bee of two distinct natures (that is one part much more <word deleted> *volatile* then the other), it [*f*.2] were a thing new and surprizing to me, for then you have anatomized the subject into four distinct principles with the spirit and fixed earth. These two middle

---

[277] oca or occa = goose (It.)
[278] Cloacina was the Roman goddess of sewers.
[279] i.e. workshop or laboratory
[280] Written as a symbol
[281] Johann Daniel Mylius (c.1583–1642), writer on alchemy
[282] *Aqua fortis*

salts must bee purified to the greatest heighth that may bee *by* repeated solutions and filtrations: as for the fixed earth I see no way to cleanse him better then you have done, and peradventure there is need of it, for I remember there is a processe goes under the name of Dunstan's in Riply's[283] printed Latin workes which bids, for want of an other basis to fixe on, to take egge shells calcined twenty four houres. So it seemes that any earth that is effete and quite deprived of his moysture may serve the turne though that of our Saturne bee the most naturall.

This is the barrennest week for noveltry has com a great while onely Edgar Duke of Cambridge[284] had like to marched of[f] this weeke, being in great danger of a gangrene in his arm occasioned by the unskilfull making or binding an issue there, the pea having made his way down as low as his elbow.

You may have heard perchance from other hands last week that the Earl of Carlisle our embassadour in Sweden has killed with his own hands in a *rencontre* the French embassadour at Stockholm, but I did not write it because there is no ground of truth in it, there having not lately been either French embassadour or agent in that place.

For want of other news the master of the rolles sonnes[285] man was faine to pistoll himself last Sunday. Having lost his mony at play, he made bold to borrow thirty guinnys out of his master's cabinet, with hopes to make himself whole againe with them at Spering's ordinary,[286] but loosing them too, he was in despaire ever to recover his mony or his reputation wherefore on Sunday evening after he had been twice at church that day he made bold with a screwed pistoll and one bullet to drive two sermons out of his head, but before he did this execution being an ingenious young *man* he writ a narrative of his life, with a dehortation from idlenes, showing how that he having so little to do fell into gaming company, which was the occasion of that sad fate he was to undergoe, so with a devout prayer to God to forgive him what he was going about he concluded, and so fell to worke.

My brother Grevys[287] had a sad misfortune lately, getting up on a young filly he intended to ride out, his breeches hitched so behind on the saddle that he could not well seat himself, which the mare finding began to reare, and as he fell of[f], lashed out a kick at him which hitting him [f.3] on the ancle broke his legge and put his foot out of joynt in which condition he was faine to lye till they could send twenty mile for a chirurgion for him. How he hath don since I have not heard, but I am much affrayed of his life.

Mrs Cornwallis[288] will not beatifie Norfolk with her presence till she has honoured my house with her company which she sais shall begin on Monday next and she will bring her sister Peg with her, but old *nalgas*[289] have no great attraction in them for old philosophers.

---

[283] George Ripley (d.c.1490), alchemist and Augustinian canon

[284] Edgar (1667–1671), duke of Cambridge was the only surviving son of the duke of York

[285] Samuel, son of Sir Harbottle Grimston (1603–1685), master of the rolls

[286] A meal at a fixed price in a tavern or eating house; the word is used here for the tavern itself.

[287] Richard Grevys of King's Norton, husband of Henshaw's sister Anne

[288] Paston was related to the Cornwallises through the marriage of his uncle Thomas Paston (1614–c.1654) to Frances, daughter of Sir William Cornwallis (d.1614). Frances' brother Thomas Cornwallis of Burnham Thorpe was married to Penelope Wiseman, who may have been a sister of Henshaw's cousin Margaret Wiseman.                    [289] i.e. hindquarters, arses [Sp.]

I am much pleased to hear your spirit does the same miracles your salt did, I pray as soon as you are better stored think of your poor friends at Agur Hall.

You ought not to expect any alteration in the atheriall water till the lampe has been under it forty dayes.

Thanks bee praised that I am this *day* delivered of my man Robert Pursly whom I fitted for a seaman *de cap en pieds* and sent him away by Sir Thomas Allen.[290]

*Unsigned*

*Addressed*: For the honourable Sir Robert Paston at Oxnead neare Norwich this [*postmark*]

*NRO: BL/Y/1/29*

## Sir John Clayton to Sir Robert Paston

**1669, June 19**. Sir Robert, my being at Denham has put me so in arrears in scribing that I know not where to begin but by beging your pardon: I was on Thirsday at the custome house in order to dispatch the two afares which you desired me to do: which I have accordingly without feare pressed them a new, as to the first I told them it was a shame to let it hang so long undonne (I mean my sister's £125) & especially since they have acknowledged the thing by paying the mony to her & that they have but ill requited her dilligence & paines in neglecting the finishing the deed for her. I find nothing by their discourse, but that they intend to deale honestly by you in all things, they are hard men to deale withall but I take them to be very just so I left the writings with them & I believe they will seale them this next weeke; as to the other of Sir George Downing I have no possitive denyall, but civill puts of [*f*] till they see this quarter over, & how monys will arise, in the meane time Sir George is nowayes disgusted for I told him the truth how things stood, & that it was not your faulte, for I had orders from you to receive £100 for him at the custome house, but as yet the monys did not arise, over & above the King's rent, but [*f.2*] that I hoped to get it speedily for him, in the mean time I dessired him to accept of ten guinies which I gave him in part of payment untill I could present him with the rest.

I cannot think, but before this you have received your wine, for it is a great while since it was shiped abord a Yarmouth vessel & the bill of lading I sent in a letter by the post to Mr John Dawson[291] to take care of it: to make you amends for oranges, Mr Burgesse has sent you a chest of lemons & some sherry by sea, & I think the Venice glasses will come at the same time: I have taken consideration & pitty upon the marow[292] & have order a stufe suit for you, which is donn by this time & shall be sent by the first oportunity, least you should fall away to an alderman's thumb ring before I see you.[293]

I have sent your letter to Sir Thomas Osburne[294] which he cannot but like. I hope

---

[290] Sir Thomas Allin (c 1612–1685), admiral

[291] John Dawson was collector of customs for Yarmouth.          [292] i.e. companion or spouse

[293] 'Hal, I could have crept into any alderman's thumb ring' (Sir John Fastolf boasting of his youthful slenderness in Shakespeare's *Henry IV pt 1*).

[294] Osborne was now joint treasurer of the navy: Clayton and Paston proposed erecting lighthouses at St Nicholas Gatt (Yarmouth), Cromer, Flamborough Head and Farne Island; the scheme was approved

togather to attempt something which will disserve your love, if not your thankes, & if wee should miss of what wee designe I hope you will not blame our forwardnes to serve you. My sister has given mee an accompt of the sense & care you have of your affaires which pleaseth mee mightily, & since you are so kind as to make me a weak instrument to serve you in't [f.3] I shall desire to steer no better way then what your owne prudence shall direct, & though in these weighty afaires I have presumed to tell you my sense, out of the great afection I have for you & the flourishing of your family, yet I never designed to be possitive but ever intend to serve you your owne way. Yesterday I went to see Mr Cheeke whom I found a whore-hoping [sic] none but himself & ten woemen; like Hercules & Dianira only I think he had not so good a distafe *I mean Hercules*: & since his last hapynes of killing his wife the women run a muck after him.[295] The chymicall glasses sure are come safe by this time & the glas bottles with stoples, which will perfect the experiment I so much long after: as for my chouse[296] of AF from adrop dispise it not, but let it be seven times rectified & dephleamed for when I come I may chance shew you a knock you little dreame of: my daughter Mis is wonderously pleased with your letter & wee must both thank you for it. I have not yet gusto'd your son with the news of his deliverance from the house of bondage, but I think I have gained his hart in it for ever, if you don't spoyle him now & teach him to drink [f.4] with your selfe & your parson I question not but the child may doe very well: I do not like your £50 which you intend for Mr Burwell, it is unreasonable unles he were your atturny generall, if you will leave it to Mr Don & I, Ile warant you wee'l bring you of[f] upon better termes, & not basely neither: I have not shewen Don yet your rebuke, which you must expect a licke for six months hence, but this afternoon upon more serious thoughts wee will agree upon the history for your chapell.

Your frind Mat Wren[297] has newly set up his coach & six, my Lord Corneberry & he & wee supped with Lord John last night & drank your health: James[298] next Munday is to enter upon the great secret of the gentle craft, one halfe of the mony is already payd, the tother part at his binding. As for your coach you were better thinke of some other way of sending for it: for the journy will quite spoyle it, if it be not canvassed all up[299] the beauty of it will be quite <spoyled> *lost* before you use it: all at Denham are yours, so is, dear Sir Robert,

*Signed:* your most affectionate servant, J Clayton.
*NRO: BL/Y/1/30*

---

but failed to make any money because of the hostility of Trinity House, and the difficulty of collecting fees (*CSPD, 1668–69*, pp 461, 629, *1675–76*, p.251, *1676–7*, pp 257–306).

295 Thomas Cheeke's first wife Dorothy Sydney, daughter of the 3rd earl of Leicester, whom he married in 1668, died a month later; in 1671 he married Letitia Russell, niece of the 1st duke of Bedford.

296 i.e. trick

297 Matthew Wren (1629–1672), political writer, formerly secretary to Lord Clarendon, and from 1667 secretary to the duke of York         298 Unidentified person starting an apprenticeship

299 i.e. with the glass taken out and the sides wrapped in canvas

# Sir John Clayton to Sir Robert Paston

**1669, June 29.** Deare Sir Robert, I confes that to the utmost of my power I have alwayes indeavord to testifie my services to you, but never to diserve such a reward as you have bestowed upon me, for which I give you my most humble thankes: yesterday I dined with Sir Thomas Osburne to the end wee might have time enuf to discourse our buisnes, which I acquainted him withall, & deliverd your letter with the other papers inclosed as you directed mee: the thing is highly aproved of as usefull & necessary, of which this post Sir Thomas will give you some short account & leaves the rest for four or five days consideration before he gives his ful judgement of it, the maine thing which wee feare is that this <th> cannot be perfected without an act of parliment, & then you know into how great dificulties & uncertanties wee shall be involved. Mr Bradford seems in his letter to intimate that it is in the King's power solely to grant this thing, I should be extreem glad that he would explane himselfe in that point, & informe us how it may be donne, & which way any imposition can be laid towards the maintenan[c]e of it, by the King's prerogative without a parliment, the next week wee shal be able to tell you more, for I am ingaged to inquire of council how far the King's power goes in this matter, & Sir Thomas will inform himselfe as to other matters especially what conserns the corporation of Trinity House, whose cheife buisnes is to consider & act things necessary to the navigation & if wee find this to be obtained through the King's favor only, wee shall doe it with that secrecy & dexterity as shall exclude all hazard of whatever other pretender can object: & I think you have put it into the hands of so worthy a person, as you may be confident to find your own termes justly & strictly performed to you: I shall not faile to [f.2] indeavor all in my capacity to sett us forwards, & shall constantly from time to time give you an account of it, as occasion shall require. Your stuf suit it seems was not donne late Thirsday so it was not sent till last Munday by the hackny coach together with a garniture[300] for it: I have complaned to Battilier[301] about your wine which you lost & have got four dozen of bottles recompence, which being it is not worth the sending to you, I intend to keep in an obscure hole till wee have the hapynes to meet in these parts agane to rejoyce in togather: yesterday came news to court from Mr Offly who is at Avignon who writes that Sir Robert Brookes parliment man & your acquaintance drowned himselfe there baithing in the Rhodanus,[302] as also news from Paris of my Lord Candish[303] his being dangerously ill of seven wounds received in a quarrell which hapned in the playhouse when Scaramuchio acted, my Lord Rochester only being in his company, it is said that my Lord Candish has killed two of the French men, the story is too long to acquaint you with every particular but so horrid you never heard of the like & much to the advantage of the English; the King of France is so inraged at it, as he intends to hang all the French that were conserned in it, there being at the least six or seven of them in the buisnes. The Duke of Richmond has a very great ag[u]e & cannot returne so soon as was expected, the

---

[300] i.e. ornamentation or trimmings

[301] William and Joseph Batelier were wine merchants and friends of Samuel Pepys; they later supplied bills of exchange for William Paston on his grand tour in 1671.

[302] Sir Robert Brooke, MP for Aldeburgh, drowned in the Rhone

[303] William, Lord Cavendish (1641–1707), later 1st duke of Devonshire

Duke of Buckingham is *tout a vous*, as Sir Thomas will informe you & so is, deare Sir Robert,

*Signed:* your most afectionate & obliged servant, John Clayton

*Postscript:* by the [?]vusuall disaster of thatcher [*sic*] your letter came not to my hands till Saturday night otherwise I had returned a speedier answer

*Addressed*: These for the honourable Sir Robert Paston baronet at Oxnead neer Norwitch in Norfolke

*NRO: BL/Y/1/31*

## Sir John Clayton to Sir Robert Paston

**1669, July 6**. Deare Sir Robert, I may cannot [*sic*] pas by the duty & praise which your pen disservs for in your two last letters you have outdonne your selfe, upon the receipt of them I imediately went to Sir [*Thomas*] Osb[*orne*] but found him go[*ne*] out to Sir Thomas Littleton's where I found him & deliverd your letter & the D[*uke'*]s which he aproves of very much, & has appointed to meet me to morrow at dinner at the Duke's, & there both to present it to him, which will speedily put an issue to this buisness one way or other, for he has tarryed all this while only for your desires & will now serve you in it cordially: what hapens farther upon the delivery by Thirsday's post you shall not faile of the accompt of it, & I beg of you not to preposes your thoughts of what the fate of it will be: for be confident you have the best advacate this day in Ingland to plead your cause; & if it be in his power will prevale for you to the hight of your expectations: as for Winterton[304] I have binn very sedulous in searching into the knowledge of it, & by a wonderfull accident have at the custome house lit upon a man, that has made me understand the very bottom of it, & the whole method of managing of it having lately transacted the very same thing for Colonel Edward Villers:[305] & as to Mr Br[*adford's*] letter it does not at all informe us of what was desired, for so far he is in the right as that it belongs wholy to the King to grant, but out of his power to impose any tax or rate for to mantaine it: the way therfor must be this, to get the subscriptions of all the masters of ships who trade to the northward to an allowance for it: otherwise it is not to be donne without act of parl[*iament*] and farther this person has promised underhand to fish the masters how such a thing will relish among them, & if it take with them, he questions not but to get mee [*f.*2] 300 subscriptions towards it if not more, his place at the customhouse giving him the advantage of doing this, as entering all those ships that deale to the norwards, & for his panes when the whole buisnes is effected he expects £100 which I think you will not think too much, for if it ever be donne it must be this way & by his particular industry or not at all: the only thing objectd is this, how far these bouys will conduce to thir preservation in the night as well as the day, of this he will make an inquiry, & next Saturday I am to meet him & to be farther satisfied in it. I have

[304] Winterton lighthouse was built between 1616 and 1618 and was owned by the Turner family; it was rebuilt in 1687 after a fire.

[305] Colonel Edward Villiers was governor of Tynemouth Castle and had recently built a lighthouse there, *see* Horatio A. Adamson, 'The Villiers Family as Governors of Tynemouth Castle and Owners of the Lighthouse' (*Archaeologia Aeliana*, XXV, (1904) pp 111–117).

discoursed all this to Sir Thomas & he aproves of it exceedingly & as for what you desire in concealing your name, you shall do it as you please, & you shal not faile of your advantage in it & if you think fitting to make choyce of any frind's name who may secure your interest to you, I will see it faithfully donne for you.[306] I have bin at my Lord Linsy's[307] according to your desires to condole for you but his gon out of towne three days after his wife's death: the King three weeks hence goes a progres to Plymouth & to my Lord Ashly's or Lord St John's, so you will be very kind in releeving us from the dullnes of this place, which time now draws neer, if nothing in which I can serve you prevent, for I assure you with all joy I think every houre upon the journy, for I am, deare Sir Robert,

*Signed:* your most affectionate brother & servant, J: Clayton
*NRO: BL/Y/1/32*

## Thomas Henshaw to Sir Robert Paston

**1669, July 31.** Deare patrone, if I were hypocondriacque, or used to have my braines often visited with black fumes from the spleen, I could easily fancy you were suddenly taken with an autumnall fit of sicknes, or invaded, and bound hand [*and*] foot by the invincible Lady Podagra[308] or her handmaid Chiragra,[309] or at best that you had taken a Bougerman[310] over night, or a journy in the morning to some kind hearted neighbours to bring home potatos, but having no other then sanguine good wishes for you in my heart, I can entertaine no other then cheerfull phansies of your condition in my imagination, and therfore doe not trouble myself to guesse at the reason why I had never a letter from you this weeke, though I am sorry to misse of the usuall *avisos*[311] from Vulcan's court, longing to heare some good news of Venus, or Diana, nor should I feare Actaeon's fate though shee were *sine veste*.[312] I am at present under great inconveniences here, not being yet furnished with a footboy, my coachman fixed to his bed this week with a terrible ague, and the best of my coach mares lyes a dying in the stable; but I shall have by it the advantage to try the energie of your febrifugum on my man: after I had given him a vomit of [*mercury*][313] *vitae* which wrought well, before the next fit I gave him a glasse of white wine one spoonfull of your spirit, which showed no manner of effect unlesse it were perchance to make his fit the more burning, this day I have given him two spoonfulls two houres before his fit, and covered him warme to see if I could dispose him to sweate, for to mee the spirit seemes not only much paler but also weaker then our former spirit used to bee on the toungue, therfore though you commend your <*word deleted*> minera never so much, this in my opinion is able to disparage it: your volatil salt goes of[ʃ] a hot iron very well (though not so quick neare as the first salt) and leaves very little signe, but no stoole behind it; the fixed salt (as I guessed by the colour) is full of oyle which

---

[306] The licence to erect lighthouses was issued to Sir John Clayton and George Blake, a customs official, on 27 August 1669 (*CSPD, 1668–69*, p.629).

[307] Paston's cousin Robert Bertie, 3rd earl of Lindsey

[309] i.e. gout of the hand

[311] Dispatches [Spanish]

[313] Symbol not reproduced here

[308] i.e. gout of the foot

[310] ? bogeyman

[312] Without clothes

smokes on a red hot iron, but the salt which remaines when calcined is is [*sic*] very white, therfor when you farther prepare this salt it were best to calcine him in a retort first to save what oyle or volatil salt comes from him.

The King went down two dayes since to Shirnesse and returnes to day, a good part of the new work there is fallen down by reason the foundation was so rotten, they must bee forced to lay good store of rubbish[314] under it before they new build the wall.

Last week Mr John Lovelasse,[315] the Lord Lovelasse's son, riding home from Oxford after a good large dose of the university Helicon,[316] fell of[f] his horse and broke his necke, he was taken up dead to every one's thinking; but a lucky handed fellow in the company laying him down again on the ground and setting both his feet against his shoulders pulled his head so strongly that his neck bone came in again and he returned to motion and sense, being now in a hopefull way of recovery.

[f.2] The King they say now goes no progresse this yeare but only hunts for a week at Bagshot, if that prove true it will spoile my journy for Worcesters shire this yeare. There goes a report about, that Candy[317] was taken after the arrivall of the French fleet and before the landing of theyr army, which though I hope is not true, is not improbable by the relation of the condition of the town in Thursday's *Gazette*:[318] if it prove so, it gives a sh[*illegible*] crisis of the King of France's fortune, and will reflect with dishonour on the conductours of that fleet and army. On the other side if the siege should bee raised, it would goe neare to cost the life of the grand signor himself as well as the vizier's, the souldiers as well as the burghers of Constantinople and Adrianople being so incensed that so many lives have been lost without taking the town, that the grand signor is retired to Larissa (the town *in* Macedonia where Achilles was borne, who is called by Virgill Larissan Achilles) for these seven or eight monthes as much for his own safety as to take care of theyr army in Candy.

Mr Walker[319] is not yet come to town, which I am glad of because I may bee first instructed what salary it is fit to propose to him, for I would not have you content with an ordinary tuition and inspection from him, but I would for the education of your son (on the successe wherof depends not only his own happines but much of the whole families too) have him make it *in* a manner his whole busines to attend and converse with him. If you should ask my judgement in the case what were sufficient for him I protest I am lesse experienced in it then yourself, only thus much I would advise that it should neither bee measured by your generosity nor Mr Walker's deserts but proportioned to what your present condition can well spare, and make him some better amends herafter according as he shall merit, or succeed in his undertaking, and yet his frequent converse with your son will retrench considerable of his idle expenses in a yeare.

[314] i.e. rubble or hardcore: the fort at Sheerness had been more or less destroyed by the Dutch in 1667, and was now being rebuilt and remodelled.        [315] John, later 3rd baron Lovelace

[316] Drinking water from the fountains of Mount Helicon (in Boetia) was supposed to bring poetic inspiration, but Henshaw is implying that the university Helicon was something stronger than water.

[317] Candia, now Heraklion, Crete; it had been beseiged by the Ottoman Turks since 1648.

[318] *The London Gazette* was the official government newsletter (P.M. Handover, *A History of the London Gazette, 1665–1965* (HMSO, 1965).

[319] Henshaw's friend Obadiah Walker (1616–1699), later master of University College Oxford

Pray tell Sir John I cannot yet heare any news of our Parma cheese which gives me occasion to gratify \*you\* with a great secret if you doe not know it, that *caseio imperiale*, which is some of such old parmesan as Dickinson sent you, sliced thin and melted on a plate, is peradventure one of the best ragousts that ever you tasted.

My good wishes of mirth and felicity attend the meeting of so many of my excellent freinds of both sexes.

*Dum fata sinunt vivite laeti.*[320]

*Postscript*: [f.3] Your spirit this day hath put back the fellow's fit for four houres already so that I hope he will misse it this day.

*Addressed*: For the honourable Sir Robert Paston at Oxnead near Norwich, this
*British Library: Add. MSS 36988, ff 95–96*

# Thomas Henshaw to Sir Robert Paston

**1669, August 21**. Dearest patrone, I am heartily sorry you discover more light, in a busines I could wish had been never but a chaos, or rather a non entity – *basta*.[321] I can give you no further account of Mr Walker because I have neither seen nor heard from him since; which I am confident is but an indication that he will bee suddainly in town, however I will not faile on Tuesday to write to him to require his punctuall resolution in the pointe, that I may put you out of doubt and procure you satisfaction to your queries about your son's expenses, before I go for Dorsetshire, whether I am ingaged to take an unwilling journy about the middle of next month, to see what remedie I find for my misfortunes there, having now a second farme thrown on my hands and almost a yeares rents behind.

The subtutour I put in my calculations was only in case Mr Walker, uppon account of an executorship he is engaged in, should have occasion to bee oftener at London then is requisit for the charge he undertakes (which I doubt is the thing makes him so long demurre before he gives me in his answer) but such an absence for a week or ten dayes in a terme or two only might bee easily made up by the choice of some ingenious young man of the same colledge to supply his place. However before you ingage, I must tell you there are many that blame him very much for his education of Mr Hales[322] for they say if he had not too severely recommended to him a corporall honesty and vertue, Mr Hales could never have been such an Amorous Lafoole[323] as to have quitted Sir George Sandys' daughter with £40,000 to marry Mrs Windibanck who had only two milles[324] to pay £1,000 debt.

I like well your trying what the salt of adrop will yeald that has been twenty times deliquated,[325] but I doubt it will bee only a few graines of volatile salt, which though its being sweet like sugar is very considerable, yet tis not easy to find which use to make of it. I should think the salt of adrop may supply the place of the red lions bones

---

[320] Live happily while the fates permit.          [321] Enough! No matter! (It.)
[322] Sir Edward Hales (1645–1695) married Frances Windebank on 12 July 1669; he later became a Roman Catholic and a Jacobite.
[323] Sir Amorous Lafoole was a character in Ben Jonson's play *Epicoene or the Silent Woman*.
[324] i.e. thousands          [325] i.e. dissolved or melted down

if they should bee deficient either in quantitie or purity, but tis only experience can truly informe you, whether the very drawing of adrop with water (which wee see makes it so different from the other in most things) may not have also slaked that thirst in the salt, which is so requisite for the union of the principles.

I am realy troubled for the indisposition of Mr Le Grosse,[326] who (I doe agree with you) is cordially and unfeignedly your freind, and that your losse will be very great when ever you are so unfortunate to loose him; I could bee more troubled for your ladies indisposition but that I have hopes she will soon bee rid of it.

Sir William Backhouse is returned from the Bath so ill that he is *reduit a l'extremité et aux abois de la mort*,[327] one of his d[octor]s tould me yesterday, that there was no manner of hope and that he veryly believed he was dead by that time. [*f.*2] I could say with Chaucer A lack A lack what aileth thee to die having gold enough and Emilie[328] but that I have been taught that Jupiter allows every man when he comes into the world a different proportion of drink which when he has dispatched there remaines nothing for him but to die: and that the proportion and expedition makes the great difference in men's ages. *Ploratur lachrimis amissa pecunia veris*.[329] If he dies I doe loose £500 by it, judge you whether I have not a just and solid cause of grief. Sir Richard Pole had lately his arme put out by the overturning of the Dutches's coach at Tunbridge, but he is already well enough to ride a woing in his coach and six as soon as decency will permit.[330]

You have met with the unfortunate story of Candia in the Monday's *Gazette*, I have nothing to adde to it but that Blancfort is in mourning for his brother[331] the Count de Rosan who lost his life in that ingagement. You will meet there likewise with the entry and audience of the Danish embassador Gulden Lew[332] (that is golden lion, the gentry of Denmark (who never yet assumed any additionall titles of honour) taking the names of their families from theyr bearing in theyr scutchions) I have nothing therfor left to say of it but that it was the most splendid I ever saw any embassador come in with; though his richest coach being as they say not yet come over, the Duke of Monmouth's coach passed for one of the embassador's three, next after the King's coach. He is vice roy of Norway and naturall son of the present king, a very handsom proper man as I have seen and much a monsieur in his mine[333] and language. His busines they say is to excuse the carriage at Berghen in the time of the Dutch warre.

---

[326] Thomas Le Gros of Crostwick, who made his will on 27 Oct 1669 (proved 21 Sep 1671, TNA: PROB11/337), was a cousin of the Pastons, having both Paston and Knyvett ancestry. In 1638 he accompanied Sir William Paston on his grand tour as far as Italy, and he was a friend and neighbour of Sir Robert who shared his intellectual interests. Sir Thomas Browne dedicated *Hydrotaphia* to him in 1658.

[327] i.e. at bay before death: a phrase from a funeral sermon by Jacques-Benigne Bossuet.

[328] This is a loose paraphrase of part of Chaucer's *The Knight's Tale*; Backhouse had married an heiress, *see* above p.42.                      [329] Lost money is wept for with real tears (Juvenal)

[330] Sir Richard Powle (1628–1678) of Shottesbrook, Berks, master of the horse to the duchess of York. He married Anne, daughter and heiress of Sir Nicholas Crisp. He was MP for Berkshire but apparently his excessive care for his appearance made him a late-comer at debates (B.D. Henning, *The House of Commons, 1660–1690* (London, 1983), III, pp 275–6 [hereafter Henning, *Commons*]).

[331] They were sons of Guy Aldonce de Durfort (1605–1665), marquis of Duras, count of Rozan and of Lorges; Blanquefort subsequently became the 2nd earl of Feversham.

[332] Ulrik Frederik Gyldenløve (1638–1704), son of Frederick III of Denmark

[333] i.e. a Frenchman in his mien

There came over a second son of the king's with him, a young man who is gon to see our universities. There is also lately come to court a younger brother of the Duke of Saxony.

The thunder which made so little noise with you, did slay severall people in Stafford and Worster shires; and this day three weekes neere Lichfield there appeared a great cloud which darkened the sun, and comming nearer the earth it discovred it self to be an infinity of ant flies which made the men as well as the cattle run roaring out of the fields for theyr lives, but the cloud fell over Lichfield town and covered the streats and houses four inches deep and shortly after died; so that the inhabitants swept them together on heaps and carried them out to avoid the inconvenience of theyr putrefaction.

On Munday I carried my wife and daughter to Greenwich to see the grunpois,[334] which though it was but a very little whale, is yet a very great fish; the skin like that of all cetaceous animalls is like that of an eele's, and the flesh as white as a conger's, the humours of his body though he was dead were in a brisk fermentation, and out of a hole where they struck the iron that killed him, there zested out bloud and oyle lik barme out of a barrell of new ale. It put me in mind of some slain innocent that bleeds at the approche of his murderers: but the stench was so uncouth [f.3] that it was able to discompose any meditations.

On Sunday I heard the Duke, after he had related to us the storie of Candia, sent by Madame his sister,[335] that a workman in a quarry of stone in Glostershire not far from the Severne going to rise a great stone (he had loosened) on one end, it sunk away downward from him and had almost carried the fellow along with it, leaving a great hole which they trying to fathom found it sixty fathom[336] ere the plummet reached the bottom, the news of this being sent to the King, one here at London undertook to goe down and give an account of it. When he was below he found great vast cavernes and a great river twenty fathom over and eight deep, into a lesser cavity where he judged there might be som rake[337] of a mine he sent in a miner with a light who was not gon far but he cried they were all made for he had found what they sought for but when he had gon a little farther, he came thundring back again ready to break his neck, saying he had met with a spirit that so frighted him, he would not venture in again for the world.[338]

The King on Thursday last had news by letter from Jamaica, that one Morgan[339] whom he had sent thither to command a small frigat of twelve guns, going with this ship and six more small vessells without ever a gun but only a few murdering peeces into a harbour on *terra firma* [...][340] from Mexico, found himself at the close of the evening incompassed with twelve Spanis[*h men of*] war; the admirall sent to him to know how he durst venture beyond his boun[*dary and as*]ked him quietly to render his ships and he and his men should have quarter for theyr [*lives ot*]herwise he would hang them all. Morgan answered his Spanish Rodomonte with a Welsh one and sent

---

[334] i.e. grampus: orca or killer whale

[335] Henriette Anne, duchess of Orleans

[336] i.e. 360 feet

[337] A vein of ore, generally vertical

[338] For further information about this cave *see* G.J. Mullan, 'Pen Park Hole, Bristol, a Reassessment' (*Proc. Univ. Bristol Spelaeol. Soc.*, 1993 19 (3), pp 291–311).

[339] Sir Henry Morgan (c.1635–1688), privateer

[340] There is a hole in the paper, probably where a seal has been pulled off, affecting four lines.

him word that if he did not surrender his ships to him he should see how *he * would order them next morning. That night Morgan turnes one of his small vessells into a fire ship, and by break of day comes up to the admirall, fires his twelve guns at him and in the smoke layes his fire ship close by his side, the admirall thinking he had taken *a prize* caught a tartar, for he had *no* sooner grappled her to him and sent twenty men abord her but she begun to blaze and quickly set fire on the admirall, the rest of their fleet being in a great consternation slipt their anchors to get a way, but the tide brought two of them uppon the admirall and there burnt with her, a fourth running on shore set fire on her selfe because she would not bee taken, a fifth the rere admirall they took and brought a way where they found so great a prize of ready money that the meanest boy of the adventurers had £50 for his share. This I had from the King's own mouth, who sais it shall not bee printed, least it by reflecting too much on the Spanish bravery should provoke them to a revenge.

At the Councill on Wedensday uppon the petition of three Devonshire men who last assizes were convict uppon the statute of Q Eliz. for paying £10 a month for for-bearing the church[341] which amounted to a great summe of mony payable to the King, his Majesty did not only pardon theyr fine but declared he would not have that statute put in execution herafter; it being his indulgence that no man ought to suffer meerly for conscience sake, but he did not meane by this to excuse those that were found at unlawfull assemblies, they being always of daungerous consequence to government.

*Unsigned*
*Addressed*: To the honourable Sir Robert Paston at Oxnead neare Norwich, this
*NRO: BL/Y/1/33*

## Thomas Henshaw to Sir Robert Paston

**1669, August 28**. *Mon tres chere [sic] monsieur*, the scene of this epistle is Westminster, and I am in a great hurry of busines if an indeavour to get 100 markes may deserve so solemne a name. The truth is in seven yeare and a half that I have served the King, I have never seen his face in anything but flesh and bloud as Capt. Bessus[342] said; last yeare there was an assignement on hearth mony for one year's wage, and because the farmers tould me they had so much in arreare to them that it would hardly bee paid in theyr time, I was so slack in my sollicitation that I did not call uppon Downing's clarkes above twenty times concerning *it*, which made so little impres-sion that I had no warrant passed, and though that is not yet payed, nor will not bee this twelve monthes, the want of passing then, by a generall order excludes me, now there is a year's salary paying to every servant by an assignment on the custom-house.[343] I cannot yet learne whether it bee one of my usuall misfortunes, or my ill information concerning expedition mony. The lords commissioners are a weeke since

---

[341] Under the Elizabethan recusancy laws fines were levied on those who refused to attend church; they were normally Roman Catholics, but the fines could also be levied on protestant dissenters.

[342] A cowardly bragging captain in *A King and no King* by Beaumont and Fletcher

[343] Henshaw was French secretary to the King; he succeeded in getting a money order for £66 13s 4d (*CTB, 3,* p.274).

adjourned and there is onely the Generall and Sir John Duncomb in town; the last goes away to Berry[344] on Monday, so that I have but this punctillio of time to indeavour to retrive it or else to bee shut out for ever; so that I hope you will excuse my hast in telling my newes though I will not wholly absolve my self from my weekly respect. In the first place I am very well pleased that you find such incouragement by your practise, that you hope well of our subject and processe; perhaps the *stomachus struthionis*[345] may show you something extraordinary, the hypostasis[346] your white fume water let fall there, which it would not doe in heate, does give you very rationall hopes of it; though I doe beeleve all the red oyle or any sediment of that colour you have yet seene will in distillation.

The shortnes of my paper last week made me forget to tell you that Will Russell[347] was married to the great heir, the Lord Vaughan's widdow, who as it is generally computed will bee worth him £8,000. The Lord Anglesey['s] and the Lord Ashly's son are plying their busines at your cousin of Rutland's[348] and tis thought they have each of them by this time got a tartar. Sir William Backhouse died on Monday last, and I doe not yet heare whether he had so much sense, or morality to take any care of his <*word illegible*> ingagements in this world, before he went to cast up his accounts in the next.

Our good freind too Sir Edward Filmer is gone to see what mushroms the Elysian fields will yeeld; he took his flight thither from France, and therfor out of respect and civility to the place would dye in the religion of the country, Catholick Romain, it being not fit that one who had alway lived like a gentleman, should bee carried [*f.*2] *sans ceremonie*, to bee earthed in a church yard at Charenton.[349]

Pargeter the goldsmith has bin detected to have bought clippings of coyned silver and to have held correspondence with those kind of rogues, he has put in bayle of £30,000 to answer at the sessions, and his estate is alredy begd at adventure.

The King begins his progresse on Munday but goes no farther then Winchester and Southhampton, the chief designe being to hunt in New Forest. Hee will defeat the Earl of Pembrook, Lord St Johns, Lord Ashly to whose houses he invited himself when he intended to goe as farr as Plimouth which dispensation he has quitted for this yeare being tould <that> by the Earl of Laudardale that he need not ride post after a town that will not run away from him, and that it is neither safe nor decorous for so great a prince to appeare in so remote a part of his kingdome with only half a score of dusty followers.

The Queen and Dutches in the meane time will goe to Hampton Court, to give opportunity to the housekeeper to cleans[e] and sweeten Whitehall.

Here is lately come over a French minister[350] to court, a great calculator and if his

---

[344] Duncombe was MP for Bury St Edmund's, Suffolk.

[345] i.e. *aqua fortis*                                      [346] i.e. sediment

[347] William Lord Russell (1639–1683) married Rachel, Lady Vaughan, daughter of the 4th earl of Southampton; he was executed following the Rye House Plot.

[348] John, 8th earl of Rutland, was Paston's cousin; two of his daughters married the future earls of Anglesey and Shaftesbury.                      [349] The Protestant cemetery near Paris

[350] Presumably the Abbé Pregnani, a Parisian astrologer and fortune teller, who acted as courier and spy for Louis XIV. He undermined his own credibility by failing to tip any winners at Newmarket (Jenny Uglow, *A Gambling Man: Charles II and the Restoration* (London, 2009) p.494).

own testimony may bee credited the most accurate chronologer that ever was, one that by strength of cabala can tell of what colour and fashon the Queen of Sheba's stockings and roses[351] were of.

For Mr Walker because I am in hast let his own letter speake for him. If you doe intend to make use of him, inclose in your next a letter to him, and I will tak care to send it.

I much rejoyce to heare your affaires at Yarmouth are so prosperous,[352] God give you successe in that and all your other affaires that wee may have a cheerfull meeting at the terme. *Mon chere monsieur, je suis de toute mon ame*

*Signed: Le tout a vous*
*Addressed*: For the honourable Sir Robert Paston at Oxnead neare Norwich, this
*British Library: Add. MSS 36988, ff 97–98*

# Thomas Henshaw to Sir Robert Paston

**1670, July 16.** *Padron caro*, I have all this while expected when you would according to your promise at parting give me notice that you were at leisure to begin our correspondence, though I was well enough pleased that you spared me last Saturday: for I had then lodging at my house for som days my brother Ducket[353] and his wife, who came up to look after his daughter att Kensington schoole who has been very like to die of a surfet of fruit but is now well again: and I could not have been so long <*word deleted*> *absent* from attending on them as to have written a prolixe letter to you. I am not a little pleased that you find your experiment of fixing the spirit on the salt of adrop to succeed so constantly, and doubt not now but if you proceed as you determine som great magnate of nature will shew it self to you; if the divine Nemesis doe not by some strange accidents withdraw it from you as a just punishment for your revealing this great Arcanum to so many after the taking so solemne a sacrament of secrecy.[354] But I am glad Mr Brickenden[355] is so highly gratified with his own discoveries in Sendivog[*ius*] that he will not accept of the obligation to bee taught a frivolous secret by you: especially since he has a better way to the wood of his own then any Sendivog[*ius*] can teach him. It would require a great deale more time then either I can spaire or the disquisition is worth to examine particularly the hypothesis he has raised out of his reading Sendivogius, though otherwise I think it not very difficult to prove that he mistakes in saying that the universall matter ought not to bee extracted out of the earth because as soon as ever it is imbibed by the nitrous magnet in the superficies[356] of the earth it is

---

[351] On her garters, or possibly her shoes

[352] Paston had issued 'encouragements' with details of his proposed development ar Southtown, *see* Paul Rutledge, 'Merchant Housing at Yarmouth' (*Norfolk Historic Buildings Group Newsletter*, Spring 2003, no.5, p.14), NRO: FX 51/1, and British Library: Add. MSS 27447, f.313.

[353] William Duckett (1624–1686), MP for Calne; his first wife had been Henshaw's sister Elizabeth.

[354] Henshaw had given a Paston a secret recipe from the mathematician William Oughtred (c.1575–1660) which Paston had copied into a notebook (now British Library: Sloane MS 2222) formerly belonging to Theodore Turquet de Mayerne, on 6 June 1668, and he had presumably shared this with Brickenden (Dickson, 'Thomas Henshaw and Sir Robert Paston's Pursuit of the Red Elixir', pp 61–5).

[355] Richard Brickenden, alchemist, and owner in 1680 of Sloane MS 1687 (British Library)

[356] i.e. outer surface

for ever after prest to serve the vegetable family only and of an universall becom a particular only & it is true indeed that where the superficies of the earth is exposed to the sun and rain it is hard to meet with this universall matter, because as soon as it is generated, the vegetables doe attract it for their nourishment but in places that are defended from the sun and rain it is to bee had in plenty, and yet it is but the same matter that is found in the bowells of the earth and of which mineralls are ingendred; for Sendivog[ius] saith per 34 tract: 6$^{to}$ *sed verissimum est quod superius non e[st] nisi ut istud quod inferius, et vice versa, id quod nascitur supra, nascitur ex eodem fonte sicut illud quod nascitur in terrae visceribus*[357] &c. and the generall theory of Sendivogi[us] is that the four elements working one uppon the other doe beget an universall sperme or matter which is carried by the wind or ayre into the center of the earth whence it is sublimed by the Archeus or internall heat and distributed to all parts of that globe where according to the severall places or matrices different things are produced as mineralls, stones &c but in the superficies of the earth *ubi radii radiis iunguntur* ie the beams of the Sol Centralis or Archeus with those of the Sol Calestis, there is a more nimble and speedie generation performed, as that of vegetables, and yet this nitrous magnet is found as well in mines as on the superficies of the earth and wheras [*f.*2] he sais that it is not in the power of art *ever* to seperate that distinguishing earthy pinguedo[358] every refiner of saltpeeter can confute that, it beeing the chief parte of theyr trade to seperate the greasy liquor which is found with all peeter. Nay Send[ivogius] at the latter end of the twelfth treatise makes it a chief piece of the great art to purge the pinguedo not to throw it away; marke the words for I say to you but not to Mr Brickenden that he does no where else so plainly discover the matter. *Num scito quod sall nitri centrale non accipit plus de terra nisi quantus opus habet sive sit pura sive impura: aquae (ie aquosa) pinguedo aliter se habet, nam nunquam habetur pura ars purgat illam per duplicem calorem et denuo coniungit illam.* What matter in the world can so perfectly square with this description as that wherof artisans make saltpeeter and philosophers their medecine and the four asteriskes that follow to illustrate the place were not put their for nothing. Hee farther urges the authority of Send[ivogius] (but does not quote the place) that the matter is neither to bee drawn out of aire <not> *nor* water, but I know no such directions in him. But I cannot immagin what Mr Brick[ende]n means when he proposes to draw the universall spirit *in puris naturalibus* without any elementall mixtures, immediately from the very rayes of the sun and moon as they pass through the region of the ayre. Can he handle sunbeames and shut up influences in a glasse? (I have heard in deed that sunbeames and musick make excellent potage) nay grant him his owne fancy that he hath Sandivog[iu]s' magnet or chalybs,[359] and that he litterally draws it *ex ventre aristis* or out of sheepsdung; yet he confesses he draws it in forme of a water from the moon, but I would faine know what letters of credence this water brings from the moone more then the water any other calcined salt draws from the moist vapours of the ayre in a cellar. I[360] but sais he I have learnt a way to make a menstruum[361] of it to dissolve gold, such as Send[ivogius] describes p 79, when I see it I will beleeve it not till then, but there is a saying in the place he quotes he should have taken better notice of, speaking of his dissolvent: *si hoc invenistis habetis rem ex qua aurum a natura productum: et quamvis omnia metella et res omnes (inter quas sunt vegetabilia) ex illa*

---

[357] See note 234 above    [358] i.e. oilyness
[359] i.e. steel    [360] *recte* aye    [361] i.e. solvent

*ortum habeant, nil tamen ita amicatur et sicut aurum* &c.) For the chalyb drawing *ex radiis solis et lunae illud quod tot homines quaesierunt et est operis nostri principium*, and the following quotations: I suppose Send[*ivogius*] does equivocally use the word *sol et luna*, somtimes for the planets, sometimes for their symbolick mettalls; and where he means litterally that the chalibs doth extract it out of the influence of sun and moon, he aimes principally at that universall magnet dispersed through the whole globe of the earth; yet he may glance at a private magnet that some artists have used, who know not an easier way, but for Mr Brick[*ende*]n's better way then all this, I feare it will not bee worth much courtship to obtein the knowledge of it, let him enjoy it [*f.3*] only I am sorry to heare som of his neighbours say he has almost undon himselfe in chimistry as well for his own sake as the reputation of the art.

But I have been much longer deteined on this subject then *I* intended, it is now time to refresh you with that little news there is. You have heard I guesse by som earlier post that on Sunday last the King publickly declared in the drawing room on the Queen's side that he had created the Lady Castlemain Duchesse of Cleaveland, her eldest son Marquis of Southhampton and the second son[362] Earle of Northhumberland, the patents are not yet past the seale and if lords should persist in enfeebling their bodies so as not to *bee* able to get heires male, yet England in a few yeares may bee so happy as to see a House of Peeres truly noble, when they are all extracted out of royall bloud, and there will bee no need of calling a way country gentlemen from the service of theyr country, either at theyr own houses or that of the Commons.

The suspicion of Madame being poysoned which at first ran in everyone's head is now taken of by the comming of the Mareschal de Bellefonde, and to requite the comming hither of so great a person, the Duke of Buckingham is to goe compliment the French King; there goe divers over with him but especially the Lord Buckhurst, and Sir Charles Sidly who will lead the muses and the graces such a dance as may instruct and civilize fair France, but *a propos* to your letter having been three times at Sir T O[*sborne'*]s and not meeting with him I left the letter for him, supposing he would write you some account of what his grace sais, but since he has failed I will speak with him as soon as I can.

The Earl of Lauderdale went Thursday morning toward Scotland lord commis[*sioner*], the parliament being to open there the beginning of next month. The Duk[*e*] of [*illegible*] went the same night toward Edinburgh by sea in a yacht. There was a young heiress snatcht up a bout Wansor last weeke by Mr Obrien the youngest and his company, but they layd there plot so ill that she was recovered that night by the lord chief justice warrant and he is faine to satisfie him self with riding a trouper in the Duke's gards, it was said at first to bee Mrs Bonfoy[363] but I have forgot her true name. The Duke has been very ill since you saw him of a cough which had taken away his sences of smelling and hearing, he is they say now something better but not out of danger of a consumption. The King carried the Mareschell yesterday to see

---

[362] He was actually their third son but the King did not recognise his brother Henry, later duke of Grafton, as his son at this date.

[363] Susanna Bonfoy (d.1693), daughter and heiress of Sir Thomas Bonfoy, a wealthy London merchant; see also below p.138.

his new launched ship the *London*, and was this morning to shew him all his gards muster in Hide Parke if the wetnes of the day did not hinder, for their fell much rain both this day and yesterday which was St Swithin's.[364] There were lately severall bullets to the number of forty shot into the King's gallery and garden, the politicks judged there was treason intended, and that they were shot with white powder[365] because no noise was heard, but at last it is found to bee an ordinary fellow that not farre keeps tame pidgeons which it seemes his neighbours cats are very lickorish of, he to bee revenged watches to kill all cats that come·over the tiles with his stoneboy[366] and som of his shot have reached into Whitehall. On Thursday night the Earl of St Albans treated the King and the Mareschell at supper, where Mr Waller the poet made one, who when the King went away waiting on him down the ston steps toward [f.4] the water his feet slipping he fell and crackt his scull, which tis feard will put finis to his poetry.[367] The Earl of St Alb[ans] has lost his mistris they say for want of being able to make her a sufficient joyntur, which is the very case of poor Tom Cheek who [word illegible] as unconcernedly at Richmond as if he had not been lately in love. To conclude there died lately in London a maiden daughter of an earle named Diana in childbed of her second son, the wicked are so uncharitable as to say it was by her brother she was both times impregnated because he is very handsom and she left him her portion for a legacy.[368]

*Unsigned*
*Addressed*: For the honourable Sir Robert Paston at Oxnead neare Norwich [*franked*]
*NRO: BL/Y/1/34*

## Thomas Bainbrigg to Sir Robert Paston

**1670, October 13, Trinity College.** Most honoured sir, at your command I returne your sonne,[369] and with him all thanks, that by your favour he has honoured me with the name of tutor for a while. I shall now begin, and for ever after will call him my master, & I hope your selfe will permitt me to petition you not to be looked upon as a discarded servant or a peice of useless lumber for ever to be cast aside; I doubt not amongst your many servants you have some whose offices are meane and their titles low, let me be reckoned amongst the meanest of 'em & I shall not faile to keep up as a [*sic*] great a sense of it as the cheifest of them all. I can assure you sir,

---

[364] The weather on St Swithin's day was believed to continue for forty days and nights.

[365] Black powder, a form of gunpowder, is made of saltpetre, sulphur and charcoal; in white powder the charcoal is replaced by fine sawdust.

[366] Presumably a stonebow which was a crossbow adapted for propelling stones (David Yaxley, *A Researcher's Glossary of Words found in Historical Documents of East Anglia* (2003), p.203).

[367] John Aubrey repeats this story lamenting 'They made him damnable drunke at Somerset-house' (Oliver Lawson Dick (ed.), *Aubrey's Brief Lives* (1962), p.470).

[368] Henshaw appears to be referring to Lady Diana Sidney, daughter of the 2nd earl of Leicester, whose will was made on 5 March 1670 and proved on 26 July 1670, and who left her property to her brother Henry Sidney, later 1st earl of Romney, who was indeed very handsome. There seems to be no supporting evidence for Henshaw's story in other sources (including the *Memoirs of the Count de Gramont* in which Sidney plays a starring role), but most unusually the will contains two bequests where blanks have been left in the registered copy for the names of the beneficiaries and the sums they were to receive (TNA: PROB 11/333).

[369] William Paston

noe person has been in Trinity Colledge these many years that has had more of affection or a higher esteeme from the generality of the Colledge then your sonne and my
master has. He goes attended with many pious prayers and hearty good wishes for
his welfare abroad, and his happy returne, and our expectations are very high of his
improovements abroad, inasmuch as we beleive that he has spent the little time of
his residence here to very considerable advantage, which I presume and hope he will
be able *to give* a satisfactory account of it to your selfe. I remaine, most honoured
sir,

*Signed:* your faithful & humble servant, Tho: Bainbrigg
*Addressed*: These to the honourable Sir Robert Paston knight & baronett at Oxnett
Hall
*NRO: BL/Y/1/35*

## Thomas Henshaw to Sir Robert Paston

**1670, October 13**. My honoured patrone, while I was in Worcester shire[370] I
received a second letter from you given September the 14, wherin I received the
pleasant news of your having accomplished our long looked for sublimate; I was
mightyly exalted at it, but durst not adventure to give you my opinion how to proceed
with a subject you had so small a quantitie of, after all your charge and attendance,
till I had consulted som of our best authours, which I could not do till my returne to
Pondhouse,[371] but for a fortnight together, wee were twice a week disappointed of
the Shrewsbury stage coach, and was last of all forced to bring up my family in the
Bromicham[372] Geehoe coach, where wee arrived Saturday last: the book from which
I hoped most particular directions is Lullies[373] *experimentor[um] liber,*[374] of which Sir
John many years since gave each of us one for a new year's gift. I have lookt for mine
as the good woman did for the lost groat but in vaine; at last I remembred one of you
had borrowed mine. Sir John went Friday last to Denham and is not returned, till I
see that book I dare not adventure to give you any rubricks how to proceed; but you
may sooner and easilier take them from the first and second of Raimund's experiments, the one of fixing sp[irit] vin[egar] the other sp[irit] of urin[e], both set down at
large by him to adumbrate that processe you are now uppon. It would bee perhaps
worth your paines too, to looke over the places I have scored in the MS poem of
Edward Noell you have of mine.

   You must not hope or attempt any dissolution of mercury till you have reduced
your sublimate into a spirit, and then I take [mercury][375] *dulcis* to bee more proper to
work on then the crude, but then it should bee prepared by your self or some artist
that will doe it faythfully, for that which is commonly sold in shops is made of Holland
sublimate wherin they use much arsenick to make it looke very white which will not
easily wash away in the [?]delinfying and (beside the danger of it if one should apply

370   Presumably at the house of his brother-in-law, Richard Grevys of King's Norton
371   Henshaw lived at the manor of West Town, Kensington, in a house known as Pondhouse from the
fishponds there, *see* Pasmore, 'Thomas Henshaw', p.177.                    372   i.e. Birmingham
373   Raymond Lully (d.1315)                                  374   Book of experiments
375   Symbol in text

it to any medecinall use) it will be apt to blunt and fix your spirit, it were not amisse to make som triall also on precipitate.

That which yet straps down my fancy from aspiring to the hope of great things is that after so much spirit spent in imbibitions[376] there is produced but half an ounce of sublimate which is too little to make any considerable trialls: and next you not having at first taken the exact weight of your basis or fixed salt wee are still uncertain whether there bee any of the fixed united with the volatile: and if it bee onely a drawing of the volatile salt out of the spirit, wee had a way before to doe it in greater plenty with more ease and speed, therfor I pray in the first place make some triall of your new sublimate putting a grain of *it* on the blade of a knife, hold it over a candle and see whether it it [sic] fly all away as soon as our other salt did or whether it leave any stoole behind it: if it goe not all up, try what it will doe on a thin plate of iron red hot.

Wee have all had our health, God be praised, though it have been a very sickly time not onely all England over but in Holland too, and most of all in France, which I heare hath made my landlady,[377] her squire and dwarfe take up a resolution of [f.2] returning to us againe shortly. My poor cousin Major Thomas Henshaw is by the second fit of an autumnall ague transported from the joyes of Barwick to the delights of another world. The circumstances of his death I know not, for my aunt is not yet com to us: he was a right honest, worthy, unfortunate man, and I am hartily troubled for the losse of him.

I was on Sunday *at* Parsons Green, Lord John is pretty well and hearty but I feare my good lady's days are not many. She was after nine weeks sicknes in her bed with Mrs Hicks sitting behind her to hold her up with pillows, she was not able to speak one word to me but gave me a sad looke and shook her head; though perhaps her speech is much hindered by her salivation, for her doctors for I know not what intention having given her 20 gr[ains] of [mercury] dulcis, it casually[378] fluxed her and has continued on her about three weeks, so that one always stands by her with a bason.[379]

The court returnes not till Saturday so there is little news. The yaughts and the Earl of Ossory are gone for the Prince of Orange and he is expected at Harwich tomorrow. The Countess of Sh[rewsbury's] belly begins to swell and she gives us a faire probability of a hopeful issue.[380] Last week there being a feire neare neare [sic] Audly End[381] the Queen, the Duchess of Rich[mond] and the Duchess of Buck[ingha]m had a frolick to disguise themselves like country lasses in red petticoats wastcotes &c and

---

[376] i.e. absorption

[377] Henshaw held Pondhouse by lease from the Rich family, earls of Holland and Warwick (Pasmore, 'Thomas Henshaw', p.177). His 'landlady' in 1670 was Elizabeth, second wife of Richard Rich, 2nd earl of Holland, and one of Paston's Montagu cousins being daughter of the 2nd earl of Manchester; see also p.118 below.    [378] i.e. accidentally

[379] Apparently her physicians had overdosed her with mercury dulcis but she recovered, see Edward Maunde Thompson (ed.), *Correspondence of the Family of Hatton*, pp 57–8).

[380] Anna Maria, countess of Shrewsbury; her illegitimate son was fathered by the duke of Buckingham who had fought a duel with her husband, who subsequently died from his wounds; the child died in infancy and was buried in Westminster Abbey which gave great offence.

[381] Audley End, near Saffron Waldon, Essex; Charles II bought the house from the earls of Suffolk in 1668 to use when attending the races at Newmarket.

to goe see the faire: Sir Bernard Gasc[*oigne*] on a cart jade rode before the Queen, another stranger before the Duchess of Buck[*ingham*] and Mr Roper before Richm[*ond*]. They had all so over don *it* in their disguise, and looked so much more like antiques then country volk, that as soon as they came to the faire the people began to goe after them, but the Queen going to a booth to buy a pair of yellow stockins for her sweethard and Sir Bernard asking for a pair of gloves stitcht with blew for his sweethard they were soon by theyr gebrish[382] found to bee strangers which drew a bigger flock about them, one among them had seen the Queen at dinner, knew her and was proud of her knowledge, this soon brought all the faire into a crowd to stare at the Queen, being discovered, they as soon as they could got to horses but as many of the feire as had horses gotte up with theyr wives, children, sweetharts or neighbours behind them to get as much gapeseed[383] as they could till they brought them to the court gate. Thus by ill conduct was a merry frolic turnd into a pennance.

*Unsigned*

*Addressed*: For the honourable Sir Robert Paston at Oxnead neare Norwich, this [*franked*]

*NRO: BL/Y/1/36*

## John Fisher to Sir Robert Paston

**1670, November 1, Westminster**. Sir, I have been so little in town, & so full of busines, that I can very hardly gain time to write letters any way, and the parliament sit but every fourth day, and have only voted the King a supply, but how much & which way wilbe debated further on Thursday. His debts at interest are deliverd in at about £1,300,000, which a committee have undertaken to satisfy the House in against Thursday, and the setting out of fifty sayle of shipps next spring (to bear up to the proportion of our neighbours & allies) is computed at £800,000 more, so that the summe now to be given to put his Majesty out of debt (besides the arreares to servants, seamen, & for provisions, for which no interest is assigned) will be above two millions, but some of the court affirm it will require double that summe to preserve the honour of the King & nation and 'tis very hard pressed to rayse it by a land tax,[384] which wilbe the ruin of our country though the north & west may scape better. I have met Mr Dickinson but can do little good with him, either for Alderman Backwell's[385] or Sir George Downing's money, your patent being so farr charged that the custom farmers cannot accept it as a security for any summe, after the assignments they have taken notice of, and it wilbe unjust for them to repay themselves before: he confesses this is a very good year, but he feares henceforward they will decline, and whosoever

---

[382] i.e. gibberish: Gascoigne was a Florentine who spoke English with a heavy accent, as possibly did the Queen.                [383] Usually used as a noun for a gaping rustic.

[384] Taxes on land fell most heavily on the rural population. A 'new model' subsidy was devised for 1671 which attempted to improve assessment and collection on both landed property and 'personalty', i.e. money, including money at interest and banking profits. However the yield was disappointing and the tax was not repeated. (Chandaman, *The English Public Revenue*, pp 149–50, 165).

[385] Alderman Edward Backwell (c.1618–1683), goldsmith and banker

lookes about the citty cannot but thinke the customs for tymber must fayle, there being such infinite stores upon the wharfes, & the houses (in all but high streets) stand more then half empty, which is but a slender encouragement to go on with the rest. Sir Charles [*Harbord*] hath not met with Sir William Adams[386] yet, nor I have not seen him; it is probable on Thursday (when the sheriffs are to be named) he wilbe about the Hall & then 'tis likely he may see him. Sir Charles presents his humble service to you & my lady & will be ready to do you all the good offices he can, as there shalbe occasion. I come late in from beyond Brainford[387] this evening, so that I have only time before the post goes to present mine & my wife's humblest service to you & my lady, and rest, sir,

*Signed:* your most faithfull servant, John Fisher

*Postscript:* The booke acquaints you with the Prince of Orange his coming to town on Sunday evening. Just as I was sealing this, young Sir Charles[388] came in & desires his service may be presented to you, &c.

*Addressed*: These present for the honourable Sir Robert Paston knightt & baronett, a member of parliament, at Oxnead hall in Norfolk. At Norwich post [*franked*]
*NRO: BL/Y/1/37*

## Richard Brickenden to Sir Robert Paston

**1671.** Honoured sir, yours dated the 15th of the last month wherin you informde me of poor Dr Lloyd's death,[389] of your approving Mr Gough[390] to stand candidate to your service, of your receiving the alderman's old present without addition (which I conceive politiquely so presented to beget another refusal but you have now orewitted him,) that letter I answerd immediatly so soon as it came to my hands; but hearing not from you since that, and having promised you in my last to give you an *accompt* of that emblematical scrowle of the philosophick process[391] which I then went to see in Oxford Library I have presumed to trouble you with theis lines if happily they can finde you out but for fear they should not they shall be shorter than otherwise I intended them. I take the painted emblems of that scrowl to be the best that ever I saw especially that of the first matter the vessell & process of the first worke which I have engaged the lybrary-keeper himself to copy out for me in black & white so soon as possible, when tis in my hands 'tis at your service, the few lines that were written by the emblems in an old character with red inke are for the most part publisht in print by Ashmole[392] in his English *Theatrum Chemicum* calld the Verses of Riply's Emblematical Scrowle, but there are some lattine verses not printed of great consequence of which when we next meet. Dear sir, you were pleased to write in your last abovesaid to me that I should get Mr Gough to transcribe for me your ways of

---

[386] Sir William Adams of Sprowston Hall    [387] i.e. Brentford
[388] Sir Charles Harbord the younger who was killed at the battle of Sole Bay in the following year and was buried in Westminster Abbey (Ketton-Cremer, 'Charles Harbord', *Norfolk Assembly*, pp 41–62).
[389] Possibly Dr John Lloyd, canon of Windsor, died 8 July 1671
[390] John Gough, who was appointed rector of Oxnead on 17 June 1671.
[391] The Emblematical Scroll on preparing the philosopher's stone was attributed to George Ripley.
[392] Elias Ashmole (1617–1692), astrologer and antiquary

making the salt of nature by several ways of magnetisme as also your *Medicina Catholica Sendivogii* for which your candor kindeness & openness to me I sende you harty thanks, and in token of my sincere resentment[393] thereof (uppon the promise of your secrecy for I have not the like kindness for any man as for Sir Robert Paston) I will send you the process of turning May-dew[394] into salt by coction according to that rule of Sendevow *Quis auram coquere nescit procul omnis dubio errabit*, & again *extracti onem saltem nostri salis armoniaci ex aqua nostra pontica non tam aperte revelavi quia non habuis licentiam scribendi a magistro natura*. I can tell likewise what farther use is to *be* made of this salt for infinite health and riches & happily may of yours if you have any quantity by you but of theis things it is not safe to write at so great distance; it should not be long but I would be with you in your laboratory but that my wife is at present much troubled with melancholy & the disturbance of hypocondriack vapours so that I can neither settle to doe anything of that nature here nor yet to remove from hence. If you have not that art allready of gaining salt of dew gett some quantity this month or the next after some eight days of dry wether without raine, and I will send you the process, & after that, other directions; but I must desire from you cordial & sincere secresy in this matter. My wife joyns with me in presenting our most humble services to you & your vertuous consort, & in praying for the health & happiness of you & yours.

*Signed:* Sir, your most obliged, most affectionate & most humble servant, Rich: Brickenden
*NRO: BL/Y/1/38*

## William Paston[395] to Rebecca, Lady Paston

**1670/71, March 7/17,**[396] **Calais**. Deare madam, according to your ladyship's commands, I take the first oppertunity of letting you know our safe arrivall at Calais. Whe[397] had a very faire passage from Dover as could be expected. I was a little sea sick but I quickly rub[b]ed of that and I thank *God* I was never better in health in my life then now, my stomach[398] is much more encreased since I got ashore; the doctor is extream kind and civill, and the best company in the world so that I am extreamely well pleased and satisfyed; a Thursday we intend to march to Paris, in the mean time we will see some fare towns neere and divertise our selves for the present w[h]ere I hope to heare from your ladyshipe and my father which to me will be the wellcomest news in the world for I have *allways* been very sensible of your great kindnesses to me and when I see England agen you shall see that you have bestown them upon one who will not be ungratefull but shall *all*ways endeavor to gaine more; deare madam, I have nothing more to say but to subscribe myself,

*Signed:* your most obedient son, William Paston

---

[393]  i.e. appreciation

[394]  May dew was thought to contain wonderful properties because it was endued with the spirit of life or *anima mundi* (Dickson, 'Thomas Henshaw and Sir Robert Paston's Pursuit of the Red Elixir', p.64). Thomas Henshaw had delivered two papers on May dew to the Royal Society in 1664 (Royal Society, RBO/3/9–10).          [395]  William Paston (1654–1732), eldest son, subsequently 2nd earl of Yarmouth

[396]  See note on dating, above p.32.

[397]  We is spelled 'whe' throughout William Paston's letters.          [398]  i.e. appetite

*Postscript:* My most humble duty to my father.
*Addressed*: These present to My Lady Paston, London
*NRO: BL/Y/1/39*


## William Aglionby[399] to Rebecca, Lady Paston

**1670/71, March 7/17, Calais**. Madam, though I doubt not but Mr Paston's letter which am sure will bee first read will have informed your ladishipp of the successe of our journy hether to; yett to confirme the good newes and acquitt myselfe of the trust you have layed uppon mee, t'is fitt I should tell your ladishipp that wee arrived heere on Sunday morning about nine of [*the*] clocke having had a verry favorable passage: all that I cann say more *is* that I am too happy to travell with a gentleman that has soe much discretion and good nature as I every day discover in Mr Paston. This place affords noe ladyes newes only heere is the equipage of an English knight that makes a great noyse for hee has allready sent before him sixe fine coach horses with a coach chariot and curry and eight stable horses and is himselfe expected here with his lady in a pleasure boat every tide, his name is Sir James Rushwood as I am told bound for Montpellier; on Thursday wee goe for Paris where wee shall expect your ladiship's commands in the mean time I rest,

*Signed:* your most humble and most obedient servant, W: Aglionby
*Addressed*: These for my ever honoured lady, My Lady Paston at the Golden Ball,[400] Suffolke Street, London
*NRO: BL/Y/1/40*


## William Aglionby to Sir Robert Paston

**1670/71, March 7/17, Calais**. Sir, *enfin le fossé est heureusement passé* and wee are safely arrived at the *rocher diamontale avec le ravissement de la belle Europe*; it was Sunday before wee sett sayle, wee stayed Thursday and Friday morning at Sir Arnold Braemses[401] who made us verry wellcome, wee received manny civilitys from Mr Housman who saw us abord though at three of the clocke in the morning: our passage was of nine houres and were carried at last uppon the backes of poore Frenchmen a good way in the sea before wee touched French ground, and then wee had a lusty walke to Calais all which wee thought better then to ride it out another tide at sea. This towne is full of expectation for the King's coming, hee has caused all the fortifications of Dunkirke to bee razed though they <caused> cost both us and him soe much money soe that now the towne may be taken in an houres time, but hee comes this spring and setts his camp before it and is to see it fortified <he> by his owne souldiers. On

---

[399] William Aglionby (d.1705), FRS, subsequently writer on art and diplomat, was employed by the Pastons to accompany their eldest son on his grand tour; for Aglionby's career as a diplomat see *Notes and Queries*, 12 S IX (Aug 20 1921), pp 141–143, and for his career as a writer *see* Craig Ashley Hanson, *The English Virtuoso: Art, Medicine, and Antiquarianism in the Age of Empiricism* (Chicago, 2009), pp 94–108. He had qualified as a doctor of physic at the University of Bordeaux.

[400] The Pastons lived in Suffolk Street throughout the 1670s and collected their letters from the Golden Ball.          [401] Sir Arnold Breames of Bridge Court, Kent

Thursday morning wee mount Rosinante by the messenger and goe *a bride abattue*[402] to Paris; if you have any orders to give us Monsieur Bataillhe[403] can convey them thither. Thus with my service to all wee left at Rochester & their ladyes, I am

*Signed:* your most humble and obedient servant: W: Aglionby
*Postscript:* Pray lett my uncle know that I am well, hee has excused mee from writing till wee are settled.
*Addressed*: These for Sir Robert Paston at the signe of the Golden Ball in Suffolke Street, London
*NRO: BL/Y/1/41*

## William Paston to Rebecca, Lady Paston

**1671, March 28,**[404] **Paris**. Deare madam, I have now seen the whole city of Paris and all that is curious or magnificent in it and I find that our money does crumble away extreamly, so that whe will make all the haste that whe can to be gone, I stay for nothing but only to deliver my Lord Embassadour's[405] letter & Sir Thomas Bond's,[406] which buisness I doe intend to despatch to morrow. The nun's letter pray tell my Lady Bedingfield[407] is delivered, she inquired after all that family extreamly and after ours, and did extreamly admire to see she said a son of Sir Robert Paston's so bigg; she discoursed very handsomely & was *very* pleasant and glad to see me. I have made the suit that I brought from London a very novle suit with alterings and putting points and ribbons, and a a [*sic*] belt and hat so that I could not have made such a suit, the taylor sees, under thirty <*word deleted*> pistols but that cost me ten pistols the altering. Pray present my humble duty to my father,

*Signed:* so I rest your most obedient son, William Paston
*Postscript:* I doe keep the shirt that you bed Ward bring back.
*Addressed*: These present to My Lady Paston, London
*NRO: BL/Y/1/42*

## William Aglionby to Rebecca, Lady Paston

**1671, March 29 new stile, Paris**. Madame, if our journy had afforded us soe much variety of matter as would have sufficed to have filled two letters I should have writt your ladiship one the last post but all being easily summed upp in the assurance that wee are safely arrived here I thought one to Sir Robert would suffize. Wee have yett seen noe body, and for ought I can perceive it is as hard or harder to have audience from my Lord Ambassadour <than> *as* from the King; for I am told that hee is in the morning at tennis, and in the afternoon with the ladyes at both which times

---

[402] i.e. hell for leather
[403] Batelier, the London wine merchant who was to supply the travellers with bills of exchange.
[404] New Style
[405] The ambassador was Ralph Montagu (c.1638–1709), later 1st duke of Montagu, a cousin of Sir Robert Paston whose grandmother was a Montagu.                    [406] Sir Thomas Bond of Peckham
[407] Margaret, wife of Sir Henry Bedingfeld the elder, was the daughter and heiress of Edward Paston of Appleton, and thus a distant cousin of the Oxnead Pastons; she had two daughters who were nuns.

he admitts of little <leisure> *company*. Wee will try our fortune tomorrow morning but doe not intend to returne often for neither our leisure nor our monny will give us leave to stay heere above two dayes more, and when wee come to Tours I am confident wee shall not have ten pistolls left. Sir John Clayton desired mee to gett him some melon seed but I have in vaine enquired for the person hee directed mee too. Wee will endeavour to see Sir Thomas Bond but I am afraid that will produce some new expense which in the scarcenesse wee are inn wee must by all meanes avoyd. Mr Paston has [f.2] a servant who lookes like an honest boy. It was impossible to gett a protestant in the little time wee have had and to keep Mr Ward longer was to encrease our charge – his coming cost us above [illegible] which might have been better saved in our pockets and hee has not done us *one* halfe pennyworth of service. I know not yett whether or noe our banquier will convert our letter of credit for Paris into one for Tours but Mr Bataillhé committed a great neglect for I left him one of our bills of exchange to send before to Mr Balmentier and when wee came hether it was not come soe that if by accident I had lost the other which was in my custody wee must have been without monny for that which I left with him is not come at all. Pray madam lett Sir John Clayton tell him of it that hee may not committ a like errour another time. As soone as wee come to Tours and are settled your ladishipp shall heare from us, in the meane time I take leave and remayne, madam,

*Signed:* your ladyship's most humble and most obedient servant, W. Aglionby.
*Addressed:* For my ever honoured lady, My Lady Paston at the signe of the Golden Ball in Suffolke Street, London
*NRO: BL/Y/1/43*

## William Aglionby to Sir Robert Paston

**1671, March 29 new stile, Paris**. Sir, wee doe on Munday dispatch Mr Ward backe again and from him you will know all our adventures. Wee have not yett, by reason that it is the holy weeke, been able to putt ourselves in a fitting equipage to waite uppon my Lord Embassadour but doe hope to putt our selves in a readynesse *by* this night – but to morrow wee must neverthelesse performe our private devotions <at> inn our inn for Mr Paston thinkes it not convenient to bee seen by my lord in his chappel before wee have waited uppon him in his chamber. Towards the latter end of next weeke wee march for Tours. I suppose I need not desire you to mind Sir John to bee punctuall in his returne to us, wee will desire Mr Valensy to send to a friend of his in Tours all such letters as shall bee directed for us and likewise entreate him to give us his letter of credit to Tours instead of that which Mr Battaillhé has given us to Paris.

I have inquired more into this new invention of sedans and find that I am not verry well able to give you a good account of it, and therefore would faine have you desire Mr Henshaw to write hether about it. The Duke of Anguien[408] has the patent heere and it will bee worth a great deale to him. I believe you might begg it in England as

---

[408] Louis, duc d'Enghien, prince de Condé, victor of the battle of Rocroi in 1643, where the French took the sedan chair of the Spanish General Fuentes as a trophy.

for a new invention and for aught I know it might bee a second custome house. It is the wish of

*Signed:* your most humble and obedient servant, W. Aglionby
*Addressed*: For Sir Robert Paston member of parlement at the signe of the Golden Ball in Suffolke Street, London
*NRO: BL/ Y/ 1/ 44*

## William Aglionby to Rebecca, Lady Paston

**1671, April 8, Tours.** Madam, I received your ladiship's letter in answer to mine from Calais, just the verry evening before the day wee were to take horse for Orleans, so that I had not time to answer it then and wee have since made such diligence that wee have not stayed in any place above a night. Wee came hether on Saturday morning by eight a clocke having gone the day before in nine houres fourscore and odd miles downe one of the pleasantest rivers in the world, and I never saw Mr Paston more pleased then hee was in this voyage – before wee sett out from Paris wee waited uppon my Lord Embassadour who received Mr Paston with all the demonstrations of civility and kindnesse that could be expected, offering him his coach and servants to waite uppon him to see the environs of Paris; wee delivered likewise my Lord Morda[u]nt's letter to Sir Thomas Bond from whom we received offers of civility and of letters of recommendation to Tours but hee was then in soe great a hurry beeing ready to go for England that wee did not thinke fitt to trouble him soe farr. Our banquier Mr Bataillhé's correspondent at Paris is [*f.*2] a verry worthy civill man and as farr as I can guesse a verry able man; hee gave us a letter of credit for Tours to a merchant whom wee have been to see and who I beleeve will be verry civill to us. We do not intend to make use of the bill of credit but uppon verry urgent occasions and wee have where withall to keepe ourselves about three weekes from the date of this letter which I hope will bee a longer time then is necessary for the returning of our new supply. I suppose by this time Mr Ward is come to London, wee parted from him verry willingly and besides the £5 your ladiship gave us towards the bearing of our charges hee has cost us above nine more but Mr Paston is soe well pleased with the servant hee has he does allmost resolve against all valet de chambres for the future. This place though it answers our expectations as to one point which is the avoyding of English <wh> there beeing not one in towne, yett does it come soe farr short in other things that I beleeve wee shall not make any considerable stay in it and indeed to say truth I was as much deceived in it myselfe as could bee; for having never made any great stay heere and seeing it a populous place I thought it might bee well provided of masters which I find it is not, the busynesse of this place beeing only trade and not breeding, soe that about a month hence wee shall goe downe the river as farr as Angers which does not swarme with English soe much as Saumur and there fixe. In the mean time Mr Paston is resolved to apply himselfe with all his might to the French tougue that hee may have an antidote against [*f.*3] the infection of his countrymen whom he is resolved to avoyd. He is in all points, madam, the best travellour in the world, undergoing all hardshipps with a pleasantnesse which I have seen in few persons of his age and quality. Hee does mee the honnour to aske and take my advice in every thing and in a word hee is master of a great deale of reason and good nature which cannot but in time make him verry accomplished; all which does soe much encrease my joy and satisfaction that I doe hardly wish to any addition to my content but the perfecting of these soe happy beginnings. Wee doe expect every day an answer <from> *to* the letters wee writt from Paris for there is nothing does soe much transport us as to see your ladiship's hand uppon the backe of a letter. I hope by this time and before Sir Robert is well of the goute and at liberty to lett us heare from him. It is the wish of, madam,

*Signed:* your ladiship's most humble and most obedient servant, W. Aglionby
*Postscript:* I suppose your ladiship will bee shortly at Oxnead and I begg that my respects to the young ladyes and Mrs Wiseman may beare you company thither.
*Addressed*: These for my ever honoured lady, My Lady Paston at her lodgings at the signe of the Golden Ball in Suffolke Street, London
*NRO: BL/Y/1/45*

## William Paston to Rebecca, Lady Paston

**1671, April 8, Tours**. Deare madam, I received your ladyship's letter at Paris *at which I was mightily transported* but I could *not* stay to answer it for as soon as ever I had paid my visites to my Lord Embassadour and to Sir Thomas Bond, whe bid *à dieu* to Paris and whe came for Orleans; my Lord Embassadeur was extreamely kind & civill, as possibly could have been expected, and called me nothing but cousen and proffered me his coach and servants to carry me wheresoever I pleased; Sir Thomas Bond was extream civill, and offered letters of recommendation to Tours; whe had extream good company [to] Orleans as could be, and after whe had stayed and viewed the town a day, which is a very large one well built and populous, whe tooke a boat and came for Tours and in eleven hours whe arrived at our city *which* pleased us very much; till whe had viewed the *town*, and found our expectations so frustrated, finding it a town only for merchandise and not for breeding, so that about a month hence we intend to set out for Angiers, in the mean time I doe intend to spend my time as well as I can, for I doe not mean to be idle, but I will ply my French mightily and will learn tenis and lim[n]ing if there bee such a master. Pray present my humble duty to my father & grandmother, my service to my uncle & aunt. So I am

*Signed:* your most obedient son, William Paston
*Addressed*: For My Lady Paston
*NRO: BL/Y/1/46*

## William Aglionby to Sir Robert Paston

**1671, April 21,**[409] **Tours**. Sir, yours of the thirtieth March came to my hands this morning and hath been eleven dayes[410] a coming; wee have heared nothing of the

---

[409] Written as 21th      [410] New Style, it was 11 April in England.

bills of exchange which you have soe carefully returned us, which is such a disappointment that if they doe not come next post wee shall make use of our bill of credit. At whose doore the neglect lyes I cannot well tell though I can guesse for my marchant from Paris writes mee word positively that hee sends mee the enclosed which were these which wee have now received beeing all that hee has received since our depart from Paris soe that the mistake must bee in England and I doubt not but Mr Batelier is both able and willing but hee must bee punctuall likewise or else wee shall suffer for it and I am sure that cannot be called punctuality, when wee receive letters written two posts after the bill is sent, and yett doe not receive the bill; I suppose our letters from Tours are with you by this time and have acquainted you with the successe of our visits to my Lord Embassadour and Sir Thomas Bond, wee should have understood our selfes verry ill if wee had omitted so essentiall a duty as our respect to the first. My lady is pleased to bee verry earnest uppon the point of relligion and order us to put away this servant and take another of the protestant relligion. Shee shall bee obeyed as farr as I have any influence and whosoever has any suspicion of my inclinations to the church of Rome does mee a great deale of injury. If I was bred up in it in my youth it was not my fault but my mother's who revolted to that church and I thinke that she having left it when I came to bee a man and having ever since lived in it with the observation of all its rites and submission to its doctrine should bee enough to cleere any rational body's mind for it is not in my power to give greater testimonys of my sincerity in the relligion of the Church of England then those which I have given and of which your whole family is wittnesse.[411] If after that the [f.2] jealousyes[412] doe still continue it were better both for the satisfaction of my lady and of myselfe that shee provide herselfe of somebody against whom that aspersion may not bee cast and in whom shee may more entirely relye, for to speake ingeniously[413] though I love Mr Paston as I would a brother yett for mee to bee in that state as to *bee* answerable for all the changes that shall or may happen in his mind and principles by travelling and conversing as hee must doe with all sorts of people is a thing which I will not undergoe. I doe not say this as if there were any likelyhood of such a misfortune for hee is as farr from it as any body cann bee and I doe and have promised uppon my honnour (which it may bee I value as much as any body) to endeavour to keep him from all change in his relligion to the utmost of my power, but still if such a thing should happen though I had opposed it with all my might yett in this prejudice that some people have infused into my lady it will still bee thought that I had a hand in it. Therefore I humbly desire you if you are satisfyed uppon the point to expresse it to mee in your next and then to committ to my care the management and getting of such servants as shall stand best with our convenience. Servants to a master that understands the language doe not use to have much influence as to relligion, much lesse to one that understands it not. I would have gott one of the protestant relligion if I could have stayed long enough to have had my choice but among all those which were offered there was not one of that relligion;

---

[411] Aglionby's parents were Dr George Aglionby (d.1643), prebendary of Westminster, and his wife Sibella Smith. The accusation that he was a Roman Catholic dogged him for the whole of his life, *see* Aglionby to Nottingham, 1704 (British Library: Add. MSS 29589, ff 433–437).

[412] i.e. suspicions

[413] *Recte* ingenuously, i.e. candidly

this servant which wee have would not stirr from Paris till wee had promised him to pay his journy back in case wee turnd him away of ourselves; and in this place where wee \*are\* it will bee verry hard if not impossible to gett a protestant one, for indeed one cann hardly gett any at all and it is not to bee expected that wee cann have that choice in a country towne as wee might have had in Paris; besides when wee come into Italy shall wee carry one with us who it may bee by his indiscretion or zeale may make us bee knocked on the head. These considerations I thought fitt to represent to you particularly because I discerne lesse suspicion in your letter then in my ladyes yett if after this you bee of opinion to have this servant who is a verry good one turned away and a protestant one taken you shall bee obeyed punctually to the utmost of the endeavours of

*Signed:* your most humble and most obedient servant, W. Aglionby
*Postscript:* My respects to my lady. I shall write to her next post. My service to Sir John and his ladye.
*Addressed:* For the honnorable Sir Robert Paston member of parlement at the signe of the Golden Ball in Suffolke Street, London
*NRO: BL/Y/1/47*

## William Aglionby to Rebecca, Lady Paston

**1671, April 23, Tours**. Madame, I could not possibly answer your ladyship's letter the last post because I received it but just an houre before the post <wh> went away for Paris and it was as much as I could doe to write to Sir Robert to lett him know that wee had not received the bills of exchange which were sent the weeke before the date of his; I am sorry I must confirme that ill newes still but soe it is that wee heare nothing at all of them and must now if they come not next post make use of our bill of credit, all Mr Paston's pockett monny and mine beeing allmost gone; I am loath to come to that extremity and soe shall if I can gett credit rather for meate and drinke. Your ladyship is pleased to recommend to mee verry earnestly the taking of a protestant servant and Ile assure your ladiship that I was as desirous of one as you could wish but wee had not monny enough to keepe us at Paris till wee could gett one, and heere it will bee a verry difficult matter, yett if I cann find one and persuade Mr Paston to part with this which hee has who is a verry [*f*.2] good servant and has hetherto showed himselfe verry faithfull and diligent. If I had had the honnour to speake of this matter with your ladyship before our depart I could easily have made it appeare that there was noe danger for Mr Paston's conscience to have his shoes pulled off by a papist; for as to any other influence uppon him hee does mee the favour to beleeve mee <too much> enough to hinder all its effects, soe that all the suspicions and feares must needs bee founded uppon my having been a Catholik which I thinke is a little uncharitable to one who has given such evident testimonys to the contrary and besides those jealousyes doe reckon ill if they should thinke to find an opposition in a servant to those persuasions which my hidden malice and desire of making proselytes must make mee use towards Mr Paston. Therefore madam pray lett mee desire your ladyshipp to sett your heart at rest for I will rather dye a thousand deaths by the hands of tormentours then ever endeavour so wicked a thing or suffer any body else to doe it, but if your ladiship should continue these distrusts I should pitty you verry much for I should measure the greatnesse of your care and disquiet by that of the tender love and affection which I know you have for Mr Paston and I should myselfe advize you rather to withdraw <you> *mee* then to keepe yourselfe in perpetuall feare and sollicitude.

Wee are heere settled for a while and Mr Paston has not ill employed his time for hee learnes French every day of mee; he learnes to draw and perspective, and hee has a fencing master and plaies at tennis which is as much [f.3] as anyone man [*may d*]oe[414] at once – the dancing masters here are none of the best which made mee advise him to deferr learning to dance till wee came to some place where he might meet with more modish ones; our stay heere will as I allwaies intended it proove a thing of great importance for his emprouvement for now I have gott such possession of his mind and soe principled him against the English that I doe not much apprehend the beeing in one and the same towne with them. Mr Paston is extremly well at present; hee was a little troubled with bleeding at the nose where uppon by the advise of physicians hee has been lett blood and purged and is now as well as ever hee was in his life. I doubt not but hee will continue soe and to that end and all other emprouvements hee shall not want the assistance and service of, madam,

*Signed:* your ladyshipp's most humble and most obedient servant, W: Aglionby
*Postscript:* My most humble service to both the Lady Claytons and Sir John whom wee desire to looke a little after our bills. My respects to Sir Robert. Mr Paston re[*memb*]ers his duty to Sir Robert a[*nd to y*]our ladyship
*Addressed:* For my honoured lady, My Lady Paston at the signe of the Golden Ball in Suffolke Street, London
*NRO: BL/Y/1/48*

## William Paston to Rebecca, Lady Paston

**1671, May 4, Tours.** Deare madam, I received your ladyship's letter the second of May, and am extreamely much satisfyed to heare that you are as willing we should leave this place as we our selves; we are just now agoing to Angiers where I hope to see some of my kindred, my cosens Osborns[415] are heare at Tours, yesterday I gave them a visit, they intend to stay a month to get a little French before they goe to Angiers, for there they will get a very little, if they intend to be in the house of their countrymen, there is some five or six in a house of an Englishman and they talk nothing but English, so that they had as good allmost to have stayed at home, for my part I intend to be in a French pension and imploy my time to my best advantage. I met there of the gentlemen of Angiers at Richelieu (who gave this account) among them was my cosin Hary[416] who I scarce knew, we are extremly civill to one another

---

[414] Paper damaged.

[415] Edward and Peregrine Osborne, sons of Sir Thomas Osborne and Lady Bridget Bertie, were at Saumur for several months; their mother joined them in October then returned to England with Peregrine while Edward remained in France until the following year (Browning, *Leeds*, I, p.68n).

[416] Henry Bertie (c.1656–1734), son of Sir Robert Paston's uncle, the 2nd earl of Lindsey, by his second wife.

and he desired mee to present his service to my father and your [*f.2*] ladyship. Richelieu is a very noble palace and the pleasant[*e*]s[*t*] *palace* <one of abode> that ever I saw and the best house in France, it cost the cardinall a world of money but he being treasurer to the King of France did not want for money. This is all I have to say at present, only my humble service to all my friends and my most humble duty to my father, so I am

*Signed:* your most obedient, William Paston
*Addressed:* These for My Lady Paston
*NRO: BL/Y/1/49*

## William Aglionby to Rebecca, Lady Paston

**1671, May 7, Tours**. Madam, I have received your ladyshipp's letter of the 10th of April and all the others except that which you writt when you sent the bill of exchange; which is a thing which I most wonder at. I have writt to Mr Bataillhé twice but cannot yett hope for an answer; in my last to him which was on the 5th instant I gave him advice how wee had been obliged to make use of our bill of credit since wee could heare noe newes of that of exchange, I tooke upp the monny *£100* on the same day that I writt and as neare as I could tooke it according to the exchange that is between London and Paris, the merchant heere made us pay halfe per cent for the returne from Paris hither; this when wee shall bee remoter from you will still encrease uppon us which added to a matter of £3 in the hundred which wee loose by every returne will amount to above £20 a yeare defalcation in our allowance which I beseech your ladyshipp to consider. Wee have been now for this month heere as good husbands as it is possible for us to bee any where and yett wee find uppon account that wee have exceeded our monthly [*f.2*] allowance by above five pistolls. Noe young man that comes abroad did ever in soe little a time emprove him selfe better then Mr Paston has done – in this month hee has learned a great deale of French; the whole art of perspective; to limm and to fence a little, soe that by that your ladyship may see that whatsoever charge you are at it will bee infinitly requited in processe of time; it is not my busynesse to flatter Mr Paston nor your ladyship and much lesse my humour, and therefore what I write you may beleeve, and if hence-forth the face of things should change your ladyship should see the wrong side of the medall as you doe now the right. Hee ownes that his stay heere for a while was and will bee a thing of great use – for by it I have inured him to French company and given him occasion to have some insight into their wayes, manners and breeding, all which hee likes well and is of opinion that hee should have avoyded them had hee gone to a place at first where there had been store of English company. Wee tooke a small journy three dayes agoe to see the pallace of Richelieu and there wee acci-dentally met with Sir Thomas Midleton[417] and his brother and Mr Bartie who were come from Angers uppon the same designe of curiosity; and at our returne wee found heere Sir Thomas Osburne's two sonns whom wee went to see yesterday and who by our example intend to passe a month heere before they goe any further. Secretary

---

[417] Sir Thomas Myddelton of Chirk and his brother Richard

Trevors[418] his sonn [*f.*3] is gone on straight to Angers, when wee see him wee shall endeavour to oblige him in all things. Wee thinke of going hence on the 9th instant to Saumur and after a dayes stay or two there goe to Angers. Saumur swarmes with English, there are my Lady Holland with Adam Loftus and my lord, Sir Robert Atkins with his lady, a coach and six horses, a pack of hounds and halfe a dozen stable horses, divers other private gentlemen, I fancy for my part that I am going to London.

I suppose by this time your ladishipp will have been a little in peine by *Sir Robert* receiving a letter from mee and none from Mr Paston but I hope before this comes to your hand you know the cause of that omission which was our letters sent back by a mistake from Paris. In one to your ladyship of the next post I endeavoured to cleere myselfe of the suspicion of popery and soe will say noe noe more now but that I have a reall kindnesse for Mr Paston as for my friend and shall behave myselfe towards him like one in all considerations and particularly in that of the wellfare of his soule which I thinke cann bee noe where soe safely guided as in the obedience to the doctrine and discipline of the Church of England as it now stands; this is a truth that I am ready to suffer for at any time – and which I hope you will doe me the honnour to bee persuaded of or else I shall hardly thinke that you give mee leave to bee

*Signed:* your most humble and most obedient servant, W. Aglionby
*Addressed*: For my honoured lady, My Lady Paston at her lodging at the signe of the Golden Ball in Suffolk Street, London
*NRO: BL/Y/1/50*

## Thomas Henshaw to Sir Robert Paston

**1671, May 13**. *Cher chevalier de Paston*, you leave me that never was your condisciple under Lilly,[419] and that have no faith in astrology, to divine by the stars what should bee the reason that I have these two last posts with great expectation and no satisfaction attended for some account of your safe arrivall at Oxnet, interlarded with the gusto's and divertisements of your reception at Huson:[420] for my part I beleeve in God, and not in old wives' fables, nor will I bee so hypocondriack as to fancy your entertaining your self with the goute, or your passing your time with a *flus de ventre*, should bee cause of it; but am more apt to beleeve it proceeded from some more gentlemanlike spontaneous lassitude, or that your nearer concernments have ingrossed this week's inke and paper. Bee it so, I am content, provided it bee no worse. In the *meane* time we have bin treating the Dukes de Longueville, Bouillon, Marillac, Monsieur le Grand[421] &c who made a trip over to see this court, and doe their reverence to our King who they *say* is *le plus honest homme du monde*. Your cousin Manchester has bid *buenas noches al mondo* and was snatcht away with a collick before he had time to think death was now at last in good earnest with him.[422] The Earle

---

[418] Sir John Trevor (1624–1672), secretary of state    [419] William Lilly (1602–1681), astrologer

[420] Probably Euston Hall, Suffolk, home of the earl of Arlington

[421] Louis of Lorraine (1641–1718), count of Armagnac, was hereditary grand squire of France, with the title of Monsieur le Grand.

[422] The earl of Manchester, lord chamberlain, died suddenly at Whitehall on 7 May. He was a cousin of Paston's mother, Lady Katherine Bertie, and was also the man who took the Paston plate during the civil war, see p.4 above.

of St Alban[s] is grown young again with the satisfaction he has in succeeding him to bee the King's lord chamberlain, and will bee as youthfull when he gets the white staffe and blew ribban as when he was Harry Jermin; the first being of course deferred till the solemnity of breaking the old staffe and throwing it into the grave of his predecessor. Chief Justice Keeling[423] on Wedensday last had an old statute executed uppon him by a writ of *statutum est omnibus semel mori*,[424] but that which is most to bee admired in it was that a man of so bilious a complexion should have so flegmatick a conveyance to the other world as a lethargy. The prentice boys persist in theyr antient zeale against bawdy houses (sure they find it hinders the trading of their mistresses and chambermaids at home) and therefor on Munday night last did demolish six neare Clerkenwell. But the Romant of the Rose is a story you will find in Thursday's *Gazette* of one Blood's[425] stealing the crown out of the Tower, as gallant hardy a villain as ever herded in that sneaking sect of the Anabaptists. When he was examined before the King he answered so franckly and undauntedly that everyone stood amazed. He told him he had bin an officer in his father's *army* and had ruined his estate for the service of the Crown, and since his Majesty would doe nothing for him he had resolved to make himself reparation out of the Crown, which he thought was more honorable then to take a crown out of a private man's pocket on the highway, and that (had he not had an aversion to murder) if he would have killed the man that kept it, he would not have given a crown to have secured the crown to himself. The King asking how long he had bin a fanatick he answered never till his Majesty turned Presbyterian and tooke [f.2] the Covenant. He knowledged himself to bee the head of the fanatick party, and said they only wanted a good summe of mony to put that designe in execution which they have in readines, which he thought to have furnished them with by stealing the crown for he thought it worth at least £10,000 (wheras in truth the crown, septer, globe, and St Edward's staffe which are all of gold, stood the King but in £6,000). He acknowledged himself to have headed that party which *was* to have surprized Dublin Castle about eight years since for which some of his complices were hanged and himself outlawed, he was chief in a plot for rising about Yorke where he rescued one of his camrade that was carrying to execution out of the hands of the officers of justice. He confessed it was he and his company that seized the Duke of Orm[on]d and he himself puld him out of his coach, but said he meant not to have kild him for that he could easyly have don at first, but to have carryed him to a place he had provided for him where he would have treated him as well as if he had bin at his own house, but would have secured him till he had ransomed himself with a good summe of mony to give himself satisfaction for £200 *per annum* land the Duke had taken from him in Ireland. This Blood went sometimes for a minister in which habit he was now taken <to> and sometime for a doctor of physick, and his son a lusty young man now apprehended with him did that while keep an apothecary's shop neare London for countenance. He makes the greatest slight in the world of death, sais he has been a dead man in law these eight years, every *man* must dye, and he knowes not but a rope is a more cleanly and expeditious passage out of the world then a feavour, a dropsy or a squirt. There was found about *him*

[423] Sir John Keeling or Kelyng died 10 May 1671.
[424] All men must die once.      [425] Thomas Blood (1618–1680), adventurer and spy

a little booke of paper wherin he had set down above sixty signall deliverances from eminent dangers. Men guesse \*him\* to bee about fifty years of age by the gray hairs sprinkled up and down in his head and beard but he sais he is not above forty five and his son twenty one. He vaunts of his knowledge of severall plots and designes <and designes> against the governement, & sais there is not an eminent malecontent in England or Scotland but he is well acquainted with him, but will confesse nothing, for sais he what shall I get to betray my freinds, which looks as if he had a mind to drive a bargain for his life. Prince Robert remembers he served under him, and sais he was a very stout bold fellow

My daughter I thank God seems a little better then she was but I feare will not last long, all she had from Sir G[*eorge*] Ent did her no manner of good, if there bee any improvement she ows it under God to my aunt's snaile water in a morning. My wife is great with child again but what joy is there in that when, on an unhelthy woman, who can beget other then funeralls and mortuaries.[426] For chymicall dispensations wee will prorogue them till you are [*f.*3] in some forwardnes. I want but one barrell full now to have collected all the dew the King has appointed. I pray once more send me up speedily De Paris' French work, as also the other book of recipes that was Sir Edmund Stafford's[427] where there are several processes concerning May dew, I will secure you them again, and if there bee any use made of them the King shall know they came from you. My most humble service I pray to my good lady, to Mrs Paston,[428] & my cousin Wiseman.

*Signed: Je suis, mon cher monsieur, le tout a vous*, T.H.
*Addressed*: For the honourable Sir Robert Paston at Oxned near Norwich, this
*NRO: BL/Y/1/51*

## William Aglionby to Rebecca, Lady Paston

**1671, May 16, Angers**. Madam, I doe not remember that in my letter to Sir Robert of the 21 April (which is that which I suppose your ladyship has received) I sayd that Mr Paston was not well but only that hee had been a little indisposed and had taken physick for prevention but was in good health at the writing of that letter, as hee is now God bee praised. I suppose by this time you have received his letters of the 21[*st*] which were sent back to us at Tours and sent away again by us the 28th. Hee is not backward in writing and is as glad to heare from your ladyshipp as you cann bee to heare from him. We have executed our designe of leaving Tours to come to Angers; not soe much because it was not a place to breed a gentleman inn (for uppon enquiry wee found out verry good masters and some of them a great deale better then they are heere), as because there were noe English there with whom to passe our idle houres. My designe was in that month's stay there to custome Mr Paston to that assiduity of life and punctuality in his exercices which is necessary for the breeding of him and alsoe by the by to make him gett a beginning in the French toungue

---

[426] Henshaw and his wife had six sons and two daughters, all of whom died apart from one daughter.
[427] For Stafford *see* F. Sherwood Taylor, 'The Chemical Studies of John Evelyn' (*Annals of Science*, 8, no 4, 31 Dec 1952).                    [428] Sir Robert's eldest daughter Margaret

without the interruption of English conversation. If the time had been well spent at Oxnead in the French language I [*f.2*] should not have endeavoured to severe him at the first from his countrymen for hee would have then done it of him selfe: this much I writt to my uncle whom I desired to communicate it to your ladyship which I suppose hee has not done else you would not have been soe earnest in desiring us to leave a place which at the verry first I never designed to stay long inn; if all the months we stay a broad are spent as well as this was at Tours I dare answer to bring Mr Paston back a verry accomplished gentleman. This I have thought myselfe bound to say in my owne justification for having made some stay in a place which does soe much displease the judgment of those who I beleeve have a great deale more experience of France and are wiser then I am. I am not at all fond of my owne conduct and am verry glad your ladyship has those neare you whose affection and abilitys are soe great as to give you the advice which wee need abroad; and I doe most willingly submitt and subscribe to all that shall come from them beeing accompanyed with your commands; therefore as much as in mee lyes I shall dispose Mr Paston to expect the spring of all our motions from thence and in all other things whatsoever you please to hint shall bee punctually obeyed; for I had a great deale rather have your ladyship's letters to show for a reason of my conduct then the allegations of my owne judgment and experience. Wee are heere settled in a pension in the pleasantest part of the towne and in a house where there are noe strangers besides ourselves, within a street or two of the rest of the English who are all in the same house as to dyet though soe crowded that some have been forced to take chambers over the way. [*f.3*] Wee have been to see them and I doe find find [*sic*] Mr Trevour to bee the prettyest gentleman of them all beeing verry judicious and having brought a good stock of French with him out of England which enables him to make his advantage of all French company as hee does. This is all I can say at present only I must add that I should bee verry unfortunate if you could beleeve that I could bee otherwise then kind to Mr Paston who is soe to mee, there beeing a great deale of cordiality between us, but however I shall bee the more incited to continue soe by your ladyship's particular command and doe thinke myselfe verry *happy* to have soe easy occasion of shewing how much I am, madam,

*Signed:* your most humble and most obedient servant, W. Aglionby

*Postscript:* My most humble service to Sir Robert and Sir John Claiton with my respects to both the Lady Claytons. Your ladyship's letter of 24 April came to mee this morning after Mr Paston had writt the enclosed.

*Addressed:* For My Lady Paston at her lodgings at the signe of the Golden Ball in Suffolke Street, London

*NRO: BL/Y/1/52*

## Sir John Hobart[429] to Sir Robert Paston

**1671, June 6, Blickling.** *Details of arrangements for collection of the subsidy[430] in their division following discourse with Mr Bendish.[431] He will send warrant to the chief constables of North Erpingham.*

*Signed:* your humble & faithfull servant, J Hobart
*Postscript:* I am heartely sory for the death of our worthy friend & neighbour Sir Thomas Rant, who dyed at London Friday last: a great loss in general to the countrey as in particuler to his friends.
*Addressed:* For the honorable Sir Robert Paston baronet at Oxnead
*NRO: BL/Y/1/53*

## Sir John Hobart to Sir Robert Paston

**1671, June 16, Blickling.** *Sends duplicates of the totals of the charge of the subsidy upon the three hundreds[432] as discussed with Mr Bendish.*

*Signed:* your most humble & faithfull servant, J Hobart
*Postscript:* Sir I have taken the freedome to sett Sir Ja[*cob*] As[*t*]ley's[433] hand & seale to the papers.
*Addressed:* For the honourable Sir Robert Paston baronet at Oxnead
*NRO: BL/Y/1/54*

## William Paston to Rebecca, Lady Paston

**1671, June 21, Angers.** Dear madam, I received your ladyship's letters daited the 26 of May, wherein I find your ladyship has received the account of our being pensioned at Angers, which is an extream pleasant place & one of the cheapest towns in France but I find that even here seting still our allowance will not hold out (as will appear by the accounts) much less when we travail, and I am faint [*sic*] to leave severall exersises aside as not having where with all to doe it, as riding the great horse[434] & playing on the guittare etc., and I beg of your ladyshipe & my father that you would be pleased to take it into consideration, or I can never hope to answer the consire[435] which you have that I should be well bred in all things, (riding alone) will be a thing that will cost above £40 a yeare here, & much more elsewhere & I doe here live as close as any body making very few extraordinarys and I am not ignorant nor insensible of my [*f.2*] father's occasions for money, yet since he has been pleased to send me abroad I cannot but inform him & your ladyship of my necessitys here in consequence

---

[429] Sir John Hobart (1628–1683) of Blickling, formerly a parliamentarian and one of Cromwell's upper house. He was appointed a deputy lieutenant in 1668. When Paston replaced Lord Townshend as lord lieutenant in 1676 Hobart became the leading figure in the opposition 'country' party.

[430] Paston was one of the subsidy commissioners for Norfolk.

[431] Alderman Robert Bendish (d.1693) of Norwich

[432] An administrative division within a county

[433] Sir Jacob Astley (1640–1729) of Melton Constable, deputy lieutenant

[434] i.e. learning to control a warhorse or charger

[435] ? concern, intention

of my design of education. This is all I have to say at present, only my most humble duty to my father & grandmother and my service to my sisters, so I am

*Signed:* your most obedient son, William Paston
*Addressed*: These present to My Lady Paston at her house Oxnead in Norfolk, near Norwich
*NRO: BL/Y/1/55*

## Sir John Hobart to Sir Robert Paston

**1671, July 24, Blickling**. Sir, I have received the favour of your letter with the inclosed duplicate, which might have been much better dispatched from Norwich to London then to have taken its way by Oxnead to your trouble, but I can well excuse my share in it since it brought mee the advantage of heareing of your & your familyes welfare, and for your sake I shall take charge of it, though it comes after I have sent away the other three hundreds to the Exchequer.

Sir, the waters which are soe strong to make a sober man drunke, may make a modest man bold, and raise his temper to the same effects that wine dose, and with this addition that wee have not only the company but authority of the divine & physician on our side, besides the ladyes who daylie increase uppon us, and that is the reason why I presume to begg once more the favour of your tent: the truth is our company is now growne soe great, & our house is soe smale, thaet the least ventulation or <cascquade> caskeade from the modest sex is beleived by them to bee heard by us, which causes an extreordinary flusshing, or els dangerous fumes: I know sir you are *the* civillest person living to that tender sex, and therefore uppon their account I am much more confident of success then from the title I can pretend to in your favour though I am really

*Signed*: your most humble & faithfull servant, J Hobart
*Postscript*: Sir I begg your honour to kiss my ladyes handes, soe doe all our company to you both.
Sir if you doe not forbid mee because every day is precious I shall presume to send a carriag for your tent tomorrow morning and take greater care then last tyme in the speedy returne.[436]
*British Library: Add. MSS 27447, f. 318*

## Thomas Henshaw to Sir Robert Paston

**1671, August 5**. Deare patrone, our doctour[437] is now come in good earnest, and is not so fat and red faced as every one reported him to bee, which makes me have the more favorable opinion of the Spanish proverb which says the divell is not so blacke as he is painted; and all amounts to this that his shape is *only* somwhat more lubberly then it was, so farre is he from being arrived at the honour of <*word deleted*>

---

[436] It is to be hoped that Hobart returned the Paston 'portaloo' in time for the visit of the King and court to Oxnead in September 1671.
[437] His brother Dr Nathaniel Henshaw (c.1628–1673), physician

a goodly portly man, yet the muses have made a bowling ally on his head, for it seemes he has been fain to scratch ha\*r\*d for a conceit but if all were as smooth within as it is without now, his fancy would run very glib: I expect him here anon to stay with me for sometime, but wee have already dined together in London, and had a compotation in good company: he is still of the same humour he was, and has had no opportunity to improve himself but with Irish tales and drolery of Dublin, he yet talkes of returning into Ireland but knows not when: he is much joyed to heare of your health and desired me when I writ next to present his most humble service to yourself and my lady. He has a designe to exhibit himself to you at Oxned for a week after the King's entertainment is over; but now wee talk of that I hope you have somebody at court will send you timely intelligence of the King's comming, for I was tould on Thursday \*last\* by some of the courtiers, that the King had said very lately he would lodge one night at Sir R Paston, as also that he would begin his progresse your way the 20th of this month.

If the name written on the glasse of powder or on the [*word illegible*] bee Giles, it has falsly usurped the honour of having belonged to old Alexander,[438] for he and all his sons did write theyr name Gill. It seems strange to me that your marle should have imbibed vast quantities of dew without changing his com [*sic*] complexion, there are but few good fellows that theyr drink will not work at all uppon them, perhaps the alteration in this may bee inward, and therfor it will bee worth the bestowing a good fire and a retort uppon him. What you say of the severall glasses you have, of the salt of rain water coagulated according to De Paris, I doe not yet conceive the meaning of, for De P. has no such practicke but if you had coagulated R[*ain.?*] W[*ater.?*] as De Par[*is*] teaches to doe water drawn by his magnet, the news were very considerable and worth making some farther trialls on, but how came it to passe you did not again proceed on the right practick of De Paris you had bestowed so much time and pains on, not without some successe suitable to the indications given by the authour? If your patience bee soe short breathed that you give over the race as soon almost as you are entered into it, if you despair because fruits doe not ripe[*n*] in the spring and you cannot stay till autumne, it is no wonder if all this time you have seen no effects of your great charge and trouble. Deare sir, I hope you will doe me the justice to remember that twenty years since or neare uppon (Sir J Clayton is my witnesse) I earnestly dehorted you both from entring on so hopelesse a study, which is a lottery wherin there are soe many millions of blankes for any never so small a price. I was unwilling to teach you the making of pomanders and angell water (which you then thought were don by chymistry) least they might ingage <*word deleted*>your esteem and affection to do, I tould you I had spent some years very fruitlesly in this prosecution though with the most serious application of all my poor abilities, that I would never again addresse myself to so coy a mistresse, that if there were any truth in the science (which I am not yet convinced there is not) to bee an adeptus (that is to have a power equall to five or six emperours together) must needs bee a most super-eminent grace of God to some singular favorite whom he knew would make a pious and a virtuous use of it, that I was too well acquainted with my own frailtys to

[438] Alexander Gil or Gill (1565–1635), schoolmaster and author of preface to Francis Anthony's *Apologia Veritatis Illucescentis, pro Auro Potabile* (1616)

dare to aspire above the rancke of the meanest of his hired servants, that since your
fate has cast you on this attempt notwithstanding all the caution I gave (though you
have always pretended[439] to have made choyce of chymistry only as your divertise-
ment for want of other recreations) I have not only in obedience to your generall
commands but uppon your frequent and constant sollicitation spent many howres
[f.2] (which else I should have otherwise employed) in the revew and considerations
of those authours, and faythfully acquainted you with all the reall or seeming truths
I could discover in so obscure and winding a laberinth, you yourself know this is all
you could expect from my service and that I did never pretend to revelations, secret
demonstrations, or recipees found in abbey walls; if I had had ten elixirs you had bin
master of them all long ere this time; therfore in justice and equity you ought not to
impute to me the ill successe of your triall, nor the losse of your time and expence; I
have often exhorted you to desist, but you could not live without a castle in the ayre,
and at this time I should not only bee well pleased but exceeding glad you would
abandon this sooty imployment unsuitable to the calling of a gentleman, you may
with much lesse charge and anxiety spend your afternoons with a chessbord or a pair
of tables.[440] To tell you the same truth I have often told you before, I have no hopes
from chymistry but to obteine an extraordinary medecine which will cure most diseases and maintain a vigorous health to the time appointed, this would gratify my
greatest ambition nor should I much doubt of compassing it had I a laboratory, operator and minera[441] to my mind; but your ayms are so vast and generous, that such
a thing would give you no more satisfaction then a cure for the itch or a gal[le]d
horsebacke, besid your minera is so poore that you will but loose your time and
patience upon it, therfore in time desist.

Sir John hath sent me the excerpta (out the bigger book) that he is bringing down
to you, I have read it over twice (though I know not whether this should not bee a
secret) all I could learne out if [sic] was, that he that will make it (that is Holden's
medecin) had need of the patience of half a douzen Jobs, and to begin very young,
for I doe not see how it can bee done in lesse then twenty years, I will give you an
instance only of an inconsiderable part of the worke. The oyle is to bee distilled 164
times in all, beside a very great number of burialls, and baptismes *in balneo* interven-
ing; for my part I will never beleeve that ever any man much lesse God[d]ard or
Holden had the flegme[442] to follow that processe κατα ποδα,[443] and if they do not
find out they [sic] abreviation Sir J. and his partner had as good have thrown theyr
mony into kanill.[444]

I know not whether Thursday's *Gazette* told you that sweet hopefull youth the Duke
of Guise[445] that *was* over here this spring is now dead of the smallpox, or that
Madame de Lion[446] that great minister of state's wife is prisoner in the Bastile for
crimes, which being kept secret, sets all the world to guesse at them. It is now again

---

[439] i.e. claimed    [440] i.e. a writing tablet for notes and memoranda

[441] The matrix in which a metal or precious stone was believed to grow; the ore of a metal.

[442] i.e. calmness, stolidness    [443] Step by step [Gr.]

[444] i.e. the kennel: a drain or gutter    [445] Louis Joseph (1650–1671), duc de Guise

[446] Paula, wife of Hugues de Lionne (1611–1671). There does not seem to have been any truth in this
rumour; de Lionne died on 1 September 1671 and, as with the death of Charles II's sister Madame, there
was subsequently a suggestion that he had been poisoned.

briskly reported at court that the King of France will besiege Colen[447] for all he seemed to disband his army. The Lady Barkly went on Wedensday last with her two sons toward France, and as soon as the King sets his face toward Norfolk the lord lieutenant her husband[448] goes for Ireland. On Thursday last in the court yard at Whitehall I saw walking in a new shute[449] and periwig Mr Blood, extraordinary pleasant and jocose; he has been at liberty this fortnight. He is nothing like the idea I had made to my self of him, for he is a tall rough boned *man* with small legs, a long pockfrecken face with little hollow blew eyes.

*Unsigned*
*NRO: BL/Y/1/56*

## Thomas Henshaw to Sir Robert Paston

**1671, August 12, Pondhouse.** Deare patrone, I shall present your kind salutation to the doctor when I see him this evening, for nothing can drive him out of town but the approching Sabbath, hee being troubled with a head that cannot endure bells nor psalmes. A freind at court the proverb says is worth a penny in a man's purse, then I cannot amount to a hape[*nny*]-worth, for I am but a country courtier, and can tosse no intelligence to you, but at the second or third rebound: I heare them talk that the King will set out for Norfolk on the 25 of September but these are not informations to bee relyed on; your surest news will bee from Norwich, the Deputy Duke[450] being to knock his eas[*e*] on the head before you. Walking on Thursday last to London I saw the carcasse of your great Cook[451] of Norfolk conveying to his long home (which to one of you that dwell a hundred <*miles*> miles off, methinks should not bee so greivous, being all your lives accustomed to the mortification of going to your long homes). The attendance was very moderate, consisting of three coaches, wherof one had but two horses, and about six or eight horsemen in a disorderly manner. I perceived the heire[452] *&* executors had the gift of parcimony, that however they should bee provided for in wit, the wealth of the family was like to continue yet some time, and that the blessing of crescere and thrivare bestowed on the old lawyer was not yet effete.

The Duke of York has lately made that compliment to the King of submitting his fancy and liberty in the choyce of a wife to his Majesty's judgement and election, assuring him he will never think of any but such a one as shall bee proposed by his Majesty.

---

[447] Cologne/Köln

[448] Sir John Berkeley (c.1607–1678), lord lieutenant of Ireland, 1670–1672; his wife Christian was a Roman Catholic.                                                                [449] i.e. suit

[450] Henry Howard (1628–1684), later 6th duke of Norfolk. The title was revived in 1660, but was borne by Howard's older brother, a lunatic incarcerated in Padua since 1645. In his brother's absence Howard functioned as 'deputy duke' and, as a great landowner, had much influence in the county. He was debarred by his Catholicism from playing an active role in public life but was frequently at court and entertained the King on 28 September before the latter went to Blickling, Oxnead and Raynham. He became earl of Norwich and earl Marshall in 1672, and finally succeeded as duke on his brother's death in 1677.

[451] John Coke of Holkham, buried there on 12 August 1671, grandson of Sir Edward Coke, lord chief justice, by his first wife, Bridget Paston.

[452] John Coke's heir was his great nephew Robert Coke (c.1651–1679), who married Paston's cousin, Lady Anne Osborne, and became MP for King's Lynn.

There has ever been as great a dispute among you gallants concerning the best in Christendome, as there has been among us philosophers about the *summum bonum*: but a greate searcher of nature hath *not* many days since been pleased to declare that the best in Christendome is at this time in the custody of Madll Caroüell.[453] Doe not you now read this to the weomen, and call me Lecheroso, because I have put in a jyg to raise your dumps. *Lasciva est nobis pagina vita proba*, or in English my life is modest though my leafe bee loose, grave dons doe often waggish pages choose.

Dear sir, I am sorry that after you have lookt so high you should now fall in a sur-reverence,[454] and that having soared to that pitch, you should at last light uppon pidgeonshite. I fear you will eare long <word deleted> proceed to *rebis humanum* because it is the doung of the microcosme. Tis true the sages doe say that a wise man can dis-cover theyr matter in *sterqulinio*,[455] when a foole cannot find it in gold, not that ever they went directly to a dunghill for it, but they knew there was there, a specificate salt but one degree removed from the universall, which nature could in a short time, by means of ayre, water and earth, reduce to its primigeniall entity, with which they saw all vegetables were either nourished or spontaneously produced, but not till it was thus changed by nature, which was a work as farre above theyr skill, as to make it as nature does of the four elements. Therfor it is no great wonder if you find more volatile salt in dovehouse earth then in most other mineras for the *stercus columbinum*[456] lying to some thicknes at top, the moyst ayre dissolves it and carries it into the earth, where it receives a considerable alteration before it bee made universall, but that volatile salt may bee had many other *ways*, the processe of Sendivogius (from which you learnt first to make it) is witnes, where hee bids take the earth of a fallow field, not but that the volatile salt and spirit of pidgeon rebis may bee made a good medi-cine, especially if it could in any reasonable measure bee made as pure and volatile as the other, which you think you *have* some rectified five or six times that is so; Sir John fell in to this very heresy seven years agoe, but after hee had taken a great deale of paines with it, he found [f.2] hee could never so free it from the merdacious s[c]ent nature had put uppon it, but that a turd would smell like a turd doe what he could unto it. Now he is with you, he has promised to use some industry to discover a good mine somewhere, which is the only thing wee want. He is very well acquainted with the smacke of peter earth and therfor may with lesse trouble make triall of severall places. There is no manner of news stirring this week, and I have not the faculty of making any. The King on Wedensday night received a lodging and a treat at Mr Demihoy's[457] at Guilford, intending to spend two or three days in hunting about Windsor, but the stag on Thursday not making sport to his mind he came away of a suddain for London and left the Duke to follow the chase.

*Unsigned*
*Addressed:* For the honourable Sir Robert Paston, Norwich, this
*NRO: BL/Y/1/57*

[453] Louise de Keroualle, later duchess of Portsmouth, the King's new mistress
[454] From having meant extreme reverence, by the second half of the seventeenth century 'surreverence' was used to mean excrement.
[455] Dunghill                                                                    [456] Dove droppings
[457] Thomas Dalmahoy (d.1682), a Scot, MP for Guildford (Henning, *Commons,* II, pp 185–6)

# Thomas Henshaw to Sir Robert Paston

**1671, August 19.**[458] Deare patrone, I have always had so great a concernment for the happines of your family, that I cannot but beare my part in the just resentment you have of your daughter's misguided warmth, though you ought withall to make your account that nature is as much to blame in this case as shee, for the *lac virginis*[459] of some young women is twice as frisking, warme, and stirring as that of others, and she was the first flower of your youthfull heate, not so well allayed with her mother's excellent temper as could have been wished: to this her grandsire's cursed gold is cause of so much woe, it having given her a false opinion that she is at her owne disposall, and the confidence to choose for her self;[460] Sir John was sometime since pleased to trust me with some jealousie[461] he had of this *amour*, which did exceedingly surprise and trouble me; you have a very hard game to play in this affair, having to deale with one who seems to *bee* both resolute and obstinate in her humour, but whether she has made herself sure to Rumbald[462] or no (unles it has been the Pyecorner[463] way) you ought to use your utmost endeavour to keep a daughter and £4,000 from going into perdition. Force and fair means, threats and flatterys, are requisite arts to bee practised uppon her: methinks the very calling this amourous flame by that homely and contemptuous name of lechery which grave and severe matrones are used to bestow uppon it, should work some good effect on that modesty which *is* borne with all weomen and from which they cannot seperate themselves, but by long time and lewd practises. She should bee often tould of the care and desire her parents have to match her to youth and beauty as well as welth and honour, and bee made sensible when she has satisfied her passion in the marriage with Rumbald, how miserable and contemptible shee will bee not only in the eyes of the world but in her own and her husband's too. Love is a distemper of the bloud (though a florid one), why should she not then bee persuaded to bleed and fast, or at least bee kept from wine, spices, and meate of too high nourrishment? – her romances and amorous books taken from her, and books of devotion and mortification left her to passe her solitude with. Why should not Sir John write to Rumbald to expostulate with him, why *he* has broken the laws of hospitality and freindship to tempt a young maiden of a quality and fortune so far above his pretenses and which he could not but know would bee *so* much against her freinds' approbation and good will, to let him know all is discovered, her parents resolved against the match, and shee penitent for her want of wit, and therfore advise him in time to desist from such fond hopes, this may possibly beat him of [*f*], or else draw such excuses from him as may justly move her indignation if she have any generosity, but youle say honest freind you might have saved the writing of this page, for I had revolved all these expedients in my thoughts and many more before I writ to you. I doubt it not, but when our freinds are in extremity wee cannot forbeare offering our remedies even to theyr doctours, who doe excuse our want of wit, because they are demonstrations of our kindnesse.

---

[458] But endorsed '17th'                        [459] Virgin's milk or mercurial water, used here figuratively.
[460] Sir William Paston had left her a dowry of £4,000 to be paid on marriage or at the age of 21; she was now 19.                        [461] i.e. suspicion
[462] Margaret Paston had secretly betrothed herself to Henry Rumbold (d.1683), a young army officer, son of Henry Rumbold (1617–1690), merchant and diplomat, and his first wife, a Spanish Catholic; see also p.10.
[463] Pie Corner was the street in London at which the Great Fire ended; the reference is obscure.

But after this dolefull tune of *lachrimae*[464] [*f.2*] you strike up such a merry gig that makes me skip again, you both promise like emperours, and with such an assurance, that my fayth waits and is expectant. What new revelation is this? and backt I doubt not with good experience; else you would not take uppon you thus; has Venus alighting at your dore left her doves to direct you to the golden branch? *Maternas agnoscis aves? Geminae cui forte columbae, ipsae sub ora viri coelo venere volantes.*[465] I have never a word to say for my self, *non audeo dicere muttum*,[466] I submit to your reasons, and betwixt hope and feare attend the issue of your experiments: though I am somewhat doubtfull of the asseveration you so knowingly make a challenge uppon, ie that no volatile salt can bee gotten out of a minera where has been no rebis, when as Sendivogius' processe which was our light, bids you [take earth][467] *in loco fertili quam probe [?]forde circa 1½ uln. sub terra, ubi terram puram sine radicibus habeas &c* it were a good peece of naturall philosophy to bee assured of the truth of this, which made easily bee tried in Sir John's presence (that wee may have two witnesses of it) since you resolve to work at one time on those three excellent subjects, Adam, Peter, and Job on the dunghill. You will now remember that *man* is the most noble creature of earth's composition that ever God <made> wrought, in whom are the four elements proportioned by nature, a naturall mercuriality which costeth right nought: that Morien told Calid[468] inquiring for the matter, it is in thee and mee O King: and other philosophers said Adam brought it with him out of Paradice, which some inferred thence was *rebis humanum*, but if you get any store of salt out of the columbine that has been exposed to the sun and rain two years together I shall much marvell.

We are still under a dearth of newes, all that is stirring is that the Duk[e] having sent one of the King's yachts to Harwich to make the Dutch fleet riding there about strik[e] saile, the yacht calling to them to strike and they not obeying, fired two or three guns at them, but Van Ghent theyr admirall presently came aboard the yacht and desired them to have patience, and said they had no instructions what to doe in this case but he would write to theyr masters at the Hague for orders in it, the master taking this either for *a* sufficient submission or excuse, was as soone as he came home committed to the Tower, and another yacht sent to doe the busines better, what his successe has been I have not yet heard, nor has the Dutch embassadour here received instructions yet from his masters, what he is to offer to the King by way of excuse, for I heare they are resolved to strike no more.

Mr Henry Coventry and Tom Rosse, who goes secretary to the embasy are not yet gone for Sweden, but are to stay till the arrivall of an embassadour from that crown who is dayly expected here, which makes people talk *of* a marriage [*f.3*] to bee proposed to our Duke with an aunt of that King's, but it is more likely to bee a treaty about receiving the Emperour into the Triple League which is prest by Hollande and not much approved by our King.

We heare the Duke of Buck[ingham] is to take Holland House of the Earl of

---

[464] Tears

[465] Do you recognise your mother's birds? When by chance a pair of doves came flying down from the sky, beneath his very eyes (based on Virgil, *Aeneid*, VI, when Aeneas recognises Venus's doves).

[466] I dare not say a word.        [467] 'take earth' is written in symbols which are not reproduced here.

[468] From an early mediaeval work on alchemy translated by the seventeenth century as *L'Entretien de Calid et du Philosophe Morien*.

Ang[*lesey*]: hee has been there three evenings successively; I saw him last night goe up with the Count[*ess*] of Shrewsb[*ury*], Sir C. Sydly, and James Porter[469] in the coach with him. This vacation they say has brought fifty extents uppon his lands and that when his debts are payd his grace will not have above £1,200 per annum.

*Unsigned:* Humble my service and respects I pray to all with you.

*Postscript:* My Lady Cornbury's[470] great belly sinkes a pace, shee tould me yesterday she sees it will now come to nothing.

*Addressed:* For the Honourable Sir Robert Paston at Norwich, this

*NRO: BL/Y/1/58*

## Thomas Henshaw to Sir John Clayton

**1671, August 29.** Deare Sir John, my wife's violent sicknes not giving mee leave to waite on Lady Morda[*u*]nt so soon again, as I intended, on Sunday she sent for me to come to her (my wife finding some good alleviation by a glister my brother prescribed her, and is now in a hopefull way of recovery, it proving but a collick and not the stone as wee feared), I waited on her ladyship in the evening. She gave me a long and particular account of the discourse between her and Mr Rumball upon her pressing him in the Countesse of Middleton's[471] name to prepare himself to attend her to Tanger, she having prepared all necessarys for his particular accomodation by the way; he first excused himself by telling her that the profit of his ensignes place there was so small that it had only maintened him in clothes, but had for some time been able to subsist on it, by reason he had by the favour of the Earle of Teviot and Colonel Norwood[472] been as a domestick at both theyr tables, which he had no reason to expect of Earl Middleton, but when her ladyship had assured him that she had disposed both him and his lady not only to allow him that priviledge, but also to accomodate him *in* the first place with all preferment should fall in theyr gift, he told her he was positively resolved not to goe any more thither, upon the assurance the Lord Arlington had given to him to provide some better employment for him heere. She replyed shee knew well enough the reason of his aversenesse, which was grounded upon an intrigue betweene Mrs Paston and him, that he would bee much out <out> in the reckoning he made of it, for her freinds had discovered all, and would bee sure to apply all possible vigilance and care they should not come together. He coloured, and at first faintly denyed it, but after finding she had been informed of all passages from Oxnead, having excused himself that no man in his condition could in prudence refuse the temptation of so faire an offer, said he was not to bee frighted out *of* England nor would he leave it till he had other busines should call him, then that of Tanger, that though her freinds might for some time put a restraint

---

[469] Presumably James Porter, youngest son of Endymion Porter; he was a groom of the bedchamber in the duke of York's household and a cousin of the duke of Buckingham.

[470] Flower, daughter of William Backhouse (1593–1662) of Swallowfield, alchemist and antiquary, widow of her cousin Sir William Backhouse, and second wife of Lord Cornbury.

[471] Lady Middleton was Lady Mordaunt's cousin, Martha Cary, who had married Lord Middleton, governor of Tangier, in 1667.

[472] Andrew Rutherford (d.1664), earl of Teviot, and Colonel Henry Norwood (c.1614–1689), were previous governors of Tangiers.

uppon her, he was resolved never to quit that interest he had, unlesse (because her ladiship told him Mrs Paston was sorry for her folly) she should tell him with her own mouth that she repented of what she had done: then he protested he would desist and never trouble her more; till then he should call any that pretended to marry her to a severe account, for he had nothing but a carcasse to loose, and that he was resolved to sacryfyse. Thus ended theyr discourse at that time, but since divers have been there who have talked of this *amour* for news, among others Lady Elizabeth Cary brought a long story, and told of the young lady's imprisonment with many other circumstances, but said she had it from a lady of Norfolk, but it is guessed she heard it of Lady Trevour to whom it might bee written by Lady Hubbard.[473] In fine Lady Morda[u]nt's opinion was that things were gone so far it was now past remedy. Leaving her I went to Lord Mord[aunt] who though he had a great deale of company with him in his garden, yet after a while found an opportunity to walk with me for a quarter [f.2] of a houre. He asked me if I had been with his wife, I told him I had and that the Countesse of Falmouth walked away into the garden to give me a privacy with his lady. Why then sais he I have something more to tell you then my wife yet knows; but doubt it is not proper for Sir Robert's knowledge. I have (said he) had Mr Rumball (who is now walking yonder with the rest) under a strict examination, beleeving that he would bee more franck with me then perhaps his modestie and respect would give him leave to bee with my wife; yet (though I find he does keep some reserve for a more pressing occasion) he does confesse to me that he has a contract under Mrs Paston's hand, which he promises to shew me, that she has given him an authenticated copie of her grandfather's will, to free him from all scruple, that her £4,000 is well secured; that he should never have dared to make any addresses to one of her quality *and fortune* had he not been incouraged by a letter from her, that she constantly told him whatever was sayd of him by her uncle or others, that he sat up with her alone in her chamber the whole night after her first day's journy homeward[474] (and said Lord John what love youth, darknes and solitude might inspire who can tell?) but that she was inspired is certain, for she foretold that she was now going to *bee* his martyr, that she should bee kept under restraint, should suffer the reproshe and contempt of her freinds, all which would for his sake bee but a pleasure and a glory to her, but that there would bee tricks and plots and letters contrived by her freinds, <but they> which would all bee counterfait or forced and therfore gave him charge not to beleeve anything of them though he should see it under her own hand, and (said he) it has *just* so fallen out, for they have lately sent me a counterfait letter from her maid; sure they that sent it tooke me for a man of a grosse understanding that could bee imposed on by so palpable an imposture, and so showed his lordship the letter to judge of. Rumbald told his lordship farther that she said to him, perhaps you may beleeve that I will prove an extravagant expensive wife, t'is true I spend my father £200 a yeare, and why should I not as things are? but when I am your wife (if there should bee occasion for it) I will bee content to weare haircloth and bee pleased with the coursest dyet in the world, and so by fresh oathes ingaging theyr eternall constancy and fidelity they took leave of one another.

[473] Ruth, Lady Trevor, and Mary, Lady Hobart, were sisters, daughters of John Hampden (1595–1643) of Great Hampden.    [474] i.e. to Oxnead

This is as neare as I can possibly remember the substance of which I was tould by them both. I was desired to keep some of this to my self, but I thought it might bee a <word deleted> *failure* of freindship to conceale any thing I knew in this case, for wounds can never be healed till they bee searched to the bottome, and I thought once to have inclosed this latter part in a private paper that you might have showed my letter and reserved the other if you had thought fit: for I had a great tendernesse to adde anything to Sir Robert and my lady's greef of which I feare they have *but* too much already, but I considered that there can never a proper remedy bee applyed till the state of the disease bee fully knowne, and [f.3] perhaps it may bee easier to them to know the worst all at once, then to bee longer wracked between hope and feare. Not any one that hath heard this lamentable story hath any pitty for Mrs Paston but only

*Signed:* your very humble servant, TH
*Addressed:* For my honoured freind Sir John Clayton at Oxned neare Norwich, this
*Endorsed:* Mr. Henshaw's letter about Peg's bisnes
*NRO: BL/Y/1/59*

## Thomas Henshaw to Sir Robert Paston

**1671, September 2**. Dearest patrone, my wife (I thank God) has been freed from the extremity she was under, ever since Sunday last in the evening; which since hath manifested it self to have been the collick, another sort of devill or tormentour, not much inferiour to that which is called the stone, yet she is scarce ever free from paine, some times in her stomack, other while in her back, sides, or belly, according as the wind blows, but for the most part so remisse that she begins to rest pretty well a nights; nor doe I expect she should bee well at ease till she bee delivered of her great belly which at farthest will bee within three weeks. Your story of the spirit of May dew is very remarkable; though I have ever observed my self that upon [?]urging[475] the feces of May dew or rain by fire there is constantly produced an armoniack s[c]ent, which seems to me an argument that the universall <word deleted> spirit had something of armoniacke in it, if it bee handled by a right ενχειρια,[476] as on the contrarie you see that niter earth even where there is some mixture of animall excrements with it, if the salt bee drawn by water yeelds good peeter without the least mixture of salt armoniack. I confesse I cannot yet perswade my self but that there is some fault in your minera, and am still loath *to* beleeve that no sal armoniack can bee drawn out of right peeter earth where there has been no animall mixtion, not only uppon the authority of Sendivogius' MS processe but because Mr James Lloyd did then never use to refine other then Indian or Barbary peeter, which in those parts is raked (at a certain time of yeare) from the surface of barren desart ground, where there are no pidgeon houses; and yet you may remember that when the doctor sent for the greasy *oyle* that lay on the top of his brother's ash tubs after the percolation of the peeter water, wee drew out of it by sublimation a great quantity (for the proportion of the matter) of our volatile salt: and all hermeticall philosophers doe assure us that

[475] or 'carying'          [476] encheiria = method of manipulation of materials (Gr.)

theyr dissolvent can not bee made of animall or vegetable matters. Yet I doe heartily adore that providence, that put it in your heart to make these trialls on *rebis colum-banum*[477] and doubt not but you may make of it the richest and noblest medicine in the world next the elixer, especially since you assure me that it yeelds a spirit salt and oyle, so much beyond *cranium hum[anum]*[478] which would even fill my heart with joy, were it not much allayed with the consideration, that although perhaps all mankind may bee felicitated by this discovery of yours, yet wee shall never bee able to make any advantage of it, so long as your operator knows as much as you doe of it. Therfore there must bee some way thought on to put a mist before his eyes, or else a strong obligation of secresy on him, but above all conceale from him the use you mean to make of it, and take heed least he picke any thing out of your discourse before him with Sir John but use French or Latine where there is anything of secrecy. [*f*.2] When this medecine comes to farther maturity it is necessary wee should have an obligation among our selves not to discover it to any without the consent of the other two in writing if they bee living. One thing I much desire to bee resolved on by your next letter, that is whether if a little of this *colum[banum]* salt layd on the point of a knife and held over the flame of a candle will vanish all away without leaving any mark or sediment as most armoniack doe; it were desirable also to know whether the heate of the sun or any other gentle heate will volatilize *it* nay the open ayre it self, as it did the former salt, which hence forward let *us* call the Romans sal for Peeter's sake, and this latter the American salt because discovered by Columbus. It were also requisite to try whether, by often sublimations per se, or else from lime bolus &c it might not bee freed from the ingratefull smell. Why should you not also essay whether by mingling the principles according to the method and proportion I not long since sent you an idea of that so by nipping them up and setting it in an athanos you might *have* an animall elixer if you cannot attaine to a minerall one. If you should abound in red oyle and can find no better use of it, I am confident you might turne the greatest part of it into vol[*atile*] salt by subliming it often from *bol[us] arm[enus]*[479] I hope by that [*time*] Sir John comes away you will bee in a good forwardnes, and rich enough to send me a little of your salt very well rectified.

Now Lord Arlington has sent you the King's gists[480] you need have no farther scruples, for he did it by the King's order, and you may relie on it that the Queen will goe no farther then Norwich, otherwise he would not have failed to send you word of it. I shall as you order me indeavour to doe my reverence in your name *to* the Lord Arl[*ington*] and give him thanks &c.

It is generally reported here that the King has promised the Duke of Buck[*ingham*] to reimburse him the mony he paid the Generall[481] for the master of the horse place: and that therfore to secure himself of it he endeavours to bring in Lord Ash[*ley*] treasurer, but I yesterday spoke with the gentleman I writ you it was said should bee his secretary, who tould me it was true Lord Ash[*ley*] might bee treasurer if he would, but mony matters was so out of order and the humour of the court so unconstant, that he knew he was too wise to accept of it. Neverthelesse it is beleeved it will bee

---

477  Pigeon dung
478  Human skull (used as a medicine)
479  Armenian clay containing iron oxide
480  i.e. stopping places in a royal progress
481  The duke of Albemarle

so, and Sir Thomas Cliff[ord] chancellor of the exchequer. The King and Duke goe next week to Windsor for another hunting bout, the Prince[482] endeavouring to make him as much in love with that place as he can, who is building, fortifying, and making considerable alterations in the castle.

Heer are lately come over some English gentlemen out of France to raise horse here for the service of that king, and Sir H Jones is to have a regiment of horse,[483] they say Scotland hath lately affoorded 5000 men for that Majesty's service. Some of [f.3] these gentlemen that are come over doe assure us that he designes to have in a redines against next campagne 120,000 men, and those great levys in Italy, Dalmatia, Germany mentioned in the *Gazettes* doe forespeake no lesse; so that a *great* diminution is like to befall mankind next summer, for either he will set this vast army to cuts [*sic*] his neighbours' throats, or else the greatest part of these wretches that hope to live of his pay will dy of hunger. The Swedish embassadour is not yet arrived. I have nothing more yet to adde to the *histoire amoureuse*, but if you have any farther commands therin shall readily obey them, and shall within a day or two give your thanks to Lady Morda[u]nt.

*Unsigned*
*Addressed:* For the honourable Sir Robert Paston at Norwich, this [*postmark*]
*Endorsed:* Twelve dos[en] silver plates, twelve ring stands, six great charger dishes for the desert[484]
*NRO: BL/Y/1/60*

## Thomas Henshaw to Sir Robert Paston

**1671, September 9**. Deare patrone, I am at this time under some tender concernments which have this day cost me the writing two letters of each a whole sheet of paper, so that if I should bee any thing long with you it would grow dark and I should loose the opportunity of sending a way my letters, for my boy has been very sick of the squirt these eight days, and I yet feare his soule may goe out that way; therfore I desire you excuse if I am at this time somewhat curt in my conversation; as also to ask my pardon of your lady and Sir John that I doe not now answer theyr letters, but you may assure my lady that what fruite I have that will fit that occasion shall certainely bee reserved for her service, but what that can bee beside grapes of severall sorts (especially moschats) I can not well imagine, and the grapes, if this wet weather doe not spoyle them, would bee very good by that time.[485] If the occasion had been now, I have some peaches, alberges,[486] nectarines, burgomots[487] of nine or ten inches about which are very good, but every one of these will bee rotten before the end of next week: and I have some pomes D'Appy which are more taking to the eye then the palate and in all great feasts *Ponuntur oculis plurima pauca gulae*.[488]

---

482  Prince Rupert, who was governor of Windsor Castle
483  For another reference to Jones's recruiting *see* Guy de la Bedoyere (ed.) *The Diary of John Evelyn* (Woodbridge, 1995), p.185          484  Note in another hand relating to the King's visit
485  i.e. for the royal visit at the end of the month
486  The name was used for varieties of both peach and apricot.          487  i.e. pears
488  There is much to please the eye, little to tickle the palate.

My wife continues so constantly in great paine and sicknes (having no ease nor rest but what is gained by force of opium) that I am not able to leave her alone,[489] not so mutch as to make a short visit to Lord John, so that I know nothing more what they have wrought uppon Rumbald but as soon as ever I can perceive my wife to have a lucid intervall, I will make a step over to fixe them in theyr promise concerning fruite, and to advise farther what may bee hoped for to the disappointement of lovers. But by no means give not your daughter her liberty nor your countenance till she gives good evidence that in good earnest she will use her best indeavours to free herself. It may bee, what cannot bee don at present, time as it does of all passions may take of[f] the edge of theyrs. I shall at this time suspend all mention of chymistry, save that your ingenious remarques on the American creature doth give me some hints of farther contemplation on it, and that I doe very much approve your intention of making some triall of the Arietine minera if it can easily bee had for who knows but Sendivog[ius] myght safely enough conceale his meaning in a litterall sence, where all the world expected an enigmaticall: at least you will by this discover which is the best of those two excellent composts.

On Sunday night last hapned a great fire at Cole Harbour,[490] but there was only consumed a great sugar house and to the value of £14 or £15,000 of sugar.

Here is a new set of highwaymen who rob every night about us, they say they are all very young, and are thought to bee sparkish prentices: this day senight they robbed both the Oxford coaches on Acton road at the backside of Holland House: one Izzard an atturny who was there, and would needs bee so valiant as to defend him self with his sword against pistolls received severall shots whereof he is since dead.

There is much talk of a specter that one night in Lincolnes In[n] fields last week fild the ayre with loud crys, and dismall lamentations, which when people were wakened and sufficiently frighted were turned into as loud laughters, and all concluded with som ravishing touches of divine musick, which for my part I think was but some wanton freak of Sir Robert Leech [f.2] and his company, or some other of the serenaders.

The little yacht which was sent to make the Dutch fleet strike, returning lately from Scotland whither he had gone to fetch us the Countesse of South Aske,[491] met again with that fleet, when firing two guns to make them strick saile, the whole fleet presently struck and saluted our yacht with each double the number of guns she had given them; which does somewhat appease the indignation wee had against the Dutch, and aggravate the cowardise of the late master of the yacht who is still a prisoner in the Tower.

*Unsigned*
*Addressed:* For the honourable Sir Robert Paston at Norwich, this
*NRO: BL/Y/1/61*

---

[489] She died on 4 October 1671 and was buried in the old church of St Mary Abbots, Kensington, as was Henshaw himself in 1700 (Daniel Lysons, *The Environs of London, 3, Middlesex* (1795)).

[490] Presumably Coldharbour, then to the east of the city of London

[491] Anna Carnegie (d.1695), countess of Southesk and mistress of James, duke of York

# [Henry Howard][492] to [Philip Howard]

**1671, September 18, Norwich**. Deare brother, since I came hither beeing nott perfectly recovered of the gout, and running a little too much about my howse, has soe disordered my foot againe, as itt is att this present wors then ever butt I noe wayse doubt in the lea[s]t to gitt perfectly well this week for since my bleeding yesterday I am much better, and can sett itt to the ground allready: Sir Robert Paston is now with mee, and in the greatest trouble and confusion I ever saw man for feare of missing of the honor of serving her Majesty as becomes him att his howse, tis true he was forced to confess in his letter to my Lord Arlington, that itt was impossible to lodge both their Majestyes att once[493] with any convenience in his howse and indeed this is noe more then I and all the world knew before as both their Majestyes have beene told before he sayd itt, butt that her Majesty should speake uncertainely of her comming to him att all to my Lord Arlington is what confounds him, and all of us, his neighbors, for really should her Majesty now deny & withdraw that honor totally from him, itt would be his eternall disgrace & mortification to all this country, where his family have beene for many descents the most antient of all the <country> gentry heere without competition. I therefore doe now in his behalfe & my owne most earnestly desire you will make his and his lady's moane in most humble manner to the Queen,[494] & beg the knowledge of the day or night her Majesty will honor him, I supose that her Majesty not supping on Fridays[495] will (after she has dined at Sir J[ohn] Hobart with the King) returne to honor my house here at night, & then if she wold pleas to honor Sir Robert Paston next day att dinner, his Majesty I presume will easily be prevailed upon to dined there with her ere she goes to my Lord Towneshend's which is lesse then twenty miles thence; & so her Majesty (whom her return to London must of necessity passe back againe thro Norwich) will againe honor my house that night where next morning she may heare masse, dyne, & after dinner returne (it being but twenty miles to my lord Arlington's[496]) whence as it is coming so it is returning but two days journy to London, if her Majesty's resolution do continue being there so soon. [f.2] But of all these particulars I first beg your lordship's pardon & next the answer since itt is to serve & oblige so worthy a person as Sir Robert Paston, who is one of my best friends & neighbors, & a worthy gentleman, who both in his owne person as well as his father & family have ever bin true & faithfull honorers & followers of the King & his interests, & I am sure her Majesty who is all vertue, goodnesse & sweetnesse will never disoblige such persons as are ever ready day & night to creep on their hands & knees to serve & pray for her temporall & eternall hapynesse, & so they & I as in duty bound shall ever pray &c. I am, dear brother,

*Signed:* your most affectionate bro[ther] & servant, H.H. &c
*Copy:* part in the hand of Sir Robert Paston
NRO: BL/Y/1/62

[492] Henry, baron Howard of Castle Rising, later 6th duke of Norfolk, to his brother Philip, later Cardinal Howard who was grand almoner to Queen Catherine.

[493] The Queen's retinue alone comprised fifty five persons; for the royal visit *see* Robert H. Hill (ed.), *The Thomas Corie Letters, 1664–1687* (NRS (1956), XXVII, pp 32–36) and R.W. Ketton-Cremer, *Norfolk Portraits* (London, 1944), pp 9–21).

[494] Written to this point in Sir Robert Paston's hand.

[495] Because she was a Roman Catholic

[496] Euston Hall in Suffolk

## Thomas Henshaw to Sir Robert Paston

**1671, December 17**. Deare patrone, I give you many thanks for your farther inlarging your self in your last letter on the magicall subject, I doe now pretty well comprehend it in my imagination, but am sorry to heare that twenty four retorts yeeld little above an ounce at a distillation, of adrop, and that after the pains and patience you have bestowed on it, your store exceeds not half a pound, therfore I conceive the best way *to* make experiences uppon it will bee to make them singly one after another, and not two at once. Uppon the triall of putrefying you may venture your whole quantity at once, for if it doe not putrefy your adrop will bee never the worse to use in any other experiment, and if it doe succeed, then you will need to make no other experiments. I have no chymicall books with me in town and if I had, neither time nor tranquillity enough of mind to read and consider them: but as I remember you will find the most concerning this red gum in books I have not, namely in some works of Riply's, published in Latine by Combacchius,[497] and which I suppose you have among the last books Sir John gave you a book in 8° also in the first authour in *Aquarium Sapientum*[498] (a book in 4<sup>to</sup> you had of me last time you were in town but one) placed before Madathanus' *Aur[eum] Saecul[um]* you will find some directions how to draw out the blood of the lion, somwhat also of the red gumme you [*sic*] among the small poems in *Theat.Brit.Chym.*[499] Your way of drawing it in three great iron pots I approve very well of, as also your resolution not to bee at that charge till you find what use to make of the adrop. I am much of your mind that all the volatile *salts* are the same, though I could wish the Roman had the praeeminence but if you have tried and found them all as easily vanish with the same, and leave as little feculancy behind as that there is no more to bee said. You say no more of your salt of deares bones since the first whether you can make it as pure and as volatill as the rest.

Heer died on Wedensday last at Worster House the Duk[e] of Sommerset a youth of great beauty and hopes aged about twenty, he was lately let goe out of his mother's constant care and inspection to come up to court the Countesse of Northumberland[500] who would not be persuaded to marry one five or six years yonger then herself. This occasion gave him the acquaintance of the chief young men about the town, and introduced him into libertys before unknown to him. Some little disorder the Thursday before began such a fermentation in his bloud as produced a violent malignant feavour, the meazells or small pocks were expected the first three days but there never appeared any evident signes of either, so that most now think that *if* any of that numerous company of doctors that attended him had prevayld to have let him bloud it had saved his life, which is so much the more deplorable in that the title and estate goe [to] his uncle the Lord John who has never like to have children and after him [the] honour will go *to* his uncle Trowbridge's children, and the land among the old duke's daughters.

[*f.*2] It is now cleare that the King of Fr[ance] his designe is on Cologne, and beside the Lorraine army marched thither, we are told the Prince of Condé is to follow

---

[497] *G. Riplæi ... Opera Omnia Chemica, ...* etc. (edited by L.H. Combachius, 1649)

[498] *Hydrolithus Sophicus, seu Aquarium Sapientum*, printed following *Aureum Seculum Redivivum*, by Henry Madathanus in *Musaeum Hermeticum* (1625).

[499] Elias Ashmole (ed.), *Theatrum Chemicum Britannicum* (1652)

[500] Elizabeth (d.1690), young and wealthy widow of the 11th earl of Northumberland

16,000 men, but the confederates of the new league are in pretty good readines to receive them, I doe beleeve our King intends to stand newter if he can. Before a French almanack of this year in a single sheet they have as is usuall with them pictured theyr King riding *in* a triumphall chariot like the sun. The Dutch in scorn of this rant have befor an almanack set the picture of a man ecclipsing the sun with a Holland cheese. They say they have also printed a *book* called the *Sermons of his Excellence Sir G Downing Embassador for the King of Great Brittain to the States Generall, preached before Sir Artur Hazelrig, Coll: Okey, Coll: Baxter &c.*[501] I am told the fame of the Duke of Buckingham's new play has reached the French court, and that that King asked Monsieur Colbert when he would write him a play, who excusing his want *of* talents that way to serve him, the King told him he would bee out of fashion for the chief minister of state in England had gotten a great deale of honour by writing a farse, these tales *se non vero son ben trovate*,[502] but not by

*Signed:* your humblest servant, T.H.
*Addressed:* For the honourable Sir Robert Paston at Norwich, this
*NRO: BL/Y/1/63*

# List of payments by Robert Paston, Earl of Yarmouth[503]
## 1672–1676

| | | | |
|---|---|---|---|
| For presents to Mrs Bonfois[504] whole family | Febry 28 (71) | To Deborah Burton of the Exchange | 100–00–00 |
| for my sister Alberty | March 16 (71) | To Madam Sherrad | 032–00–00 |
| for my sister Alberty | March 17 (71) | To Mr Lably | 050–00–00 |
| part of it a debt of Sir William Paston's | March 18 (71) | John Le Roy alias King – jeweler | 025–00–00 |
| Sent to pay my brother Yarmouth's tutor | March 19 (71) | Mr Robert Tuttell[505] of Crostwick | 080–00–00 |
| | March 20 (71) | Mr East the watchmaker[506] | 040–00–00 |
| Treats for Mrs Bonfois | March 24 (71) | To Jonson the cook | 060–00–00 |
| When the King came to Oxnead | March 26 (71)[507] | Mr Langly pewterer | 060–00–00 |
| | | | £467 00–00 |

[501] Downing had arrested Okey and other regicides, and sent them back to England to be executed. This action was widely deplored since Downing had formerly been chaplain to Okey's dragoons.

[502] *recte* trovato, i.e. even if it's not true it's well conceived (It.)

[503] This table appears to be in Sir Robert Paston's hand, but the remarks in the left hand column (and possibly the dates in brackets) were added after his death by one of his younger sons. Some of the page totals are wrong.

[504] It appears that the Pastons attempted unsuccessfully to woo the heiress Susanna Bonfoy (and her uncle Nicholas Bonfoy) for a marriage with their eldest son William early in March 1671/2, *see* NRO: AYL 92, book of evidences, 1683, where she is described as the niece of Nicholas Bumphrey, and TNA: C111/120/514 particular of estate of Sir Robert Paston, 4 Mar 1671/2. This latter mentions a proposed settlement; although Susanna is not mentioned it is too early for William's marriage with Charlotte Howard. Susanna married Sir Julius Caesar on 3 September 1672.

[505] Robert Tuthill was a gentleman servant in the household of Lord Yarmouth's cousin and friend Thomas Le Gros of Crostwick; he is named in Le Gros's will as one of his trustees and executors (TNA: PROB 11/337).

[506] Probably Edward East (c.1602–1696), clockmaker to Charles II

[507] *recte* 1672

[f.2]

| | | | |
|---|---|---|---|
| against the King's coming to Oxnead | March 27 (72) | William [?]Tysy for hatts | 020–00–00 |
| for the King at Oxnead | May 15 (72) | Peter de la Haye the King's confectioner | 040–00–00 |
| | May 17 (71) | To John Workhouse the ?T atturny for busness at the tryall at Yarmouth | 090–00–00 |
| my sister Alberty's debt | May 18 (72) | To Mr Ruttland semster | 100–00–00 |
| Sir William Paston's debt | May 19 (72) | To Mr Davy Knight brewer | 060–00–00 |
| | May 20 (72) | Anne Andrews widdow | 015–00–00 |
| | May 31 (72) | Mr Levar | 045–00–00 |
| Sir Will Paston's debt | July 1 (72) | Richard Allen[508] | 090–00–00 |
| | | | £460–00–00 |

[f.3]

| | | | |
|---|---|---|---|
| For a jewel for Mr Chiffins and my Lady Yarmouth at her wedding | July 2 (72) | Mr King the jeweler | 300–00–00 |
| | Octbr 21 (72) | Mr Francis Jefferys vintner | 100–00–00 |
| for teaching my sister Alberty and brother &c | Janry 25 (72) | Mr Gorg | 100–00–00 |
| | Sepbr 29 (73) | Mr Goff minister of Oxnead for tithes[509] | 105–00–00 |
| | the same day | to Francis Darvoe | 071–00–00 |
| My sister Alberty's cloaths | July 27 (74) | To Mr Eaton | 091–00–00 |
| For childbed linnen for my Lady Yarmouth | Febry 16 (74) | To Lady Clayton my mother, with severall endorsements to the value of two or three hundred pounds | 103–00–00 |
| for his care of my Lord Yarmouth in the smallpox | Feb 16 (74) | To Francis Rawlins | 100–00–00 |
| | | | £985–00–00 |

[f.4]

| | | | |
|---|---|---|---|
| Against my brother's wedding | May 19 (75) | ?Mr Gossling Caseman – 2 bonds joyned in an assignment | 366–00–00 |
| | May 22 (75) | To Mr Bullard for the charges of the tryall of Yarmouth | 177–00–00 |
| | May 20 (75) | Mrs Smith linnendraper for linnen for Oxnead | 150–00–00 |
| | June 9 (75) | To David Jolly shoomaker | 174–10–00 |
| wedding linning for my brother Yarmouth | July 15 (75) | Mrs Katherin Eaton | 454–00–00 |
| | May 27 (76) | To my Lady Clayton for mony advanced on the orange farme | 304–00–00 |
| | May (76) | Mr Wake Exchangeman for ribband for my brother | 100–00–00 |
| | | | £1725–10–00 |

*NRO: BL/Y/1/64*

[508] Richard Allen was a servant of Sir William Paston who had received an annuity of £8 p.a. under his will (TNA: PROB11/311).

[509] John Gough was still owed money at the time of his death in 1684 (NRO: ANF218, f. 241, no.144).

# Thomas Henshaw to Sir Robert Paston

**1671[/2], January 6**. *Mon tres chere* [*sic*] *monsieur*, I wish you many returnes of a happy Christmas and a merry new yeare, I for my part having been fourteen years accustomed to a serious private and studious life, sweetned by the conversation of a good woman who always bid me welcom, and never interrupted my contentment by a minute's ill humour, cannot yet find the least satisfaction in that great variety of court scenes, nightly parades <of young beauties> of young beauties in the drawing roome, sumptuous fare, and gay conversation which I am dayly incombred with. You that are a philosopher will quickly smell out my disease and tell me I was too old ere I was accustomed to it: I know it and therfore will retire as soon as I can, and had don it sooner, had not the King interposed this parenthesis of some monthes, uncertain in number; that which would most powerfully have inclined my genius next to the enjoying your company (which is above all to me) had been to have pusht on to the end whether this pleasing dreame hath been so long a leading us. What you say as to water adrop I must referre to experience, only according to the best idea I could ever conceive of this processe, I think you need not feare to mingle the [*symbol*]$^{510}$ when it is well rectified, with the other principles especially if you first fixe the spirit on the salt alcaly of the subject which is all I can imagine necessary to bee hinted till farther trialls. Before I proceed to the diurnall part of this paper, which will give you a strange view of the uncertainty of humane affaires, give me leave to wonder that you tooke no more notice of the modest hint I gave in my last, which I gathered from inquiry of the most sober and knowing persons I am acquainted with, that either this ambition of the King of France for frontispiciall disticks was either a story published at first uppon no sure foundation or if it were his mind is now so much altered that he is ashamed to own it, and therfore I cannot thinke it fit to make any attempts that might have the least reflection on so worthy a person as my honored *friend* Sir John Knyvet though it were but to disparage his intelligence to the reputation of his poetry.

Here is designed a preparation of a most magnificent fleet against next spring, the Duke himself intending to goe the great admirall, the two other squadrons are to bee commanded by the Earl of Sandwich and Sir G Ascough, the number of ships fifty wherof six of the first rate (which is more then any king of England was ever master of) beside thirty fire ships. Sir Edward Sprag is to bee a vice admirall and Sir R. Holmes another, the Earl of Ossory goes captain of a ship, Mr Digby was appointed to bee the Duke's second in a first rate ship [*f.2*] but has given up his commission, t'is said he was *picqué* that he was not a flag officer, but since Sir R. Holmes hath quitted his flagg to desire to bee the Duke's second. The present necessity uppon the King for this great preparation hath enforced him to put a stop on all assignements he had given the *banquiers* for great summes of monys he had taken up of them, during the space of one yeare commencing the first of this Jan: which though it bee a vast disappointment to all that had any mony in theyr hands especially to merchants who will bee thrust uppon great difficultys by it, yet all objections having been heard and debated in Counsill no other equivalent expedient could bee found to serve the King's occasions. On Munday will come forth a declaratory order which will let us quondam

---

$^{510}$ Unclear symbol

monyed men know in what condition wee are in, for you always find that as bare of wool as I am, I passe by no bryar but some of my fleece hangs at it, I had lately sold a small parcell of land for £700, two I payd debts withall the rest I put in Backwell's hands, and now I must pray God it light not in hucksters hands. This morning the news was at court, that the Dutch having better considered whether they are able to wage warre with the most puissant King of France, have chosen De Witte theyr plenipotentiary and send him to France with *carte blanche*, to make a peace with that King uppon a*ny* termes he will require. This humiliation of the Hollanders would bee pleasing enough to all theyr neighbours, if it would so appease that great Leviathan that he would bee content to sport him self next summer only in his owne waters and save us the charges of putting a fleet to sea.

The Duke of Albemarle was this weeke reported to bee dead, he has been dangerously sick of a cold and some disorder but tis hoped he is in the way of recovery. Mr Harry Jermin has been sometime under a melancholy dispensation and has talked much against the vanitys of the world and threatened to enter into a retird life, but as it is a certain symptom in young men that either they want money or health when they grow devoute of a suddain, the lat[t]er hapned to him he having been dangerously ill since, they say it came by a bruise gotten by a falle from his horse at Newmarket, this ripening into an impostume and since breaking there is better hopes of his recovery, this advantage he hath had by it that pitty hath soften[ed] most men's harts to speake as good words of him as ever I heard of any young gallant which perhaps if his prosperity had continued they would not have afforded him.

[f.3] If you cannot find your Rumelius and think you have great occation for him I will borrow Dr Hodges his for you but you must not keep it so long as you did last time. My bro[ther] Ben begs your leave that he may wayt on you at Oxnead for two or three dayes he being desirous to have some excuse to goe into Norfolk that he may wayt on my Lady Petahouse[511] going and comming, though she hath already satisfied him how little hopes he can have of her, but he desires you would make no mention of his comming till he bee with you.

*Unsigned*
*Addressed:* For the honourable Sir Robert Paston at Norwich, this
*NRO: BL/Y/1/65*

## Thomas Henshaw to Sir Robert Paston

**1671[/2], February 10.** Dearest patrone, on condition you will forgive my last week's omission, I will excuse yours of this; I was this day senight ingaged at an enterteinment which did not release me till ten at night. Your late indisposition and the distemper of this comfortles weather have bound up your hands from the practicke and a hundred other occasions have almost driven the theory of chymistry quite out of my head, so that I have no more at this time to say on that subject, but that my brother is returned with a great deale of gratitude for your kind enterteinment, but not a grain of volatile salt in his pocket you promised to send me by him.

---

[511]  ? Peterborough

I suppose the goute by putting stronger impressions might easily obliterate some of no greater importance then that was, but I hope you *will* shortly think of some other opportunity to conveigh a little of it to me, for I should bee very unwilling to goe without so good an alexiterium[512] to Denmark, where all manner of cordialls will bee no more then needful, and in order to it Sir John Clayton has (the better to incourage me) threatned to bestow on me a large cellar of bottles furnished with severall sorts of strong water. The *Gazette* has informed you that Sir G Downing for coming home[513] contrary to the King's expresse order is prisoner in the Tower, but I can adde that the King has given to Sir John Davys of Barkshire his place of commissioner of the customes and requested his other place of teller in the exchequer, what [f.2] should cause Sir G so peremptorily to disobey the Kings command wee doe not certeinly know, but it is guessed that it was an apprehension *he* had least the common people who hate him for the last warre should doe some violence uppon him. Here is a new Dutch embassadour (Van Beuning) arrived immediately after Sir George, who they say brings great submissions of the Hollanders along with him, but though it were true, they have so sleighted and provoked the King hitherto that I doubt theyr humiliation comes too late, for wee see all preparations toward a warre notwithstanding goe on vigorously, nor are they behind us diligence, for wee are tould by that time wee are fitted to come out, they will bee ready with 120 saile. The French wee heare now will help us but with 30 saile only, and the great summe of mony so much talked of that lately came from France proves to bee but £54,000 sterling. I am extremely defeated in my expectation that my brother would have looked after my little affaires in my absence as he promised, for now the Duke has commanded him and his new company to attend him at sea in Capt. Harman's ship one of the first rate.

This week produced a wedding between your cousin the Lord Norris[514] and Mrs Lee, and the next week will bee honoured with one twixt the Earl of Laudardale and the Countesse of Dysar[t]. I should the last week have given you account that Coll Desbrough, Major Genll Kelsy are returned into England *cum permissu superiorum*[515] procured as is said at the intercession of Mr Bloud which makes others talke that Lambard and Overton are also to [f.3] come shortly. Last night in the French embassadour's pacquet came the Duke of Monmouth's commission for a regiment of [*word illegible*] men, each company is to have two lieutenants, three sargeants, five corporalls beside captain and ensigne, some say there are bills of exchange for mony too.

*Unsigned*
*Addressed:* For the honourable Sir Robert Paston at Norwich, this
*NRO: BL/Y/1/66*

---

[512] A preservative against contagion or poison: Henshaw had been appointed secretary to the duke of Richmond on an extraordinary embassy to Denmark.

[513] i.e. from Holland where he was ambassador

[514] James Bertie, Lord Norris, later 1st earl of Abingdon, married Eleanora, daughter of Sir Henry Lee on 1 Feb 1672.

[515] With permission from on high

## Horatio, Baron Townshend to Sir Robert Paston

**1672, August 12, Raineham**. Sir, you have performed like a man of honour your self, & so deserve above, what titles, even the highest, your countrie out of their inclinationes & good opinion of you, give you by report heere belowe.

I am glad the Duche East India fleet are not so secuer but that fire on water may reache them. As to your fine daughter[516] I thinke you are much in the right, & if I may be so happy as to be able to serve her there, or anywhere els, I shall be most ready, as you know I have always bine to my power to serve you, & ever will be, as becomes sir,

*Signed:* your most faithfull humble servant, Townshend
*Postscript:* My most humble service to my lady, your sonn & his lady, with my wife's both to you & them.
*Addressed:* For the honourable Sir Robert Paston knight & baronett at his lodgings at the Golden Ball in Suffolke Street, London
*NRO: BL/Y/1/67*

## Horatio, Baron Townshend to Sir Robert Paston

**1673, August 10, Rainham**. My lord, that you are so, is as welcome to your friends as it can be to your selfe & I wish the good news of your being Baron of Paston & Viscount Yarmouth had come but one day souner & L[*ieut*] Colonell Howard & I had cellebrated the good news with one of the glasses of the first rancke in my poore house. He went a way this morning before I could get up but wee stood in no need of seconds for I am resolved never to drink more to that picke,[517] though wee should have bine glad of the honour of your lordship's compennie; notwithstanding my resolve, our brother Howard hath prevailed with mee to come to the camp and waite upon Generall Shomburge, but I shall make no staye, my lord I shall conclude with the same freedome, as well as the same reallity, as I use to doe to Sir R. Paston, hopeing the latter may be matter of excuse for the former subscribeing, my lord,

*Signed:* your lordship's most obedient humble servant, Townshend
*Addressed:* These for the right honourable the Lord Viscount Yarmouth at his lodgings at the Golden Ball in Suffolke Street, London
*NRO: BL/Y/1/69*

## [?] P. Howard to Rebecca, Viscountess Yarmouth

**1673, August 11, Yarmouth**. Madame, being so much conserned in all the honnors the King has done you and your famelye I could not omitt the giveing your ladyship this troble to assure you no parson has a greater joye in the honnor done you nor a greater respect for your ladyship in perticular to whome I wish a continewance of your happiness and that you may advance in all things as in this and

---

[516] Paston's eldest son William had married Charlotte Jemima, daughter of Charles II and Elizabeth, viscountess Shannon, on 17 July 1672.     [517] Probably peak or height

never knowe a more unhappye hower. We are all in paine heare for the success of our fleet which we believe certainelye engaged after which I hope we may be released from this campe[518] that I may have the libertye to assure your ladyship in parson that noe man living is more then myself,

*Signed:* your ladyship's most humble and faithful servant, [?]P. Howard
*Addressed:* For the right honourable the Viscountess of Yarmouth
*NRO: BL/Y/1/68*

## Margaret, Lady Bedingfeld,[519] to Rebecca, Viscountess Yarmouth

**1673, August 18, Beckhall.**[520] Madam, to whish and pray that your greatnes may increase till it comes to equalle the measure of your goodnes, your enimys can not in justice deny it to you, nor your frends in modesty aske more. I hope your ladyshipe will long enjoy the fruits of your labours, with the life of my dear Lord Paston, in the naming whose title (to confess a truth) I find my harte transported in spite of my age and mortifyd resolutions. May your ladyship have ever from the family all thanks. I whish my self at present as a Paston considerable, but being a poore papist I can only serve you with a good harte, and whisper to my frinds and acquaintances about Norwhich to the advantage of your concerns and how they may pay there respects, in order to which I am just now a sending to the dean of Norwhich[521] to dine with me tomorrow that I may season him befor *he* returns to his wife's frends, that they may not hinder [*f.2*] others, to my Lord Marashall[522] we will be carefull to speack, but I would be glad you would either lett him or us know the punctuall day you would have us meett you, but madam you will have to[*o*] many great affaires to be any longer troubled with

*Signed:* your ladyship's most humble servant and kindswoman, Margarit Bedingfeild
*NRO: BL/Y/1/70*

## Sir Robert Kemp[523] to Robert, Viscount Yarmouth

**1673, August 22, Norwich.** Deare sir, you know my hearte is really yours, but withall you know the multitude of my rurall employments, and some additionall, upon the death of your worthy kinsman,[524] which pleades my excuse, if my pen kisseth not your handes soe often as itt should doe: att present, itt must congratulate your fair deserved accession: I doe assure you, noe man in England, wishes more

---

518 The coming naval battle with the Dutch was expected to clear the way for a joint Anglo-French invasion force, part of which was waiting at Yarmouth. But the battle of Texel, fought on 11 August (Old Style) was inconclusive leaving both fleets exhausted but with the tactical advantage to the Dutch.

519 See above p.110n

520 Beckhall was near Dereham. The main Bedingfeld seat at Oxburgh had been badly damaged in the interregnum and was now the home of Margaret Bedingfeld's son, Sir Henry Bedingfeld the younger.

521 Herbert Astley, dean of Norwich; his wife was a cousin of the Hobarts.

522 Henry Howard, Earl Marshal, later 6th duke of Norfolk

523 Sir Robert Kemp (1628–1710) of Gissing, future MP for the county of Norfolk

524 Probably Lord Yarmouth's cousin William Paston of Appleton

prosperity to your person, family, and concernes, then myselfe: if I bee not one of the first that come and tell you soe att Oxnead, beleave it is because next weeke I goe with my wife beyond Bury and returne not, of three weekes, after which time I will attend you: as soon *as* the needes will give leave, I shall presents you with a dish of carpe, but if in the meane time, your occasions should be extrordinary, by the company you bring with you, and that ther stay will not bee of any continuance, I pray att your owne freedom take the liber[t]y of my pondes, for whatever is mine, is att your service. My humble service to your lady, your son and daughtr, the post onely tarryes till I subscribe my selfe, my lord,

*Signed:* your affectionate humble servant, Robt Kemp
*Addressed*: These to the right honorable Robert Lord Viscount Yarmouth and Baron Paston present. Leave this letter att the Golden Ball in Suffolke Street, London
At Ublesten[525] in Suffolk by Yoxford post
*NRO: BL/Y/1/71*

## Thomas King[526] to Robert, Viscount Yarmouth

**1673, September 6, London**. My dear lord, in obedience to your lordship's commands I waighted on Mr Dickenson & showed him the paynnes I have taken to serve your lordship & the publick. He semes to approve of what I have done & I have left the copie for him to amend or draw up what he thincks better to satisfie your lordship – to which I shall agree. I hop[e] it will prove not only good for the kingdom but wilbe worth £40 or £50,000 to your lordship.

It wilbe so farr from being a [?]boon from his Majesty to your lordship as it wilbe your honor to proposse it being a thing much to his Majesty's advantage.

I hop in five or six years to build your lordship as good a street as is upon Yarmouth Kea – if your lordship hath the houses I hop your lordship will thincke it reasonable I may have the profitt of the fishing vessells which is all I desire & that I hop your lordship will covenant to.

If your lordship will approve of that is lynd out & writ to your sonn to engage my Lord Treasurer[527] & Mr Secretary Coventry to [?]posses the King may get that order or something like it signed by the King your work with great facilitie is don without halfe the truble or charge you had *to get* the act of parliament. Your lordship need not acquaint the town of Yarmouth with your design – they cannot apprehend the depth of it – but being a greater advantag to your ground then to Yarmouth side <may> they may opposse it – pardon this presumtion from, my good lord,

*Signed:* your lordship's devoted humble servant, Tho: King
*Postscript:* I desire the your honnor of a lyn in answer to your servant
*Addressed:* These humbly present to the right honourable My Lord of Yarmouth
*NRO: BL/Y/1/72*

---

[525] *recte* Ubbeston, Suffolk, the home of Kemp's mother-in-law
[526] Thomas King (d.1688), MP for Harwich, who was involved in a number of proposals to build commercial premises to promote the fishing industry, etc. (Henning, *Commons*, II, pp 684–6).
[527] Thomas Osborne (1632–1712), earl of Danby and later 1st earl of Leeds, became lord treasurer on 19 June 1673; his wife was Yarmouth's first cousin Bridget Bertie.

## Girolamo Alberti[528] to Robert, Viscount Yarmouth

**1673, September 25, Chelsea**. *Although the continual loss of his letters does not encourage him to write by post he is sorry Lord Yarmouth should complain of his silence as he has written several times; my Lord Marshall and his son have visited him and they have drunk Yarmouth's health; news of the marriage of the Duke of York to whom my Lord Marshall has spoken about Yarmouth; differences with Spain; wishes him a good journey from Oxnead.*[529]

*Signed: vostre tres humble tres ob[eissant] fils*, Gir Alberti
*NRO: BL/ Y/ 1/ 73*

## Draft petition from Robert, Viscount Yarmouth to Charles II

**1674, April 2**. If his Majestie will be graciously pleased to allow <the Lord Yarmouth> *my* accompt of <his> *my* farme of the customes of wood, earth, glasse and stone ware as the [*word illegible*] hath bene or shall be truly stated for the two yeares and a halfe of warr ended at Lady Day last, and for the future abate £1,800 per annum <*word deleted*> out of the £3,800 per annum which was the inhanced rent by reason *& upon no other consideration then* <of> the fyring of the citty of London <*word deleted*> *I am* willing to pay presently to his Majesty *upon possessing such a release or graunt* £2,000 as a testimony of <illegible> *my* gratefull acknowledgement of his Majesty's *justice &* favour to <him> me.

*Signed:* Yarmouth[530]
*Endorsed:* My Lord Yarmouth letter to the King
*NRO: BL/ Y/ 1/ 74*

## Robert Paston[531] to William Paston

**1674, October 7, Paris**. Dear brother, I hope you will pardon me for not writing to you from Calais but I had soe little time there that I could hardly write to my father; we were intertained by the Duke de Sharoe[532] governour of Calais twice very handsome and all the garisons towns that we passed; the drums trumpetts and fiddles were still sent us by the governours and <som> they either came *themselves* or sent some gentlemen with complements to my Lord Plim[ou]th[533] who is very kind to me: I have seen yet soe little of the town of Paris that I can give very little account of it: the Prince de Conde came last week to Paris and hase sent [*f.2*] his armei to there winter quarters: Mr Jarrard[534] my Lord Jarrard's sone came to waite on <La> my

---

[528] Girolamo Alberti di Conti had married Margaret Paston, eldest daughter of Lord Yarmouth, in the summer of 1673. He was the Venetian Resident in England from 1670–1675 when he returned to Venice with his wife. For his dispatches see *CSPV*, vols 36–38 (1937–1939).

[529] This letter is very faded and is written in Italianate French which has been summarised.

[530] Not in Yarmouth's hand. The King responded to this petition by abating £1,800 as requested (*CTB, 4, 1672–1675*, pp 516–8).    [531] Robert Paston (1656–1705), second son of viscount Yarmouth

[532] Louis Armand, duc de Charost, governor of Calais

[533] Charles FitzCharles (1657–1680), earl of Plymouth, illegitimate son of Charles II

[534] Charles Gerard (c. 1659–1701), later 2nd earl of Macclesfield

Lord Plim[ou]th last *night* who came *with* the prince: he saws [sic] that Teureine[535] is still in the feild and does expect every day to fite: this is all the news that he tells us of. Pray present my humble service to <your> *my* sister and tell her I send her many thanks for her goose pie: if there be any thing that I can serve you in while I stay att Paris if you will imploy me you obleige

*Signed*: your most affectionate and loving brother, Robert Paston
*Postscript:* Pray if you write direct your letter *A Monsieur Mesnard demeurant dans la rue de chantre, a la ville de Sainte, pres le Pallais royall, A Paris*, and inclose mine in this.
*NRO: BL/Y/1/75*

## Thomas Gooch and Thomas England to Robert, Viscount Yarmouth

**1674[/5], January 4, Yarmouth.** *He has been unanimously elected lord high steward to succeed the late Earl of Clarendon.*[536]

*Signed:* your lordshipp's most faithfull and most humble servants, Thomas Gooch, Tho: England, bayliffs
*Addressed:* The right honourable Robert Lord Paston Viscount Yarmouth present these att the Goulden Ball in Suffolke Streete neare Charing Cross in London [*postmark*]
*NRO: BL/Y/1/76*

## Roger Flynt[537] to Robert, Viscount Yarmouth

**1674/5, January 6, Ludham**. My most honoured lord, it cannot be expressed with how much pleasure I receive your lordship's kind resentment[538] of my hearty endeavour to serve under your concernes. I did make a bold adventure without your lordship's privity, haveing noe other ground but a full assureance of your great forwardnes to serve your country. And yet not knowing what particular dislikes your lordship might possibly have to that employ, I must say as Erasmus did to Budaeus,[539] *Verebar hercle ne ipso officio inofficiosus fuissem.*

As for your lordship's kind mistakes of merritt in me, I shall make it my endeavour that you be no longer deceived. I thinke by this time your buisines is past the seale of St Nicholas,[540] & it is ordered that a select number of aldermen shall wayt upon your lordship & present you with it at your comeing to Oxnett.

I must acquaint your lordship with one thing which I know will be acceptable, that your election was so free that noe one person did openly oppose it; one or twoe of the fanatics would have taken advice, I shall tell your lordship of whome when I next see you, but it was instantly over ruled, & it passed clearly without opposition.

[535] Henri, vicomte de Turenne, marshal of France     [536] He died on 9 December 1674.
[537] Roger Flynt, rector of Beeston Regis, Runcton Holme and Runton     [538] i.e. appreciation
[539] Guillaume Budé (1467–1540): I was afraid, to be sure, that in my very duty I had been undutiful. I am indebted to Dr Robin Darwall-Smith for this translation.
[540] i.e. the seal of the corporation of Great Yarmouth

We returne our most humble services to your lordship and most honourable lady, beseeching the Allmighty to powre downe upon your heads and your honourable family the blessings of both hands, and that you may still continue the delight and ornament of your country. I am, my lord,

*Signed:* your honour's most obliged and most obedient in all services, Ro: Flynt
*Addressed:* Present this to the right honourable Robert Lord Paston Viscount Yarmouth at his house in Suffolke Street, London [*postmark*]
*NRO: BL/Y/1/77*

## Robert Paston to Robert, Viscount Yarmouth

**1675,**[541] **February 6, Saumur**. My lord, I received your lordship's letter with more satisfaction then any thing I ever did before, because that the contin\*u\*all fear that I had, ever since I understood your lordship's displeasure, is now quite extinguished; I tooke the more care for to give your lordshipe a very full account how this mistake happened, because that I <ever> \*have\* had a great care heitherto of displeasing your lordshipe, and I hope that God will give me his grace for to continue in the same as long as I live. I doe give your lordshipe abundance of thanks for the kinde and good advise your lordshipe was pleased to give me, <of> not for learn [*sic*] so many [*f.*2] exercises att on[*c*]e, and particularly your lordshipe was pleased \*to mention\* riding the great horse. I did not desine to have learnt that exercises hear but that \*my\* Lord Plimmouth did perswade me very much to ride hear, to beare him company and for to recompense me for it he has given \*me\* his honor that when he comes into England, if ever he has any command, I shall be his second captaine; and in the mean while \*he\* <and> has promised me that if he makes his <campaine> campaine the next year in France he will take mee with him; ther is yet another reason that makes [*me*] rather chuse to learne hear becaus I pay [*f.*3] but 10 crowns by the month and att Paris they pay 20: if these reasons does not satisfie your lordshipe, if [*your*] lordshipe will let me know by your next letter, to the contrairy, I will leave it of imeadiately. Your lordshipe bid me send <your lor> you word if I should \*have\* neede for a bil of credit; which question that I might the better satisfie your lordshipe, I asked Mr Cheek; and he says it is very nessairy for me; your lordshipe has left my goeing to Angeir to my own discretion; therfore haveing <he> got the advise of Mr Cheek, and the leave of my Lord Plimmouth, I doe on the 20 of this month [*f.*4] intend for to put my selfe into some pension in Angeirs where there is not one English and sett my selfe close to the learning perfectly the French language; which I find very easie for <alth> although I am in a town wher ther is a great many English, yet I can read allmost any book in French as well as if it was English and can understand, and can make my selfe be understood any thing that is in common discourse. My cosin Cooke[542] present his humble service to your lordshipe, and my mother; he is thinking with in three months to \*goe\* down to Lions; and to stay two or three months there; and goe then for Rome:

*Unsigned, continuation sheet missing*
*NRO: BL/Y/1/79*

---

[541]  New Style dating; in England it was still 1674.
[542]  Unidentified, presumably a cousin of Robert Coke of Holkham.

## Robert Paston to Rebecca, Viscountess Yarmouth

**1675, February 6, Saumur.** Madame, I received your ladyship's letter which joyed me very much, when I read that the mistake of the bill of credit was at an end; I did defer writing to your ladyshipe untill I did hear that your ladyshipe was reconciled to me againe, for I did fear that in my time of disgrace a letter from me to your lady-shipe would not have not [*sic*] bin soe wellcome as I hope now it will. I am a goeing to live at Angeirs for two or three months to learn the language but it is by the consent of my Lord Plim[*ou*]th who is [*f.2*] very kinde to me, and has promised me on his honor that when he comes into England, he will be very much my freind; he is *the* most altered in every thing for the better, as it cannot be imagined; insoemuch that the last post Mr Cheeke writt to the King, and did give him a very good charecter of him, which I hope will make the King more kind to him; I will be shure to kepe my intrest with my lord when I am att Angeirs as your ladyshipe advised me. My brother Paston writt me a very kind letter by my father for which I have returned him thanks by a letter in this packett. I shall trouble your ladyshipe [*f.3*] noe longer, only I shall beg that your ladyship will have as good an opinion as ever of him who is:

*Signed:* your ladyship's most dutyfull and obedient son, Ro: Paston
*Postscript:* When your ladyshipe writes to me a gaine direct *your* letters *A Monsier, Monsier Giulliaume de Voulger, merchand banquier, rue du post destin a Paris*
*Addressed:* For the right honorable the Lady Yarmouth
*NRO: BL/Y/1/80*

## Robert Paston to Robert, Viscount Yarmouth

**1675, February 28, Angiers**. *Brief description of Anjou [in good French].*

*Signed: vostre tres humble et tres obeissant fils,* Robert Paston
*Addressed: A Monsieur, Monsieur le Comte de Yarmouthe*
*NRO: BL/Y/1/81*

## John Gough[543] to Robert, Viscount Yarmouth

**1674/5, March 22, Oxnead.** My noble lord, your honour's expressions of kindnesse to mee are so great that I must now study what course to take that I may in the least wise merit them, and yet I conclude when I have *done* the best I can, all your favours must be ascribed to the large bounteousnesse of your nature & not the poor worth of my services. I am so very sensible of my condition, as to assure my self that by reason thereof the best of my performances can be neither in themselves nor their desert <in>considerable, but what they want in quantity Ile endeavour to make up in quality, that is, in the faithfulnesse and sincerity of them. In testimony whereof and in answer to your lordship['*s*] demand of my opinion concerning the young gentle-men with submission I make this return.

---

[543] John Gough, rector of Oxnead from 1671, and tutor to the younger Paston children

My lord what I said in a former letter I do now upon better experience speake that nature has not been niggardly in furnishing Mr Jasper with abilityes of mind for a scholar. The truth is, my lord, his reason & judgment are in my opinion more then ordinary for his years, & his temper so even that whatsoever school he be put to where he may be followed close & lookt after there is no doubt but he will in time make a good scholar. But time must be allowed & that no short one seeing he is now so backward. The greatest fear I have is least when he does *manum ferulae subducere*[544] get from under the severe discipline of a school, & live more at freedome he will love his pleasures too much, & neglect his study. The ground for which fear is the great disinclination I find *in* him to any learned profession, he having upon all occasions when I have discours't with him upon that subject declared against beeing a scholar though I have wrought so much on him as to make him resolve to submit himself wholly to your lordship's and my ladyes designment. As for Mr Thomas I apprehend the case between them to be much different, for though he has a neat wit & very good parts yet there must be a very discreet mixture of kindnesse & roughnesse to bring him to exert them. Too much roughnesse I perswade my self must do him hurt & yet to[o] much yeilding to his humour will make him extreamly perverse. I confesse he puts mee sometimes to my wits end what course to take with him, but I humbly conceive were he so place't where <*words deleted*> *the person he is entrusted with* would have a diligent care of him, so resigned to the care of a scholmaster as not to hope for any favour when he does amisse, & yet to be kept rather in a fearfull apprehension of danger then to feel much he would thrive well in his learning & make a very fine man. But if I mistake not his temper, there must be a great deal of care & prudence used in the managing of him. My lord I have freely spoke on most serious thoughts of them.

[*f.2*] I cannot say but I may have erred in my judgment, 'tis a humane frailty & if I have done so I crave your honour's pardon for it as well as for the freedome I have used; and I beg your lordship to be so favourable in the interpretation of what I have writ as to have regard to my reall design in it which was to satisfy your honour's demand to serve you in your children & to benefit them.

I would gladly wait upon your lordship at London in my return, but I doubt my time which I have took for my jorney will not give mee leave to ride so far out of the way, wherefore I beg your honour's excuse if I in these circumstances decline so obliging an invitation unlesse by taking London in my way I may in any wise bee serviceable to your honour and then I shall make that way my choice, as beeing very forward to lay hold of any opportunity wherin I may testify that I am, right honourable,

*Signed:* your honour's most dutyfull chaplain & obedient servant, John Gough
*Postscript:* I crave my most humble service presented to my noble lady, to Mr Paston & his lady.
*Addressed:* These to the right honourable the Lord Viscount Yarmouth at the Golden Ball in Suffolk Street, London, humbly present
*NRO: BL/Y/1/82*

---

[544] To withdraw the hand from underneath the rod, to be no longer a schoolboy.

# Sir John Holland to Mr Barnard[545]

**1675, April 1, Quidenham**. Mr Barnard, I know that I shall not need to sollicit you to promote the election of Sir Robert Kemp, your neighbour, nor give you reasons to induce you to it, you knowing his worth & fittnesse to serve his county in parliament. And after he was proposed <by my Lord Townsend> soone after the death of my Lord Richardson, by my Lord Townsend, with the approbation of most of the gentleman of this county: twas believed that there would have been no opposition. But it is now & have been for some time reported, that there are some persons that endeavour to give some disturbance, by proposing Sir Nevill Catelyne,[546] a very worthy gentleman, but I doe know that he hath by letter under his owne hand to my Lord Townsend declared that he will not be ingaged heerein: but on the con<*letters deleted*>trary will promote the interest of Sir Robert Kemp all he can. And I am so confident of his ingenuity & worth, as I assure my selfe he doth & will abide by it, whatsoever is reported. But it is yet said (I heare) that there is an intention to set up some for him at the day of election, contrary to his desires & engagement: which I should be sorry to se[e] because I am very sensible of the ill effects of a contested election which our neighbour county[547] feels & complains of.

I heare some of the clergie are very active & looked upon as the cheife promoters of this intended opposition. I am heartily sorry for it, even for the clergie's sakes (for whom I have ever had a kindenesse & due respect) for (if they will well consider it) they cannot but judge that this setting up a person (how deserving soever) against his will & ingagement (which he himselfe have no reason to take well from them) in opposition to the lord lieutenant, all the deputy lieutenants, most of the justices of peace, most of the gentlemen & persons of greatest interest and quality in the county, will be looked upon but as an affected affectation, to shew their spirit, power & interest which have ever untill now wisely closed with that of the gentry, which truly (Mr Barnard) I doe very much feare <will> may turn at one time or other extreamly to the prejudice of the church & clergie.

I heare it is given out (as many other things are falsely enough) in prejudice to Sir Robert Kemp, that he have been heard to say, that had he a hundred livings to dispose off, that he would not give any one of them but under a condition of resignation, & that this have been much resented; whether he have said this or no I know not: but this I know that it have been said that one of the eminentest lawyers for learning & place, that this county have had,[548] made this his practice, & how soone this may be brought again into practice (by this example) by those who never intended it, when patrons shall se[e] that those who they out of kindenesse & respect to their persons & parts, have presented freely, shall bandy against them in the choyce of a knight of the shire, purely [f.2] upon the account to put an affront upon them & to let the world se[e] <that> how little power & interest the lord leiutenant & gentle-

---

[545] Probably Edward Barnard, rector of Diss; for another copy of this letter *see* British Library: Add. MSS 27447, f.342.    [546] Sir Neville Catelyn (1634–1702), later MP for Norfolk

[547] The election for a new member for Suffolk in February 1673 had been so hotly contested that a double return was made to the House of Commons leaving them to decide that Sir Samuel Barnardiston, a member of the country party, had been elected (Henning, *Commons*, III, pp 392–3).

[548] Probably Sir Edward Coke (1552–1634), attorney general

men have in the county if they oppose. I doe (out of my tender respect to the clergie
in generall) heartily wish that they would timely weigh the consequence of this opposition, & I doe desire that you (who are well knowing & knowne amongst the
bretheren upon whom I have ever looked as upon a person sober & discreet) would
use your interest & perswasion to those of your acquaintance & others that are active
heerein timely to give over this attempt; which I am confident they will in the end
miscarry in, and get the opposition highly resented.

And now (Mr Barnard) whether you will use my name heerein to any of them,
having freely delivered you my sense, out of out of [sic] no other end than out of my
respect to the clergie in generall, I leave it frankly to your owne choyce & discretion,
and remain,

*Signed:* your very affectionate friend, J Holland
*Headed:* A copy of Sir J. Holland's letter to Mr Barnard
*NRO: BL/Y/1/83*

## Robert Paston to Robert, Viscount Yarmouth

**1675, April 2**. My lord, this morning I received a pacquet of letters from your lordship wherein I did find a bill of exchange for which I doe returne my humble duty
and thanks to your lordship for the care you have take[n] that it might come safe to
my hands and in soe good time; your lordship ordered me to send you word how the
marchand has used me, he has dealt by me as he does to every body ells, for, for the
£42 ster[ling] I doe receive a 168 crowns and that is just crown for crown, the
exchang of money never being known soe low before now, my *marchand* did just
now receive and accept of my bill of exchange and has promised to pay within tow
or three days; I am extreamely troubled to hear how ill my uncle Sir John Clayton
has dealt by your lordship. I hope he will *make* his peace <with> againe very speedily for till shuch time as I heare soe I shall obey your lordship's commands in not
writing to him. According to your lordship's orders I have writt a small account of
the towns I have seen on the Rivire Loire and more espeacially of the town of
Angiers; Orleans was the first town that I came at on the Loire, where we stayed three
days; this town is situated in a very pleasant <con> country, very rich for corne, fruits
and more particularly for wines which is the great trade of this town, it *is* very well
walled, but within I did not find any *thing* that was courious, or worth remarking,
ther was three or four churches and a libreary that strangers are advised to see for
very fine pieces of workmanshipe and the image on the bridge of the Pucelle
D'Orleans, all which I did se[e] without any admiration being things very common;
after having spent three days in this town, we hired a boat for Saumur, but I never
did se[e] shuch boats in my life, they being nothing but five planks nailed together
without any pitch, or anyshuch *thing* to hinder the water from coming into the
boat, but in this pityfull boat we made a shift to git to Blois that night, we made noe
stay hear, therfore I had not time to se[e] anything but the castell which one sees more
for antiquity sake, then for any other reason; the next night we lay att Amboise, this
is a pityfull *place* there being nothing to see in it but the castell, which *is* a very

strong place and stands very hiegh, soe that from this castell one may se[e] ten leagues round, they carried us into a little chappell, where they showed us a paire of the largest hornes that ever was yet seen I beleeve by man, there are a great many people that does not beleeve them reall, but counterfited, the next night we lay at Tours; this a very well bult town and strong, there is tow or three very pritty churches in it, hear is allsoe a very fine maile,[549] and on[e] of the finest sources in France, this town is very considerable for trade, the greatest manufactor in this town is silks and stuffs which are made better heare then in any other town in France, the next night we arrived att Saumur, this town is but little within the walls but its subburbs are large and well bult, it is a poore town, and there is not one person of quallity that lives in it, hear is tow colledges one for the catholiques, and another *for* the protestants, the best church in this town is fallen down lately, ther is *allsoe* a very handsom church for the protestants: there is a very fine meddow att the *end* of the town, where all the people walk every night; between this town and Angiers ther was noe town that I saw worth takeing notice of, I shall *therfore* now give your lordship as good an account of this town as I can; this town is situated in a very rich fine pleasant country and upon allmost as fine a rivire as the Loire by name the Maine, which falls about a league below the town into the Loire, it is walled very strongly with slate and very deep ditches, there belongs to this wall eighteen strong towers, and three bastions, hear *are* two fine churches, and three very fine <mostreys> monastreys, a very long bridge which joyns the town on this and the other side of the rivire together, the walls of the houses in this town are [f.2] bult commonly with slate, this town being the only place in France where ther are slate quarres and all France has there slate from hence, it is impossible to imagine the quantitys that are sent to Paris every year from this town, I went to see these slate quarres the other day that are about a league from the town, I <word deleted> *saw* one that was above 330 foote deepe, there <is> *was* in this quarre above 100 men at work every day in the yeare there, above three or four horses that work day and night without seasing for if the[y] should neglect two houers to draw up the water, they would be filled full, thear are as many men more about of the <mine> quarre at work for to shape the slate, I did se[e] a man split a slate allmost as thin as a paper, hear is a castell which is walled allsoe very strong, but within it is gone all to ruine; here is a very plaisant maile where about three a clocke after dinner is all the compagnie in the town; as for the spending my time heare, as soon as I have done my exercises, I retire my selfe to my chambre where I spend the rest of the day in doing something or other, because I have not any acquaintance in this town to divertise my selfe with; I am in love with France every day more *and more* now I begin to speake a little French; I have received one or tow very kind letters from my Lord Plimmouth, he is very well and *has* given me command when I write to your lordship to present his service, and Mr Cheek the same; my *lord* has sent to me, to come and kepe my Easter with *him*, which I shall not faile to doe; I doe make it my busness to gain his lordship's favour, which at present I doe think I have as much as another, if I should *find* him very desierous for to have me returne to Saumur againe, pray my lord advise what I should doe by your lordship's next; I am very glad to hear that all our familie is soe well againe: I shall not trouble your

---

[549] i.e. mall

lordship any longer only to desire that your lordship *would beleeve* that there is none that endeavours more to please and obey your lordship then,

*Signed:* your lordship's most dutyfull and obedient son, Rob: Paston
*Postscript:* Pray my lord present my most humble service to my brother Paston and his lady, and to my sister Mary.[550]
Pray lord with my humble duty give this letter to my mother.
*Addressed:* These for right honorable the Lord Viscount Yarmouth Yarmouth [*sic*] at the sign of the Golden Ball in Souffolk Street, London
*NRO: BL/Y/1/84*

## Thomas Gooch and Thomas England, bailiffs of Yarmouth, to Robert, Viscount Yarmouth

**1675, April 26, Yarmouth.** *They beg him to accept his patent from the hands of George England esq.*

*Signed*: your lordship's most obedient & humble servants, Thomas Gooch, Tho: England, bayliffs
*Addressed:* This to the right honourable Robert Viscount Yarmouth, London
*NRO: BL/Y/1/85*

## John Hurton[551] to Robert, Viscount Yarmouth

**1675, April 26, Oxnead.** My lord, this letter had been sent by the Friday post if extraordinary busines had not cald me abroad that day, so as I could not speak Mr Wharton[552] as since I have, and doe find him wholly conformable to your lordship's desires, though 'tis beleaved most of those persons (whether of the clergy or laity) that are right for the Church of England, are for Sir Nevill Catilin; as on the contrary they say all the godly party whether Presbyterians, Independents or Quakers are for Sir Robert Kemp. As to the truth of this I can say nothing, but 'tis most certainly true that the good success Mr Cook had at Linn[553] puts the Catilins into a mighty stock of confidence, so that if those great persons please to take the pains to encourage Sir Robert Kemp's party with their presence, perchance 'twill be no more then needs. I remember the election which was in the first year of the late King which is fifty years, and I have taken notice of many elections since, but did never hear that men's minds were so strangely moved as in this; this day fortnight will (sure) put an end to these heats. The coach horse continues still in an ill case with that filthy humour; John Waden told me neer five months agoe he was sure he had cured him, but if he works no better cure on him then this, I doubt he will not doe your lordship much service in the coach. Haply he may make a very good stallion if your honor please to employ him that way, for here has been none in the paddocks ever since your lordship was here, save that little one which was Mr Paston's, and he's long since sold. Mr Gough

---

550 Mary Paston (c.1664–1676), second daughter of viscount Yarmouth
551 Lord Yarmouth's steward at Oxnead                    552 Edmund Wharton, rector of Sloley
553 Robert Coke of Holkham had been elected for King's Lynn on 21 April 1675.

came home the last Friday. Mr Francis since his late pretended sicknes, seems to be troubled with a disease they call the greedy worm. One day I went out with him and his dear friend that watcht with him night after night when he was in as great danger of death as I am now: I waited on them till they markt out thirty trees, which since they have got home and made fit for the fire. A very great deal of wood they yeild, yet I'm very confident if I would have let them alone, they'd have markt a hundred. The other day he comes again and (as if I had done him an injury in staying their proceedings) he tels me if I please I may make him amends by letting him have an old ash is blown down in the park: I told him then I must first see it. Tis a very great tree, and though haply 'tis good for nothing but the fire, in good faith I had rather ride forty miles to see him fairly laid in a grave, then part with the tree, but if your honor please to give it him I shall not oppose. He's also bawling at me for money which I delay to pay as long as I can, because they that are wiser then I say he cannot live long. Mr Bulwer I suppose will wait on your honor before this letter, he went from Norwich on Wednesday last. God send your lordship much health and happines and a good journey home. My lord,

*Signed:* your honor's most obedient servant, J Hurton
*Addressed*: These present to the right honorable My Lord Viscount Yarmouth at the Golden Ball in Suffolk Street, London
*NRO: BL/Y/1/86*

## Robert, Viscount Yarmouth to the Bailiffs of Yarmouth

**1675, April 29**. *Mr England has delivered their patent which he received as a mark of honour and favour and has desired his noble friend Sir William Doyly,*[554] *to methodize som proposition that may be of advantage to the towne.*

*Signed:* your much obliged humble servant, Yarmouth
*Copy endorsed:* My answer to the bayliffs' letter of Yarmouth sent with the patent of my beeing steward
*NRO: BL/Y/1/87*

## William de Grey[555] to Mr Blome and the rest of the gentlemen and freeholders in the towns of Thompson and Tottington

**1675, May 1**. Gentlemen, freinds & neighbours, I have bin hitherto so well assured of your kindness to me upon all occasions whatever that I neede not doubt it now tis requested in a business that so much concernes the publick good, and that is in the choice of Sir Robert Kempe for our next knight of this shire; you cannot but know he is recommended to us by our lord lieutenant (who alone hath done such service for this countye that I think we should seeme mighty ingratefull if we should not endeavour to maintaine his interest), by our collonell Sir John Holland, and by most of the gentry besides in this countye, and let me, who have bin long acquainted with

---

[554] Doyly was MP for Great Yarmouth.    [555] William de Grey (1652–1687) of Merton

Sir Robert assure you I think him a man of unquestionable worth and abilities, one
that hath a reall value and respect for the clergye, and one that hath not only professed but alwayes evidenced a perfect kindness for this whole countye in generall; so
farr from being a fanatick, as some have most falsly reported him, that if there were
no other testimonies to shew the unreasonableness of this report, then his father's and
his constant suffering in the late rebellion for their loyaltye, we might judge it sufficient; but before this election was ever thought of, I have heard him earnestly maintaine the principles of the Church of England in most publick discourses; and when
I justifie these things to you upon my owne knowledge, I hope you will so farr credit
me in it as to think I would not offer to put so notorious an abuse upon those who in
publick undertakings I must profess I wish as well to as myself. Pray consider these
things and then judge whether you have not more reason to give your votes for this
gentleman then for another, who is pretended to be set up against him, that to my
knowledge is engaged in honour & conscience not only to oppose his owne election,
but to promote that of Sir Robert Kempes. My desire is that those that are satisfyed
with these reasons would come hither to Merton upon Sunday the ninth of May, the
day before the election, by three of the clock in the afternoone, or else meete me the
same day at Hingham by five of the clock in the afternoone exactly, that we may from
thence goe to Norwich, & give our votes together for Sir Robert Kempe, which maybe
a meanes to prevent the inconveniences of a contested election, and preserve still this
countye in that unitye and agreement it hath continued in many yeeres: those that
shall goe along with me upon this score I'm confident will never have cause to repent
them of their choice, and let me end with this assurance, that their kindness & respect
to me shall be ever most thankfully acknowledged by him who is, gentlemen,

*Signed:* your most affectionate freinde & faithfull servant of his countrye, Will: de Grey
*Addressed:* These for his much esteemed freind Mr Blome and the rest of the gentlemen
& freeholders in the tounes of Thompson and Tottington
Pray let this letter be communicated to them by speediest opertunitye
*NRO: BL/Y/1/88*

## John Gough to Rebecca, Viscountess Yarmouth

**1675, May 7, Oxnead**. Right honourable & most honoured, the state of this country
in the present conjuncture is somewhat turbulent; both partyes concerned in the election are very active to make their particular and different interests. The Catlines on the
one hand seem stiff in maintaining the freedome of their election & do what they can
for Sir Nevill whom their adversaryes cannot charge with any unfitnesse for the place
& whom they think as the best qualified and fittest to be intrusted with the concerns of
the county. On the other hand the adverse party drive on with all vigour to maintaine
my L[ord] L[ieutenant]'s honour & to promote the designe for Sir Robert Kemp; each
party talk high for themselves but Sir RK's are now most confident, possibly fledged
by the late successes, & hopeing great advantages from the triumvirates appearing at
Norwich. The truth is the defeat at Lynne raised Sir Nevill's party very much and had
they been happy in having the shelter & countenance of a person of honour in the
county they had continued firm & likely enough encreased their numbers; but this

successe made their opposites more vigorous & watchfull, & finding no way else to keep up a cracking cause they came to the last *&* worst argument, that is, menaces. Tis confidently talkt (though Ile assert nothing) that many have been threatened <*words deleted*> unlesse they would go the way their drivers pleased, and there goes about a letter under an honourable person's hand wherein the clergy seeme to be threatened with beeing brought under the bondage of bonds of resignation unlesse they desist. By this or whatsoever other means many have been brought off from Sir Nevill, though not so many but that still they talk of making their party good, & truly I am in the mind if Mr Cook appear 'twill be a very hard pluck[556] between them. I am confident the grandees are very much afraid of a miscarriage though they will not seem to be so. And if they should carry it as like enough with much contest they may yet, there are wise men that think they have extreamly lost themselves by this buisnesse in the affections of the country & now that there is room to receive another, who will stand by them, into their hearts. In relation to my self, right honourable, be assured that I have so much honour & <duty> owe so much duty to my lord as not to go against his mind. I must freely confesse to your honour that my judgment leads mee to Sir Nevill but seeing my lord's promise is pass't & so his honour engaged to Sir Robert Kemp I have so much duty as not to be against him; which compliance against my own judgment is I think a pregnant argument of my dutifullnesse. This my determination I have openly declared & very lately was forced with some passion to do it in order to the vindicating my lord's honour against an unhansome & ungratefull [f.2] story of which you will hear more by a letter that bears this company. For as a sufficient confutation I let the relater know that I would have been for Sir Nevill had I not been under the obligations I am & nothing kept mee from beeing in that party but that I know my lord does seriously espouse the interest of Sir Robert Kemp, & I had in the first placed [*sic*] resolved with myself to move <*illegible*> by his lordship's directions, and therefore declared myself in my vote not to be a Catline.

Right honourable, the young gentlemen & Misse[557] are in good health & present their duty. They so little proffit in their learning that I am ashamed of them & though I do what I can, & scould at them more then I would or indeed should every day yet it signifyes nothing. Their minds are so much upon their pleasures that the book is a toyle & irksome, I hope your honour will consider of disposeing of them shortly for what they will learn here is inconsiderable. Far be it from mee to grudge my pains if thereby I might serve your honour, but when I lose my time & they get nothing it is no little trouble to mee & puts mee upon beseeching your honour for their good & my ease to beg a release. Right honourable, I beg my most humble *service* & duty presented to my lord & my most humble service to Mr Paston & his lady and Mrs Mary, from right honourable,

*Signed:* your honour's most dutifull chaplain & servant, John Gough
*Postscript:* On Munday your honour shall receive an account of the election
*Addressed:* These for the right honourable the lady Viscountess Yarmouth at the Golden Ball in Suffolk Street, London
*NRO: BL/Y/1/89*

---

[556] i.e. a tussle or bout     [557] Elizabeth Paston, youngest daughter of viscount Yarmouth

# John Hurton to Robert, Viscount Yarmouth

**1675, May 7, Oxnead.** My lord, Mr Gough tels me your honor would have an account from me how things stand now in reference to the election. This I can say, the heats not only continue but are much increased: every week, almost every day brings forth one new thing or other. There is now much discourse of a letter said to be written by Sir John Holland full of threatening expressions against the clergy in case they continue to oppose this party. I know not how to beleeve such an unworthy thing should come from so worthy a person, but they that report it say they have the originall letter written with his own hand. Both parties shew very great confidence but this party would make us beleeve they are sure to carry it, though I am above half afraid the people of Rome were not more afflicted after the battell at Cannae, then many of this people are to hear of such mighty opposition. They are no children that speak and confidently beleeve that had your lordship appeared for the other party they had carried it against all those great persons; notwithstanding, some of the party (I would fain find them out) have made your honor most base unworthy returns. Two daies since (not more) come hither two of the clergy, and one (falling into the common discourse which has taken up all people this six months) sayes he was resolved to know of Mr Hurton whether it was true that is reported. The report is that Sir Robert Kemp being lately at Norwich was told by Mr Linsted that my Lord of Yarmouth had written to Mr Hurton to make all his tenants and friends for Sir Robert Kemp, but that lately his lordship had written to him again, to goe to all those that were made for Sir Robert Kemp, and to let them know his lordship now left them at liberty to take which party they best lik't, and this Mr Linsted had from Mr Hurton's own mouth. The author of this damnable fals report perchance we shall never know, but the end is doubtles to advance their own reputation, if they carry the cause, with most base slight and dishonour to your lordship. Mr Courtais was the man that told us this story, and because he was not willing to tell us who told it him, I could not be at quiet in my own mind till I went to him this morning and told him I must acquaint your lordship with it, and that he must need tell me from whom he had it. He told me very freely Sir John Potts[558] told it to him and Mr Ransome and Mr Faucet, adding that he did not beleeve it, but who told it to him he did not tell them. It had been much fairer if Sir John Potts had sent for me to enform him of the truth, rather then to tell it to others, and then say he does not beleeve it, for be it never so fals, comming from the mouth of such a person, though haply he does not beleeve it, there are enough that will. In the mean time 'tis most certainly true, I have not exchanged one word with Mr Linsted these last twelve months, and if I had, 'tis strange I should communicate such a thing to him who is little more than a meer stranger to me. By Munday night we *shall* see how things will goe, though I confes already, it passeth my understanding how the other party should be able to ballance this, considering the chief persons in the county have been so long engaged for Sir Robert Kemp. Never had any person a greater praise then Sir Nevill Catilin; had he declared himself sooner, no

---

[558] Sir John Potts (d.1678), of Mannington; his wife Susanna Heveningham was first cousin to Sir William Paston and sister to William Heveningham the regicide.

doubt it had been much for his advantage. But I shall hold your lordship no longer. My lord,

*Signed:* your honor's most obedient servant, J Hurton
*Addressed:* These present to the right honorable My Lord Viscount Yarmouth at the Golden Ball in Suffolk Street, London
*NRO: BL/Y/1/90*

## Account of the Norfolk county election sent to an unnamed member of parliament

**1675, May 10, Norwich**. Sir, I shall here give you an account of the proceedings of this day in order to the election for a knight of the shire for Norfolk. There were twoe persons in nomination, Sir Robert Kempe was one putt upp by the power of the lord leiutenant[559] & some deputy leiuetenants &c of the county accompanied with his owne activity & forwardnesse. The other was Sir Nevil Catlyne putt upp by a loyall party of gentry, clergie & comonalty much against his owne will and inclinations.

The lord leiutenant accompanied with many of his collonells, captaines & justices of the peace mett together att Norwich on Saturday last, and takeing notice that the King's Head was a house where many of the Catlynes used to meet together & dyne on Saturdayes, appointed the landlord of the house to prepare a dynner that they might there freindly meete & dyne with those gentlemen that were freinds to Sir Nevil Catlyne. About noone thither they came butt with soe great a number as many of their owne company were forced for want of roome to remove from thence to another place. The Catlynes to avoyd disturbance went away & dyned together att another house.

This house was before that tyme taken upp for the service of Sir Nevil Catlyne's freinds and intended to bee their cheife place of randezvous upon the day of election. After dynner the Catlynes returned to the King's Head where many of them stayed till about seven of the clock att night & then parted with full assurance of haveing that house for their reception this morneing. Butt about nine of the clock att night on Saturday the lord lieuetenant[560] soe managed the buisinesse as by his power hee prevailed & tooke upp the house for Sir Robert Kempe. This morneing the lord leiuetenant was placed in a chaire proportionable to his greatnes in the markett crosse over against the King's Head gate where many of the Catlynes expected their randezvous & entertainement, butt comeing thither unexpectedly found the lord leiutenant & his party there, what disorder & disadvantage this might *putt* upon Sir Nevil Catlyne's party may bee easily understood.

Sir Nevil Catlyne was yesterday seised on att church by many of the freeholders of the county & was this morneing brought into towne with about 4000 horse, butt finding themselves thus disappointed of the King's Head were necessitated to goe to the White Swann which is on the backside of the butchers' shambles, a house taken

---

[559] Lord Townshend
[560] Where contracted this has been extended to leiuetenant, the writer's usual spelling.

upp for some of the Catlynes, butt very incomodiously situated to bee made use off as the cheife house of entertainement upon the day of election.

After the towne was filled with the great numbers which the power & terrours, industry & art of the lord leiuetenant, deputy leiuetenants, their collonells, captaines, justices had drawne & driven thither to vote for Sir Robert Kempe, contrary to their owne judgments & inclinations as they themselves publikely & generally declared, and those alsoe which continued stout for Sir Nevil Catlyne declareing for a free choice & their birthrights against this powerfull imposition; the writt was read in the usuall place by the sheriffe & the knights mounted their chaires, the multitudes which followed each of them seemed to bee much equall butt the party for Sir Nevil Catlyne the greatest of the twoe.

Whilst the knights ridd about the high sheriffe withdrawes himself to the grand jury chamber in order to the setling of such a method in the carriage of the buisines of the day as all things might bee equally & indifferently administered. Sir John Hobart & Sir John Holland managed the discourse on the parte of Sir Robert Kempe & made their severall speeches, the effect whereof was, that they desired onely an impartiall neighbourly & honourable way of proceeding. After a full debate betweene them & the gentlemen on the parte of Sir Nevil Catlyne for ascertaineing of what was then agreed on, itt was thought *fitt* the agreement should bee putt in writeing, Sir John Hobart offering himselfe to bee penman, the other party expecting the agreement should bee impartially sett downe & observed by Sir Robertt Kemp's party according to what the twoe Sir Johns had declared yeilded thereunto.

[f.2] And when Sir John Hobart had done writeing the agreement the gentlemen that were on the parte of Sir Nevil Catline desired that itt might bee publikely read to the end that if there were any mistakes they might bee tymely corrected. Butt the two Sir Johns could not bee prevailed withall to stay soe long and soe went imediately out of the roome, the agreement being left behind them to bee coppyed out & to bee observed stricktly on both sides. When a copy thereof was written the gentlemen which stayed caused the same to bee examined with the originall which was of Sir John Hobart's writeing, there were severall articles found defective and one materiall article wholly omitted which was to this effect that for the dispatch of the country there should bee two penmen & two persons to sweare the freeholders att the poll on each side butt those to bee placed soe nere together as the clerkes on either side respectively might see all persons that came to the poll to the intent that if any person should come twice or oftner to the same poll hee might possibly bee discovered. The omission of writeing this article was very ill resented & greately to the discontent of the Catlynes butt the two Sir Johns being gone off the chamber upon confidence that this article & all others agreed off would bee stricktly & honourably observed according to the true intent thereof were for the present <satisfyed> *qualified*. Butt contrary to their expectations assoon as they gott off the chamber imediately sett upp twoe distinct polls for Sir Robert Kempe att one where of the lord leiuetenant himself personally acted as cheife instrument and Sir John Holland att the other which continued for some tyme before itt was taken notice of by those gentlemen that were on the parte of Sir Nevil Catlyne or that any clerks could gett thether. Butt assoone as notice was taken of the said twoe distinct polls sett upp for Sir Robt Kempe, some gentlemen addressed themselves to the sheriffe whom they found in the grand jury chamber with Sir John Hobart & diverse other gentleman whoe appeared for Sir Robert Kempe and there complayned of this practice as a breach of article & very unjust & dishonourable, Sir John Hobart to excuse himselfe objected that when thinges were referred to writeing, the writeing was the onely rule to judge by, and this article was not in the writeing, *Ergo.* This objection made a warme debate & amongst other things itt was replyed that Sir John Hobart was the person intrusted to write the agreement & that though itt was his fault to omitt the writeing this article yett itt could nott enter into their thoughts that hee did itt with designe to breake itt, and that this his objection tending only to the mending one fault with another was an aggravation of the offence. Att length the sheriffe beeing present & privy to the before mentioned agreement was desired to declare his sense as to the justice of this complaynt, whereupon he did openly averre that the agreement was as above mentioned and that the breach thereof was without his privity or knowledge & contrary to his likeing. How to remedy this abuse was the next question itt tending to the great damage of the one party & <*illegible*> sinisterly *to the* advantage of the other. In conclusion att the sheriffe's proposal gentlemen on both sides accompanied him to the lord leiutenant's boath[561] and acquainted him with the agreement aforesaid, and that <though> Sir John Hobart had omitted (though trusted with the pen) the writeing of this article. The lord leiuetenant declared that hee was not privy to the agreement & seemed troubled for the breach of it & expressed his readines to comply to any course that should bee prescribed as a meanes to the strict observance of itt for the remainder of the day.

   Butt whilst this was thus in debate the gentlemen that were for Sir Nevil Catlyne finding the disadvantage that they were upon & expecting noe releife therein did <for> *from* that tyme sett upp twoe distinct polling places and soe that discourse ended for the present. Whilst the lord leiuetenant & Sir John Holland were acting their partes att their polls Sir John Hobart [*f*.3] attended with the sheriffe's men *& holberds* came many tymes to Sir Nevill Catlyne's poll & disordered & disturbed the freeholders there & affronted & behaved themselves very rudely towards them. Notwithstanding all these passages Sir Nevil Catlyne continued his poll till late in the evening & then accompanied with many of his freinds retired himselfe. Soone after the lord leiuetenant & that party went into the grand jury chamber & delivered the sheriffe their bookes & pressed him to cast them upp & alsoe the bookes taken by Sir Nevil Catlyne & accordingly the number should appeare to returne the writt. The gentlemen that were on Sir Nevil Catlyne's party being retired & hearing of this agreed that some person should bee chosen to goe to the sheriffe & acquaint him how that Sir Nevil Catlyne's poll was continued till late in the evening & that there were a considerable number of freeholders still in towne that had not polled, and that of them some had already offered themselves to the poll that day butt were hindred by Sir Robert Kemp's party & likewise to remind him of the breach of the agreement aforesaid & to desire that the bookes might bee sealed up & the poll adjourned till next morneing & then the bookes to bee opened againe & the poll continued. This was delivered by the gentlemen that were selected for that purpose. But Sir Robert

561 i.e. booth

Kemp's party were soe prevalent with the sheriffe as hee imediately cast upp the bookes & returned Sir Robert Kempe for knight of the shire.

Itt's much observed here that many of those persons that came to the poll for Sir Robert Kempe cryed out that they came for the lord leiuetenant's sake & others for this collonell, captaine or justice butt rarely any man said hee came for Sir Robert Kemp's sake. The fanatticks were generally for Sir Robert Kempe & alsoe the greater parte of the Roman Catholics (for feare as is supposed of sequestration).

And now good sir, whether you will communicate to your brethren of the House of Commons how the malitia of Norfolk governe their poor countrey men or whether you will <publiquely> publish this paper to any of them I leave itt to freely to your owne choyce & discretion with this assurance that if these irregularityes bee brought in question in the House of Comons, this relation will seeme butt a shadow to what will appeare by the proofes. Sir your letter gave the fullest account of the Lord [*blank*] of any I have mett with, I have noe more tyme butt to subscribe myselfe, sir, your humble servant

*Unsigned, anonymous, copy or draft*
*NRO: BL/Y/1/91*

## Margaret, Lady Bedingfeld, to Rebecca, Viscountess Yarmouth

**1675, July 25, Beckhall.** Madam, I had just now the honnour to receive your lady-ship's letter, which was of all things most welcome unto me – Ile assure your ladyship I was strangely transported with the visitt I made at Oxnett, which was at that time lik to a terrestriall paradise: the gardians so sweet: so full of flowers, and so pleasant; the hous so cleane and appeared so magnificent, yet graced with haveing those fine children in it, whosoever looketh uppon them will think my lord and you the happiest parents in the world: and in *what* parts soever they were mett, they would be known to be yours by their hansomeness and civility: indeed Miss and my cosen Thomas are both prettier then I can express, nor did I ever in my life find anything in poetry or painting half so fine as what I saw that day at your ladyship's house – where I wish you and my lord settled in peace: but I doubt you'le make it so late that the beautie of the summer will be over first. For news out of Norfolk I can send you none, but what I suppose you have heard perticularly, the price Sir Robert Kemp payed for his honnour was above £1500, Sir Nevill who went without it, £6[*00*] or £700, their continuous and unseparable frindship between our great neighbours and yours.[562]

[*f.2*] Mrs Michell[563] is in the heigh of her progress at the two Sir Johns' houses. Some says but tis not beleeved that Seamer[564] the Speaker sueth Sir John in the behalf of a grandchild of my Lady Craffs,[565] but I tier your ladyship quite out before I make the protestation to live and die

---

[562] i.e. the Townshends and Hobarts

[563] Possibly the sister of Dr John Collinges (HMC *Lothian*, p.131).

[564] Edward Seymour (1633–1708), speaker of the House of Commons.

[565] Dorothy, baroness Crofts (d.1663), was a first cousin of Sir John Hobart, and a half-sister of his first wife Philippa Hobart; she had no children by William, baron Crofts (d.1677) but had been married previously twice or three times.

*Signed*: your ladiship's most faithfull and affectionate servant, Margaret Bedingfield
*Postscript*: My husband[566] beggs my lord and you might find his humble service hier. Your ladiship writt nothing how your little grandchild thrives.[567]
Sir Joseph Colston is newly dead. I must not forgett to be just but to give everybody their due. Mrs <Sheppard> Cooper[568] and Mr Goff dose their parts (I think) very well.
*British Library: Add. MSS 36988, f. 106*

## John Gough to Rebecca, Viscountess Yarmouth

**1675, August 13, Oxnead**. Most honoured madam, I exceeding lament the unfortunate accident that has befell my good lord,[569] and the ill newes has struck us all into a great damp as it must needs do to all that have any honour for or dependance upon the family. Our most hearty prayers shall attend the endeavours of the chirurgions for his happy recovery, & I hope that God in mercy will give us a gracious answere in his lordship's most desired restauration. I am in great hopes from the account that I had from Mr Clayton[570] that by tomorrow's poste wee shall receive some comfort, God grant wee may find so. But, madam, I do most earnestly beg your honour with patience to bear this affliction & in the use of means to trust in God's goodnesse for a blessing on them. Bee nott, good madam, out of measure dejected, I know your love to be so great as that you cannot but be sorrowfull & I am very well assured you will not be wanting in any point of duty towards my lord, but madam I beseech you too have some regard to your own health & to take care least by overgreiving & overwatching you endanger your own health. I do most heartily wish his lordship's recovery & I assure my self no means will be wanting in order thereunto, but I would not have his lordship's health be succeeded by your honour's sicknesse which will be matter of greife afresh to us all. Honoured madam, I pray God comfort you under & strengthen you to bear his hand & give a happy issue to your present trouble. I crave *my* most humble duty to my lord & to let him know that while I have breath my prayers shall still be for his lordship's welfare in this world & in that which is to come. I have no more but to assure your honour that I am

*Signed:* your honour's most dutifull chaplain & most devoted servant, John Gough
*Postscript:* I crave my most humble service to all & my thankes to the honoured Mr Clayton for his kind letter.
*Addressed:* These to the right honourable the Lady Viscountess Yarmouth at the Goulden Ball in Suffolk Street in London, humbly present [*postmark*]
*NRO: BL/Y/1/92*

---

566 Sir Henry Bedingfeld (c.1614–1685) the elder
567 Charles Paston (1673–1718), eldest son of William and Charlotte Paston, grandson of viscount Yarmouth and also of Charles II.    568 Housekeeper at Oxnead
569 Several shots had been fired into Lord Yarmouth's coach by highwaymen, one of which wounded him.    570 Probably George Clayton, Lady Yarmouth's younger brother

## William Windham[571] to Robert, Viscount Yarmouth

**1675, August 15, Felbrigg**. My lord, since I have heard of your being wounded
upon the road, by persons who came to rob you, I have been continually between
hope & feare of your being better or worst then is reported & doe very heartily pray
for & long to heare of your recoverye; for as noe bodye rejoyces more at your good
fortune than myselfe, soe this unluckie accident doe very much affect & trouble

*Signed:* your lordship's affectionate and obedient servant, Will Windham
*NRO: BL/Y/1/93*

## John Gough to Rebecca, Viscountess Yarmouth

**1675, August 16, Oxnead**. Most honoured madam, the news by Saturday poste
has mightily revived mee and I cannot tell how to expresse my thankfulnesse to your
honour for the care you took to let mee know it in any proportion to the comfort I
receive from *it*. I must confesse when I had the first newes of my lord's mishap from
Mr Clayton, though I hoped it would prove no worse then hee represented, yet when
I reflected upon the extraordinary danger his lordship was engaged in I was trem-
blingly afraid of some worse news, and truly since it proves so good as could reasonably be expected in such circumstances I bowe my knees in thankfulnesse to the father
*of mercyes* for so wonderfully delivering my lord from the jaws of death, & for
giving us so fair hopes of his lordship's speedy & happy recovery. I pray God make
us dutifully sensible of & thankfull *for* so great mercyes to the family & our beeing
so, will be the best course we can take for the continuance of them, & the addition
of further blessings to it. I hope this letter will find your honour chearing up after so
sad an event seeing through God's goodnesse things succeed so well, & to understand
so much will bee matter of rejoycing to mee seeing in your honour's greife I cannot
but sympathize. The news was not rife in the country till Saturday poste came in,
since which time severall have sent to understand how my lord is, Major Doughty[572]
came at nine a clock on Saturday night not beeing able to rest till he understood what
condition my lord was in, & see*m*ing much satisfied at the good newes. He desired
mee to tender his humble service to both your honours & his best wishes for my lord's
good health. I beg my most humble duty to my lord from, right honourable,

*Signed:* your honour's most dutyfull chaplain & obedient servant, John Gough
*Postscript:* The young gentlemen & Miss present their duty to my lord & your honour
& are very glad to hear that their father had such a deliverance & is in so fair a way
of recovery. Poor Mr Thomas presently fell a crying at the first newes & could not in
a great while be comforted so much as to stop his tears.
*Addressed:* These to the right honourable the Lady Viscountess Yarmouth at the
Goulden Ball in Suffolk Street in London [*postmark*]
*NRO: BL/Y/1/94*

---

571  William Windham (1647–1689) of Felbrigg
572  Major Robert Doughty (d.1679) of Aylsham; see also pp 20–1 above

# Sir John Holland to Robert, Viscount Yarmouth

**1675, August 16, Quidenham**. My lord, whylst I was in full expectation to heare of your lordship's arrivall at your sweet Oxnett (the summer being soe farr spent & our meeting at Westminster drawing on) my Lord Chamberlaine[573] giving mee heer a visite upon Fryday last, told me that your lordship had binn sett upon about Kensington by some highway rogues, & that you had binn robbed, & dangerously wounded; newes very unwelcome to mee & coming from such a hand, did very much surprize mee, yett hearing nothing from Mr Fisher, nor finding any thinge therof in the *Gazett*[e], nor from any other hand, I ame in some hope my lord's inteligence was mistaken, but I cannot be at ease untill I find it contradicted by your owne hand, which I hope & long for.

The routing of Crequi[574] since the loss of Turenne comes to us heere confirmed of all hands & whether slayn or gott into Treves is uncerteynly reported; wee cannot mourn much heere that Monsir's ambition have received so considerable a check, but wee are somwhat alarmed with the newes of that disorder the citty of London was in, occasioned as wee heare by the dangerous discontentment that the silk weavers & others have taken up against the French inhabiting in the citty & suburbs, robbing them of as they conceive of ther trade & livelyhood: & that for the quietting of them his Majesty was returned to Whyte Hall, with the greatest part of his gaurds, & the citty generally & yett dayly in armes; but of this I have as yett received nothing of certaynty by any letter which makes mee think that Mr Fisher is out of town; & whylst I think I have the greater apprehension that what my Lord Chamberlaine *told mee* touching your lordship's condition may be true, I pray satisfy heerin, my lord,

*Signed:* your lordship's most humble servant, J Holland
*Postscript:* I humbly kiss my ladyes hands
*Addressed:* For the Lord Viscount Yarmouth at his house in Suffolk Streete, London
[*postmark*]
*NRO: BL/Y/1/95*

# John Gough to Rebecca, Viscountess Yarmouth

**1675, August 23, Oxnead**. Most honoured madam, I cannot tell how sufficiently to expresse my thankfulnesse to your honour for your great kindnesse in acquainting mee every poste with my most honoured lord's condition. There beeing nothing in this world dearer to mee then my lord's welfare I was very desirous to know how the case was with him <and> *as* I am very joyfull to understand it is so well & that there are such promising hopes of his speedy & perfect cure: and your honour having vouchsafed to gratify mee herein has obliged mee to return my most humble thanks for the great kindnesse. But madam if my obligation to your honour be great, as indeed it is, then how great is both your honour's & mine to God who has in so wonderfull a manner preserved his lordship & continues his favour in blessing the means

---

[573] The earl of Arlington
[574] François Crequi, maréchal de France, was routed at the battle of Konzer Brücke on 11 August; Turenne had been killed on 27 July 1675.

used for my lord's cure. Truly madam the mercy is too great to be competently acknowledged in one act but it must be *the* businesse of our future life. But yet your honour's piety deserves commendation in pitching upon so good a way of testifying our thankfulness to God. For there can be no better way of shewing our gratitude to <God> *him* then that wherein we renew & confirme our promises of beeing his & commemorate him who was the fountain and spring of all blessings & such wherein in testimony of our debt we pay an acknowledgement to him in charity to the poor, which are things that for my part I shall be ready to correspond with your honour in, but for that your honour mentions of a form I confesse I do not understand how lawfully here we can use any other then that of the church, which is certainly the best & for the present will be sufficient, seeing in the generall thanksgiving the church gives leave in one place to insert what is most suitable for the occasion & the particular matter of our giving thanks. And though in private there is no prohibition of any man's private form yet in my apprehension in any consecrated place which in a sense is a publick place no form may be used but what has the stamp of publick authority, but herein I shall submit *to* a better judgment & stronger reason. Most honoured madam, I am not onely for my lord's sake glad that he is so well, but for your honour's too, and I pray God to continue & encrease your comfort in the life health & prosperity of both your honours which is the hearty constant prayer of, right honourable,

*Signed:* your honour's most humble servant, John Gough
*Addressed:* These to the right honourable the Lady Viscountesse Yarmouth at the Golden Ball in Suffolk Street in London, humbly present
*NRO: BL/Y/1/96*

## John Gough to Robert, Viscount Yarmouth

**1675, August 23, Oxnead**. My noble lord, it is scarce imaginable with what horrour the first news of your lordship's disaster struck mee, and that which in no mean degree increased my trouble was a fearfull expectation of more tragicall newes by the following poste for I could not perswade my self (though I wisht heartily it might prove so) that considering the number of rogues your honour was assaulted by & the many shots discharged at you when confined to the narrow compasse of a coach where they could scarcely misse you, your honour should escape so well as was then represented. But now, my lord, seeing the first newes so happily & beyond expectation proves true, since the black cloud is blown over & succeeded by a bright sunshine, and since I have the happinesse continued of tendring my humble service to your honour in a letter, whom I was once mortally afraid I should never write to or see alive more, I hope your lordship will give mee leave to change my stile as well as I have my countenaunce to rejoyce with your lordship for this signall deliverance & to congratulate you upon occasion of this bless't issue in a businesse which look't so fatally at first. I do in all humble prostration adore that mercifull providence which preserved you in & delivered your honour from so imminent danger, and which has been graciously pleased to continue you longer in this life to the great comfort & benefit of the family & the great joy of your friends. I know your honour can never forget this so eminent deliverance, and I hope you will alwayes remember to be thankfull to the authour of it. Since the protection of your lordship was so remarkable it is very congruous your honour's acknowledgement for it should bear some proportion to the obligation and I doubt not, considering your pious inclinations, but as your lordship has in this mercy been made a <particular> *singular* instance of God's goodnesse so you will be an eminent & illustrious example of thankfulnesse.

My lord, I'le be no further troublesome but to say that you have my most hearty prayers for your perfect recovery, long life, & prosperity, and that I am, right honourable,

*Signed:* your honour's most dutifull chaplain & obedient servant, John Gough
*Postscript:* Captain Barber presents his most humble service & best wishes for your lordship's perfect recovery.
*Addressed:* These to the right honourable the Lord Viscount Yarmouth at the Golden Ball in Suffolk Street in London humbly present
*NRO: BL/Y/1/97*

## John Hildeyard[575] to Robert, Viscount Yarmouth

**1675, August 29.** My lord, this day fortnight my Lady Smith[576] engaged mee to officiate in her chappell for the welcome of her friends into Norfolk, where I first heard of your lordship's disaster, and having the next day informed my selfe from your true and my most constant friend Sir Henry Bedingfeild, wee did most hartily condole with you but many dayes did not passe before that worthy gentleman gave mee an happy allay to my greife and now the very remaynes thereof are vanquished and by your perfect recovery wholy swallowed up into joy. Witnesse our offering up of prayer to God this day in your behalfe, wherein I did most delightfully beare my share; I assure your lordship all your friends are much joyed at your deliverance: and your very enimyes (if any such you have) must acknowledge God's hand in it; who by *this* preservation hath owned you in his speciall care; the benefitt of our prayse and your thankfullnesse will I doubt not redound to the comfort of your posterity. For your solemne acknowledgement of God's mercy in this deliverance testifies, to the great satisfaction of all good men, your piety to the world, in this world of irreligion and impiety; wherein thinges of this nature are rather attributed to I know what chance or good fortune then to him who is the onely preserver of men and covereth the heads of his servants in the day of danger therefore doe his saynts blesse him and are alwayes talking of his power, but not to be too troubleome to your lordship our desire of seeing you at Oxnead is now doubled and amongst others, when your occasions will permitt, I am ready with all syncerity to ofer my testimony of beeing to your selfe, your lady, and family, right honourable,

*Signed*: your most humbly devoted, J Hildeyerd
*Addressed:* These to the right honourable the Lord Vicount Yarmouth at the Golden Ball in Suffolk Street in London, present [*postmark*]
*NRO: BL/Y/1/98*

[575] Dr John Hildeyard, rector of Cawston and later prebendary of Norwich and JP; he signed his name both 'Hildeyerd' and 'Hildeyard'.    [576] Alice, widow of Sir Owen Smith or Smyth of Irmingland

# John Gough to Rebecca, Viscountess Yarmouth

**1675, August 30, Oxnead.** Most honoured madam, I know your honour will be desirous to understand the circumstances of our yesterday's religious performance, and I think it a peice of my duty to informe you in all particulars of it. At the usuall time for celebration of divine service wee assembled in the chappel, a place most suitable for the occasion & private businesse of thanksgiving that day to be performed, but yet the day beeing such as is appointed for God's publick worship, & wee having a full congregation of the parish and of many others in the judgment of others whom I consulted as well as my own the churches form only could be used, & to make use of any other could not consist with our duty of obedience to the King, the church & that tender regard we ought to have to your honour seeing the following the directions of a private form would no doubt open the mouths of such as wish you ill. Notwithstanding that wee might not be wanting in our service to the solemn of [*sic*] occasion of our meeting I collected the<m> substance of the prayers in the form your honour sent me into a narrow compasse and inserted them in the proper place appointed by the order of the church, giving our hearty thanks to Almighty God for his mercifull protection, preservation & restauration of my lord to his perfect health & praying for the continuance of such his mercyes to his person & the whole family. After this we used the thanksgiving for deliverance from enemyes. Then in the communion service we made use of the last prayer in the thanksgiving for the King's birth & returne onely changing what the nature of our buisnesse required a change of. Thus madam in our service we obeyed the church, complyed with the present occasion & defeated them of an opportunity of mirth who perhaps lay at catch for one. And as on the one hand we have solemnly performed the duty of thanksgiving which God's great mercy towards us required so on the other hand we have done it in that regular justifiable way that nothing but malice I think can quarrell at; and if there be any that shall do so, I doubt their next quarrell will be against God & all religion. After the sermon seasonable for the time wee proceeded to the holy communion, & had a pretty good appearance, near about thirty in all, whereof the strangers were Dr Hildeyerd & his sister, Mr Curtis & his wife, Mr Bulwer & his wife, Mr Wharton & Captain Barber, the rest of the family & parish. The communicants all dined here & wished my lord & your honour health in a glasse of wine. After all had dined order was given [*f.*2] that all should repair to church, that so neither God might be dishonoured by the intemperance of any, nor occasion administered to calumnious tongues. Thus most honoured madam I have given you a relation of the whole management from the beginning to the end & I hope your honour will well approve of what has been done seeing I have used what care I could that we might decently solemnly & devoutly acknowledge God's great goodnesse to this family in his late signall deliverance <to> of my lord which I pray we may be alwayes so mindfull of as continually to thank him for both with our lips & in our lives; and that God would be pleased to continue such his mercyes to my lord & the whole family, blessing them with health, peace, prosperity, honour, & a long life here & everlasting life hereafter, was our prayer yesterday, is mine today & shall be still the prayer of, madam,

*Signed:* your honour's most dutifull chaplain & obedient servant, John Gough

*Postscript:* Dr Hildeyerd has writ to my lord this day & Mr Wharton I presume will do the like; for the other buisinesse of your honour's letter I have done something in it with Mr Bulwer & will go on to performe it with as much speed & caution as I can. *Addressed:* These to the right honourable the Lady Viscountesse Yarmouth at the Golden Ball in Suffolk Street in London, humbly present
*NRO: BL/Y/1/99*

## Thomas Bulwer to Robert, Viscount Yarmouth

**1675, August 30, Buxton**. Right honourable, the newes of your lordshipp's fallinge into the hands of those barbarous wretches and their puttinge your precious life into soe great jeopardy was soe great a surprise to us here as even to cast us upon the brinke of confusion, but gatheringe out of the relation some glimerings of comfort as to the hopes of your recovery made us & all this parte of the world to enter, as it were, into the lists with Almighty God by our humble wrastlings with him for your lord-shipp's life, and now blessed be the great God of heaven & earth, who hath heard us & granted us the desires of our harts & hath not denyed us the humble requests of our lipps, and therefore in acknowledgement of & thankfulnes for soe gracious a returne to our praye[r]s, wee did yesterday, accordinge to your lordshipp's & my hon-ourable ladyes intimation (soe pious & soe religious), meete at Oxnet where we went into the house of the Lord with praise & were thankfull unto him & spake good of his name & after a very good sermon preached by Mr Wharton wherein he discreetly tooke notice of the occasion, wee received the cupp of salvation & called upon the name of the Lord, and then falling to our owne refreshments with an excellent good dinner out of your lordshipp's most noble bounty, wee then went to Buxton church, where Dr Hildeyard made another excellent good sermon & soe we closed the day with joy & gladnes of harte for soe signall, soe gracious, & soe wonderfull a deliver-ance, and to God alone be all the glorie for ever.

Now my good lord as to Yarmouth, I received a letter from my sonne England[577] wherein he tell me that himselfe and partner with the wholle corporation were very much saddnd at your lordshipp's being wounded & that they were all most earnest supplicants to God for your recovery & withall desired me to returne your lordship his most humble thanks for yours current and for all your favours to him, and saith that as to the corporation takeinge leases he cann say noe more then he did in his letter to me, which I left with your lordshipp, and that he finds they are rather more coole in that proposall then otherwise but wherein he cann or may be in any sort be servicable to your lordshipp, he assure[s] me he will not be wantinge in any manner, to the utmost of his power. I doe verely beleve, that when your lordshipp come into the country you will have some addresses made to you about it. I did write to him that your lordshipp would not tye them to any hard covenants in their leases as to building or otherwise, but only to leave at the end of the lease what buildings should be erected in the meanetyme. My lord I have bene too tedious, I shall only add the tender of my own with my wives most humble duty & service to your lordshipp, and

---

[577] Thomas England of Yarmouth, husband of Bulwer's daughter Ann; for the England family of Yarmouth *see* Arthur Campling (ed.), *East Anglian Pedigrees* (NRS (1940) XIII) pp 68–69.

to the right honourable your good lady and all yours, and so presume to subscribe my selfe,

*Signed*: your lordshipp's most humble & obedient servant, Tho: Bulwer
*Addressed*: For the right honourable the Lord Viscount Yarmouth at the Goulden Ball in Suffolk Streete present [*postmark*]
*NRO: BL/Y/1/100*

# Edmund Wharton[578] to Robert, Viscount Yarmouth

**1675, August 30**. My most honoured lord, a numerous companie of your faithfull friends mett yesterday in that place dedicated by you to the worship of Almightie God, to celebrate his praises, and offer up to him our sacrifice of thankesgiving for your happie deliverance. And although wee were not corporally present with you, yett were wee in spiritt and in affection, and heartily joined with you in eucharisticall acknowledgements to the gracious preserver of your person for the exhibition of his power in so great a miracle of mercy. It did mee good meethought to behold so fervent, so unanimous a devotion; and what the father speakes of the primitive ages, when the fires of zeale, and the flames of holy love, and the heats of piety were most considerable, our Amen to every praier was like a clap of thunder, so loud noise did it make, and yett a sound so musicall. The whole service was by your worthy chaplaine and my deare brother Mr Gough performed with so much decencie and a gravity so becoming that had you been present with us, I know you would have strangely been affected with the comeliness and order of our religious deportment, had it not in some measure elevated and influenced your devotion. But that, I am sure, was high; and none, I thinke, can be more deeply sensible of a mercy, or more gratefull for it, than you are to God for his preservation of your person from so apparent danger, and from the violence of such desperate men. It was the Lord's doing, and it is marvellous in our eyes. So wee all said yesterday, and so for ever shall wee thinke.

And <that> thus having first offered up to God our oblation of praise for your wonderfull deliverance, give us now leave in a civill complement to congratulate your recovery, and to pray once more for the continuance of this health, and the prolongation of your life. That your daies may be many and your yeares prosperous [f.2] and happie: that you may be a comfort to your friends, and an instrument of God's glorie: that hee would every day please to crowne you with some favour, and to eternity continue his loving kindness towards you. Thus wish they all, and amongst them all his desires are not the faintest, his petitions not most cold, who is, my noble lord,

*Signed*: your honour's most affectionate and yett most humble and most devoted chaplaine, Edm: Wharton
*Postscript*: I present my humble service to my most excellent lady, and send my hearty thankes to her for the favour of her last letter. My wife also desires her honour to accept of the tender of her service.
*Addressed*: These present to the right honourable the Lord Viscount Yarmouth at the Golden Ball in Suffolk Street, London [*postmark*]
*NRO: BL/Y/1/101*

---

578  Edmund Wharton (d.1717), rector of Sloley and vicar of Worstead

# Robert, Viscount Yarmouth to Rebecca, Viscountess Yarmouth

**1675, September 15**. My deare hart, according to my promise this is the second
to you on the rode, the last from Littlebury[579] sent by a flying *coachman* is in certaine whether itt came to your hands from thence, wee dined att Newmarkett, and
from thence by sunsett gott safe to Thetford where I was entertained with the ringing
of the bells and immediately by a most civill visitt from the mayor in his formalityes
with all his brethren who stayed with mee about halfe an hower to drinke the King's,
the Duke's and the Lord Marshall's healthes, the doctor of the towne who is now with
mee att mutton and onions came along with them. Mr Gough & & [sic] Kilby mett
mee heere, & to morrowe I am informed by Mr Gough more persons then I desire
intend to meet mee on this side [of] Norwich. I heare I am expected tomorrowe
morning att Sir John Holland's butt I will nott stay long having soe great an appetite
to see my owne home. Mr Gough who presents his service to you tells mee miracles
of <her> *Betty's* learning, wee are all well thankes bee to God, and I am now better
then I have beene all the journey, the approach to my native soyle I presume gives
mee som vigor; your daughter Mary presents her duty, Mr Fisher his service who
cheeres mee [f.2] up on the rode, Mr Gough tells mee the towne of Yarmouth are
highly civill to mee that they designe six personns to com over to mee that they
designe mee a present, all this will bee matter of new accompt to you. The best
welcome I can have att home will bee to receive a letter from you though of the date
of the day I parted with you, those next my beeing *with* you will bee the greatest
alleviation for your absence. My service to all that are kind to you, adieu till Friday,
I am

*Signed*: your most affectionate friend and servant, Yarmouth
*Addressed*: These present to the right honorable the Lady Viscountess Yarmouth att
the Golden Ball in Suffolke Street, London [*postmark*]
*NRO: BL/Y/1/102*

# John Fisher to Rebecca, Viscountess Yarmouth

**1675, September 17, Oxnead**. Madam, the fortunateness & circumstances of our
two first daies journy were fully imparted to your honour by my lord's own pen, but
yesterday admitted of so much variety of pleasure & content, that tis a subject
copious enough for many penns, & yet omit many materiall circumstances fit to be
observed by the curiosity of exact ones, that I should not adventure to blemish it with
the unpoliteness of mine, were it not my duty to give some account of our progress,
& of the charge I received from your honour at our departure from London.

No sooner did the morning appear, but my lord was awakened with the melody
(not of Thetford town, for they were abroad at a wedding, but) of artists that fell in
with us by providence, for the skilfullest musicians are said to frame the sweetest
music out of discords, & ours was wholly of that composure, which wrought its
desired effect, for it enlivened & quickened us to be gon (though we were loath to
part with that corporation, who had been so civill overnight) and at the first mile &

579 Littlebury, Essex

house we came at, my lord was congratulated for his happy deliverance by an honest worthy gentleman, who saluted him at the coach side, & welcomed him into [*the*] country with a good bottle of sider, and gave us directions for our right way to Quidenham, but there is no pleasure to beat always in troden pathes, and therefore to make the way the more delightfull, we lost it awhile (the design being so laid at first, by placing our guide to ride backwards) that we might not come to that sweet place before our sett time, to inclose my lord again withindores, who we found so much refreshed with the open ayre of Norfolk.

At our alighting from the coach, the good old gentleman[580] (pitty it is that ever he should be old) who had been a little indisposed before, revived with the sight of my lord, betwixt whom there was such chearful & friendly embraces, that the mutuall affection which ran in their bloods was easily discernible, but the kindnes of his first word had like to have killed us, for as master of the place, he gave present orders to make us prisoners for that night, so that our names were no sooner up, but we might have layen in bed till noon, for there was no going further that day; this was evident enough when we came within, where the noble lady was ready to receive us, and a provision, not for a meale, but rather for a week's entertainment. My lord used all the arguments he could to have broke his fast there & so away, but a buck had been sent for fifty miles, & must be eaten before we parted, and it was not long ere a dinner came upon the table, such as for the variety of all sorts of flesh, fish & foule in per-fection, that are now in season, with severall sorts of liquors sutable, that it looked more like a preparation for his Majesty than a kinsman, and had not a letter come in unexpected (yet opportunely) at the third course, which gave intimation that divers persons of quality intended to wait upon my lord in the road, when he came near Norwich, all persuasions for his appointment of being [*f*.2] at home that night & impatience to see this sweet place & his dear children, had been of no force, if Sir John had not been sensible of the civility designed by those gentlemen upon the way, which till then we knew nothing of, but would looke unhandsomly to disappoint them, and for this reason (unwillingly enough) we got off soon after one a clock, and made all the convenient hast we could. At Attleburgh our company began to increase, beyond Wymondham more came in and so all the way till within a mile of the citty, where our number was compleated (where I must not forget my old master[581] who seemed as young and was as brisk as any in the company) consisting of baronets, knights, esquires, gentlemen & clergy, aldermen & townclarke of the citty with divers other substantiall cittizens, those of my Lord Marshall's family that were in town & severall from the bishop,[582] with his coach & about six coaches more. All saluted my lord at meeting, expressing their great joy to see his lordship in the country so well recovered, who appeared to them like a resurrection, the former reports hereabouts being that his wounds were mortall and that his coachman (who was hired above a week before) was at that time killed. They made no stop or delay to his lordship, for they fell into excellent order before they came to St Stephen's gate, and the van being

---

[580] Sir John Holland: he was then 71 but he outlived Fisher and both Lord and Lady Yarmouth, dying on 29 January 1701 at the age of 97; he was first cousin to Lord Yarmouth's father.

[581] Fisher began his career under Sir Charles Harbord (1596–1679), who was surveyor-general to Charles I in the 1630s.     [582] Edward Reynolds (1599–1676), bishop of Norwich from 1660

led by near forty of the orthodox clergy (habited according to their function) the rest followed in their course to the number of about 300 on horseback, before my lord's coach, which was followed by all the other coaches, & so passed slowly through the citty, the bells ringing, the inhabitants genrall looking out at their dores or windows, and a lane of ordinary persons of the citty on both sides of us from one gate to the other, all with cheerful countenances, who made their observances that they did not see a factious or presbiterian looke in all the train. Most of the horsemen & severall of the coaches accompanied my lord up the hill at Catton, where my lord alighted in the feild to return them his thanks, and those of the citty went back again, & about twenty attended him home & supped with his lordship. Our stay at Quidenham made us a little benighted, yet the sun would not leave us till we had passed the citty, and then deputed the moon to show us light hither, where the governess of this place had so artificially enlightened the house, that we could see the inside on't at half a mile distance, and at our approch to us seemed as noonday. His lordship was long looked for & and met at the gate about eight a clock by the young lady & mistris here, supported by her two brothers who conducted my lord & their sister in with abundance of joy & satisfaction on all parts, where his lordship found the house & everything in that order & decency, with such an entertainment for himself & the company that attended him, that exceeded all we had seen or could see elsewhere, and I cannot express it otherwise, than by saying, we were arrived at Oxnead, where with my most humble service presented to your honour, I remayn, madam,

*Signed*: your honour's most obedient & faithfull servant, John Fisher
*Addressed*: These present for the right honourable the Lady Viscountess Yarmouth at the Golden Ball in Suffolke Street, London [*postmark*]
*NRO: BL/Y/1/103*

## John Fisher to Rebecca, Viscountess Yarmouth

**1675, September 29, Yarmouth**. Madam, though we set out from Oxnead yesterday before the usuall time of the posts bringing the letters, yet my lord so ordered it, that your honour's letters met him at Coultshill[583] bridge, where Capt Harbord[584] came into his coach, Mr Tasburgh coming from Norwich before we came from Oxnead, who went also in my lord's coach, severall neighbours on horseback, which increased upon the way, & at Ludham, Major Waldegrave & Mr Huby[585] stayed in their coach till my lord came by. So that we entered Flegg with these two coaches & about forty horse, & came to Mr Call's[586] at Mautby about two a clock (my lord having eaten nothing that day) where a very excellent dinner was set upon the table in three minutes after my lord got in, with beer, wine, & evrything sutable,

---

583 i.e. Coltishall, which is on the river Bure
584 John Harbord (1637–1711) of Gunton, son of Sir Charles Harbord
585 Huby and Waldegrave appear to have been gentlemen of the Earl Marshal's household; Huby was probably John Huby, gentleman of Norwich, whose will was proved 1 Feb 1679 (TNA: PROB 11/359; British Library: Add. MSS 27448, f.100), and Waldegrave was presumably one of the Waldegraves of Stanninghall, a Roman Catholic family.
586 Andrew Call or Calle (d.1698), rector of Mautby

that feasted the whole company, to my lord's great satisfaction & theirs; & Mr Call & his wife desire their humble services to be presented to your honour.

In little more than an hour, we went from Mautby, & within a mile, Sir Nevill Catelyn with his father in law Mr Houghton, his neighbour Capt Cooke,[587] & and others in his coach, & and sevrall on horseback, fell in with us, & at Caster (two miles from Yarmouth) Sir William Adams in his coach waited for my lord's coming, and there, at Alderman Rowe's house in the street, the whole body of the corporation of Yarmouth attended his lordship's coming (& it was so layed, that they stayed not a quarter of an hower) *vizt* the old bayliffs, & the new, the three knights of the town, most of the aldermen & common councell, & other merchants, who saluted my lord (who came out of his coach to them) with a glass of good wine in their hands, & <immediately> *presently* the bayliffs tooke their coach, & went immediately before my lord's, the aldermen – common councill, with the rest of the townsmen & about fourteen clergy rode all before the coaches, which we estimated at above 300 *some say above 400*, my lord's servants followed immediately after his own coach, & after them, the three coaches that attended my lord, & the three knights' coaches of the town, *vizt* Sir Thomas Meadow's, Sir George England's & Sir James Johnson's,[588] with severall servants after them, which with my lord's made up near fifty horse more, and in this order we passed slowly over the deanes[589] to the north gates, the bells ringing & the street & market place set very thick with people, & and so we marched to the further end of the town on the market side, all the great gunns firing, as we passed by the sevrall forts, & near the further end of the town by the south gates, we turned down to the key side, where the haven lay very full of shipps all with their flaggs & streamers out, & such as had gunns firing them, as we came along by them, to the new elect bayliff Mr Thaxter's house, where my lord allighted, & received the visitts [f.2] of all the townsmen, of those that came along, & such as could not get horses to attend him upon the way, & soon after was entertayned there with all the gentlemen that came with him, & some of the cheife of the town at a very great supper, & there lodged, and about ten this morning his lordship with most of the other gentlemen in coaches went to the town hall by the church, where the bayliffs & aldermen, all in scarlett, were sat at an assembly, for choosing a scholemaster, & making my lord a freeman of the corporation, the instrument whereof, sealed with their common seale, & inclosed in a handsom square silver box they presented his lordship with, & so went to church, where my lord was placed in their gallery, betwixt the two old bayliffs, & prayed for by the preacher, by his particular title of their high steward. After sermon, the bayliffs, aldermen & common councell walked on foot to their other town hall (being their place of judicature near a mile off) & my lord & the other gentlemen in their coaches, where my lord was again placed betwixt the two old bayliffs, whilst the new ones took their oathes & divers others of the officers of the town, & severall other cerimonyes were performed as is usuall & then the new bayliffs tooke their places, of each side next my lord, & immediately the assembly brake up,

---

[587] Captain (later Sir) William Cook (c.1630–1708) of Broome
[588] Sir Thomas Medowe (1644–1688), alderman, knighted 1660; Sir George England (d.1677), and Sir James Johnson (b.1615), military contractor, both knighted on the King's visit to Great Yarmouth in 1671.
[589] A sandy area surrounding the town of Yarmouth on the north, south and east sides

& my lord came to this chief bayliff, Mr Thaxter's, where his lordship & all the gentlemen & ministers were entertayned with a magnificent dinner, the junior bayliff (Mr Bradford) being a bachelour entertayning his company (which were such of the aldermen & common councell that gave way for those gentlemen that came with my lord to dine here) at an inn, who, as soon as they had dined came all to attend my lord, and upon the whole matter, shew as much kindness to him, as could be imagined, the cheife of the town in their unanimous hearty expressions, & the common people in their shouts & acclamations. Sir Henry Bacon,[590] the two Mr Kevitts & some other gentlemen came in here this morning, and we hope soon after the letters be come in tomorrow, to get away for Oxnead.

Sir John Holland hath busines all this weeke upon his new purchase, on the further side of the country, & comes away for London the next, & so hath excused his coming to Oxnead by a very civill letter. I believe our Shottisham friends[591] are rather in Suffolke but without doubt at St Faith's fair,[592] next weeke, we shall hear of them. From Blickling my lord hath had two civill messages & Sir John Hobart will wayt upon his lordship at his return.

It was sunset before we had dined, & late before I could begin this, which I must breake off abruptly (being called for by the company) with my hearty wishes for your honour's good success in all your affairs above, for the advance & prosperity of your noble family. Thus presenting my most humble [*service*] to your honour, I remayn, madam,

*Signed*: your honour's most faithfull servant, John Fisher
*Addressed:* These humbly present to the right honourable the Lady Viscountess Yarmouth
*NRO: BL/Y/1/104*

## Robert, Viscount Yarmouth to Rebecca, Viscountess Yarmouth

**1675, September 29, Yarmouth**. My dearest deare, yesterday I came to Yarmouth, Captaine Harbord, Jack Tasburgh and Mr Fisher in the coach with mee and about forty horse which increased on the way. I was entertained att Maultby as I passed with the company very handsomly att Mr Call's from whence about foure in the afternoone I came on, Sir William Adams and Sir Neville Cataline, Mr Haughton, Major Waldegrave, Mr Huby falling in with their coaches; att Castor three miles from Yarmouth the baliffs and the corporation mett mee att an aldermann's country howse where I alighted and saluted them, soe wee proceeded following the bayliffs' coach and with eight coaches and five hundred horse I beleeve att the least, I was conducted first into the markett place where the great gunns fired all along the walls then comming along the key all the gunns from the shipps in the haven fired as wee passed along and the horse making a lane on both sides I was brought to the new bayliff's howse and had severall kind shouts att my lighting. Itt was don with as much height of kindness as any subject could receive. This morning

---

[590] Sir Henry Bacon (d.1686) of Herringfleet and Gillingham
[591] The two Sir William Doylys
[592] A large cattle fair held at Horsham St Faith each 17 October

I went with the bayliffs and aldermen to their guild hall where they were all in their scarlett gownes, they presented me with the instrument of my freedome in a silver box with the townes armes upon't, and then I went with them to church where I satt betweene the two bayliffs, after that was [*f.*2] don wee passed through the towne, the gunns firing, to their other towne hall where the new bayliffs and all the other officers were sworne in my presence from whence I returned to a most noble dinner where about three and fourty gentlemen satt downe att itt. *Itt is* now allmost six of the clock that I steale into my lodging chamber from the company to write to you, though Mr Fisher has promised mee to doe itt. Mr England desires mee to have butt a little patience, and tells mee the growth of the towne in shipping and trade must necessarily throwe them upon mee, itt is nott now the time to conclude anything. I find them nibling butt pray gett Mr Fits[593] to com downe if possibly the next week which must one way or other doe mee good. I forgott to tell you the first night I had a noble entertainement. I received the enclosed from Mr Dickinson, itt is in an odd straine butt pray pacify him with good words. I meane to write to him on Monday. Tomorrowe I intend to goe from hence about tenn or eleven of the clock if I can gett of butt doe expect to receive your deare letter first. Pray excuse mee to Sir John Clayton and Mr Henshaw whose letters I have received butt cannott answer them this post, your letters after I have read them over tenn times I committ to the fire, I have now nothing more to say. On Friday I am for Beckshall. I doe nott thinke these favors don mee soe extraordinarily will relish with som of this country neither [*f.*3] shall I much concerne my self for itt. My service to my son and daughter, I am sorry that that [?]trap in St Jeames his street must ly whether I will or noe, till the next post farewell. I am deare hart

*Signed*: your most affectionate servant, Yarmouth
*Postscript*: My cosin Windham came and dined with mee againe butt his wife[594] is nott com from Raineham, he has invited mee Tuesday next
*Addressed*: These present to the right honorable the Lady Viscountess Yarmouth att the Golden Ball in Suffolke Street, London [*franked by Yarmouth, postmark*]
*NRO: BL/Y/1/105*

## Robert, Viscount Yarmouth to Rebecca, Viscountess Yarmouth

**1675, October 1**. My deare hart, yesterday I received your deare letter att Yarmouth where my entertainement was prodigious and my comming away was licke my comming, the bayliffs that were new chosen carried mee three miles, foure or five coaches and a great number of horse, nothing could bee with more kindness nor with greater pomp, the gunns fired againe as I came back and in the morning all the gunns in the haven gave mee my morning's wakening. I gott home about eight of the clock att night, and am now this morning att nine going for Sir Henry Bedingfeld's, therefore I have butt very small time to write but Mr Fisher is now writing the second part

---

[593] Thomas Fitch (c.1637–1688), building contractor, responsible for building wharves on the Fleet, Blackfriars, London, etc. (*ODNB*)

[594] William Windham's wife Katherine was the sister of Lady Townshend.

to the same tune. The coffee howse man[595] writt itt up to Sir Joseph Williamson.[596] The story you write mee is strange concerning *8*,[597] I had noe letter from ▽ soe I doe suppose he had nott spoken with *8* or had nothing to say. I pray you gett Mr Fits to com downe if possibly itt will advance my work to som purpose for the trading increaseth soe much and the shipping as itt is impossible butt I must now reap advantage on the other side or any that undertakes the worke. Jack Tasburgh who is now with mee desires to have his service presented to you. The clock strickes nine and I am nott ready therefore I must conclude that in all this progress where everyone had their liberty of lickquors nott a man was observed to be distempered; neither have I had halfe an one since I came into the country. I am glad deare Charles is well, present my service to my son & my daughter, and pray remember pore Robin's bill: I thanke you for all the variety of newse, all your children heere present their dutys, Betty has as much of beauty & witt as is possible & good nature to boot. God send good newse in your letter tomorrowe, I am

*Signed*: your affectionate servant, Yarmouth
*NRO: BL/Y/1/107*

## John Fisher to Rebecca, Viscountess Yarmouth

**1675, October 1, Oxnead**. Madam, on Michaelmas day at night I gave your honour a hasty accompt of my lord's most kind & noble reception at Yarmouth, which continued at the same heigth to the end, about one a clock yesterday when, after (breakfast as they called it, but more truly) a very great dinner for my lord & all the gentlemen with him, the old & new bayliffs & severall of the aldermen (who never left his lordship) we marched off in the same way & like parade as we came in (though not with so many horse), passing by a new great ship, just fitted to be la[u]nched as we came away, and thus we went along the market side of the town, the new bayliffs & sevrall of the townsmen riding before my lord's coach, & the old bayliffs with the knights of the town & others following my lord's coach, in their own, and without the gates, an honest gunner (who saluted my lord (at his allighting at the bayliff's dore) when he came in, with above twenty pottgunns[598]) bad his lordship farewell again with the like number, and thus we were sent away with a powder, which is one signall testimony of the affection of the town, but in truth, their extraordinary kindnes & love to his lordship was so fully demonstrated throughout their whole entertainment that 'tis hard to judge wherein they could possibly have exceeded it, for 'twas so hearty & unanimous, that there was not a dissenting brother in the whole body of the magistracy, nor a sower looke in man, woman, or child, throughout the whole town but all in as high a measure of rejoiycing as could be imaginable, and least my lord should not be satisfyed or well pleased with the variety of provisions, for which they had ransacked the earth, water & ayre, they would not let the fourth element escape,

---

[595] Richard Bower, government informer at Yarmouth, who sent regular information to the secretary of state (see *CSPD* between 1666 and 1683), and kept a coffee house for the better gathering of information.

[596] Sir Joseph Williamson (1633–1701), FRS, MP for Thetford, and secretary of state for the north

[597] This is the first instance of the Pastons using cipher and the only instance from 1675, making it impossible to decode.                                  [598] i.e. mortars

but before his lordship was quite risen from dinner, or just turning about from the table, for a fourth course, they brought in a man to shew his lordship the experiment how fier might be eaten without damage or hurt, for such whose stomacks were prepared for it, or were not satisfyed with those daynties we had received, but this countryman of ours gave us our fill of this immediately, & we left him to his own peculiar diet, nobody that I saw being willing to tast on't. But now I am got back again into the town, I must not omit their generosity in clearing my lord & all his followers of all charges for horsemeat[599] & other expences in the severall inns, which was an additional demonstration of their kindnes, & the more acceptable, by being unexpected. My lord would have gratified severall officers of the town, but we were informed, it would not be accepted, nor the offring it well taken, so his lordship ordered 5s to the servants in the bayliff's house where he lay & had received all their civillyties, & £10 more for the poor. And now I am got on to the deans again where, at the rayles, being the extent of their jurisdiction a mile out of the town, the old bayliffs & knights, with Sir William Adams & others, tooke their leaves of my lord, the new bayliffs & severall aldermen, justices &c riding on still a mile further to Caster (where we first mett them on Tuesday) & would have attended his lordship yet further, but that he [f.2] persuaded them to the contrary & there with mutuall embraces & a bottle of excellent wine, they sang Loth to Depart,[600] but by this time 'twas two a clock, & and the length of my lord's journy made us breake off, & so with their hearty good wishes for his lordship's health & prosperity, they returned back to the town, & we hastned hither, dropping Major Waldegrave & Mr Huby in their coach, when the way parted for Norwich, & severall others of our horsemen, where their wayes went off, Capt Harbord where we tooke him up at Coulshill bridge, & Capt Tasburgh (who presents his humble service to your honour) with some ministers & others attending my lord hither, whether we gat very safe & well (thanks be to God) by seven a clock last night.

I know my lord gives your honour his judgment of the temper of the town, as to his own affair there, which is not yet ripe for him to close withall, for as their trading increases (as it doth very much, they having augmented their shipping this year about eighty sayle) they wilbe the more straigthened for room within the town, & they have no addition but on my lord's side. Therefore my lord's opinion is, if Mr Fitch were there, he might be a great attractive to bring them in to better terms than they seem now to offer, which certainly is very probable & rationall.

My lord calls away for me to wayte upon him & Capt Tasburgh to Beckhall which makes me the sooner, with the presentment of my most humble service to your honour, take leave & rest, madam,

*Signed*: your honour's most faithfull servant, John Fisher
*Addressed*: These present to the right honourable the Lady Viscountess Yarmouth
*NRO: BL/Y/1/106*

---

[599] i.e. fodder
[600] A popular song sung at departures; there is a version arranged by Giles Farnaby (d.1640).

## John Gough to Rebecca Viscountess Yarmouth

**1675, October 1, Oxnead**. Most honoured madam, your honour had by Wednesday poste as exact an account of my lord's jorney to reception and entertainment at Yarmouth as Mr Fisher's and my own observations could make beeing put together. I know that my lord's attendance out of the country had been much greater if the ill weather had not prevented it, but as it was I know your honour will think it very well there beeing not lesse then threscore & five horse and three coaches that out of the country waited upon his lordship. The reception his lordship met with from the town of Yarmouth at Caster was as splendid as they could make it or as we could desire it; and the horsmen marshalled themselves in so very good order that made the appearance very glorious; when wee entered the town his lordship was welcomed into it with innumerable companys of the inhabitants crowding the streets, with bells ringing, & guns firing at every fort & from the ships. I told[601] to the number of seven & thirty great guns besides the five & twenty potguns discharged at his lordship's allighting & severall more from the ships in the haven. To be short madam (because your honour has before had as full an account as Mr Fisher's time would permit & wee could think of) the reception of his lordship was much beyond what ever any subject ever had from that town & so splendid that I could not see how they could have done more to expresse their affections. And yet which is most of all the chearfull meen of all faces & joyfull acclamations of the people at his lordship['s] entrance into the lodging destined for him shewed that all that was done was not barely artificiall & complementall but sincere & cordiall. The entertainment his lordship found was suitable to his reception, and they were not onely kind & respectfull to his honour, but testified their kindnesse to him in their liberality & kindnesse to all that were related to him, so that it was enough to entitle any person to the kindnesse of any of the town to say that he belonged to my Lord of Yarmouth. And this their kindnesse did not stop at men but descended to our very horses, they beeing all made a town charge by the order of the assembly as the bayliff told mee and wee in the evening found true. And madam, as the town on their part exceeded in generosity so all my lord's attendants were very respective & civill to them & not withstanding every one was at liberty to call for & might have what they would, yet I neither saw nor knew of any one that run into any excesse so as to dishonour God & to reflect any the least dishonour to my lord. The clergy I am sure who having a table prepared purposely for them, demeaned themselves with that great temperance & sobriety so as their enemyes could not blemish[602] them, even Mr Harly who thrust himself into the company, being advised by mee on the rode to keep a watch over himself for my lord's honour, was very carefull [of] [f.2] the counsell I gave him. When wee came away there seemed in all a generall satisfaction; they mightily pleased with their high steward & hee as well with them. His lordship was attended out of the town by the principall men of it, the new baylifs waiting upon him on horsback, the old ones with the knights *of the town* following his lordship's coach in <to> two coaches. A ship was just ready to be lau*n*ched at his lordship's passing by the haven. Five guns from the most northerne fort gave his lordship a farewell & the same five & twenty potguns

---

[601] i.e. counted          [602] i.e. discredit or defame

did the same without the Northgates. The knights of Yarmouth & the old bayliffs took their leave about the middle of the deans but at the bounds of their jurisdiction, the new bayliffs with severall aldermen and justices intending to waite upon my lord four miles further, were by *my* lord's interest prevailed with to return when they had accompanyed his lordship so far as Caster (the place where they <word deleted> *first* received him). There they wish't his lordship health & prosperity *in a glasse of wine* & so took leave. There is one thing that I must not omit of their great civility to his lordship which was this, when I enquired of Mr England (who is my lord's very great honourer) what gratuity would be proper & honourable for his lordship to reward the ringers & gunners with, he answered that his lordship was to be desired by no means to think of any such thing for the town having determined that his lordship should come to them without charge to himself, they had in their assembly appointed those persons a very good pay for what they did, but he added that what his lordship should think fit to give to the poor would be kindly received. So that my lord what he designed to bestow otherwise, converted into the poor's box & shewed his respects to the town & charity to them in a donation of £10 to them. Thus madam from this imperfect relation I have given your honour, you may be able to guesse at the great honour this country has done my lord. God grant it may end in his glory & the good of this noble family, which I am very sure it will do if your honour depend upon God in the use of lawfull & proper means for such an end. And as I do humbly advise & confidently assure my self that your honour will be diligent in the use of such means, so my prayers shall never be wanting that they may not faile of such an end. The young gentlemen & Misse present their duty to your honour. I crave my most humble service to Mr Paston & his lady & the little sweet gentleman, from most honoured & right honourable,

*Signed*: your honour's most dutifull chaplain & obedient servant, John Gough
*Addressed*: These to the right honourable the Lady Viscountess Yarmouth at the Golden Ball in Suffolke Street in London [*postmark*]
*NRO: BL/Y/1/108*

## John Hurton to Rebecca, Viscountess Yarmouth

**1675, October 4, Oxnead**. Madam, it will be needles[s] for me to give your honor an account of my lord's noble reception and entertainment at Yarmouth, it having been given already by one that could doe it much better. I shall only say, the expressions of that town were so full of love and honour to my lord, and of such exceeding kindnes to his lordship's friends and servants, as I cannot think the heart of man can desire more. I used the means to speake with Atwood's wife in Yarmouth, where I found her full of tears and lamentations for the sad and deplorable fate of her most unhappy husband. After I had discourst the busines with her, she told me nothing can be done in it till the bonds are paid, which she sayes amounts to near £5,000, but when those are discharged, she promises to doe all she can for your honor's satisfaction. What lies in me to doe shall be done: though I must confess my hope is in an extreme languishing condition for what has been told me by others, whose concerns are much greater in Atwood's ruine. This day I have been abroad about my busines, and at my return finding the house full of my lord's friends, I could scarce gain time to present these few lines to your honor, with the most humble duty of, madam,

*Signed*: your honor's most obedient servant, J Hurton
*Addressed*: These present to the right honorable My Lady Yarmouth at the Golden Ball in Suffolk Street, London [*postmark*]
*NRO: BL/Y/1/109*

# Susan Cooper[603] to Rebecca, Viscountess Yarmouth

**[*1675*], October 4**. Right honourable, I hope your honour hath by this received great satisfaction in my lord's entertainment at Yarmouth for by the relation of all it was extraordinary free & handsom, I know your honour hath the full relation of all but the pleasure I have in hereing make me so rejoyce that I cannot pass it by in silence. On Saturday last Sir John Hubbord[604] knowing my lord was from home came to give his vissitt, for his lordship went to Beckhall the day before, Sir John with all his prudence could not but think it must needs apeire as it was: done one purpos yet for all this my lord was pleased to <*word deleted*> think of returnning the vissitt this afternoone but I think his honour is prevented by verie much companie that did come in this morning as my Lord Richardson,[605] Sir Robert Yallop[606] & very many more; indeed I think it is noe reason my lord should returne such a visitt for shure Oxnead is much neerer then Rainnam for he could visitt there the last weeke for his lordship[607] lieth sick of the gout but the saing is fulfilled, burds of a feather will flock togeather, this day one of the knott brook loos[e] & sent my lord a presant of teall, it is Mr Smith who hath nether come nor sent till this day, I know your honour hath a much parfect*ter*, acount then is possible for me to give, for I am forst to write a line or two & then [*f.2*] begon therefore I beg your honour's pardon for the faults in this paper & what ever ells I have at any time bin flighty inn.

Mrs Paston,[608] Mis & the two gentlemen are very well, Mis & the two gentlemen desire thire dutys should be presented to your honour, Mis begins to be mighty wild but not such words as she had before. I thank God my lord is finly well & I belive is better then if his honour should meddle with phisick, haveing so much companie continually his lordship cannot a tall observe himselfe, he is very merry & when his honour had the flux it was not with grip[e]s so that I hope it may doe him good. Your honour is pleased to say my lord liks all things, if it be so I have great satisfaction for I desire to be noe longer at Oxnead then while I can give my lord & your honour content. I pray God give your honour health & so good end to all those great concerns as hath keept your honour now from Oxnead so that I may hope to live to se[e] your honour againe in Norfolk, this is the harty desire & prayers of, madam,

*Signed*: your honour's ever obedient servant, Sus: Cooper

---

[603] Susan Cooper, housekeeper at Oxnead. She and Francis Rawlins were the only two of his servants to be mentioned in Lord Yarmouth's will.
[604] i.e. Sir John Hobart          [605] Henry Richardson (1650–1701), 3rd baron Cramond
[606] Sir Robert Yallopp (1637–1705) of Bowthorpe          [607] Lord Townshend
[608] Mary 'Mall' Paston who had accompanied her father from London

*Addressed:* These for the right honourable the Lady Viscountess Yarmouth at the Golden Ball in Suffolk Street, London
*British Library: Add. MSS 27447, ff 347–349*

## Roger Flynt to Rebecca, Viscountess Yarmouth

**1675, October 8, Ludham**. Right honourable, amidst those many congratulations wherewith I doubt not but your honour hath bin saluted upon his lordship's safe arrivall and noble reception in this county, I should betray my duty of gratitude for your many favours if I should make no memoriall of the great occurrences in this place relating to your owne concernes. It would exceed the volume of a letter to declare all the particular kindnesses betweene his lordship & his country, I shall guesse at some passages wherewith your honour may be as yet unacquainted.

Had his lordship's comeing bin more publickly knowne, and not at such time as Starbridg Faire,[609] when most of the horses of the citty were out of towne, <I am assured> I am assured that the twoe hundred and thirty horse which attended him into the citty had bin multiplied to at least a thousand.

Soe soone as his comeing into the country was knowne at Yarmouth, it was determined in an assembly that both the bayliffs and one of the new-elects and halfe the aldermen should wayt upon his lordship at Oxnead, and invite him to their towne on Michaelmas eve, whoe were pleased to doe mee the favour as to call in at my house by the way, & his lordship did double the honour upon me, himselfe vouchsafeing me a visit in goeing to Yarmouth, whereof I doe not a little glory. I must not omitt the handsome treat which Mr Call gave him at Mautby where he largely testified his gratitude to soe honourable a patron.

From thence his lordship advances towards Yarmouth with a traine of about twoe hundred horse, and was mett at Caster by both the bayliffs new-elects, and aldermen with above twoe hundred horse *more* soe thatt when our forces were joyned together his lordship was conducted into the towne with very neare five hundred horse and eleven coaches. All the persons were of quality, the order of the cavilcade very decent and uniforme, the bells ringing and [*f.*2] gunnes merrily roaring from their forts all along as he passed by. He was conducted on the deanes side from the North-gate to the South-gate and from thence round by the keyside, from whence the gunnes out of the shipps did kindly thunder out their salutations; every one of which (being in number so neare as I can guesse, betweene seaven and eight hundred) did brave it in their flaggs, pendants and streamers, as allso the custome-house and many other houses of quality were all sett forth with the ornaments of the sea to wellcome his lordship to that place which he honours with his title.

And that all this may appeare to be somewhat more then an externall and formall ceremony that treble shout of acclamation which the people gave his lordship so soone as he appeared out of his coach did declare the vigorous soule of joy which was in the hearts of all the people. He arrived at the new-elect's house, Mr Thaxter, now bayliff, whoe indeed expressed very great affection to his lordship and much satisfaction in the election of his lordship to the high stewardshipp of that towne. Truly

---

[609] Stourbridge fair, Cambridge

madam, I did with some curiosity observe the faces of the beholders, and could not discerne the least shadow of a cloud in the eye of any one person, but all the people abundantly satisfyed and over-joyed at the presence of his lordship.

Their treating his lordship at their feast was ample and splendid such as became them to give, and I hope was pleasant to his lordship to receive.

On Michaelmas day his lordship went to church, and by the way at the towne-hall was received by the bayliffs, aldermen and common councill men, all in their habits; and there presented with his burgesse letter of freedome in a handsome silver boxe, which should have bin better, if they had had any better artist.

The next day after breakfast, his lordship takes his leave, and was conducted out of the towne with the old bayliffs as farre as the uttmost limitts of their jurisdiction, and by the new with a considerable number of horse as farre as Castor, where was a most kind parting betweene his lordship and the towne whoe excused themselves because being fishing time they could doe noe more; which yet was so much as I protest I never saw the like given to any subject in my life.

In my private discourse with divers of the aldermen, I find so much satisfaction given to the towne by his lordship's deportment that I doe not doubt but a short time will produce some good effects out of [f.3] this mutuall kindnes on the other side of the haven: some overtures are allready made wherewith I have acquainted his lordship and whereof I doe hope your honour will shortly heare more.

And now madam, I doe presume to assure you that the eyes and hearts of the whole county are so fixt upon his lordship that whensoever he shall have any occasion to make use of their service, he may be assured of any thing he will please to command.

Now the God of heaven powre downe his blessings upon his lordship and your selfe, and your honourable family in this life, and augment them to eternity in a better. So prays, madam,

*Signed*: your honour's most humble and obedient servant, Ro: Flynt
*Addressed*: Humbly present this to the right honourable the Lady Viscountesse Yarmouth at the Golden Ball in Suffolke Street, London [*postmark*]
*NRO: BL/Y/1/110*

## Margaret, Lady Bedingfeld, to Rebecca, Viscountess Yarmouth

**[1675, October].** Madam, I am sory my letter writt in haste should be so slowe a coming as I find by yours of the 30th, which I had the honor to receave by the hand of the <hand> favorite of Norfolk, who I must bragg was our gueste, though to his lordship's sufferance in all kinds, I had mine in beeing deprived of the felicity of hearing his stories, beeing just deaf as I was when you were in the country; two or three days after I heard again, and have not bin so deaf till now, which in one more *considerable* might be imputed to witchcraft, but I submitt to mortification. Now in earnest madam, I think my lord came downe in the criticall time, and I wish from my harte that you and the King's grantchild with the father and mother (who I begg may find my humble servis) had bin all here togather that you might have seen what a generall disposition of kindness there was in the people to my lord. I think you should do well to have it told att courte as newse what a lovefitt the country is fallen into to my Lord of Yarmouth, but this not to come imediately from yourself, but rather to seem coole in it. What passed at Yarmouth I shall not need to repeat, the canons were loud enough to reach to London. Many thanks for the concern you had of my sonne and husband; in what place soever they are, all the servis [*f.2*] they are able of doeing is but to whisper to all persons what worth, what witt my Lord of Yarmouth is master of, with the sweetness and candide nature, truth and constancie to his freinds, then perswade them to compare him to others, where they find the contrary very transparent. My lord hath not had the fortune to be knowne enough, but those that hath his true caracter, lett them refuse to love him that can.

On Fryday Sir Phillip Woodhouse[610] and Sir Jacob Astley with other gentlemen came on purpose to waite upon him. The Dean also with much respect who bro*u*ght a present of oisters; I expected divers of a lower form who was desirous to come, but were kept of by a false alarum that we were full by my Lord Townsend beeing here, and it seems he sayd some such thing to Mr Rawlins that he would have mett here, had not the goute hindred him, and that goute was one reason I took to perswade my lord to send, for I must confess madam it was my fault if any, my lord's sending thether, but I am confident he will be no looser by it, but put the two Sir Johns to new consults. To goe himself had bin below him, but this sending whilst he wore the laurell on his browe is but *to* triumph in a civill way. I could give you more <more> substantiall reasons, if fitt for paper, but I hope you will believe none studys more my lord's and your ladyshipp's [*f.3*] reputation then madam

*Signed*: your ladyship's humble servant and kinswoman, M Bedingfield
*Postscript*: My husband presents his humble servis to your ladyship
*British Library: Add. MS 27448, ff 212–213*

## Edmund Thaxter and Thomas Bradford to Robert, Viscount Yarmouth

**1675, November 22, Yarmouth**. *The common council was highly pleased with his letter of thanks for their reception.*

*Signed*: your lordship's most humble servants, Edm: Thaxter, Tho: Bradford, bayliffs
*Addressed*: For the right honourable Robert, Lord Viscount Yarmouth att Westminster, London, these
*NRO: BL/Y/1/111*

## John Gough to Rebecca, Viscountess Yarmouth

**1675, November 26, Yarmouth**. Most honoured madam, I intended when I came hither to have been at home last night & thence to have writ to your honour where I might have been better accomodated with instruments of writing then I now am. I went to Norwich on Tuesday last & beyond expectation & contrary to the generall report I found that Mr Jay[611] was then alive but in great danger of death upon which

---

[610] Sir Philip Wodehouse (c.1608–1681), 3rd bt, of Kimberley
[611] Christopher Jay (c.1605–1677), MP for Norwich

account men were busy to make partyes underhand in order unto a new election. There were three persons in nomination *viz* Mr John Hobart,[612] Alderman Paine,[613] & Alderman Bendish; no mention in publick discourses of Sir N.C.[614] who yet had great endeavours used on his behalf in private; now I presume the prorogation of the parliament (if the recovery of Mr Jay does not) will hush such discourses for a time. On Wednesday Dr Hildeyerd & my self set out for this place & got hither by night. All people seem<ing> *to* continue in the same heat of affection & honour for my lord as formerly, & their respects so far as I can learn rather grow then decrease. The letter his lordship *sent* met with an extraordinary kind reception as I am confident your <are> *honour* is not now to be told having learnt it *already* from the return the town have made to it, which I doubt not but his lordship has some dayes since received. The great kindnesse my lord expresses to them & the offers he has made to serve them has put them upon thinking upon some advantageous motion to make to him, & they have fixt upon a businesse wherein they will crave the King's favour by his lordship's intercession of which his honour will hear in due time. All persons we have visited shew us a great deal of kindnesse. I know tis upon account of the relation we are in to his honour & I doubt not but we shall meet with the same dealing from the person we are to visit this morning, whom as soon as we can get free of we are for Oxned, from whence your honour shall hear more by Munday poste, beeing now so straitened in time as only to adde that I am,

*Signed*: your honour's most dutifull chaplain & humble servant, John Gough
*Postscript*: The doctor presents his humble service
*Addressed*: These to the right honourable the Lady Viscountess Yarmouth at the Golden Ball in Suffolk Street in London humbly present
*NRO: BL/Y/1/112*

## John Gough to Rebecca, Viscountess Yarmouth

**1675, November 29, Oxnead**. Most honoured madam, in my last from Yarmouth I omitted to acquaint your honour that in our journey thither we called at Mr Flint's hopeing to have enjoyed his company, but hee beeing at that time from home wee were faine to go without him; and though we fully intended to have seen him in our return back yet Mr Bayliffs kindnesse kept us at Yarmouth so long that we could not possibly do it without being benighted home. The expenses we were at in this jorney I defrayed my self finding Brown not much inclined to put it upon account, and indeed I was not very urgent for it beeing a little sensible of the reckonings hee makes when they are paid that way, and yet though he had ready money his bill for one man and three horses (for the doctor & I did not eat & scarce dranke in the house all the time) for the space of one whole day & <three> *two* nights came to £1 2s 4d, a reckoning so unreasonable that I shall not be very ready to commend anyone to the house & were I perfectly at liberty should scarce be induced to go *to* it myself. This with two shillings we gave away at the places of our entertainment comes to £1 4s 4d which I have disbursed & shall scarce get Mr Hurton to repay mee without your honour's order.

612  John Hobart, MP for Norwich 1654–1660, called 'Commonwealth Hobart' by Lord Yarmouth.
613  Miller, 'Containing Division in Restoration Norwich', p.1027          614  Sir Nevill Catelyn

On Friday night I came home & met with your honour's letter to which I can make
no other return then that I had heard of the prorogation of the parliament to the
mentioned time but could not perceive at Yarmouth any thing of disrelish of the
people at it, onely they seemed concerned that there was no Bill pass't for encreasing
the navy. It was generally thought that so long a prorogation was but a prelude to a
dissolution, which should it happen I hope this country will take care that they bee
not overreacht again by the tricks of the caball. The pretences of some persons' avers-
nesse to stand are here lookt upon but as pretences many beeing of the mind that the
two Sir J's[615] will joyne interest for knights of the shire, possibly Sir R will sit still
having pretty well paid for stirring already. I am glad to understand your honour's
indifferency in relation to [blank] it is a matter in my judgment of great weight &
deserves a most serious consideration. I do not question but Yarmouth will be found
very kind & whether they will not take it ill that any aimes should be another way
when my lord had bespoke them I leave to your honour's consideration. If you fix
that way there must be great care in pitching upon a second knight such as the
country may have some liking *to* otherwise the party may be disunited & occasion
given those that watch but for such an opportunity. The letters after perusall I sealed
& sent according to direction yesterday. I could not seal them with the arms of the
family none here having such a seal, but borrowed an unknown seal which I set on
them. Mr Flint by the messenger has returned an answere which I send this poste;
Mr Wharton was taken ill on Saturday. Major Doughty is at Norwich & I have his
returned back but will send it inclosed in a new paper with a new superscription by
the poste this night. I crave my humble duty & service to my lord & be pleased to let
him know that I will send the book by Mr Lant who comes for London
on Thursday next. My most humble service to Mr Paston whom I will serve
with all zeal & affection if their be occasion, to his lady & Mrs Paston, from right
honourable,

*Signed*: your honour's most dutifull chaplain & most humble servant, John Gough
*Postscript*: I wish your honour could make sure of Mr Bulwer before he comes out of
town.
*Addressed*: These to the right honourable the Lady Viscountess Yarmouth at the
Golden Ball in Suffolk Street, humbly present [*postmark*]
*NRO: BL/Y/1/113*

## John Gough to Robert, Viscount Yarmouth

**1675, December 8, Oxnead**. My lord, by my letter to your lordship this day se'n-
night I gave you a breif account how affairs stood at your town of Yarmouth, &
withall by the same bearer sent the book your honour desired, both which I doubt
not have come to hand before this time. Our news here in the country is little or
none, people seem generally dissatisfied that the parliament should quarrell themselves into a prorogation at this time when the condition of the kingdome in respect
of its navall force required their assistance, for want of which they fear at Yarmouth

---

[615] i.e. Sir John Hobart and Sir John Holland

the Dutch at sea will be too strong for us, the French almost equall us & both much endamage us in our trade. The parliament men are now coming down, Sir John H is expected at Norwich tomorrow & intends to keep his Christmas there. Here was a report that Sir William Doyly was dead but hearing no more of it I conclude it to have no more truth in it then that of Mr Jay. The very mention of Sir William's name puts mee in mind to intimate to your lordship a businesse wherein you may extreamly, I think, oblige the town of Yarmouth. Tis my lord in a money matter due to the town for wounded men & seamen's widdows wherein Sir William Doyly is concerned[616] & from whom they have a long time in vain expected payment of it, but have never been able to get above £200 & now there is almost a thousand due. By the non-payment Sir William has much lost himself & I am very confident could your lordship procure it 'twould be one of the greatest obligations you could lay upon them. The town indeed looking upon it as an affair too mean for your lordship's notice will not move you in it but if your lordship could with convenience effect it 'twould be the more acceptable for beeing voluntary, & would <*word deleted*> without doubt gain you much honour respects & affections from the inhabitants of all conditions; but I know not whether your honour can without prejudicing your own affairs stir in it & therefore I do but only move it & your lordship may do as you think fit. My lord, before I conclude this letter I must request your lordship to bestow upon mee about thirty young oaks which I would plant at Swanton; I would have begged some few ashes too but finding your stock of those is brought so low I should be very rude & undeserving to mention it. The young gentlemen & Misse are in health & present their duty to your lordship & my lady, to whom I crave my most humble duty & service who am, right honourable,

*Signed*: your honour's most dutifull chaplain & obedient servant, John Gough
*Addressed*: These to the right honourable the Lord Viscount Yarmouth at the Golden Ball in Suffolk Street in London humbly present [*postmark*]
*NRO: BL/Y/1/114*

# Owen Hughes[617] to Rebecca, Viscountess Yarmouth

**1675/6, January 17, Norwich**. Madam, this address may seem too late, when I consider the mighty obligations your ladyship has placed upon me, but your goodness is such that you imitate heaven thereby, that accepts of duty and services, when hearty, at any time: I protest unto your honor, such are all my devotions to you, and only such are worthy the lady, who is the great patroness of merit and virtue, and compassionates the unreasonably and unduely oppressed with the influences of an excellent nature and noble disposition, a kind of sympathy and resentment: this (madam) I early discovered, which indeed rendered me somewhat bold and confident in the frequent applications I made to your ladyship: yet I found by the best experience that I never had cause to goe out of your ladyship's presence but joyfull, easy and better satisfied than before; which gives me reason to beleive that this countries primitive hospitality

---

[616] Doyly was one of the commissioners for sick and wounded.
[617] Dr Owen Hughes, bishop's commissary in Norwich and Norfolk archdeaconries

and debonair humor seeme only to survive in your noble lord and your self, for none can be met with, or heard of elsewhere; and tho possibly from better hands your ladyship has been informed of the transactions and affairs of this place, I humbly begg your ladyship's pardon, if I faile in the account I am about to give because, beeing too much upon the stage, modesty perhaps or partiality may be objected against me: I have formerly acquainted your ladyship that for beeing loyall, and appearing against the phanaticks I had enemies round about me, and especially what an inveterate and causelesly malicious adversary I had raised up against me, one Turkington[618] a parson; which puts me in mind of the old saying, corruption of the best is the worst; he had his first incouragement from Dr Pepper,[619] a man of equall principles, parts, and reputation with himself, whome he promoted to be surrogate, that he might have a more convenient station to affront and abuse me, and whereunto he gave him commission, and indeed he did it sufficiently the last generall court at Licheham, and was commanded thereunto by my Lord Townshend, which Turkington owned and declared in the face of the country at the sessions last Wedensday morning: after many insufferable provocations I caused that daring and insolent fellow (tho he was countenanced by the civil magistrate to fly in the face of the ecclesiastical) to be bound over to his good behaviour. When he appeared I mooved the bench to take cognizances of the cause, and to heare the evidence: which assoon as they pretended to doe, I had a view of their partiality and design; for when the first witness begann to speake, it was ordered that the depositions <were> *should be* taken in writing, a new devise, foreign, and nere practiced before in that place: but the design was to daunt the witnesses, and to see whether by their testimonys they could advance the action against me of *scandalum magnatum*,[620] God be praised they failed in both; for the four witnesses, who were all grave, worthy and stout clergymen, gave as convincing, manifest and clear evidence as could be given, and all good, and indifferent men that were then present asserted that they never heard fuller and plainer. Sir John Hobart espoused the quarrell, and made it my Lord T[*ownshend'*]s but first in open court Turkington delivered him a letter, which he read behind Sir Robert Baldock's[621] back and would *not* answer to his name the six or seaven times called before he gave the letter into his own hands: his good worship was the only man that plyed me with language, but God knows very little to purpose, the great improovement of his rhetoric consisted in the [*f.*2] kindred distinction between my politic and personal capacity, *viz* that the abuse was upon Hughes, not the commissary or officiall, or the justice, which cunning distinction was the occasion of the best [*sic*] King's martyrdom, and of Sir John's advancement to be a lord,[622] to which when I was ready desperately to reply, Sir Robert Baldocke, who is now one of the tribe, proposed *it* as a point of weight and

---

[618] John Turkington (d.1698), vicar of Gateley and rector of Horningtoft

[619] Dr Robert Pepper (d.1700), chancellor of Norwich

[620] Defamation of a peer was called *scandalum magnatum*; Lord Townshend had commenced an action against Hughes in the House of Lords in the previous November (*Journal of the House of Lords*, volume 13, 15 November 1675). Hughes had apparently said that Townshend was 'an unworthy man & acts things against law & reason' (NRO: NNAS C3/1/9/12). For further letters from Hughes, Pepper and Turkington *see* NRO: MC1601/33, 46, 61, 76; *see also* Rosenheim, 'Party Organisation at the Local Level', p 719n).

[621] Sir Robert Baldock (1625–1691), recorder of Great Yarmouth

[622] Hobart had been a member of Cromwell's 'other house'.

prudence, that they should doe well to defer the debate of that buisness untill they had dined and then resume it in the chamber where they *were* then to be: which after they had done a very little time, the grand result was, that Turkington was bound over without good cause, and that he was to be dismissed forthwith, without giveing any acknowledgement; nay Sir William D'Oyly was of opinion that he should be dismissed, because a clergyman with reputation; meaning perhaps that they ought to thank him for abusing and affronting one whome the Lord T[ownshen]d had called without cause sawcy and pragmaticall[623] fellow. I was forced to be my own advocate, and whether I said to purpose your ladyship will heare time enough. The whole story of my Lord T[ownshend']s treating me at his house was openly repeated by Turkington, which insted of his defence he was advised unto immediately before, and the words that are laid to my charge declared: viz: that I said my Lord T[ownshend] is the unworthiest patron of the clergy, if he commanded Turkington to abuse and affront me openly as he did, and then added that my lord in his own house called me sawcy and pragmatical fellow, and commanded me out of his house, out of his dors, but mentioned not the least tittle I gave my lord of provocation. When the leading men gave their opinion, most by far of the other[s] followed, those that said nothing gave consent by stupid and unmanly silence, whereof some of the wisest have protested to me that I had very hard measure: and now since the Lord T[ownshend's] pleasure has influenced the (or rather his) justices against their own honor and reputation at sessions, only because I was concerned, what must I expect from a jury at the sessions? I am unjustly accused and prosequuted, therefore shall not be afraid to stand it to the last. Madam, if the power continues in the hands it is, wee are not like long to use our reasons, or assert our liberties and birthrights; the proceedings are growing soe arbitrary that justice itself is to seek for habitation amongst us; wee must be flatterers and idolaters if wee expect common favors: our prospect is, as if wee were beginning the foundations of a heptarchy in Norfolk; the actions of one side are soe exorbitantly high, that it will not endure the least chec[k], and of the other soe meane and low that wee seem to submit thereunto: the Presbiterian faction, that most dangerouse and restless sort of mankind, behave themselves as tho they *were* killing and takeing again possession; and my little misfortune at sessions they take as a sign and effect of their power and interest. It is openly affirmed that the Lord T[ownshend] is not the man he was, and it may be Sir John has confessed him to reformation or the opinion of some of his greatest relations: but when Sir J. comes to have his prayers heard, and to be lord againe, the regall honors must truckle to the Hogan Hogan Mogan[624] preferments of a Commonwealth. But there is one honorable person left of Norfolk, that may be made the great and happy instrument of our salvation and his sacred Majesty may yet here secure himself thereby, and he may free the countrie from pride and oppression [f.3] and can your ladyship goe a neerer way to celebrate and aeternise your family, name and memory! Methinkes I allready see day appeare, and am all hope; how can I doubt when your deare lord is a stepping to govern the [word illegible].

---

[623] i.e. officious or meddlesome

[624] A corruption of the Dutch 'Hoge Mogenden', i.e. 'High Mightinesses', the title of the States-General. It was used as a humorous or contemptuous term for those of humble origins holding office and affecting grandeur.

In the mean time our grandees are upon a more considerable attempt which may better be called a subject of revenge, and as far as I can guess thereby design to lessen the power of *the* King, and the influence and common priviledges of the court, and withall infringe a statute by their too forward subscriptions: and all this because against the Lord T[*ownshend's*] approbation, Mr Pell was lately made high sheriff of Norfolk: to effect this design they have mustered from all parts all such as are lyable and capable by reason of their estates to undergoe that office, to subscribe to such and such propositions; that they may be noe more imposed upon by the courtiers, and put upon unnecessary charges, either to get themselves of[*f*], or if they hold to have their expenses defrayed by reason of the intended contribution, to which they have procured allready about thirty subscribers;[625] the tenor of their subscriptions is this: that if any one of the subscribers or their heires shall for the future be made high sheriff of this county, there shall be coach and horses provided for him, thirty men with darke stuff liveries, lined with blew, hatts and saddles proportionable; at the sheriff's table if any eat the ordinary is to be 4s a meale, the liveries to be renewed every third yeare, soe that the sheriff must be a gainer if he be a subscriber thereby: soe that if his Majesty intends in some measure to mortify one that he suspects, or a phanatick, by making him sheriff, they subscribe it shall not be soe, wee will beare him out; if the courtiers design it, they oppose and practice against it. If a non-subscriber, or one that has not listend to the address of Sir John, and Sir John has a cause to try either at sessions or assize, by the correspondency they have with one another, and the power they have over all justices both the sheriff beeing beforehand menaged, it is very unlikely, be the cause ne'r soe just, it should goe for such a one, besides it is not considered how tenants may be disobliged thereby, who usually had the liveries after they had served at both assizes; and it is strange that so many wise men should ingage to be at the expense of £5 or £6 yearly to gratify and doe a kindness (probably) to some that they *are* nothing related unto, and noe way acquainted with: especially they themselves being a far of[*f*] from the pretended danger: but I feare there is more in the design then I can fathom: God knows, what may be done upon occasion with the militia and *posse comitatus*, the subscribers by these (I doubt indirect) means allways securing both in their hands: I pray God grant the King and his Councell resolution and courage, wise and understanding hearts, that all contrivances against them may be searched into and timely prevented, that the overthrow of church, king and state, law and liberty may not again happen in our daies.

Madam, all yours at Oxnead are very well, I presumed in Christmas time to take some diversion there a day or two, I should yet joy in Norfolk were it consistent with my good lord's and your ladyship's occasions to make most of your residence in that pleasant and stately place. The bishop is as well as he has been these many yeares, and is like to continue still disapointing.

---

[625] Townshend had attempted to have John Pell excused from the expensive and time consuming office of high sheriff of the county. When this was unsuccessful and Pell was appointed, Townshend organised a group of local gentry to enter into an agreement to subscribe towards the sheriff's expenses (*HMC, Lothian*, pp 122–124). Although the subscribers included, as well as a number of future whigs, several men who later served as deputy lieutenants under Lord Yarmouth, the subscription was seen, particularly by the high Anglican clergy, as highly partisan and possibly illegal. (Rosenheim, 'Party Organisation at the Local Level', pp 713–722); Miller, 'Sir John Holland', pp 864–65).

Madam, I have now presumed too much on your ladyship's incomparable patience, I humbly therefore begg pardon, and hope that your excellent temper, rare charity and eminent goodness will not long continue [?]me under censure and mortification, and that because oppression [*sic*], all worthy and honest men are possessed with the just respect they have for the grandeur of his genius and what is in your bosom (madam) that may restore us to our witts and selves again. God workes ordinarily by means and naturall causes, therefore now if ever solicitation and importunity too are necessary and I know your ladyship can soe well menage both, that they will be judged the products of prudence and pious zeale, of honor and resolution. Madam, I glory in the title of beeing

*Signed*: your ladyship's most obliged and devoted servant, Ow: Hughes
*Postscript:* My most humble service to my good lord, and the truly virtuous <madam> *lady* Mary Paston
*NRO: BL/Y/1/115*

## John Gough to Robert, Viscount Yarmouth

**1675/6, February 28, Oxnead.** My noble lord, beeing to preach at Norwich on Friday last, that task hindered mee from writing to your lordship this day sennight as I thought to have done, but to make recompence for that impediment my beeing there furnish't mee with some unexpected matter to fill up this letter. For I happened there into <som> *some* company who did talk very confidently of a great peice of news which I could then scarcely tell how to beleive, though I understood it very well notwithstanding its beeing veiled under Arcadian names. Twas that the great Demagoras[626] was fallen under some great displeasure of his good king in so much as he was in danger to be deprived of the office he held & to be brought a peg lower, & that Philanax[627] was like to succeed in his room; the former I understand has received a confirmation by the last pacquet boat, but of the latter I hear no certainty though men are very inquisitive now to know. And indeed I perceived the company spake it rather as what they hope then what they had then any certain ground to beleive, and for the love I have to loyalty & consequently to the name of Philanax I do joyn with them in their wishes & shall be glad to hear that a person whose very name speaks him to deserve so well may be honoured with such a trust. This my lord for forreign news. Our news at home is that we have now orders to return to my Lord Archbishop[628] the number of the inhabitants in our severall parishes, & the number of all dissenters under what name soever they passe, and this to be done by Easter when the bishop does intend to visit his diocesse himself (which is more then he hath done these severall years & which the great indisposition of his flock too much wants) & see that these orders & others of the church be carefully executed, which proceedings put us here in a great deal of hope that the cloud that has been sometime upon this poor distracted church will, through God's mercy & his Majesty's great wisdome & care, in some little time be blown over. I am very sorry that my Lady

---

[626]  Lord Townshend          [627]  Lord Yarmouth, who was appointed lord lieutenant on 6 March.
[628]  Gilbert Sheldon, archbishop of Canterbury; however the moving force behind this census was Henry Compton, bishop of London, and it is known by the latter's name.

Danby's gentleman met with such cold encouragement in his journey to Oxnead, but it was such as no foresight of ours could have prevented, we coming home in the night knew not any thing of his beeing sent till the next morning, nor never heard any thing of his disaster till on Saturday following Mr Robert Doughty sent mee a letter to tell mee of it. And it beeing then to[o] late for us to make an apology for it here in the country, my lady being gone the Friday before for London, I let your honour know it by my last letter to my lady that what was needfull might be done in it, and having done thus what I could I hope neither my Lady Danby will be displeased nor your honour damaged by an accident which <nothing> *no care* could have prevented. My lord I'le be no further troublesome then to beg my most humble service to my lady, Mr Paston & his lady & to Mrs Paston, wishing you from my heart an affluence of blessings here in health honour prosperity & comfort <here> & blessedness here-after which that God in his mercy would grant is the constant & fervent prayer of, my lord,

*Signed*: your honour's most dutifull chaplain & humble servant, John Gough
*Addressed*: These to the right honourable the Lord Viscount Yarmouth at the Golden Ball in Suffolk Street in London humbly present
*NRO: BL/Y/1/116*

## Robert Doughty to Robert, Viscount Yarmouth

**1675[/6], March 6, Tuttington**. My lord, last night I received your lordshipp's letter of the 2nd instant for which I retorne my most humble thankes. On Saturday last I mett with many of your lordshipp's hearty freinds in Norwich, on the after-noone, the cheife of them retired themselves to a private chamber where they debated the present state of Norfolk's affaires, and out of the great honour they have for your lordshipp, commanded me to offer itt to your lordshipp, as their humble request, that your lordshipp would please to suspend your positive determination concerning the continueing of old deputy leiuetenants & commanders till your comeing into Norfolke & have had an account of their deportments & have seene their faces, least itt should render his Majesty's service & your lordshipp's honour att too cheape a rate, by admitting such as will never bee cordiall or faithfull to the just interest of either, and to acquaint your lordshipp that it's their sence that if Shaftesburyes freinds Sir John Hobart, Sir John Holland &c <you> should bee by your lordshipp made deputy leiuetenants or collonells, you would fix in them a stronger interest then ever they yett had, to the discouragement of the loyall party & your lordshipp's firme freinds, and the ill consequence that may ensue thereby your lordshipp may easly foresee, nor doe they thinke itt safe that any person who have lately appeared of Shaftesbury's party should bee in commission of the peace, hee being as ill thought of here as att Whitehall. The fanaticks seeme generally dissatisfyed & feare they shall not bee soe kindly used as they have been, th'other party cry out they are glad to see the King is King of Norfolk againe. My lord, the change seemes to most & the best very gratefull & by your lordshipp's courage & prudent management all the opposite combination will drop asunder like a rope of sand. They begin already to see that your lordshipp will have more persons that are your hearty freinds then you can find imployments for. Norwich & Yarmouth were very hott for bonefires & ringing of the bells, butt the prudenter sort of your lordshipp's freinds did not thinke itt convenient.[629] May itt not bee convenient your lordshipp should write a letter to the bayliffs of Yarmouth <&> I know itt will bee kindly taken. I shall give your lordshipp noe more trouble att present butt that I am att all commands,

*Signed:* your lordshipp's most devoted servant, Robt Doughty

*Postscript:* Pray my most humble service to my Lady Yarmouth. If my L[ord] [Townshend] doth not take his chastisement humbly here is a spiritt will innumerate the extravagances [of h]is government.

Mr Warkhouse[630] tells mee hee intends to write to your lordshipp this post.

[f.2] It's reported the L[ord] T[ownshend] is turned out for tyranizeing *in* his country, caballing with Shaftsbury, Sir S. Barnediston sr. Most beleive the whole story true & condemne him exceedingly. Some are infidells & will not beleive his caballing because as they say hee has offered to forsweare Shaftsbury & all his works &c: it's likewise reported L[ord] [Townshend] is appointed deputy of Ireland, butt comes downe to settle his affaires in the country before hee goes upp to take his command. Dr Hughes is to give a justyfyeing plea & the good men of Yarmouth promise to prove itt without other helpe. Sir John Hobart declares hee will goe to Thetford assizes to drive on the combination.

*Addressed:* For the right honourable Robert Lord Viscount Yarmouth att his lodgings in Suffolke Streete, London [postmark]

*NRO: BL/Y/1/117*

## John Gough to Rebecca, Viscountess Yarmouth

**1675/6, March 8, Oxnead**. Most honoured madam, it is scarce expressible with what raptures of joy the news of my lord's promotion is received by a great many persons in this country, the prisoner could not more welcomly receive a release from his fetters, nor the slave with more joy hear of his redemption, then they do of the change of the leiutenant of the county & that his Majesty has been pleased to place that trust on so honourable a person from whose loyalty & justice they do & very well may promise themselves the preservation & promotion of the King's interest, & the countryes rights & priviledges. And in so universall a joy I must be both stupid & ungratefull should I not bear a part seeing my relation to so honourable a personage & my certain knowledg of his great worth & merit, makes it an act both of gratitude & justice to do so. And I am sure in relation to this most fortunate event I am defective in neither, as I ought not so I will not give place to any in rejoycing & thankfulnesse to God for his great blessings to this family & particularly for the honour his Majesty has in this last act conferred upon it. None with more heartinesse wished, with more earnestnesse prayed, for your honour & happinesse *than myself* & now such a great accession of honour has befallen you, none with more pleasure delight & comfort resents it. And though I do not seem so forward publickly to expresse it in a letter of congratulation to you yet I must entreat your honour to impute that to that

---

[629] i.e. suitable or appropriate

[630] John Warkhouse, attorney, was Doughty's son-in-law (Blomefield, *Norfolk*, VI, p.279).

great extasy & ravishment that the confirmation of the news in my lord's Saturday letter put mee in which was so great that I could not take my thoughts in any kind off from it & so wholly took possession of my mind that I had much adoe to settle my mind to my sermon on Sunday or to return an answere to my lord's letter on Munday. But madam, though all your own family your friends & the loyally disposed party of the county are joyfully affected with the news, yet there are not wanting those that are dejected at it. The fanatick party at Norwich are much dissatisfied & they say begin to cry out popery (God knows with how little reason) & it's feared that there are some who underhand encourage them to it & do cunningly instill into them idle jealousyes & fears. It is said though I cannot assert it upon my own knowledge that Sir [John] makes it his businesse to dissuade men from taking commission under my lord, and that he has been with several [f.2] persons for that purpose, and as if that were not enough to satisfy his malice I hear that his zany Mr H[erne]⁶³¹ rides up & down to put people into fears & to worke them into discontents & disaffections to my lord, but as I doubt not but his lordship's conduct will confute their storyes & defeat their aims so I hope his lordship's speedy coming into Norfolk will put a stop to their ill & unhansome practises. The young gentlemen & Misse are very well & present their duty to your honour. Mr Thomas has been a great while very good & is mighty studious & industrious, indeed he now deservs commendation & it would be injustice not to let him have *it* & your honour may be pleased some way or other to take notice of it for his further encouragement. I have no more but to crave my humble duty & service to my lord & to say that I am, right honourable,

*Signed*: your honour's most dutifull chaplain & obedient servant, John Gough
*Addressed*: These to the right honourable the Lady Viscountesse Yarmouth at the Golden Ball in Suffolk Street, London, humbly present [*postmark*]
*NRO: BL/Y/1/118*

## Sir Henry Bedingfeld the younger⁶³² to Robert, Viscount Yarmouth

[*1675/6*] **March 13, Oxborrow**. My lord, I cannot unridle the meaning of soe large reports of your succeeding my Lord Townshend, and that neither from your lord-shipps nor by your order I should have any notice; my lord being assured that letters are intercepted I have secured this by a private cover and begging your lordshipp's pardon for the freedom of speech I desyre this letter may bee burnt and not kept amongst your papers, and from henceforth I shall signe instead of H:B: Thomas Blunt.

My lord, pretending business att the assises I thought I might doe your lordshipp some service by discovering the behaviour of our countye men att this great nick of change, and I hope it will bee acceptable to you to know, first,

That undoubtedly Sir John Hobart and Sir Robert Kemp's partye are designing

---

⁶³¹ Clement Herne (d.1694) of Haveringland; through his mother he was a cousin of Sir John Hobart, and he was one of his most ardent supporters.
⁶³² Sir Henry Bedingfeld (c.1636–1704) the younger, of Oxborough

all micheife to supplant your influence on the county and debauch most part of the deputie leiftenants and milicia officers to refuse future comissions in a compliment to my Lord Townshend. [*f.2*] Their act of subscription is much fortifyed and the Prester Jacks[633] have putt itt into a method for future practice which certainlye will conduce to the advantage of succeding shreifs of that fraternitye.

I found all out of the pale of presbitrye infinittlye satisfyed that your lordshipp is our governor, but the aforesaid partye cannot conceale their affliction, nor some of them from muttering that the Church of England and the papist joines to the suppression of other dissenters, Sir John Hobart drol[*l*]ed[634] much with me in the interest I have in your lordshipp, my Lord Treasurer and Mr Coke, my replyes I hope were modest itt being my business to prevent their plotting, and discovering their temper which I am sure I effected.

My lord though I doubt not of your lordshipp's putting all into a good posture yet I hope you will not bee displeased if I speake my foolish opinion, first that your lordship would consider a litle before you dispose of comissions, and if itt might bee secure not to displace Sir John Holland yet, but with all kindness draw him to you whereby he might desert [*f.3*] the other partye and this you may doe by making his peace at court for his foolish speech[635] and I am persuaded he would bee much joyed to redeeme his creditt, he is soe considerable a man with the vulgar as his sooden departure may influence the reckoning of discontent. Sir Robert Kempt and others will dye att my Lord T[*ownshend's*] foot, but lett them goe.

If your lordship wants comissioners I have two or three neighbours I willinglye would ingage to your service. I begg you would nott displace Mr Le Strange[636] clerke to the leiftenantcye till you have well weighed the employment or spoke with me.

My lord I should bee most joyfull to serve your lordship but I feare itt's only from my closett, my qualification[637] denyes my entrance any where else, and my loyaltye and seale to the court renders me odious and suspicious to the countrye, besydes the honour of your lordship's kindsman and friend makes my Lord T[*ownshend's*] partye to look on me as if they had the collik, but my lord I am at all times readye to performe what your lordshipp shall comand.

*Signed*: My lord, your obedient servant & kindsman, H:B: junior
*Postscript*: My humble dutye I beseech your lordshipp to my ladye
*British Library: Add. MSS 27447, ff 503–4*

## Robert, Viscount Yarmouth to Rebecca, Viscountess Yarmouth

**1676, March 28**. My dearest deare, after the misfortune of parting with you wee have had none this day, eleven of the clock brought us to Hoggsden,[638] and five & an half to Littlebury, Mr Fisher having calculated all to a minute, att Littlebury I had

---

[633] i.e. the two Sir Johns: Prester John was an oriental king in mediaeval legend.
[634] i.e. jested or joked                                                  [635] Above p.14n.
[636] Edward L'estrange (1640–1715), son of Sir Nicholas L'estrange of Hunstanton. He subsequently became a personal friend of Lord Yarmouth; see their correspondence in the British Library, Add. MSS 27447, 27448, 36988. Those volumes of Paston letters also include Yarmouth's original letters to L'estrange, with postmarks, which cannot have formed part of the Oxnead muniments.
[637] He was a Roman catholic.                                              [638] Hoddesdon, Herts

a visitt from Mr Lucy, my Lord of Suffolke's steward & Mr Sayer[639] the King's cooke, Mr Lucy having brought too exelent bottles, wee first celebrated his Majesty's & then your health, neare Bishop Stafford[640] wee mett my Lord Townshend's horses driving up to bring him downe. Som too howres after our arrivall, & pleasant enough passing our time, coms in Robin with the box soe long looked for, & my scarfe & Dr Lake's[641] books which I thanke you for remembring & I hope I shall use for my owne satisfaction. My equippage I thanke your care was noble, every body well fitted, my horses both for coach & saddle in exelent plight, and have performed there journey exeeding well. Just now I have supped with good boyled beefe, veale & pulletts, and am now going to bed, to morrowe morning you shall know how I slept for I will nott close my letter till then, butt Mr Fisher desires mee now to present his service. I hope you have seen my Lord Treasurer before he coms out of towne, however I know you'l see my Lady Danby & promote my request of his seeing Oxnett. I pray present my service to my son & daughter, & to Sir [f.2] George Wakeman.[642] I hope they have this day prosecuted the method agreed on as the business amongst us & att least left som farther impressions on my Lord Treasurer's promises to us before his comming away in which I am sure Mr Brent[643] will bee assiduus to fix it to all intents & purposes for att the very present wee can hope for noe more morall security then wee have till the King's returne. Thus much for this night butt pray before I sleepe lett mee not forgett my dayghter Mary whome God preserve.

And now I bid you go[o]d morrowe having nott slept very well butt according to the usuall rate of [?]mine I have given Robin Pysar a crowne of my owne benevolence, and att London promised him a badge to weare as my porter which I desire Wickes the goldsmith may make him. You shall heare from mee againe as soone as I can, soe *adieu* for I am just entering the coach, my horses all well, I am for ever

*Signed*: yours to death, Yarmouth
*NRO: BL/Y/1/119*

## Robert, Viscount Yarmouth to Rebecca, Viscountess Yarmouth

**1676, March 29**. My deare, this day has beene as propitious as the first dayes journey, I passed Newmarkett without stay where Sir Will Doyly's son & Mr Lane his brother in law[644] came to meet mee & Mr Peckover[645] informed that my cozin Coke, Sir Edmond Bacon[646] & Captaine Coke[647] were gon before to Barton Mills to bespeake my dinner & to dine with mee soe I went on and there mett them where they stayed for mee with much civility about five of the clock or half an howre before I tooke my leave of them they returning to Newmarkett and I comming on for

---

[639] John Sayers, master cook of the King's kitchen, d.1683    [640] Bishops Stortford, Herts
[641] Probably sermons by Dr Arthur Lake (c.1567–1626), bishop of Bath and Wells
[642] Sir George Wakeman was physician-in-ordinary to Queen Catherine and a Roman Catholic. He was later accused by Titus Oates of plotting to poison the King but made a strong defence and was acquitted. He seems to have been one of Lord Yarmouth's proposed partners in the expected farm of the excise, see p.207n below.    [643] Robert Brent [?of Lark Stoke, Gloucs], possibly a secretary of Lord Danby
[644] Mr Lane of Watlington in Northamptonshire    [645] A gentleman servant of Lord Yarmouth
[646] Sir Edmund Bacon (d.1685) of Thornage, Norfolk, and Redgrave, Suffolk
[647] Captain, later Sir, William Cook of Broome

Thetford; about three miles from thence I was mett by young Sir Henry Bedingfeld & Sir Thomas Garrett[648] who are now with mee drinking your health att Thetford, tomorrowe I heare Sir John Holland will meet mee att Larling ford,[649] Sir Will Doyly with severall others att Windham and they tell mee above too thousand horse in a body will carrie mee through Norwich. You shall have an accompt of all by the first post. I was received heere by the corporation in their formalityes & the bells ringing. I have now noe more to say resolving to bee [f.2] in the coach by seven in the morning & the post is now gooing of [f] soe that I must seale my letter with the services of all with mee. My horses have traveled rarely well hetherto & noe disaster. My service to all my friends, I am to the last breath

*Signed*: your most humble servant, Yarmouth
*Addressed*: These present to the right honourable the Lady Viscountess Yarmouth att the Golden Ball in Suffolke Street, London [*postmark*]
*NRO: BL/Y/1/120*


## J. Hurton to Rebecca, Viscountess Yarmouth

**1676, March 29, Oxnead**. Madam, my lord's reception the last time though very noble is believed to be no way comparable to what this will be. The countrey seems ambitious to pay his lordship very much honour and respect. As for the sullen fanatics let them goe by themselves, I'm confident here will be no need of them. Mr Bulwer has alwaies shown a very great honour for my lord, and I know not how to doubt of it. My accounts shall be quickly ready; glad would I be, your honor would be as quickly here to examine them. All possible care is taken to content my lord, and if all things be not to his lordship's mind the fault shall not be mine, for I have resolved to contribute my best care and pains to that end. I would be exceeding glad to pay Mr Gough and all men els, but while expences run at this very high rate, all the money that can be raisd upon Lady rent[650] will never answer them, and to doe such other things as of necessity are to be done. However I have paid him £10 upon your honor's importunity, I hope that will satisfie him till we are able to doe more. For the town of Yarmouth, I had occasion to be lately there, and to speak with divers of the principall and divers others, and can say I found them to express very great kindnes and honour for my lord: one of the chief aldermen having great plenty of wine, I went to, to buy a tun of it, but he said he had none good enough that he would commend it to my lord. It was a piece of integrity I was much taken with. I think I have taken notice of every part of your honor's letter, and shall now only say a word or two of Mrs Cooper. Yesterday she was in much better condition then she has been in since last Wednesday night which is now a week, in all which time she never was out of her chamber, save that on Thursday morning she would needs goe to chapell, as I said before, but was fain presently to goe to bed. This last night she could take

---

[648] Sir Thomas Garrett or Garrard, 2nd bt, of Langford
[649] Larling is at the ford of the river Thet and is twenty miles from Norwich. The inn, the Angel, made it a convenient place for the gentry to rendezvous and form a cavalcade to welcome the lord lieutenant.
[650] Rents were often paid in two instalments on Lady Day (25 March) and Michaelmas (29 September)

no rest, which I perceive has much indisposed her; yet we all hope the worst is past. I am, madam,

*Signed*: your honor's most obedient servant, J Hurton

*Addressed*: These present to the right honorable My Lady Yarmouth at the Golden Ball in Suffolk Street, London [*postmark*]

*NRO: BL/Y/1/121*

## Robert, Viscount Yarmouth to Rebecca, Viscountess Yarmouth

**1676, March 31, Oxned**. My deare, from Thetford I presume you heard from mee and yesterday morning foure miles from thence mett mee Sir John Holland whome I tooke into my coach and carried as far as Attleborough, wee discoursed matters with great civility butt still to the point of the letter formerly written butt protests never any thing went soe neare him in his life as to thinke that prejudice may bee layed upon him on a score where he intends candidly: att Attleborough Sir Francis Bickley[651] mett mee with his coach whome I carried too miles further in mine and soe parted. Sir Phillip Woodhowse sent his sonns to Attleborough from thence all along personns of quality mett mee and about three mile from Norwich I was mett first by Sir Will Doyly's coach & Mr Suckling's who was the kindest man in his salutes in the world, Sir Austine Palgrave[652] & Sir Carlos Rich the stokin man[653] & his son a very handsome young man on horseback, and then the bishop's coach with the chancelor & his chaplaines and five or six horses of his servants with pistolls, abundance of my cosin Cooke's tennants and then five & forty coaches with the prime of the gentry, abundance of the clergy and som fifteene hundred on horseback, a world of people on each side of the way and Norwich streetes soe thick crouded on both sides that the coaches were long a passing, the balconies were crammed and all the windowes and a generall shout from one gate to the other the trumpetts before mee and my sumpter and all my servants looked very well, the mayor[654] and aldermen on the guild hall in the markett, to tell you truth itt was beyound expression and had the [*f.2*] King himself beene there he could nott have beene more honored then his commission; by my coach side by the mayor's appointment foure of the towne beadles in liveries attended the side of my coach to keep of the croud who stood six rowes deep in most places and the markett cross soe thronged that I never saw a greater concourse which gives mee an evident testimony that I have an interest in my country. Austine Briggs who was there has sent mee a most handsom complement. I did expect to have found more blue men[655] then I doe, Mr Bulwer mett mee beyound Norwich, Sir Will Doyly and his son are now with mee, he is my steady friend and I honor & love him of his owne accord he told mee I must make Sir Jacob

---

[651] Sir Francis Bickley (d.1681), 2nd bt, of Attleborough

[652] Sir Augustine Palgrave (c.1629–1711), of Norwood Barningham

[653] Sir Charles Rich of London, of the Mulbarton family, probably accompanied by his son in law Sir Robert Rich of Roos Hall. The Rich papers in the Folger Shakespeare Library contain an agreement between Charles Rich, hosier, and John Wells, framework knitter of stockings, whose stock he has bought, 1672 (X.d.451 (28)).                    [654] John Manser (d.1694)

[655] i.e. looking depressed or dismayed

Astley lieftennant colonell of the horse, he beeing major before. I intend tomorrowe to send to my Lady Anne[656] for my coz Coke has shewne mee all the civility he can & Peckover is left att Newmarkett purposely to give mee warning as soon as my Lord Treasurer's intentions appeare. Yesterday's encounter was enough to have elevated an ambitious hart butt I was soe weary of the sport that I never was soe glad in my life as when I was gotten to Catton hill where I aleghted and saluted everybody though many were turned of before, till I was ready to drop downe and with riding bare headed soe long I have gotten a cold. When I came home which is the sweetest place in the world had I money to make itt <soe> a little finer, I found my children & Mrs Cooper pritty well and they with the gentlemen are now taking their pleasure to see an otter hunted in the pond whilst I borrow this time to write to you. I am glad the sick lady[657] will bee my friend & that you thinke she may have power to shew itt, I should [be] glad to heare that they gett any opportunity on Tuesday to speake to my Lord Treasurer about the business amongst us or if nott that they keep itt in warme clothes till his returne. I wish my Lady Clayton would gett mee creditt [f.3] for a sute of brisk[658] hangings for the roome over the little parlor and that they might be sent sent [sic] downe by the first carts, [?]Ridges is now att Holcom furnishing the dining roome for a lodging for my Lord Treasurer soe very little is the howse in receipt, I have many melancholy thoughts coms over my spiritt som times. On Sunday God willing I shall receive[659] and on Tuesday or Wedensday bee sworne and I hope proceed with that vigilance and circumspection as to shew every body I will be just & civill & I find by Dr Hylierd & Mr Doughty now with mee that all my friends approove the methods I chuse, I resolve to heare all & governe myself. My service to my daughter Paston & my son & Charles & the little one,[660] would you were all heere, pray God make the sick lady's words true, pray keep a friend of Mr Brent, my duty to your mother & my service to all my friends, I am with the greatest passion in the world

*Signed*: yours, Yarmouth
*Postscript*: Your children present their duty. Betty's ravished with her things butt her coat is somwhat too little.
*Addressed*: These present to the right honourable the Lady Viscountess Yarmouth att the Golden Ball in Suffolke Street, London [*postmark*]
*NRO: BL/Y/1/126*

## John Gough to Rebecca, Viscountess Yarmouth

**1676, March 31, Oxnead**. Most honoured madam, the account of my lord's reception into his country I'le there begin where my Thetford letter ended. Between five and six of the clock on Wednesday evening Sir Henry Bedingfield junior & Sir

---

[656] Lady Anne Coke (1657–1722), daughter of the earl of Danby and his wife Bridget Bertie, cousin of Lord Yarmouth. She had married Robert Coke of Holkham in 1674.

[657] Probably the duchess of Portsmouth who had recently miscarried but went to Newmarket to support Lord Danby in a 'falling-out' with the duke of York (HMC 6: 7th R.I., p.467), and see p.206 below.

[658] i.e. smart or cheerful, although the word is more commonly used to describe people.

[659] i.e. the sacrament

[660] Lord Yarmouth's granddaughter Charlotte who was born on 14 February 1676

Thomas Garret in a coach with their attendants well mounted, Sir William Doily's second son & his son in law Mr Lane, Mr Lestrange, Mr Doughty & myself set out of Thetford toward Barton to meet my lord, & by that time we had gotten about two miles on that rode we joyned his honour's coach & after congratulating his honour's health & advancement we mounted again & conducted him to the inne, where his lordship was received with the ringing of the bells, the town musick, & the magistracy's complements upon the occasion. Thursday soon after seven we set out of Thetford, Sir Henry Bedingfeld beeing in my lord's coach & his own following empty & Sir Thomas Garret on horsback, *who* some *space* out of the town took his leave beeing obliged to be that day at Newmarket. Before we came at Larlingford Sir John Holland came in & having with a great deal of civility accosted his lordship was received into my lord's coach & his own followed. Here Sir Henry B left my lord at this time not thinking fit to go so far as Norwich in company for some private reason though he formerly, as he told mee, had thoughts to do so. We had Sir J['s] company to the inne at Attleboro where after Sir Frances Bickley was come in his coach to waite on his lordship Sir J took leave & in his coach returned to Quidenham. Finding at Attleboro that by the time of the day we should be earlier at Norwich then his lordship's appointment was the night before, which I gave notice of by letter to Major Doughty that night, his honour was pleased to stay there near two hours. Soon after twelve we set forward on our jorney, Sir Francis Bickley riding in my lord's coach & his own following. Two miles distance from that town Sir F took his leave & returned home & about the same time & distance came in Sir Phillip Woodhouse's sons on horsback to make their father's excuse & to attend my lord to Norwich. By that time we got to Windham we had increased the number of our horsmen to above thirty, & understanding by some of them that we were yet too early his lordship ordered to drive very slowly. At which rate of procedure when we had got <Eaton> *Cringleford* on our backs his lordship was saluted by half a dozen coaches & severall gentlemen on horseback. The coaches were old Sir William Doily's & his son's, Sir Charles Harbord's, Sir John Pettus's,[661] Sir Thomas Riche's and the dean's of Norwich. Some distance from them other coaches at severall times met us as Mr Aid's,[662] Mr John Harbord's, Mr Peck's & last of all, the bishop's of Norwich with his chaplains in it & severall of his servants well mounted & with pistolls & holsters. All this time our number of horsmen as well *as* of coaches encreased & such a cloud of dust was raised that I could scarce hold open my eyes, & yet we were not come within sight of the main body of the gentlemen that came to pay their service to my lord. But about a mile & half from Norwich we came at them, where first stood the coaches to the number of about thirty four in very good [*order*] & the owners of them by to complement his lordship in his passage; then of gentlemen on horsback a very great number who were marshalled in rank on each side as *we* went only leaving a way between them for his lordship's coach & retinue. As soon as his lordship was pass't the coaches they struck in in good order & followed but by the forward zeal of some horsmen, they were at first put into some confusion, but before they came [f.2] near the citty by the great pains of Major Doughty & Captain Cook they were marshalled

    [661] Sir John Pettus (d.1698) of Rackheath was a second cousin of Lord Yarmouth; his mother was a Knyvett.        [662] John Ayde of Horsted whose wife was one of Lord Yarmouth's Knyvett cousins

into a very becomeing order, they went four a breast generally, the gentlemen leading the van, then the clergy amounting to near an hundred, then the sherifs of Norwich with some of the aldermen & their attendants & lastly my lord's servants imediately before the coaches, all the other coaches to the number of forty four following my lord's. The horsmen were computed altogether 1500. The train of horsmen & coaches was so long that many were out at Maudlin gates before all the coaches were in at St Stephen's. The streets & windows & balconyes of the citty were all crowded with spectators, the market place particularly so full that we could scarce passe it & there the mayor, aldermen & common councill in their formalityes attended his lordship. As his lordship's coach pass't by, the streets rung with acclamations of people to welcome his honour, as well as the steeples with the sound of bells. When we were got quite through the citty some of the horsmen went off at Maudlin gates. The greatest part with all the coaches came near Catten & there wish't his lordship health & well to Oxnead. Six coaches attended him further, but as their rodes parted broke off so as but three of them came quite home, Sir William Doily's and his son's two & Major Doughty's the third. Many horsmen of the neighborhood to the number of thirty or more came home and supped here. My lord (God be thanked) came very well home & with as much honour from the country as he could wish. It did so much rejoyce mee to see it as that I scarce was my self & I wish to your comfort that your honour had been a spectator that you might not have been beholding to the defects of my pen for this relation. Which as far as my memory & informations serve mee is a true one & madam, I can adde too a very modest one, I beeing not willing to write the rambling reports of all, but speak what I truly think without lessening the countryes kindnesse or stretching any thing beyond the bounds of truth. I conclude madam with telling your honour two things which my lord having in his letter forgot commands mee to write. One is that your honour would out of the hogshead of nog draw <and> as many bottles for the use of Mr Paston's lady as shee shall desire, his lordship beeing willing shee should have it since shee has a liking to that <the> kind of drink. The other is to desire your honour that my lord's commission for the viceadmiralty now in Mr Bret's hands to be sealed may with the first <the first> opportunity be dispatched hither. No more, but my most humble service & the assurance that I am, right honourable,

*Signed*: your honour's most dutifull chap[*lain*] & humble servant, J Gough
*Addressed*: These to the right honourable the Lady Viscountesse Yarmouth at the Golden Ball in Suffolk Street in London, humbly present [*postmark*]
*NRO: BL/Y/1/122*

## Sir William Doyly to Rebecca, Viscountess Yarmouth

**1676, March 31, Oxnet**. Madam, this brings your ladiship the welcome newes of my lord's safe arrivall last night at Oxnet. He was mett on the roade by severall gentlemen of eminent qualitie in divers places, but more especially betweene Wimundham and Norwich in which trayne I was, and about forty coaches more fild with gentlemen of the best rank, together with about fower scoare clergymen and above a thousand gentlemen on horseback, who roade in good order before my lord through the citty. The streets, the windowes and balconyes were strangly[663] fild with spectators, soe that from without the citty towards Windham, and through the citty in every street till my lord gott almost to Catton, every place was fild, in my whole life I never saw (excepting only at the King's coming in) a greater parade, many shouts and great acclamations weare made, every man rejoycing and the ladyes makeing their curtesies, which my lord answered with low civilities (as having beene their old servant) bare headed, this hath given his lordship a great cold, and more wearines, and least I should be offensive to your ladiship, Ile humbly take leave to remaine

*Signed*: your ladishipp's most humble servant, Will D'oyly
*Addressed*: To the right honourable the Lady Viscountess Yarmouth at her lodging at the Golden Ball in Suffolke Street, humbly present these
*NRO: BL/Y/1/124*

## John Fisher to Rebecca, Viscountess Yarmouth

**1676, March 31, Oxnead**. Madam, the happines of our first two daies journy, your honour hath received from my lord's own hand, & the noble reception that my lord found into this country yesterday, is so fully related to your honour in this inclosed from Sir William D'oyly, that I can make no addition to it, yet I cannot satisfy his lordship without putting your honour to the trouble of taking off this cover, before you can reap the satisfaction of so welcome a relation, wherein Sir William is not only too modest in expressing the method, number, & splendour of that extraordinary appearance (because his own kindnes went farr in the contrivance of it) but may make your honour's apprehension of the journy my lord received by the gratefull returns he made to the civillitys of so vast a company, to be greater than in truth it is, whereby my lord tooke a little cold, & was hoarsh upon it this morning, which is so much abated in eight hours distance, between the writing of Sir William D'oyley's letter and this, that it's plainly discernable it will not stick at all by his lordship. Severall gentlemen have sent to his lordship today, to know how he is after his journy, but Sir John Pettus only came & Major Doughty to dine with his lordship today, most being willing to adjourn their visitts till after Sunday be past, that they may not disturb his lordship in his preparations against that day, whereon 'tis publiquely known he intends to receive the sacrament. I shall not trouble your honour further at this time, but with the presentment of the humblest service to your honour of, madam,

*Signed*: your honour's most faithfull servant, John Fisher
*Postscript*: I must not forget the particular kindnes of my old master & his family who came with five coaches yesterday to meet my lord, & Sir Charles himself is just now come in to afford my lord all the assistance he is able in his best advice, whosoever happen to fall off, in this ticklish time of tryall.
*Addressed*: These present to the right honourable the Lady Viscountess Yarmouth at the Golden Ball in Suffolk Street, London post [*postmark*]
*NRO: BL/Y/1/123*

[663] i.e. greatly, remarkably

## Susan Cooper to Rebecca, Viscountess Yarmouth

**[1676], March 31**. Right honourable, the generall joy I se[e] for my lord's coming to Norfolk fills me so with gladness that I beg the leave to wish your honour joye too, I hope now it will not be long before your honour will compleat all & come downe to Oxnead for my owne part I cannot I cannot [*sic*] think it comepleat till then.

Mis[s] & the gentlemen desirs me to present thire dutys to your honour, I have received all thire things except one sute of coleburtine[664] for the gentlemen. Mr Rawlins finds he hath but owne & two suts of laist.[665]

I hope my lord will pardon all that he hath meet with amiss for now it pleaseth God to give me a little more health nothing but my lord & your honour could a made me doe what I have done though it is very little. Be pleased to give me leave to returne your honour my humble thanks for my most fine peticoat, I vallue it much the more because it was your honour's. My time is short thirefore I beg your honour's pardon & leave to subscribe my selfe allways, madam,

*Signed*: your honour's ever obedient servant, Sus: Cooper

*Postscript*: Here I send your honour a note of what puter[666] I received. I think here is a very sivell man for a porter when his cloaths is sent downe thire should be a porter's stalf[667] likewise for there is none to be had at Norwich

*Addressed*: These for the right honourable the Lady Viscountess Yarmouth at the Golden Ball in Suffolk Street, London [*postmark*]

*NRO: BL/Y/1/125*

## M[argaret, Lady] B[edingfeld] to Rebecca, Viscountess Yarmouth

**1676, April 2**. Madam, I hope your ladyship has received satisfaction in the relation you have had of my Lord Lieutenant's triumphant passing through Norwich. I wish his detractours had but seen how filled the streets, doores, windows were with persons of all ages and sexes, the very high wayes and hedges were lined with men: and they tell me that there was so many gott uppon trees for a sight of my lord, that the poor boyes hung on bowes together as moles. That all may be the better known at Newmarkett, wee have this day sealed up in a letter Steevenson's[668] verses, that whilst they are new the King migh[t] have a sight of them. I hope their mouths are pretty well stopped for lying, the very night before, t'was reported at Norwich that none would meet my lord but the papists with the rascallity of people: and in this corner of the country that if Sir Henry B[edingfeld] did not drive them his owne self none would goe, but they'le find my lord can stand on his own bottume, and besids gentlemen had those they call substantiall men which carrieth most sway: many more he would have had if the justices had not sett that very day uppon busines, a mess of chief constables wee lost and at least fifteen more such by them, which vexed me and made everything els uneasy, but your ladyship's two letters were cordials especially

---

664 Colebertine was a kind of crocheted lace on a squared ground.    665 i.e. lace
666 i.e. pewter (with a Norfolk accent)    667 *recte* staff
668 Matthew Stevenson (d.1684), poet, author of *Norfolk drollery* etc.

that which had your secreet in't, which I swere madam I will never open my lipps of, but to pray that you may have many more such, in the meane time you had need to be thoroughly armed with patienc[e] to stay till the fruitt be full ripe for if you should strive to gather before, your harvest may be the less worth. Our three neighbours things are pretty well, the game must be played with care every were. My lord will have account of all tomorrow by my husband who is as well as my selfe,

*Signed*: your ladyship's humble servant, M:B.
*NRO: BL/Y/1/127*

## Sir John Holland to Robert, Viscount Yarmouth

**1676, April 3, Quidenham**. My lord, I acknowledg your lordshipp's favour in that tender regard you have expressed in all your proceedings, notwithstanding my early declared resolution against all engagements in relation to the militia; but I doe with truth profess, that since his Majesty have beene pleasd to appoint you lord leiutenant, I doe now declyne the service with much regrett, having a very quick sense of my obligation, being soe neerly related to you in bloud, & having received soe many evidences of your affection, but never a cleerer then your lordship's so kind *and frendly* carriage towards me upon the present occasion, which can never bee forgotten & your lordship shall find that I will alwayes have honour for you; & bee pleased still to preserve your wonted affection & favour to, my lord,

*Signed*: your lordship's most faithfull & humble servant, J Holland
*Addressed*: For the Lord Viscount Yarmouth, Lord Leiutenant of the county of Norfolk
*NRO: BL/Y/1/128*

## Robert, Viscount Yarmouth to Rebecca, Viscountess Yarmouth

**1676, April 3**. My deare hart, on Saterday morning Sir William Doyly left mee after he and I & Sir Charles Harbord and Major Doughty had consulted som methods in order to my affaires, I retired into my chamber & stirred nott out that day, though Mr Arminger[669] & Mr Spelman[670] & another gentleman came hether. On Sunday I received the blessed sacrament & prayed for you & my pore family, I doe expect Sir Henry Bedingfeld today for he writt to mee on Saterday that he would com, on Saterday I sent Rawlins with a complement to Holcom to my Lady Anne who was pleased to receive itt very civily and my Lady Bridgett & my Lord Dunblane[671] who is very well againe and gotten on horsback that day; my Lady Anne is mightily commended for her kindness & goodness to her neighbors, and Mr Arminger tells mee is certainely with child, hee is one of her nearest neighbors and frequently there. On Wedensday I am to goe to the sessions to take the oathes in the morning & to dine with the justices of peace and if I heare intelligence of my Lord Treasurer's comming

---

[669] William Armiger of North Creake
[670] There were branches of this West Norfolk family at Narborough, Congham and Holme.
[671] Lady Bridget Osborne, later countess of Plymouth, Peregrine, viscount Dunblane, and Lady Anne Coke were children of Lord Danby, the lord treasurer.

shall goe on towards Holcom, the sessions must be adjourned to whitsun week by my motion that the deputy leiftenants may have time to sweare and nott bee surprised for from this week should itt determine is neare three monthes to the next sessions, I shall see all faces that day how they looke for which I shall nott bee concerned if I spy a blue man or too. I am infinitely glad to heare what you tell mee between ▽⁶⁷² [*Lady Danby*] and you, pray prosecute those affections for I knowe noe reall instances butt from thence though *13* sett the wheles att work itt is an exelent game you play if itt be acceptable and you can performe itt to bring *36* into friendship with ▽ [*Lady Danby*] & *88*, and I am glad to hear that *88* and *36* who I looke upon to have a contriving head doe promise such friendship & such handsom thinges. You may be sure that upon good occasion *600* [*I*] will bee ready to com att few howres. [*f.2*] I am very glad that ▽ [*Lady Danby*] will encourage *60*, if soe the business will certainly take which cannott depend any longer then midsummer, butt I have nott one word from any of the partys concerned to whome I pray present my service especially to my couzin Peregrine Bertie⁶⁷³ & his lady, desire H[*oet*]⁶⁷⁴ to write to mee, you never speake a word whether *8* will bee att Newmarkett.

Present my service to my son & daughter Paston & pray lett my daughter draw of what bottles she pleaseth of the nogg for she spoke to mee of her lickeing itt before she came away, remember mee to pritty Charles & Charlotte. Mrs Cooper is well againe and therefore there needes none of the matters you spoke of besides I must bee up & downe & shall nott settle till you com. I am now going abroad into the park to take the ayre and shall nott close up my letter <till> untill I have seene Sir Henry Bedingfeld with whome I shall nott forgett to discourse what you told mee.

Pray write mee word if *9* or *6* or *50* will doe as you would have & whether upon *700*'s [*your*] motion ▽ [*Lady Danby*] thouht itt might be considerable to ✧ [*my Lord Treasurer*].

Young Doughty⁶⁷⁵ that is my secretary I could nott have beene better fitted in England for besides his writing a very good hand and understanding the law perfectly he is an handsom respective man & a creditt wheresoever he comms.

Sir Henry Bedingfeld presents his service to you, he has transmitted the whole relation to Yarmouth⁶⁷⁶ of my reception to those that will both shew itt my Lord Treasurer & the King, all other thinges he will performe to his best power. My cousin Windham, Jack Tasburgh, Major Waldegrave, Mr Moutham & others doe now drink your health.

[*f.3*] I have now noe more to say butt that [*I am*]⁶⁷⁷

*Signed*: your most aff[*ectio*]nate servant, Yarmouth
*Addressed*: These present to the right honourable the Lady Viscountess Yarmouth att the Golden Ball in Suffolke Street, London [*postmark*]
*NRO: BL/Y/1/129*

---

⁶⁷² This cipher is used from April to August 1676; there is no key extant but it has been possible to identify those persons whose names occur frequently. See appendix 1.

⁶⁷³ Peregrine Bertie (c.1635–1701), deputy searcher of customs, London, 1676–1783; he was Lord Yarmouth's cousin, and a brother of Lady Danby (Henning, *Commons*, I, 644–645).

⁶⁷⁴ Peter Hoet was a London merchant.

⁶⁷⁵ John Doughty, son of Major Robert Doughty of Aylsham

⁶⁷⁶ *? recte* Newmarket                                                    ⁶⁷⁷ Paper torn

# Robert, Viscount Yarmouth to Rebecca, Viscountess Yarmouth

**1676, April 5, Norwich**. My deare hart, by the paper you will find I am in a taverne where I dined with the justices of peace after having in the sessions publickely taken my oathes. Wee were forty att dinner, amongst whome Sir John Hobart & Sir Robert Kemp who with great civility came to mee and with as much expressions to mee as was possible for civility to express have declined what I as civily by another hand tendered. Sir John Holland writt mee a very civill letter to the first tune, Sir Phillip Woodhowse, Sir Jacob Astley, Windham & the rest stick to mee soe this week I shall give out commissions to the deputy leiftenants, and then together proceed to the setling the militia in such a way as I hope will give content to the King & country. The business you write I shall hint to *19* [*Sir Henry Bedingfeld jr*] somwhat of what your letter to day sayth which was delivered mee on the bench by Mr Newton, but I must before hand tell you that if *15* goes out ✧ & ▽ [*my Lord Treasurer & Lady Danby*] designe *4000* comming in and soe *600* [*I*] shall disoblidge ✧ & ▽ [*my Lord Treasurer & Lady Danby*] in striving against the streame butt those prickes you will feele best att London; *19* [*Sir Henry Bedingfeld jr*] nor *24* [*Sir Henry Bedingfeld*] have noe interest in the point you hint butt if any thing were that way Sir George Wakeman were a proper person by one I have hinted to him that has appeared my friend in ⊗ family I know *19* [*Sir Henry Bedingfeld jr*] & *24* [*Sir Henry Bedingfeld*] have personall civilityes to *15* & soe has ⊗ therefore itt's a nice matter to touch yett I shall make my discourse as I find itt proper. I wonder I heare yett nothing of my Lord Treasurer's comming into Norfolk yett Sir William Doyly tells mee he heares my lord will bee att Holcom on Friday night, as I have intelligence I shall moove on to Beckhall. They have promised to send to informe mee besides Peckover att Newmarkett is to com as soone as any certainety appears. I am sorrie the lady I left sick coms nott into the party from whose nobleness [f.2] much might bee expected yett *700* [*you*] having don such a peece of service may rationally expect that *36* who is discreet & *6* may doe *600* [*me*] som service in som point or other. I have this day gotten pore Oakes a pension of £15 a yeere and £7 10s advance in hand. I am gooing now to give the bishop a visitt & soe hoome againe to my sweet howse. Pray present my service to my daughter & my son & to Charles & the little one & to my daughter Mary. You may now tell ▽ [*Lady Danby*] that the three personns are out[678] butt I would nott have carried itt otherwise then I did for £100.

All heere presents there service, young Doughty is the most fitt for the place in the world, Mr Fisher presents his service who has beene very usefull to mee & I thinke perfectly honest. One of Sir John Hobart's reasons was why he desired to accquiess his having contracted <an> a great debt his beeing opprest with a sute for half his estate upon which the last Thursday writts of ejectment were served on the tennnants & his having beene once so unfortunate in the regiment he has as if my Lord Townshend had continewed he thought to have quitted it. I must confess he behaved himself civily, soe did Kemp & Sir John Holland & I am nott very sorry itt coms of soe.

[678] i.e. Hobart, Holland and Kemp

I have now noe more to say butt that you love mee soe well which I prize above all other thinges. I hope the 𝒦 [*the excise*]⁶⁷⁹ business will doe & that the partys concerned are sedulus in itt. Adieu till the next post, I am

*Signed*: your most passionate servant, Yarmouth

*Addressed*: These present to the right honorable the Lady Viscountess Yarmouth att the Golden Ball in Suffolke Street, London

*NRO: BL/Y/1/130*

## Robert, Viscount Yarmouth to Rebecca, Viscountess Yarmouth

**1676, April 7**. My dearest hart, the last accompt you had of mee was from Norwich. I onely made the bishop a visitt which was most kindly taken of him & his lady, the pore man is in great paine somtimes butt I doe nott see butt that he may live som yeares. From thence I went home, where yesterday I received your deare letter which is the pleasure of my life. I am surprised with the kindness of ▽ [*Lady Danby*], and att the policy of *600* [*myself*] pray God send a good issue, I have written this inclosed to my Lady Danby, pray seale itt with your owne seale and lett itt bee sent the same night itt comes to your hands.⁶⁸⁰ This morning comes in a messenger from Holcom with six barrells of pickled oysters from my Lady Anne Coke butt my cousin Coke told mee att Barton Mills he had ordered them for mee, in the steward's letter which came along with them I find my cosin Coke nott com home butt watching the motion of my Lord Treasurer as I doe (which the letter sayth is uncertaine) & soe to goe meet him att Holcom, I beleeve your intelligence is best & that he will bee there on Saterday com sevenight. *19* [*Sir Henry Bedingfeld jr*] & *24* [*Sir Henry Bedingfeld*] have given an accompt to ⊗ of *700* [*you*], butt as to the business of *15* I thinke itt most improper for their hands I can make use of them att any time & you find by ▽ [*Lady Danby*] that if I should interfare with *4000* or ▽ & ✧ [*Lady Danby & my Lord Treasurer's*] designes for any body itt would fall ill upon *700* [*you*]: Sir Peter Gleane⁶⁸¹ has written [*f.2*] a wonderfull franke and civill letter to mee to desire my favor with an excuse of taking up his commission which is soe well expressed as I have in as much civility complied with him and answered his letter the coppie of which I keep by mee. The session is adjourned to Whitsun week that the deputy leiftenants may then meet & take their oathes of which pray lett Sir William Adams who is att London have notice from your brother George his commission for deputy leiftenant

---

⁶⁷⁹ The excise which produced nearly half of the income of the Crown had been farmed by George Dashwood, a wealthy London merchant, and partners, since 1674. Danby intended to change the terms for the next farm which ran from June 1677 to maximise the profits in order to produce a surplus which could be used to make a settlement with the merchants who had lost by the Stop of the Exchequer in 1672. A number of ideas were floated in 1676 involving an increased number of excise commissioners and sub-commissioners, and a proposal was put forward that these posts should be given to ex-cavaliers and members of the court party (Browning, *Leeds*, I, pp 209–11, III, pp 4–6). Lord Yarmouth's coded entries between April and early August 1676, and the letter from Robert Brent (below p.236) make it clear that he expected to benefit by the new arrangements, and that he went as far as to offer positions to prospective customs officials. The farm was eventually granted to Dashwood again, with a fresh set of partners and revised conditions. There is no evidence that Lord Yarmouth was involved in any way in the new farm.

⁶⁸⁰ For this letter *see* British Library: Egerton MS 3338, f.74.

⁶⁸¹ Sir Peter Gleane (1619–1696), a deputy lieutenant and colonel of militia to 1676

beeing ready for him. I received a letter from Don which Ile answer by Monday's post beeing now going to dine att Rackey[682] pray lett Lewis send him home the Duke of Richmond's seale[683] and the press which was left behind beeing of noe use to mee, in his letter he tells mee on Monday he was att Lombard Street att a reconciliation dinner between Sir John & his mother where according to the usuall way Sir John was on his maribones[684] and his mother is to reconcile him to you & you to mee to putt him in new capacityes of betraying & undooing all my concernes. You know how tenderly I love you and by all that love I doe conjure you never to speake to mee in itt & then I will, as I did before this was don, bee formally civill to him butt having in my owne mind & thoughts suffered soe deeply by the recollections onely of the insolent use of my obligations that man has made I doe [f.3] solemnely resolve and to take of all discourses in the beginning that shall bee made mee of itt I shall when either your mother or your self begin the discourse take an oath never to see him more if I can avoid him. Therefore you had better leave itt as itt is, for the world shall never alter mee in the least in that point and therefore pray informe your mother soe much and desire her to mind her word soe farr as nott to leave any concernes of ours in his menage and this I begg att her hands and att yours that itt may proceed noe further then a decent outward civility betweene brother & sister, as soone as he sees any loopehole of sunshine then he appeares, butt in cold weather licke a tortoise undermines and goes into the ground. The children are well & present their service. I have made the blue & white laced bed in the inner chamber to the parlor chamber bee putt up in my dressing roome where I now ly, I long to heare som newse of *600* [*myself*] & *36* & *6* meeting. I have now noe more to say but that I am

*Signed*: your most affectionate servant, Yarmouth
*Postscript*: Peregrine Bertie & my son have written to mee by this post which I have answered. My service to Mr Brent.
*NRO: BL/Y/1/131*

## Robert, Viscount Yarmouth to Rebecca, Viscountess Yarmouth

**1676, April 9, Holkcom**. My deare, my Lord Treasurer kept his intentions very private soe that yesterday morning I had onely notice that he would be att Holcom last night Peckover came on purpose to mee from Newmarkett soe I did immediately take coach after I had recieved your letter by the post, and with Sir John Pettus with mee came to Holcom where I mett my Lord Treasurer, my Lord Lindsey & my Lord Fretswell & my Lord Latimer.[685] My lord tooke my comming very kindly & told mee hee feared my bringing people to meet him which was the reason he was soe private, he seemes to bee very sorry he cannott see Oxned this time butt sayes hee will com

---

[682] i.e. Rackheath, home of Sir John Pettus

[683] Henshaw had been appointed secretary to the duke of Richmond when he was sent as ambassador extraordinary to Christian V of Denmark; however Richmond died a few months after his arrival there and Henshaw continued as envoy in Copenhagen, much against his inclination, until May 1674 (Pasmore, 'Thomas Henshaw', pp 186–187).                    [684] Marrowbones, i.e. his knees

[685] Lord Danby, his brother-in-law the 3rd earl of Lindsey, his half-uncle John Frescheville, baron Frescheville of Staveley, and his elder son Edward, viscount Latimer.

on purpose. My Lord Lindsey speakes very obligingly of you & wee have your health every meale. My Lord Treasurer goes away on Tuesday morning for Newmarkett, my Lady Anne Coke went out of her owne chamber to lodge mee in itt, and they are all very civill to mee. This day came Alderman Backwell on som business to my Lord Treasurer, dined heere & is gon, I told him in his eare I hoped he would doe our business, he sayth if he deales with any body in that kind itt shall be with us but still runns on that tis a deare bargaine and if ∇ [*Lady Danby*] doth nott spurr him up I feare he will fayle us: I doe smell out [*f.2*] they have a mind that my couzin Coke should have the command of the horse which if itt bee I must doe itt without dispute and my son may if he has a mind to the trouble have Hobart's or Gleane's regiment. I borrowe a moment to give you a word, the howse is crammed with people and I have much adoe to gett pen or paper but Mrs Fleet[686] lends me a scurvy one, they all present their service to you & on Wedensday by the post I shall give you a more particular accompt. Itt is now Sunday seven of the clock *att night* and the post from hence is ready to goe, soe that I must conclude myself,

*Signed*: your must humble servant, Yarmouth, in great hast
*Addressed*: These present to the right honourable the Lady Viscountess Yarmouth att the Golden Ball in Suffolke Street, London
*NRO: BL/Y/1/132*

## Robert, Viscount Yarmouth to Rebecca, Viscountess Yarmouth

**1676, 12 April**. My dearest deare, in my blotted and hasty letter from Holkham I promised you the farther accompt by this dayes post, my Lord Treasurer was very kind to mee all the while and I pushed my humor to be soe good company that I gave him som diversion, I was lodged in my Lady Anne's owne bed and my Lord Treasurer & my Lord Lindsey lay together, the howse was very full of company & severall gentlemen I presented to my Lord Treasurer as old Sir Henry Bedingfeld, Sir Jacob Astley, Captaine Coke of Broome and many others besides Mr Deane, my Lord Lindsey and I had severell discourses by ourselves and he pretends[687] to have commended your policy & wisdome soe far to ∇ [*Lady Danby*] as to have made up the breach, I perceved by his discourse that matters can never sitt aright with ✧ [*my Lord Treasurer*] till that *15* and others followe him out of the power they now have, he tells mee my Lord ✧ [*Treasurer*] is perfectly kind to mee which my Lord Treasurer himself expressed much at Holkham, and att our parting made mee promise to write to him and told mee how ready I should find him to serve mee in anything: butt I doe verily believe *15* is designed by them all for *4000* & therefore I cannott imagine what you meane when you said that ∇ [*Lady Danby*] named the next to that for *600* [*me*], for the next to that is *100*: itt was impossible to have opportunity to entertaine my Lord Treasurer long with intreagues, the affaire of Mr Coke's executor[688] and business of the settlement of differences betweene them taking up all

---

[686] Mrs Jane Fleet, housekeeper at Holkham                    [687] i.e. claims

[688] The will of John Coke who died in 1671 had led to lawsuits between his sisters and their husbands and his heir Robert Coke of Holkham, supported by his father-in-law Lord Danby (NRO: LEST/EF 8/13/10, 16–40, LEST/EF 10/1–24).

the time that was nott spent in discourse of publicke natures and divertisements of going to the seaside & cards, yett I lost noe opportunity to informe *him* that 700 & 600 [we] would bee noe unprofitable servants; mee thoughts *he was* a little shie of 6 & the brother butt I doe suppose that when ▽ [Lady Danby] informes ✧ [my Lord Treasurer] of the whole matter my Lord Treasurer will have reason to thanke 700 [you] and I am confident 600 [I] will find som effects if thinges worke aright: 19 [Sir Henry Bedingfeld jr] att Newmarkett informed ⊗ of all who spoke the kind-liest in the world of 600 [me] and the King & & [sic] my Lord Treasurer had all the information of the countries civilitie to me [f.2] which pleased them all highly. I hope the letter I writt to ▽ [Lady Danby] will please her,[689] Mrs Fleet was mighty civill to mee, I gave her a guinney at parting, my cosin Coke and my Lady Anne & my Lady Bridgett coms hither the next <weomen> week and I must have a fiddle & som weomen to keep her company, she sayth she had allwaies a mighty mind to com to 700 [you] butt was faine to comply with ▽ [Lady Danby], my Lord Dunblaine playes the best of the violin I ever heard and my Lord Latimer was very kind on Tuesday morning. After parting I went immediately to Beckhall where wee have the best friends in the world, wee remembred you often and soe att night I came home where I found old Sir Will Doyly who shews his friendship most handsomly to mee & usefully: butt now as I am writing is com in to dinner Sir Jacob Astley, Sir Nevile Cataline, the deane, Thomas Wood & severall others. The corporation of Yarmouth had been heere this week butt hearing I was from home deffered itt till next week and doe intend to present mee a tunn of exelent wine. Mr Flynt says positively his son shall begin the work this yeare and I hope well from that, Sir Nevil Cataline brought they tell mee 400 horse to meet mee & in that croud itt was impossible to name perticular personns butt som of the cheif. Your children presents their duty to you & are very well. Sir Will Doyly brought his eldest grandchild who is the prittiest bred boy I have seene & speakes French very well and now I must goe to these gentlemen who expect mee and therefore till the next post am

*Signed*: yours for ever, Yarmouth

*Postscript*: You know I leave all thinges to your best conduct next under God's: pray speake to Lewis that Mr Henshaw's seale & press bee sent home. Noe pleasure licke your letters.

[f.3] My service to Matt Snelling,[690] excuse mee to him this post. My duty & service to my Lord Marshall when you see with all the compliments you can make.

*Addressed*: These present to the right honorable the Lady Viscountess Yarmouth att the Golden Ball in Suffolke Street, London

*NRO: BL/Y/1/133*

---

[689] By this small slip of the pen Lord Yarmouth reveals that ▽ was a woman making it possible for her to be identified as Lady Danby.

[690] Matthew Snelling (c.1621–1678), miniature painter and courtier, who was born in King's Lynn, and was a friend of the Earl Marshal.

# Robert, Viscount Yarmouth to Rebecca, Viscountess Yarmouth

**1676, April 14**. My dearest deare, thy deare letters are the greatest pleasures I can receive besides the cordiall testimonyes in them of your affections to my interest, which alwayes involves yours with a deeper concerne in my imaginations then anything that can otherwise relate to my owne satisfaction. Yesterday I thought to have beene alone, butt besides som that came in to dine with mee, and Sir Robert Kemp that with great civility came to give mee a visitt in the afternoone, the towne of Yarmouth sent ten or eleven of the cheif of them amongst which was Sir Thomas Meddowes, Mr Collier,[691] Mr England and the rest unknowne to you, they made mee a speech of congratulation & of great respect to mee, and att supper after they had divertised themselves with drinking, walking and looking about the howse, I entertained them kindly and this day att dinner, and after dinner having sett a bottle att every mann's trencher, we parted with that they call starke love & kindness. In this time I was nott negligent to prosecute my long intended designe and Mr Dawson who was heere has found out a thing, which he sayth will infallible doe my business & the easiest thing in nature for the King if he respects his owne advantage to graunt and my Lord Treasurer in a word to doe. I inclose Dawson's paper who besides this promiseth by Mondayes post to write to you fuller about the matter, in short, the towne has turned the King's officers out of the custome howse in the towne & att present they are faine to hire a private howse, now if the King will please to build the custome howse on my side, where a yeare or too agoe I built a key I will give his Majesty the ground & key: and itt stand in *a* much more commodious place of the haven there then any other part of Yarmouth. Dawson imagines that all the commissioners of the custome howse will bee for itt and once you knowe the commissioners of the treasury were [f.2] for itt had nott Sir John Dunscomb and the towne clapt up an agreement which now is voyd & the King in one of the best ports of England voyd of a custome howse of his owne, *500* or *600* [I] will build a noble one and Dawson will undertake to doe itt if an order bee butt procured from my Lord Treasurer to reimburse him out of the customes of the towne of which he is receiver of [?]in part, this he sayes without more adoe will effect my business to the greatest advantage I can imagine and presently make my side built all over, now how easy a matter is this if a man had any favor. England, Mr Bulwer's *son*, is my constant friend and has desired mee in a weekes time to send him proposalls that he may endeavor for to serve mee, which I desire you forthwith to gett Mr Bulwer to draw up: att £1,000 a yeare quarterly payments besides the present rent of £300 as itt now stands for under £1,300 a year quarterly payments itt shall never goe for a lease of 99 yeares and then they shall build itt after their owne fancy with a covenant to leave what itt is built in tenentable reparation att the end of the terme. Butt Dawson sayth the custome howse way will bee more for my advantage & I am sure itt's the more easy & facile way and may presently bee don butt in this allsoe which must bee kept very private, you must use Mr Bulwer to draw up the paper after you have received Dawson's fuller instructions by the next post, as he promised mee. Your letters are infinitely full of variety & pleasure pray God any thing succeed as you would, by that time this comes to your

---

691 Probably John Caulier, bailiff in 1678

hands, everybody will bee in towne and then your prospect will bee the better. Yesterday according to the advice of Sir 24 [*Sir Henry Bedingfeld*] I sent over my man Rawlins to [*f*.3] Raineham to make a compliment to my Lord Townshend & my lady, my lord received him very kindly: and asked for my Lord Leiftenant and enquired much after your comming downe, soe did my lady (who is ill and suspected to bee in a consumption), after they had given him his skin full of wine he came home the same night. My Lord Arlington and my Lord of Ormond are to bee there the next week.

I have allready issued out severall commissions, as to Sir Jacob Astley I have made him colonel of Sir John Hobart's regiment and deputy leiftenant, I have given Sir Nevile Cataline & my cosin Coke & Captaine Coke of Broome & the Doylys theirs & Sir John Pettus his, I shall send you up a coppy of Sir Peter Gleane's letter on Munday for my Lord Marshall to peruse (which though itt's very civill to mee) I beleave he will nott think itt fitt after that to trouble him itt itt [*sic*] and if he should itt would bee to noe purpose, it will falle I believe to Sir Will Adams to whome I find the puls of the citty beates most.

Mr Peckover tells me my couzin Coke waves totally any thing in the militia but the deputy leiftenancy which I am nott ill satisfied in itt beeing soe noble a command for my son I meane the regiment of horse butt however Ile keep the commission under my thumb that ▽ [*Lady Danby*] may have noe more pretences to quarrell a while.[692]

I doubt nott butt att our meeting in Whitson week, before which time I desire Sir William Adams & my cousin Windham (who Rawlins perceives they have no great gusto for att Rainham) may be heere, I shall give a good accompt of the settlement of the militia which beleeve mee is noe light task, and perhapps wee may shew that the affaires of the cuntry may be driven on without the help of those sages who are nott att leysure. I am wonderous carefull & am faine to putt a guide upon my lipps & actions, though I doe expect som kind of tricks to be played mee, yett I hope the great wonder will presently cease & the [*f*.4] scabbie opinions dry & fade especially when their wings are clipped.

You wright mee word to tell you how Oxnead lookes, I tell you sweetly, Mrs Cooper performes her part very well, the children looke very well, Mis growes tall and handsom and full of witt, Thom plyes me with Latin letters butt Jasper is the worst and I knowe nott what he can be good for, which makes me have the worst opinion of him. You must get Mr Bulwer to gett mee a power from Sir Robert Clayton's[693] trustees to make all leases good which I shall make of improovement att Yarmouth which will bee better then to runn in any others' names. I am very glad you speake soe hopefully of the business of 𝒦 [*the excise*] which must now be determined & confirmed betwixt this and middsummer or nott att all.

Pray get Mr Brent to gett the commission of my vice admiraltie dated as early as possible that I may not bee putt to sweare againe for that, and Dr Hughes who I

---

[692] Lady Danby was an overbearing and imperious woman; she was disliked by Lord and Lady Yarmouth who were obliged to court her and to flatter her.

[693] Sir Robert Clayton (1629–1707), banker, who arranged Lord Yarmouth's mortgages and loans, *see* above pp 9–10.

supposes waites on you att London must informe mee of the power & convenience of itt which I understand is much, he desired he might have my letter to you butt went away when I was att Holcom. I distributed your letters all butt Mr Fisher's who is gon with Sir Charles Harbord for a day or too towards the seaside, els I had answered Mr Snelling's motion about my Lord Candish,[694] butt I shall I hope by the Monday's post gett a letter from Sir Charles to send up for that purpose. Heere is a very handsom fellow that is porter & wants his livery which Mrs Cooper desired mee to mind you of. The picture for the cleaning the frame & all the man, I mean Mr Cross, was to have £5 for. I hope ▽ [*Lady Danby*] will be reall[695] & that ✧ [*my Lord Treasurer*] will find his interest in *36 6*. The children presents their duty: my service in the Pal Mal, I have heard from my son butt once, never from Captain Kirle or Sir George.

*Signed*: With all the facultys of sowle & body I am yours, Yarmouth
*Postscript*: Sir Will Doyly will waite on you & bee heere by Whitsuntide. Remember me to Mall I pray.
*NRO: BL/Y/1/134*

# Robert, Viscount Yarmouth to Rebecca, Viscountess Yarmouth

**1676, April 17**. My deare hart, my Lady Anne Coke deferrs her journey hither till you com home butt her husband coms hither this night. I have heere sent you inclosed the two notes signed for Sir Robert Clayton and the last post I writt a letter to your mother to desire her to continue her kindness to you and that she will nott deliver us over into the power of Sir John. I have allsoe written to Sir George Wakeman about the business of 𝒦 [*the excise*], which if ▽ [*Lady Danby*] be a friend to, may be brought about and I should be very loath itt should now goe into other hands. As soon as my cousin Coke is gon I hope I shall bee private for som while for I am weary with company. Pray God send ✧ and ▽ [*my Lord Treasurer & Lady Danby*] to bee kind to us and to thinke itt their interest to promote *600* & *700* [*us*]; I am sorrie to find that *88* hath yett noe progress in comming to court. I wonder you never writt mee one word of the Frenchmann's comming downe[696] by this dayes coach when I am told of itt by other letters. I doe asure you if I had looked all England over I could nott have a better secretary then I have chosen, he writes a most faire hand and doth the commissions most neately besides he is very understanding in all points of the law and capable of any business. I hope Mr Brent will look that my commission for the admiralty be full & nott defective as the other was and that either in words specified in the graunt or some private order itt may intitle mee to the proffitts in the King's right. Now my Lord Treasurer [*f.2*] and ▽ [*Lady Danby*] are com to towne I doe expect to heare that somwhat mooves in the matters of *15* and the rest for itt's noe time to delay. My picture every body sayth is the likest

---

[694] i.e. Lord Cavendish who was one of the leaders of the 'country' party in parliament
[695] i.e. honest, sincere, loyal, etc.
[696] i.e. to be tutor to Lord Yarmouth's younger children. This Frenchman was the natural philosopher Gideon Bonnivert who wrote a description of Lord Yarmouth at this date (British Library: Sloane MS 1928, f.47; and see Sloane MS 1009, f.139, letter to Bonnivert at Oxnead, 9 May 1676).

in the world, itt shall be hanged in your closett, my velvett cap I have received too. I wish you could gett any thing effected handsomly as to the business I writt you in my last concerning Yarmouth, in which Mr Brent may be a proper instrument. I have written to Sir William Adams to com downe as speedily as may bee for I doe perceive the citty have most mind to him for the colonel in Sir Peter Gleane's place, the coppy of whose letter I have inclosed that you may lett my Lord Marshall see to hinder him from interposing in a matter where heel fayle and that I would nott have him. Ile warrant you wee shall doe well enough in time, the business is nott soe unfathomable butt to bee comprehended & for the expence I hope som way will bee found out by his Majesty's kindness to defray itt.

The children are well and present their dutys to you, Betty growes tall & is very handsom & extreame witty and entertaines mee with very pritty discourses, wee are wonderous great.

I thanke God I have had noe gout since I came and have nott drunke six glasses of wine in my owne house since I came butt nog and shall endeavor to husband my body as well as I may [f.3] now the Philistines com butt my couzin Coke hath much given over that sport as they say[697] which I doe nott find. Pore Mrs Sadler[698] growes wors & wors is faine to bee bound in her bed and her mind runns that the King has sent mee downe to kill her.

Sir John Hobart has this week had a mischance by fire to the value of £200 or £300 att Langley Abbey, the barnes and outhowses beeing burnt downe, alsoe Mr Scarborrowe[699] att North Walsham had too or three howses burnt downe this week.

And now I have told you all the newse I knowe here I hope I shall heare what you knowe from *London* for, as I have told you before, in your letters are the perticular pleasure of my life when I am absent from your conversation. Remembrance to my son & to my daughter, to little Charles and Charlotte, pray God send matters to steere well, God beeing the guide I am

*Signed*: your most humble servant, Yarmouth
*NRO: BL/Y/1/135*

## Robert, Viscount Yarmouth to Rebecca, Viscountess Yarmouth

**1676, April 19**. My dearest hart, I have had all the terrors imaginable about you but the Frenchman who came the last night has in som part lesened my feares as well as Sir George Wakeman's letter, pray God by tomorrowes post I may bee sett att ease. My cousin Coke <has> and Captaine Coke and three or foure more that came along with him have beene heere since Monday and very well pleased, yesterday I had noe less then thre[e] & twenty gentlemen satt downe att my table, amongst whome was Sir Christopher Calthorp[700] my Lord Townshend's nearest relation who in spight of mother brothers and all the machines in the world to divert stickes to mee

---

[697] Coke was noted for his heavy drinking, see also p.298 below.

[698] Probably Lord Yarmouth's neighbour Mrs Susannah Sadler of Lammas (NRO: ANW, admin. act book, 1668–1681, f.73).                    [699] Henry Scarburgh (d.1687), of North Walsham

[700] Sir Christopher Calthorpe (c.1645–1718) was Townshend's first cousin; their mothers were daughters of Sir Edward Lewknor of Denham.

in the principle of serving his prince, he is a most popular man and has given mee more creditt then can bee imagined, hee received his commissions from mee as deputy leiftenant & colonel of a foot regiment. Captaine Coke will ride over on purpose to tell Sir Peter Gleane his owne, this day my cousin Coke is gon of otter hunting, calls in att Sir John Pettus his [*house*] in the afternoone and coms home att supper. I perceive by *19* [*Sir Henry Bedingfeld jr*] that my Lady Anne had sett her hart on comming but the gentleman was positive against her & Mrs Fleet that she should nott com till you came home, soe I sent her yesterday a tame doe for a present which her husband sayth will bee very acceptable to her, to morrowe I thinke after dinner they goe home. Heere is Sir Austine Palgrave and a coach full com in with him as I am writing. Att Raineham this week will be my Lord Arlington & the Duke of Monmouth itt's sayd and the Duke of Ormond. If my ✧ [*Lord Treasurer*] doth nott vigorusly followe the business of *15* hee undoth himself, itt is fitt my Lord Treasurer should knowe my cousin Coke told *mee* that my Lord Townshend lately should say that the King should never have penny of money in parlament as long as he was treasurer and threatens terrible thinges the next parlament, Hobart my cousin Coke mett as he came to mee going to Raineham where I presume som of the male-contents are to meet to urgg an interest against ✧ [*my Lord Treasurer*] I hope their power will be too small to doe any feates of malice. [*f*.2] What you sayd was literally true to my Lord Marshall and that you may ashure him that itt onely concernes Sir Jeames Johnson which I told of before is one of his back friends and mine, I shall doe noe materiall thing without his privity and he may trust mee to distinguish betweene men. You make mee hope well of the business of *K* [*the excise*] butt I hope itt may every whitt bee don as well without mee since I have appeared in itt both to the King & my Lord Treasurer before my comming away that noe stone might be unturned and att Whitsuntide the world if I bee alive must nott prevent my beeing att Norwich for I have a task there to doe which is to acquitt my good behavior one way or other. I long to heare you have seene ✧ [*my Lord Treasurer*] who you will nott find a man of many words beleeve mee ▽ [*Lady Danby*] is the point that mirrors the other in great measure. I hope Peregrine Bertie had the letter I writt in answer to his.

I pray lett mee have notice exactly when that my Lord Marshall comes into the country that I may meet him with my friends, Snelling sayth itt will bee three <six> weekes hence.

I doe protest itt has hindred my repose the thoughts of your sickness and shall long to heare that early gooing abroad has nott hurt you.

Heere has beene noe hard drinking and I have strangely preserved myself from itt, I doe ashure you.

Mr Fisher is this day gon after Sir Charles Harbord towards Thetford and presumes from thence they shall bee called to London; hee has beene very instrumentall in Sir Christopher Calthorpe's business which I must tell you is the greatest counterstroke has beene [?]given and more then that of my cousin Windham who is the brother in law,[701] all the artifices will amount butt to a little I plainely see as particularly my Lord Townshend has taken whome[702] to him the booke of

---

[701] Windham was the brother-in-law of Lord Townshend.        [702] i.e. home

presidents[703] kept by the clarke of the militia pretending itt to bee his owne which would nott looke well should I make a bussle about \*itt\* butt Ile begin my owne records my self and I hope shall nott need any of those helpes which are, itt may bee, taken away to make mee [f.3] seek for them and to bee denied. Wee have wanted raine heere most mightily butt now God bee thanked wee have itt powre downe upon us which is a great comfort to this country. I know you looke after the Yarmouth affaire, could itt bee don handsomly itt would putt a great face of encouragement to builders and what were itt for the King to give mee a patent to have the custome howse on my side during the lease I make him for nothing which may be 99 yeares butt I suppose you have ere this consulted Mr Bulwer. Pray keep Fisher in hart concerning the business of *K* [*the excise*] and none can bee more serviceable to mee in itt then he if itt fadges[704] which I hope in God itt will, for I am sure ✧ [*my Lord Treasurer*] can have soe great an interest in none as in us. Pray if possible lett Mr Brent gett the date of my vice admirall's commission as early as that of my patent otherwise I must sweare anew for that as they tell mee.

I shall give you a further accompt of Monsieur by the next who speakes nott one word of English and therefore Mr Gough & I cannott imagine how hee should teach the children. God of heaven keep you and send us a quick meeting & that thinges may goe well, I had a letter from my son which Ile answer by the next post having now noe time, my service to all my friends. I hope ✧ & ▽ [*my Lord Treasurer & Lady Danby*] stand firme, I long to heare how the business of *8* & *6* & *36* mooves, I am my dearest hart,

*Signed*: thy most passionate friend & servant till death, Yarmouth
*Postscript*: Pray write mee word if you have never seene nor heard of Sir John since my comming.
*NRO: BL/Y/1/136*

## Robert, Viscount Yarmouth to Rebecca, Viscountess Yarmouth

**1676, April 21.** My deare hart, yesterday after dinner my cousin and his company left mee, I carried him as far as Major Doughty's and about five of the clock he went for Holkham & I home, he was extreamely satisfied with his entertainement and told som persons, Mat Peckover for one, that he never was soe pleased with any visitt in his life. I had a letter yesterday from *19* [*Sir Henry Bedingfeld jr*] who acquainted mee that the Duke of Ormond & my Lord Arlington came nott to Raineham as they were looked for and nobody was there butt Sir John Hobart & my lady. I am sorry for ▽ & ✧ [*Lady Danby & my Lord Treasurer's*] apprehensions of *24* [*Sir Henry Bedingfeld*] who I dare sweare for to bee much their servants [*sic*] I wish those things were better examined what though he has been civil to *15* heeretofore I am sure he was allwaies a great hater of his friend and never had any esteem there; whatever error has beene layd to his charge is out of som mistake or folly & you know

---

[703] This 'booke of presidents' was published as R.M. Dunn (ed.), *Norfolk Lieutenancy Journal, 1660–1676* (NRS XLV, 1977), and is now British Library: Add. MSS 11601; Yarmouth started a new journal published as B. Cozens-Hardy (ed.), *Norfolk Lieutenancy Journal, 1676–1701* (NRS, XXX, 1961), which is now NRO: NRS 27276.    [704] i.e. if it comes off

how passionately zealous he is & was ever for our interest and has lately shewne itt att Newmarkett & therefore pray putt in a good word for him lett them love him if they doe nott think to trust him butt for *24* [*Sir Henry Bedingfeld*] & the lady the world has nott people Ile sooner answer for and their counsell was good to mee, and I am well satisfied I have sent as I did and would doe it againe tomorrowe if I had nott don itt; by those thinges noe man looses butt gaines ground. As for Dr Heuse[705] I cannott but admire hee should tell you so many lies, first Sir William Doyly nor Mr Windham never mentioned the name *of* Dr Peper to mee nor any man els butt Dr Hyliard who excused Dr Peper when I discoursed Hughes' business with him, then as to the session of Norwich nothing could bee with more respect, all proceedings did stop att my word butt when I desired them to goe on because I had a mind to sitt som time on the bench; when I went away Sir Philip [*f*.2] Woodhowse, Sir Jacob Astley, Sir William Doyley with all the coaches that were there which was but three went with mee to the place where wee dined, the corporation sent to mee to know when they should waite on mee and I beeing resolved presently after dinner to goe away itt was deferred by my desire till my next comming to towne; when I told Mr Gough of this he was amased & I doe find the pore doctor has foibles which I pitty and will serve him as farr as I may butt these thinges are plaine downeright lyes, and pray lett mee heare noe more of them: nor doubt you butt Ile carry myself with all circumspection and looke for all thinges fitt for my place which I find none butt are ready enough to give mee, and I am sure noe lord leiftenant in England has had soe much butt now I am resolved to dine att home butt two *dayes* in a week publickely that is Tuesdayes & Fridayes then I have given out I shall be glad & ready to receive my friends, the rest for gooing to mine & privacy with my owne family & children, for the slavery & expence denies the other way. I have beene soe pressed with company that I have nott had liberty to stirr into the park in foure or five dayes. I am very glad ▽ [*Lady Danby*] is soe kind as to <visitt to> visitt you in your sickness which has made mee all most mad & from Beckhall they sent over on purpose and yesterday from your owne letter I sent them the good newse of your health which I have reason enough to pray for & doe soe when I pray for anything: butt pray write mee word when you first see ✧ [*my Lord Treasurer*] for I doe nott find you have seene his face yett I am glad that ▽ [*Lady Danby*] is soe communicative [*f*.3] to you, as to tell you *600* [*I*] shall bee remembred in somwhat. I doe suppose the matters of *6 36* & *8* and *700* [*you*] & ▽ [*Lady Danby*] are nott soe fitt for a letter.

I should bee glad to heare any thing certaine of the matter of 𝒦 [*the excise*] which must now presently worke or never. God almighty bless you & your endeavors & send us with speed & with joy to meet, and lett mee ashure you that any business you take in hand will thrive the better for Sir John's nott knowing of itt. I hope by this time you have had a letter from Dawson as he promised mee who tells mee the timber trade increaseth mightily. If Yarmouth has a beginning you'l see a fine matter of itt and I hope in God itt will by this meanes or som other if that they will give £1,000 a yeare improvement for itt for 99 yeares.

I have given your sons great caution & the tutor great care who speakes nott Latine very fluently himself butt perhapps may teach itt better, but Mis[s] who has the most

[705] Dr Owen Hughes

witt in the world will bee att itt with them and has in two dayes loaded herself with French.

Sir Charles is gon towards London & will endeavor to serve my Lord Candish all he can possibly: pray bee you extreame kind to Sir William Doyly who I doe ashure you has shewne himself my friend, I wonder Windham has nott beene to see you, my sonn's commission shall bee ready for him.

I hope tomorrowe againe I shall heare of the confirmation of your health which will be the best newse you can sent to, my dear hart,

*Signed*: yours most passionately, Yarmouth

*Postscript*: I hope your mother received my letter. The children presents their duty to you. Pray remember mee to Mr Pettus when you see him. Thanke my daughter Mary for her last. Marke your sheets when more then one with 1:2:3 on the top of the paper. *NRO: BL/Y/1/137*

## Robert, Viscount Yarmouth to Rebecca, Viscountess Yarmouth

**1676, April 24**. My dearest dearest deare, I went on Saterday on the rode to meet thy deare letter which alwayes coms as a cordiall to mee. I am very much cheered up with ▽ [*Lady Danby's*] kindness to you which I hope will hold for certainely soe free a trust as matters you dare nott write and the expressions of an intention for pore Mall are great thinges, I will say my prayers as you direct and leave all events to providence. The leauge betwixt ▽ [*Lady Danby*], *13*, ✧ [*my Lord Treasurer*] and *600* [*myself*] & *4000* will produce good effects. Sir John Pettus with his lady & children are gon this day for London, he was heere with me yesterday to take his leave & to receive my commands for you, butt I onely desired him to see you as soone as he came to towne, he told me his wife had heard abroad that *600* [*I*] was to be *15* which I laughed him out of the impossibility of: I am glad to find every one was soe kind to you in your sickness, pray God increase itt and may every one love you as well as I. I would faine have Sir Charles Harbord doe my Lord Candish som considerable service in which he promiseth faire and that my Lord Candish might com about to our friends, but for the matter of *36* & *6* & ▽ [*Lady Danby*] I feare itt may breed som ill bloud for when those thinges are nott accepted they turne to perfect hatred & animosity which may perhapps touch you though contrary to all reason.

I shall be infinitely glad to heare of the business of 𝒦 [*the excise*]: I had nott a line from any of them this post butt doe expect now suddainely to be out of our paine one way or other. I hope Sir George Wakeman had my letter I sent him by the common post as well as that I writt him in yours and that he stayes to give mee som significant answer. On Friday Mr Flynt my good friend and som of the Yarmouth men will bee with mee to propose som beginning which the matter I writt to you of if it should hitt would fix to the purpose & goe on with a driving pace. I am hugely glad that *13* resolves to make <*word deleted*>⊗ kind to ✧ [*my Lord Treasurer*] and if that ✧ [*he*] apprehends itt to be [?]by your contrivance itt must needes make him as well as ▽ [*Lady Danby*] esteeme you butt you has never [*f.2*] yett told mee that they have seene ✧ [*his*] face. By Mr Warkhowse who coms from hence on Wedensday my some commissions shall be sent (butt to what purpose did you write

that long doubt to what I sayd) when you know that if ✧ [*my Lord Treasurer*]
would butt have hinted he would have had itt soe itt must have beene don, but my
cousin Coke has noe mind to trouble himself in the militia farther then deputy leiftenants for early or later itt's noe matter for all the commissions beare date one day.

I am this day beginning a work which I thought nott to have told you of till you
see itt, itt's the alteration of your lodging chamber, which I was faine to forsake for
the wind & cold & ugly flore, I am beating out an alcove into the inner chamber for
the bed to stand <itt> in which shall shall [*sic*] be handsomly enough don, and leave
a handsom passage to your closett beyound itt and as much to answer the uniformity
on the other side. When itt's a little forward I must have som pritty cheap stuff to hang
itt within from the lower cornish, straining itt according to the fashion, and I remaine
yett in dispute whether I shall not wainscott the rest of the chamber with broad pan-
nells, and paint all white & gold in the seames; their shall bee too halfe pillasters
turned to support the alcove and an handsom square cornish on the top, for the
hiegth of the roome will nott beare an arch, neither is the Dutchess of Portsmouth's
arched butt goes in just as this will doe, their will bee a yard of each side the bed and
more and as much from the feet of the bed to the step rising out of the chamber, the
roome shall bee new flored, & I intend a small marble chimney peece, the gallery
allsoe & my dressing roome shall bee new flored, and all this 300 deales will doe,
which I sent John Griffin for this day to Yarmouth, and by that time itt's finished
which will be three weekes hence I hope to see you heere. The roome that must bee
your inner roome is that where the pintado[706] bed stands which will have a dore
opposite to the dore that goes out of the chamber towards your closett and both dors
shall have handsom frames sutable to the worke of the alcove which will bee neat and
very warme for I wonder hetherto you have nott been killed with itt.

[*f.3*] I doe expect Sir Henry Bedingfeld tomorrowe, I heare my cousin Coke comes
to Norwich this night & that my Lady Anne coms alsoe and that he goes from thence
into Suffolke, I shall send & see.

Heere was one Lumbert an aturney with mee to tell mee Blacklowe's executor suc:
mee in the exchequer, I thought all that had been payd, he has promised to write to
Mr Bulwer this night & to bee with him in a few dayes in the meane time pray
acquaint Mr Bulwer with itt. I have been damnedly troubled about Lewis Micko
which your mother writt mee word of, I shall answer her letter by the next post. She
sayth she will nott subject mee to Sir John & that she knowes enough of his unworthy
dealings towards [*me*] & beleeve mee when I contemplate them in the park alone somtimes itt is the greatest amasement to mee to mee[*sic*] in the world, if he can heel rout
all *700* [*your*] pretences I am sure of itt; he is an hyppocriticall falsharted man & of
soe tyrannous insuting a nature as I abhor his complexion.

My children thanke God are very well, pore Robin I hope is soe too, pray God keep
you soe who are the onely comfort of my life excepting those that I have had from you.

Mr Gough & Major Doughty present their service to you, soe doth Mr Peckover
of whome I wish you yould mind my Lord Latimer butt if my Lord Treasurer or my
Lady Danby could gett a knight's place at Windsor[707] itt would bee the heigth of his

---

[706] Pintado was fine cotton cloth imported from India painted or dyed with spots or patterns of flowers.
[707] The Knights of Windsor, also called the Poor Knights, were originally impoverished military

ambition and he is ours body & soule. I had a letter from young Knyvett out of Suffolke who with Sir John Rowse[708] is gooing a ramble this summer to the Bath and they intend to see you att London. The children present their dutys to you & I am

*Signed*: yours for ever, Yarmouth

*Postscript*: Pray write mee word how the match goes on with my Lord Howard[709] & when. The church is most neat & prayers duly sayd in the chappell, though God forgive mee I am writing whilst they are att them, my chaplaine Mr Paston[710] gave mee a very good sermon yesterday.

[*f.*4] The history of my Lady Trevor's courtliness to you is pleasant for I beleeve she wishes you hanged for meeting you there where I am sorrie she coms att all butt I presume you have had experience of the affections of that family and know her, I am glad Mr Fanshaw gave her a wipe[711] which wipe I hope my Lord Treasurer will putt in practise.

I know nott whether ever I told you the widdowe Paston[712] Will Paston's mother was dead.

Everybody sayth my picture is the likest in the world.

Pray write a letter to Nurs Port to thanke her for washing my laced linning for amongst eight maides that are heere nott one butt she can doe itt.

*NRO: BL/Y/1/138*

# Thomas Henshaw to Robert, Viscount Yarmouth

**1676, April 24, Pondhouse**. My deare lord, yours of the 12 current I received some days *since*, but having nothing else to write you of, I deferred it till I could tell your lordship certainly the day of my setting *out* for Ireland, which is now resolved on to bee Monday the 8th of May; this had like to have been changed into another voyage, for Denmarke, *but* not to have stayed there beyond six monthes, onely to have settled some articles for the security of our merchants (during this warre between the Northerne Kings) in the Balthick seas but this designe is now either layd aside or deferred till my returne; and I feare by the next letters from Copenhagen that wee shall heare poor Griffenfeld's head has flown off his shoulders,[713] for this is the very day appointed for his publicke triall. Not only every age, but every yeare almost, affords us some eminent example of the inconstancy of fortune, the more frequently to warne us not to bee too fond of her smiles and caresses; wee may even at

veterans who received a salary and accommodation at Windsor Castle. Charles II increased the number from thirteen to eighteen. Paston's suggestion implies that Peckover had military experience but there is no evidence for this.

[708] John Knyvett, son of Sir John Knyvett (d.1673), and his first cousin Sir John Rowse or Rous of Henham; both were cousins of Lord Yarmouth whose grandmother was a Knyvett.

[709] Henry Howard, later earl of Arundel, and 7th duke of Norfolk; he married Lady Mary Mordaunt on 8 August 1677 but later divorced her.

[710] theclergydatabase.org.uk contains a James Paston, rector of Finningham, Suffolk, at this date, but no-one of that name held any of Lord Yarmouth's livings. [711] i.e. a put down

[712] Agnes, widow of William Paston of Appleton

[713] Peder Schumacher (1635–1699), Count Griffenfeld; he was pardoned on the scaffold and sentenced to life imprisonment.

home bee edifyed by some petty precedents of it, since Sir John Duncombe is layd by and Sir John Earnly[714] on Saturday last appointed to bee chancellor of the exchequer, and some theruppon talke as if fortune or her great minister would ere long exchange a secretary too.

I have not seen Sir John since I had your letter and therfor can say nothing of him, I suppose he is following his great designes, neither was what I writ in my last about him any more then to give your lordship a bare narrative of what past, not to undertake any plea on his behalf, which is beyond my skill, and would bee too pragmaticall a thing for my humour. I am [f.2] glad your lordship finds so much leisure in the midst of so much businesse as to look sometime into your still house.[715] I should bee glad to heare of some experiment to satisfye us what effect on [mercury][716] or other mettalls this strange & unexpected alteration of our subject is able to produce. If I write no more to your lordship before I goe for Ireland (whether as I hear the lord lieutenant[717] is this day goeing) I shall not faile dayly to pray for your lordship's happines in this world and the next, and that God would send us a happy meeting, as being, my dear lord,

*Signed*: your lordship's most faithfull and most obedient servant, De Caningcourt[718]
*Postscript*: My daughter humbly kisses your lordship's hands and thanks you for your kind remembrance of her.
*Addressed*: For the right honourable the Lord Vicount Yarmouth at Norwich [*postmark*]
*NRO: BL/Y/1/139*

## Sir Thomas Medowe to Robert, Viscount Yarmouth

**1676, April 24, Yarmouth**. My lord, since my returne hither from your honour I have had conference with this bearer Mr Thomas Parris about the fort at the peers where hee is appointed cannoneer as alsoe about the magazine under his custody and for what ammunition he hath belonging to this countie of Norfolk, to all which he is purpossly come to attend your lordship to render a perticuler accompt of them severally and what part of that (which belongeth to the countie) is disposed of, and by what orders I held it my duty to represent these lines by him and alsoe to returne your lordship my most humble and harty thankes for your noble faviours lately received and to assure your lordship that I am, and allways shall be, ready to expres myself as really I am, my lord,

*Signed*: your lordship's most humble and faithfull servant to command, Tho: Medowe
*Addressed*: These for the right honourable Robert Lord Paston Viscount Yarmouth & Lord Lieutenant of the county of Norfolk in Oxnead, humbly present
*Endorsed with sketch of a throne on a dais under a canopy, or possibly the bed described in BL/Y/1/138*
*NRO: BL/Y/1/140*

---

[714] Duncomb had presented a petition on behalf of sellers of coffee whose shops Danby proposed to suppress as centres of sedition; he was replaced by Sir John Ernle, a Danby supporter, and other opponents of Danby were expected to lose their positions (Browning, *Leeds*, I, pp 194–197).

[715] i.e. his laboratory                                    [716] Symbol not reproduced here

[717] Arthur Capel (c.1632–1683), 1st earl of Essex, lord lieutenant of Ireland 1672–1677

[718] Possibly a play on the name Pondhouse in French: Etangcourt

# Edward Warnes[719] to Robert, Viscount Yarmouth

**1676, April 24**. My lord, whereas one Richard White, who styles himselfe Messenger, did with much violence & injustice as this bearer who was an eye-witnes thereof can testify, take a distresse upon some lands of mine in Thrigby & exacted severall summes of money from my tenant there in my absence: and likewise from many others in those parts (by common report) wrongfully, to the dishonour of his Majesty, the breach of the publike peace, & oppression of his Majesties loyall subjects. I am advized by my counsaile (it beeinge likely that the common lawe in its proceedinges against that person in that case may receive some obstruction) to make my addresse to your honour who is lord lieutenant in this county, to grant your warrant to bringe this fellowe before you, and uppon cause shewne to compell him to answer theise misdemeanors before the judges of assizes at their next comeinge into this county.

Assuredly if these thinges be not rectified the people will be much dissatisfied as beeinge not assured of their property in their goods, & security of their persons, such haveinge authority (it may be) from his Majesty to do lawfull thinges, abusinge that authority to affright the people to satisfy their tort & covetous desires. Which if your lordship be pleased to interpose your authority to redresse, you shall promote thereby his Majesties honour, & oblige very much the countrey's thankfullnes to your lordship, for it is not alone the cause of him that is, my lord,

*Signed*: your honour's most obliged servant, Edward Warnes

My lord, the \<chase\> case was thus – the rent payable to his Majesty for my lands was 6[*illegible*] per annum, which for twenty-eight yeares last past was satisfied & paid & acquittances under the hands of the lawfull receivers given & acknoweledged paid for, which acquittances I have ready to produce. Now this rent was by this fellowe in his Majesties name demanded of my tenant in my absence for sixteen yeares last past (that is, ever since his Majesties restauration) which together with the fees which he exacted, \<which\> was 40 shillings. He violently brake up my tenant's house, & threatened beinge armed to slay both horse and man, rendinge & tearinge & cursinge with that execrable oath, which I am afraid & tremble to name G[*od*] damne – and all this with tumult, commandinge the people in his Majesties name to assist him, and said he would fine the towne, and by theise practises exacted & had of my tenant beinge thus affrighted 40 shillings. Nowe is not this iniquity worthy to be punished by the judge? Job 31.28.[720]

My lord, this I say farther if you doe not rectify this wronge, I will endeavour this rectification, if there be any *ius & fas*[721] in England.

*Addressed*: To the right honourable & truly noble My Lord Viscount Yarmouth, Lord Lieutenant of Norfolk

*NRO: BL/Y/1/141*

---

[719] Edward Warnes (d.1700), rector of Great Hautbois

[720] 'This also were an iniquity to be punished by the judge: for I should have denied the God that is above.' Job 31.28.          [721] i.e. what is right by law and religion

# Robert, Viscount Yarmouth to Rebecca, Viscountess Yarmouth

**1676, April 26**. My deare hart, Sir John Holland has beene with mee since Monday in the evening and made mee a most civill visitt and expressed great affections to mee, and I doe find that if a letter were writt by the King's command that hee should keep in, he would doe itt and this *24* [*Sir Henry Bedingfeld*] thinkes would bee of great consequence & the greatest blowe to the caballs of the other side in the world, and would alsoe take him of[f] from ever speaking more in parlament what might be interpreted ill provided hee might have a kind expression to testify that the King passeth by all that's past, I doubt nott butt this may bee of consequence too my Lord Treasurer's interest as I may menage the matter, pray lett my Lord Marshall and my Lord Treasurer bee consulted in the point & lett mee have their speedy thoughts.[722]

Sir John Hobart came heere to give mee a visitt yesterday and is amased att my Lady Trevor who he says could have informed my Lady Danby otherwise he having written a letter to a friend (who I suppose to bee Bragg) wherein he mentions my usage of him with all the respects and candor imaginable and soe I have carried my self to them all of which in a small time when matters are a little riper Ile give my Lord Treasurer an accompt [*f*.2] and I doubt nott butt to menage all thinges with all prudence and zeale to the Crowne. Sir John & his godaughter[723] were very kind and hee would have had her home to Quidnam, I shall have a care of fals friends for my owne misfortunes have taught mee circumspection.

My couzin Coke is att Norwich butt nott my Lady Anne who they say is breeding *sume nott* and Mrs Fleet is very ill of somthing in her brest licke a cancer. Many discourses were between Sir John Holland & I concerning the former lord leiftenant which is nott soe fitt for a letter butt I find great testimonyes of Sir John Holland's integrity to my Lord Marshall & mee and I doe beleeve if by my Lord Treasurer's meanes I could sett him right in his Majesty's favor I should doe my Lord Treasurer & in that my self a curtisy and give the others a most unexpected defeat.

My Lady Bedingfeld who complaines that you doe nott answer her letters will write to you. I am infinitely pleased att the great kindness ▽ [*Lady Danby*] shewes you, pray God keep the same mind att work. My couzin Coke talkes of nothing more then his reception heere, I hope in God *K* [*the excise*] will goe on for the other can answer noe great expectation of which I shall informe myself butt the other is the considerable.

Sir John Duncomb's putting out makes us beleeve severall will followe of which I expect to heare by your next, I wonder *88* is in noe manner [*f*.3] of play: yesternight Mr Warkhouse brake his shoulder with a fall from his hors, so that all his business had beene lost att London had I nott lent my secretary[724] for tenn days, his father supplyng his place in the meane time, hee'l bee with you before this letter, pray encourage him for hee is an able and fine fellowe, I doubt[725] the Frenchman you sent downe is butt a dull fellowe & neither speakes Latine well, nor French pleasantly.

Pray God I may find som civility concerning Yarmouth for som of them dine heere

---

[722] Danby eventually arranged for Holland's son to be awarded a secret service pension of £200 p.a. for his father's lifetime, 29 Aug 1677 (Henning, *Commons*, II, p.559).

[723] Presumably Yarmouth's youngest daughter Betty, as Mary was in London with her mother.

[724] John Doughty, who was Warkhouse's brother in law                         [725] i.e. I fear

on Friday: and your letter tomorrowe would be *a propos* if itt had somwhat in itt of that affaire.

I doe nott desire more company till you com yourself neither know I what to do with weomen and just now the howse above is all in rubbish for a forthnight.

Sir Henry Bedingfeld who now stands by mee gives you his service, you know he is one of the best friends wee have in the world; butt I will dispute itt with him to you who am for ever my dearest till death,

*Signed*: yours most passionately, Yarmouth
*Postscript*: I humbly kiss my Lord Treasurer's & my Lady Danby's hands.
*NRO: BL/Y/1/142*

## Sir William Doyly to Robert, Viscount Yarmouth

**1676, April 27, Westminster**. My lord, last night I got hether in safetie, and this morning I waighted upon your lady, whome I found in most perfect health, soe are all the rest of your lordshipp's familie. I doubt not but your lordship have heard of the remoovall of Sir John Duncombe *in* whose place Sir John Earneley is to succeed, others also (are said) will be remooved, to all which your lordship (I doubt not) will be noe stranger when you have red my ladyes letter by this post, for as she told me her ladyship did this day dine at my Lord Treasurer's. The talke now of our Norfolk affaire is wholly at an end, all men being fully satisfied with your lordshipp's proceedings.

This day the Dorsetshire jury gave in theire verdict against the Lord Digby,[726] and gave £1,000 in damage against him for the scandalous words against the Lord Shaftsbury, some few days (I suppose) will produce more businesse; for discourse through the towne, I shall be forsed to continue in towne untill the end of the terme, but I forget not Thursday in Witson weeke if I may receive a line or two from your lordship I shall take it for a most especiall favour, I have undeceived some persons heere that did beleeve Sir John Holland, Hobart, and the rest in Norfolk were dis-placed by your lordshipp's procurement, but they know better, my sonns are your lordshipp's most humble servants, soe is by tenn thousand obligations,

*Signed*: your old infirme but most faithfull old servant, Will: D'oyly
*Addressed*: For the right honourable the Lord Viscount Yarmouth, Lord Lieutenant of Norfolk and Norwich at Oxnett, Norwich [*postmark*]
NRO: BL/Y/1/143

## Robert, Viscount Yarmouth to Rebecca, Viscountess Yarmouth

**1676, April 30**. My deare hart, on Friday heere was a great deale of company from Norwich whome I entertained very civily, I doe ashure you I doe keep up his Majesty's interest and I hope you'l find I have a great interest in this country which

---

[726] John, Lord Digby, later 3rd earl of Bristol, MP for the county of Dorset, lost an action for *scandalum magnatum* against Lord Shaftesbury; his damages and costs were covered by a subscription from the gentlemen of Dorset (Henning, *Commons*, II, p.213).

joyned with my Lord Marshall's and my cousin Coke's will nott bee shaken easily besides the many props wee have besides. I am most infinitely pleased with your letter on Saterday which I received after I came home from the seaside where I was by six of the clock on fishing, and had many thoughts of you along the shore in my contemplations, after having passed foure or five howers there I went to Parson Thexton's[727] and eat our fish & stayed the heat of the day, came home by North Walsham where the bells gave me a peale, and I sent in to see Mrs Hogan[728] & soe came home before prayers and read over your letter three or foure times. Itts most exelent newse that the business of *K* [*the excise*] has any hopes in itt and that L[729] had hopes that the next day itt would bee concluded amongst them butt I can take noe alarums, butt this way itt must proove great and the other way nothing. I am glad ✧ [*my Lord Treasurer*] is soe just to us. I never heare from H[730] which makes mee beleeve he stayes to give mee the good newse of a conclusion which I doe confess will bee most welcome to mee and more then any other newse, butt you doe amase mee & sett of thinking when you say there is another besides *10 12* & *8* that doth business I cannott imagine where to fix itt, itt cannott bee *88*: I am very glad you hopes to open the eyes of ▽ ✧ [*Lady Danby & my Lord Treasurer*] as to *6* & *36* for they cannott doe better. The remoove of Sir John Doncomb gives alarums I believe to many others of whome I expect in a post or two to heare somwhat, I beleeve my Lord Campden's[731] comming is nott for nothing, and *4000* will be *15* I doe verily beleeve I have written to *24* [*Sir Henry Bedingfeld*] what you mentioned in letter & nott to *19* [*Sir Henry Bedingfeld jr*] whome you confound with *24* [*Sir Henry Bedingfeld*] whose interest is the most in the places you speake of. I have sent away the letter & before I close this may perhapps give you som accompt of him as to the Dutchess of Lauderdale: ✧ [*my Lord Treasurer*] ⊗ he told mee [*f.2*] that his son had heard by Mrs Deareham[732] they had noe opinion of him att Wallingford Howse[733] which went to his hart. I would faine have you sett *19* [*Sir Henry Bedingfeld jr*] right there if itt bee possible without burning of fingers, Ile answer for him that he shall make what declaration they please that hee is perfectly [*sic*] ▽ & ✧ [*Lady Danby & my Lord Treasurer*] and that he has som interest with ⊗ butt if they have new [*?*]propps[734] and that their bee more black gennises[735] in the way then wee know of I know nott what to say. As to the business of Yarmouth, they had beene heere on Friday butt one of the principall[*s*] having a ship to arrive which he doth howerly expect they sent mee a letter that as soone as itt coms the next day they com, butt if I can gett the custom howse there the business is don, and methinkes Mr Dickinson might draw up a paper from Dawson's reasons to present the King who presently of course refers

[727] Robert Thexton (d.1709), rector of Gimingham and Trunch

[728] Mary Hogan (d. c.1698, of North Walsham). Lady Yarmouth had some cousins called Hoggan and it is likely that Mary was one of this family. In 1679 the Paston children paid her a visit, see p.360 below.

[729] i.e. Lee, an associate of Peter Hoet below

[730] Peter Hoet, a London merchant, involved in the re-leasing of the excise

[731] Baptist Noel, 3rd viscount Campden, was married to Lady Elizabeth Bertie, Lady Danby's sister and Paston's cousin.

[732] Probably Frances, wife of Richard Dereham, later 3rd bt; through her mother, who was a Danvers, she was a cousin of Lord Danby.

[733] Wallingford House, Whitehall, was occupied by the lord treasurer.          [734] ? proposals

[735] ? geniuses

itt to my Lord Treasurer and this you may doe by my lord's owne consent as Mr
Brent will putt you in a way, itt beeing as much for the King's advantage as mine. I
beleeve my Lord Lindsey would doe itt for you if he bee soe kind to mee, for then
this summer would make a large progress and his Majesty may doe itt with greater
or less kindness to mee as he pleaseth, butt these are discourses, doe nott you thinke
that I push you on beyound your own time, for I know you to bee the most diligent
& eager persuer of matters of this nature in the world. I am mightily encouraged since
you applaud my designe for your chamber which shall bee my whole pastime within
dores to make itt very commode by the end of this month for if itt pleaseth God I
desire you to lay your designe to bee heere to keep our wedding day which is yett a
large space of time, to sett all wheeles att work and to fix somwhat which may make
us com to towne in the winter into a small habitation of our owne if the business of
𝒦 [*the excise*] goes on that certainely doth itt for anything els I desire to bee surprised rather than to beleeve itt. Pray keep up your cajoles to 13 & his madam. Huby
was heere on Friday and Austine Briggs who is very kind to mee and takes itt kindly
to bee continued in his employments for which he has his commission.

[*f.*3] I sent to see Windham's wife butt she was gon to Raineham. My Lord
Townshend came to Norwich on Saterday night to Briggs his [*house*] butt Kilby that
saw him light saw neither wife nor child who went perhapps at Chappelithfield[736] for
Sir John Hobart came to him a quarter of an hower after hee came in. I doe suppose
they will bee all att Blickling this week, of whome Ile take noe further notice unless
they take itt of mee, & though I meane to returne Hobart his visitt, Ile stay till the
other bee gon.

Here has beene both cherries and roses therefore pray make hast downe for itt's a
most sweet place & 𝒦 [*the excise*] may make itt sweeter.

To salute my vice-admiralty there is a boat taken in the sea by Paul Clark worth
som £20 which as soone as my commission coms I shall speak with and use itt either
there or att Yarmouth for fishing: my man Rawlins sayth that Mr Phillipps told him
my Lord Townshend made one yeare £700 of itt but that must be in time of the
Dutch warr for now I do nott believe itt's worth £100 butt Ile endeavor to putt itt in
the best method to avoid being cheated. I am now gooing to write to my Lord
Treasurer & my Lord Great Chamberlaine,[737] pray doe you seale them both and
remember Paine has a seale or too of mine which must nott bee lost.

I have had a little spell of the gout soe last night I took guacum[738] which workes
nott soe well as itt uses to doe butt I thank God I can sett my foot on the ground and
I hope itt will away as formerly. Sir Henry Bedingfeld writt mee a letter today, hee
will by the next post write to his mistress as he calls the Dutchess of Lauderdale[739]
concerning 600 [*me*] and he pretends to have as much interest there as any man on
the earth. He has allsoe written to 19 [*Sir Henry Bedingfeld jr*] to write to his
friends to speake well & confirme all old thinges with ⊗. By the next post I shall send

---

[736] Chapelfield (originally Chapel in the Field) was the Hobarts' house in Norwich.
[737] Lord Arlington
[738] Gum guaicum from the tree *lignum vitae* had a number of medicinal uses.
[739] Elizabeth, duchess of Lauderdale: as Elizabeth, countess of Dysart she had been an active member
of the royalist secret organization the 'Sealed Knot' during the interregnum, and Sir Henry had been living
with the court in exile, where he presumably met her.

you a letter for *4000*, I could now butt finish one for my Lord Treasurer[740] which pray seale and [*f.*4] give him after you have read itt: Don[741] writes mee word hee is going for Ireland the 8th day of May present, by the next post I shall write to him, butt should bee very glad you would in the meane time keep up the old interest with his daughter for I verily beleeve hee has a most kind inclination for mee in all thinges.

The weather heere is so extreamely hott that I must needs have a little stuff sute for every day which I would have the Quaker make att a price, drawers & all, and the next post Ile send him up measures, I had once one made for £5 by a Quaker which pleased mee most extreamely; I reserve my new sute till Whitsuntide that I goe to Norwich and the stuff one I weare is hotter then cloth. Pray bee very kind to Sir William Doyly for I doe ashure you he is soe to mee in many respects, and try what you can doe to sett *19* [*Sir Henry Bedingfeld jr*] right in the opinion of ▽ & ✧ [*Lady Danby & my Lord Treasurer*] for I know he may bee serviceable to them and I hope *600* & *700* [*we*] will arrive to that creditt as to bee beeleeved by them in what they say. When I take the penn in my hand to you I can never leave of[*f*], meethinkes I am conversing with you which to mee is the pleasantest conversation in the world & the greatest joy I have in itt and the expectation of your letters are the best expectations I have and the reading of them the pleasantest moments especially when your hopes are cheered up. I hope L & H[742] stop their hands to write mee that 𝒦 [*the excise*] is concluded. Pray present my kind service to Mr Brent and know if I must receive & sweare againe for this vice admiralty. I beleeve verdict against my Lord Digby will bee a leading card to that against Dr Hewse,[743] Sir Henry Bedingfeld has tryed to stop itt with my Lord Townshend butt he is inflexible. My Lady Anne Coke is certainly with child they say & he is mighty kind to mee and in all his discourses of mee. Pray present my humble service to *13* whom I shall shortly write to. Your children are very well & present their duty, Mrs Cooper, Mr Gough, Major Doughty and

*Signed*: he who loves you above the world, Yarmouth
*Postscript*: My service to my son & daughter & to Mal
*NRO: BL/Y/1/144*

## Deposition by inhabitants of Cawston

**1676, May 4**. These certify that upon the day and year above written beeing Ascension Day and the day on which of ancient custome the parish of Cawston use to go their perambulation, wee John Hildeyerd doctor of laws & rector and John Lomb churchwarden with severall others of our parish of Cawston went the bounds of the said parish. And in this perambulation wee went unto a stone standing in the lane leading from Cawston to Norwich commonly called a dowle stone[744] which is just by Mr Hirn's house and sent John Lomb & Harold Gamble to demand drink of Mr Hirne which his predecessors had alwayes granted unto the parish of Cawston at that stone in acknowledgment of their civility in not passing in their perambulation

---

[740] For this letter *see* British Library: Egerton MS 3329, f.94     [741] Thomas Henshaw
[742] Lee & Hoet                 [743] Dr Owen Hughes          [744] A boundary stone

through his mansion house. The servants of the said Mr Hirne lock't the gate & denyed their master saying hee was not at home. Whereupon wee sent for an iron crowe to make a mark upon the brick wall, where anciently when there was a mud wall was a gate. And this wee did because the judge at the last assizes at Norwich enquired if wee had in our said perambulation made any such marks, which had been done but so small as they could not be well seen. And whilst John Lomb was making this mark Mr Hirne came out & spit upon the handle of his staff, and with much fury ran to John Lomb & violently laid him over the pate with an oaken stick, then gave him a second blow. Dr Hildeyerd after the first blow demanded what he meant beeing a justice of peace. Hee replyed he would strike him for digging downe his wall and then struck a second, making a third blow at Dr Hildeyerd. The doctor struck Mr Hirn & throwing away his cane boxed him. To which wee standing in the king's highway in the above mentioned lane give testimony & set our hands

*Signed*: John Dewing, Gilbert Margatson, Anthony Atthill, William Dewing senior, William Dewing junior, John Fairchild, Edward Bradfield, Richard Giles, Harold Gamble, Thomas Godfrey, William Garwood
*Copy in the hand of John Gough*
*NRO: BL/Y/1/145*

## Owen Hughes to Robert, Viscount Yarmouth

**1676, May 5, The Black Boy on Ludgate Hill**. My lord, my obligations to your honor are infinitely beyond any acknowledgements that can be made in the bounds of a letter; it must be the buisness of my whole life to express them, this I assure your lordship that your lordship has placed your favors upon a man that is truly sensible and resolved to be gratefull and your lordship has my life and fortunes to command in every thing, that may be thought to conduce to your honor's service. And though my little concern and the methods of prudence have kept me yet in some distance, yet my love and steadiness are as true and fix't, as if I were admitted to mor plausible and nere priviledges. To serve your lordship I would be content to be a hewer of wood and drawer of water; and sometimes those little things serve the family to good purpose: and I could have chearfully sung my *nunc dimittis*, when your lordship completed the restoration of your county.

My lord I am related to your honor as vice-admiral of Norfolk which is my conquest, pride, and will be my reputation – but 'tis a [?]little unfortunate to me, that your lordship's patent is not yett in your hands; for 'tis not safe to act without it, neither can it be ante-dated: the present state of that affaire looks towards some profitt and advantage, for I am informed that there is a vessell stranded nere Paston, which prooves a derelict: upon that account your lordship will have the greatest right and claime to her: there is another at Monesly[745] that has the same fate; this last is allready secured, t'other I most humbly advice may be regarded upon the same score; for your lordship may command any of your servants publiquely to take notice thereof, as by commission from your lordship (or my self) and to take possession

[745] Mundesley, Norfolk

thereof for the use of the admiralty.

My lord, the things of this prosequuting world are uncertaine; but 'tis most certaine, that I am, and ever will be, my very good lord,

*Signed*: your lordship's most faithfull, obliged and humble servant, Owen Hughes
*Addressed*: These to the right honourable Robert Vicount Yarmouth, Lord Leifetenant of Norfolk, att Oxnead in Norfolk, humbly present [*postmark*]
NRO: BL/Y/1/146

## Robert, Viscount Yarmouth to Rebecca, Viscountess Yarmouth

**1676, May 5**. My deare hart, I have beene confined with the gout to my chamber since Monday butt of nights gott downe into the parlor and am soe lame of one foot that I cannott sett to the ground, itt is a cold and windy humor, I have this day sent for Dr Hawse[746] to com to mee and will take of him som gentle physick. This day is com to dine heere my Lord Astley,[747] Sir Phillip Woodhowse and Sir Jacob Astley butt I cannott gett downe staires, this windy gout has strangely mooved my spleene & made mee melancholy against which your letters are the best antidotes. I am well pleased that the business of 𝒦 [*the excise*] is lickely to tugg throwe soe many difficultyes, butt I wonder Backwell[748] should be soe much his owne enemie as to injure himself by discouraging Dashwood sure that was folly, I wonder the long captaine could never spare me one letter yett: my son writt to mee the last post and lookes on the business as good as don (would I could heare itt were soe though). Pray remember mee to Mr Brent and lett him <him> knowe his chadfish[749] he gave mee is the best meat I did ever eat. You speake of a patent for the vice admiralty, I thought itt had onely beene a commission from the commissioners of the admiralty, Mr Doughty comes out of towne to morrowe I hope hee'l bring itt with him, for itt will bee necessary I have itt betweene this and Whitsun Thursday when I am to bee att Norwich. Itt's a strange scene altered you write mee from *10* & *12* to *8* and yett all this to bee for ✧ [*my Lord Treasurer's*] advantage too & for the contrary to *15*, & that *6* & *36* should bee of *15* is a thing past the beleeve of *600* [*myself*], and makes him[750] rove mightily in his fancy to fathome the intreauge which I doubt may not proove soe well to ▽ & ✧ [*Lady Danby & my Lord Treasurer*] as is imagined; what I writt to my Lord Marshall about Sir John Holland you may give him private notice nott *to* exasperate ▽ [*Lady Danby's*] fury, in attempting thinges contrary to their [*f.2*] sense who cannott judge of matters concerning the country soe well as wee. My Lord Townshend came to Norwich on Saterday night, Sir John Hobart mett him butt went

[746] Probably John Hawys or Hawse of Norwich, doctor of physick (*The Visitation of Norfolk, 1664* (NRS, IV (1933), p. 97)). It is difficult to distinguish him from Dr Owen Hughes, who was a doctor of laws, because Lord Yarmouth used the same variant spellings for both names. References not relating to Yarmouth's health have been indexed under Hughes.

[747] Isaac, 3rd baron Astley of Reading; he was a cousin of Sir Jacob Astley, and Wodehouse was Sir Jacob's father-in-law.

[748] Backwell was one of the merchants who had lost heavily by the Stop of the Exchequer and stood to gain when the excise was farmed under revised conditions.

[749] A fish known as the river herring

[750] i.e. me; Lord Yarmouth uses the third person with all the ciphers, including his own.

home that night, the next morning he went to Christchurch[751] with Sir Peter Gleane, Captaine Rookwood & his couzin Townshend[752] in his company, all right men for the Church of England, and tooke som paines though too late to profess himself noe lover of the presbitery, on Monday he went a fishing all day att Captain Rookwood's & on Tuesday home by Mr Neaves & Sir Henry Bedingfeld from whome I just now I [sic] received the inclosed which you soe desired me to gett for the Dutchess of Lauderdale, I hope [?]she will diserve your favor. I know nott if the ring that father gave mee was amongst that parcell, I should bee glad to weare itt if itt were.

I am very glad you have itt in your mind to doe somwhat about Yarmouth for that's the onely thing will doe my business suddenly[753] for the Yarmouth *men* will baffle & baffle[754] & never doe any thing and the King mythinkes should bee glad to improove an estate hee is concerned in. Heere is Mr Flynt & England now heere butt all our discourse is words, and if this were don I would make them pay for their convenience.

I have now noe more to say to you, your children are well & present their dutys to you, soe doth Mr Gough, Major Doughty, Mrs Cooper, Mr Hurton, Mr Peckover; a line from you would revive to [sic] promise that you will endeavor to gett him in at Windsor or in som place.

Pray God send us with joy to meet & speedily, I am my deare hart

*Signed*: yours till death, Yarmouth

*NRO: BL/Y/1/147*

## Robert, Viscount Yarmouth to Rebecca, Viscountess Yarmouth

**1676, May 10**. My dearest deare, I came this day of my chamber, went into my coach, tooke the ayre in the parke, came home and eat my dinner with a very good appetite. Yesterday heere was much company with mee, Dr Smith, Mr Corie,[755] Mr [?]Bark, Captaine Bladwell,[756] Major Waldgrave and many others and this day I am nott free though itt's one of my private dayes, I have taken physick and had Dr Hawse with mee and intend to take more and empty my body most bravely of which I have beene noe ill husband for I have observed all the temperate methods I can. I am much concerned to find such delayes in the K [*the excise*] which makes mee begin to feare least itt should slip from us and the newse of seven shares more is nott over pleasant, by degrees Ile observe all your commands and have now written a letter to my Lord Lindsy which peruse, seale and give him; I long for Mr Doughty's returne whome wee expected the last night by the flying coach but certainely will bee heere this night, I hope I shall thence have a full narrative of such perticulars as you will nott trust the common post with, you invite mee to patience, alas my deare I have beene beene [sic] bred up in that schoole long enough to attend a good issue in any matter with all the delay imaginable: I should be very glad to heare further of the

---

[751] i.e. Norwich Cathedral
[752] Thomas Townshend of Norwich                    [753] i.e. speedily
[754] i.e. quibble, shuffle
[755] Francis Corie, MP for Norwich, or his cousin Thomas, the town clerk.
[756] Sir John Bladwell (c.1616–1680) of Rougham, deputy lieutenant

business of *6 36* ✧ & ▽ [*my Lord Treasurer & Lady Danby*] for *24* [*Sir Henry Bedingfeld*] & *19* [*Sir Henry Bedingfeld jr*] I know they will doe anything they can, *24* [*Sir Henry Bedingfeld*] dines heere on Friday next, and then wee shall have variety of discourse, that which you sayd ⊗ sayd to Mrs Brumley of *600* [*me*] was a great while agoe and nott lately, all that's now in my mind is to settle the militia in this country soe as to give his Majesty and the Duke a good accompt of itt which I doubt nott butt I shall bee able [*f.2*] to doe in a short time. Yesterday the children were invited to Captaine Harbord's to dinner and to a bull-bayting where they were most kindly treated, I am glad Mr Henshaw is soe kind as to trust his jewell[757] in your hand, this is a most sweete place pray God send you hither to mee, itt lookes soe greene and sweet that the very aire is a balsome. I intend this week to send over to Halcom butt defferr itt a day or two that my gardiner may carrie my Lady Anne a pound of cherries.

I thanke you for the care you have of mee and all my affaires of which since you have faire hopes I will nott dispaire nor dispond, all I feare is that Sir John should smell any thing about the exise from my son of which pray satisfy mee for Ile have nothing to doe with him in any matter. I have broken more braines about him then hee's worth, and as to the religious part can forgive him, butt never to deale for a penny one way or other, and I hope there's noe such thing butt what my spleene and gout creates. Mr Eldred who has beene long languishing died the last night, my last letter was soe long that this shall bee shorter, my service to my son & daughter, to Charles & Charlotte, your children present their dutys and I am whilst I breathe

*Signed*: your most affectionate servant, Yarmouth
*Addressed*: These present to the right honorable the Lady Viscountess Yarmouth att the Golden Ball in Suffolke Street, London [postmark]
*NRO: BL/Y/1/148*

## Robert, Viscount Yarmouth to Rebecca, Viscountess Yarmouth

**1676, May 12**. My deare hart, your letters are such cordialls that they are able to sett a gouty man on his leggs againe – I goe now abroad and take the sweet ayre every day, butt I have a great deale of company dayly heere, and Sir John Hobart, though I have nott have nott [*sic*] had time to returne his first visitt, has made mee a second and a long one, butt I suppose itt was about the business of Dr Hyliard and Mr Hyrne who is very ill of an unlucky blow in the head which hitt him with the iron pike in the end of the [?]cane and give him a dangerous hurt, but this was in the doctor's defence. Sir John Hobart is civill in the matter and I fancy all will end in a composure of differences between Hyrne & him, butt give me leave to tell you, parsonns are silly animalls in the menagement of their owne affaires, and though I am the doctor's friend I have shewne him his imprudences in this which he has thanked mee for, butt as to the meritts of the cause itt's of his side. Just now is com in Sir Henry Bedingfeld & my lady, and my couzin Windham, and som others to dinner and I have the largest <bream> *turbott* sent mee for a present that has beene seene and I have had many

---

[757] His only surviving child Anne who stayed with Lady Yarmouth while Henshaw was in Ireland.

presents. As to my neighbour I knowe him well enough and shall answer all civilityes but noe trust nor confidence: itt's a strange piece of service you have don ✧ & ▽ [*my Lord Treasurer & Lady Danby*] with *6* & *36* for *8* must needes have lost them, had nott the tide <turned> [*f.*2] beene turned by you which to mee itt appears was absolutely don. I doe expect Mr Doughty to morrowe night with som impatience that with freedome I may read your history, I am infinitely pleased to heare the business of *K* [*the excise*] is in soe happy a way, I hope after soe many confirmations wee shall nott bee baulked butt that a post or two will say itt's don. I thanke God I am very well though I hault a little, Dr Hawse his wife has altered a roome for mee, the doctor has with soe much kindness invited mee, as I shall ly noe where els, and doe hope I shall give a good accompt of the militia, as good an one as any that has gon before mee if nott a better, a little time will doe itt; I am hugely pleased with the hopes that Sir John Earnly will doe that business judiciously of the custome howse for Yarmouth: I will now goe downe & close up my letter when I have discoursed Sir Henry & my lady, onely first I have sent to see this day the family of the Henninghams[758] and tomorrowe I send to Holkham, and shall send my Lady Anne a baskett of cheries and som pease from this pore place.

Your & my old & best friends Sir Henry & my lady present their services, wee drunke your health this day att a very good dinner which my peavish adversaries pride themselves in hoping I shall nott be able to maintaine. [*f.*3] *24* [*Sir Henry Bedingfeld*] & *19* [*Sir Henry Bedingfeld jr*] will doe all in their power to keep thinges warme where they have begun, and are the cordialest friends in nature.

My couzin Windham dined heere as he came home nott having seene his wife, he has thanked mee againe & againe for his deputy leiftenantship and professes his readiness to shew his integrity to the Crowne & mee. On Sunday by the permission of God I doe intend to receive the blessed sacrament & to take the oathes att the session on Thursday where there will bee deputy lieftenants enough therefore I wonder you should take care for Sir John Pettus who is att London and defferred his journey som time to attend mee. Till Monday I hartily bid you farewell, my service to all my friends:

*Signed*: my dearest I am yours for ever, Yarmouth
*NRO: BL/Y/1/149*

## Robert, Viscount Yarmouth to Rebecca, Viscountess Yarmouth

**1676, May 15**. My dearest deare, on Saterday betimes Mr Doughty came and delivered mee your pacquett of letters which was very welcome to mee as alsoe the newse of your health, butt when I heard that on Thursday night a man was to ly with you what do you thinke I thought then? Pray give mee a perticular accompt of the young gentleman,[759] how he behaved himself and how this favor came to bee accorded you though the new cote is somwhat of the matter. I wish with all my hart I could heare that the shuffles about the business of *K* [*the excise*] were over and that some con-

---

[758] Lady Mary Heveningham, widow of William Heveningham the regicide, and her son Sir William Heveningham of Ketteringham. William Heveningham the regicide was a first cousin of Sir William Paston, being the son of Sir William's aunt Bridget Paston.          [759] i.e. his grandson Charles Paston

clusion were made though I licke well that the gratuities bee adjusted for then noe bodie will have reason to complaine, butt the lord knows on what tearmes these new men com in. I doe wonder that none of my partners would vouchsafe to sett pen to paper butt keep mee totally in the darke, and my cousin Peregrine Bertie in his letter speakes nott one word of itt, I am most hartily glad to find you soe full of hopes and comfort for indeed you have don great thinges and I doe hope ✧ & ▽ [my Lord Treasurer & Lady Danby] will esteeme them soe and in the business of 6 & 36 and 8; I have had noe letter from my Lord Marshall. That which you writt about my Lord Plimmouth I doe very well approove butt you must have a care nott to disoblidge the other[760] who I beleeve will allwaies bee cheif in the favor of his Majesty, butt I doe wonder how you steere betweene my Lady Lindsey[761] & my Lady Newburgh & my Lady Wentworth & my Lady Harvey[762] & the Dutchess of Lauderdale & my Lady Trevor, I would faine be satisfied a little in these matters: on Saterday morning I sent [f.2] John Gammon over to my Lady Anne Coke with a baskett of cherries of about a pound and half, and som such licke parcell of pease, my Lady Anne fell on them in bed and itt was the kindliest taken that ever you heard, they gave the gardiner a peece and returned the inclosed letter[763] which you may shew my Lady Danby if you please.

It will please 24 [Sir Henry Bedingfeld] highly when I give him an accompt of the success of his letter and I am glad allsoe that itt did him good with ▽ & ✧ [Lady Danby & my Lord Treasurer].

I thanke God I goe abroad every day now I have taken much physick which I beleeve has disturbed mee butt I hope to find the effects of itt now.

This afternooone I am going to the great Zar of Muscovy my nieghbor[764] to returne one of his too visitts where after halfe an howres dissimulation on both sides I will com home againe. I take great care of your chamber which will be very commode & warme, I doe nott wonder that you allwaies catched cold in itt. The alcove and betweene the wainscott & the cornish will take up soe much as is in the inclosed note of anie prittie stuff to hang itt which I hope your brother George or Mr Rutty will furnish. Thomas Reeve measured itt and makes mee beleeve they will understand this note att London, I make the joyner work all the hollie days for dispatch.

On Thursday morning I goe to Norwich where I must sweare againe for the new commission having received[765] yesterday and prayed for you att that instant, Sir William Doyly writt to mee this day that hee's com downe on purpose to attend mee, and that he left you in health on Wednesday night.

[f.3] My perewig is the basest one that by the next flying coach itt must bee sent

[760] i.e. the duke of Monmouth

[761] Elizabeth, wife of Yarmouth's cousin Robert Bertie, 3rd earl of Lindsey

[762] Probably Elizabeth, widow of Sir Daniel Harvey (1631–1672); she was the daughter of Edward, Lord Montagu of Boughton, and was a cousin of Lord Yarmouth.

[763] See Robert Coke to Lord Yarmouth, 13 May 1676, commenting that no other place in Norfolk could have produced cherries so early (British Library: Add. MSS 27447, f.359). The variety was probably a black cherry known as Kerroon or Carone. I am indebted to the Royal Horticultural Society for information on early-fruiting cherries.

[764] Sir John Hobart of Blickling                    [765] i.e. having received the sacrament

up againe and either the [?]ld knave must give Lewis my money or another soe that I must weare my old one att Norwich.

Your children are well and present their duty to you, tomorrowe I expect Sir Will Adams and severall others. I have now nothing more to say butt that I am for ever

*Signed*: your most humble servant, Yarmouth

*Postscript*: I am glad you remember Yarmouth business, heere was Watts yesterday and sayth if such a thing could bee don everybody would presently build there. I shall by the next write to my cousin Peregrine, my service to Mrs Henshaw & Mal. *NRO: BL/Y/1/150*

## Robert, Viscount Yarmouth to Rebecca, Viscountess Yarmouth

**1676, May 17**. My dearest deare, yours I received with many politick instances of which I am as much aware of as your imagination can suggest cautions to you, and if I were to tread over againe the steps I have yett made they should bee in the same path, ▽ [*Lady Danby's*] fancy can never bee helped itt's soe extravagant butt every day will give <[?]her> proofes of the cooleness there but a man in my post must act with decency and soe I will and my owne method in that will bee my best guide. You cleerely mistake *13* letter, I conclude with you nott to make any request that any should bee putt out[766] butt I must give an accompt who they are that have diserted the service and those I hope my Lord Treasurer will see shall nott stand, though I have private reasons why I wish Sir John Holland might for he has shewen great respects to mee butt if itt bee nott thought fitt I cannott help itt, when I have beene att Norwich whether tomorrowe I am to goe I shall knowe better how matters will stand, and soe bee able to give a better accompt of itt, you need nott doubt my vigilancy in all thinges insoemuch as itt allmost makes mee madd till I have setled the affaire which I hope I shall doe and disoblidge as few as is possible. Heere was yesterday a great deale of company, Major Gray & his nephew Captaine Gray, Sir William Rant, the Prestons, Sir Will Adams who I have made colonel of the citty regiment, hee being the man they pitched on with most favor and desire, and severall others; Mr Briggs his letter might containe what itt pleased butt what you write was quite out of the way of anything that passed, butt if an [?]ass bee [f.2] to interprett I cannott help neither sayings nor writings. Dawson was heere yesterday from Yarmouth and is in the same mind that if I gett what hee writt to you effected, the business is don; to his knowledge there are those that would immediately begin even this summer and itt would bee all speedily built, I thought you had designed Sir John Earnly should have don you som favor in itt, butt I heare you speake of him noe more.

As to the schoole att Walsham[767] all the care shall be taken that can bee and without an universall approbation I shall nott bee my owne chooser, heere are som parsonns com this day with one that the bishop putt in their as lecturer whome they

---

[766] i.e. out of the commission of the peace

[767] Yarmouth's great-great-grandfather Sir William Paston had founded a grammar school at North Walsham in 1606, which is now Paston Sixth Form College, North Walsham.

recommend, there is lickewise the usher of Norwich schoole, men both they say very fitt for the employment.

On Monday in the afternoone I was att Blickling where I saw her ladyshipp and Windham's wife butt they made their retreat presently & Sir John & Windham & I stayd about an howre together taking a pipe and Sir John drunke your health, and I came away as wise as I went.

My son's letter gave mee a cold pye,[768] I see their is an universall plott to beat us of[f] and these monied *men* dive into our project to cast us out for others, I doe now dispaire though Sir George Wakeman in Lewis' letter sends mee a confident message, and that you say Mr Brent is vigorous in the matter, yett I doubt itt's a lost game, [f.3] I shall bee glad to heare otherwise by the next post and som good newse of the reallityes of ▽ ✧ [*Lady Danby & my Lord Treasurer*] 6 36 8. I am glad you intend to goe to ⊗ to make my compliment there which I am sure you will doe in as good termes and better then I can direct.

Pray God send us suddainely now to meet, your lodging goes on apace and I doe hope you will approove of a dull contrivance if there could bee a bed sutable to the hanging & the furniture that's now there would furnish another roome and if you thinke to order itt soe send me word by the next.

I <burne> burne all your letters when I have read them over & over and keep none by mee, I had forgott to tell you Sir William Henningham was heere yesterday att dinner, I hope his Majesty will find wayes to support mee for his owne honor for this way cannott hold out els. I shall consider of what you saye of May <day> the 29th[769] which will bee more taken notice of with som few friends and the county people att a bonefire then the other formall way which will bee both troublesom & chargeable, decent thinges shall bee don butt I that feast twice a week constantly, and on the other dayes am never empty need doe no more. We have drunke your bed-fellowes health heere, I meane little deare Charles who you writt mee word was to ly with you, and to cuccold mee, I doe desire to know how he behaved himself.

[f.4] You never putt in a word of pore Peckover who is a little blanck to find that other people are remembred and hee neglected, who is the most zealous man in the world for your cawse and mine.

From Norwich on Friday you will have butt a short letter from mee for I shall bee verie busie butt on Monday you shall have a long one, I am every day in your chamber with the workmen and the alteration will I thinke make that convenient which noe screene before could cure.

I thanke God my gout is gon & I have swinged my body with physick, but my owne salt which while I live Ile never neglect soe long againe Dr Hawse beleeves the best medicine in the world for the scurvey and pray doe you take itt. Sir George Wakeman has a glass full which I desire you to gett of him for itt's most laborious to make. Pray present my harty service to him and for 𝒦 [*the excise*] tell him I am *courage de brebis*,[770] I asked once or twice what's become of Mr Cheek & his lady?

Remember mee to Mr Brent and tell him if he doth retrive our game hee's the

---

[768] i.e. a wake-up call          [769] 29 May was the King's birthday, and also Paston's own.
[770] From *courage de brebis tantost venu tantost failly*: i.e. the courage of a sheep, sometimes coming, sometimes failing.

best man ith' world and better if he sends mee downe an instrument for the custome-howse att Yarmouth, pray lett Mr Bulwer butt fix the £33 now due to Suckling[771] and then wee shall for treat for the principle afterwards. I am with all imaginable fervency

*Signed*: yours, Yarmouth
*Postscript*: Your children are well present their duty, Gough, Cooper, Hurton, Mr Peckover the same. My love to Mrs Mary: my service to Mrs Henshaw.
*NRO: BL/Y/1/151*

## Robert Brent to Robert, Viscount Yarmouth

**1676, May 18**. My lord, when I confesse I received your lordship's letter I know not with what face I may expect your pardon for my silence unless it be (as the truth is) that I dayly expected an oportunity of sending your lordship an happy conclusion of your great affaire which was one part of the comands of your letters and put by your lordshipp into my province wherein I have endeavoured to act my part but *very* feebly for want of your lordshipp's presence here, the want whereof made the major part of your partners[772] *courage de brebis* yet have made the best of a bad markett, and have at last concluded with the country gentlemen (haveing first tryed many wayes of raising the whole money) upon these termes. *vizt.* first that those of the country gentlemen now lending as have bin farmers shall have their owne farmes & then will remaine about fourteen countyes (besides the home farme) out of which your lord-shipp & partners have preference besides Norfolk allotted to your lordship only to choose six, the rest with the home farme [*f*.2] is to be divided into eighteen parts whereof your lordshipp & partners to have six & the country gentlemen twelve, but the government of the whole is to be equall between them and your lordshipp & part-ners who are all to raise their shares of the money. This being the substance of their agreement they all goe tomorrow to my Lord Treasurer to give & receive mutuall assurances of compliance and performances of your lordshipp's former proposalls save only that the country gentlemen doe desire to alter that part of the proposall which allowes £500,000 per annum in case the duty be not continued, and insert this in its roome – that in that case they will abide by my Lord Treasurer's judgment what shalbe given and <in that case> they ascribe two reasons of this alteration, *vizt.* 1. that the duty may not clearly appear in parliament what it will be without the addi-tion, 2. because they think themselves safe in my Lord Treasurer's justice not to impose more then the reall value in proportion upon those foundations I laid believe my Lord Treasurer will consent to the alteration if he consent & stand by the originall [*f*.3] proposall which I assure your lordshipp he hath great temptations to waive, & nothing but the considerations of the King's service being equally served by the one as by the other can have any place with him in this affaire to prefer your lordshipp's party *to* which I doubt not he hath a particular kindnes for your lordshipp's sake, and I hope it will shortly appeare soe, when we shall desire your lordshipp's presence

---

[771] Robert Suckling held one of Yarmouth's mortgages which had been renewed in 1675 (NRO: AYL 91).     [772] i.e. in the exise

to the confirmation of this busines; in the mean tyme I have undertaken another for your lordshipp's service, that of New Yarmouth[773] of which I have the mapp from my lady and will take the first & best oportunity of moving that matter to my Lord Treasurer and give your lordship an accompt of it; begging your lordshipp's pardon for this which with my most faithfull humble service is writ in hast & sent as hastily by the post from, my lord,

*Signed*: your lordshipp's most obedient humble servant, Rob Brent
*NRO: BL/Y/1/152*

## Robert, Viscount Yarmouth to Rebecca, Viscountess Yarmouth

[*1676*].[774] Pray lett my Lord Marshall knowe that Captaine Brandsby has never appeared heere att [*sic*] that I am informed this day privately that Sir Jeames Johnston who is as great a rouge to my Lord Marshall as lives and a dispiser of all the world butt my Lord Townshend has beene dealing with Brandsby nott to accept a commission that England might com in which I for my part should bee glad of, butt I shall desire my Lord Marshall's orders beeing wholy to bee disposed by him. Brandsby is this day gon for London, I wish my Lord Marshall would send mee his order in itt.

*Unsigned but in Lord Yarmouth's hand*
*Addressed*: These present to the right honorable the Lady Viscountess Yarmouth at the Golden Ball in Suffolke Street, London
*NRO: BL/Y/2/15*

## Robert, Viscount Yarmouth to Rebecca, Viscountess Yarmouth

**1676, May 19**. My deare hart, yours came to mee att Norwich whence this comes to you where I have againe taken the o[a]thes and beene verie busie and am soe now att this howre, I wonder how you thinke I bestowe my time that you send mee to Cristchurch to prayers where I have nott time to goe nor yett to see any person. Heere are with mee these deputy leiftenants, Sir Phillip Woodhowse, Sir Jacob Astley, my cousin Coke, Mr Windham, Sir Nevile Catalyne, Mr Coke of Broome, Sir Will Doyly, Sir Will Adams, Phil Harbord,[775] and before I stirr, which will bee tomorrowe, I hope I shall have setled most part of the militia, though the first private muster cannott bee till the 3[r]d of July and the great generall muster att which I must bee my self nott till the latter end of harvest. I am glad $X$ will gett [?]$D$ to doe that same you write of though the next I shall returne a list of the justices of peace in the county to him.

The greatest difficulty I am licke to meet is in the towne of Yarmouth where Sir Thomas Meddowes who I had designed all the kindness in the world useth mee peremptorily standing upon termes that unless Huntington bee putt out he will nott serve, I shall find others in his place, every body cries out upon this unhandsom way

---

[773] i.e. Lord Yarmouth's proposed development on the west side of the river Yare, then in Suffolk, opposite the old town of Yarmouth.

[774] This letter is undated but has been placed in May 1676 because it appears to relate to the settlement of the Yarmouth militia.          [775] Colonel Philip Harbord (d.1687), eldest son of Sir Charles

of his proceedings butt they are the stubbornest ill naturd people in the world, I have taken my methods soe as to displease as few as I may butt itt's impossible to please all. I am amased att the passage in your letter concerning 𝒦 [*the excise*] and Lewis comming downe tomorrowe, butt more att my [*f.2*] comming which I hope in God you may divert, there's nothing butt may bee acted in my absence and it will bee an horrible trouble and charge without there bee somwhat in the bargaine which seeme nott to hint that may make amends.

Currance[776] did send me a subpoena which I ordered Mr <Bulwer> Hurton to send itt up to Mr Bulwer to take care of.

Dr Hawse has invited mee to dinner tomorrowe from whence I goe home, they are the mightiest kind to mee in the world and present their service to you, all heere doe the same, on Monday you may expect from mee a long letter. I am now in the middle of my affaires faine to borrowe a moment. The mayor and the corporation have made mee a very civill visitt and are much pleased in the choise of a colonel, if the custome howse business bee don itt will infalibly doe mine att Yarmouth, if nott I dispaire.

My service to all, I am for ever

*Signed*: yours, Yarmouth

*Postscript*: My cousin Thomas Knyvett[777] I have made colonel of Sir John Holland's regiment of which Sir Nevile Catlyne gives him an accompt this day.

*Addressed*: These present to the right honourable the Lady Viscountess Yarmouth att the Golden Ball in Suffolke Street, London [*postmark*]

*NRO: BL/Y/1/153*

# Robert, Viscount Yarmouth to Rebecca, Viscountess Yarmouth

**1676, May 26**. My dearest deare, yours I received for which I give you many thankes, and doe now passionately long for the time of our meeting, I find that itt is time that must make any thing *work* unless wee are soe happy as to conclude this business of 𝒦 [*the excise*] which must needes proove very considerable, I am glad *4000* is in with us, twill strike the surer stroke butt how to putt of [*f*] the other three I cannott imagine without making them commissioners of the exise or som other recompense butt if this bee transacted without my privity what have I to doe with itt, I long to heare itt's finished once, I am very glad to find Mr Brent after having mooved the treasurer hopefull to doe the business of the customehowse att Yarmouth which will goe a great way in my affaire and certainly finish itt in a little time, pray sollicitt him to moove with as much speed as possibly. I am sorry to find ✧ & ▽ [*my Lord Treasurer & Lady Danby*] flagg in the business of *6 & 36 & 8* which may bee for their prejudice in the fixing *15*, who will never bee a true friend to *600* or *700* [*me or you*], butt I hope they flag nott in their kindness & esteeme for *700* [*you*], nor in their good intentions to *600* [*me*]; *40* I am sure is a fixt truehearted man. Mr

---

[776] John Corrance (c.1616–1694) of London and Rendlesham, Suffolk, brother-in-law of Sir Ralph Hare of Stow Bardolph. Corrance was one of Lord Yarmouth's mortgagees and brought a suit against him (see TNA: C5/465/83, NRO: NRS 4018, and Henning, *Commons*, II, p.135).

[777] Thomas Knyvett (1656–1693) of Ashwellthorpe

Corrance is the greatest Jew in nature thus to persecute mee, and itt's hard the hearing could not bee putt of [*f*], God's will be don in all thinges. I am sorrie ▽ [*Lady Danby*] coms before you com, I hope som what will alter or differ itt, as to your mother pray use your artifice to stand itt of [*f*] till about midsommer and certainly by that time you'l bee heere or send those that should com before you; your appartement will bee very neat and cleane and warme, this day the marble chimney peece was sett up and the joyner has sett up a great deale of the allkove and the wainscott, I wish the stuff were heere to hang itt for in a forthnight it will bee all don. As to what you writ of Barney[778] itt may be, butt his father is now in an humor to give away most of the estate from him to his eldest brother's son and is att the greatest fewd imaginable with him. I shall enquire further of the matter, but doe nott think itt lickely butt what agents they have is uncertaine. Mr Peckover is gon from Norwich into Suffolk this week with my cousin Coke who returnes to morrowe and then Peckover sayd he would com hither, and I shall know of him more butt I hope God will provide for my daughter at last on whome I rely for all thinges having noe visible hopes but what heaven menages which may be is the most certaine.

[*f*.2] I doe expect Sir Nevile Catalyne heere this day who went to Yarmouth to remonstrate to Sir Thomas Meaddowes his simplicaty[779] & ungratefullness butt hee is positive I heare soe I have contrived a way which will please the town better and make Sir Thomas be left alone to him self & his penitence which [*is*] to make Sir [*sic*] Thomas England colonel and Baly Thaxter leiftenant colonel, the two captaines as they now are, and young England another captaine. This is a peece of policy amongst our selves contrived to disappoint the other party: Sir Jeames Johnston is att London and is nott one that loves Meddowes unless this unites them, when this is don all is almost over.

On Monday Ile have a great bonfire butt I shall invite noe body butt som of my neare neighbors and the cuntry people to tipple, I hope you'l see his Majesty and shew him Charles.[780] Itt was a strange story you write mee of Harry Savile I am sorrie for it but princes must be handled with reverence otherwise there's noe dooings and he having faltered in that kind before methinkes should have been more cautious for I doubt this relaps will hardly bee pardoned.

That which you write mee <mee> of *10* is strange newse, pray tell mee what will becom of <*word deleted*> *12* & ☐. I am soe sick at your being in that stinking howse that I pray for your deliverance out of it hither, this place now is very sweet and whilst itt is in the perfection I faine would have your company; I doe butt now begin to bee well for I have beene as odd for one that has nott beene downe right sick as any man could bee, I believe itt a mighty fitt of spleene & scurvy. On Saterday after I have your letters I intend to goe see my cousin Wyndham and the next week Ile goe to Beckhall, I shall bee informed from you of my Lady Danby's motions this way which I presume will nott bee soe suddaine, I hope you'l perswade her to stay till you com.

---

[778] The Barneys or Berneys of Reedham were one of the most ancient gentry families in Norfolk (Blomefield, *Norfolk*, XI, pp 121–132; Edward Maunde Thompson (ed.), *Letters of Humphrey Prideaux*, p.166), and a marriage alliance seems to have been contemplated for Mary Paston; see also p.381 below.

[779] Simplicity i.e. lack of judgment

[780] Charles Paston was the King's grandson and also his godson.

I have nothing els more to say to you yett am I loth to leave of [*f*] writing: pray againe endeavor to stave of my journey to London, with all your artifice.

[*f.3*] I dined on Wedensday at old Wood's[781] att Braken Ash and was well treated there, and I hope I have made such a remonstrance to the old mann as will moove him to pay his sonn's debts, methought I found him very kind and complyant, however I have don a kind thing which Thomas Wood and his lady are infinitely sensible of.

If you have any fancy for the painting of the wainscott of your chamber more then bare white and a gold streek write mee word by the next that I may give instructions to Sterling about itt. Remember mee to my son & daughter, to the little ones, to Mrs Henshaw and Mal, pray bid Mal write to mee for somtimes she has newse you have nott.

I must now have don and doe confirme myself to bee with all the passion in the world,

*Signed*: yours, Yarmouth
*Postscript*: Mr Gough, Major Doughty, your children & all presents their dutys & service to you.
*NRO: BL/Y/1/154*

## John Gough to Colonel William Paston

**1676, June 5, Oxnead.** Honourable sir, the favours I have received from your family are so many and great that I should be unpardonably guilty should I not acknowledge them and very ungratefull should I not be ready in any capacity I can to serve it. And truly the service of it is in itself so great an honour and I have found it to mee so beneficiall that 'tis not to be wondered at if I am very ambitious both to be continued & further engaged in it. For this reason sir I have taken the confidence to become your humble petitioner that I may have the honour to be listed into your service and as my lord is pleased to own mee his chaplain at home, you would vouchsafe to take *mee* for yours in the field that so I may have the favour in the same capacity to serve his lordship in his household and you in your regiment. In this request sir my lord has vouchsafed to grant mee his consent & there is nothing wanting to compleat my aim but yours, which by this paper I do most humbly crave and do almost beforehand assure my self that you will give it to, honourable sir,

*Signed*: your most humble & obedient servant, John Gough
*Postscript*: I crave my most humble service presented to your honourable lady and the sweet young gentleman
*Addressed*: These to the honourable Collonel Paston at the Golden Ball in Suffolk Street in London humbly present
*NRO: BL/Y/1/155*

---

[781] Thomas Wood (1626–1699) the elder, of Bracon Ash

# Hamon Thurstone[782] to Robert Doughty

**1676, St John Baptist, Norwich**. Sir, you have formerly done to me reall & great favors, I have payd you with nothing but thankes, & that you have had from a sensable true hart, pray helpe me this once more.

My master the good Lord Yarmouth have often bedd me aske him ought wherin with convenience he might doe me good, I have been a great sufferer in the warr a great many thousand pounds, I am poor you see what I doe to live, I am growen very ould & would faine leave this imploy, but then I feare I should want to eate. Upon a certificate & my petition about five yeares since to the justices at sessions they granted me a pention of £10 per annum, & truly with a great complement that the tresury was then lowe but after they would left the pention hyer, & now it is most apt my lord appearing to serve his countrie I know will doe it for me, good sir please to motion it to him I know he will not be angrie, it is the only thinge that I shall ever aske, & it is to keepe me in my age, pray let my lord know according to his commands I delivered the muster roll & all other concernes of the hundred to Capt Doubty.

*Signed*: Sir, your most humble obliged servant, Hamo: Thurstone
*Addressed*: Present this to Robert Doughty senior esquire, Ayelsham
*NRO: BL/Y/1/156*

# Edmund Thaxter, George England, Richard Huntington, and Thomas England, to Robert, Viscount Yarmouth

**1676, July 3, Yarmouth**. May it please your lordship, wee having had a sight of that scandolous libell \*wrote\* by one Bowers[783] our late coffee man to Mr Secretary Williamson might be prompted to vindicate our reputations & to cleare ourselves from the unjust aspersions therein most falsly cast upon us: butt considering your lordshipp's creditt cannot wee hope ours will not be eclipsed or the least impaired by the most untrue suggestions of so malitious, envious & abject a person. Wee wholly decline it & choose rather to give your lordshipp some short account of the employment & deportment of this fellow since he lived att Yarmouth. About twenty yeares since he came to this towne in a most forlorn and impoverishd condition having scarce where withall to cover his nakedness: but by some meanes got to be an inferior officer in the excise under one Mr Greensmith & others then commissioners for that purpose but stayd not long in that imployment for in a short while for most notorious

---

[782] Hamon Thurstan, d.1694, a former royalist soldier, who is buried with his wife in the churchyard of St Stephen's, Norwich (Blomefield, *Norfolk*, IV, p.62).

[783] Richard Bower, a government agent who ran a coffee house in Great Yarmouth, had written to Williamson complaining that the Great Yarmouth magistrates made no attempt to suppress meetings of nonconformists, being nonconformists themselves, and had obtained commissions in the militia. Bower waited on Lord Yarmouth and subsequently wrote to him complaining about the situation in Great Yarmouth and professing his own attachment to the loyal party (*CSPD, 1676–7*, pp 155–7). Lord Yarmouth resented Bower's interference and presumption and encouraged the Great Yarmouth magistrates to fine him for selling ale without a licence. He was subsequently prosecuted by the magistrates for libel, but at Williamson's request Lord Yarmouth persuaded them to drop the proceedings. (*CSPD, 1678*, pp 1–2, 9–10; Gauci, *Great Yarmouth*, p.143)

& palpable unfaithfullness in the discharge of that office was turned out, & soon after he procured himself a land waiter's place in the customs & he behaving himself as little faithfully in this as in the former employment was for breach of trust after a short continuance discharged thereof. Next he listed himself for £8 per annum in a troop raised for plunder & decimation under Col[one]l Brewster & complyed most exactly with all the proceedings of the usurped powers & authority in the late troublesome & rebellious times: after his Majesty's most happy restauration he scrued himself (by what means wee knowe not) into severall places (successively) of publick trust but behaved himselfe so treacherously in all as he could not long keep any but was dismist for manyfest falsness & fraud in the execution thereof; and being <being> by these ill practises so well knowne he thought it vain again to attempt any employment of the like nature & therefore betoke himselfe to keep a coffee house, procures the publick intelligence & by caballing with some few persons of his owne humour, have ever since bin a buisy & troublesome man & in as much as in him laid, disturbing or incourraging the government of the towne, according to the apprehensions he had of the persons in whose hands it happned to be lodged: particularly he discovers much dissatisfaction with your lordship's late settlement of the militia in this corporation by complaining of the persons intrusted & most incessantly disswading severall (who wee humbly conceive are duly & legally assessed) [f.2] from appearing in their armes when summoned which courses of his unless timely prevented by some examplary punishment must unavoidably be highly prejudiciall to his Majesty's service in this place. Wee humbly submitt the premises to your lordship's prudence & pray your lordship's speedy consideration of some course effectually to punish the past & prevent the future ill behaviour of this insolent fellow whereby both the civill & military gover[n]ment of this place will in all probability be mannaged with much more ease and chearefullness then now it is.

*Signed*: Wee are your lordshipp's most faithfull & most obedient servants, Edm Thaxter, George England, Richd Huntington, Tho: England
*Addressed*: These for the right honourable Robert Lord Paston Viscount Yarmouth att the Golden Ball in Suffolke Street neare Charing Crosse, London [*postmark*]
*NRO: BL/Y/1/157*

## George England, Edmund Thaxter, Thomas Bransby, Richard Huntington, and Thomas England, to Robert, Viscount Yarmouth

**1676, July 7, Yarmouth**. May it please your lordshipp, in obedience to your lordshipp['s] command wee mustered our severall companies on Wedensday the 5th instant, & notwithstanding the great endeavours of Bowers & his complices wee had a very full and chearfull appearance; 120, 90, & not less then 80 in a company, very few defaults & as few complaints from whence it may be reasonnably concluded that our assessments were generally to the content & satisfaction of the inhabitants: what was amiss wee are very confident will be in every respect amended when your lordshipp commands another muster. The muster master had three yeares arrears & his present wages payd him with all readiness & found the arms & all things in as good a posture as could be expected from so short warning, thus much wee thought it our duty to signifie to your lordshipp not knowing but some use there of *might be made* in the prosecution of that daring & bold coffee man, of whom we gave your lordshipp some account on Munday last. Wee are with all due observance,

*Signed*: your lordship's most faithfull and most obedient servants, George England, Edm: Thaxter, Tho: Bransby, Richd Huntington, Tho England
*Addressed*: These to the right honourable Robert Lord Paston Viscount Yarmouth present att the Golden Ball in Suffolke Street neare Charing Crosse, London
*NRO: BL/Y/1/158*

## Robert Coke to Robert, Viscount Yarmouth

**1676, July 9, Godwick**.[784] My lord, since Mr Bedingfield's being out of commission for the peace,[785] that part of the country is likely to bee at a losse, Captaine Gibbons[786] being the onely justice of the peace thereabouts, who is too remote from Wells which is a contentious sea port towne, the dayly disorders that happen there make it necessary that some gentleman who is near them have a commission to keep them quiet & to determine the differences that arise among them. Mr William Armiger of North Creak who is a counsellor at law & I presume not unknowne to your lordship is a person very fitt for such a trust, I therefore beg of your lordship to use your interest with my Lord Chauncellor[787] to get a commission for him. I know him to bee an honest gentleman, & make no question but hee will manage the trust with prudence, & <and> except your lordship obtaine this favour for mee I shall find the townesmen of Wells very troublesome neighbours. Your lordship hath been pleased to bestow so many favours upon mee, which have een made mee presume to beg this. My wife & sister[788] present their services to your lordship & my Lady Yarmouth, which I desire your lordship to accept of, from my lord

*Signed*: your lordship's humble servant & kinsman, Robert Coke
*Addressed*: To the right honourable Robert Lord Viscount Yarmouth these present
*NRO: BL/Y/1/159*

## Edward L'estrange to Robert, Viscount Yarmouth

**1676, July 12, Norwich**. My lord, I have here inclosed sent your lordship the names of the deputy lieutenants that mett yesterday in the litle grand jury chamber in the castle of Norwich, as also an extract of their orders; the chiefe of their time being spent in signing of severall captains' muster rolls, and receiving an account of the hundred stores; all which I shall enter into your lordship's booke: the five Yarmouth captains appeared with compleat and full muster rolls, and for their encouragement

---

[784] Godwick Hall, near Tittleshall, was built by Sir Edward Coke in 1585.
[785] Christopher Bedingfeld, *see* Lord Yarmouth to Lord Danby, 5 June 1676 (British Library: Egerton 3339, f.111).    [786] Captain (later Sir) Francis Guybon (c.1639–1705)
[787] Heneage Finch (1621–1682), lord chancellor, later earl of Nottingham
[788] Probably his sister-in-law Lady Bridget Osborne, later countess of Plymouth

had £8 allowed to every company for to buy new trophies: I desire to receive your lordship's commands in a line or two, whether I shall keep the duplicates of the severall muster rolls which are to be returned by the captains, or deliver them to your lordship's secretary (who demands them of mee): here is order taken by Sir William Doyly, amongst the gentry to attend my Lord Chief Baron,[789] which I hope will answer your lordship's expectation: if your honour be pleased to let mee receive your commands in a letter, if it be directed to Alderman Briggs in Norwich for mee, it will come safe to my hands, for I shall (God willing) give my attendance here the next week at the assizes: this with the tendure of my humble service to your lordship, and right honourable concernes concludes mee, my lord,

*Signed*: your lordship's as most obliged so most faithfull servant, Edward L'estrange
*NRO: BL/Y/1/160*

## Robert, Viscount Yarmouth to Rebecca, Viscountess Yarmouth

**1676, July 16, Sunday morne eight of the clock**. My deare, after parting from you the sad thoughts brought mee asleep and Mr Snelling and I scarce waked till <ten> seven of the clock brought us to Hoggsdon, and ten to Bishop Stafford, where we found my Lord Marshall's artillery ready to receive him butt wee played too howres att pickquett before he, Madam Child, my Lady Frances his daughter and Mr Crane's sister of Rising came, then wee went to dinner where wee were very merry and my lord the kindest man to mee & my concernes in the world, wee had your health began by the lord & lady, who sayth he will com to Oxnett when the assizes are over, till when I beeleeve shee stayes about Newmarkett, my lord will bee att Norwich on Wednesday and my Lord Howard both, who followes after; wee came on the rode as farr as Littlebury where I now am, & they went on for Newmarkett. I doe hope in God my Lord Treasurer will write mee somwhat which I may shew to encourage the deputy leiftenants, and all my friends [f.2]. I hope the writt to sweare the justices coms by Sir William Doyly or som other way. I am just now taking coach for Thetford having nott as yett mett any sinister accident. Pray God keep you merry and in hart & pray lett my Lady ▽ [*Danby*] know that though wee doe what wee can with Sir J H[790] as she directed yett our reliance is on her, I need nott mind you of anything. On Tuesday morning I hope to heare from you for in this world there's nothing can consolate mee for my absence from you but that. Remember mee to my daughter Mary & Mrs Henshaw, Mr Snelling presents his service.

*Signed:* I am for ever yours, Yarmouth
*Addressed:* These present to the right honorable the Lady Viscountess Yarmouth att the Golden Ball in Suffolke Street, London
*British Library: Add. MSS 27447, ff 360–361*

---

[789] William Montagu (c.1618–1706), chief baron of the exchequer; he was Yarmouth's half great-uncle, being a younger half brother of Yarmouth's grandmother, Elizabeth, countess of Lindsey.
[790] Probably Sir John Holland rather than Sir John Hobart

# Robert, Viscount Yarmouth to Rebecca, Viscountess Yarmouth

**1676, July 17.** My deare hart, on Sunday night I came early to Thetford where I am lodged and treated equally as well as att Mrs Ainsworth's,[791] I mett a letter from my Lord Cheif Baron and this day I have sent to him to Bury to acquaint *him* that I and severall gentlemen stay heere for him and to desire him to com to morrowe morning through this towne, where is Sir Will Doyly who gave mee your letter & the *dedimus*;[792] heere is Sir Will Adams & Lee and Hoet will bee heere this night and about Windham[793] my friends will meet which I heare will bee very numerous, I heare my Lord Townshend will nott appeare butt itt's yett uncertaine; all the militia officers will bee to meet my Lord Cheif Baron and and [*sic*] such a noyse of trumpetts as will outdoe the sheriffs. I am glad my Lord Treasurer promiseth mee a letter on Tuesday's post to bee att Norwich in the middle of the assizes which as itt is powrefull & vigorous will exalt or debase my reputation. I heare my cousin *Coke* will bee very splendid att the assizes with new liveries and he very fine, my Lady Anne Coke's great bellie goes on for certaine, Mr Doughtie my secretary tells mee that upon the last present of frute which went on Friday to my Lady Anne, she tooke itt extreamly kindly and sayd she either had or would write to your ladyshipp. All this day wee are idle for Mr Doughty is gon the second time to my Lord Cheif Baron from mee who had appointed mee to meet him att Attleborowe butt I have pressed him againe to com this way and shall have his answer perhapps before I seale this letter, he writt mee one very respective letter which I sent to my friends att Norwich who were in som incertainety of the time of his comming. I am a little surprised att 5 comming to tell you the story of □ for now she must expect to bee interested in the affaire and I that pay soe deare doe humbly desire to pay butt one and reserve 5 favors for som other opportunity when ∅ turnes [*f*.2] up trump for I cannot abide wheadles espe-cially when they cost what I am nott able to satisfy therefore I desire to stick in the right rode where there are soe many more powerfull instruments though 5 may cast out small words somtimes in this can neither doe good nor harme.

I shall menage all your hints with the best of my discretion and give you an accompt. I doe heare that the towne of Yarmouth who intend to meet the judge in great numbers doe make Bowers lead a very uneasy life and if repentance could retract a dangerous scandall I presume hee would give noe more intelligence of that kind till the next time. Pray keepe faire with your mother I tell you without her downe right assistance □ can never bee gon through. The coachman that came downe with mee if he had or doth goe directly to London will be there to morrowe night, which will *bee* sooner then the common post butt he gooing to Bury to try to gett fares for London I rather chose the common way which is the surest way. Little Snelling is stepped over to Bury[794] this day and nott yett returned, all your children are well

---

[791] Elizabeth Aynsworth kept the very successful Reindeer Inn at Bishop's Stortford, having previously been a notorious procuress at Cambridge (Henry B. Wheatley, *The Diary of Samuel Pepys*, (London, 1896), VII, p.137n).

[792] *Dedimus potestatem*: a writ generally to commission a private person to act in place of a judge

[793] i.e. Wymondham.

[794] Snelling had a home at the household of his stepfather at Little Horringer Hall, near Bury St Edmunds (*ODNB*).

att home I heare, I have now noe more to say till Mr Doughty coms back from Bury and soe subscribe myself,

*Signed:* yours eternally, Yarmouth

*Postscript:* All heere present their service to you; mine to Mall, Mrs Henshaw, my son & daughter, Charles & Charlotte.

My Lord Cheif Baron coms through this towne of Thetford in the morning where the mayor & corporation & my self & severall gentlemen are ready to receive & attend him

*Addressed:* These present to the right honorable the Lady Viscountess Yarmouth att the Golden Ball in Suffolke Street, London [*postmark*]

*British Library: Add. MSS 27447, ff 362–363*

## Robert, Viscount Yarmouth to Rebecca, Viscountess Yarmouth

**1676, July 19**. My deare hart, since my last att Thetford I must acquaintt you that my Lord Cheif Baron came next morning thether by eleven of the clock where I receved him with Sir William Adams, Sir William Doyly, the mayor and all the corporation in their formalitys, he entered into my coach, his owne followed and the rest, onely he and I in mine. Wee made som short stay att Atteborowe where Sir Francis Bickley mett us with his coach then wee went on, and above five mile from Norwich mett us a noble body of horse of the prime gentlemen in the country and som thirty coaches, the horse marched on and as wee followed wee gathered to about forty or more coaches; about too miles from Norwich came the sheriff who the affections of the gentlemen to mee had quite robbed of all the traine butt the blue boyes and of gentry one\*ly\* Windham & Walpoole appeared with him. I delivered up my Lord Cheif Baron by his own consent on debate into his hands and entered my owne coach, with my couzin Coke, the high sheriff was soe civill as he came riding back from his owne company to my coach side and alighted to salute mee so I lighted too and my couz Coke and returned his compliment, then wee made a stay to lett them march in att St Giles his gates and came into St Stephen's gates and soe through the markett place downe to the towne howse to the judge, whome frome thence I waited on up to the castle where hee read his commission in <which> one of which their was a mistake and I putt in by the name of Earle of Yarmouth (which caused severall people on the place to salute mee for the new honor; which caused such private inquisitions of my friends as I was faine as well as to my unckle[795] to severall of my friends to tell them absolutely itt was nott butt I had reason to beleeve itt would be soe). My Lord Cheif Baron was ravished with his reception and I doe beleeve will doe me the right to say never yett any judge was ever received licke him, and will sett itt out and indeed itt [*f.2*] could nott bee higher nor more splendid. About eleven of the clock att night came in my Lord Marshall, who this morning I carried my cousin Coke to visitt as he was comming to mee butt went back on our comming to the Duke's P[a]lace[796] and after-

---

[795] William Montagu, the lord chief baron

[796] The palace of the duke of Norfolk was built in the mid-sixteenth century to the east of modern Duke Street on a site stretching down to the river Wensum in the middle of the city's cloth and dyeing district. In spite of vast sums spent on it subsequently it never overcame the disadvantages of its site. The King stayed there on his visit in 1671 but it was never completed and was demolished after 1711.

wards dined att our ordinary and was my guest from whence he went to see my Lord Cheif Baron, with whome I was on the bench most part of this afternoone. He is mighty kind to mee, and on Saterday goes to Oxned till Monday. He has on the bench whence I came to write this, made great compliments to you in the high sheriff's hearing who sate next us and charged mee to lode my letter with his service to you, I supped with him last night and on Friday my Lord Marshall & I dine with him, and now whilst I am writing I breake of[f] abruptly for my Lord Cheife Baron is just now com in to Dr Hawse, he to give mee a visitt, and soe expecting yours tomorrowe, I am

*Signed:* yours eternally, Yarmouth
*Postscript:* Heeres all the world in towne, Sir John Hobarte & Sir Robert Kemp whome wee see nott
*Addressed:* These present to My Lady Yarmouth
*British Library: Add. MSS 36988, ff 115–116*

## John Gough to Rebecca, Viscountess Yarmouth

**1676, July 19, Oxnead**. Right honourable & most honoured madam, about ten a clock yesterday my Lord Chief Baron coming to Thetford we presently set forward in our rode to Norwich having in company my lord's own coach, the judge's & young Sir William Doily's; nothing new occurred till we came to Attleboro & there Sir Francis Bickly & Mr Potts (son to Sir John) came in their coaches, upon whose coming both their lordships who were in my lord's own coach alighted & staid there about an hour. After which we went forward & met with few besides some of my lord's own servants from hence. When we got so far as the end of Windham[797] common their lordships were saluted with a good body of horse consisting of gentlemen of good quality drawn up in a very hansome order & about eighteen very fine coaches (no tumbrells[798] I assure your honour), thence we marcht on, some horses before the coaches & some behind (though the greatest part kept behind) till we came to Eaton where the high sheriff with about eight gentlemen & his forty liveryes met their lordships & after about half an hour's stay their lordships parted, my Lord Cheif Baron going along with the sheriff & entring in at St Giles his gates & my Lord Lieutenant with his friends going another way & entring in at St Stephen's. But at this parting the horsmen were ordered to march before which they did four in a brest & I beeing all this while behind the coaches had opportunity to tell[799] the coaches & found them to be in number two & thirty besides my lord's coach. In this order they marcht through the citty by the guild hall & so came by the close up to Cunsford[800] house where whether my lord alighted or not I know not having struck out of the company a little before beeing quite spent with the violent heat & the great cloud of dust that was raised. The gentlemen on horsback to speak modestly were above three hundred<s> besides such citizens & country men whose curiosity lead them to the sight, and I think it was worth their payns to see it. Tis said that of the eight gentlemen that came with the sheriff three were such as ought to have done otherwise but

---

[797] Wymondham          [798] i.e. carts          [799] i.e. to count
[800] Either Wensum Lodge owned by Robert Coke, or the Earl Marshal's garden house in King Street, north of Conisford Gate.

I beg your honour's pardon if I do not name them though I shall not easily forget them. Most honoured madam, this is the best relation of the parade that my memory will serve mee to give, & which I hope your honour will take in good part from, right honorable,

*Signed*: your honour's most dutifull chaplain & humble servant, John Gough
*Addressed*: These to the right honourable the Lady Viscountesse Yarmouth at the Golden Ball in Suffolk Street in London humbly present
*NRO: BL/Y/1/161*

## Sir John Holland to Robert, Viscount Yarmouth

**1676, July 20, Quidenham**. My lord, your lordshipp's of the 18 instant from Thetford was a very seasonable and returne favour, & had your lordshipp beene pleasd to have intimated about what time you conceived you should have passd by at Larlingford, I would infallably have wayted upon your lordshipp & my Lord Chiefe Baron upon the road though with the toothach, which have beene my constant companion this fortnight. My lord, though from the clerk of the assizes I heare that I am still continued in the commission of *oyer & terminer* & soe might have appeared with confidence enough upon the bench, yett knowing this to bee a very criticall assizes & considering how all my words & actions have beene watched of late & how innocent soever intended, yett how sever[e]ly construed & censured, & that my being left out of the commission of the peace (is sayd) to bee by the express directions of his Majesty, I know not how my appearance at these assizes would have beene taken above for I beleeve it was *as* well intended, that I should have beene left out of that commission as of that of the peace, but that those directions were forgott, which I presume will be supplyed before the next assizes.

My lord, my sonn gives mee an account of my Lord Chiefe Baron's great civility to him at Bury & of his favourable enquiry after mee which (in this conjuncture and under his lordshipp's circumstances) I have great reason to have a gratefull sense of; I have therfore by my sonn addressed to his lordshipp as well to excuse my not wayting upon him as to give him a short account of my self & my condition; which your lordship may please to take an oportunity to improve to my advantage; for I looke upon him as a person of great generosity & prudence & so I heare hee have approved himself hetherto through out the circuite.

My lord, I just now received an intimation from Mr Corey[801] of my Lord Marshall's arrival ther, upon whom I intend to wayte as soone as the assizes are over, which I presume will determine with the weeke & that I may find your lordship at the Duke's Palace upon Munday at dinner, wher (God willing) I resolve to bee; howsoever if your lordship makes any stay I intend to kiss your hands before your return, your lordshipp having by the constancy of your kindnes obliged mee forever to bee, my lord,

*Signed*: your lordshipp's most faythfull & humble servant, J Holland
*Addressed*: For the Lord Vicount Yermouth, Lord Leiutenant of the county of Norfolk
*NRO: BL/Y/1/162*

[801] Thomas Corie (1613–1687), town clerk of Norwich

# W. Thursby[802] to Robert, Viscount Yarmouth

**1676, July 20**. My lord, upon the perusall of your papers & the consideration of your case I thinke the letter from Bower to Mr Secretary Williamson to bee full of scandalous reflexions in some little upon your lordship but very much upon the commission officers & justices & the magistrates of Yarmouth, the latter of which he sayes connive at non-conformist meetings, that those meetings take confidence by the militia officers & justices being such as joyned in the late rebellious government & thirdly that your lordship is influenced by Sir William Doyly by whose good will the churches freinds shall neither have favour or command.[803] These are three principall remarkes in the letter; bad enough, very saucy & censorious & such (I thinke) as would receive a smart check if your lordship should promote the hearing of the cause at the councell table & such for which the writer of the letter ought to bee bound to the good behaviour either at the sessions of the peace or by the judge of assize or bee bound over to the King's *Bench* to answere there such false reflecting expressions upon the magistracy of the towne & county.

These wayes (my lord) I conceive the writer of the letter might be proceeded against, but I beseech your lordship to consider whether it bee not possible hee may justify himselfe in the two first particulars & thereby mitigate his offence something, for few great townes in England (even London) those who have done most towards the suppression of conventicles but have shewn some remissenesse in their prosecutions of conventicles therefore tis possible hee may make some instance hereof & call it connivance in the magistrats of Yarmouth, though it were unmannerly for so meane a fellow to doe soe. And in like manner for the second particular that many of the commission officers & justices are such as have joyned in the late rebellious government. Everybody knows there may bee instances hereof in every county & almost every judicature of England & tis almost impossible to bee otherwise, those who had hands & hearts in the rebellious government being soe numerous, yet to mention this as a reflexion or reproach is expressely an offence against the Act of Oblivion & punishable as a misbehaviour in a meane person against the King's officers & magistrats in commission. And tis a bold reflexion upon your lordship to informe a secretary of state that you are influenced by (Sir William Doyly) a man who favours not the church. Yet all these cannot otherwise bee punished by law then by being openly reproved & put to find securityes for the future behaviour which may more properly be done at the sessions or assizes then at the councill table where theyre time ought not to bee taken up in such offences punishable elsewhere. And therefore I humbly advise your lordship rather to have this sawcy letter transmitted from the Secretary to the justices of the peace or the judge of assize to bee considered of & punished by them then to trouble the King & Councell therewith where though it has been unhappily taken notice of yet as to your lordship's concerne therein (being a person soe eminently known & soe transcendently above the slaunder & detraction of soe meane a fellow) I'm sure it cannot affect you, but as to Sir William Doyly & the justices & commission officers & baylifes of Yarmouth who are expressly

---

[802] William Thursby of the Middle Temple, a leading counsellor at law
[803] Doyly was one of the MPs for Great Yarmouth where the electors were largely nonconformists.

slaundered &c I conceive it very reasonable your lordship should have the slaunderer punished (on theire behalfes) in the face of the country. All which is most humbly submitted to your lordship's owne wisdome by (my lord)

*Signed*: your lordship's most faythfull servant, W Thursby
*Addressed*: These for the right honourable the Lord Viscount Yarmouth humbly present
*NRO: BL/Y/1/163*

## Robert, Viscount Yarmouth to Rebecca, Viscountess Yarmouth

**1676, July 21.** My deare hart, my Lord Chief Baron has gotten great fame by his way heere of administring justice and this day the two great tryalls of the doctors passed where they were both cast on their croopers,[804] my Lord Marshall sayd all that could bee for Dr Hewse,[805] the words were sworne (though Turkinton the witness was made the greatest roage in nature) yett £4,000 damages were given my Lord Townshend, I was there all the time, ther coms a message from my Lord Townshend that if Hewse & his wife would butt promise to hold their tounges for the future he would remitt all. Hewse would doe nothing without my Lord Marshall's consent & mine, butt the proposall beeing made by Major Doughty I beleeve itt will end handsomly: then came on Dr Hyliard's which would nott beare water, and my Lord Cheif Baron finding itt makes a proposall which hee tooke an answer to before he gave directions to the jury: that if great damages were given and Hyrne purged of forgery they should be remitted: soe £300 given Hyrne, which att the barr he frankely remitted as well as all causes depending for the riott, the doctor and he made mutall promises to live in amity and Hyrne came immediately to my chamber whith the doctor where I told him he had don a thing which from hence forward oblidged mee to bee his friend and in great kindness wee all parted: heere never was knowne such an appearance att an assizes since Norwich was a towne, and this morning the gallery at Dr Hawes his [*sic*] was as full of gentlemen as itt could thwack[806] and I have had as great respects as [*f*.2] is possible for a man to expect. This day my Lord Marshall, my Lord Howard and som twenty other gentlemen dined with the judge who begun your health himself, to morrowe he goes with mee to Oxned and on Monday betimes must be on the bench where I beleeve the assizes will last till Wedensday or Thursday, I doe nott thinke my lord & the ladyes will have time to see Oxned this time. Yesternight att my Lord Howard's garden[807] was above fifty coaches, the walkes as full as Springarden,[808] and in I went and saw dancing on the bowlingreene by torch light. Mr Le Strange is much concerned that I having desired him to wright, should by mistake keep his letter in my pockett[809] till the next post. Their will bee noe need of counter subscribers I presume this will fall of itt self & the other is nott thought the way. Pray excuse mee to my son till the next post, noe letter came from my Lord Treasurer, in hast I am

*Signed:* yours most affectionately for ever, Yarmouth

---

[804] i.e. on their rumps or buttocks                    [805] i.e. Dr Owen Hughes
[806] i.e. crowd or cram            [807] Presumably at his house in King Street, see note 800 above
[808] Spring Garden was a pleasure ground in London.            [809] ? *recte* his letter in his pocket

*Postscript:* If their be any faults pardon them I had nott time to read my letter
*Addressed:* These present to the right honorable the Lady Viscountess Yarmouth att
the Golden Ball, Suffolke Street, London [*postmark*]
*British Library: Add. MSS 36988, ff 117–118*

## Robert, Viscount Yarmouth to Rebecca, Viscountess Yarmouth

**1676, July 24.** My deare hart, on Saterday my Lord Chief Baron having invited mee
to dinner came along with mee in my coach about three or four of the clock to Oxned
where I enterteined him with all the respects of the place with which he is sufficiently
satisfied. Yesterday beeing Sunday he heard a good sermon heere and severall gentlemen came to waite of [*sic*] him att dinner, after dinner hee and I went out into the
park and I shewed him the spring in the wood, hee is extreamely well pleased with
his reception and with the place & with your children, this morning he was gon by
fowre of the clock, on Wedensday I goe to waite on him to take my leave for on
Thursday he goes away. I heare my Lord Marshall goes away to morrowe butt I have
sent Snelling this day to Norwich to invite him to morrowe to dinner & Sir Edmond
Bacon who has promised mee a visitt and is as extravagant in his kindness to mee as
hee is in his other discourses to others which makes people thinke and nott without
reason that his braine somtimes is a little touched butt he has a great deale of witt
and to mee is very oblidging. This is a most sweet place and I have nott observed itt
sweeter then att this time nor this day when I happen to bee alone with my children
without interruption for most people expected mee at Norwich upon the returne of
my Lord Cheif Baron who has gained himself immortall fame in his carriage of all
matters more especially in that of Dr Hyliard's and now itt happens that since the
tryall the acquittance Mr Hyrne signed is found by the falling out of the two brothers
the Earles,[810] butt however, the doctor has purchased his peace and having beene
fairely used att an advantage ought nott to breake out on a nice [*f.2*] score. I saw Sir
John Hobart & Sir Robert Kemp on the bench twice butt wee looked couldly one
upon the other and the salutes were such, Sir Peter Gleane came and made mee a
very civill visitt and Sir John Holland sent mee by his son a civill letter, my cousin
Coke & I were very kind. My Lord Treasurer's letter was very full and very kind,
pray present my humble service to him, tell him that I did communicate itt and had
itt read in publicque to all the deputy leiftenants, and itt relished well for mee and
was as kindly taken by them. My Lord Cheif Baron when he comes to towne will lett
the King & my Lord Treasurer know that those that love the Crowne heere are more
numerous by farr then those that observe their own methods & thinke to serve the
King by new wayes which he desires nott to bee served by.

   This night I wright to Dawson to speake to Dunster[811] to give in a report speedily
if hee be still there, for Major Doughty has engaged severall to build as soone as
the customehowse goes up, which you must sollicitt Brent & the treasurer in for the
time is now almost past. I pray God that my son & I may have Norfolke & Suffolke
upon reasonable penniworths, which my son writes mee word Peregrine Bertie is still
confident on.

---

[810] Sons of Serjeant Erasmus Earle of Heydon        [811] Giles Dunster, surveyor-general of customs

Bowers the coffee man shall rest till I com up, I have those of the towne of Yarmouth that watch him & will ferrett him; for they have putt downe his coffee howse and now understanding he sells alle and mum[812] they send this week to levy his twenty shillings for the first offence according to the statute, and the next offence is the howse of correction. I hope you will speake to my ▽ [*Lady Danby*] that wee have noe trickes playd us in 𝒦 [*the excise*]. Yesterday I had by a post which cost mee two shillings a letter from my cousin Wolstan [*f.3*] Paston[813] which as I suppose came onely as a convoy to one of my Lord of my Lord of [*sic*] Barkshire's[814] inclosed itt still to tell mee tha[*t*] by a late opportunity he had of addressing he had recommended my former business, as Sir George W or other that converse there might knowe upon enquiry, itt were worth the while to gett Sir George Wakeman by the by to ask Mr Coleman[815] whether my lord had troubled himself lately to write about any such matter which he may say hee beeleeves has long intended to bee done, I leave itt to your discretion for I hate to make many partys in one matter.

I shall write to my Lord Treasurer when the assizes are don and give him a full accompt of all thinges. Your children presents their dutys to you, they are very well and Betty growes a brave lusty girle and thinkes she shall never see you, when I am alone I am as melancholy as can bee but allwayes, my deare hart,

*Signed:* yours eternally, Yarmouth
*Addressed:* For yourself
*British Library: Add. MSS 36988, ff 119–120*

# Robert, Viscount Yarmouth to Rebecca, Viscountess Yarmouth

**1676, July 28**. My dearest hart, thy deare letters are the greatest joyes I have heere, I thinke to com away from hence on Thursday next unless your letter by that post which shall bee called for att Norwich att [*sic*] meet mee on the rode should desire my stay. I have written to Yarmouth to Mr Dawson about Dunster's business butt yett have nott had the answer butt if none of them com today shall send over thither on purpose about that and Bowers business. I have sufficiently examined the business of 𝒦 [*the excise*] and shall have customers[816] enough if itt falls into my hands, I have sent for Jey of Norwich to com over to mee and will make my tearmes with him[817] and if he have another county through Peregrine Bertie's and my meanes wee'll have som of the profitts; butt I doe beeleeve that will bee hard to procure for him, I wish wee fixed nott our owne soe & therefore itt was nott amiss to keep an hand of <of> interest for the home farme. Sir John Pettus is very kind to mee and has beene heare this two dayes, I would faine have his lady[818] & you friends; my Lord Marshall is by this time in towne, I shall speake to Mr Snelling butt he must first bee in towne; I

---

[812]  Mum was beer brewed from wheat malt and flavoured with aromatic herbs.

[813]  Wolstan Paston, will proved 1681 (TNA: PROB 11/368), was one of the Pastons of Appleton.

[814]  Charles Howard, 2nd earl of Berkshire, he was the father-in-law of Sir Henry Bedingfeld the younger.

[815]  Probably Edward Colman, secretary to the duchess of York          [816]  i.e. customs officials

[817]  *See* Christopher Jay to Lady Yarmouth, 28 July 1676: he agrees to terms discussed at this meeting and understands from Lord Yarmouth that the customs on tin are to be let (British Library: Add. MSS 27447, f.367).          [818]  Sir John Pettus's wife was Mary, daughter of Nicholas Burwell of Grays Inn.

would nott have you insist too much on the commissions mistake for those are things soe ordinary as itt's butt a frivolous matter to mention itt; this is a most sweet place if God were pleased to give mee where withall to support my condition. Heere's licke to bee a great deale of company with mee today, Wood, Peyton,[819] Sir John Pettus, Brickenden and divers more, I have a good pasty of venison for them and now I talke of venison pray forgett nott Mr Bulwer's on Saterday the 5 of August, which you may thus performe, Mr Fisher has a warrant for a buck in Copthall park which hee'l deliver into your hands and lett him have one heere or els Will Cheffins will give halfe a buck att the first word butt itt imports Mr Bulwer for the creditt of the feast. I wonder you wright [f.2] mee nothing of my Lady Danby's comming for I heare she is expected att Holkham to morrowe, but I presume because you say nothing she will nott com soe soone, or els she keepes her journey very private. I am glad to heare you say ✧ & ▽ [my Lord Treasurer & Lady Danby] keep up their interest butt all is soe uncertaine in this world that noe man knowes which way to turne himselfe butt he that has his coffers well lined and cares for nothing butt himself. What you sayd of Lewis' letter was truth. I had in the gallery att Dr Hawse's every morning thirty or forty gentlemen. I am infinitely glad my daughter Paston is soe kind to you for differences att home are wors then abroad. Mr Le Strange thankes you for your thankes for his letter, pray lett your answer to this com to Norwich where Ile make provision to receive itt, if I bee advanced farther. Heere is soe much company I can say noe more, Sir John Rowse, Sir William Adams, Dr Hewse, Sir Francis Mannock,[820] that my howse is a small court, butt nothing is [to] mee licke your company; my service to my son & daughter, my daughter Mary, Mrs Henshaw, Charles & Charlotte. Mr Jey will doe what I please hee'l take £100 a year for Norfolke and if Peregrine Bertie gitts him another countie hee'l take £500 per annum for all & Peregrine or els I alone if nott Peregrine & I shall devide or keep the rest of the proffitts, Jey writes concerning the tinn business himself I have noe more att present. Mr Doughty parts now for <Norw> Yarmouth & on Monday you shall heare further from

*Signed:* yours for ever, Yarmouth
*Addressed:* These present to the right honorable the Lady Viscountess Yarmouth att the Golden Ball in Suffolke Street, London [*postmark*]
*British Library: Add. MSS 27447, ff 368–369*

## Robert, Viscount Yarmouth to Rebecca, Viscountess Yarmouth

**1676, July 31.** My dearest deare, on Friday the bishop of Norwich died, I am sorrie I heard nott of itt time enough to write by that post: my Lord Chief Baron and I endeavored to have given him a visitt butt hee was soe ill that he desired our excuse, I hope the bishop of Exeter[821] will succeed him. Heere are now with mee Sir John Rowse, Colonell Knyvett, Captaine Knyvett and young Bedingfeld, which are soe

---

[819] Possibly Thomas Peyton of Rougham, whose daughter was married to Thomas Wood the elder of Bracon Ash (Blomefield, *Norfolk*, 5)     [820] Sir Francis Mannock (d.1686), of Gifford's Hall
[821] Anthony Sparrow (1612–1685), bishop of Exeter, a high-church Anglican who succeeded as bishop of Norwich.

good company they make mee merrie in spight of my hart, your children are very fine children and Mis[s] very pritty and the wittiest in the world, wee all have beene hunting this morning and had very good sport, I wish you had the buck with you. As to my Yarmouth affaire I sent Mr Doughty over on Friday, who spoke with Mr Dawson & Mr Dunster the surveighor who is mighty civill to mee and told Mr Doughty that if I had nott sent hee must in justice have given in his report that my side is the properest place for the King to build a custome howse on, he promised to com over to mee this night or to morrowe and farther promised to make such a report by letter if I should require him as I should desire butt sayth hee shall doe itt personally more significantly. I shall press him to doe both, for hee is to goe from hence to Wells, and from thence to Lynn where his circuit ends which may bee som time before he coms to London, I have promised him a gratuity if itt takes effect, and I am ill befriended if what is convenient for the King should bee hindred. I will either bring or send itt by the Wedensday's post which will bee butt att London one day before mee.

My Lord Townshend and his lady have beene att Blickling most part of the last week and on Saturday came my couzin Windham to waite on mee and told mee my Lord Townshend had commanded him to present his service to mee and bid him lett mee know hee was my humble servant to which I tooke little notice & diverted all the discourse made that was nott soe much as asking him one question good nor bad of any of them. Mr Snelling went over to visitt Mrs Ramsey who told him my Lady Townshend, my Lady Hobart & Mrs Windham were there the day before & my Lady Hobart was saying noe man had beene soe well received into the country as I, butt I knowe them all and shall gard myself from all their falshood & envy as well as I can. To morrowe I writt to Sir Henry Bedingfeld to com & dine with mee, and then wee shall talke somwhat together as toe ⊗. This is a most sweet place and I am lothe to leave itt butt noe place without you is pleasant to mee and besides I have [f.2] a vast resort of company that my howse is licke a little court yett I may protest I know of noe man has beene drunke heere not I my self half way nor a quarter. Everybody heere allmost has fluxes and I have had a great one, Sir Edmond Bacon had licke to have died att Norwich of itt and fell into cramps and convulsions els he had beene heere. As to the business of the verdict against Dr Hewse, the jury had never given itt butt that they were assured my Lord Townshend would remitt great damages and nott small ones, butt I <will> beleeve my Lord Cheif Baron will soe certify as that the doctor will have a new tryall if itt bee nott quickly made an end of, itt is the nature of all sorts of people that are out of play to magnifye every thing butt the truth of this story & the insignificance of the parson that was the wittness will appeare in itts due time.

My cousin Cooke's steward writt a letter over heere to Mr Hurton to borrowe som hangings of nine foot deep to which I made Mr Gough returne a very civill answer that I had none of that size butt what I was ashamed to send butt that I desired the steward might com over and chuse anything himself that was for his turne to acco-modate them, they doe expect my Lady Danby this week. I shall bring up som spiritt of scurvy grass for my Lord Campden and for our selves for the world has nott a more soveraigne remedy.

Pray present my service to my sonn & my daughter, to Charles & Charlotte, to my daughter Mary & Mrs Henshaw, as to what you write mee concerning your mother I am very glad she is soe kind to you, pray present my duty to her, and as to Sir John I should very well approove you should both ask for his wife & children, & even bee civill to his person, butt to have anything to doe with him is butt to betray ourselves. I told you before itt would com to a whining story and that he thinkes reasonable to purge all his falshoods, his contempts, now his particular joy that wee were fallen out that he might noe more bee troubled with us, for my part I am resolved to have nothing to doe with *him* further then speaking to him & eating & drinking with him, lett him either bee distracted or sober he shall stand on his owne feet, the world shall nott stirr mee from this and when I tell you any other story remember I dissemble; I hate and abhor the remembrance of his ingratefull returnes to mee, the disowning the curtesys I have don him, and laying on the farmers,[822] his baseness to you, a thousand perticulars to mee which I cannott now remember, his using mee in his owne howse as if I [f.3] had com on begging for a meales meat insoemuch that your owne mother and his wife were ashamed att itt, I have sayd enough and the less fury and transport I am in the more resolute I am in the point butt this needs noe way appeare butt in the want of that intimacy which used to bee, and for a formall civility I shall bee content with itt. As to □ I doe nott approove writing to him, nor to have any letters shewed ∇ [Lady Danby] of my magnifying myself or upbraiding his delay, I could nott reconcile itt to my reason and doe thinke the thing in itt self would rather hinder then further the matter.

I have sent your sister Nurs[823] her note inclosed signed by my hand, I have soe many services desired to bee inserted into the letter that I shall onely say your children presents their duty and all the company their service with great devotion, Major Doughty & Gough will have theirs in by name: on Thursday morning I intend to bee in the coach God willing by foure of the clock and perhapps if I find my time serve may call att Sir John Holland's. I shall take order for your letter which I expect att Norwich and soe I besheech God send us a good meeting on Saterday in the evening; by Wedensday's post you shall have another from mee and soe I am for ever my dearest hart

*Signed:* yours most passionately & unalterably, Yarmouth
*Postscript:* I send you my Lord Barkshire's letter which keep till I com for I have nott answered butt meane to doe itt from London when I can say anything to the matter.
*British Library: Add. MSS 27447, ff 370–371*

---

[822] i.e. of the wood farm in which Clayton was concerned

[823] Lady Yarmouth's elder sister Mary married Peter Nourse. Their daughter Mary Nourse married James Fraser (1645–1731) in 1681. Fraser was, with Lord Yarmouth, one of the parties appealing for the renewal of the greenwax grant in April 1681; he was acting as Lord Yarmouth's secretary in 1682, and became secretary of the Royal Chelsea Hospital, probably royal librarian, and a noted book dealer (*ODNB*; British Library: Add. MSS 27447, f.461, 27448, f.128v, 36988, ff 197, 227; *CTB, 7*, p.125).

## Robert, Viscount Yarmouth to Rebecca, Viscountess Yarmouth

**1676, August 2**. My dearest hart, this is my last from hence, Mr Dunster the King's surveighor and Mr Dawson is heere with him and wee are agreed thus that I procure a letter from Charles Bertie[824] to him for his report of Yarmouth which he will answer the post after as effectually as I can desire, soe you must desire Charles Bertie by the next Mondayes post to write him this letter and send itt to the secretaryes of the custome howse *&* itt coms to him immediately they keeping correspondence with him from towne to towne and he has now left Yarmouth, and is gooing towards Lyn and soe further itt will bee six weekes before he coms to London and if I should stay all that time there were noe hopes of effecting *any* thing this yeare. He promises to speake all the advantages of itt that's possible and I have promised him if I gett the order for the building the customehowse and that any effect succeeds, I would give him £20; I have this day a great deale of company with mee itt being the last day, to morrowe I intend to call att Sir John Holland's and doe beleeve I shall com noe further then Thetford and the next day to Littlebury and on Saterday night I hope to waite on you, I shall call for your letter to morrowe att Norwich. Few words are now best, I have left my chipher with Sir Henry Bedingfeld who has promised mee his lady should keep a correspondence with you and that I should find the effects of what hee would suddainly have ⊗ informed of, I have now noe more to say butt that I am

*Signed:* your most affectionate humble servant, Yarmouth
*Addressed:* These present to the right honorable the Lady Viscountess Yarmouth att the Golden Ball in Suffolke Street, London [*postmark*]
*British Library: Add. MSS 27447, f. 372*

## Edmund Thaxter and Thomas Bradford to Robert, Viscount Yarmouth

**1676, August 7, Yarmouth**. May it please your lordship, yours of the 2nd instant is before us and according to directions wee sent for Bower on Saturday last and *read* over to him the coppie of the letter which he sent to Sir Joseph Williamson and demanded of him whether he writt any letter to that purpose which he evaded by this answere, his memory was treacherous, and saide what I have writt I have writt; and being pressed by us to declare what cause wee had given him to abuse us in that lyeing and shamefull manner, at which he seemed not at all troubled but justifyed himselfe therein by referring himselfe to his originall letter; upon which wee demanded sureties for his good behaviour which he refuseinge to give wee sent him to gaole; and after some tyme he tendred us sufficient bail which wee tooke himselfe in £100 and his sureties in £50 a peece. But more seriously peruseing your lordship's letter finding that not fully to answere your honour's commands wee this day levied 20s upon his goods for selling beere without licence and after that wee suppressed

---

[824] Charles Bertie (1641–1711) was Lord Yarmouth's cousin, brother in law to Lord Danby and his right hand man.

him and then sent for three witnesses which wee were informed could testifie something materiall against him for diswading of persons from receiving commissions and findinge armes here; but their testimonies agreeing all in this that he  had the Act 14 Car[o]l[us] 2 in his hand and did reade the clause therein by which corporations are chargable to finde their usuall number of souldiers unless the leiutenants finde cause to lessen the same, and soe delivered his opinion that he conceived by that Act the number of souldjers in corporations might be diminished but not increased, which wee humbly submitt to your honour's further consideration; and do assure your lordship wee will have spies contynually upon him, and if wee finde him tripping shall seveerly punnish him. Returning your honour our humble thankes for your great care of us, assureing your lordship wee shalbe punctuall observers of all comands sent by your honour unto

*Signed*: your lordship's most humble servants, Edm Thaxter, Tho: Bradford, Bailiffs
*Postscript*: Pleas to peruse the inclosed & if your honour judge it fitt to be delivered seale it, and cause the same soe to be, els keepe it by your honour
*Addressed*: These for the right honourable Robert Lord Paston Viscount Yarmouth att his lodgings att the Golden Ball in Suffolke Streete, Westminster, London
*NRO: BL/Y/1/164*

## Edmund Thaxter and George England to Robert, Viscount Yarmouth

**1676, August 14, Yarmouth**. May it please your lordship, this day sevennight wee gave your lordshipp the trouble of a letter & therein an account of our proceedings against Bowers which wee heare by Capt Huntington came safe to hand & that your lordshipp was pleased to express satisfaction in what wee had done. Wee were this day intended to have commenced an action of debt (as the act of parliament direct) against him as an unlicensed coffee-seller for we are well informed that he never tooke any licence for the uttering of that liquor & consequently have exposed himself to the penalty of £5 a month, but he have prevented or rather delayed our designe by his journey to London, for thither wee are told he sett forward on Satterday night for what purpose we knowe not but doubt not but your lordshipp's eye upon him will frustrate any attempt which may give him or his faction the least shadow of a conquest in his insolent undertakings; our zeale in this matter proceed[s] from an apprehension of the indignity offered to your lordshipp & the mischeife that must unavoidably attend the goverment of this place if impunity follow such actions. Wee are truly glad your lordshipp have the originall letter & pray the favour thereof as soon as is possible.

*Signed*: We are your lordship's most faithfull & most obedient servants, Edm Thaxter, George England
*Addressed*: These to the right honourable Robert Lord Paston Viscount Yarmouth present, London
*NRO: BL/Y/1/165*

## Giles Dunster to Thomas, Earl of Danby

**1676, August 19, Hull**. May it please your lordshippe, in obedience to your lord-shipp's commands signified be the honourable Charles Bartie[825] esquire that I should informe your lordshipp what place in Yarmouth is convenient for the building a new custome house, I doe humbly offer to your lordshipp's consideration that if his Majesty please to build a new custome house on the south side of the river against the present old customhouse where the right honorable the Lord of Yarmouth hath already built a kye may be a great incouragment to the building of that side of the water which may much increase the navigation and trade of that towne; the old customhouse dos belong to the corporation, and hath beene lett for many years at £4 per annum; about a yeare past the corporation demanded £16 per annum, the commissioners for manageing his Majesty's customes not thinking fitt to give so great a price, ordered theyr collecter to take another which accordingly he did at £12 per annum, but at my comeing to Yarmouth and findeing it remoute from the business at the water side did with the aprobation of the sayd commissioners take the former customehouse from the corporation at £12 per annum for one yeare or more as the commissioners shall thinke fitt.

I am of oppinion that some of the marchants on the north side of the river will thinke it a trouble to goe over the bridge to make theyr entrys if a customehouse be there erected which is no more then those that live neare the Exchange of London should complaine that a customehouse is not there built to ease them of the trouble of going [f.2] into Thames Streete. This is all I have att presant to say, submitting the whole to your lordshipp's more serious consideration doth humbly crave leave and remaine,

*Signed*: your lordshipp's most humble and faithfull servant, Giles Dunster
*Addressed*: To the right honorable Thomas Earle of Danby, Lord High Treasurer of England, these present, Wallingford House
*NRO: BL/Y/1/166*

## Robert Doughty to Robert, Viscount Yarmouth

**1676, August 25, Tuttington**. My lord, your lordship I suppose is satisfied, as well as your freinds here how necessary itt is, to his Majesties service, to have a freind sher-iffe of this county, & that the office may bee the lesse ungratefull to have itt soe managed as not to make itt burthensome. In order to which I have by the earnest pressure of the clubb[826] drawne the inclosed & present itt for your lordship's & my Lord Marshall's advice, butt I shall not comunicate itt till I receive your lordship's answere, I have alsoe inclosed a copy of subscription & reasons against itt (least your former papers should be mislayed).

Your lordship may consider whether itt bee not fitt to write to your collonells that the charge of armes in the severall troops & foote companyes bee compleated, and that notice bee given to the persons new charged to have their armes in readinesse, and that there bee private musters of every troope & foote companys on such dayes

---

[825] *Recte* Bertie    [826] Presumably a club of court party supporters

as the respective captains shall thinke most convenient before Michaelmas. And the rather for that some neighbours are soe kind, as to report that your lordshipp is weary of the trouble & burthen of the militia imploy, & have begged of the King to bee discharged. I wish your lordshipp, my lady & your wholle family all prosperity, as I am, my lord,

*Signed*: your lordshipp's most devoted servant, Robt Doughty
*Postscript*: If your lordshipp writes on Tuesday night, please to direct your letter to bee left for mee att the posthouse in Bungay in Suffolk, for I shall bee there Weddensday & Thursday
*Addressed*: These present for the right honourable the Lord Viscount Yarmouth att the Golden Ball in Suffolke Streete, London [*postmark*]
*NRO: BL/Y/1/167*

## John Dawson to Robert, Viscount Yarmouth

**1676, August 28, Yarmouth**. Right honourable, I have yours of the 26th with the coppy of Mr Dunster's letter inclossed and shall bee very redy to serve your lordshippe to the uttermost of my power. I doe not yet heare of any letter come to our balliffes nether have I any (as to your buisnes) from the commissioners, if any thinge come to mee I doubt not but to get it represented in your favor by the officers that are in port but you may bee confident the towne will appeare agaynest you: but I am sure thay can give noe other reason then that it will bee troublesum to goe over the bridge to the custome howse: when I heare of any letter come to the balliffes or any other thinge that relates to your honour's service I shall not faile to give notice thereof and your lordshippe may be confident that I will allway appeare

*Signed*: your honour's most humble servant whilst John Dawson
*Addressed*: For the right honourable my Lord Viscount Yarmouth Lord Leiftenant of the County of Norfolk at the Golden Ball in Suffolke Street these, in London [*postmark*]
*NRO: BL/Y/1/168*

## Edmund Thaxter, George England and Richard Huntington to Robert, Viscount Yarmouth

**1676, September 8, Yarmouth**. May it please your lordshipp, your second of the 5th instant was this morning given us by the hands of your secretary whereby wee receive abundant satisfaction as it further evidence[s] your lordshipp's great care of us & immoveable resolution to stand by us in the trouble most unjustly given to your lordshipp & ourselves by Bower's impudence & implacable malice.

What your lordshipp was pleased to communicate as the result of a debate had att [*blank*] is matter of much hearts ease to us especially for that my Lord Treasurer is pleased to espouse our quarrell & to give himselfe the trouble to understand the injury offered us & the nature of the offence committed by that daring fellowe in order to which wee doe most readily comply with your lordshipp's advice & shall not faile by next post taking our rise from your lordshipp's information to pay our thankes to his honour & give him a summary account of the whole matter, having first by inclosure committed it to your lordshipp's perusall & shall likewise consider of something to be drawen up stating our case by way of petition which may be presented to King & Councell if your lordshipp upon sight thereof shall so thinke fitt for wee are equally sensible with your lordshipp of what ill consequence it would be to us & the successive goverment of this place if wee should in the least flinch or for feare of trouble not prosecute this matter with the greatest vigour imaginable & sure wee are if a good cause will afford incourragement wee shall not want it.

Wee can learne little of Bowers or his faction of the event of his London journey farther then that wee heare he publickly brags & declare[s] wee shall all appeare att counsell table the 6th of next month. He carryes the flagg on the maintope & remitts not the least of his undaunted confidence, nor were wee tender upon the receipt of Sir Joseph's letter (a copy wereof wee sent you last post) to countenance the same thing: but Sir Joseph & Bowers seem to interfer the one saying his Majesty had not nor could not appoint a day, the other taking upon him to <appoint> nominate the 6th of October which inclines us to beleive that they are not so absolutely resolved upon the matter as they pretend besides wee thinke that Sir Joseph should be att a loss for the originall letter but bee it or be it not, or be it when it will except it be in [f.2] fishing season which will last till the first of December, wee shall endeavour to looke our enimy in the face & hope for such an issue as may not onely be a terrour to him but affright others from the like daring attempts.

*Signed*: Wee are your lordshipp's most faithfull & most obedient servants, Edm Thaxter, George England, Richd Huntington
*Addressed*: To the right honourable Robert Lord Paston Viscount Yarmouth
*NRO: BL/Y/1/169*

## Edmund Thaxter, George England, and Richard Huntington, to Robert, Viscount Yarmouth

**1676, September 11, Yarmouth**. May it please your lordshipp, by last post wee gave your lordshipp *an account* of what wee received by the hands of your secretary, & then promised what will be found enclosed *viz*: a letter to my Lord Treasurer, to the effect your lordshipp advised, as likewise a petition which as your lordshipp see occation may be presented or omitted. Whether your lordship will lett the petition see light before the 6th of October, the day Bowers pretend to be appointed for a hearing, is submitted to your lordshipp's better judgment. In the meane while wee cannot but acquaint you with what have happened since our last. A certificate on the behalfe of Bowers is sett on foot & subscribed by some whose names your lordshipp shall know if desired in your next, although severall of them with much sorrow & reluctantcy *as* <are> ashamed of what they have done have since recanted & offered to enter their protests upon record as being much surprized in what they have done. With <*word deleted*> our hearty thanks for your lordshipp's most endearing & obliging expressions in yours of the 7th instant wee are as becomes us,

*Signed*: your lordship's most faythfull & most humble servants, Edm Thaxter, George England, Richd Huntington

*Postscript*: It is told us that Bowers & his faction are very sick of their proceedings & would compound but more of that if your lordshipp please hereafter

A copy of the above mentioned certificate

Yarmouth    These are to certife that Richard Bower of the said towne gent. is a person well knowne to us & of a sober life & conversation, truly loyall, obedient & conformable to his Majesty's laws ecclesiasticall & civill & to our knowledge was never contentious but living <pri> peacably & quietly among his neighbours. In testimony whereof wee subscribe our names:

*Endorsed*: This is the balifs of Yarmouth letters, and an inclosed for my Lord Treasurer and a petition to the King: paid Sept the 11

*Addressed*: These to the right honourable Robert Lord Paston Viscount Yarmouth present att his lodgeings at the Golden Ball in Suffolke Street, London [*postmark*]
*NRO: BL/Y/1/170*

## Richard Huntington and Benjamin England to Robert, Viscount Yarmouth

**1676, September 11, Yarmouth**. May it please your lordshipp, an account being given herewith and in former letters of what concerns Bowers & his impudence wee have onely to returne our most thankefull acknowledgement of your lordshipp's most noble kindness in furnishing of us with venison against our Michaelmess solemnity as likewise for the joy your lordshipp is pleased to give us of our approaching trouble-some office during which wee humbly pray your lordshipp's advice & assistance as that which is absolutely necessary & will be highly acceptable to us, with full assurance that wee shall not faile in all respects within our power to evidence that wee are friends to Sir John Clayton (whose company wee have bin honoured with) & his concerns[827] & likewise

*Signed*: your lordship's most faithfull & obedient servants, Richd Huntington, Ben: England

*Addressed*: To the right honourable Robert Lord Paston Viscount Yarmouth present
*NRO: BL/Y/1/171*

## Robert Doughty to Rebecca, Viscountess Yarmouth

**1676, September 15, Tuttington**. Right honourable, by the best information I can gett, I have collected the names of the subscribers which I doubt is not perfect, diverse of them itt's supposed are weary of their bargaine, & will willingly come on the other side, I hope most of the persons named in in the colonell's list will follow

---

[827] Sir John Clayton had built a lighthouse at St Nicholas Gatt, an approach to Yarmouth between sandbanks. Clayton surrendered his warrant to Henry Bowyer, who was probably his brother-in-law, in 1682. Bowyer applied for permission to build a second lighthouse at St Nicholas Gatt but this does not appear to have been granted (*CSPD 1682*, p.293).

his example, and I doe not *att* all question butt that other gentleman (under the degree of knights) will much <much> outnumber the covenanteers.

Our county sessions are on Tuesday fortnight, which may bee a good tyme for promoteing this designe, I formerly wrote to my lord about the augmentation of Capt Thurston's pension (his old tenant), if my lord please to write a letter to bee communicated to the justices, itt will bee effectually accomplished. Here's great expectancy of our bishop's arrivall amongst us.

Yarmouth men I find very resolute in Bower's buisines, I shall give noe particulars because I knowe your ladyshipp will have a full account from themselves. Wee expect Mr Dunstar dayly butt have noe intelligence of him, I hope your ladyshipp has considered of instructions, whether to proceed upon the old or by an new commission. I am very gladd of your ladyshipp's recovery & shall alwaies pray for the continuance of itt.

*Signed*: I am your ladyshipp's most devoted servant, Robt Doughty
*Postscript*: I wish my lord would please to consider of a letter to his deputy leiuetenants to appoint private musters for horse & foote as they shall thinke fitt
*Address*: These present to the right honourable the Lady Viscountes Yarmouth att the Golden Ball in Suffolke Streete, London
*NRO: BL/Y/1/172*

## Robert Doughty to Robert, Viscount Yarmouth

**1676, September 22, Tuttington**. My lord, upon your lordshipp's last meeting your deputy leiuetenants, the charge of horse & foote armes were very imperfect & few or noe duplicates returned, nor any account of the hundred stores. To the end therefore that the militia may bee speedily compleated & the hundred stores supplyed to bee in a readinesse for his Majesties & countrey's service, if your lordshipp please (in regard of your absence) to recommend the care thereof to your deputy leiuetenants & alsoe to require them to appoint twoe private musters att tymes most convenient for the severall troopes & foote companies betweene this tyme & Christmas & that strict notice bee taken of defaulters & they proceeded against as your deputy leiuetenants in discretion shall see cause for, that the militia may bee fitt for a generall muster tymely in the spring, where your lordship intends personally to bee, & that the severall commanders or colonells of horse & foote deliver to your secretary for your lordshipp's use, a copy of their respective muster rolls. If your lordship please to write your pleasure to your deputy leiuetenants next post, I'le take care itt shall bee directed to them all as in your last, & this day senight delivered to Sir William Adams & Colonell Harboard & take their advice in communicateing of itt to the rest. There will bee eight or nyne of your deputy leiuetenants meete (of course) att sessions the Tuesday after which may then putt all matters of this affaire into an orderly way of settlement according to your lordshipp's commands.

Wee heare nothing yett of Mr Dunstar's comeing to Yarmouth, nor can I yett give your lordshipp any account concerning the lamping,[828] though I am willing to hope well.

---

[828] i.e. flashing: this must refer to Clayton's lighthouse in which Lord Yarmouth seems to have retained an interest.

As to the sherivalty itt growes now something late for our freinds to compasse what they inclyned too, the tyme of choice for the new sheriffe being soe nere att hand, butt that I submitt to your lordshipp.

Why might not the sheriffe bee sent for by the Councell to produce the subscription, and the King & Councell in some eminent manner to declare their dislike thereof.

Your lordshipp has answered nothing in reference to Capt Thurston's pension which is now £10 per annum, hee would gladly by your lordshipp's favour itt might bee improoved to £20, he's aged & forc't to give over his trade by poverty, I desire a word of your *lordship's* meaneing herein. My lord I shall improve all arguments & interest I can to promote your Yarmouth designe, my most humble service to your lordshipp & my lady I am

*Signed*: your lordshipp's most devoted servant, Robt Doughty
*Postscript*: If the subscription bee burnt or taken away by the Councell all their confederacy is att an end & the country att your lordshipp['s] beck.
*Addressed*: These present to the right honorable the Lord Viscount Yarmouth att the Golden Ball in Suffolke Streete, London
*NRO: BL/Y/1/173*

## Edmund Thaxter, George England, Richard Huntington, and Thomas England, to Robert, Viscount Yarmouth

**1676, September 22, Yarmouth**. May it please your lordshipp, wee have the honour of yours of the 19th instant & therein full evidence of your lordshipp's great care & endeavours to prevent the disturbance which Bowers might give us in the height of our business: if he effects not that as it is more then probable he will not, wee shall be but little sollicitous what may be the event of his utmost prosecution, being well assured that this his violent & malicious dealing will certainly come upon his owne pate, when the merritts of our case come to be impartially controverted.

Wee are much obliged by your lordshipp's proposalls for intelligence, but the widdow whose concerne it is to be thrifty have very luckily mett with an opportunity for her supply; however wee are bound to returne our thankfull acknowledgement of your lordship's condescencion & favour therein, & doe most heartily wish you a speedy freedome from your present distemper, some of us can experimentally sympathize with your lordship having to purpose felt the tortures of the goutt. Bowers & his party for ought wee can heare are very silent, some others of the subscribers begin to think they have done more then amiss in signing the certificate. Having nothing further at present worth your lordship's cognisance,

*Signed*: wee are your lordshipp's most faythfull & most obedient servants, Edm Thaxter, George England, Richd Huntington, Tho: England
*Addressed*: To the right honourable Robert Lord Paston Viscount Yarmouth present at his lodgings at the Golden Ball in Suffolk Street, London [*postmark*]
*NRO: BL/Y/1/174*

# Edmund Thaxter, George England, Richard Huntington, Thomas England, to Robert, Viscount Yarmouth

**1676, September 25, Yarmouth**. May it please your lordshipp, the continued & most obleiginge intercourse which your lordshipp is pleased to vouchsafe us must ever be had in gratefull remembrance & particularly wee acknowledge your lordshipp's indefatigable care evidenced by your lordshipp's letters of the 21st & 23rd instant to prevent a disturbance in our present concerne, and wee are more than satisfyed that whatever briskenesse Bowers & his party may outwardly make shew of, that they are cold att the hart, & could wish that all things relatinge to this buisnesse were as if they had never bin, for wee are well assured that unlesse he rake hell & scume the devill (pardone the expression) for evidence he can never make goode his malicious accusation. But although his hart faile him, & his certificate too, as certainly they must, yet wee suppose a bare cessation of armes on his part will not be admitted by your lordshipp as satisfaction.

As opportunity presents wee will acquaint our justifyinge subscribers with your lordshipp's pleasure. Our curate it is like in time may be brought to pray the benefitt of his clergy though not in the strictest sence, it may without breach of charity be thought he is more active in secular affairs than is consistent with his coat and interest, & did wee study revenge wee might without any hazard to our eye sight by an over curious & narrow search finde enough against him to make his hart ake but wee desire to be kinder to him than he deserves.[829]

In pursuance of your lordshipp's advice & direction in order to Bowers his conviction, wee this day uppon an information against him for sellinge of coffee without licence summoned him appeare before us, which he presently obeyed, uppon our tellinge him that wee were informed he sold coffee & that without licence, he replyed the one was evident & the other true, wee then told him the penalty of the law must be levyed on him, his returne was that he did expect no lesse, & although he promised uppon our prohibition not to utter coffee more, yet wee thinke to morrow to levy by warrant £5 as the forfeiture of one month.

We are not a little pleased that Bowers his insolence proved so comicall to give my Lord Marshall and your lordshipp so pleasant a diversion, wee question not but your lordship have that mad bull in such a net, as that the more he strives the more he will be entangled & if that a chaine will reduce that wild creature your lordshipp calls a baboon, there may be some hopes of Bowers his reformation, & by what may be the consequence of his impudence he will experimentally verify the proverbe, it is ill dallyinge with edged tools.

As to his pedigree wee pray your lordshipp's repreive 'till next opportunity least for want of time wee doe him an injury by takeinge it too low, but wee are much affraide that his gentility after all our pains will prove to be of the Welch race, not farther to trouble your lordship att present, wee are with all due observance

*Signed*: your lordshipp's most faithfull & most obedient servants, Edm Thaxter, George England, Richd Huntington, Tho: England

[829] Probably the royalist poet and satirist Luke Milbourne (1649–1720); he was rector of Osmandiston but appears to have held a further living in Yarmouth (*ODNB*).

*Addressed*: These to the right honourable Robert Lord Paston Viscount Yarmouth att his lodgeings att the Golden Ball in Suffolke Streete, London, present [*postmark*] *NRO: BL/Y/1/175*

## Richard Huntington, George England, Edmund Thaxter, and Thomas England, to Robert, Viscount Yarmouth

**1676, September 29, Yarmouth**. May it please your lordshipp, by what wee wrote on Munday in answer to your lordshipp's of the 19 & 21 instant, your lordshipp might have expected to have heard from us againe last post but beinge delayed by some accident in the execution of our warrant uppon Bowers wee thought it convenient not to trouble your lordshipp 'till wee could give some satisfactory account thereof. Yesterday by the hands of three constables wee sent a warrant for the levyinge of £5 as the forfeiture of one month for sellinge coffee without licence & for want of a dis-tresse to take his body according to the direction of the Act. He suffered the distresse to be taken with a greate deale of outward calmenesse, but doubtlesse he had a hart full of gall, yet made no reply, save that if wee tooke all away he & his family must come to us, an expression wee thinke much beneath that undaunted courage resolu-tion or rather impudence wherewith the gentlemen [*sic*] have hithertoo seemed to proceede, but wee hope law & justice & a regular governement will ever have strength to grapole with its insolent opposers, the distresse we are by law to keepe fourteen days, & then expose it to sale & render the overplus, & if he can finde any flaw in our proceedings there is no doubt but wee shal heare from him, for although his purse may be humbled yet wee beleive his spirit to be as high as ever, for it seemes he has declared his skin shal be pluckt from his flesh, & his flesh from his bones, ere he will make any voluntary submission. How far this act may be construed revenge with his abettors wee are not concerned, beinge conscious it have another principle, a due & just execution of the law accordinge to our duty & a complyance with your lordship's earnest desire [*to*] that purpose; yet wee must surely expect all the trouble that the malice of ill disposed men can give us in this matter.

There was some discourse he had procured the King's pardone, & therefore before the distresse taken, wee sent to him to know the truth thereof that we might forbeare our intentions, but findinge it not so wee executed our purpose as above, & doe humbly desire your lordshipp's care to prevent any thinge of that nature least the governement of this towne in generall & wee in particular be foreclosed of the satis-faction wee may in justice expect by his exemplary humiliation or other punishment, but wee forbeare to trouble your honour with many words in this point beinge so assured of your lordshipp's thorough apprehension of the whole matter as not to stande in neede of a remembrancer.

By what search wee have as yet made in our heralds office heere, wee can give your lordshipp no farther account than before, other than that our gentleman is Yorkeshire borne, his father *a* writing schoolemaster, his employment & course of livinge since he came hither which was about twenty yeares since the same wee informed your lordship in that narrative, wee att your lordshipp's command gave att the beginninge of this controversie.

Our ould bayliffs this day tooke leave of theire place, & the new ones installed, att whose festivall solemnitys your lordshipp's health was dranke with that respect that becomes us, with earnest wishes of your lordshipp's health & prosperity wee are

*Signed*: your lordshipp's most faithfull & most obedient servants, Richd: Huntington, George England, Edm Thaxter, Tho: England
*Addressed*: These to the right honourable Robert Lord Paston Viscount Yarmouth present att his lodgeings att the Golden Ball in Suffolke Streete in London [*postmark*]
*NRO: BL/Y/1/176*

# Deposition at the session of Sewers held at the King's Head,
Norwich before Sir John Pettus, Sir Charles Harbord, Robert Houghton, Jacob Preston, John Ayde, Henry Negus,[830] Robert Doughty the elder, Edward Warde, John Page, George Ward, John Berney, esquires, John Mingay and Isaacke Mootham, gentlemen

**1676, October 2**. *Deposition by jurors empannelled at Ludham as to need for a floodgate at Great Yarmouth costing at least £1,000 to prevent influx of salt water tides which are overflowing good marsh land; various objections raised including possibility that the level of water in streams between Horning and Coltishall, etc., will be too low for the watermen who frequent them with keels and wherries.*
*NRO: BL/Y/2/1*

# John Doughty to Robert, Viscount Yarmouth

**1676, October 2, Oxnead**. My lord, I received your lordshipp's to your deputy leiuetenants & have shewne itt to Sir William Adams & Collonell Harboard before itt was closed as your lordshipp comanded, who will observe your lordshipp's orders therein. My father will take care to promote the matters of Sir William Mason's, Mr Oakes' & Little Oliver's[831] petitions as effectually as hee can, which I shall give your lordship a particular account off.

My lord, Sir William Adams had his generall muster the last Tuesday in Chapley Fields in Norwich, where hee appeared very glorious in apparrell, as well as curtious & noble to his soldjers, haveing presented all his inferior officers as well by comission as otherwise with large skey coloured scarfes which they all generously putt silver fringe on to the value of 50s or £3 a peece. There were five of the seaven deputy leiuetenants present (Mr Jay & Mr Corye being att London). After the muster was over Sir William treated the officers of his owne company & halfe a score gentlemen that trayled pikes under him as volunteers (amongst whom was Mr Huby) att the White Swann att an noble supper to which hee was please[d] to invite mee, the rest <doeing> of the captaines doeing the like to their respective inferior officers. I had an account the last Saturday of Major Bendish of all the inferior officers in the regi-

---

[830] Henry Negus of Hoveton
[831] *See* letter from Lord Yarmouth to Edward L'estrange on the same subject (British Library: Add. MSS 36988, f.124)

ment & how many soldiers in every company which I shall (adding the commanders) ingrosse in parchment & send to your lordship by the first carefull hand. I am promised the muster rolls of every particular company this weeke.

My lord, my father received a letter the last Fryday from Mr Bayliffe Huntington, in which hee desired proposalls for your lordshipp's estate att Yarmouth, & promises the utmost of his assistance. Inclosed are copies of letters sent to him this day, which I have adventured to send your lordshipp, though without my father's privity or order. My lord, itt were convenient that some person should bee appointed to draw upp a charge for Collonell Paston's troope, his captain leiuetenant I thinke somewhat too remote to draw upp a charge for the hundreds hereabout, & that your lordshipp would please to thinke of some briske young gentleman for his cornett.

My father I shall accompany tomorrow to the sessions, what passes there I shall give your lordship a full relation according to the duty of, my lord,

*Signed*: your honour's most faithfull & ever obliged servant, Jo Doughty
*Addressed*: These present to the right honourable my Lord Viscount Yarmouth att the Golden Ball in Suffolk Streete, London [*postmark*]
*NRO: BL/Y/2/2*

## Edward L'estrange to Robert, Viscount Yarmouth

**1676, October 4, Norwich**. My lord, I have here inclosed sent your lordship an account of the orders passed at this meeting of the deputy lieutenants: Sir William Adams having delivered your lordship's letter the deputy lieutenants in obedience to your honour's desires, did take care to have all things setled in the militia according to your lordship's orders, and as they hope to your satisfaction: as to the business relating to Mr Hamon Thurston's petition, there is none as yet delivered into the sessions, but so farre as I can understand it may be brought in to morrow, which if it be, in compliance with your honour's desires, will be much favoured.

In answer to your lordship's very kind letter of the 27th past, I am bound to acknowledge your honour's extraordinary kindness to mee, in proffering your assistance if any *thing* of advantage shall happen within your lordship's power. My lord, I have received such high obligations from your honour that I have onely to begg this favour; that your lordship will beleeve it is impossible for mee to be otherwise then, my lord,

*Signed*: your honour's as most obliged so most faithfull servant, Edward L'estrange
*Postscript*: My lord, I begg the acceptance of all duty and service which I humbly tendure to your honour, and right honourable family.
*NRO: BL/Y/2/3*

## Richard Huntington, George England, Edmund Thaxter, and

## Thomas England, to Robert, Viscount Yarmouth

**1676, October 6, Yarmouth**. May it please your lordshipp, wee have the honour of yours of the 3rd instant purportinge[832] your lordshipp['s] approbation of our proceedinge against Bowers, wee heartily wish that that gentlenesse & moderation which your lordshipp & wee have hither to used toward him might be effectuall to reforme him without any farther rigour or severity, but so far is he from any such consideration as that he seemes to take fresh courage, & to bid defiance (whether out of despaire or presumption wee cannot say) to what have already bin or can be done to him.

Ever since his suppression he had sold a liquor called bocquet, & yesterday he beganne againe to sell coffee, & this day he had the impudence to come to Mr Bailiffe Huntington for a licence, but he denyed him with as much reason as he had confidence to desire it, uppon which he went away with a thrate to apply himselfe to King & Councell for right & justice. He still continues to utter coffee & att his house with all companys that come thither, the differences & divisions he *have* made are the common subject of discourse. And disputes pro & con are there maintained & managed with heate & passion, which may prove of very ill consequence, as they tende to the creatinge & encreaseinge of factions and animositys in the towne, & although wee cannot heare he gains many proselytes (so ill doe all who have not so far engaged themselves as they cannot well filler [sic] resent his impudence) yet he brags att a greate rate, & uppon any reprehension or wishes of submission by such who are more sensible of his miscarriage, than himselfe, he declares the towne is highly obleiged to him, that he have bin so sparinge in his complaints for that he could have wrote ten times more & so he will make them know before the buisnesse come to a close, & openly publishes his intentions of hastinge to London to speede a heareinge, with many such like bravados, which wee looke uppon as the effect of rashnesse, if not of right down madnesse, rather than any thinge else, however your lordshipp may perceive heereby, that he is as yet a very unfit subject for mercy & compassion, he seemeing hithertoo voyde of all sence, & so doubtlesse will continue, 'till cauterized & brought to feele farther smart than yet he have done. His ruine & destruction if the governement & quiett of this place may stand & be enjoyed without it, is not the thinge wee aim att, but such satisfaction as shal be judged in some measure adequate to the indignitys & injurys done to your lordshipp & the magistracy of this place, & without that wee must expect to be dayly bearded by him, contempt to grow uppon us, disturbances to be promoted amongst us & all the mischeifs in nature to befall us. All which wee humbly submit your lordshipp's consideration, & remaine as becomes us,

*Signed*: your lordship's most faithfull & most obedient servants, Richd Huntington, George England, Edm. Thaxter, Tho: England
*Postscript*: Wee this day received your lordshipp's order relatinge to the embargos & it shal be duely observed.
*Addressed*: These to the right honourable Robert Lord Paston Viscount Yarmouth

---

[832] i.e. setting forth

present att his lodgeings att the Golden Ball in Suffolke Streete in London [*postmark*]
*NRO: BL/Y/2/4*

## Sir William Adams to Robert, Viscount Yarmouth

**1676, October 9, Sprowston**. My lord, the great honour I received by your letter makes me blush at my omition in not giving your lordship some account of our obedience to your commands, & the circumstances of the citty's muster under that command your lordship has honoured me with. But (my lord) I was so sencible of my insufficiency for either which made me so remiss, that nothing but my strong presumption upon your candour & pardon can make me capable to absolve myself. Yett since your lordship is so kindly pleased to accept of what has bin done in loyalty to our King, & honour to your lordship I may with more confidence presume upon your pardon & return my humble thanks for your noble resentment of our well intended endeavours (mine in perticular). I am satisfied your lordship has had a full account from more experienced persons of the concern of that day, so that I shall adde nothing more then to assure your lordship that as the number is rather encreased then lessoned, so the comportments not inferior to the former appearances. My lord, I must conclude with this truth, that next to the duty I owe to his Majesty, the greatest & onely inducement of all my designs that way is to testifie the honour I must owne due to your lordship by maney & great obligations which shall ever be acknowledged by

*Signed*: your lordship's most obliged & humble servant, Wm Adams
*Addressed*: These for the right honourable the Lord Viscount Yarmouth in Little Suffolk Street, London [*postmark*]
*NRO: BL/Y/2/5*

## John Doughty to Robert, Viscount Yarmouth

**1676, October 9, Oxnead**. My lord, on Saturday last my father received a letter from Mr Bayliffe Huntington, which mentions that hee hath acquainted some freinds with your lordshipp's proposalls, who thinke the improovement of £1,000 per annum cannot bee made by them, that on Thursday next there will bee an assembly, & in the interim desired to receive an answere for his better information, of the reasons for such improovement, which my father has sent him this day, butt whether hee will thinke itt convenient, then to offer itt there or noe, is yett uncertaine. Mr Bayliffe Huntington <had> had his doe att Michaelmas, the other will deferr his till Hollomas.[833]

I have spoken to Mr Warkhouse as your lordshipp commands, who will take care to call for the justices fees, the tyme to <putt> make an addition of the justices will not bee till the next Hillary terme, against which tyme your lordshipp shall have a note of such persons as are fitt to bee putt in comission.

I shall wayte upon Colonell Harbard & acquaint him with your lordshipp's order

---

[833] Hallowmass or All Saints (1 November)

to mee to advise with him about a cornett tomorrow morneing. I shall take what care (I possibly can) to compleat the charge for the colonell's troope. My lord, my father desires his most humble service to your honour & my lady, & will use his utmost endeavours to propagate your Yarmouth concerne or anything that your lordship shall please to intrust him. I have noe more to add att the present but that I am my lord

*Signed*: your honour's most faithfull & ever obliged servant, Jo: Doughty

*Postscript*: My lord the inclosed presentation Mr Gough has diligently inquired about & is informed att all hands that the bishopp has not anything to add to itt, only to give a lycense to teach the schoole, & if your *lordshipp* pleases desires itt may [*be*] signed.

*Addressed*: These present to the right honorable the Lord Viscount Yarmouth att the Golden Ball in Suffolke Streete, London

*NRO: BL/Y/2/6*

## John Doughty to Robert, Viscount Yarmouth

**1676, October 16, Oxnead**. My lord, I have shewne your lordshipp's letter to my father, who resolves (since tis your lordshipp's pleasure) to bee for Yarmouth to morrow morneing, from [*whence*] he will give your lordshipp an account concerning Bowers, and alsoe as to your lordshipp's other concernes there, though as hee feares to little effect.

My lord, as concerning the sheriffes my father alsoe intends this weeke to conferre with Sir Nevill Cattelyn & Capt Cooke & some other freinds about itt, & by Monday post to give your lordshipp some account thereof. They all apprehend itt to bee of dangerous consequence to the King's service & the interest of his freinds for a sub-scriber or any of that party to bee sheriffe.

My lord, as to a cornett for Colonell Paston's troope I have acquainted (according to your lordshipp's comands) Colonell Harbard with itt, butt hee can nott as yett name a fitting person <as yett> for that place, who itt's convenient should live within the hundreds where the troope arise, in regard the captain leiuetenant live soe remote & ought to bee a person of an estate & creditt in the country. My father hopes to find out a person proper for the office & right to your lordshipp's interest (which if hee can) will give your honour an account off very speedily. My lord, Mr Gough writes fully to your lordshipp this night concerning the schoole master of North Walsham, Mr Fisher presents his service to your lordshipp & my lady & doe intend to wayte upon your honour on Sunday next att dynner. I intend to goe along with my father to Yarmouth, from whence your lordshipp shall receive an exact account of what passes from, my lord,

*Signed*: your honour's ever obliged & most faithfull servant, Jo. Doughty

*Addressed*: These present to the right honorable the Lord Viscount Yarmouth att the Golden Ball in Suffolke Streete, London [*postmark*]

*NRO: BL/Y/2/7*

## John Doughty to Robert, Viscount Yarmouth

**1676, October 18, Yarmouth**. My lord, my father has this day discoursed Mr Bayliffe Huntington, Sir George England &c about Bowers buisinesse. They declare they are resolved to proceed on their petition att the councell table, which they have lodged in your lordshipp's hands, and that though they apprehend Bowers intend not any further prosecution, yett they doe & seeme to desire their petition might bee speeded, least they should bee mistaken, & his proceed. This night they intend to discourse Sir Robert Baldock[834] (who is in towne) about itt, & to give your lordshipp a letter this night of the result.

My lord, my father has alsoe spoken with Mr Bayliffe Huntington about your lordshipp's concernes att Yarmouth, who sayes, that this present difference in the towne concerning Bowers gives such a disturbance as nothing can now bee effected therein, in regard Bowers' party will oppose itt, butt hee thinkes that when that's over there may bee some proposalls made to your lordshipp which shall not want his endeavours to the utmost for your lordshipp's service. I am very confident your lordshipp will find him very right, & that hee desires to preferr your lordshipp's buisines att a right tyme for effect. My lord, my father beggs your lordshipp's excuse for *not* writeing this post. I have onely to add my most humble service to your lordshipp & my lady from, my lord,

*Signed*: your honour's most humble & most faithfull servant, Jo. Doughty
*Addressed*: These present to the right honorable the Lord Viscount Yarmouth att the Golden Ball in Suffolke Streete, London [*postmark*]
*NRO: BL/Y/2/8*

## Matthew Peckover to Robert, Viscount Yarmouth

**1676, December 4, Oxnead**. My Lord, not farre from El[*ve*]den a messenger from the corporation of Thetford *I* met <me &> *who* inquired <how far> wheare the Hearte[835] was, presently appeared severall persons upon theire horses & Sir Thomas Garrett his lady, & Mrs Tasburgh, Captaine Harboard's <& his> lady, Captaine Cropley[836] in theire coaches; *thus* accompanied to the entrance of Thetford towne, wheare stood the mayor & his brethren in theire habitts, & solemnely attended the corps the length of theire liberty, the bells tolling all the while: before wee came to Larlingford Mr Bryan Holland in Sir John's coach with severall gentlemen a horseback joynd with the company to Attleburgh, he excused his sister's <Holland> not appearing from her indisposition of health; the company increased much before the Hearte came to Wymondham, wheare the streetes were hugely fild & the bells chymed all the time of theire passage from thence theare was an increase of persons

<hr>

[834] Sir Robert Baldock was the recorder of Yarmouth.

[835] Lord Yarmouth's second daughter Mary (Mall) died of smallpox in November and was buried in London (HMC 6: 7th R.I., p. 467, HMC, *Rutland II*, p. 32), but her heart was brought to Norfolk to be buried at Oxnead. The cavalcade that met the heart was unusual in that it included many ladies. Mary is portrayed in the painting 'The Paston Treasure' in Norwich Castle Museum, surrounded by many symbols of death and decay.

[836] Presumably William Cropley, brother-in-law of Captain Harbord

<&> upon horseback, & coaches, the Lady Mary Heveningham & Sir William upon his horse met at Hethersett, then came Mr Manock & his lady in theire coach, Mr Woods <& his> Lady Maidstone,[837] Lady Yallop, Sir William Rant, Capt[ain] Rant, Sir Edward Ward, Captaine Ward, Mr Calthorpe, Sir William Doylie, Sir Nevill Catelyne, Mr Windham with six horses in his coach, *Sir Henry Bedingfeld sen, Mrs Aldrich, Mrs Browne, Mrs Aldr. Man, Col Harboard, Berny, Suckling, Ward, Gooch &c, severall gentlemen & <word deleted> *ladies* I did not know, the recorder of Norwich[838] his coach, severall aldermen in coaches, & a horseback, Mr Deane in his coach, & prebends, & cannons upon horses, *40 clergymen*, all sorts of people, otherwise disagreing here united to doe your lordship honour; about [?]50 coaches & betweene two & three hundred horsemen came through Norwich upon Saturday at one of the clock, wheare the streetes & all the balcones & windowes were filled with people, the bells in every parrish they passed by chyming, except St Peter's in the markett place, for the rest of the solemnity I referre your lordship to a better account, humb[l]y kissing my noble ladies hands, your pardon is begd for this rude one <from> *by*, my lord,

*Signed*: your lordshipp's most humble & most obedient servant, Matt Peckover
*Address*: For the right honourable the Lord Yarmouth at his house in Suffolke Streete, London [*postmark*]
*NRO: BL/Y/2/9*

## Edward Warnes to Robert, Viscount Yarmouth

**1676, December 4**. My lord, although in regard of naturall affection you cannot but sorrowe for the departure of so eminently a dutifull daughter, as that deceased lady was, yet you may with greater cause rejoyce (as some present at the relation made of her at her funerall did, I assure you) that shee lived so vertuously & made so comfortable an end, for as the preacher then said, her death was blessed because she dyed in the Lord. And you may be assured of her, what our Saviour said in the gospell Matt. 9. 24, The maid is not dead but sleepeth. Be pleased to read what is written in the booke intitled the Wised[om] of Sol[omon] from the 1st to the 10th [*verse*][839] is worth your observation.

My lord, shee is better bestowed then if you had matched her to any earthly potentate, and her portion is in the inheritance of the saints, her soule is conveyed by the ministery of angels into Abraham's bosome and is in that heavenly society which is beyond any prince's court, Hebr. 12 from the 22 [*verse*]. It was said well by that preacher in St Paul's words, Eye hath not seen &c what God hath prepared in mercy for her. Allthough you have (I question not) but done sufficiently what Syracides saith Eccles'us 38 16 [*verse*], Let tears fall downe over the dead &c, yett be pleased to read further & considder what he saith from the latter part of <that> verse the 17 there, as allso [*verse*] the 16.

My lord amonge the many comforts God hath given you, certainly this is not the least: that God hath pleased to make you <instrumentall> a happy instrument in

---

[837] Elizabeth, viscountess Maidstone, was the sister of William Windham of Felbrigg.
[838] Francis Corie          [839] Warnes uses a symbol for 'verse' which has not been reproduced here.

bringinge into this world a childe that hath now increased heaven. Considder what David saith in that case 2 Sam. 12, 22, 23 [*verses*] While the child was yet alive I wept &c but nowe tis dead wherefore should I do soe? I shall goe to (her) but (shee) shall not returne to me. And in what the Ap[*ostle*]le 1 Thes. 4, 13, 14 [*verses*] Concerninge (her) that is a sleepe that you sorrowe not as others which have no hope. For if wee beleeve that Jesus died, & rose againe, even so allso them allso that sleep in Jesus will God bringe with him. God grant that wee may so live, as that death may make us blessed, is the prayer of him that is, my lord,

*Signed*: the unworthy servant of the Church of Christ & your lordshipp's most devoted in all duty, Edw Warnes

*Postscript*: My lord, what I doe heere write doe I suppose equally concerne that worthy person, your noble lady, to whome with the presentation of my humble duty & service to her (blessinge God who inabled her to be so assistant both in the happy education, and comfortable departure of the newe deceased lady (notwithstanding the danger of the distemper) to doe her so much good), I doe desire this to be communicated: beseechinge Allmighty God to blesse you both with longe life & many happy days for God's glory (which is the great end of all) & allso for both the churches & the commonwealthes good.

*Addressed*: For the right honourable & truly noble Robert Lord Paston Viscount Yermouth, Lord Lieutenant of Norfolke, London

*NRO: BL/Y/2/10*

## John Hildeyard to Rebecca, Viscountess Yarmouth

**1676[/7], January 8, Norwich**. Madam, the forwardnesse Mr Mazey the schoole master in Norwich shewed to take Mr Thomas into his care hath been fully intimated to my lord and your honor by other pens. On Munday next Mr Thomas will enter the schoole and I am requested by Mr Mazey to give my lord and you thankes for the honor you have don him in putting that trust into his hands, hee very solemnely promiseth to *have* soe speciall and particular care of him, that neyther my lord nor you shall think him placed in any circumstance to his disadvantage; and I willingly undertooke to doe this least your honor should think mee not mindfull of what I promised when with you at London, I have engaged Mr Mazey to keep him stricktly to his booke, not to suffer him upon any pretense of beeing sent for to goe into towne, to take him up into *my son* Jack's form nor will I be unmindfull of minding Mr Mazey of these & all other things to Mr Thomas his advantage as often as I shall come to Norwich. My wife presents *to* your honor <with> her service and to my lord as doth, madam,

*Signed*: your most faithfull and perpetuall servant, J Hildeyerd

*Postscript*: Madam, when his Majesty had made my lord lieutenant of Norfolk by the request of most of our orthodox clergy I presumed to move my lord that they might be exempted from armes but there were some advised the contrary and prevailed: I am soe satisfyed that some in comission of the militia doe in this affaire deale soe hardly by the clergy that I feare they have their designe thoroughout the county in making them clamorous and I have since I came to towne mett with soe many complaints under this oppression (as they call it because noe explicit law commands it) and those complaints now much accompanyed with reflections that I durst not out of my service to his lordship omitt the signification of it. They of the militia have beene so severe that they have generally laid the clergy up to what the parishes report the livings worth which seldom is lower then the utmost penny: some clergy men protest they are layd more then their livings can be valued at, and some that are but curates laid for their curacy. All this pretended to be by my lord's consent and order. Wee are certainly informed that *the clergy of* both Cambridgeshire and Bedfordshire are by their lord lieutenants exempt from armes, a moderation heer may please, an exemption eternally oblige.

*Addressed*: This to the right honourable lady the Lady Vicountesse Yarmouth at the Golden Ball in Suffolk Street in London [*postmark*]
*NRO: BL/Y/2/11*

## William Cooke to Robert, Viscount Yarmouth

**1676[/7], January 22**. My lord, Sir Neville Catelyn did me the favour to shew me your lordship's letter full of grace & kindenes which with former obligations would speake me the rudest man alive should I omitt that diligence & attendance I justly owe to your lordship's commands & concernes: being very sensible that I am master of no other qualifications for that character your lordship have honoured me with than those of unfayned alegiance to my sovereigne & duty to his lieftenant. We hope, my lord, there was no fayleure in the lieftenancy this sessions, although there was one of your lordship's deputyes in towne & very assiduous on the bench, who did not looke into the grand jury chamber. My lord, notwithstanding the militia is in a good posture yet tis possible some of the old ferment may maligne your lordship's prosperity, however I beseech your lordship to believe that your lordship having pleased to take soe unworthy a thing as my selfe into your vessell & make me part of your cargoe I am resolved to sink or swim, live or dye with your lordship. My lord, I humbly kisse your hands & rest

*Signed*: your lordship's most obliged & obedient servant, Wm Cooke
*Addressed*: Present these to the right honourable the Lord Viscount Yarmouth in Suffolke Street by Sharen Crosse, London [*postmark*]
*NRO: BL/Y/2/12*

## Sir Nevill Catelyn to Robert, Viscount Yarmouth

**1676[/7], January 26**. My lord, I humbly beg your lordship's pardon that I have been so late in my return to yours of the 4th of January which I received att Norwich sessions from whence I was hastily called into Suffolke upon some service to my Lady Bedingfeild so that I have not been master of my own time ever since; I received your lordship's commands whilst I was attending att Norwich sessions which I communicated to Mr Cooke who was there present from whom I presume you have received an account of himselfe, for my own part I doe faithfully assure your lordship that ever since you have conferred the honnor upon mee of deputy leiftennant I have never mist any publique meeting except last Michaelmas sessions when the court beeing at Newmarkett (which though so neare mee I had never seen) I was prevailed upon by some of my neighbours to make an excursion thither not without some hopes that I might kisse your lordship's hand there but you may rest assured my lord that for the future my pleasure shall never take place of my duty. I wishe your lordship has not been too kind to mee in the character you have honoured mee with to the King but this I am sure off my lord that were my head as right as my heart neither his Majesty nor your lordship should bee deceived in your expectation.

My lord, wee have so honest loyall and gentile an high shirriffe[840] this yeare (who appeared amoungst us this sessions) as I doubt not but with a little incouragement such a grand jury may bee found against summer assizes as will breake the neck of the Norfolke Covenant[841] by presenting it as a publique nuisance which doubtlesse tis and a very great one too, but in my observation it begins to dwindle in its reputation daily and had wee the influence of your lordship's presence amoungst us it would quickly bee nothing; my lord, I dare take up noe more of your minutes then whilst I am subscribing my selfe,

*Signed*: your lordship's faithfull humble and most obedient servant, Neville Catelyn
*Addressed*: These for the right honourable Lord Viscount Yarmouth att his house in Suffolk Street, London [*postmark*]
*NRO: BL/Y/2/13*

## Richard Huntington and Benjamin England to Robert, Viscount Yarmouth

**1676/7, February 26, Yarmouth**. May it please your lordshipp, for the effectuall imparting your particular letter to us together with the enclosed directed to our corporation in generall, wee called a common councill this day seven night on purpose, at which both were read and received with that observance & respect as is due to so undeniable an evidence of your lordshipp's affections & kindness and unanimously agreed by all then present that in regard they concerned matters of moment & importance, it was not convenient to give their resolve on a suddaine, but to adjourne the debate for that time & to reassemble the week following & then to give such an answear, as a deliberate & serious consideration on the whole matter should direct. In pursuance whereof they this day mett againe at our common hall, & determined their thoughts touching your lordshipp's proposall and have desired us as bayliffs in their name & behalfe, first in all humble & hearty manner to pay their thankfull acknowledgement of your benigne & favourable intentions as a signall & pregnant instance of your well wishes toward us, & then to acquaint your lordshipp that the immense sum of money required to make an improvement sutable to expectation is unspeakably beyond their purse & creditts & the very ill circumstances they are in, by reason of their many & great debts, doe render them utterly uncapable even upon

---

[840] Christopher Layer of Booton
[841] i.e. the subscription for the expenses of the sheriff; the word 'covenant' was highly emotive and designed to arouse hostility among royalists.

any termes of so great an undertaking and consequently impose an absolute necessity upon them of declining the advantage your lordshipp most obligingly give[s] us of preference and preemption, for which & other favours particularly for that your lord-shipp will please to countenance the renewing the Act[842] for our peeres (which will equally concerne your owne interest as ours and without which both must inevitably come to ruine) wee are greatly your lordshipp's debtors & doe againe in behalfe of the corporation repeat our thankes & in their name subscribe ourselves,

*Signed*: your lordshipp's most faithfull & humble servants, Richd Huntington, Ben: England, bayliffs

*Addressed*: These to the right honourable Robert Lord Paston Viscount Yarmouth present att his lodgings in Suffolke Street, London

*NRO: BL/Y/2/14*

## Sir Francis Bickley to Robert, Viscount Yarmouth

**1676[/7], March 5, Attleborogh Hall**. My honoured lord, I have received your lordship's most gracious letter, together with a commission for my selfe as one of your lordship's deputy lieutenaunts for this county of Norfolke, which I have embraced as an especiall marke of his Majesty's and your lordship's grace and favour and shall not fayle (God willing) to take an oportunity to be sworne at Thetford assizes about the 22th [*sic*] of this instant March and after that, I shall make it my whole study how I may best outwardly expresse my duty and loyallty to his Majesty and my obedience and service to your lordship as my superiour under him, so long as I shall live. And by how much the more conscious I am to my selfe, of my owne unworthinesse to deserve it; by so much the greater ty, doe I hold my selfe obliged upon all occasions and at all times to manifest that I am, my lord,

*Signed*: your lordship's most humble, most faithfull and most obedient servaunt, Francis Bickley

*Address*: These for the right honourable Robert Viscount Yarmouth at London [*post-mark*]

*NRO: BL/Y/2/16*

## John Hildeyard to Rebecca, Viscountess Yarmouth

**1677, April 11, Cawston**. Madam, I was willing to deferre my answer to your honor's letter that I might more then complementally returne therein the thankes of my brethren; but there hath beene noe occasion yet for the clergy to see and feele the effects of my lord's great favour towards them, the evidence of that cannot bee untill the next muster, therefore I would not deferre too long to lett your honour know that both my lord's intentions and your honor's intimations of befriending them have begott universall sense of gratitude in the clergy towards you both and have I verily beleive given an happy stop to that dissatisfaction which was too fast spreading amongst them. Nor can I ever bee mistaken in representing my lord and yourselfe true and harty friends to the whole junction for upon all occasions you have ever owned

[842] The Act for the maintenance of the piers at Great Yarmouth

your selves great lovers of, as well as in communion with, our English church, the great and true motive of my listing myselfe among your honors' servants and it is such a reason as will make it impossible for any thing to lessen my affectionatenesse in doing your honors' service. They that love and pray for the peace of Jerusalem shall prosper; I know you doe both therefore the God of peace multiply upon you and yours his blessings both temporall and spirituall is and ever shall bee the constant prayer of

*Signed*: your honor's most humbly devoted, J Hildeyerd
*Postscript*: Myne and my wives most humble service to my lord
*Addressed*: This to the right honorable the Viscountesse of <Great> Yarmouth at the Golden Ball in Suffolk Street, London, present [*postmark*]
*NRO: BL/Y/2/17*

## Richard Huntington and Benjamin England to Robert, Viscount Yarmouth

**1677, April 20, Yarmouth**. *They acknowledge receipt of his warrant which they will execute with due diligence but at present there are neither Ostend nor other privateers in their road or harbour.*

*Signed*: your lordshipp's most faithfull & humble servants, Richd: Huntington, Ben: England, bayliffs
*Addressed*: These to the right honourable Robert Lord Paston Viscount Yarmouth present att his lodgings att the Golden Ball in Suffolk Street, London [*postmark*]
*NRO: BL/Y/2/18*

## Sir Peter Gleane to Robert, Viscount Yarmouth

**1677 June 8**. My lord, I receyved by Sir John Holand an intimation of your contin-ued favours towards mee by taking notice of Mr Leigh's unkindness. I might justly give it another tearme, but that I shall leave to the standard by[843] to doe; were it not for your lordshipp's greate trouble I would give you a particular of his proceedings agaynst mee, it is only upon the accounte of my buying of a marsh, a limbe of my estate that has bine my families this hunderd yeares & could not have bine without it, but much to my disadvantage, which marsh he & his tenant Smyth had a desiere too, I not knowing of it, till it was offered mee to buy; & this only is the cause of his displeasure: his purse (my lord) was filld when mine was emptied, that makes him promise himsealfe conquerer & boasts accordingly; the justness of my cause I am well assured you will espouse, which will give mee courage to receyve his atacques, who is not only master of the sinnews of warr, but law it sealfe. But he shall find that *a* just cause shall keep up my courage and the prospecte of your favour will add to my mettall, and ever confirme mee in my resolutions of being, my lord,

*Signed*: your most thankfull & obedient servant, Peter Gleane
*Addressed*: For the right honorable the Lord Yarmouth at the Golden Ball in Suffolke Street, these [*postmark*]
*NRO: BL/Y/2/19*

[843] *recte* ? standers by

## Edward L'estrange to Robert, Viscount Yarmouth

**1677, June 18, Gressenhall**. My lord, the deputy lieutenants being to meet at Norwich, about the beginning of July, at the quarter sessions then to be holden; and not knowing whether your lordship intends to be in the country before that time, I have thought it my duty to certify thus much to your lordship, that so I may receive your commands against that time, which shall be ever faithfully executed by, my lord,

*Signed*: your honour's most obliged & obedient servant, Edward L'estrange
*Postscript*: My lord, I pray present my humble duty & service to your right honourable lady, and honourable relations
*NRO: BL/Y/2/20*

## Sir Peter Gleane to Robert, Viscount Yarmouth

**1677, August 13**. My lord, I did not thinke I should be so unhappy (when I had the honour last to receyve a letter from you) as to have occassion to give you the trouble of so many lines upon the subjecte I am forst upon; the unkindnesses (of Mr Leigh & his tenant Mr Thomas Smyth of Waxham, who I heare was formerly your lordshipp's tenant, or neer neighbour) are so greate to mee, that the King's lawes (as theye order the matter) cannot protecte mee from there violence, but I am forst to make use of my arms, & many servants to gua[r]de mee from them: I have my lord upon my free-hold a dequoy that has bine there fortie yeers & above, which is a greate eye sore to Mr Leigh & Mr Smyth, and theye study all the ways possibly to distroye it. Mr Smyth first caused shooting in every corner aboute it to fright the fowle from it, when that would not doe, he sent his servants secretly in the morning when the fowles came from there feed to fright them out of the quoy, one of whose servants my servant took *in* my dequoy, & by threatning to have him punished brought him to confesse he had never done it, but by the perswassion of his master Smyth, who commanded him to fright the fowle out of my quoy; & in hopes the pardoning that offence I should have had more neighbourly doeings I did soe, & never did doe anythinge agaynst him: but now he finds out peopell for his purpose that are not Christians, or that have no Christian names that I can learne, and therefore can make no use of the King's lawes to protecte mee, and these are persons imployed under the pretence of mowing fodder in the fenns fast by my quoy but theye bringe alonge with them stones & slinges to throw them into the dequoy to fright the fowle, and this did not only there buissness in frighting away the fowle, but indangered the lives or mischeiffe of my servants, who works aboute the quoy, and are in that feare, that upon there exami-nations before a justice of peace, did confesse that theye durst not follow there buiss-ness without a guarde, so that I am forst to have other servants with gunnes to guarde them whylst theye are aboute there buissnes: my lord I sent a letter to Mr Smyth, after I understood this violence, a copie of which I have heer sent you, he would neither send mee an answere nor the names of those persons he set on worke: my lord I thought it my duty to let you know what I am forst to doe to defend my ser-vants, & my owne intrest [f.2] besides my feares of what may follow upon such greate provocations: my lord my loyallty has left mee but a small estate, I contracting a greate debte in his Majesties service, I should be glad to keepe that littell I have, and beleeve mee (my lord) although my quoy is but a litell helpe to mee yet that litell is greate where there is but a small estate, and to take a way my livelyhood is hard for flesh & blood to indure: I desiere your favour my lord, that you would advise some neighboring justice to him as Major Doubty or Mr Negusse to perswade him to a neighbourly & quiett living: I will assure your lordship that there shall never be any provocation given on my parte, nor my servants: I never yet made any returne to him of unkindness neither would suffer my servants, but my lord I can hold no longer, I doe therfore most humbly beg your love of mee: you may prevent mischeiffe that may follow, if he still goe on in this darke & pevish way, for his landlord or his owne coursses in law & equity let them proceed vigorously, I desiere no favour in that: were theye as well assured (as I am) of my Lord Leiutenant's favour towards mee, theye durst not be so bold to doe by mee as theye doe, but thinke I am under a frowne: my lord I will ever study to answer by my servisses all your favours & smiles to mee, and your helpe by this grant will everlastingly fix mee

*Signed*: your lordship's most humble and obedient servant, Peter Gleane

*Postscript*: **1677 August 9**. Mr Smyth, I hope you have no knowlidg of that mischeife that is done mee by your Hickling workmen that are in your marshes by there throwing of stones into my quoy & frighting those fowles that were in it, I desiere to be freindly & neighbourly towards you, and although wee are in law & equity for matters of *meum & tuum*, let us be freindly if you please, I begg it. And doe mee that neighbourly kindness, as to give mee the names of those persons that works in your marsh; the grant of this kindness will shew your inocencie of the mischeife theye have done mee, and obblige mee to be your neighbour & freind, Peter Gleane

*NRO: BL/Y/2/21*

## Robert Paston to Robert, Viscount Yarmouth

**1677, August 16, Bruxells**. My lord, after that night's rest at Ostend finding our horses in very good condition, we marched with a good convey to Bruges where we rested the next day; we were received with all the cerimony due to a person of my Lord Ply[*mouth's*] quallity. The town & country pleased extreamly having never seen anything soe neat but the next day getting to Ghent I thought myselfe in paradise, it being [*a*] noble large town, well situated, good buldings and in a very rich furtile country: which though harrased by continuell wars does not discover halfe the pauverty and misery, as does the very best parts of France; we by the assi[*s*]tance of a good strong convey the next day got to this town all of us very well, after having bin severall times by the way allarrumed by French parties: of [*sic*] our arrive here we found the greatest chang[*e*] imagenable, all the pe*o*pall in a very great confusion and consternation, the Prince of Orange having [*f.2*] the 11th by a concell of war raised the seige of Charleroy, noe body knows the raison, some says because Monr Lux[*em*]b[*ur*]ge[844] had cut of[*f*] their provisions, others upon some dispute between the Duke de Villa Harmosa but the peopell here will have it that it is a plot of our

---

[844] François Henri de Montmorency-Bouteville (1628–1695), duc de Luxembourg, marshal of France

King's, and my Lord Ossory was sent over on purpose to perswade the Prince to it: against whom they are all here soe inraged that they goe up and down the streets swering openly if they had him here they would serve him as de Witt was,[845] they threaten all the English soe here that we dare not appear in public for fear of being knocked of [*sic*] the head; we intend tomorrow by five in the morning to steal out of this disordered town, and follow the Prince, who is within halfe a day's journy, they say is in that dispair that noebody knows what he will doe; he has left the Spanish army, and the Duke de Vaudemont who was his great freind left him this day and came heither where *he* was formerly very well beloved but had the gates shutt upon him at first they biding him goe back with the Prince to [*f*.3] Charleroy: the Duke of Lorraine is in a worse condition being surrounded by Mon[*sieu*]r Crequi and Marshall Shomburg soe that he cannot escape without fi[*gh*]ting upon great disadvantage, they are soe near that they scermish all day long. All these misfortunes happning togather <makes> *putt* the whole contry in disparation: pray my lord present my duty to my mother and beleave me <my>

*Signed*: your lordship's most dutyfull and obedient son, Rob: Paston
*Postscript*: Pray address mine to Sir Richard Bolstope[846] the English agent at Bruxells
*Addressed*: These for the right honorable the Lord Viscount Yarmouth in Suffolke Street, London [*postmark*]
*NRO: BL/Y/2/22*

## John Doughty to Rebecca, Viscountess Yarmouth

**1677, August 22, Norwich**. Right honorable, my lord went out yesterday about five in the afternoone accompanied with my Lord Bishopp, Sir Thomas Garrett, Sir John Pettus, Sir Charles Harbord, Sir Henry Bedingfeild junior, both Sir William Doyleys, Sir John Rous, Colonell Knivett, Colonell Harbord and severall other of the cheife gentry of the county about 24 coaches & 100 horse. About a mile from the citty this company mett Mr Paston whom I went before to meet upon intelligence that hee was att Wymondham to salute his happy arrivall in Norfolk & the tytle (as I hope & thinke there's no doubt) of burgesse of Norwich in the roome of Mr Jay who dyed in the forenoone; Sir Neville Catlyne was much noysed to bee the person that wou'd stand, butt hee voluntarily & with much satisfaction as hee protested refused itt upon my lord's motioning itt to him, & has promised to use all his interest aswell as vigilance to effect it; Sir William Adams I had almost forgotten who will alsoe bee very assisting. All that has been spoken as yett (which not a few) are very complyable & there is [*?no*] feare (as farr as I can judge) of the event, the mayor,[847] Alderman Bendish, Briggs, & severall others are fixt already. There is *noe* tyme lost to compasse this buisinesse, & everybody very well pleased. Colonell Paston's equippage is very noble & great & [*?so*] is my lord's six horses your ladyshipp was pleased to send downe. The judges were mightily pleased with their reception, butt came not in till itt was darke, my lord has presented them with a noble present both of fish & flesh. Madam, never did any*thing* hitt soe well & soe seasonable as Mr Paston's comeing

---

[845] Johan de Witt, grand pensionary of Holland, and his brother were lynched by a mob in 1672.
[846] *recte* Bulstrode
[847] John Richer

downe, I hope both for his his [*sic*] honour's advantage, I have been with severall persons that have very good interest here <which> that are my very good *freinds*, they all have promised mee both their *owne* & those votes they can ingage, which are considerable. Madam, there shall not bee a minitt's tyme lost in the furtherance & compassing of this buisinesse as farr as lyes in the weake endeavours of, right honourable,

*Signed*: your honour's most devoted & humble & faithfull servant, Jo: Doughty

*Postscript*: Madam, I cannot write more att large for the post will bee gone.

*Addressed*: These present to the right honorable the Lady Viscountesse Yarmouth in Suffolk Street, London [*postmark*]

*NRO: BL/Y/2/23*

## John Fisher to Rebecca, Viscountess Yarmouth

**1677, August 22, Norwich**. Madam, my lord's time hath been wholly taken up to day with attending upon the judges all the forenoon, & giving a visit to the bishop this evening that he will hardly have leisure to write by this post, & therefore commanded me to give your honour an account, that the neighbouring gentlemen came unanimously in to him yesterday to wait upon the judges & bring them into this town, which though late (by reason my Lord Chief Justice[848] dined at Euston) was don with that solemnity, as they confessed they neaver saw the like any where, there were above twenty coaches, besides very many gentlemen on horseback. They went out a mile further than usuall, where they were forced to stay almost two hours before the judges came, and whilst they were thus staying, the high sheriff came up to the same place too, otherwise he had wayted with none but his own servants. By that time wee were come a mile out of town, wee met Colonell Paston with Sir John & Mr Clayton & Capt Pettus, who having drove hard & their horses hot, went a way into the town to rest their horses & provide themselves quarters; and all attended the judges *this forenoon* at an excellent sermon in Christchurch & afterwards at the sheirhouse, where after the commissions were read, & the grand jury sworn (which consisted of severall baronetts & justices (that came freely off the bench) & other gentlemen of quality), my Lord Bertie[849] (who setts here upon the gayle)[850] gave an extraordinary good charge[851] & then they returned to dinner. The judges invited my lord to dine with them this day (who sent them in last night, a buck, and a noble present of fish) but his lordship, having promised the gentlemen to dine with them, excused it till to morrow, & at the ordinary at the King's Head, they had a whole buck sent in by Mr Coke, and the commission of sewers was then to be opened, which Sir Charles Harbord tooke a particular care of, & the gentlemen do seem very forward to do Mr Paston all the right they can in the drayning & meliorating of his marshes at Mautby, which are now so much drowned, as they are becom little or nothing worth.

The first newes we met with here yesterday, was the death of [*f.2*] the old

---

848   Sir Francis North (1637–1685) lord chief justice of the common pleas, 1674–1682
849   Vere Bertie (d.1681), baron of the exchequer, cousin of Lord Yarmouth
850   *recte* gaol, i.e. a commission of gaol delivery
851   An admonition or address by a judge to a jury

Alderman Jay, and my lord being pleased to express his willingness that Mr Paston should stand for the next election of his place in the House of Commons, we find the sence of severall of the cheif persons that wilbe concerned therein, to be very inclynable to promote Mr Paston's interest, as the likelyest person they can choose to promote theirs at court, & most probable by his relations to make a good party for them in parliament, in both which places their trade & manufactury will make it necessary for them to pitch upon as good a friend as they can, but it's impossible to be certain what a popular election will do so long beforehand, as after the 3rd December next. I shall trouble your honour no further but with the presentment of my most humble service, ever remayning, madam,

*Signed*: your honour's most faithfull servant, John Fisher

*Postscript*: Dr Hildeyard is now by mee & presents his humble service to your honour. And Sir Charles Harbord gave me a particular charge *to add* his, most humbly & hartily to your honour, & to acquaint your ladyship that the ladyes of this country are in a longing expectation of your honour's presence here amongst them.

*Addressed*: These present to the right honourable the Lady Viscountess Yarmouth over against the Golden Ball in Suffolk Street, London

*NRO: BL/Y/2/24*

## Robert, Viscount Yarmouth to Rebecca, Viscountess Yarmouth

**1677, August 29**. My deare hart, I cannott butt be troubled till I heare you have beene abroad for itt seemes you have beene wors then you have let mee know, itt makes mee hope for to morrowes post; I am glad you are, or seeme to bee satisfied with the progress in [*Brunskell's*][852] business butt I must heare som further newse from [*you*] before I shall beleeve itt hath any other leggs then delay. Sir John Pettus writes to mee butt cannott give mee hopes of any expedition, God's will be done, for all the hopes of my enemies is now to see mee fall for lack of the ingredient which makes all thinges moove cheerefully, may they be disappointed. I saw a letter from [*daughter Paston*] to [*son Paston*] wherein she sayth you sent for the brother to speake with him about [*that business*] and that you spake to [*daughter Paston*] to reconcile [*you*] to [*Lady Shannon*][853] butt sayd that [*daughter Paston*] durst nott write noe more to [*son Paston*] by the open post, [*daughter Paston*] sayd allsoe that [*Lady Danby*] had sent to [*Lady Shannon*] about [*that business*] by which [*son Paston*] thought [*that business*] might be in a faire way. This day your son and too brothers are gon to Yarmouth & Maultby and meet mee on Thursday att noone att Sir William Doyly's att Shottesham on Thursday att dinner. On Tuesday next hee treates all the officers that are in commission of his regiment of horse wheresoever and

[852] Percival Brunskell of Bowes, Yorkshire, was a clerk of the Rolls Chapel and was prime mover behind a scheme to obtain a grant of a moiety of the revenue of greenwax out of the exchequer to a partnership of receivers consisting of the earl of Peterborough, viscount Yarmouth, Henry, Lord O'Brien, Sir Francis Compton, Bernard Greenville and Henry Fanshaw, with himself as surveyor (*CTB, 4, 1672–1675*, pp 862, 869, *CTB, 5, 1676–1679*, pp 795, 945, 993–4). A new cipher was used by the Pastons from this point, with a key (British Library: Add. MSS 27447, ff 303–4, see below p.386).

[853] Elizabeth Boyle (c.1622–1681), viscountess Shannon, daughter of Sir Robert Killigrew, and mother, by Charles II, of Charlotte Jemima, wife of William Paston

entertaines them all wherefore pray for us that none of them bee disguised[854] with nog that day. On the Thursday next weeke by all I can perceive my son intends to goe for London which he sayth is to bring you & his lady hether butt I find itt's to learne som little experience to menage his regiment which is very quickly shewn them. I have nott yett had one syllable from [f.2] either of your brothers concerning the farme when they begin I am prepared to answer them. I hope against Sir John coms that [*Peregrine Bertie*] will bee in towne butt that's too good newse to bee true though you dare nott send him the letter wee intended him yett meethinkes you should adventure to through another after him to find where he is. You still flatter mee with hopes of seeing you suddainely, God graunt itt in his mercy. On the next Saterday Sir Will Adams has invited us all and on Monday Sir Henry Bedingfeld; I sent yesterday to visitt my Lord Chief Justice at Norwich who returned mee many compliments about my entertainements butt Baron Bertie & Harrie Bertie were that day gon to Yarmouth, and Mr Finch[855] to see his cousin of Blickling, Mr North[856] stayed att Norwich where my Lord Chief Justice will nott have don his worke till this night att the soonest. Baron Bertie condemned three and saved one att your soon's[857] request and other gentlemen's. Pray write mee somwhat how [*Mrs Knight*][858] is accepted by [*Lady Danby*] and what reallityes[859] are betweene [*Lady Shrewsbury*] & [*the Duchess of Portsmouth*] and [*Lady Danby*] & [*my Lord Treasurer*]. You have promised mee a long letter tomorrowe which I shall meet as I goe through <Shottesham> Norwich to Shottesham. Your soon's hopes att Norwich encreaseth dayly and I doe nott much feare the success; my coachorses thrive bravely and are licke to last this seven yeares in a thriving condition if I bee able to keep them, they are the best conditioned finest creatures I ever saw and as handsom as is possible, they must bee spared att first & used gently butt now [f.3] I visitt them dayly in the stables too or three times a day. Noe man loves a good horse better than myself and I must needs have sent downe by the first [?]six leather cases to buckle up their tayles and to preserve them from the dirt, Lewis sent down topps with the harness, I imagine these may cost about six shillings a peece. I made the cases of glasses bee opened in my chamber this morning allthough Mrs Cooper told mee you would nott have them opened till you came; they are fine ones, butt I find many sands and bubbles in them, there was butt three small drinking glasses broke of all the parcells. All your children presents their duty to you, and long to see you, soe doth with passion my deare

*Signed*: yours till death, Yarmouth
*Postscript*: Pray name Mr Fisher, Mr Gough & Peckover in your next, itt rejoyceth them that you honor their names in your letter, pray dispose the inclosed.
*NRO: BL/Y/2/25*

[854] i.e. drunk

[855] Presumably one of the sons of Heneage Finch, the lord chancellor, whose mother and Sir John Hobart's grandmother were members of the Bell family of Beaupre Hall.

[856] Possibly Roger North (1653–1674), brother of the lord chief justice; their sister Elizabeth was the second wife of William Paston, 2nd earl of Yarmouth.     [857] i.e. son's

[858] Mrs Mary Knight (c.1631–1698), singer and courtier. She may one time have been mistress to Charles II and he granted her a pension of £200 for life in 1672. She sang in the last court masque 'Calisto' with the daughters of the duke of York in 1675. Her father Sir Stephen Knight (c.1591–1664) is buried in Norwich Cathedral.     [859] i.e. sincere expressions

# Sir Peter Gleane to Robert, Viscount Yarmouth

**1677, September 1**. My lord, the greate trouble you have taken in my private afayers to compose a difference that would royle flesh & blood, and the progress your lordshipp has made in it, is enough to testifie greater kindness from your lordshipp towards mee, then the world will beleeve I deserve; and the reports I meet with (that I should slight your lordshipp since your coming into this county as lord lieutenant) and my own feares will not sufer mee to be at any quiett till I doe sularge[860] my sealfe, upon that subjecte that gives occassion for their beleefe & my jealousie, that I deserve not that favour your lordshipp is pleased to shew me; the not taking new commissions from you; the not attending upon you, when you fierst came into the county as lord leiutenant; my absence from Oxnead when you have bine there, and my absenting from publique meetings (to my charge) but not from my Lord Leiutenant: my guilt is such in some of these particculars that it will become mee to give my reasons for my neglect in some measure: for the fierst I humbly thank your lordshipp you did early receyve satisfaction that it was only upon the account of freindshipp, and the infirmities that attends age, made mee doe that, and no backwardness to loyaltie nor disrespecte to the person that came in with the King's comission: I had honour & love to both, and doe protest it to be true, in the presence of God; but I was willing, & am still soe, to let the world see that I can sufer with my freind;[861] and (my lord) freindship & loyaltie are so neer a kin, that I hope I shall not be thought to decline the one, for the other: I only begg to be rightly understood by your lordshipp: from the censures of the world, my owne innocence will defend mee; I am no longer my freind's freind then he is freind to my prince & to the government which I ever will be constant too, with liffe & fortune, iff there has bine errors of judgment comitted since I receyved this inclosed justification from him, I am harttely sorry, but I remember he is a man, & may have passions & faylings as one: I ought not to forsake him barly upon that accounte; if my breade were at stake I should not, but when he [*f*.2] shall fayle of his principalls in this letter, I forsake him, if he were my father, but never will <but> upon an other accounte: and (my lord) as I hope for mercie, the same love I have for your authority & you, only he was my fierst acquayntance. Deare my lord, doe not sufer mee to fall into my prince's displeasure for a punctillio of honour, I'lle asure you he shall be no longer my freind, then he is my King's freind. I feare nothing but the King's & your displeasure (and doe not know <but> *what* whispring may doe in this case) that would destroye mee, sooner then a bullet: when your lordshipp has red this inclosed, honour mee so farr as to seale it up in a paper, & send it to mee, this is all the satisfaction I give my sealfe for the censures I undergoe: that he is the King's freind, as well as mine & no longer the one, without the other; as for not attending your lordshipp at your coming into the cuntry, I may truly answere, I was hindered by sickness, and did wright to my friend [?]Tom Holand to exscuse mee to your lordshipp, the copie of which letter I have by mee; and as for my neglecte of wayting on you at Oxnead I cannot exscuse, no more then I can exscuse my neglecte at Raynham for I <*words deleted*> I have not bine there this four or five yeares, only in generall, my private misfortunes makes mee dwell at homme so much, that I am

---

[860] Probably solace or relieve, from *soulager* (Fr.)        [861] i.e. Lord Townshend

a strainger to my next neighbour: and my naturall disposition makes company a burden to mee,[862] I am not ashamed, upon this occassion, to speake this truth: for my absenting from publique meetings or asizes & sessions, the differences that are amongst us keepe mee from them, I am not willing to meet with disputes that may arise from thence, but wayte till the heate of differences be alayed, which I most harttely wish & pray for. I hope my lord by this time I am righter in your lordshipp's opinion. If these thinges should be often whispred to you, the assurance of which will give me liffe, if not I am deade as a dore nayle, I will take that corage as to beleeve (that maugr[e] my enemys) <that> I am in your lordshipp's favour, and I will never fayle of being constant. My lord,

*Signed*: your lordship's most humble, faythfull & obedient servant, Peter Gleane
*Postscript*: What ever your lordshipp does in relation of compassing the differences that are between Mr Smyth & my sealfe, I shall say amen too, and be infinitely obliged to you.
If Townshend were not, I would never be at rest till I were imeadiately under your command, rayther than not be, I would be *a* corporall.
*NRO: BL/Y/2/26*

## William Paston to Rebecca, Viscountess Yarmouth

**1677, September 2, Oxnett**. Deare madam, I received your ladyship's most obliging letter, & am very glad to here (both by my lord's letter & myne) how kind my Lady Danby is; I have been extraordinary kindly received by all the country; & more particularly at Yarmouth where nobody could be more kindly received. My lord has used his interest with very good successe here at Norwich concerning my being burgesse <here> soe that I think there will be noe dispute at all of it, as Major Doughty & Mr Buller & all tells me; for wee have *not* only prevailed upon the right party, but alsoe upon the heads of the phanatiks. Sir Hary Bedingfeild has informed us [f.2] of news that I hope will not displease your ladyshipe; which is of his being trustee to Climent Paston's estate & William Paston's of above £3,000 per annum; & that both are setled upon my lord & his heirs in case they dye, there is but three between *my lord* now, whereof two are Clim's sons & one Will Paston's; the former *sons* Sir Hary informed my lord that theyr father was in a deep dropsy when they were borne & that Dr Brown did informe *him* that they could not live to be men; & the tother was soe sickly he was *not* likely to live a yeare. My commission is to be executed a Mondy come sevennight, I hope matters will [?]goo ver[y] well; I beg your ladyship's pardon that I have noe more to say only that I am

*Signed*: your ladyship's most obedient son, Will Paston
*Postscript*: My duty to my grandmother
*Addressed*: These to the right honourable the Lady Viscountesse Yarmouth att her lodgings in Suffolk Street over against the Golden Ball in London
*NRO: BL/Y/2/27*

---

862 However Gleane's retiring disposition did not prevent him from standing against Lord Yarmouth's candidates in the county elections of 1679 and 1681, and winning.

# Richard Huntington and Benjamin England to John Dawson

**1677, September 6, Yarmouth**. Sir, wee thanke you for your care to prevent dis-apointment to those gentlemen who were this day designed by desire of the corpora-tion to waite upon his lordshipp: they must take some other opertunity but it cannot possibly be the next week by reason of our sessions. Wee pray leave our most humble service to be presented to his lordshipp att his returne. Wee are

*Signed*: your affectionate friends & servants, Richd Huntington, Ben: England, bayliffs
*Addressed*: To Mr John Dawson att Oxnead Hall present, or in his absence to my lord's secretary
*NRO: BL/Y/2/28*

# Robert, Viscount Yarmouth to Rebecca, Viscountess Yarmouth

**1677, September 12**. My dearest hart, by thy last to mee I find Mr Atturney[863] peremptory and I doe believe hee will find out ways to delay the passing the matter till [*the King*] and [*my Lord Treasurer*] be gon, butt *who* can doe more then is possible to bee don in any thing, pray God send mee better newse for this putts mee to a stand what to beleeve. Your son had a great appearance of comm[*issione*]rs of gentlemen[864] at Ludham as ever was on such an occasion, and his business is licke to goe on. Yesterday morning beeing Tuesday they went from hence in the morning betwixt eight & nine, they dined att Beckhall and stayed there till two and then went on for Oxborrowe where there resolutions were to goe away on Wedensday morning & to reach London on Thursday night butt I believe itt will bee Friday which makes mee the more perticular in my relation; your son gave away £10 in the howse, to Mrs Cooper 40s and to Nurs Port a guinney. Yesterday the bishop & one of his sonns in law came and dined with mee, hee was infinitely pleased with the church & chap-pell, and every thing els and talked with mee very sincerely & honestly, and I doe fancy he will proove a very good man, he stayed till five in the afternoone and then I carried him som part of his way & soe parted kindly. To morrowe I goe to Stanninghall[865] to dinner, and intend by the way to meet your letters on the rode. What you write mee word that [*Lady Danby*] sayth concerning 10 beeing soe melancholy I wonder att, butt I believe 9 is nott a mann much pleasing to her. Little deare Charles his pritty letter pleased mee very much. Pray God after all [*my Lord Treasurer*] keepes stedfast to his word and that [*the King*] and hee doe not find som way now att the brink to destroy [*Brunskell's affair*]: [*Sir John Clayton*] coms up with full designe to animate [*f.2*] [*Peregrine Bertie*][866] in [*that concern of ours*] and if hee can carrie itt without having more scrutinys putt upon't then is ordi-nary in such cases itt will bee worth his paines, pray my service to him & my thankes

---

[863] Sir William Jones (c.1630–1682), attorney-general
[864] i.e. gentlemen who were commissioners of sewers        [865] Home of Colonel Philip Harbord
[866] Peregrine Bertie was not only Lord Yarmouth's cousin but was also the brother-in-law of Lord Danby, and for this reason it is possible that he had been persuaded to take a part in Lord Yarmouth and Sir John Clayton's scheme for the erection of lighthouses; Clayton had been granted further letters patent on 23 January 1677 but thereafter the scheme hung fire. (*CSPD*, *1682*, pp 293, 350).

for his letter,[867] what's nott don in [*that concern of ours*] & [*Brunskell's affair*] before [*the King*] goes will scarce goe on I feare afterwards. I am glad you say that [*Lady Shrewsbury*], [*Lady Danby*], [*Mrs Knight*], [*the Duchess of Portsmouth*] & [*you*] are very kind, pray God som effects may followe; pray what becomes of 4 & that gang, are they in with [*the King*]? I suppose before this coms to your hands they will bee with you from whome you will have a large accompt of all thinges heere, heere are Mr Gulston's[868] papers signed & sealed, pray send mee noe accompts till you com your self, itt's enough that I approove & others doe admire att your spiritt & vigor in the prosecution of the affaires of your family.

Heere's a letter inclosed I suppose from my sonn's wife which I send as itt came to mee with a pin through the seale.

Your children all presents their duty to you and are well. Betty is growne mighty sober & reserved, she thinkes she shall never *see* you, all heere present their service and wish for your comming butt above all hee that is

*Signed*: yours till death, Yarmouth

*Postscript*: My duty to your mother. I am glad you have a chaise of your owne. Pray lett Lewis keepe his horse to com downe with you, he sayth he is his owne butt hee was bought with my money, if itt appeares nott soe on accompt Ile allowe him his prise for him. Dr Hughes is very sick butt has writt to mee that hee will allwayse bee what he has professed.

*Addressed*: For your selfe

*NRO: BL/Y/2/29*

## Robert, Viscount Yarmouth to Rebecca, Viscountess Yarmouth

**1677, September 19**. My dearest deare, your letters are the pleasure of my life and you are the subject for which I desire to live, in the hopes you give mee that things may mend, the first prospect is over by this time, Monday morning I prayed for, butt when I know the varietys of appointments and the treasury chamber and that dayes doe seldome hold there, I feare itt may bee longer putt of[f] or that the first hearing may bee fatall, butt thinges can bee noe better nor wiselier ordered, lett the success proove what itt will. I will goe out in the morning to attend your letters which I all-waies doe read with the greatest pleasure in the world, God send good tidings, Mr Russell will bee a pleasant messenger butt pray lett his journey be ordered att London that hee may nott be putt on my choyse for a reward butt by agreement before hee coms. You tell mee of great friends that will stick close to the matter in hand, pray God [*the King*] & [*my Lord Treasurer*] doe nott fayle upon the suggestions of Mr Atturney who noe doubt has mustered up all his rethorick to oppose the matter; I am glad to find that [*Mrs Knight*], [*Lady Danby*], [*Lady Shrewsbury*], [*the Duchess of Portsmouth*], 9, [*my Lord Treasurer*] are soe kind to you, pray God continue itt, I am sure you deserve the kindness of all the world that converses with

---

[867] Peregrine Bertie to Lord Yarmouth, 8 Sep 1677 (British Library: Add. MSS 27447, f.380): will take no steps in the business until Sir John comes to town otherwise will be 'a grate ignoramus in it'.

[868] William Goulston (c.1641–1687), later MP, who married the niece of John Morris, partner of Sir Robert Clayton the financier, and was employed in his business.

you. Sir Peter Gleane has beene with mee since Monday night and is soe highly satisfied in my reception of him that he is this morning gon the most pleased man in the world and the most full of expressions to my service, he is a man of honor & integritie, and itt's noe ill thing to have such a friend.

What you write about Hurton is nott soe complaineable if he is a gripple[869] fellowe and will nott lett everie groome have soe much over measure as they sell att the ale-house for drink butt what I command is don, and when you com to give him his *quietus est* you'l see if his grippleness bee to my proffitt or his owne. In the meane [*time*] my fine horses are menaged with all the care the directions of the Dutchman left which is nott according to English rules butt they are very fine and £50 better then when they came hither, and as for a gentleman of the hors itt shall [*f*.2] bee none butt Rawlins, who now doth looke after what you speake of and understands an hors and is a handsom usefull man on horsback. I every day make itt my *owne* business to looke after them and see they have their due watering & ayrings everie day. I pray send downe by the carts well tied up the surveigh on Yarmouth which is in a long deale box & lett itt bee sealed up; itt's a strange thing of [*Peregrine Bertie*] & [*Sir John Clayton*] that for a business of that advantage, they should make fruitless journeys.

Just now I have turned away the coachman who though the best driver I ever had yett soe insufferable a rouge for drinking & debaucherie that Miss and the weomen beeing gon of ayring to Dr Hylierd's with the grays, hee was drinking att Runton till three in the afternoone, and when he had his horses made ready for him hee gott up and gave Rawlins all the ill language in the world, threw him his livery, jumped of [*f*] the coachbox & Rawlins was faine to drive them home that little part of the way they were gon, soe that now I have neither coachman nor postilion, and I must have both, and they must bee experienced in driving for every one cannott drive these horses; therefore lett Lewis immediately looke out and lett them bee sent by the first opportunity for I am a prisoner to all occasions till they com more then that Leonard, who prooves an usefull servant for everything, can drive mee abroad with too horses, can ride postilion with these horses which the postilion could nott & can shave mee upon an occasion.

Busby I had lickewise turned away for for [*sic*] all the warning I gave nott one drop of drink in the howse of any kind butt nogg that is to bee drunke, soe that I am forced to send to Beckhall for the beere I drinke butt as he was quitting the howse Mis[*s*] came to mee in a greevous compassionate fitt and reprived him att least till you com butt there's nothing more necessary in the world then to dissolve this family[870] and when I goe to London againe to leave noe more then just to keep the howse which three or foure att the most may doe and if they will give entertainement lett itt bee out of their owne bordwages.

[*f*.3] Mr Peckover has beene very usefull to mee and is ready to lay downe his life for you, soe I have sent up his measure and if to his <cote and> cote and breeches you add a silke or slight sattin wastcote I find itt will oblidge him strangely and on my conscience hee will well in som kind or other deserve itt.

Pray lett this coachman bee one that will dress his horses himself & the postilion a light fellowe that has beene used to ride postilion & to dress horses and lett them bee well recommended.

---

[869] i.e. niggardly, usurious     [870] i.e. his household

My service to my son & daughter, thanke them for their letters Ile write the next post, I had a letter allsoe from your brother George which I shall answer butt I cannott thinke of anything till I have read my doome in [*Brunskell's affair*].

I am glad you gave that answer as to my farme which is the greatest concerne of my life to dispose in som way that the creditors may have satisfaction and Mr Bulwer must bee consulted and som method advised before I dispose itt and nott to tye my self up as I was to the pleasure of Sir John, butt wee'l see both this business and [*Brunskell's affair*] over before wee meddle butt wee may thinke on't.

Pray kiss deare little Charles a 100 times for mee, I read his letter to severall that were heere. My duty to your mother,

*Signed*: I am my dearest yours till death, Yarmouth
*Postscript*: Your children are well and presents their dutys, all heere are your most humble servants.
*NRO: BL/Y/2/30*

## Robert, Viscount Yarmouth to Rebecca, Viscountess Yarmouth

**1677, September 28**. My deare hart, I was yesterday nott a little disturbed to see my pacquet returned mee, which came with a letter of Captaine Lulman's the post-master heere *inclosed* and the carefullest of my concernes of any man, he to demon-strate sends mee the letter with the London marke upon't as you will find when you receive itt. I have this day written to Colonel Whitley[871] to desire that I may have right don mee for this mistake, and Captaine Lulman writes too, and you may send to him. I would nott open the packquett by Mr Fisher's advice, that Whitley might see itt, nay I had inclosed itt in a letter to him butt for feare hee should bee gon to Newmarkett, from which place I have not heard one word, but am in the mind to send over Mr Doughty to waite on my Lord Treasurer. I can find by your two last letters your humor mightily changed would you confess itt, the rubbs you have encountred & the delays you meet with beeing able to discourage any one butt my Lady Yarmouth who lives under the character now of a lady that does great thinges for her family. I am very glad to find that Mr Atturney has signed anything sure this must bee the bill and nott the warrant, for the warrant is signed by none butt the King & the secretary. I beseech God wee may heare of itts progress for from this step methinkes itt should pass the broad seales before the tearme.

Yesterday Sir Jeames Jonston, Mr England & Alderman Hall were with mee from the towne of Yarmouth, and Sir James in his florid stile complemented *mee* highly from them, they did acknowledge all my favors, and desired not to prejudice my inter-est and for all matters betwixt us desired they might be referred to whome I pleased, soe they have chosen Sir Robert Baldock and I Major Doughty & Mr Bulwer, and I hope in time wee shall yett gett that in a way of improovement.[872] I doe wonder that in none of yours you give mee noe hints of my Lord Treasurer whether he coms for Norfolke, or whether my Lady Anne bee com or what [*Lady Danby*] doth doe in

---

[871] Colonel Roger Whitley (1618–1697), deputy postmaster
[872] This probably refers to a dispute over mooring posts erected by the town on the west side of the river Yare.

their absence, I am sorrie to be in the darke for these matters though for those of
[*Brunskell's affair*] I can stay, you writt mee nott word when [*Brunskell*] [*f.2*] was
to goe to Newmarkett, and as to the atturney's beeing as you hope kinder then was
expected, I cannott fathome itt for he must followe his directions & orders without
he has an influence to stop them.

I am glad to heare *my son* is very kind to you, nott one word of [*Lady Shannon*]
[*Lady Danby*] [*Mrs Knight*] [*Lady Shrewsbury*] [*the Duchess of Portsmouth*]
[*my Lord Treasurer*] or any of them in this letter, I am glad you say the King stayes
butt a forthnigtgh att Newmarkett butt I cannott conceive hee will leave his pleasures
there soe soone.

I was mightily kindly used the other day att Sir Will Rant's, I beleeve they will
proove very good neighbors. Your children are all well and presents their dutys to
you, all heere are your humble servants. My humble duty to your mother I would
faine see her hand againe, God send us better newse, I suppose [*Peregrine Bertie*]
& [*Sir John Clayton*] moove nott till the King returns. I doe suppose Robin comes
over with the Prince.[873] You say the newse is neare us by beeing att Newmarkett butt
that half way fetcheth quicker to you then to us for wee heare nott a word yett from
thence. I have noe more to say butt that I am for ever my dearest deare

*Signed*: thyne most passionately, Yarmouth
*Postscript*: If the pacquett coms to your hands before Whitley sees itt keep the superscription & lett Lewis goe shew it to Whitly & find out the author of the mistake for
soe itt will proove & meere one. Pray send downe the lining for the chariott.
*Addressed*: These present to the right honorable the Lady Viscountess Yarmouth over
against the Golden Ball in Suffolke Street, London [*postmark, franked: Yarmouth*]
*NRO: BL/Y/2/31*

## Note of resolutions of deputy lieutenants concerning militia

**1677, October 2, Norwich Castle**. *Present: Sir John Pettus, Sir Jacob Astley, baronets,
Sir Nevill Cateline, knight. Ordered that Mr Henry Daynes of Raydon be discharged from finding
any proportion of foot arms under Capt Barney, and be charged for the future one third part of a
horse & arms complete under Capt Sir William Doyly junior. The muster being put off till next
spring, the order to treasurer Augustine Briggs to pay £40 11s 6d to clerk Edward L'estrange is
cancelled and L'estrange is fully discharged.*

*In L'estrange's hand*
*NRO: BL/Y/2/32*

## Robert, Viscount Yarmouth to [Sir Robert Howard]

**1677, October 19, Oxnead**. Sir, your letter directed to me to Yarmouth came to
my house twenty miles from there just now, & found me newly out of a feavour, which
put me in much danger of my life, & terminates in a violent fitt of the gout, which
deprives me of all motion, & makes me utterly uncapable of obeying the Order of

873 i.e. William, Prince of Orange, later William III

Councill, which I must represent thear by some friend. I am utterly ignorant what my testimony might have proved usefull in things altogether remote from my knowledg, however at any time wherin I had not been totally disabled from motion, I should have paid my obedience to the Councell's commands, and to yours as being sir

*Signed*: your most humble servant, Yarmouth
*Copy, not in Yarmouth's hand*
*NRO: BL/Y/2/33*

## Robert, Viscount Yarmouth to Rebecca, Viscountess Yarmouth

**1677, October 22**. My dearest deare, thy deare letters, the testimonys of thy kindness, are the best cordialls soe great a distance can afford mee & the best pictures of yourself which I can looke upon. I knowe nott what to say to the contents of itt, you have preached confidence soe long that were cowardly now to feare though this solemnity of the assembling the judges is a matter I cannott interprett any good meaning in, for itt is for them to argue all against itt or els to protract itt till they have leysure to heare itt which may nott bee till God knowes when, for I feare Saterday you spake of will bee too soone and other Saterdayes proove too late. My mind is troubled enough about itt and the more because I know yours is twice as much, God putt a good issue to itt for itt's death to expect with feare; may to morrowe give mee better light & further hopes of the lickelihood of itts growing towards a conclusion. On Friday night was in one with a letter to mee from London, I thought itt had beene Mr Russell, butt he prooved a messeger from the Counsell, who brought mee a civill letter from Sir Robert Howard with an Order of Cou[n]sell, and had made the most fri[e]ndless journey in the world, first to Yarmouth, then to Oxned, the Order was dated a month before and I noe notice till the 21 of October to appeare there on Wednesday next, which if I had beene in health I would nott have don, soe I writt to Sir Robert Howard the coppie of which I send you as allsoe his letter, and a coppie of the Order of Counsell. You had best lett Lewis step downe to the Counsell or Robin, and speake to Sir Robert Southwell who signed the Order to gett mee excused by letting them know if occasion bee how ill I have beene & am still of the gout butt people that are summoned there appeare nott often att the distance I am att; I am of opinion my Lord Treasurer will hoyst him out of his place.[874] I sent away John Gammon with these papers to young Sir William Doyly, with a letter of my owne to him to desire him to com over & explaine matters a little to mee, withall I told him that Sir Robert Clayton did alarum you att London that procesers would com out against mee for his father & him, & that this stopped all the [f.2] current of my business with Sir Robert butt hee was gon to London on Tuesday before. My letter was promised to bee sent up by Mr Cock to him, and I doe desire you to send to him & shew him these papers, which keep by you, and lett's know what he sayth & desire him to write to mee who have beene his good friend as you may promise to bee for hee is one that is very instrumentall to serve my family.

I have returned you the acquittance signed & sealed. Mr Bulwer & his wife who

---

[874] Danby had brought charges against Howard of misuse of government funds etc., but he escaped with a severe reprimand (Browning, *Leeds*, I, p.246).

dined heere yesterday com up to London on Monday next from hence, and will bee in towne on Wedensday; I shall give him a paper of instructions and hee is the fittest man to model the way of the assignements and to discurse Dickinson for an agreement according to Dickinson's proposalls which letter I hope you keep safe and ready to produce. I am very glad att what you tell mee concerning [*Peregrine Bertie*] & that itt will bee putt in a posture to try what itt will doe speedily. I writt in my last that I know nott if Ayde will bee willing to seale to anything of hazzard butt as I remember [*Sir John Clayton*] himself propounded an easier way and that none of us need bee named in the patent butt I resolve nott to have my name used. Must I never doe anything butt that I must bee the packhorse to carrie itt through after I have seised the opposition lett [*Peregrine Bertie*] if hee be convinced of the reallitys of the thing struggle itt through.

As to Robin I have written my mind bothe to you & him; lett him com or nott com yett as hee thinkes the journey may hinder his proffitt or advance his pleasure. The bishop ends his visitation this week att Northwalsham having beene out neare too monthes, I intend to invite him on Friday to dine heere in his way home; I had a letter from old Sir Henry Bedingfeld by which you may see that my sickness was taken notice of att Newmarkett. If I could but carrie them the good newse to Beckhall that my affaire were concluded itt would be a cordiall to them, there's nothing they watch for more then my good and prosperity and are our friends upon all accompts, and do nott onely doe [*f.3*] what they say butt are still[875] contriving how to act for us. The next post I shall write you somwhat about the shreeves in which I m[a]y gett my Lord Cheif Baron to help me, & my Lord Treasurer if need bee.

You promised mee somwhat of the histore of [?]9['s] retirement butt have sayd nothing of itt since. I thought the Lady Mary[876] had beene of yeares beyound a governess, and that if one my Lady Villers would bee the woman.

I can now make shift to gett into my charriott which is very pritty with the new lining putt into itt, I have great care of my health, because I long to live to see you.

My sonn's business att Norwich I thinke is fixed beyound the power of any opposition that's now to bee raised, and that of the commissioners of sewers licke to end as well. Pray present my service to him & his lady & the children, I hope he is gotten abroad before now.

Sir Nevile Catlyne & Sir Will Adams are com for London. I pray for God sake & mine looke after your owne health which is the joy of my sowle. Don Henshaw has never written to mee since I came downe though I have beene sick, itt's that damned £45 that betrays mee to perdition in his thoughts, which slavery of owing friends money especially I hope to be rid on.

I did nott thinke when I began that I should have spun out my letter halfe soe long having nothing of novelty heere. My Blickling neighbors are as if they were dead to mee I heare noe words of them, I sent this day Mr Doughty to Holcam to

---

[875] i.e. continually, constantly

[876] Lady Mary (1662–1694), daughter of the duke of York and later Queen; she married William, prince of Orange on 4 November. The match was largely Danby's doing and was very popular, as the country mistrusted the King's Francophile policy.

complement my cousin Coke, who goes to morrow to Newmarkett butt returnes againe as soone as Sir Robert Carr's race is over with Robin Coke, for £400.

Pray present my duty to your mother and tell her I long to see her hand, dispense my service where you thinke itt materiall and to yourself take all the facultys of the hart & sowle of him that's yours to the last,

*Signed*: Yarmouth
*NRO: BL/Y/2/34*

## Robert, Viscount Yarmouth to Rebecca, Viscountess Yarmouth

**1677, October 26**. My dearest deare, with thy deare letter I received many others to informe mee of Monday's success which now depends on my Lord Chancelor's civility to us of which I hope the best because you have formerly told mee hee was a friend to itt; my Lord Privy Seale[877] is a brave advocate where he undertakes a cawse and soe itt seemes he behaved himself in ours; I hope wee have noe more tenter-hookes to hang upon after this greatest test is past which have beene putt upon itt; and yett I made my observation of your last that itt was nott soe brisk as the former ones, though Sir John Pettus was brisker then his usuall stile. I have returned answers to all that writt except to Mr Hildersly[878] who gave mee a very good accompt, butt his was an answer to mine. I had one from Sir John just to the matters in hand without any reflexions by which I perceived a reservedness, though it were full enough to the purpose, yett Brunskill, Hildersly & Pettus made our case better then his seemed to doe, itt must now bee pushed on apace els itt's lost and I hope it will yett answer som of those expections you have putt on itt of which I would faine heare you say a word because I know nott what recoupts and cutts of may be in the orders for our patent of inspection & collection and how these emoluments are to bee appro-priated to us, which is to bee Mr Brunskill's contrivance and the King's kindness allowed by my Lord Chancelor. By this time I suppose Sir Robert Howard's business is over, I cannott imagine the intreage of my summons much less of yours, I am sorrie you were soe troubled att itt, that I beleeve itt putt you in ill humor when you writt, butt you did well [f.2] nott to thinke of appearing, butt I would nott too much declare any dislike becawse Sir Robert Howard has allwayes comported himself civily to mee and in my Yarmouth affaire was very brisk for mee.

My Lord Bishop who carries himself licke a bishop to the satisfaction of all the right clergy ends his visitation this day, and dines heere where there will bee a confirmation. He yesterday told Dr Hyliard that he was obliged to give mee an accompt of what he had don, he dined one day att Raineham but my Lord Townshend was soe ill of the gout that he could nott com down and the bishop onely saw him butt in the church their was a confirmation; but their happned a pritty acci-dent. The clergy about one hundred beeing informed the bishop dined att Sir John Hobart's went out of Walsham to meet him butt he never came more there soe they missed him; the chancelor had pressed him, though he were invited to another place,

---

[877] 1st earl of Anglesey
[878] Stephen Hildesly, sub-commissioner of excise for Norfolk, etc.; his name is included in the key to this cipher but the symbol is never used.

to goe dine att Mr Windham's, where when they came was neither steward meat or drinke, att last he gott a cup of beere, and som little morsell which was prepared for the servants, & left them noe dinner butt came away a little unsatisfied with the chancelor's importunity. My Lady Danby's letter is very kind, pray seale the inclosed and give itt her from mee. I write this in the morning, when the bishop goes I will close up my pacquett and if I have anything more to say you shall have itt, onely you having the narrative of the business which [*f.*3] concernes the shreeves, must show itt my Lord Cheif Baron and take his directions and perhapps my Lord Treasurer who need butt lett Mr Ramsey putt him in mind of itt att the time or som other a word doth itt, and he will doe himself service in itt and my Lord Cheif Baron will oblidge us all.

The bishop has dined with mee and the chancelor and severall of the clergy, wee had a confirmation in my chappell, my children and all my family and severall others were decently confirmed, he used me with great respect as I did him for I thinke him a very good man and one wee shall have much comfort in, he is zealous for my sonn's election which I thinke wee need nott doubt.

The post calls, God send mee good newse from thy deare hand, God preserve thee in soule & body, my duty to your mother I saw none of her letters the last post, pray God send Peregrine Bertie well in [*that concern of ours*].

*Signed*: I am from my soule thine, Yarmouth
*Postscript*: Your children presents their dutys.
*NRO: BL/Y/2/35*

## Robert, Viscount Yarmouth to Rebecca, Viscountess Yarmouth

**1677, October 29**. My dearest deare hart, thine I received early on the rode where I usually goe to meet with thy deare letters which are in thy absence the greatest cordialls I can receive. I am glad to heare you say you are as well as ever were in your life, which makes my health the better, last night I tooke my salt of which I find prodigious good effects soe as I hope I shall never leave a medicine soe long that I have had soe good experience of; I am glad you are satisfied in the progress of [*Brunskell's affair*], may wee com to an end of itt once I hope now matters tend to a settlement & that [*the King*] will be as good as his word, if my Lord Chancelor & my Lord Treasurer bee satisfied with [*Brunskell's*] paper then sure wee shall quickly runn our patent on. I shall bee glad to heare further allsoe of [*Peregrine Bertie*] & [*Sir John Clayton*] what they doe and how they go on in [*that concern of ours*] which beleeve mee will bee a fine thing if itt can bee accomplished butt I feare wee shall meet with as many rubbs in that as wee have don in this, otherwise why goes itt nott dayly on? I am mightily satisfied in having Mr Rutty's name in as trustee for mee itt cannott bee better, but I pray speake to [*Peregrine Bertie*] that in the articles he may order itt soe as that wee may accompt quarterly, for this is of another nature then the wood farme and brings in money every day, and these long reckonings are very unprofitable as well as uneasy. The match of the Prince of Orange was congratulated in Norwich with bonefires and ringing of bells, and itt is universally pleasing to the nation, and if my Lord Treasurer has beene the instrument of itt hee has don for himself a great worke. You have nott writt mee one word this many dayes of [*Lady Shannon*], I doe suppose that does licke all thinges there com to nothing.

[*f.*2] I am sorrie my sonn's distemper has kept him soe long within dores, pray present my service to his lady and him and the sweet children. Sir Charles Harbord had my daughter's letter whereupon on Friday last they both went to Norwich where they mett the commissioners which were many that appeared as Moutham, Mr Haughton, the Wards and several others besides Major Doughty who is the carrier on of the worke & the maine pillar of all. Itt is licke to succeed very well & speedily, the objections putt in were butt too and those unmateriall ones and they are now about to send for an ingineer to see the most convenient place for clapping downe the floodgates, and ordering how to sett the wheele att work. As for his election att Norwich nothing can seeme fairer or better layd in the world, and Thomas Corie who has beene with mee these too nights, and brought som papers which he conceives may doe mee good in my Yarmouth reference sayth he thinkes there can bee noe pretence in the matter against him. Mr Bulwer has these papers up with him, and will extract what may bee for my benefitt against the meeting which is agreed the 14 of December; he & his wife came away this day for London, they will wayte on you; I gave him a paper of instructions, which hee is to consult you in, the first is about Dickinson's business, som others there are allsoe which I desire hee & you will make the best way in you can. He has beene very instrumentall about my sonn's affaire, and this Rutty who your brother George sayth is written to is the only person wee now openly heare of that opposeth us.

I must desire you to lett Lewis goe to Riches shop and gett mee the largest paire of thred stockings he can and send them downe by the Norwich coach, I can gett none heere and I have butt one paire which I now weare night and day and I feare with plasters & lying in them they will bee worne out before I can have [*f.*3] others. I doe wonder you never writt mee word of Windham & his wife, I suppose they are att Sir Joseph Ashe's[879] in the country and never com to towne. Remember mee to Robin, tell him I shall bee glad to see him as soone as you & hee thinke fitt for his convenience and hee shall bee the more welcom for bringing mee downe any newse wherein your satisfaction may beare a part.

I doe intend to make a visitt to Beckhall as soone as I can have any newse from you of my owne concernes that's good that I may rely on and not have fobbs to allay itt afterwards as wee have had in this after the joy given for the success.

I am very glad you find [*Mrs Knight*] soe good and constant a friend, I doe suppose by the newse you write that som new intreauge is driving on I [*word illegible*] for the faire lady that cannott brooke the ayre of Sussex[880] which is butt a melancholy place, how doth her lord take itt who used to bee very chagrin on such accompts. Wee doe doe [*sic*] imagine heere the great nuptialls are over privately butt I beelieve not soe; I doe nott find by yours many servants named for soe great a princess to attend her butt I doe suppose there will bee noe want of company. I am hartily sorry

---

[879] Windham's father-in-law Sir Joseph Ashe (1617–1686) lived at Twickenham.

[880] 'Lord Sussex is parting with his lady and going to travel; he would have carried her into the country, but that life she liked not, so would not go.' (HMC 6: 7th R.I., pp 467–8); Anne (1661–1722), countess of Sussex, was the daughter of the King and the duchess of Cleveland.

I can divert you with noe newse from hence for heere wee all are in a calme, I doe nott soe much as knowe how my kind neighbors doe of the other side of Aylesham nor what they project but the newse of the sealinge of the patent, iff itt prooves to bee soe, will bee nutts[881] there.

I told my Lord Bishop the other day the story of Mr Haylett[882] and hee resented itt very handsomly and has commanded Dr Hyliard to give him notice and putt him in mind that he may enquire whether Haylett reades all the common prayer or weares the surplice & the hood, which he never doth, soe that I shall att least make him doe what he should doe, for having don what he should nott have don.[883]

My deare I have noe more to say butt that your children presents their dutys and I heare Burton[884] is an exelent schoole master and keeps Thom to itt as I desire hee should.

I have heere inclosed the <coppie> *letter * of Sir William Doyly's [f.4] to mee which is very full & satisfactory, these are butt ordinary kindnesses to friends therefore doe nott press to much on the point of jealousy.

Pray tell mee how *14* steeres his course and what hopes *60* gives him, I doubt if that coms on itt will nott bee well for [*you nor me*]. Has [*Lady Shrewsbury*] any thing to doe in matters of concerne or with [*the King*]?

Butt I trouble you too much with my impertinency and therefore will now release you till the next post, pray present my duty to your mother, and dispose my service as you see occasion presents itself, God Almighty have thee in his protection and bless thee with thy hart's desire and send us once together againe is the prayers of my dear hart

*Signed*: thyne for ever, Yarmouth
*Postscript*: Pray keep Sir William Doyly's letter safe by you, you see what he owes to my kindness.
*NRO: BL/Y/2/36*

## Robert, Viscount Yarmouth to Rebecca, Viscountess Yarmouth

**1677, November 5**. My dearest deare, I received thy deare letter by which I was glad to find manner of prog[r]ess in our affaire of soe long dependance for I was affraid of a totall dash to all our hopes. I find by yours you were nott well when you writt which is the greatest affliction to mee in the world to suspect, by the next I hope I shall find you in a better temper; upon what score this champion my Lord Privy Seale fights our battles soe bravely I doe nott knowe, butt I find hee has gained by meritt great applause in his steady promotion of itt and there's noe better man to drive on a business then himself. I long to heare the King has signed the warrant which I will allowe two or three counsell dayes for and as many more for the warrant of the moiety though I doe suppose Mr Brunskell's industry looses noe time, pray God send us good newse for my feares & jealousies will remaine till the broad seale

---

[881] i.e. a source of pleasure; he is presumably referring to the Bedingfelds.
[882] William Haylett, rector of Hevingham and Stratton Strawless
[883] 'We have left undone those things which we ought to have done; And we have done those things which we ought not to have done' (*The Book of Common Prayer*).
[884] John Burton, schoolmaster at Norwich (Blomefield, *History of Norfolk*, 4, pt II, chapter 41)

is passed which I hope may bee this month; I have written to my friends this week and have troubled your pacquett with severall letters which I desire you to seale and lett them bee delivered if you licke them. I suppose Mr Henshaw is now att this time of the yeare in towne and I have written him somthing will please him. You spoke a bold word of our keeping our Christmas heere together, O that itt might bee, if itt bee God's good pleasure. In your last letter had nott one word of the intended visitt from [*daughter Paston*] to [*the King*] therefore I doe suppose there was noe such matter performed. This night as I had notice yesterday from Sir Henry Bedingfeld coms my cousin Coke hither, and young Sir Henry with him, he stayes heere tomor-rowe and returnes [*f.2*] to Godwicke on Wedensday, and on Thursday has a feast of roe venison att his parke att Elmham where many of his friends meet him as Sir Henry Bedingfeld himself for one, itt is a kind of collection for the benefitt of the keeper; he dines at Beckhall as hee coms hether, and I doe suppose intends to bee shortly att London. I received my too paire of stokings by the coach which by reason of the bad wayes came nott in till Sunday, the cotton stockings are very fitt I have them now on and the thred ones are of the same size, too paire more of the cotton ones will bee as much as I shall need this winter. I am glad you have putt the papers into my Lord Treasurer's hands butt Ramsey must mind him of them; if the sub-scriber can bee fixed in Suffolke and there's none will hinder a man of that office itt will bee such a bob to the subscription as never was given them.[885]

I have sent Sir George Wakeman a <swan> swan pye, if you think fitt by your next Ile send [*Lady Shannon*] a very good one. I keep the rest of the good thinges in hopes yett [*sic*] you will com & eat them heere.

Pray pardon my blotting, itt is the quality of my inke I now write with, I have noe more now to say butt that

*Signed*: I am thyne for ever, Yarmouth
*Endorsed*: My Lord Privy Seal   88, Mr [?]Frouds sifer   Z, my Lord Chancellor   W, Mr Bedingfeild the Pr[i]est[886]   D
*Addressed*: Yourself
*NRO: BL/Y/2/37*

## Robert, Viscount Yarmouth to Rebecca, Viscountess Yarmouth

**1677, November 7**. My dearest deare, thyne I received wherein you chide mee for beeing melancholy and doubtfull upon the delays of this matter butt since you will have mee otherwise I will thinke of itt noe more, since you have such confident hopes of itt[*s*] progress; Brounskell's letter seemes to impute this delay to the want of a counsell day and the Prince's marriage. You speake of sending Robin out of towne on Tuesday morning soe that I expect him heere to morrowe, if the first warrant were signed Sunday or Monday, otherwise I doe suppose you'l stay him a day or two, you talke of dropping one after another better, pray God graunt you may. On Monday after dinner

---

[885] Lord Yarmouth wanted one of the subscribers to the expenses of the sheriff of Norfolk to be named sheriff for Suffolk; to give a bob to = to make a fool of.

[886] Presumably Thomas Bedingfield, Jesuit confessor to the duke of York; these additional ciphers also appear on the back of the key, p.386.

came my cousin Coke hether with young Sir Henry Bedingfeld, Dick Godfrey,[887] and one Captaine Tubbing[888] with him, and stayed till this morning after breakfast which was about eleven of the clock and then departed, and truly they plied the cup att that rate that I who onely satt by could nott chuse butt pittie a young man soe given to itt, that I doubt itt's an hard task for him to live one day without an excess in that way. He has gotten the new way of despising marriage, more especially a mann's owne wife, butt payed mee this visitt with much respect and though he were sent for to London resolved nott to goe till he had beene here. He is gon this day to Godwick and on Thursday has a venison feast att Elmham, and on Wedensday sevenight setts out for London, and meanes to bee there on Saterday sevenight att night. By a note of the shreeves putt into the bill for Suffolke I find Gascoigne Weld stands second and I hope my Lord Treasurer will fix him for I looke upon that as a matter of greater concerne then Peirson beeing sheriff of Norfolk.[889] Ramsey has Peirson's agreement with Verdan[890] to take him of[f] of all charges, and I have made Mr Doughty this day send Verdan up Peirson's letter to my cousin Coke to shew his willingness to <see> accept the thing which Verdan I beleeve will bring to you, for the shreeves are nott pricked[891] as he writes till Friday next, butt for Godsake if itt bee [f.2] possible keep Gascoigne Weld on for Suffolke, itt will make all that party tremble & give my Lord Treasurer & mee a formidable reputation heere. I can doe noe more then represent these things, Pierson's name is nott amongs[t] the three for Norfolke which is the best way for my lord that resolves to putt him downe just when the King p[ric]ks; I suppose Windham cannott chuse be fond of beeing shreeve though he justifyes the subscription therefore I presume he rather doth itt to amase Sir Nevile Catyline. I sent over to see his children the other day, and I heare the family of the Ashes com downe with him to winter heere, all formall civilityes and neighborly kindnesses Ile preserve with him as hee doth with mee, butt noe confidence in the least measure.

I am very glad [*Peregrine Bertie*] has hopes to drive on his affaire by [*Lady Danby*] butt I suppose will be long before the conclusion. I troubled you with a great many letters last post butt having leysure enough I thought fitt to write them and I hope you approove them.

Your children heere presents their dutys to you, and are well, Thom I heare studys well att Norwich, there's nothing on the face of the earth I long more for then to see you, which God graunt mee newse of. My duty to your mother, all heere present their services to you, and I am till death

*Signed:* yours with all the passion in the world, Yarmouth
*Postscript:* Present my service to Mr Brounskell, thanke him for his letter till the next post
*Addressed:* These present to the right honorable the Lady Viscountess Yarmouth over against the Golden Ball in Suffolke Street, London [*franked: Yarmouth*]
*British Library: Add. MSS 28621, ff 30–31*

[887]  Richard Godfrey, customs official at King's Lynn

[888]  Presumably Captain W. Tubbing of Sir Jacob Astley's regiment (HMC, *Lothian*, p.125)

[889]  Gascoigne Weld was one of the signatories to the subscription for the Norfolk sheriff's expenses (HMC, *Lothian*, p.124), which would of course be no help to him if he were appointed sheriff of Suffolk. The new sheriff for Norfolk was Thomas Peirson or Pierson of Wisbeach.

[890]  Samuel Verdon, attorney, later clerk of the peace, a strong supporter of the court party

[891]  The sovereign pricked with a bodkin the name of the new sheriff from a list of candidates.

## William Paston to Robert, Viscount Yarmouth

**1677, November 24**. My lord, I am very much rejoyced to understand your businesse is now at an end,[892] & I doe give your lordshipe much joy of it, it will be a very
considerable one, more then you are or can be aware of: my mother has been most
sedulous in it & deserves very much your kindnesse; never did poore *woman* labour
more for her family's good. Mr Brunskill & Major Doughty was this night at my
mother's where after a long debate, it was agreed that in case there should be any
dispute in the setling of articles your company here would be very requisite; but my
mother was very tender of giving your lordshipe such a trouble as knowing how
inconvenient it would be to you. Therefore she will endeavour all means possible to
have matters dispatch[ed] without you. I saw my Lord Treasurer tother day at
Whitehall who inquired very kindly after your lordshipe & commanded me *when*
I wrote to you to present his service. My Lord Pembroke I heare this night has killed
a man.[893] The Prince of Orange is at Cantarbury today expecting stille a fair galle
for Holland & will not come to town. This is all at present from

*Signed:* your lordship's most dutyfull son, Will Paston
*Postscript:* My wife presents her humble duty to your lordshipe, Charles & Charlotte
are very well. My service to my sister & brother Robert & my brother Jasper & to
Mr Gough
*NRO: BL/Y/2/38*

## John Gough to Rebecca, Viscountess Yarmouth

**1677, December 10, Oxnead**. Right honourable, I cannot but begin this letter
with congratulating your honour in the late successful issue you have <luckily>
*happily* met with of your vigorous and painfull endeavours; an issue which I hope
will, and heartily wish it may, recompence your honour's past and present cares with
a plentifull harvest of comforts to yourself & family. Beleive mee madam there is none
in the world can wish better nor in his capacity will do more in furtherance of this
family's honour and prosperity then my self, and therefore as I am alwayes bound to
pray for its further advance so your honour will think I must have my share of joy in
its present hopefull prosperity. I received your honour's desire both from my lord and
Mr Robert in reference to Mr Jasper's receiving the holy communion this Christmas,
which request I do most readily comply with, and humbly thank your honour for
making it. I assure you madam I own my self bound both by the duty of my place
and the particular respects I have for him to serve him as much as I can in so good
a design & your honour need not doubt but I shall do it. Considering the great danger
of unworthy receiving I shall not admit him but upon good grounds of hope for his
competent fitnesse, but hee beeing before hand seemingly and I hope really desirous

---

[892] Royal warrant to the attorney or solicitor general for a great seal to revoke the grant to Thomas
Aram of the office of surveyor and receiver of the fines, issues, amerciaments, recognisances and other for-
feitures set and forfeited in the courts of justice in England and Wales, and grant same to Henry, earl of
Peterborough, Robert, viscount Yarmouth, etc., 23 Nov 1677 (*CTB, 5, 1676–1679*, p.795).

[893] His victim apparently survived, but Pembroke, who was married to the sister of the King's mistress
Louise de Kerouaille, subsequently committed at least two murders.

to partake in so sacred an ordinaunce I do almost promise my self that hee will in a good degree fit & prepare himself for it. My lord, through God's goodnesse to him, continues in a pretty good condition of health. Though his lordship be not so well as might be wish't yet I hope through God's blessing hee is in a fair way towards it, and is as well as reasonably can be expected for a person that is in a kind of cours of physick. Pray God blesse the means used for his recovery that they may answere expectation. Mr Robert is this morning gone for Yarmouth attended on by Mr Wharton & Mr Doughty & two servants. The unexpected suddennesse of the parliament's *meeting* will I hope hasten my honourable colonell's journey hither, where I doubt not but hee will meet with that kindness from Norwich which hee expects. I crave my most humble service to him & his lady & leave to say that I am, right honourable,

*Signed:* your honour's in all duty & service, John Gough
*Addressed:* These to the right honourable the Lady Viscountesse Yarmouth over against the Golden Ball, Suffolk Street, London
*NRO: BL/Y/2/40*

## Thomas Townshend to Robert, Viscount Yarmouth

**1677, December 12, Norwich**. My lord, I have beene with very little ease a long tyme under an apprehension of your lordship's displeasure & censure occasioned by some officious reports brought to your lordship to ill purposes. But how unworthy soever such informations might justly have rendred mee in your lordship's opinion, yet they have mett with such goodnes aswell as greatnes of mind as could not admitt those prejudiciall impressions against an old friend & servant as in like cases are usuall & naturally consequent (as some friends to whom your lordship has pleased of late to speak favourably of mee have assured mee) upon whose creditt I am encouraged thus in all humillity to kiss your lordship's hands, to acknowledge your noble favour of such gentle constructions & to excuse the seemeing neglect of those dutys of honor & service to your lordship att Oxnead which I ought & (till such imaginary prejudices) no man has in all tymes beene more forward to pay. I dare not trouble your lordship with much apologie, onely I wish it might bee considered, whilst supposeing all true your lordship (has said you) have heard I were not obliged in modesty to withdraw, but some say the world was made for the presumptuous, if so, my success in it will cleare mee from being suspected of that number.

My lord, I know my selfe & all my concernments so much beneath your lordship's thoughts as I presume not to enter upon a perticular vindication though I have good hopes I might cleare my selfe of any *ill* thing supposed to bee writt or spoken by mee how cunningly soever insinuated, or if not, I am sure I can & will most humbly begg pardon, & thereby att least convince some men of the folly of theire attempts to seperate mee from your lordship's countenance & favour, as *amongst others something like it* has beene too successfully done in more publick matters <by promoting divisions>. But no industry of that kind can prevayle with mee to part from those honorable thoughts of your lordship's generous goodnes, person, & family, which I have ever with so much esteeme & gratitude reserved in my heart. My lord, it wilbee a great increase of obligation upon mee in all these & every respect, if your lordship will pardon this, which I begg in all sincerity in behalfe of

*Signed*: your lordship's very humble & obedient servant, Tho: Tounshend
*Addessed*: These present to the right honorable the Lord Viscount Yarmouth att Oxnead
*NRO: BL/Y/2/41*

## John Doughty to Rebecca, Viscountess Yarmouth

**1677, December 14, Oxnead**. Right honourable, yesterday was the court of admiralty kept att Cromer to inquire concerning the shipp that stranded there, & to whom itt should belong. Dr Hughes behaved himselfe with great moderation & prudence as became his place, and the jury being sworne & haveing their charge of what to inquire, Sir John Hobart told the doctor that hee claymed the shipp as tenant to the dutchy of Lancaster & had in his grant all wrecks & that the doctor had noe right to keepe courts of admiralty, & to that purpose insisted on an act of parliament for his authority, which hee mistooke in the construction. Sir John had prepared a wholle sheete for a speech, butt the *doctor* would not lett him goe on, butt sent the jury away to make their verdict, whereupon Sir John protested in open court against the wholle proceedings & tooke his leave after haveing excused himselfe to the doctor if hee had said anything misbecomeing, which was onely in defence of his right, & soe desired mee to present his service to my lord. Sir William Rant & Mr Herne who came as agent for my Lady Wyndham[894] (in whose mannor the shipp was stranded) were both present, butt said nothing att all; upon the shipp's comeing ashore, my Lady Wyndham seized her as hers in the right of her mannor, & Sir William haveing a mannor adjacent claymed alsoe, upon which there arose a great contest, butt upon consideration & the advice of freinds they agreed to devide her, finding their titles too weake for contention. My lady by consent unladed the shipp <which was>, & carried the goods to her owne house which were 4,000 deales, 400 balkes & 150 masts & then left the shipp till the court <were> should bee over. The jury (who were very honest men & such as wee informed ourselves of their inclinations) brought in a very good verdict as well as honest, that the shipp was seized floating & soe belonged to the admiralty as Dr Hughes gives your honour an account of this post, all the dispute which is like to arise, is with Sir John Hobart whose grant I have sent for a copy *of* to London this day. The shipp is seised for my lord & I have wrote to Mr Dawson to gett a customer to buy itt, the other goods must lye a yeare & a day [f.2] to see if there will come any owners who if they clayme within that tyme must have their goods againe, paying all charges, butt the shipp being perishable may bee sold by the law & the money returned if there comes the right owners & challenge her. My father hired all Sir John Hobart's liberty of the dutchy above seven yeare & never had any such thing as wreck, neyther was itt in his grant then butt Sir John has renewed his grant since & has wreck added *as hee sayes* which if hee has, itt is beleived that the grant may bee annulled, because the *King* is deceived therein & noe rent increased

894 Lady Frances Windham, widow of John Windham (d.1665) of Felbrigg. She was a daughter of the 1st earl of Anglesey.

though more in grant then formerly, which is a perfect deceipt & against the law. Sir John has in this buisines runn *between* the barke & tree (that is) Sir William Rant & my Lady Wyndham, & been privy councellor to both, & now would *betray* & cutt them both out.

Madam, itt was my lord's comands to mee to give your honour a full account of this buisines, wherein I have been very tedious butt I hope for your honour's pardon being desirous to give your *honour* all the satisfaction I could as becomes the duty of, right honourable,

Signed: your honour's most obedient & faithfull servant, Jo. Doughty
*Addressed*: These present to the right honourable My Lady Viscountesse Yarmouth
*Endorsed*: The accompt of Cromer bisness
*NRO: BL/Y/2/42*

## Dr Owen Hughes to Rebecca, Viscountess Yarmouth

**1677, December 14, Oxnead**. Madam, it was yesterday my good fortune to be a little serviceable to the King and his vice-admirall of Norfolk at a court kept at Cromer for the admiralty: where for his lordship's sake I mett with a great civility, and respect from the most rough sort of people, the sea-men, and mariners; and indeed his lordship's name has in it charm enough, even *to* compose and temper the most rude and unpolished sort of mankind: what I incountered in the concern of Sir John Hobart was indeed very cordeal, and pleasant; who before the court menaged himself like an angell of light, and did nothing or said any*thing* with any transport, or the least intimation either of passion, or prejudice: but when I had ended a little address I made to the jury, he was pleased to endeavor to illustrate himself, by telling me plainely, that he protested against the whole court, as illegally kept, and the whole proceedings thereof, assuring the jury that the ship was his, and the whole lading by virtue of a right devised to him by the King, and soe indeed by way of t*h*reatning the jury (haveing had good success by such kind of arts upon the Couvenant) to bring in their verdict agreeable to his pretences: but they were too stout and honest to beleive what he alleged, by way of begging the question, against their experience, sense and reason: and indeed *did* give in a verdict quite contrary to his great expectations; and such an one as may turn to good account both as to my lord's interest and reputation; Sir John designed to harangue the court, and bestow amongst the understanding persons there some floating flowers of rhetoric; but beeing therein disapointed, he found himselfe soe uneasy, and as it were rustled, that he could by noe means recollect himself with the appearance of an argument, and indeed the gentleman was n'er so inconsistent before. Sir John is a gentleman of much gallantry and parts – but my lord's good angell has the prerogative of his, as Augustus his genius had of Mark Antony's; who was fading, low and flatt, when ever the emperor was but mentioned in his presence: and many good angells allways soe guard and attend his lordship, that every opposition and affront may sett of[*f*] and illustrate his lordship's unblemished honor noe less than yesterday's did!

Madam! it may looke immodestly in me to give your ladyship an account of my own behaviour in the late contrast [*sic*]; I wholy leave it to the character of others there present: this only Ile presume to say: that what I said or did was with a hearty design to serve the King and his lordship, and whatever I was guilty of amiss, I shall be most ready to begg pardon for, and 'tis my great happiness that I am in such excellent and noble hands, that will give it, as soon as asked: it is my delight and comfort, my glory, and the greatest value that I can putt on my self, that I am in the service of his lordship, wherein it shall be my utmost endeavor to menage my self somewhat becomeing the mighty obligation your honor has placed upon, and which long since have rendered me, madam,

*Signed*: your ladyship's most thankfull and obedient servant, Owen Hughes
*Address*: These humbly present to the right honourable the Lady Viscountess Yarmouth
*Endorsed*: The accompt of Cromer bisness
*NRO: BL/Y/2/43*

## John Gough to Rebecca, Viscountess Yarmouth

**1677, December 14, Oxnead**. Right honourable, by my lord's particular command as well as by my own inclination I am obliged to acquaint your honour with the transactions and result of the Court of Admiralty holden at Cromer yesterday. In order whereunto I must crave *leave* to remind you of what I suppose you have heard before, that there were three persons who had put in their claims to the vessell that was there driven on shore (*viz*) Sir J Hobart, Sir William Rant and my Lady Windham, all which by what they had done before the court wee expected would make some opposition against the proceedings and the judg had therefore prepared himself for them. About ten a clock yesterday wee got to Cromer & beeing come near the town Dr Hughs ordered us that were in his company to ride before, himself coming hindmost with the admirall's mace born before him by the marshall John Woden. In this order wee rid till we came to the house where the court was to be kept where wee had not been half an hour, but two servants of Sir John's came and in his name desired to know when the court would be opened for that Sir John was desirous to be present at it. Twas answered that it would be done presently, but if Sir John would hasten it should be deferred till his coming. The servants returning with this answere to theire question, Sir John presently appeared accompanyed with Sir William Rant & Mr Hirn as representative for my lady. And this their appearance was no lesse then wee expected for wee understood before hand they were all in town & had bespoke a dinner at the other house of reception. When they were come & had taken their places proclamation was made for all persons summoned to make their appearance; but it so happening that one of the constables not appearing & by the precept the jury beeing allowed liberty untill twelve of the clock there could be no further progresse made as yet (it beeing now not past eleven) & the remaining hour was spent in various discourses not relating to the businesse. About twelve all summoned persons were ready & the jury called & sworn after which the judg gave them a large charge & instructions how they should proceed in this affair. The names of the jurors & of the constables were taken by Mr Hirne as they were called, who I presume by his practise was appointed their register. The doctor's charge beeing

ended and the jury going out, Sir John stands up & desires he might be heard a few
words, and beginning his [*f.*2] formall speech (for I saw it penned in a sheet of paper
which he had in his hand) with some complements to the judg & pretty taking
claws[895] to the jury he afterwards pretends that hee would give them some light both
as to matter of law and matter of fact about this ship enquired of, and soon after falls
a quarelling with the power & jurisdiction of the court & cites an ancient peice of a
statute to invalidate the power of the admiralls in such cases as these. The clause of
the statue he desired might be read (for wee had a statute book there) that the jury
might hear it, & accordingly it was done, and he received an answere to his argument
in two particulars, one was that it was now the thing to be enquired about whether
the vessel were in such a condition *seized* as that the admirall had no power to
meddle with her according to that clause of the statute, and secondly if the statute
were taken in the true sence of it there was a plain concession of power to the admiralty to make enquiry in their courts upon such occasions as this present was. Many
words pass't to & fro between them but at last Sir John leaving his law would come
to the fact & represent how the vessel was seized. As soon as he was entred into this
second part of his discourse the doctor took him off & told him that he went about
to forestall & instruct the jury which was a thing that he could not admit of it especially considering that all the jurors were his neighbors, many of them such as were
his or my Lady Windham's or Sir William Rant's tenaunts and on <home> whom
they might have influence & therefore he could not permit him to go on so least they
might not deal impartially in the case. When Sir John saw he could not shew his elo-
quence & flatter the jury with fine words but was thus interrupted, hee proceeds to
his claim & sayes the vessell was lagen[896] (as they call it) & therefore the right was in
the lords of the soil. To which the register quickly made answere that if shee were so
as hee said then shee must needs belong to the King by law. This beeing blown off
Sir John said that 'twas thought the vessell was a wreck & then plainly said that hee
claimed under the King in right of the Duke of Lancaster & offered to produce his
<charter> *patent*, but to this 'twas returned that it seemed strange that his Majesty
should make two grants of the same thing. But if he had any right 'twas a thing that
the common law was to determine, they had nothing to do with it in this court, but
their businesse was now to enquire [*f.*3] of matter of fact how & where the ship was
seized, & therefore they should not look upon the patent. Sir John beeing thus
defeated in all these attempts flyes to his last reserve & calls all present to witnesse
that he protested against the court and all proceedings in it. To which hee was briskly
answered that if he had a mind to protest he should have brought with him a publick
notary to enter his protestation. Here all discourses broke off, but wee did observe
that throughout the whole *businesse* Sir John whether through passion <of> or fear
or whatever cause else was in a very strange trembling, his fingers & hand quaking
when he lift it up & his tongue faultring when hee spoke; on the other side the doctor
discovered nothing of passion or heat but calmly discourst the businesse. Contrasts
beeing now ended the jury were commanded to withdraw into a room together &
witnesse swore & sent to them to informe them what they knew in the present case;

---

[895] i.e. ? clause
[896] Lagan is cargo that is lying on the sea bed, but which can be reclaimed.

and the jury ordered to bring in their verdict by four a clock. Sir John & his company now departed. The jury by three bring in their verdict, Sir William Rant & my Lady Windham's son were present when it was brought in & read publickly that the vessell after her taking was flotson in the King's stream. Thus madam, begging pardon for the tediousnesse of this letter and <faults> *imperfections* of this relation, I subscribe myself

*Signed*: your honour's most obedient servant, John Gough
*Addressed*: These to the right honourable the Lady Viscountesse Yarmouth over against the Golden Ball in Suffolk Street in London humbly present
*Endorsed*: The accompt of Cromer bisness
*NRO: BL/Y/2/44*

## John Gough to Rebecca, Viscountess Yarmouth

**1677, December 17, Norwich**. Right honourable, after my most humble duty & service I have onely to desire you to hasten Colonell Paston into the country, his presence his [*sic*] absolutely necessary that hee may tell the citty hee depends upon their kindnesse. I find by the intelligence I have that here are some engines at work to oppose or divide his interest. But he has yet much the better end of the staff if hee can hold it. Mr Briggs was on Saturday last nominated for burgesse *by the court of alderm[en]* but declines it & vows to mee that hee will not appear & if they should set up another to represent him & so to choos him hee will not part with sixpence to entertain them neither will hee abate them the allowance for maintenaunce of the burgesse. However this notwithstanding I cannot engage his zeal for the collonell but as he declare hee will not hinder the colonell so I cannot prevaile with him to use his interest for him.

*Signed*: I am your honour's faithfull servant, John Gough
*Addressed*: These to the right honourable the Viscountesse Yarmouth over against the Golden Ball in Suffolk Street in London
*NRO: BL/Y/2/45*

## John Doughty to Colonel William Paston

**1677, [December] 17, Norwich**. Honored sir, by my lord's comand, I came hither today to heare how affaires stand here & to give an answere to the inclosed queries, as to petitioning itt is a thing against all manner of reason & honour after haveing desired itt of my lord as a favour not to thinke that without a petition itt should availe which were very much to lessen my lord. Mr Corie has seen them, and as to the prejudice itt is a cleere mistake for the markett att Norwich is on Tuesday & the letteres comeing in on Monday is onely a preparation for Tuesday & to give the merchants an account what may probably bee the effects of the ensueing markett, soe that there will be a double answere to the Saturday & Monday letters yett notwithstanding as full a post on Weddensday, butt to say itt will bee advantage to the post office before experiment is past *is beyond* a modest man's assertion, & to gett *itt* now for an expedient were very much for your & as well as the King's interest. Here are tricks a playing to frustrate your buisines, butt I hope wee shall out ballance them, yett itt were *fitt* you should keepe itt as *a* kindnes under your own dispose if they doe not ingage for your, as their owne interest. Notwithstanding I begg you would please to hasten downe, in the mean <tyme> *tyme* there shall bee nothing wanting to promote your interest & especially in the endeavours of, sir,

*Signed*: your most affectionate humble & most faithfull obliged servant, Jo: Doughty
*Addressed*: These present to the honourable Colonell Paston over against the Golden Ball in Suffolk Street in London [*postmark*]
*NRO: BL/Y/2/46*

## John Doughty to Colonel William Paston

**1677, December 21, Oxnead.** Honoured sir, notwithstanding there has been very strange stratagems & tricks used by the Rayneham & Blickling caballs to give you a disappointment att Norwich, yett all things have soe happily wrought as will not onely frustrate their jugling consultations and expectations, butt bee much for your honour; my Lord Townshend sent his secretary Phillipps to Norwich this weeke to blow the coales who is as much rayled att as can bee wished & a true reward for his industry. The mayor has been very false & base aswell as one <man> of his brethren who was very little suspected, aswell as sufficiently obliged to the contrary. The coman people are in a rage against them both for itt, & there are a great many honest persons who *are* extraordinarily active and honest to your concerne, insomuchas I beleive your *interest* is driven on att that high rate, as att the day you will scarce find an opposite <att the day> worth your jealousy.

The parliament setts on the 15th of January being Tuesday, the Weddensday come sevenight following is the court day, & day of election, & itt is absolutely necessary that such care bee taken, as the writt may bee taken out that day *the setting is* or att furthest soe as to bee here on Saturday morneing to deliver *itt* to the sheriffes to give due notice. If your honour thinkes I may bee serviceable to you herein, my lord will give mee leave to goe to London about itt & come downe post with the writt, I am all forwardnes to serve *you*, & if I may bee butt usefull, please [*do*] not spare mee, my lord is extreame vigilant in your concerne & your presence here will bee very necessary & I hope you will please to speed your journey soe as to bee here on this day sevenight. I can onely assure your honour there <there> is noe industry wanting [*f*.2] to promote your concernes, which I question not will answere your expectation very much to your honour & reputation, I wish all prosperity to your undertakeings, & am sir,

*Signed*: your honour's most obliged faithfull servant, Jo: Doughty
*Addressed*: These present for the honourable Colonell Paston
*NRO: BL/Y/2/47*

# Robert, Viscount Yarmouth to Rebecca, Viscountess Yarmouth

**1677, December 21**. My dearest deare, I am sorrie att the hart to find by yours that [*Brunskell's affair*] goes on so slow, as I feare itt will bee impossible to pass by Christmas; the warrant for the moiety in [*my Lord Treasurer's*] hands sure cannott followe the paces of the other if the sollicitor & scruples new arising bee remooved. God he knowes how passionately my mind is sett to see you in the holidayes. Itt's impossible for you to thinke what artifices have beene practised to disappoint my sonn's election at Norwich, which will all proove a meanes to make itt the surer, and his party is soe fortified itt's morally impossible he should fayle for they threaten the very aldermen to pull them in pieces if they offer to impose any other upon \*them\*. Alderman Briggs has showen himself now what I ever doubted him to bee, and I have nott stuck privately to send him word that he is a jugling white livered fellow which has soe startled him that now he absolutely de[c]lines standing himself (which was our onely realle danger)[897] and itt's beleeved will com to recant his caution and yett declare before the day for my son, which will neither doe us good nor harme. Itt's of absolute necessity my son coms away and itt's wished by his friends that Friday next may bee the day of his entry into Norwich, which if it should bee that wee may have notice tomorrowe as I writt for great numbers in Norwich are prepared to meet him and to bring him in with that honor never any burgess was brought in. When he coms neare Norwich I would [*f.*2] have him mount on horsback to which purpose his owne great horse heere shall bee led and <accoutred> accoutred by Rawlins, and a sober gelding wee have heere handsomly accoutred for himself. I would have nothing stay him further then Saterday unless itt bee the hopes of comming with you the Monday or Tuesday after and then my daughter might com in with this traine which I would have avoided and she and you leave Norwich, and trust to our private conduct. The common people who are soe madd for him and have the power of election in their hands must be treated and if £150 or a brace bee spent[898] hee coms of[*f*] well, I have layd all [*?*]services for all frugality and cunning they have att Norwich all the artifices from Rainham & Blickling att which they rayle sufficiently: and all will bee to his honor, if he receives opposition, hee will carrie itt three to one butt itt's thought by most now they have shewne their teeth and can doe nothing, they will acqueess and nott disturb.

Hee is infinitely beholding to a number of friends and for all wee can sift out Sir <*word deleted*> John Pettus has beene faithfull enough to him. Gett your brother George to write a letter to Sir Will Adams who is now att London, in Essex or at Iselam my Lady Mainard's[899] howse to be heere att the election. Som body must bee left in trust to gett out the writt the first day of the parlement's sitting and bring itt downe, which perhapps must cost Doughty [*f.*3] a journey on purpose. Pray lett my

---

[897] It is clear that Briggs had ambitions to stand himself in spite of his protestations, and he was rewarded for coming into line at this point by being returned unopposed a few months later after the death of Francis Corie. He apparently had considerable support from the 'presbyterians, independents, anabaptists & others' (NRO: MS 453).

[898] Apparently both sides gave 'wine, & strong beer, & plentifull entertainments' (NRO: MS 453).

[899] Katherine, widow of Sir John Maynard (d.1665), née Rushout; she was Adams's sister-in-law, and her daughter Mary married his second son William Adams.

son take his leave of the King and of my Lord Treasurer and intimate that he is resolved on all hazzards to endeavor to serve the <Crowne> Crowne.

I hope [*my Lord Privy Seale*] whome you often mention will bee in a capacity to bee relied on since hee has promised to be [*your*] friend, you have written mee nothing a great while of [*Lady Shrewsbury*]. Your son Robert presents his duty to you, soe doth Betty, The clothes are com – they fitt the children well, Thom has his on all ready for he came home licke a ragged colt. Mr Peckover is att Norwich and spends his money for to tugg my sonn's friends & interest together, which are soe sure as hee may depend as much as on any event that is to succeed on more then thrice probable grounds.

My duty to your mother, pray lett your son gett Sir John Pettus' testimony of Alderman Briggs' encouragement to your son which although itt was don with a cold meane enough yett was binding, Colonel Harbord will doe the same from Sir Charles, and Dr Hylierd will [*word illegible*] more than any of them Mr Fisher being by, butt say nothing of my rubbing him up to [*word illegible*] to my son whose case has afflicted mee more then my disease till these two last dayes has given mee fresh assurances & such as I never had before.

I had nott time to write to him now, present my service to him & my daughter whome I passionately long to see though att the worst time of the year.

The note of the admiralty fee I have, butt the note of my affections to you noe paper is long enough to hold nor like to express how much I am yours,

*Signed*: Yarmouth
*Postscript*: [*f.*4] Upon all if you can order soe as to com out the week after Christmas first week I would have you com together and will excuse him soe longe.
*NRO: BL/Y/2/48*

## John Hildeyerd to Colonel William Paston

**1677, December 21**. Honoured sir, I went this day to take an account how your affaire in Norwich stood, and was very diligent to take the best measures I could, what storyes soever common rumor may bring up to towne lett none disturb you; by discovering one they have prevented themselves in all others *trickes* (that beeing disappoynted with a witnesse) I doe *not*, I dar[e] not, I will not flatter you in this affaire but from infallible grounds I desire you would not despaire of successe. There can be nothing that is future of greater certainty than that the commons in Norwich are resolved to chuse you for their burgesse. I was with more then ten this day, they are all zealous and leading men, therefore pray sir noe way despond but hasten your coming downe and lett your friends have timely notice, the appearance that will carry you into Norwich will fully silence your enemys, who have shewn their teeth and their faces together, but with great advantage to your interest, which shall alwayes be most cordially promoted by

*Signed*: your most humble servant, J Hildeyard
*Postscript*: My most humble service to my lady and also to your owne
*NRO: BL/Y/2/49*

# Robert, Viscount Yarmouth to Rebecca, Viscountess Yarmouth

**1677, December 28.** My deare hart, by my letters which you received on Wedensday you will find my son's comming on Friday is a surprise to us all, the country having expected him butt on Saterday att the soonest, and now none of the country gentlemen can have any notice butt those that are very neare yett what might bee don is don, hee will com in nobly. I have sent him from hence too horses very richly furnished, his silver trumpetts and the trumpetters in their liveries, and two trumpetts more, everybody is ready to goe meet him. Robin & Jasper were att Sir Henry Bedingfeld's butt I sent a messenger on purpose to them to goe this morning and meet their brother. I rejoyce att noe mann's death[900] butt I doe infinitely rejoyce in the Duke of Norfolkes comming to his soe well sutable dignity and that that great title soe worthily bestowed on that family may bee worne by one that meritts itt as much as any of his ancestors. Itt's a strange mistake that should make you apply your-self to [*my Lord Privy Seale*] for a letter of the nature you speake of, for a pore Independent's speaking a word to Peckover. Such things should bee never taken notice of, itt makes men inquisitive into what is taken up by chance and lett fall by ignorance, neither must this letter bee produced. He is fixed soe fast as nothing in humane con-jecture can hurt him and the defection of the mayor if he could have invented a strat-agem to have nayled all interests policy & knavery together could never have found out such another. I am glad still to heare that the first patent makes approaches towards the broad seale, I wish the other may doe soe, and that you may have the luck to [*f.*2] adjust itt with my Lord Treasurer without rubbs, for I long to see your face. They that writt you word my sonn's concerne att Norwich made mee ill were out of the story for I could see through that concerne, and att the worst itt was three to one of his side as now itt is forty and I beleeve they will all agree to choose him without opposition. Briggs is damnably humbled and has written a letter to Hurton to demand a charge hee'l answer and cleere himself, in every point, butt I knowe him.

I expect Sir Joseph Ashe and Windham at dinner; Sir Joseph was never here. All my people are runn after the colonel, you tell mee nott who coms with him nor any-thing neither doe I suppose you can have any accompt by this post of his reception. I doe from my hart beseech God in his good providence to putt an end to your busi-ness, for till I see you I doe nott live butt languish. I am very glad that you see any life in [*Peregrine Bertie's*] [*concern*].

I will wright to the Duke of Norfolke the next post to give him joy of his honor, pray present my duty to your mother, your daughter Bettie presents her duty to you, soe doth Thom who is a brave boy. I believe nothing in the world could have the operation on mee as to heare you were comming. I wonder what my Lord Lindsey should act capable of an impeachment; if the King suffers his lord leiftenants to bee used soe none will bee safe. I have had all my cuntry neighbors this two dayes and £20 in money & money's worth was distributed to the pore, now I expect better company. I am extreamely temperate and drinke nott a gotch[901] of small beere in a day yett I gett little ground of my disease [*f.*3] but the doctor sayth hee will cure mee.

---

[900] The 5th duke of Norfolk, who was confined as a lunatic at Padua, died on 13 December 1677 and his brother the Earl Marshal inherited the title.    [901] i.e. a big-bellied earthenware pot or jug

I have noe more to say at the present butt to tell you that I am soe presented by everie bodie with provision that I am ashamed, Mr Smyth sent mee the other day the noblest present I have seene, my Lady Smyth sent too fatt pigs, t[w]o fatt turkees, too fatt geese and six huge fatt capons.

I thanke God I find the honor & kind respect of my neighbors butt where Blickling has an influence the devell is nott licke itt. This business of my sonn's as I doe expect itt should proceed will mightily flatt their harts to see itt carried soe as they can make noe lead against him that dares soe much as appeare though all the endeavors and cunning plotts and inventions have beene used. My service to my daughter, to Charles & Charlotte, God preserve you safe & well that I may speedily see you who am

*Signed*: yours for ever, Yarmouth
*NRO: BL/Y/2/50*

## John Hildeyard to Rebecca, Viscountess Yarmouth

**1677 [December] 28, Norwich**. Madam, I am in great hast yet would not omitt this post because I thought it would be acceptable to your honor to heare Mr Paston past this evening thorough Norwich beeing mett and conducted by such a number of citizens not to name the gentry <and> *as* I say he is satisfyed in coming downe. The great shouts and acclamations that weer given at the three great places of the city seeme to be an excellent omen. I have resolved to stay heer in towne at Norwich about a week and am as diligent to serve Mr Paston as I would be to serve my self in the greatest affaires of life; wee shall *have* great opposition. The post is going and therefore I can add noe more but assurance that I am to my outermost power,

*Signed*: your honour's humble servant, J Hildeyard
*Addressed*: This present to the right honourable the Lady Viscountesse Yarmouth at the Golden Ball in Suffolk Street, London
*Endorsed*: Dr Hylands letter about my sons passing throwe Norwich on Fryday
*NRO: BL/Y/2/51*

## Thomas Clayton to Rebecca, Viscountess Yarmouth

**1677 December 28, Norwich**. Most honoured lady, this evening the colonell our most hopefull branch of your most honorable family was conveyed into our cyty with two or three hundred cytyzens & gentlemen one horsbacke which mett here two miles from the cyty & was receyved through our streets with acclamations of joy as if the King, God bless him, had come amongst us. Madam, I <nor> nor the rest of the loyall cytyzens do not question but he will cary it for the burgisse of this towne but there is a p[h]anatick crew that will opose all things that's just & good: but blessed be God we out number them. Madam I make bould to give you this slender accont assureing your honour that I am whylst breath last,

*Signed*: your honour's most faithefull servant, Tho. Clayton
*Addressed*: These for the honourable lady Rebecca Viscountess Great Yarmouth in Suffolk Street, present, in London
*NRO: BL/Y/2/52*

## Robert, Viscount Yarmouth to Rebecca, Viscountess Yarmouth

**1677, December 31.** My dearest deare, on Friday your son came to Norwich about foure of the clock where he was mett on the rode with a very great number considering the small notice, and the suddainess of itt, there was about one hundred gentlemen and three hundred citizens on horsback, the bishopp's, the deane's and some other few coaches, hee had a [?]claret about the markett cross, and much respect shewn him, and as to his election though noe man can make sure of matters where the event onely warrants the title yett according to all humane prospect hee carries itt cleere. On Saterday Sir Joseph Ash and my cousin Windham came and dined heere, Sir Joseph was very good company, butt Windham looked a little blew I doe suppose to find his pretence flatted, which he would willingly have accepted if the citty had thought fitt to have made choyce of him, butt wee were all very civill one to another, the colonell was very to mee, and now I have all my children heere that are left mee,[902] and they are all very merry and recover my pore hart a little; Thom sayd this day att dinner he was the best of them all which made mee laugh. To morrowe night I expect the Norwich fidlers, and on New Yeare's Day I have invited all my better sort of neighbors and ther wifes. Young Sir Henry Bedingfeld will bee heere, your sonns were mighty kindly used att Beckhall and Robin told mee that when they came away my Lady Bedingfeld gave Jasper a guinny which she forced on him in respect he was her valentine the last yeare and she had had nothing to present him; they are allwayes forcing kindnesses upon us. I thanke God I find myself begin to gett a little ground of my scurvy, butt I am the [f.2] most regular person in the world to the doctor's prescriptions, and your company will bee the most soveraine remedye nature can apply. I pray keep your word and lett my daughter com with you, make itt a running journey and soe the less ceremony, butt I understand she longs to see this place and takes itt ill she is balked of her desires soe often.

I am glad to find [*Brunskell's affair*] goes so well, I hope time will conclude itt. May the tenn dayes you spoke of putt such an end to itt as you wish, that I may bee soe happy as to see you quickly: my duty to your mother, my service to my daughter, to deare Charles & Charlotte. I am glad yett that any life is to be found in [*Peregrine Bertie's*] [*concern*] sure a bolt or a shaft must now bee putt to itt speedily. All heere are well and present their dutys to you, your son will write himself and therefore att the present I shall say noe more, butt that with much passion I desire to see you who am my deare

*Signed:* yours till death, Yarmouth
*Postscript:* Pray send the inclosed sealed to the Duke of Norfolke and the other to Sir John Pettus nott of the Temple butt the other[903]
*British Library: Add. MSS 28621, ff 32–33*

---

[902] William, Robert, Jasper, Thomas and Elizabeth
[903] Sir John Pettus (c.1613–1685), natural philosopher and politician, later buried in the Temple church; the letter was intended for his cousin Sir John Pettus of Rackheath, deputy lieutenant of Norfolk.

# Robert, Viscount Yarmouth to Rebecca, Viscountess Yarmouth

**1677[/8], January 7**. My deare hart, by your last I find you have a cold which I am very sorrie for knowing how that disease use to stick by you, I pray have a care of yourself as I have of mine more then ever, in hopes to see you once againe, and could I butt fancy the articles and moiety could be finished before the parlament I should rest contented, butt I am soe affraid new rubbs should delay that that I am under disorder for itt. Itt doth behoove [*Mrs Knight*] & [*William Chiffinch*]904 to stir up [*the King*] to command somwhat extraordinary in the dispatch, els after the parlament you will find itt very hard to drive on, butt I trust in the providence of God who has brought itt soe farr. I received this letter from Sir John Clayton with the sad accompt of the catasthrope of that business; you speake strangely of itt in yours as if [*my Lord Privy Seal*] were now possible to act any thing without [*my Lord Treasurer*] in a thing that's wholy in [*my Lord Treasurer's*] province, itt's nott to be thought of as long as [*my Lord Treasurer*] is soe, and then you speake of leaving out of [*Peregrine Bertie*] for which there's noe reason, nor a possibility of seperating [*Sir John Clayton's*] interest; you see what [*Lady Danby's*] o[a]thes coms to, and I wonder if [*Peregrine Bertie*] knew the contents of [*Sir John Clayton's*] letter why hee should yett dreame [*my Lord Treasurer*] will doe itt, since my thinkes nothing can bee more positive then what he writes. I have sent you my answer inclosed, you must gett [*Peregrine Bertie*] & Charles Bertie to putt a push for all, and soe bid itt farewell, butt if they thinke they can fortifye themselves by adding any to their number that may effect the thing, I am for a little rather then loose all. I am glad [*Brunskell*] stands to the valew of his matter for there's the great danger, that the paines should nott bee well payd for when itt's don [*f.2*] butt itt seemes he rather increaseth then deminisheth. The first patent is nothing, when the moiety has passed the broad seale then you may call that share your owne and I hope you lay in for [*the King*] to make good his word. I spake to your son about what you writt, he will write the next post from Norwich I suppose for I thinke hee will goe thether tomorrowe and ly there all night; hee is mighty vigilant in his affaire and my opinion is after all the mighty stories that have been raised the bugbeare will bee allayed, and if nott that a part of the malicious phanatickes dare shew their teeth, we shall carrie itt three for one. Just now as I write there are severall Norwich men com in amongst whome Alderman Freeman, our party is very strong and I believe the mayor & his venerable companions and som others are sick in their stomacks for what they have don. On Thursday, Mr Doughty coms from hence in the Norwich hackney coach to bee att London on Saterday before the parlament sitts, to gett out the writt the first day and to com post away with itt, that if possible the election may be on the county day which will bee about six dayes after the parlament sitts. Tomorrowe here will bee Sir Nevile Catlyne & Bendish, soe I am full allwayes, I hope [*Brunskell's affair*] will pay all els twill go very severe: I have newse of the thinges that com by the next post you shall have an accompt of itt. My duty to your mother, dispence my service where you please, your children presents their duty and I am

*Signed*: yours for ever, Yarmouth
*NRO: BL/Y/2/53*

904 William Chiffinch (1602–1691), courtier and keeper of the King's private closet; his cipher is '*12*'; he is not listed in the key to this cipher – for the means by which he was identified *see* p.388 below.

## Robert, Viscount Yarmouth to Rebecca, Viscountess Yarmouth

**1677[/*8*], January 14**. My deare hart, your last letter surprised mee to find that a person who never coms att mee should give soe fals an accompt upon hearesay, and correct the doctor's proceedings, and alarum you with unnecessary feares; as to the purging part God knowes itt's rather much too gentle then too strong, and gives mee spiritts butts takes away none, and this is nothing butt *hiera picra*,[905] of which I am faine to take a larger dos itt is soe weake and innocent a medecine. Itt is in vaine to tell you that within these three dayes I have found that amendment which I never found greater in any distemper of my life, butt before I was still mending, butt this day is the third time I have taken the King's dropps,[906] from which I have found a most sensible releife and by the grace of God intend to take them every day in the morning excepting som dayes when I will take the *hiera picra*, and in the afternoone I take Dr Hawse his decoction; my appetite coms againe in som measure, since I tooke these dropps, the hardness of my thighes abates, and yesterday Mr Bulwer & wife dined heere, and I presume will tell you they found mee as merry as ever I was in my life. They com on Thursday next for London, and come downe againe as soone as this tearme is don which will be the [*blank*] of February, and about that time I faine would alter my will and dispose those prospects God Almighty has given of advantage to my wife & children and sure by that time somwhat will be don and somwhat will be left to hope for. There's nothing in the world can content mee more then your [*f.*2] <?> sight but for God sake, leave nott this conjuncture of time to any incertainetyes outt [*of*] the consideration of my present condition, which at the worst was nott immediately dangerous and promises now as much as I can feele or guess a disposition to health againe and for all I know my body may bee better som yeares after for the course I now runn through. My son had his freedom on Friday and Robin in the hall att Norwich[907] with a deale of civility, and on Saterday the sheriff one Alderman Vin gave him and his company a noble entertainement. This snowy day he is gon to Sir Nevile Catlyne's, wee are in as good a posture to our election as we can well wish, butt in these matters lyes and storyes will be every day putt abroad licke weedes that rise up and fall without rooteing; butt I hope Mr Doughty's returne will bee soe early att least on Saterday, as that the pennance of expectation may be of[*f*] on Munday, of which I cannott in reason doubt a good issue. What Mr Fisher writt to Alderman Briggs who is now officious as a bee, I presume was out of a good intention. My sonn's suspicion will loose him friends if he entertaines that humor which hee is too subject too. You write mee too good newse I feare to bee true, as concerning what relates to us, butt I would faine ask you one question? What prospect has [*Brunskell*] of raising the *10*[908] for [*the King*] and in what time, for upon that is the creame of the jest. I am very glad that [*William Chiffinch's*][909] match is licke to on with [*Lady Shrewsbury's*] son & especially on the tearmes you mention,

---

[905] i.e 'priestly bitters', often used to mean a purgative drug composed of aloes and canella bark.

[906] The King's drops were popularly claimed to be a volatile extract of human bone, from a recipe sold to Charles II by Dr Jonathan Goddard.

[907] Lord Yarmouth's sons were made freemen of Norwich on 11 January 1678.

[908] '10' represented some kind of gift or sweetener for the King which was to be obtained by Brunskell.

[909] 'Lord Shrewsbery is like to marry Mr. Chiffens his daughter' (HMC, *Rutland II*, p. 45).

which you are a brave artificer in and have sufficiently nott onely mine butt the admiration of others, God almighty prosper your great paines & send you to draw som effects from your toyle in ease and tranquility. I doe confess to see once an howse of mine owne where I might [f.3] breathe free in London, and order my family regularly, have a stable to my self & keep my horses att halfe the rate the rouges now have would be a pleasure to mee, butt I dare nott hope itt though itt's noe bad castle in the ayre to imagine. What fixeth mee most to itt is that you may have a retreat when I am gon ready, butt these thinges depending on the success of [*Brunskell's affair*] noe more att the present is to bee sayd of itt. Your brother George and Mr Peckover ly leiger[910] att Norwich to keep the people in right minds, and evry day wee have som new people com over to us; itt's hard to say whether there will anyone else [*sic*] will ride, butt I wish rather there would that by the difference in number wee may understand our owne interest. Our good friend Sir John Hobart is this day with his lady gon towards London, they say he has pittied Mr Paston for pretending to stand for what his interest will never carry, butt there's noe doubt he has with all his diligence imaginable corrupted as many as he could, and that Collins[911] to whom [*my Lord Privy Seal*] writt is the damdest vilest rouge in nature and nott fitt to bee suffered in the country, and the most malicious knave to our interest. For the contest att Yarmouth betweene Sir Thomas Meddowes & Huntington I am nott much for either if my power could putt in a third; Meddowes will bring fifty men for my sonn & the other will bring as many as he can butt as for Huntington's putting up or working for my Lord Ranala's[912] interest itt is a thing impracticable if hee would, som people indeed thought hee had worked for his brother Major Huntington,[913] butt itt is for his owne soe you may lett [*Lady Danby*] [*know*] or els I am greevously mistaken. Pray gett mee another bottle of the King's dropps and Ile give [*William Chiffinch*] an accompt of the good I have and shall receive from them, and I hope [*Brunskell*] will pay [*the King*] his fee in the 10.

[f.4] I want another paire of such drawers as you sent mee extreamely, Mr Doughty I feare will bee com away before a paire can be procured.

You tell me allwayes stories of [*Lady Danby*] which I dare sweare she never thinkes of and for [*my Lord Treasurer*] when his opportunity will come God knowes what other matters she pleaseth her self in talking I know nott butt [*I*] desires to bee nott in the verge of the court.

The newse you write concerning peace is welcom to mee for then I hope the parlament will nott sitt long.

Don presents his service to you & is most exelent company, your children their dutys, my sonns have both writen to you, Major Doughty, Mr Gough and all here present their service and prayers for your appearance heere; when you see Sir John Holland scatter noe words butt you may extoll the King's kindness, I have written an

---

[910]  i.e. in camp, or engaged in a siege

[911]  Dr John Collinges (c.1624–1691), presbyterian, ejected minister of St Stephen's church, Norwich, and at one time man of business to Sir John Hobart (Henning, *Commons*, II, p.552)

[912]  Richard Jones (1641–1712), earl of Ranelagh

[913]  Robert Huntingdon (d.1684), a commissioner of the excise, but formerly major in Cromwell's own regiment, *see* G.E. Aylmer, *The Crown's Servants, Government and Civil Service under Charles II, 1660–1685* (Oxford, 2002), pp 166–167.

answer to his last which I sent you up by this post to the howse dore. My humble duty to your mother and dispose my service elswhere as you please,

*Signed*: I am my dearest joy thyne till death, Yarmouth

[*on same sheet*] Madame, I could not omit this opportunity to assure your ladyship that I never saw any one so much recovered in his health as my lord has been these three or four last days, and I doe verily beleeve the King's drops have much conferred to it, so that I doe not at all doubt but he will bee able in a short time to goe up to London.

*Signed*: I am your ladyship's most humble and obedient servant, Tho: Henshawe
*NRO: BL/Y/2/54*

## Robert, Viscount Yarmouth to Rebecca, Viscountess Yarmouth

**1677[*/8*], January 21**. My deare hart, I had a fitt of the spleene in my last letter, which your last to mee cured, itt brought good newse which concernes mee the more to joy in, because you are to bee partaker in itt. I am well pleased to find [*Brunskell*] and [*his affair*] holds the valew, and that [*the King*] shews him self soe kind as to speake to the sollicitor[914] himself for the dispatch. I hope by tomorrowe's post to heare somthing of itt, and that [*my Lord Privy Seal*] has received [*the King's*] commands for the moiety which I doe hope maybee in som forwardness by the sitting of the parlament, and that I may heare that blessed newse of your comming downe, which will give mee the greatest satisfaction imaginable, to see that person who is to mee the dearest and most tender object in this world. I am much satisfied by yours to find that [*Brunskell*] knowes where to get the *10* for [*the King*] as soone as the broad seales are passed, but yett I heare nothing of the articles one with another, I hope well that [*the King*] upon *10* will performe his promise to [*Mrs Knight*] for the which you must lay the way cunningly. I am glad there is som hopes of peace in the middst of the alarumms for warr, wee now must suddainely know the issue of that expection. Your sonn's party are very strong & vigilant & the malicious opposers, the phanaticks, I hope will see the King's friends overtop them, and then they have layed themselves sufficiently open to my lash especially the mayor who defies the Duke of Norfolke att soe base a rate as itt's fittest for him to bee acquainted with all the circumstances from Sir Henry Bedingfeld's penn, who is instructed for itt by Dr Hyliard, the most vigilant and zealous man in the world in the promotion of the affaire. Dr Collings has been industrious against us and is a rouge nott fitt to be suffered in this country. I am glad you keep up so good an interest in [*my Lord Privy Seal*] and that [*f.2*] he coms to visitt you. I rejoyce much in the prosperity of the Duke of Norfolke's family and their civilitys to you which pray keep up and part nott with one of our friends that's worth the keeping. I writt particularly about my Lord of Barkshire and my lady, as allsoe about Mr Cheek and his lady who I heare lies neare you in Suffolke Street butt you say nothing of any of them. I am well pleased with the match between [*William Chiffinch*] & [*Lady Shrewsbury*], I thinke itt may bee of good consequence to [*us*]. I doe suppose if their bee no warr, att least if itt bee

---

[914] Sir Francis Winnington (1634–1700), solicitor-general

staved of[*f*] this summer, the parlament will nott sitt long, if the King getts his wine
duty renewed. Wee have traced out Sir John Hobart's affectionate proceedings in
your sonn's affaire, who has perswaded old Commonwealth Hobart[915] att Norwich
to ride against him, and sayd hee would rather ride for him himself then hee should
fayle, sure these people are backed from som above for all their support is new
framing of lyes, which every day brockes anew as the last is that your son is gon to
London and left the field; Verdon the atturney has been very active in his behalfe.
When my Lord Cheife Baron coms downe, he must have instructions from the King
by my Lord Treasurer's means to breake the subscription by the King's command
as a thing hurtfull to the governement and a combination which howsoever intended,
may proofe pernicious in the effects by fortifying a faction from whence ill consequences may arise, and have apparently don soe. You may tell Mr Fisher that I have
a week since written a letter to the howse dore to Sir John Holland in answer to his
that I sent you, butt I heare by the Knyvetts who are now heere, that hee is nott yett
gon to London butt they know nott very well. Your son is very merry heere & well
pleased, your brother George is very active in his concernes, hee is gon to Norwich
this morning and hee & Mr Henshaw I feare com for London on Thursday next in
the hackney coach. Robin presents his duty to you & sweet Betty, they are all well
God bee thanked. [*f.*3] I would bee glad to know how squars goe[916] with 4 and would
nott loose all interest there which my Lord of Barkshire can give you an accompt of.

How doth Sir George Wakeman & his wife & family, is there no [?]ghipps anywhere. I saw in your sonn's letter Mrs Lee came to see you, is shee friend or foe? I
hope [*Peregrine Bertie*] will keepe [*Lady Danby*] warme in [*that concern of
ours*] against the end of the session. I suppose by this time Mr Bulwer & Mrs Bulwer
have beene with you; mee thinkes itt's a long time betweene Saterday night and
Tuesday morning for the letters which are my greatest delight & satisfaction. Mrs
Cooper & Mr Gough and the rest presents their duty & service to you, my duty to
your mother, my son told mee hee writt to you somwhat in his letter which if itt could
com now betweene this & the election, would be as seasonable for his Majesty's
service as justice to his promise.

Mr Huby sayth that the Duke of Norfolke sweares hee will undoe the mayor of
Norwich, and truly if by letter from the King or otherwise as law shall appoint he
were turned out of his mayrolity itt would bee for the safety of the King and county
for hee is the impudentest phanatick in the world. I have now noe more to say butt
that his Majesty's dropps agrees well with mee and I mend butt I goe on licke
[*Brunskell's affair*].[917]

*Signed*: My deare I am yours for ever, Yarmouth
*Postscript*: Pray enquire and send mee word how Hobart & h[*is wife*] are att London,
Mr Doughty w[          ] Your son presents his duty till next [          ] be
given his wife to whome my son [          ][918] [*f.*4] Your son beggs this key may imme-
diately be sent his wife for his clothes and beggs your pardon to the next post.
*NRO: BL/Y/2/55*

[915] John Hobart of Norwich who had sat in parliament under the Commonwealth.
[916] How squares go = how events proceed        [917] Slowly?
[918] Side of paper torn, at least a dozen words are missing.

# Robert, Viscount Yarmouth to Rebecca, Viscountess Yarmouth

**1677[/8], February 4**. My deare hart, I have received both your packquetts of letters, butt that which was written last came first. Mr Doughty came in att night, who satisfied mee most infinitely in the assurance he gave mee of the very good posture of health you are in, which I pray God long to maintaine. I thanke God I doe find I sensibly mend and doe hope that when I gett free of this distemper I shall bee better then I have beene a good while, I am very regular, and for my sweating doe nott feare that I will run myself upon any thing that shall bee dangerous butt if I doe for experience sake make the tryall itt shall bee moderately & with caution, and as I find itt doe with mee soe proceed or lett it alone; itt is nott money cast away to have such a thing by one upon any occasion for one's self or others. [*Brunskell*] did nott *<<speake>>* to Mr Doughty speake those thinges of [*Brunskell's affair*] which you you [*sic*] seeme to hint butt spoke fairely of itt as if in all itt would proove worth £40,000 a year, and Mr Doughty and I both are in feare that the moit[*e*]y will nott pass a great while and yett he says itt was resolved to be putt on when the parlament had voted money. This will bee an hard pluck for us and soe many thinges intervenes as makes mee doubtfull of everything butt God's good time must bee waited for, pray God <the> [*the King*] may doe what [*Mrs Knight*] makes [*you*] expect and that [*Brunskell*] may gett the *10* in any time, though Doughty sayth hee hopes to doe itt this vacation, itt seemes wee are seven that are to share eequallie for all hee knowes. I hope that our former articles with Sir John Pettus will have a respect to him for his pittance besides he is a man that will bee serviceable to mee on all accompts butt I heare of noe articles and yett you told mee once you were agreed how thinges should bee in all this; I know very well you doe all you can, I doe butt only ask to informe my judgement.

The election at Yarmouth[919] will bee on Monday com sevenight, and wee must live in suspence [*f.*2] another week[920] in all which time wee must expect new historyes every day, the mayor is the strangest inveterate fellowe in the world, and has taken one Baniers who for rude words spoke against my son was sent by the court to ask his pardon which he did soe uglily as if my son had nott prevented him with a slight dismission, expecting the election would then have beene over in a day or too, hee would have run into ruder expressions then before. This mann since is wors then before, is soe dangerous a talker as is nott to bee suffered, and this man has the mayor in meere contempt taken into preferment and walkes with him everywhere as his gentleman usher; the advers party are very busy, and old Hobart the Commonwealth man is one that governes their intreauges and caballs butt our friends on the other side are resolute and watchfull, and if wee doe nott decline ourselves wee out number the others by many, soe that I thinke the feare's nott great, and I wish with all my sowle itt were com to the proofe. Sir John Hobart may tell Bernard Greenevile[921] what hee pleaseth butt hee has his hopes still to frustrate my sonn's pretence and has beene as busy himself and his steward Brewster in his absence as they can bee. The

---

[919] Sir William Doyly the elder had died at the end of 1677.      [920] i.e. until the Norwich election

[921] Bernard Grenville (1631–1701), brother of the earl of Bath and one of the grantees of the greenwax

history of the freemen coms to nothing,[922] and was grounded on a mistake to our advantage; they are nott yett resolved who to putt into the chaire against us, butt the mayor declares whosoever goes in hee will followe itt as a testimony of his zeale to phanaticisme; Puckle an independant that is now receiver for the present tax is one that stickles[923] all hee can against my sonn's election and I heare is gon up to London and makes itt his braggs hee will bee receiver againe for all that I can doe. You know what you have [*word illegible*] for Bendish who is a true loyall person and [*f.*3] if they were persons that would understand how ill people heere are *un* satisfied to see the money runn through such a notorious fellowe's fingers, sure the other matter would worke; this fellowe is brother to [*word illegible*] Puckle, doe in itt as you see cawse.

Robin by my approbation has written to Peregrine Bertie to see if hee may gett a company in the gards of this new levie, hee is one that I see watcheth all oportunities to make his fortune and discourseth the point with soe much reason as gives mee all the satisfaction in the world.

Itt was told mee that the business of the mayor was written in Mr Cobbs[924] his letter the other [*?day*] to my Lord Duke himself who was nott to take any notice butt that itt came as a private hint from [*Sir Henry Bedingfeld*] himself, & what would bee for his service to have now don if any mistakes arrives from hence they com from a good intention, butt I have nott heard from thence of any answer, but I thinke itt had better com the other way.

I have *sent* Mr Doughty to Norwich this morning to Mr Bendish to secure a fellowe[925] who I have information from one that heard him say Oliver Cromwell was a better bred man then the King and did att the same time and other[*s*] use many seditious speeches. I thought to have sent my owne warrant to have clapped him up butt was advised to proceed this way and soe to informe the secretary of state and gett him forthwith to send downe a messenger from the Counsell for him, for if hee bee left to an indictment att the sessions hee will com of[*f*] with a small scratch; people heere are soe bold in talking against the governement that if I have nott som instructions to suppress them they will bee as ready for actions as words. Till the next post I can give you noe [*f.*4] perticular accompt of what is don in the matter butt if you have opportunity you may prepare Secretary Williamson to have a messenger ready for these thinges are noe longer to bee borne. My duty to your mother, your sonns present you with theirs and are gon this day to dinner to Mr Windham's, I pray God send us a speedy & joyfull meeting butt I commend you to make all sure before you com as passionately as I desire to see you; I doe expect by tomorrowe's post to heare that money is voted and I hope when they have dispatched that affaire they will rise in som short time, if a peace should now appeare itt would be strange or if a warr should bee fenced of[*f*] any longer. Whatever my Lady Baker[926] bee yett pray have a care in discourses of my Lady Hobart & Trevor nott to say more then what you allowe they should heare againe. Bettie presents her duty to you and all your

---

[922] The mayor's court had admitted over 300 freemen to vote against Paston (Evans, *Seventeenth-Century Norwich*, p.257).                                                    [923] i.e. takes an active part

[924] A nephew of Sir Henry Bedingfeld the elder whose sister married William Cobb of Sandringham
[925] John Adcock, see below p.321.

[926] Lady Anne Baker, sister of the earl of Anglesey, lord privy seal; she was a nonconformist (HMC, 11th R. VII, p.15), as were Lady Hobart and Lady Trevor.

servants their wishes for your comming hither. For my lodging pray leave itt to my owne ease & convenience which I find much best in the place I am in which is soe farr from cold that itt is the very warmest part of the howse.

Sir John Rowse and his lady are now at Mr Ayde's and are to dine heere tomorrowe; I must begg your pardon for thus tiring you out, and am whilst I live,

*Signed*: yours most passionately, Yarmouth
*NRO: BL/Y/2/56*

## Robert, Viscount Yarmouth to Rebecca, Viscountess Yarmouth

**1677[/8], February 6**. My dearest deare, thy deare letters are the onely joy I have in thy absence to comfort myself with, may thy deare company compleat my happiness in God's good time, butt I cannott advise thee to com before the broad seale bee fixed to the moi[e]ty, which I hope [*the King*] will nott make delay in because of the parlament's sitting and I hope the party may prevaile soe with [*my Lord Treasurer & Lady Danby*] and [*the Duke of York*] if need bee as to gett itt dispatched out of hand. Itt will bee a great comfort to mee to heare any thing of itts progress, as itt is to heare that [*Mrs Knight*] is confident [*the King*] will doe all thinges in a genteel manner, butt how wee shall make itt goe beyound [*my Lord Treasurer*] is a scruple I knowe nott how to remoove. I had a letter from Mr Brounskell and am pleased they are soe forward in taking a place for the office, which I hope will suddainely fetch [*the King*] 10, butt for the artickling and settlement I see there's nothing don; I suppose your private conference with [*Brunskell*] makes you soe confident that the thing will admitt of those latitudes you speake of. Heere is inclosed too letters to the Duke of Norfolke, one from my self, another from my son which I by his desire penned for him, according to the stile of that family and indeed to the great obligations I have to him. What Mr Cheek discoursed with you is nothing butt talke and hee has a way to represent thinges somtimes in a little envious way though he wishes the concerne never soe well, and itt is the way of the world soe much that now I doe nott wonder somtimes to find itt in my best friends. I am sure earlier nor humbler applications could nott [f.2] have been made and all has beene don on their part that can bee butt God knowes the interest is butt small. I am glad the day approcheth, and I have all the reason imaginable to beleeve wee shall carrie itt. On Monday my son & Robin went to my couzin Windham's to dinner, where they mett my Lady Townshend, who was mighty complesant and swallowed both your health & mine, & begun my daughter Paston's health her self, Mrs Windham extreame kind and my Lady Townshend asked Robin when you would bee in the country; Sir Joseph Ash and my lady & all were mighty kind to them and Sir Joseph waited on them out to the coach in a great shower of raine and sayd hee would com hither before hee coms for London. This day your sonns are gon to Sir William Adams to dinner, wee pass our time pleasantly enough, and honest Bob (who is a most pritty gentleman) fetcheth guinneys out of every body's pocketts, and is a great favorite of the weomen, the two brothers are very kind and my son makes Robin ly with him, they present their dutys to you. My infirmity keepes mee within dores butt I thank God I find my hardness of my flesh remoove from one place to another, and I hope I shall this spring gett rid of itt; my cousin has beene in the same condition with mee and itt's pleasant to he[ar] his accompt soe sutable to what I find, I have a good hart, and am pleasant enough somtimes though the nature of my disease loves quiett & solitude: on Tuesday next is the election att Yarmouth which will bee soundly tugged for, both partys beeing confident of their owne strength.

[f.3] I have yett nott taken any of Rafaell's dropps that were sent mee last. I wonder if [*William Chiffinch*] ever told or shewed [*the King*] my letter, pray ask [*Mrs Knight*] to whom my service make insert a line of comfort. I have nott yett read Dr Goodall's[927] letter butt pray thanke him and tell him I shall write to him speedily. The cradle[928] is nott yett com hence Ile bee cautious before I begin to any thing that way, which my owne reason told mee would bee proper to make mee more agile & nimble, butt I shall allwayse submitt to better judgments. I have nott yett [?]tried to swallowe the clove of garlick which I know a good thing, itt is partly because I take every day the decoction & the King's dropps and find itt enough to contend with, and Mrs Cooper doubts the other is too robust for my stomach. Young Sir William Doyly takes itt every day. Would Lewis would ask him how itt doth with him for as I remember I heard him commend itt much, he is an honest man & my friend nott-withstanding that his reputation has beene sacrificed to som that doe nott understand matters soe well as myself.[929] I am glad Sir John Holland is soe complesant to you, itt's a signe that hee has heard you are a lady of success and understanding. I am glad there's more orenges comming for I eat now and then a civill[930] orenge cutt in the middle and pricked full of sugar which they say [is][931] not ill for the scurvey. My service to my daughter [P]aston & to little Charles & Charlotte; Sir John Rowse and his lady, Ayde & his,[932] Captaine Harbord & his dined [h]eere yesterday, Mis Betty is gon to day to Colonell Harbord's [to] dinner, they all present their duty to you, and I could [e]ven prate all day, for I am with all the passion imaginable [n]ow telling your picture before mee that I am

*Signed:* yours, Yarmouth
*Postscript:* [f.4] I have this day written a very kind letter to Mr Rutty; remember mee to Major Doughty who is a most kind reall friend and pray use him most kindly. You never answer concerning Sir Robert Clayton, I feare there's som [?]ghip but I cannott imagine why. Pray peruse & seale and send the Duke of Norfolke's letters.
*British Library: Add. MSS 28621, ff 34–35*

## Robert, Viscount Yarmouth to Rebecca, Viscountess Yarmouth

**1677[/8], February 8**. My deare hart, thyne I received which withe the Kinges answer made us all very merrie, to see that his Majesty will be King of England. Sir Henry Bedingfeld dined heere, and of all friends I never knew such that are soe

---

[927] Dr Charles Goodall (c.1642–1712), physician

[928] The cradle was some kind of exercise machine – Lord Yarmouth later writes of 'pulleying'.

[929] Doyly was one of the tellers of the exchequer and was guilty of misappropriation of funds although he was not prosecuted (Stephen B. Baxter, *The Development of the Treasury, 1660–1702* (Cambridge, Mass., 1957), pp 151–156).

[930] i.e. Seville                    [931] A small strip is missing from the left side of this page.

[932] Ayde's wife Elizabeth was a Knyvett and so a cousin of Sir John Rous and of Yarmouth himself.

tenderly sollicitous for our good and soe joyfull when any thing happens to our advant\*a\*ge; hee told mee what hee writt which was calculated onely from himself and made knowne to bee without the least of my privity, itt's his own nephew and one that has most privately the Duke's ear in all matters of secresy, and hee sayth he chose him because many times the Duke lays by letters som time without reading or considering them, and this hee knew would bee strongly impressed on him; butt itt was don out of friendship to us, as severall markes given us every day can sufficiently proove & make good, & now I must give you som trouble, which is if you please to shew my Lord Treasurer these papers first and then to lett them bee delivered to Secretary Williamson.[933] The phanaticks are soe insolent in Norwich and talke att that rate that itt's noe longer to be suffered, and therefore yesterday I secured one Adcock, a taylor, a desperate talking seditious rouge. Mr Bendish (whose letter I send you that you may see what wee had licke to have gotten had wee proceeded by way of indictment att the sessions) was very active to take the information, and both the shreeves were ready to execute the warrant and when they had delivered him over to the jaylor, the bells [f.2] rung too howres afterwards. The fellowe is a pritty sub-stantiall man in his trade and worth the fleecing if nott the hanging, a messenger from the Councell I would have sent downe for him; there are severall others that I shall make out thinges against and if som tenn leading people were out of Norwich itt would bee the most loyall citty in England. The bishop who yesterday I sent to see how hee did assures mee as soone as the election is over [he] will shew his power and rout Colling and [I] will shew mine if I have such encouragement in this as I expect. I would have you caress Sir Joseph a little in the point and desire him that I may have such a returne as I may shew both to the citty & country. I hope my Lord Treasurer will lett Bendish bee receiver this time for that Puckle is detestable to the loyall partie, and imploys independants who have beene som of them most zealous against my sonn's election, and I hope you will keep my couzin Coke firme to his promises, & gett my cousin Peregrine Bertie or sombody to lett my Lady Danby know the true integrity of this man.

Itt's impossible for mee to conceive the industry you worke with, because [you] hints that they were to meet [the Duke of York] att [Lord Peterborough's] chamber, and [Sir Henry Bedingfeld] vowes that noe man in the nation is more relied on then [myself] by [the Duke] butt what may be produced from thence I know [not] nor how [you] has layd the scene. I am glad to find that you still say [Brunskell's affair] will hold to the first expectations. I did expect what you writt mee from my Lady [f.3] Hobart, the malice of that family is too well knowne to mee on all occasions, I wish I may have more cawse to sett their spleenes att work for they are licke the rest of their religion irreconcilable.

I had a letter from John Fisher this week with the King's answer writt out in his daughter['s] faire hand. I doe suppose our Norfolke baronetts went out on the weaker side when the Howse divided.

I suppose when you speake to mee in your letter that [you] had tried in all places against the time to effect what [I] had formerly mentioned you did try [my Lord

[933] For Lord Yarmouth's letter to Williamson, enclosing Bendish's letter, see *CSPD, 1677–1678*, pp 634–5.

*Treasurer*] who is partly engaged to doe som good, butt I beleeve that when [*Mrs Knight*] has [?]itt for [*the King*] will bee the surest time.

Our party att Norwich are very strong and vigorous now they say that Mr Hyrne of Heverland[934] will ride which they make a mightly laughter att all over Norwich, they say Sir John Hobart has lent him Chapple'ith'feild to treat his friends att, this is soe ridiculous a story as if all falls as this must doe our danger will bee small, I am glad the day approcheth, I never was soe weary of any business in my life, and shall nott embark in the licke kind againe.

All heere are your servants, your sonns presents their dutys. I am glad you have putt Major Doughty's business into hands that will mind itt.

You mention [*Peregrine Bertie*] & [*Sir John Clayton*], & then you say [*Lady Shrewsbury*] & [*William Chiffinch*] are in the intreauge, which I understand nott beleeving itt to bee rather som other affaire then that of [*Peregrine Bertie*] & [*Sir John Clayton*].

Pray, if you can, lett Major Doughty see the information and Williamson's letter before itt bee delivered [*f.4*] that hee may bring mee som accompt of itt, as well as of other matters, he lodgeth at [?]Mr Bacon's[935] in Old Southampton buildings.

If a secretary be Right Honourable putt in Rt before Honorable butt I thinke itt is nott soe.

My duty to your mother. I am glad of what you writt mee from Sir Robert Clayton.

*Signed*: I am yours, Yarmouth
*NRO: BL/Y/2/57*

## Robert Coke to Robert, Viscount Yarmouth

**1677[/8], February 11, London**. My lord, the last year my Lord Treasurer was pleased to bestow upon mee the receiver's place of Norfolk which I hope his lordship will continue to mee, if hee should not, it would *reflect* upon my credit, which makes me more zealously endeavor the continuance of his lordship's favor to me in my pretence to this place againe. There is one Mr Bendish who by severall hands hath sollicited for this place for him selfe,[936] I hope your lordship will excuse mee if I humbly claime your lordship's favor before him, having the honnor to be related to your lordship and my sufferings in the late times being equall if not beyond anything that hee can say for him selfe in that case. As for one Puckle with whom I am reproacht, I kn<o>*e*w nothing of the man but that hee gave mee good security, which I could get nowhere else, I thought my selfe in that pinch obliged to accept, but now I have more time to seek else where, and if I can find any body that will take the imployment upon those termes, I shall readyly lay him aside which I had done before had I received your lordship's commands to dismise him, and if your lordship will recomend any person to me as my debutie let him com to me and give me good securitie <I will accept> I will accept of him. I hope your lordship nor any body else

---

[934] Haveringland    [935] Probably Thomas Bacon, brother of Francis Bacon, the recorder
[936] See letter from Thomas Knyvett asking for the place for Alderman Bendish's son (British Library: Add MSS. 27447, ff 357–8).

doues thinke that I am any waies inclined to favor or imploy any mane that is or ever was disloyall or disafected to the goverment, which good opinion I beg of your lordship to continue of, my lord,

*Signed*: your lordship's most humble and most obediant servant and kinsman, Robert Coke
*NRO: BL/Y/2/58*

## Robert Bendish to Rebecca, Viscountess Yarmouth

**1677[/*8*], February 15, Norwich**. Most honoured madam, yesterday I was at Oxnead to waite uppon my good Lord Leiftenant and the collonell to consult the manadgement of our very hopfull election of our honoured freind the event of which your honour will understand by next post. I then shewed my lord a letter that I had wrote to your ladishipp in order to my business which you had soe kindly & industriously manadged with my Lord Treasurer then suposing your intrest had fixed it for mee. But I found a letter from Captain Cook[937] to my lord, by which I perceive the seane is turned and that there is a necessity of some complyance with the captaine, towards which my lord promised to engage your ladyship to compose the whole matter, a favour which makes mee blush to have such a trouble imposed upon a person of your honour who have done soe much for mee alredy. I ame in good hopes you may make an easie composition, because my Lord Lieutenant & your oune honour, together with faire promises from my Lord Treasurer & Lady Danby & Mr Cook's favour to minde them thereof may reasonably bee put in the ballance.

Myn humble request to your honour is for to fix my perseverance, as to exclude an other from puting a baffle[938] upon mee. I doe presume you need not make a finall conclusion for what I must give the captain untill you know what supply will be given his Majestie and how long to continue; I purpose to bee at London the weeke after our election to bee advised & directed by your ladishipp, or to concent to what you shall agree untou, in case you shall aprehend a necessity to fix the business before I come upp. I humbly begg your acceptance of my most humble thankes & leave to subscribe my selfe, madam,

*Signed*: your faithfull servant to command, Robt: Bendish
*Postscript*: Mr Smallwood writeing my sonn of Captaine Cook's pretensions to the receiver's place tolld him that it will bee very easie for mee to agree with the Captaine.
*Addressed*: These present to the right honourable Viscountes Yarmouth at her house in Suffolke Street
*NRO: BL/Y/2/59*

---

937 Bendish seems to be confusing Robert Coke of Holkham and Captain William Cooke of Broome.
938 i.e. discomfiture, or an affront

## John Gough to Rebecca, Viscountess Yarmouth

**1677[/*8*], February 18, Norwich**. Most honoured madam, the glory and triumphs of this day here are inexpressible, but the welcome noises and vaunting wee are here in, makes mee utterly unable to do that right to the burgesse of Norwich which I ought. I can begin onely with the narrative of this day what did precede I must leave to other relations. Last night I came to town late and early this morning waited upon the collonell. A very great number of country gentlemen (whose names would fill this paper to write them) attended him at his lodgings & accompanyed him into the market place with such shouting as daunted the adversary. Those of the country went before, the collonell by himself in the middle & the citizens followed after. When wee came to our booth after some short stay the collonell mounted the chair & then there appeared so great odds that our adversaryes seemed but a handfull in comparison. In opposition to him, that *Dutchman* Scotish merchant Alderman Cockey rode & with his hat in his hand as if he had been saying grace invited the company to his side but not a man at all stirred but instead of doing so they hiss't & clap't their hands at the contrary party in so great a degree that we could not hear their noise. At length wee came to the poll about ten of the clock, and it went on sometime with a great deal of scorn to the faction but when Cockey got into the chair again there was a bold honest fellow that face't him to the booth with a Holland cheese & a blew apron upon a pike staff which so daunted his fanatick impudence that hee durst appear no more. The villanous party was at the first coming headed by the mayor and Mr Hobart but all of them deserted their booth before twelve in the noonday. The collonell's poll held till near five afternoon [*f*.2] and he has carryed it above three to one, the number of the fanaticks are not quite <[*?*]three> *six* hundred & fifty but the collonell has above 2200, the certainty of the books I cannot learn but I speak the least on our side so that we carry it by almost 1,600 men which is with as much honour as I could wish. And really madam I must say in the behalf of this honest citty that there were never men in the world more industrious & vigilant then our friends have been, never men that would venture their <purses> *persons* & engage their purses then they, never men that have shewed & will own more loyalty to their King then they do & therefore by all means let them be encouraged and all is at the King's devotion in this county. I must crave your honour's pardon for this hasty scribble, my head is full with noise & my mind with joy & I can say no more beeing in hast to give my lord this news, but that I am, right honourable,

*Signed*: your most dutifull chaplain & obedient servant, J Gough
*Postscript*: The certain number for the collonell is <2063> 2163 and on the other part 672.
*Addressed*: These to the right honourable the Lady Viscountesse Yarmouth over against the Golden Ball in Suffolk Street, London, with speed pray
*NRO: BL/Y/2/60*

## Robert, Viscount Yarmouth to Thomas, Earl of Danby

**1677[/*8*], February 20**. My lord, I respited my giveing your lordshipp any accompt from this place till the election att Norwich was over, where through the instigations

of some great persons in the country & the maliciousnes of a phanatick mayor & some
of the same sect not fitt to sett on the bench, or beare any rule under his Majesty,
whose goverment they hate as much as they dare shew, a greater opposition was
raised in noyse then in effect. They had much a doe to procure one to ride, butt att
the last they mounted a mungrell alderman partyperpale[939] betweene an English &
a Dutchman, a strong Comonwealths man, who after hee had suffered much by the
emblem of an Holland cheese, which some of the multitude carryed before him on
a pike with a blew apron to shew his profession, hee came to the polle & polled six
hundred voyces, and wee twoe thousand one hundred & sixty odd, & might have
polled twoe or three hundred more, who were were ready att the booth dore, which
made mee infinitely satisfyed to find the loyall party soe numerous & unanimous, &
the other party soe weake & inconsiderable; and now my lord I have an opportunity
to make this great citty the interest in the world to his Majesties service, if I may have
the liberty to purge this bench of the goates, & keepe the sheepe, and to assist the
bishopp in removeing a most seditious infuser of ill principles, a conventickling
doctor[940] who stands already excommunicated, butt has staved & fenced by appeales
& other querkes of the law. I doe most humbly beseeche your lordshipp that the
judges that come this circuit may have orders from his Majesty to declare against the
subscription, which for what end soever designed, I find itt produceth dangerous
effects & keepes upp a combination & confederacy of good & badd men mingled. My
lord, I humbly beseech your lordshipp to represent these things to his Majestie, that
I may speedily knowe how to act effectually, and to make the duty I owe to the
Crowne more significant in this place. I must tell your lordshipp the sneakeing of
these people upon this blowe, was nott suitable to their impudence & confident assurance to have laye[d] my reputation low by their victory, which they promised themselves to the last. I am infinitely pleased to heare that the King's businesse goes on
soe hopefully above, whether I send upp one to receive your lordshipp's commands
how hee may the best improve himselfe in the circumstances of his duty to his
Majesties concernes, and as soone as my health will permitt mee, I will come myselfe,
butt my lord I have been strugling betwixt life & death of a long growing scorbutick
distemper & I feare itt will bee long of removeing, itt has reduced mee to great
weaknes, butt I thanke God my heart & my head are not yett touched, my appetite
I cannot yett recover, nor my motion, which the gout had crippled before, & this has
added to that weaknes, yett I hope shortly to waite on your lordshipp. In the meane
tyme I humbly acknowledge your lordshipp's favours to mee & my wife with all
thankes imaginable & doe begg your lordship will owne mee as, my lord,

*Signed*: your lordship's most obliged kinsman & humble servant, Yarmouth
*Postscript*: I humbly kisse my Lady Danby's hands
*Endorsed*: Copy of my letter to my Lord Treasurer.[941]
*Copy in John Doughty's hand but signed by Lord Yarmouth*
*NRO: BL/Y/2/61*

---

[939] A heraldic term meaning divided into two opposite parts.    [940] Dr John Collinges
[941] For Danby's reply to this letter *see* British Library: Add. MSS 36540, f.27.

# Robert, Viscount Yarmouth to Rebecca, Viscountess Yarmouth

**1677/8, March 15**. My deare hart & sowle, such is the hast of the freemen of Norwich our friends to bee att their new election that I was forced the last night to send you a pacquett of letters; Shreeve Vin[e] of Norwich was heere and undertooke to conveigh them by the flying coach this morning to bee with you on Saterday night. By the perusall of the letters to Mr Secretary[942] you will see one is to bee showne the King, the other with the inclosed concernes the business of Bowers in which if the secretary doth nott doe somwhat to humble the insolence of that fellow I must afterwards downe right fall on him.

I am mightily pleased with the Duke's favor to Dr Hyliard[943] for which he has sent him his thankes as I advised him and the doctor will steere himself by my compass. Itt was Sir John Hobart's dooings by Hyrne to putt in a barr there which I admire my Lord Chancelor should disowne or Mr Harris doe of his owne accord butt time will discover the mistery and itt will bee noe ill card to trump for my advantage and will bee a surprise to those who thinke they have absolutely prevented itt.

Your letter tells mee of the advance of [*Brunskell's affair*] to the sollicitor butt your former spake of a warrant which was in my Lord Treasurer's hand signed by Sergeant Raymond, which my Lord Treasurer was to gett the King to signe and allsoe to signe itt himself. I hope Mr Greenvile's commands from the King will work with the sollicitor who I feare is too full of other business to make any quick dispatch without great importunity. I am glad to heare you still speake comfortably of itt and confidently as to the valew, and of [*Brunskell's*] 10 for [*the King*] but I know nott when, and of [*Mrs Knight*] beeing in the same mind as what [*the King*] has sayd. You tell mee young Mr Eliott was to see you and delivered up the note, itt's good to have such a thing nott ly out against a man upon record though I understand nott how itt could have affected mee for a [?]bargaine [?]paper[944] formed in the mann's lifetime.

[*f.2*] Old Frank Dornay died yesterday morning, Howse has offered to resigne up all his interest to mee which is nott worth the medling with. There wants half a crowne of £5 for his mony and he has given away more then what hee has to satisfy if the will stands I am to have an accompt of all proceedings and he is to be buried this day or tomorrowe; he was a very child before he died and lived as long as nature could sustaine him, wee cannott compute his yeares att less then ninety. I hope Sir Robert Clayton will bee soe kind as to free mee of the develish trouble of Suckling which you must endeavor.

Pray lett Thom Reeve know where the man lives in Chancery Lane that sells the fine ground glasses for spectacles, itt is a mathematician's shop on the left hand gooing out of Fleet Street, they are about three shillings sixpence the paire, and lett him chuse mee too paire that have noe sands in them for fifty yeares of age and gett a black case to them, these I have are full of specks.

---

[942] Lord Yarmouth to Williamson, 15 Mar 1678 (*CSPD, 1678*, p.45).

[943] This may relate to Hildeyard's becoming a justice of the peace. His arrogance in this office gave widespread offence and in 1682 Humphrey Prideaux described him as the greatest disturber of the public peace in the county (Edward Maunde Thompson (ed.), *Letters of Humphrey Prideaux*, p.124).

[944] This is the last line on the page and the bottoms of these words are missing.

The Quaker att Arundell Howse gate sells som for twelvepence a paire that are very good butt nott soe finely ground as the others, he may fitt mee with both for I would very faine light of [sic] very good ones. Lewis Miko may lett the pheasants eggs alone, I have this morning taken Dr Goodall's dropps, I am better butt nott cured, my swelling & hardness shifts from place to place which is a signe itt will goe away, I eat good store of broths, little flesh meat, my appetite is nott com to itt butt am very harty God bee thanked and shall bee much revived to see you. I am glad that att last the[re] is any hopes that [*Peregrine Bertie*] & [*Sir John Clayton*] will signe articles.

My service to my son & daughter, to deare Charles & Charlotte, pray give my Lord Treasurer this inclosed, I am quite tired with writing & [sic] well as you with reading butt never in expressing how much I am

*Signed:* yours for ever, Yarmouth
*British Library: Add. MSS 28621, f. 37*

## Robert, Viscount Yarmouth to Rebecca, Viscountess Yarmouth

**1677/8, March 22**. My deare hart, yours I received. The men att Norwich goe on and have chosen diverse new aldermen butt the mayor refuseth to sweare them soe I beleeve at the last itt will com to bee determined att the counsell table or som other court of judicature, and if the King doth command these new chosen men to bee sworne itt will make the best alteration for his advantage that ever was on such an occasion in any citty. The conviction of these aldermen is that in the booke of record appointed to register their names of the subscriptions they were nott found as others were that had don itt,[945] butt I am quite weary of these matters onely I shall bee ready beeing engaged in this to assist my friends in making good their elections according to law. Here is just now com in Captaine Pettus who brings mee the newse of your health. All the cautions you gave mee in your letter I had before hand performed with [*Sir Henry Bedingfeld*] who promised to write to the Duke of Norfolke himself and thinkes there can bee noe greater advantage then the turning out these men. My closthes are com hom very fitt and very much to my purpose. I tha[n]ke you for your care and kindness in all [f.2] thinges butt am sorrie thee delayes you meet should discourage you, I cannott forsee how [*you*] will bee able to carrie through [*the King's*] intention by [*Mrs Knight*] when [*Brunskell*] has provided 10 without [*my Lord Treasurer's*] privity which I feare will confound all the project, butt I know you are a great contriver, I hope wee shall heare Mr Solliciter has given his report to the warrant by to morrowe. Robin is with you before this time, my duty to your mother. Dr Hawse was with mee the last night & this morning hee approoves enough of my bathing with water milke & herbes when the weather is warmer. My

---

[945] Many of the dissenting aldermen had failed to subscribe their declarations against the Covenant as required by the Corporation Act; this was hastily rectified so that they could stand in the forthcoming annual elections, but was ruled to have come too late. The mayor refused to swear in the new aldermen and was summoned before the Council which ordered new elections to be held. (Evans, *Seventeenth-Century Norwich*, pp 258–9, Miller, 'Containing Division in Restoration Norwich', p.1045).

duty to your mother. I am weary with writing and therefore till Monday's post begg your pardon,

*Signed*: who am yours for ever, Yarmouth
*Postscript*: My service to my son & daughter Paston, to Charles & Charlotte
*NRO: BL/Y/2/62*

## Robert, Viscount Yarmouth to Rebecca, Viscountess Yarmouth

**1678, March 25.** My dearest hart, by your last I received a paper which you say the Duke of Norfolke and Mr Bendish drew up which contained as much as the world can say. The mayor and aldermen are very brisk and I doe suppose the brisker because they see I have yett nothing from London, the honest party have proceeded as far as they can butt the mayor's refusing to sweare them putts andnd[946] to their business; if these elections which are now made bee confirmed, his Majesty doth himself the greatest right imaginable, if nott as itt's none of my fault Ile endeavor to make itt as little my trouble as I can for I now perceive that every mann's business that I cannott compose as I would if I must lay itt to hart will suddainely breake mine and in my troublesom office, where various applications of diverse concernes are made, I must learne to doe as other men in more troublesom places doe lett things in their mind runn indifferently. A man as occasion requires labor[s] more or less in any matter butt to runn himself into quarrells with familys (though they doe not carry themselves soe well as might be expected) is noe prudence nor policy and in your last letter I presume you would nott have mee runn the course you mention, to draw an old howse on my head which had better stand rotten then directly tumble, and there's noe moderation in the distinction between cooleness and proclaiming open defiance; and pray doe you observe the same methods, winke att thinges you cannot help. To morrowe Mr Cory & Mr Bendish will bee heere and fully informe mee of all the transactions att Norwich since I writt last soe you shall know further. Jasper has a mighty mind for the sea and to goe a volunteer is as good a way for the hopes of future preferment as any is and will bee noe very great charge att first; I heare Sir Thomas Allin goes and hee weare a good man to goe withall, itt may bee inquired [*f.*2] what recommendations would but sute the occasion best for in those tearmes I looke ont as an easy matter, and itt's all can be expected the first time of seeing the sea. You still cheere mee up with hopes, now you say [*the King*] calls on the sollicitor himself and on Friday you tell me my Lady Peeterborowe[947] & yourself were promised the warrant & then I hope Sunday the King and my Lord Treasurer may signe itt and Brounskill's expedition runn itt through by Easter day. I shall by the next post write a letter to my Lord of Peeterborowe as you directed mee, by that time hee may bee com to towne. Upon consultation this day with Mr Cory & Mr Bendish they desire if there bee noe order allready make upon the last paper, thatt itt may bee made according to this inclosed by Mr Doughty.

Pray by the very next post write a letter to Mr Hurton who is impatient for the

---

[946] *recte* an end

[947] Penelope, countess of Peterborough. Her husband was one of the greenwax grantees, as was her nephew Lord Ibracken.

passing his accompt, give him som consolation that you are comming downe else hee'l com up now our Lady Day is past and hee is a moross animal.

My duty to your mother, I know nott how enough to acknowledge her inclinations for my satisfaction. I doe confess I doe long for your ba[*u*]bles[948] and mine if they could be compassed or som of them att the present.

Pray see if [*Peregrine Bertie*] & [*Sir John Clayton's*] business bee quite rayled[949] of what [*the King*] said to [*Mrs Knight*] I know nott how it can ever pass if [*my Lord Treasurer*] & [*Lady Danby*] opposeth and cannot conceive any stratagem for [*you*] to moove by.

My service to my son & daughter & to Charles & Charlotte, pray God send you hither for I love you as my owne sowle,

*Signed*: Yarmouth
*Postscript*: Remember mee to Robin
*NRO: BL/Y/2/63*

## Robert, Viscount Yarmouth to Rebecca, Viscountess Yarmouth

**1678, March 29**. My deare hart, both thyne by the post as allsoe that by Thom Reeve came the same night to my hands; by the first I find your extreame diligence in prosecuting the Norwich affaire, which when itt's over any way shall teach mee to bee quiett by all arguments butt that of necessity. I doubt nothing will bee effected the first counsell butt for that the Norwich men are pritty well satisfied that itt's a time of great business, which admitts nott of every consideration, and they can stay if they bee nourished with any hope att the last. By your last letters by Thom Reeve who sent mee them comming home late last night, and promised to be heere this morning, butt I have nott yett seene him, I find your apprehensions which may have somthing in them butt sure itt's too remote to lay any such little stratagemms when they knowe by whose meanes I came in, and how the game playes quite contrary heere, butt itt's prudent to have an eye and to prevent what one can, to which purpose after the post letters to morrowe I doe intend to send over to [*Sir Henry Bedingfeld*] to com hither on Monday or Tuesday next and to consult all thinges with him you desire. I am sure hee'l contribute all his power in anything; the Duke of Norfolke has given you the greatest testimony he can in writing that letter himself which you carried my Lord Treasurer as from mee, I have written to him the inclosed which you may shew Sir Henry Bedingfield [*the younger*] if you please and lett him deliver itt or send itt your self. I have sent to Mr Huby to ascertaine the time of his entry[950] and shall make what friends I can to meet him. Ile send my owne coach and servants, butt I feare shall nott be able to goe my self for I am very weak and nott well able to endure a coach soe long a way, butt perhapps he may rather chuse to com in privately. I shall observe the motion with the best industry and advice I can practise or give myself.

[*f.2*] As to [*Brunskell's*] business I thinke wee are little beholding to Mr Sollicitor

---

[948] For a list of Lady Yarmouth's jewels in 1679 see NRO: NRS 4013.
[949] ? arranged          [950] i.e. the duke's entry into Norwich

for his favor in itt, for now you say there's never a Counsell day till after Easter, butt [*William Chiffinch*] doth use somtimes to have papers putt into his hands by the Secretarys for his Majesty to signe att other times, for surely [*my Lord Treasurer*] will nott gett [*the King*] to doe itt *himself*, you say [*Lady Danby*] is for the dispatch, for the concerne they have in itt, butt alas that's butt little to the concernes they have allwaies on foot. I have ruminated on what you tell mee and shall discourse the matter at large with [*Sir Henry Bedingfeld*] who may either give som guess att the strength or debility of their interest though if any thing els turne up trump [*I*] sees nothing butt wors prospects from the persons you name, butt from [*the Duke of York*] hee will endeavor to fix all he can. I doe againe apply myself to [*you*] for a contrivance in [*Brunskell's*] 10 to fix what [*the King*] has promised [*Mrs Knight*] without [*my Lord Treasurer's*] opposition; now the parlament is adjourned is the time to spurr on [*Brunskell's affair*] otherwise for all I knowe itt may hang betweene wind and water till wee starve. I pray keep faire with [*my Lord Treasurer & Lady Danby*] and allsoe with their relations, for I cannott beleeve what you tell mee of yett though I knowe what you say as to the meritts of the cawse to bee true.

As to what you write concerning Mr Secretary I am amased you saw my too letters; both or one mentioned Adcock the other had as much submission *to* the hint you gave mee and as effectuall an argument in the suddaine stop they putt to their proceedings beyound my expectation, butt a man must swallowe all thinges from these great ministers. Pray endeavor by my Lady Catharine Obrien[951] to make him my friend and to tell mee what faults I must mend, gett allsoe your son to goe see him who if he bee nott humored may doe us twenty sorts of disadvantages, therefore till wee are past our pikes lett's have nor harbor any peekes[952] though on never soe just scores. Old Hobart's wife att Norwich who was on my sonn's side in the election against her husband and daughter[953] has taken a message I sent her by Dr Blinkhorne[954] so kindly that she resolves to wayte upon you, she sayth itt hath revived her, she told Dr Blinkhorne that a debate [*f.3*] arising amongst themselves hearing you were to com downe before Easter whether they should com and meet you, itt was resolved they should, nott withstanding their relation to the Hobart family.

Pray in your next satisfy mee upon a loose conjecture when you think this patent for our moiety may pass the broad seale, and when [*Brunskell*] sayes after that the 10 will bee ready, tell mee allsoe if [*Peregrine Bertie*] be quite throwne of [*f*] after all promises, I beleeve that somwhat els is promised him and there's an end.

My duty to your mother, my blessing to my son, my service to my daughter & the little ones. Remember mee to Robin, as soone as I find [*Lord Peterborough*] is returned Ile write to him nott before. Your children presents their dutys, Thom growes a great boy, their clothes are bad, pray remember to spiritt up Hurton, my sickness has picked my pockett of all my money and hee is a most moros cur as ever was endured with any patience butt when you com enter reformation. Robin

---

[951] Lady Catherine O'Brien, Lady Ibracken, sister and heir of the duke of Richmond. Her husband died later in 1678 and she married Sir Joseph Williamson in February 1679.

[952] i.e. piques                              [953] Barbara, wife of Herbert Astley, dean of Norwich.

[954] Presumably Dr Simon Blenkarne, *see* Clive Wilkins-Jones (ed.), *Norwich City Library, 1608–1737* (NRS, LXXII, (2008), p.91n)

Tomlinson is licke to proove a servant good for all thinges. I wish you would send mee a suit of clothes to give him of cloth, he has been very usefull to mee in my sickness and has and doth sitt up many a night.

I am glad to heare you say [*Brunskell's affair*] is great, pray tell mee when [*Brunskell*] sayth [*we*] are licke to have any effects of itt.

*Signed*: I have now noe more to say butt that I am yours whilst I am Yarmouth
*Postscript*: I have nott heard from my son Paston a good while.
*NRO: BL/Y/2/64*

## Sir Joseph Williamson to Robert, Viscount Yarmouth

**1678, April 6, Whitehall.** My lord, upon receipt of your lordshipp's of the 1st Aprill together with the enclosed, giveing an account of the mayor of Norwich's disobedience to his Majesty's commands, I tooke leave to acquaint his Majesty in Councell with it the first councell day which was yesterday; upon which *an* order was immediately issued commanding the mayor to appeare at the board, to answer this contempt. The day is sett Friday next, but in case your lordshipp cannot upon so short notice be here yourselfe (if you desire so to be) or that the persons necessary to attend the cause on your lordshipp's or the citty's part, cannot be here early enough, it will no doubt bee put off till the following councell day.

I must beg your lordshipp's excuse that I did not with the last order & letter that was sent you in this businesse, acknowledge likewise the favour of your lordshipp's letter, which had at first brought the notice of this abuse to us. I doe it now, and pray you to believe I am with esteeme, & truth, my lord,

*Signed*: your lordship's most humble & faithful servant, J. Williamson
*NRO: BL/Y/2/65*

## Robert, Viscount Yarmouth to Rebecca, Viscountess Yarmouth

**1678, April 8.** My dearest hart & sowle, itt was betwixt tenn & eleven of the clock before Robin & his major came in hether, his major is one of the civilest modestest persons I have mett withall, and an able souldier, I hope I shall gett them as many men as they desire. On Saterday night the Duke of Norfolk came into Norwich, where my secretary was ready with a complement from mee; on Sunday morning early I sent my coach for his grace who came to mee to dinner, with my Lord Thomas his son, Mr Corie & Major Waldgrave, Sir Henry Bedingfeld mett him heere att dinner, the Duke was mighty kind and eat his meat which was very good hartily. Hee was vexed the mayor was gon for London and sayd that hee had nott com soe soone butt onely to doe his worke for him, butt now resolves to bee himself att London on Wednesday night, gooing early from Norwich to morrowe morning butt hopes to heare the mayor is clapt by the heeles, soe well he has prepared his way, who som report heere is gon up to bee knighted! About five in the afternoone the Duke returned and an hower after when wee were att chappell coms in a messenger from the Counsell, who by missing his way betwixt Norwich and this place had allsoe

missed the Duke in his returne, butt after I had perused his orders, read the secretaryes letter and your letter, and refreshed the messenger with wine & victuals, I sent
him back to the Duke with my secretary in his company by whome I send the Orders
of Counsell & allsoe your letter to mee which expressed soe much obligation to the
Duke for him to peruse and to direct the messenger how to proceed in the mayor's
absence and to consult who is fitt to appeare att the Counsell, if any bee necessary
besides his grace himself, butt to this matter I doe expect a returne by the comming
back of Mr Doughty who I expect time <eno*u* gh> enough to send you the
accompt by this post. Yesterday Mr Corie[955] the other burgess for Norwich beeing
now dead, wee debated the matter for another parlament man and wee concluded
that if Briggs will stand there's noe [f.2] opposition to be made, and that's Sir Nevile
Catlyne's owne sence butt if he declines itt, seriously and in his discourse heere he
did (which wee shall knowe this day), I hope the other will carrie itt without dispute,
whome I resolve to assist butt nott so publicquely as to bring my name or reputation
in question, lett the matter goe how itt will; this morning Robin & his major are gon
for Norwich there to see how they can accomodate themselves. Yesterday wee had
six or seven came in heere, and I have sent to Yarmouth, and to Norwich. The major
I thinke returnes noe more hether, beeing resolved to doe what hee has to doe soe as
to com away by the Friday's coach, butt Robin I doe suppose will com and see mee
before hee goeth up. And now is the first time I can really say I find a reall amendment in my health and I impute itt to the salt of scurvygrass, and my weekely purge
which I take yesterday, I stirred more then I have done a long time and with great
ease of breathing, and the hardness & swellings in my body strangely softned and
amended, for which I hartily thanke God, and doe now see a little light of health
againe which I hope this month will much contribute to; your short letter on Saterday
night which sayd thinges were prittely well concluded gave mee to understand the
sollicitor has cutt of[f] som of our pretences, and yett you seeme to say you hope that
thinges will end well att last, butt I am growne beyound confidence in anything butt
the providence of God Almighty, which I hope will never forsake us. I am very glad
as you neglect nothing that you study wayes how to gett [Mrs Knight] to make [the
King] upon 10 make good his promises without beeing intercepted in itt by [my
Lord Treasurer] and now I stop till Doughty's returne.

Mr Doughty coms in now and brings mee my Lord Duke's letter and accompt
from Sir Henry Bedingfeld and your letter, and this inclosed from Mr Corie, butt my
Lord Duke's letter to you by the messenger will bee with you before this. Mr Doughty
is going back to Norwich, for this night they are to debate what the citty will doe in
order to the charge of those that are to appeare for them, which my Lord Duke has
promised Verdan [f.3] if he coms post to doe himself, in case they shall not agree out
this night, butt for all I know they may putt Mr Doughty on the journey. The Duke
will bee in towne on Wedensday night and I would nott have itt putt of[f] further
then Friday, you will bee informed of the conveniencyes of making Briggs parlament
man which Sir Nevile Catlyne will bee satisfied with, the Duke knowes all Mr Briggs'
circumstances, and all is endeavored to prevent trouble and charge to noe purpose.

Pray God send mee good newse of my owne concernes and that I may bee in

[955] Francis Corie (c.1596–1678), MP and recorder for Norwich

peace from these troublesom affaires which are as bad as any other difficultyes. My duty to your mother, my blessing to my son & daughter & theirs, your children present their dutys to you and all heere their service &

*Signed*: I am yours for ever, Yarmouth
*NRO: BL/Y/2/66*

## Abstract of the order of the Privy Council to the Lord Lieutenant of Norfolk

**1678, April 9**. *950 seamen are to be pressed and conveyed to Harwich*
*In the hand of John Gough*
*NRO: BL/Y/2/67*

## Robert, Viscount Yarmouth to Rebecca, Viscountess Yarmouth

**1678, April 14**. My deare hart & sowle, I am glad to find by yours that you have received my letters, and that Mr Doughty gott soe soone to towne, and that my Lord Duke of Norfolk has taken soe much paynes to rout the mayor who I feere will after all his unbended stiffness submitt to sweare the new elected aldermen and soe save himself, butt I resolve after this push to withdraw my self from all thinges that doe nott immediately concerne my place for att this rate a man shall never have a quiett hower, if either hee will give care to little thinges or subject himself to the humors and concernes of others' occasions, soe much as to lett the issues have any impression uppon him; I faine would study my owne ease and quiett butt the way to that is soe uneasy difficult and uncertaine, that without God Almighty's blessing itt's never to bee looked for; I know nott whether to rejoyce in the newse of your last letter, I am soe full of jealousies and feares soe many disappointments in the persuance of this matter have occurred that after all morall certainety still our feathers are plucked if our winges bee nott plucked, therefore in all the faire prospects you give mee my expectations cannot soare high, till I see somwhat of the reallity of itts effects. [*Brunskell*] you say is brisk and confident of his former assertions, and that hee shall gett *10* for [*the King*] butt wh[*illegible*] [*Mrs Knight*] is confident [*the King*] will perform [*me/my*] *3000*, that's well butt how shall the contrivance of man carrie it through unless [*my Lord Treasurer*] bee a friend & who dare trust to that. Your ingenuity I admire and your affections are such as noe difficultyes nor dispaires can tire out, and in this criticall time I desire [*you*] to essay the uttermost point, for any after game though such a friend as [*Brunskell*] is nott to bee layd aside in the hopes of future thinges yett the gaining them is soe difficult, and the time in compassing them soe long as they are scarce worth the endeavor. I am very glad att the newse you tell mee the person is gon who in your last you hinted had soe great an influence on [*the Duke of York*] for lett itt bee [*the Duke*] or [*the King*] they may lurke a whole in a corner and doe mischeif soe butt when a cloud obscures the sun itt never hurts with burning; however I should bee glad to heare som more of that story since itt's dubious to you which way the matter goes. Yesterday the sessions were adjourned hither, where the clerk of the [f.2] peace[956] came, and the [?]sier[957] of the court, and fowre justices of the peace *viz* Mr Negus, Major Doughty, my cousin Ayde and Dr Hyliard who in my little parlor see mee take the oathes and subscribe according to law and my vouchers Mr Peckover and Rawlins swore they see mee receive the communion soe that's over for my commission in the first patent as collector, I would the second were as well passed, and that I may nott sweare for nothing. I hope [*my Lord Treasurer*] will have noe trickes in the warrant to retrench us any further, nor protract us any longer, and what's left out of our patent cast behind you as lost. Wee wonder heere att the suddaine newse of the choyse of a new speaker,[958] sure the old one[959] is nott sick of soe good a place to bee made a lord; your newse of the French and Dutch concluding a peace without us is of a strange nature, and I cannott imagine what will bee the event of itt, whether itt will hasten the warr or oblidge us to doe as they doe, a little time will determine. To morrowe by the grace of God I intend to goe to Beckhall, where I shall discourse [*Sir Henry Bedingfeld*] upon severall thinges; young Sir Henry Bedingfeld will bee there as Ned told mee who came the other day to dine heere and is a most pritty gentleman; hee is going over into France to travel with Ann[960] Paston's sonn who stayes for him att Paris. Yesterday being Saterday (for I write now Sunday beeing to goe abroad in the morning) whilst wee were att prayers in the morning happened a most unfortunate accident heere to my man John Allen who licke an unscilfull gunner, having charged a crazy gun with twice as much powder as needed, and instead of killing a jackdaw I feare has killed himself. Mr Flynte was heere who saw the wound when newly made, and sayes itt hath beaten out one of his eyes, butt the brechpins of the gun beeing iron shott into his head and wee feare has broken the bone in the forehead above the nose and the bone on the other side the eye and stuck their soe fast, that Rawlins with all his strenth could nott pull itt out, butt tugged soe hard that att last the boy giving a good tugg himself, pulled itt out and threw itt on the ground, his face a miserable spectacle, and when som whites of eggs and flax had been applied, wee lapped him up warme and in Major Doughty's chariott with one with him, I sent him immediately away to Norwich to one Dr Blinkhorne who is an exelent surgeon as well as a learned man & a doctor and my very good friend & your sonn's, who yesterday could make noe prognosticks of him till the tumor bee a little downe & the wounds may bee inspected; tis great pitty, hee was a good servant and a good cooke and I have great miss of him beeing under more then ordinary tendance myself; hee is lodged att the Maides Head in Norwich att the present hard by the doctor's howse, who will use all meenes that's possible to him.

[f.3] I writt a civill letter to Sir John Holland upon his comming downe and had as civill a returne, Sir Robert Kemp sent his servant to see how I did, butt of my Blickling neighbors I heare neither newse nor noyse: they goe for London to morrowe and I suppose meet Sir John Holland and Sir Robert Kemp by the way, as they came downe soe they goe up.

---

[956] Isaac Moutham                    [957] ? usher                    [958] Sir Robert Sawyer (c.1633–1692)

[959] Sir Edward Seymour: an arrogant and contentious supporter of the court party; he feigned illness to avoid a formal censure but he briefly resumed the speakership.

[960] Agnes Paston (d.1676) of Appleton; she is described as Ann or Agnes in the Paston genealogy (CUL: MS Add. 6968).

As to my owne health I am strangely mended, my swellings and hardness allmost all gon, my bellie mightily fallen away and yett my strength and spiritts much better, butt my appetite still loathes all sorts of meates both flesh & fish, butt pottage & pudding and buttered lofe and cawdle[961] I eat butt nott very much itt cleares som of the humor remaines yett behind which I hope will goe away too. I have noe thirst upon mee and never drunke soe little beere in my life and what I doe is high of the scurvy grass, thus have I given you a true accompt of my present state, which som good newse from you & the hopes of seeing [*you*] would noe question make much better.

My Lord Townshend has had a severe fitt of the gount [*sic*] & stone both together or rather the strangurie,[962] butt as I heare was left somwhat better on Friday by Sir Thomas Browne who was sent for to him. All heere presents their dutys and service to you, your children are all well, Robin will bee at London I presume as soone as this, and his business was very well don heere. My duty to your mother, my blessing to my son & my service to my daughter, which allsoe I pray dispose where you thinke itt necessary, butt keep to your self the very hart and sowle of

*Signed*: Yarmouth
*Postscript*: [*Mrs Knight*] is the best friend in the world if thinges coms to pass, butt I feare [*Brunskell's*] 10 and the manner of bringing the other to effect. I had a letter for the lords commissioners of the poll money[963] which I send up to Mr Doughty to informe himself of the nature of my answer which I must have on Saterday night beeing to returne them my answer before Mayday. I thinke my farme that I have now is noe [?]office butt what I pay rent for by way of bargaines and my debts are more then my personall estate
*NRO: BL/Y/2/68*

## Abstract of instructions from the Commissioners of the Admiralty to the Lord Vice Admiral of Norfolk,

**16 April 1678,** *for the pressing of seamen*
*In John Gough's hand*
*NRO: BL/Y/2/70*

## Copy commission of Robert Bendish as conductor of pressed seamen, with instructions

**22 April 1678**
*NRO: BL/Y/2/71*

## Warrant by Robert, Viscount Yarmouth

**1678:** *appointment of pressmaster who is to deliver pressed men to the conductor, Robert Bendish of Norwich.*
*Draft*
*NRO: BL/Y/2/69*

---

[961] A warm drink of thin gruel mixed with wine or ale, sugared and spiced, and given to sick people.
[962] A disease of the urinary organs
[963] A tax raised in preparation for a military campaign against the French.

## Copy commission of Matthew Peckover as agent at the port of Harwich

**22 April 1678,** *with instructions as to the receiving of pressed seamen, 24 April 1678*
*NRO: BL/Y/2/73*

## Robert, Viscount Yarmouth to the Lords of the Council and the Commissioners of the Admiralty

**1678**. *Copies of letters with details of his actions and the estimated cost of employing pressmasters, conductor, and agent, amounting to £5 5s per diem.*
*NRO: BL/Y/2/74*

## Robert Bendish to Rebecca, Viscountess Yarmouth

**1678, May 1**. Madam, yours of the 27th April past came to myne hand upon Fryday the 30th. When wee had gonn through three of the four greate wards[964] of the citty & had laid aside six of the very worst of our 24 (which hapned to the greate contente of the loyall party): but the fourth ward beyond the water (being the sinke of the citty for fanatiques) they elected the past mayor an alderman (& chose agayne Cockey, whom wee turned out in the fore noone) so now the bench consists of 19 persons prety well fixt for the goverment of church & state and five don baked [*sic*] ones. Your honour may beleive that wee who are faithfull subjects to his Majesty have laid out the best of our endeavours & interests to quitt our bench of backing freinds to loyaltey but wee must endure what wee can't helpe; we must alwaies acknowledg my Lord Lieutenant & your ladyshipp's have been eminently instrumentall towards the rec-tifieing our goverment thus farr, in soe much as I for my part am exceedingly ashamed it hath proved so chargeable to my lord, to reimburse that most reasonable expense shall bee myn especiall care soe soone as ever I can find such an oportunity as I may probably conjecture may prove efectuall. I beg your ladyship's acceptance of my most hearty thanks for all past & continued favours which with all respective regards tendred to our good burgess Collonell Paston concludes mee

*Signed*: your honour's obedient & humble servant to command, Robt Bendish
*Postscript*: My wife & her daughter presents their most humble service to your honour & wee all doe much joy to heare that your teadious & troublesome business gives your ladishipp soe hopefull a prospect of Norfolke sudainly

Aldermen new chosen
Mr Buckenham,[965] Mr Gardner, Mr Osborne, Mr Winn, Mr Helwis, sheriffs, Mr Parmenter, Mr Sheldrake, seven
Aldermen put oute
Mr Hawes, Mr Thacker, Mr Payne, Mr Wigett, Mr Wenman, Wrench & Todd, seven in all [966]

---

[964] The wards were Conesford, Mancroft, Wymer, and Over-the-Water; see also John Gough to Lady Yarmouth, 29 April, 1 May 1678 (British Library: Add. MSS 27447, ff 387–390).
[965] Hugh Bokenham withdrew and was not sworn (Miller, 'Containing Division in Restoration Norwich', p.1027).
[966] For an analysis of the aldermanic elections *see* Evans, *Seventeenth-Century Norwich*, pp 262–265.

[*f*.2] Since the writeing of my letter wee have elected Mr Jehosafat Da[*v*]y newelect mayor though in the morneing it was hotly reported that the commons wold choose Cockey, but it was soe contrived that if he had been sent upp to our court with any junior alderman (as the custome is alwaise to send upp two & the senior is alwaise taken), yet in this case wee were all resolved to have chosen any man who had been sent upp with him, rayther then have had a mayor who had soe eminently opposed the collonell's election for a parliament man, & who was rejected for an alderman in the fornoone & chosen againe in the afternoone & if he had been chosen newelect next day, would have been soe high an affront to our lord lieutenant as wee abhoured it. J Davey is an honest right man for church & state & was a fast freind in the collonell's election. Mr Corey is soe tyred with this daies worke which concluded but at seven this evening, as he heartily begg your ladiship's pardon for not answering yours by this post. R:B

*Endorsed*: Mr Bendish letter of Norwich bisness
*Addressed*: To the right honourable Viscountess Yarmouth at her house in Suffolk Street, London post [*postmark*]
*NRO: BL/Y/2/75*

# Robert, Viscount Yarmouth to Rebecca, Viscountess Yarmouth

**1678, May 17**. My deare hart, I am very glad to find you soe well satisfied in [*Brunskell's affair*] I am sure you have reason els meerely to give mee the comfort of a whipt posset. I am allsoe very glad that you have still hopes that [*the King*] will performe his promise to [*Mrs Knight & us*], and that [*Brunskell*] will gett the 10 for [*the King*]. I doe beeleeve [*you*] doth all that may bee with the sollicitor for dispatch butt what civility hee should shew us in our patent when hee must stick to the instructions of the warrant I knowe nott. I am much concerned that a villaine who has personally affronted [*me*] in mine owne howse to that degree as nothing butt his beeing my sonn's servant made mee att that time forbeare him should now bee soe audacious (I having remitted soe much as acquainting his master with his carriage to mee) should now invent lyes and stories to create fewds and ill resentments amongst us, with the historie of the mares. As to my son Paston's fine stone-hors[967] hee never had any butt of this roage's owne contrivance, & selling one was my cousin John Bedingfeld's, as for the hors called Baxter hee is an old rude hors fitt for shew and service of a souldier, and nott for my son Paston's owne saddle, and hee had som of my owne mares, and I thinke itt impertinent in Mr Robert[968] to lay in my letters the fault upon the judgement of any man who had my approbation and the ma[s]ter of the horses leave that my mares should be covered by him; butt this I am sure of, the hors which is now a fine hors was a surfetted hors and by the care of Mr Rawlins (for the groome is a roage in graine) has recovered to bee £10 better then hee was; as for my son Paston's owne hors since this rouge is gon from hence, and my groome has the looking to him, hee is soe apparently mended as I never saw and is as quiett and gentle as a lam and soe good a conditioned hors as

---

[967] i.e. stallion    [968] i.e. 'Master Robert', his son

hee will bee fitt for him to appeare on any where and therefore these objurgations that com to mee from the vice of my owne civilityes and expence are soe hard from my owne children as I digest them uneasily. For Rawlins hee has a just recompence for leaving his old master for new ones, for I never saw noe man soe fond or observant and soe doting especially on my son Paston as hee soe observant of all his commands, as I that love my [f.2] son soe well as I doe was very well pleased to have my owne service putt after his concernes, butt men that [are] over officious out of love meet somtimes with such rebukes; butt as for the groome whose impudence to my owne person and knavrie to his master is beneath mee to write histories upon, though this unjust occasion awakens mee, I doe [here]by make itt my request to my son that hee will soe much regard the decency to his father & his owne honor as to free him self of him, for I never will write to him about that nor anything els till this bee don, for itt is a dangerous and a most wicked rouge. As for the twelve shillings which was written for to Mr Robert I have examined the matter and itt was thus: the Welchman the groome could nott well carry up too stonehorses, and soe Rawlings hired a man to carrie up Mr Robert's horse and this was that crime for telling him what hee had hired him for, and for nott paying him out of his owne purs, and next time hee will doe well to honor som body with his confidence that may act with more prudence and leave my servants to my owne governement. I could better have been content to have swallowed the relations of these matters from the messenger's returne who gave us as well as the pore silly fellow could express itt the history of our chiding, butt when itt coms to your eares I must (though covering of mares is noe discourse for you) vindicate the truth and tell you by the by, I am nott a man to brooke this usage and that you'l find when such little artifices are used by low people noebodie knowes where to lay itt. Thom Reeve I doubt is none of the hartiest to us, for though hee owes us mony which hee never intends to pay, and that his daughter was kept heere for foure yeares, for the use of all that digest an ugly whore, hee has reason to bee angry that that play must last noe longer. As to the caution you have given mee of my daughter, there's reason enough for itt, I have therefore taken those circumstances into my observation and to my view I never saw a greater amendment [in] the carriage of anybody then in your daughter's since Mrs Hunt waighted on her. As for the amours of her and her gallant, which are owned enough to make itt noe scandall, itt is a fals ly that there is any practice of them there, and greater caution is used then you imagine with her, who has soe great a spiritt as if either Gough, who uses all the respect imaginable to her, or Mrs Cooper tells her of any [f.3] visible faults shee can take them downe, and bee ready to trample them under her feet, butt shee is very good natured and of a sweet temper, good words doth any thing with her, rigor & constraint nothing att all.

Butt I must tell you of another grevance, and that this my younger children have thought itt from som that has been soe sely[969] as to putt itt into their heads that itt has beene beneath them, when I have noe stomach nor dine in the parler, to dine att the steward's table and to lett the best of my servants sitt downe att the same time with them, butt if I had made them prentices, as my father did, they must have wiped shoes att [sic] satt with the skullions, and that I shall serve your son Jasper yett, if he

969 i.e. silly, lacking in judgement

ever dares againe keep a correspondence by letters with his sister and his brother Tom wherein such stuff is write with all the intreages of the family as never was heard, and noe longer ago then yesterday he writt to his sister that att London you could nott gett bread; you may see whether when wee want itt[970] to putt itt into his and the rest of their mouthes, whether these thinges are fitt for our own children to upraid us with. I had sent you this letter butt itt's burnt, butt I shall now make itt my business to intercept som that you may see the stiles and know that what is called Norfolke's talke coms out of the traytors in our owne family. The Duke of Norfolke has sett my servant att his owne table, and I hope I have committed noe crime to boyes and girles in what I have don: these thinges are pritty to bee written to Norwich schoole for the boyes to discourse and for my servants to heare, indeed Mr Gough and Mrs Cooper have often desired me to breake of[f] this correspondence butt were nott soe free as to tell me the inconveniencys of itt which upon the occasion you gave mee to sift into the bottome of thinges I have now found out; dispatch him as soone as you can, a dungbote is to[o] good for such a rascall. Pray lett my Lady Clayton to whome my duty see this, I referr myself to her judgement if I deserve these usages; I knowe you have a coupple with you that shall never speake a word to any of your children or anybody else a word in your honor or mine, I meane those I told you of before ever you entertained them. After I have seene my daughter Paston heere, I shall surfett as few as I can with the [sic] [f.4] I have hitherto wanted my self for the pleasure of others, if this had nott beene of meere necessity and to prevent danger for the future I had nott mentioned them butt itt's high time to putt and end to these dooings which shall make mee valew you & myself the more.

Yesterday beeing a fine day I went and dined with my Lord Bishop att Norwich where I was most kindly made [much] of by my lord and lady and five of his daughters who are very pretty weomen, your health was drunke three or foure times, and I have invited them all to dine with you on your wedding day the 15th of June.

After I had parted from them I went to Alderman Bendishes and there came to mee Mr Briggs who to say the truth in his speech at his election[971] did our family in a long and particular mention as much honor and more then is ordinarily declared on such a subject, which when I thanked him for [it] hee sayd hee had don nothing butt what hee was oblidged to doe, and was sorrie hee fell short in itt; hee says hee will bee very right to the King's interest, and the next week will com over to see mee before hee goes for London.

Mrs Bendish and Mrs Craddock[972] who are your and my worthy friends and assertors of all our concernes, as is the alderman you may bee sure, sayd soe many kind thinges as this paper will nott hold. Sir Charles Harbord's recovery is very strange and I thinke of noe great consequence.

I have received from one Mr Horner, formerly my tennant, soe many presents of vast fish as I know nott to doe in requitehall. I[f] you could send mee any little toy of gloves or thing that's new to send his wife 'twould bee just; this morning I sent his present to Sir Henry Bedingfeld, to entertaine his sonn Carrill[973] & daughter withall,

---

970   i.e. bread     971   Briggs was elected MP for Norwich on 13 May 1678.
972   Elizabeth Cradock, niece of Sir Thomas Browne (NRO: ANF, 1711–12, f.2).
973   Richard Caryll of Harting, son-in-law of Sir Henry Bedingfeld the elder

£10 would nott have bought them att London. In hopes I shall live to see you, I live and you are that I desire most to live for

*Signed*: who am yours, Yarmouth

*Postscript*: The story of [*Lady Danby*] is <strage> strange. I am glad [*Lady Shrewsbury*] [&] [*Mrs Knight*] has undertaken to doe that for [*you*]. I find by [*Peregrine Bertie's*] letter hee is discontented and by Sir John Clayton's, that hee would proceed if the other had a mind to itt butt sombody has cooled him, and certainely the thing must bee great.

*NRO: BL/Y/2/76*

## Robert, Viscount Yarmouth to Rebecca, Viscountess Yarmouth

**1678, May 20**. My deare hart, by your last I find you would faine perswade mee the clawse is nott soe bad as I thinke itt, butt I thinke onely what a clawse of revocation is which is to render itt att the power of his Majesty to call in when hee pleases,[974] which is don on every pretence, butt still you give mee som hopes that [*the King*] if he has *10* will take away the clawse but how *10* should bee procured in any time is past my belieife. You say [*Brunskell*] will write to mee, I writt to him, butt have had noe answer. I am cheered up to heare you say that you will pull hard for itt to keep your wedding day heere; God Almighty graunt itt, for I hope you doe nott thinke that any thing butt the hopes and support of our family which wee have depended on from this thing, could have made mee brooke soe long an absence, which I doe with as much regrett as you express for yours, which greeves mee, besides the addition of my owne. You speake of sending little Charles downe, I shall bee very glad to see him butt betweene the 29th of May & the 15th of June is butt a small time. I am very glad att what you saye of [*Lady Danby*] itt will bee well if that impetuous storme which soe unjustly has tossed us can bee layd. I cannot think the parlament will sett long enough to make the lawes which this prorogation has cutt of[f], I am glad [*the King*] lookes about him for on my word there's an ill spiritt in som men who I hope will bee defeated in all their projects. Yesterday wee received the blessed sacrament heere and I with my pore weak leggs made a shift to walke to the church and without the help of any one butt my stick, I cannot yett gett my appetite to meat, butt I am much in the ayre in my little charriott and this fine weather I give my fine coachorses grass by turnes keeping two allwaies in the stable to carrie mee abroad; they are the best conditioned creatures in the world, and will com to my charriott's side and putt their heads into my lap and eat oates or bread out of my hand, and I feed them abroad myself every day, which is a great recreation to mee and a pleasure to mee. By all I can foresee there will bee a peace, and Sir John Holland writes mee word that itt will bee endeavored att their meeting, for to recall the prohibition of French commodityes, butt what humor the Howse will meet in or what measures they will take, is very uncertain as all the productions of great assemblys are.

[*f.*2] I can perceive Sir John is much mollified in the way of his stile as doth nott write soe angrily of thinges, as somtimes hee was wont to doe. You tell mee that [*Mrs*

---

[974] *CTB, 5 1676–1679*, p.993; the king revoked it in the following year, *CTB, 6, 1679–1680*, pp 54–6, 121, 147, 620, 660.

*Knight*] was to carrie [*you*] to [*the King*] in a day or two soe perhapps tomorrowes post may informe [*me*] of somwhat concerning [*his*] resolve, butt I know [*you*] is soe prudent as to have good warrant and assurance from [*Brunskell*] of the 10 before [*the King*] be further promised itt; and [*I*] thought itt a good argument to bee used to [*the King*] that all clawses should bee taken of[*f*] that hinders the progress of 10 for [*the King*], which cannott well bee don where the foundation and ground of itts rise is limmited and bound up with restrictions. Ile sweare [*Mrs Knight*] is a good friend, if any of these thinges com to pass that way & I am very glad [*William Chiffinch*] continews soe too, and [*the Duchess of Portsmouth*] and [*Lady Shrewsbury*], who can bee in noe great concerne now or have much interest I feare. I heare nott one word of the Harbords, neither did their wifes know any thing on Saterday night, soe I have nott received little Charles his present of the bezoar stones[975] you sent mee, from him; pray desire him to write mee som coppies of directions how to take them, with his owne hand. Remember mee to my son Paston and my daughter, and I hope I shall have that favor from him as hee will nott countenance a villaine that in my owne yard had the impudence to carrie himself most insolently to mee in language and demeanor, and is such a roage as hee disgraced his master heere, went up of his owne accord, without soe much as having the civility to speake to mee or let mee know of itt, and owes every creature heere money soe that hee has left weeping eyes for his departure, I suppose his character will com to him from other hands. I have taken the paines to open a letter from Jasper to Betty, which was well sealed and made up by Lewis which I heere send you inclosed, there is noe great harme in itt, onely one straine to the old tune, which is nott fitt for him to observe much less to send downe hether. Pray present my duty to your mother and lett her know I give her thankes for all her kindness to mee & mine; and shall bee very glad to see her heere this summer. Bid Lewis looke about & speake to Mr Bernard Greenevile to see if in the mewse or anywhere there about he can find out an old lame cart hors for a stalion, I am encouraged to breed, now knowing my defect all this while, and yett I have bred some very usefull & good ones, butt never have wintered them as they should bee. Bernard Greenevile may easily accommodate mee and an horse that is for noe service is a proper for that use as the best, Lewis may give mee some accompt of itt.

[*f*.3] From the Counsell and vice-admiralty I have noe returnes, I expect som to morrowe, for I am loth to send away the men to ly upon the King's and country's charge, before they are sure of a vessell to receive them, and halfe of them will bee sure to runn away, now what ever use there may bee of the land men a navy must be sett out to sea, and therefore meethinkes they should consider the prosecution of their owne orders.

I should bee glad to heare that there were any accomodation betweene the Duke of Norfolke and my Lord of Arundell and his younger brothers, which Thom Corie told mee hee thought would bee; I hope you pay your devoirs to her grace, which is the onely way to be great there;[976] hee is now as Sir Henry Bedingfeld tells mee

---

[975] A concretion from the stomach of an animal, generally a ruminant, thought to be an antidote to poisons but taken for other medicinal purposes.

[976] Soon after his accession to the title, the duke of Norfolk had married his mistress Jane Bickerton; as he had previously promised he would never marry her, this led to a dispute with his sons.

disparking Croxton Parke and will nott save by itt £20 a yeare, and leave himself never a parke in Norfolk. I wish you may find [*my Lord Treasurer*] & [*Lady Danby*] kind if [*I*] doth any thing out of [*Brunskell's affair*] as [*Mrs Knight*] tells [*you*] for els there will bee a rubb nott to bee passed over, pray lett [*me*] know if [*Mrs Knight*] comes at [*my Lord Treasurer & Lady Danby*]. Your daughter Betty and son Thomas who is now att home presents their dutys to you, soe doth all heere, and with all the facultyes of my body and the sincerity of my sowle

*Signed*: I am yours, Yarmouth

*Postscript*: As for [*Peregrine Bertie*] I knowe noe more can bee sayd to him, you saw his letter, if the thing should bee worth nothing in time of warr there's defalcations in the conditions and now peace is lickely to ensue, the signing of artickles were noe prejudice butt what's to bee sayd to a man that's unwilling to doe anything. [*Sir John Clayton*] writes itt's none of his fault, hee has sollicited the other and has had forty promises and nothing don.

*NRO: BL/Y/2/77*

## Robert, Viscount Yarmouth to Rebecca, Viscountess Yarmouth

**1678, June 5**. My deare hart, yesterday I went betimes in the morning to Beckhall to dine with my friends there, where I mett young Sir Henry and my Lady Anne,[977] my cousin Carrell & his lady and was most kindly made [*much*] of, in the afternoone wee entertained ourselves with discoursing in the garden, with plaing att chess, and at six of the clock I came away and gott home in very good time, butt in the morning I had ordered the post to meet mee upon Causton heath in the way, where I stayed half an howre for him, and there I read your deare letter, which brought mee the newse of the broad seale's beeing fixed to the patent, which I was very glad of, upon what conditions soever, that somthing is don to answer all your care and long patience, butt you tell mee such fine thinges as I cannott conceive how you can sett soe many wheeles on worke, though I licke well the hands you employ for I thinke that lord whose lady you were going to visitt an honest man and one that will nott betray any confidence putt in him. Your visit to ⊖ quite alters the position of affaires in your letter before which told mee that [*my Lord Treasurer & Lady Danby*] were coole butt itt seemes [*you*] finds itt otherwise, and I am glad they were kind & civill upon [*your*] comming. You speake hopefully as to the business with [*the King*] and that itt stands in a faire way butt I doe nott perceive [*Lady Shrewsbury*] has yett felt [*my Lord Treasurer's*] puls[*e*], which is the maine hinge the dore must open upon, butt [*Lady Shrewsbury, Mrs Knight & William Chiffinch*] doe bravely if they can worke itt through stitch.[978] Your mother writt mee a very kind letter, I am sorry shee has beene ill, butt she tells mee she thinkes itt impossible you should bee heere by the 15th of this month, butt this month she thinkes you may, God send the happy time that I may see your face againe never to part till for good and all, though truly for this grevous sickness I have had I thinke itt well I was in a place where I had roome to change lodging and the benefitt of much ayre, which att London I could

[977] Lady Anne Bedingfeld (d.1682), wife of Sir Henry the younger, was a daughter of the earl of Berkshire.     [978] To go through to the end or to complete something

nott have had, and then itt might have cost mee my life as itt was tenn to one itt did nott heere, butt now I thanke God I begin to grow finely well againe, and I hope when I have [f.2] recovered a little more strength I may bee the better for what's past, and my body cleered of the scurvy which has soe long infested mee with a kind of languishing. Young Sir Henry Bedingfeld told mee that my Lord of Arundell was to bee last night att [*Castle*] Rising and that he was to meet him as this day att Mr Ost's[979] att dinner, soe I have sent over Mr Doughty on purpose to make him my complement to enquire after my Lord Peterborowe, and my lady, and his owne lady.[980] The footman that came downe sayd that my son Robin was to com with him that they came post and would come noe further butt in Robin's letter yesterday I find nott a word of itt. My Lady Bedingfeld yesterday told mee a great secrett, which Sir Harrie was upon oath nott to lett mee know, nor you must take noe notice of onely in paying great civilityes to the Dutchess of Norfolk, for that's the way to oblidge the Duke who in this shewd an apparent testimony of his kindness to the family, for when itt was reported att London that I was past hopes of recovery, he went to the King and the Duke to begg that the leiftenancy might in case I died bee conferred on my son which was promised by the King.[981] This you may trust your son withall, butt if either of you att the present takes any notice of itt to him you ruine the creditt of Sir Hennry Bedingfeld, butt you may from mee make great expressions to him of somthing which my family must ever owne to him; there are nott better friends in the world nor more studiously cordiall to us then our Beckhall friends, I find the effects of itt every day. I carried yesterday with mee Mr Gough and Dr Hyliard, you tell mee in your last of Mr Fisher's writing to mee butt I had noe letter from him. Yesterday foure from Norwich came heere to invite mee to their guild on Tuesday com sevenight, which is the day the new mayor[982] takes his place & office. I heare nothing further of Charles his comming, for when I see him I am sure you cannott bee long after him. I entertained my Lady Bedingfeld with the history of him of his Majesty's birthday, and they were mightily pleased att itt, butt my Lady Anne commends him above all thinges in the world. I gasp after your letters every day and am now longing for tomorrow morning againe, for since my eyes are deprived of the happiness of seeing you, your conversation by penn is the pleasantest thing in the world to mee. Pray lett mee know how squares goe with 4 and whether you see my Lord & Lady Barkshire somtimes, and whether the match is broken of[f] betwixt the Duke of Grafton and my Lord Arlington's daughter, [f.3] wee heare heere hee is married to my Lady Northumberland's[983] daughter for certaine. I am resolved nott to have any 15th of June till you com and then to keep itt and only privately to remember itt on the day by mourning for your absence which I hope will nott now bee long, butt I doe commend you for making sure of what you can. Itt seemes

[979] James Hoste (1633–1679), of Sandringham

[980] Arundel had married the Peterboroughs' daughter, Lady Mary Mordaunt

[981] However the political situation changed in Norfolk when Lord Arundel, the future 7th duke of Norfolk, converted to Protestantism early in the following year.          [982] Jehosaphat Davy

[983] The duke of Grafton, an illegitimate son of the King, had been betrothed to Arlington's daughter Isabella since 1672, but his mother the duchess of Cleveland attempted to break the engagement so that he could marry Lady Elizabeth Percy (1667–1722), later duchess of Somerset, who was the greatest heiress in England. At the insistence of Charles II however, Grafton married Isabella in 1679.

[*Peregrine Bertie*] will now goe on with the affaire, I cannott imagine upon what bottome [*Sir John Clayton*] goes when hee endeavors to oppose a thinge his owne advantage is concerned in, or which way could he carrie itt by other hands and avoid ours; I doe beleeve hee may have a private confidence in Charles Bertie, butt his cunning is allwise methodised in soe strange a manner as itt's past my conjecture. Pray see if you have nott a small paper I left of Brounskill's which has the title of demonstration on the outside, I would gladly peruse itt if you could find itt; I had a short letter from him to informe mee the seale was passed, and that hee did still desire those thinges which were left out, as to popular actions & informations might still bee insisted upon to be gotten in: by privy seale or otherwise.

My dearest hart I have noe more to say att this present butt that Betty and all heere present you their duty & service, Hurton is upon the spurr to meet you, my service to all my friends. I hope my letters to my Lady Danby & my Lord Bathe are sent to him. Remember mee to my son Paston & my daughter, to Charles & Charlotte, and beleeve mee till death,

*Signed*: yours Yarmouth
*Postscript*: Wee very much want som leather carpetts to cover and save the turky carpets[984] from wine sauce and the fire from tobacco pipes.
*NRO: BL/Y/2/78*

## Sir Robert Kemp to Robert, Viscount Yarmouth

**1678, July 6**. My lord, tho' I have not given you the trouble of a letter a great while, yet I have made it my busines to enquire after your health from time to time, as being very much concerned for you, and the intelligence of your welfare have bin very acceptable to mee. I doe assure you, my lord, that noe man loves you better then myselfe, nor wisheth more happines to your person and family. And since I have not had the content to attend you here, I had kissed your ladyes and son's hands oftner in every sessions, but that the publike, and distance of my lodging, hath taken upp soe much of my time. Your son is of an excellent temper, and I am much pleased with his conversation and beleive him to bee a very worthy person: in one word, to give him the best commendation I can, his humor is very like his father's. Wee are finishing the money bills, which hath bin the work of this two last days, so as I can give you no newes from parliament, since Sir John Holland writt to you, who went away yesterday morning: for other intelligence, I can learn nothing certain: I hope we may have a recess by this day sevenight, so that I may leave this towne, the beginning of the weeke following. Wherever I am, noe circumstances ever did, or shal alter the value I have for you, as becomes my lord,

*Signed*: your lordship's most affectionate humble servant, Robt Kemp
*Addressed*: These to the right honorable the Lord Viscount Yarmouth att his house att Oxnead, Norfolk [*franked, with postmark*]
*NRO: BL/Y/2/79*

---

984 Turkey carpets were used to cover tables.

## John Doughty to Rebecca, Viscountess Yarmouth

**1678, July 19, Norwich**. Madam, the inclosed will give your honour a full account of this daye's proceedings about the bishopp.[985] The persons to bee bound for their good behaviour are the heads of the faction, butt noe proofe can as yett bee found against any, butt onely suspicion of the combination. My lord will write to the secretary next post, and in the meane tyme wou'd have your honour to acquaint my Lord Treasurer with the transactions & know his pleasure what *in* his lordship's judgement is further to bee done. The bishopp was concerned very much att the letter and <resents> *acknowledges* my lord's resentment & freindshipp in the matter with great satisfaction & thankfulnesse. The post stayes on purpose for these letters, soe that I am forced to bee short in this relation more then otherwise were the duty of, right honourable,

*Signed*: your honour's most obedient faithfull servant, Jo. Doughty
*Addressed*: These present to the right honorable the Lady Viscountes Yarmouth over against the Golden Ball in Suffolke Street, London [*franked and addressed by Yarmouth, postmark*]
*NRO: BL/Y/2/80*


## Thomas Corie to Robert, Viscount Yarmouth

**1678, July 22, Norwich**. Right honourable, in obedience to your lordship's comands I delivered your letter to Mr Mayor upon Saturday morne last, who sent out warrants to apprehend the six persons therein named, five whereof were brought before him that day, *vzt* Dr Collings, Annyson, Skowldinge, Balderston & Nockolls. Collings gave suertys to bee of the good behaviour, and to appeare att the next quarter sessions of the peace to bee holden for this citty and county in the penall summe of £500: the other fower prayed tyme till this day att two afternoone to give their answers, att which tyme they appeared, & Nockolls gave the same security and in the same summe, butt Annyson, Skowlding & Balderston refused to give suertyes for the good behaviour, and by a warrant under the hand & seale of the mayor were sent to the gaole, untill they should enter such security as by your lordship's (& your deputy lieutenants of this citty's) order was required. As for John Crumwell hee is gone from his house & the constables retorned their warrant that *Non est inventus*[986] soe that another warrant against him shall issue: it's believed hee is gone to a towne in Norfolk called Taisburgh within six miles of this citty, to the house of one Robert Cullier, one of the same gang. Mr Mayor summoned all the justices of the peace of this citty to appeare this afternoone, butt not a man of them did, butt Mr Bendish, by which your lordshipp may judge how they stand affected to his Majesties government both in church & state. Our worthy recorder[987] being twice sent for on Saturday last by the mayor to advise in this affaire, refused to come, nor would hee

---

[985] There were rumours of a plot against the bishop's life and a number of arrests were made.
[986] He is not found.
[987] Francis Bacon had been made recorder in the previous May, following the death of Francis Cory. Bacon's brother Thomas stood against William Paston in the Norwich election of 1679.

assist this day. Mr Mayor would have given them further tyme, & to make their applications to your lordshipp, if Mr Bendish & myselfe had not interposed, and att last
prevayled with him to goe through stitch with his buisines, and not to suffer your
lordshipp's order to bee baffled by theise turbulent fellowes. My lord, I have some
other matters to give you an account of, when I have the honour to kisse your hands.
In the interim, I pray your lordshipp to accept of the most entire & humble services
of

*Signed*: your lordship's most obedient & obliged humble servant, Tho: Corie
*Endorsed*: Copy of Mr Cory towne clerke of Norwich's letter about Collings &c [*in
John Doughty's hand*]
*NRO: BL/Y/2/81*

## Robert, Viscount Yarmouth to Rebecca, Viscountess Yarmouth

**1678, July 26**. My dearest sowle, yours I received wherein expecting to find som
accompt of [*the King*] [*Lady Shrewsbury*] [*Mrs Knight & yourself*]. You had
had a new alarum from [*the Duchess of Portsmouth*] and that you had diverted
itt by [*the Duke of York*]; I wonder what makes them bite att thinges of that incer-
tanety and distance, however I am very glad the thoughts of itt are layd aside.
Yesterday heere dined [*Sir Henry Bedingfeld*] and his lady, and one Mr Greene
and his lady, a fine woman, and I doe assure you they are the best and most stedfast
true friends in the world, I showed him the passage concerning [*the Duke of York*],
att which hee is wonderfull glad, & has promised mee this day before the post goeth
away to send mee a letter to his name sake for [*the Duke*] to see, and thereafter if
[*you*] or [*my Lord Treasurer*] shall advise mee I shall write to [*the Duke*] my self
as occasion shall require. Butt I must tell you wee were all surprised, for Mrs Hunt
having dressed up Betty in her new clothes, she appeared licke a little angell and in
the judgment of all the ladys and men as one of the greatest beautys they ever saw
and were she in your handling one weeke I am confident would bee a surprising creature. I doe assure you she is farr a finer women then she you writt to mee about, my
Lady Bedingfeld thinkes if she were att London itt would bee dangerous for her to
bee seene, if this were my sentence alone I should suspect myself butt itt's universally
allowed heere. Itt is surprising newse to mee what you write to mee about my Lady
Sophie,[988] sure itt cannott bee soe and if itt should com to a breach, that Secretary
Williamson and my Lord Treasurer will not bee soe great butt I suppose itt will nott
goe soe high. I wonder my Lord Latimer and his lady should now bee out of the way
when soe great a solemnity is approching as this great marriage.[989] As to the business
of [*the King*] [*Mrs Knight*] [*Lady Shrewsbury*] [*my Lord Treasurer*], [*I*] has
a good pretence butt whether [*my Lord Treasurer*] will nott defeat itt is the question, and [*f.2*] [*the Duke*] had putt in a generall word to [*my Lord Treasurer*],

[988] Lady Sophia Osborne, Danby's youngest daughter, had married Donough, Lord O'Brien at the
age of twelve in the previous year. Williamson was influential with O'Brien's parents and later married his
mother, Lady Catherine O'Brien.
[989] Latimer's sister Lady Bridget Osborne married the King's illegitimate son, the earl of Plymouth, on
19 September 1678.

butt I doe suppose my doome will suddainely bee pronounced, for [*the King*] going on Monday, a delay is a civill deniall. The passage which concludes your letter I wonder att that [*Lady Shannon*] and [*you*] are agreeing the affaire which will secure all, [*you*] is wise and knowes my circumstances too well to imbark in anything [*where*] the issue may nott bee of advantage to mee, and therefore I leave itt to discretion, butt [*Lady Danby*] & [*my Lord Treasurer*] will quickly appeare whether the professions made to [*you*] have any thing in them by this time [*?Mr Bedingfield*] sure is ready to stirr about, which may bee of advantage att this criticall time, for before this coms to your hands, all that is to bee don will apeare whether itt will or will nott be performed as promised. You hope to send me good newse by the next post, pray God I may heare itt tomorrowe. On Tuesday before dinner, I intend God willing to goe to Norwich if my health permitts and to goe out and meet the judges. Sir Henry Bedingfeld who is every day dooing us service has don mee a great one this weeke, hee has made Sir Roger Potts pawne his sowle to bee true to my interest and abandon the gang hee has beene engaged with, hee and his lady should have mett heere yesterday att dinner, butt hee is extreamely ill att the present of fainting fitts; hee confesseth Hobart to bee one of the falsest men alive, and I shall have all the caballs and mischeefs out, that their malice sett att work in the election, and other stories nott fitt for a letter. This comming over of his will much amase them; I have sent you his letter of excuse to Sir Henry Bedingfeld for his nott comming yesterday, though itt seemes his coachman has had a misfortune. Pray keep Pott his letter, as allsoe Thom Corie's which I heere inclose to shew you how squares goes att Norwich & may goe better if the D[*uke*] of Nor[*folk*] will butt say goe on, which I have noe reason to doubt butt that hee will, itt beeing suggested to him by those hee relys on that itt concernes him as much as myself. The little ones presents their dutys to you, Charles rides every day before Rawlinns ten or twelve miles, is mighty fond of mee and very good company, and the little one[990] picks my pocketts of all the sugar plumms.

[*f.3*] Pray present my service to my daughter and my son, pray lett them know what persons have beene and sent to see the children,[991] butt my Lady Pettus, that should give the cheif accompt, has nott yett found her coachman nor her saddle nag though she told mee should would [*sic*] mount on purpose to see them. Sir John has beene twice with mee, I have written to your mother as you desired mee, and to Sir John, both which you may peruse & seale, and having spun out my letter as farr as my thread will reach I shall need none to bind up my affections to you, which are wound on the bottome of your own diserts and my inclinations, which fix my hart and sowle to bee allwaies

*Signed*: yours, Yarmouth
*Postscript*: Remember mee kindly to Robin: thanke him for his letters.
I have this day written to the towne of Yarmouth about the remooval of the stakes; I am undon as to that business if you have lost the letter which Huntington & England then bayliffs writt to mee for my consent to place them there that fishing time.

---

[990] Charlotte, born 1676
[991] Yarmouth's grandchildren were of particular interest to the county because they were also the King's grandchildren.

I beg your pardon for breaking open my Lady Bedingfeld's letter, I never read the superscription and thought it had beene from Sir Henry to mee. The inclosed to his namesake I am confident has all the calculations for [*the Duke of York's*] view which you must address as directed. Pray send downe som Warwickshire cheeses. *NRO: BL/Y/2/82*

## Sir Thomas Higgons[992] to Robert, Viscount Yarmouth

**1678, September 18, London**. My lord, I was so unfortunate at [my] arrivall in England as not to find you either in Suffolk Street or at Parson's Green, at both which places I was to wayt upon your lordshipp. If I had then had the happiness to find you I should have given you some account (& such as I am confident would not have been displeasing to your lordshipp) of my lady your daughter at Venice, whom I left <very> well satisfyed with her condition, & very happy, were it not for the sense of your displeasure, & that of my lady her mother, the continuance of which so long I imagine may in part proceed from your not being informed how well she is. And therefore since I can not have the honor to doe it my self by reason of many businesses & the continuall expectation I am in of being commanded by his Majesty into Italy, I have engaged this gentleman Mr Berners of St Maryes[993] who is my son in law to wayt upon your lordshipp with this letter, & the inclosed, which lately came in one to my wife from Mrs Alberti, who I can assure your lordshipp is used with all respect imaginable by her husband's friends, & commands what ever she desires, having money, & cloathes, & all things suitable to a woman of quality, nor doe I know any lady here who goes better dressd than she or in finer clothes. In the [*f.*2] house where she lives (as I am told by those who know it, it not being permitted me nor the minister of any forreign prince to go into the houses of the state's secretarys) there is all the plenty that can be, & a constant good table where she is mistress. Her unckle with whom she & her husband live is a man of reputation & in a charge of the greatest trust in that government being secretary to the Consiglio de' Dieci with whom all the secrets of that state are deposited. Besides what they have in Venice, they have a house & estate in the country which they have enjoyed a long time being ancient gentlemen. So that though she have not mett with a match so good my lord as your daughter might have deserved, yet there is no reproche in it, she having marryed a gentleman, a man of parts, & one who useth her worthily. And therefore I can not doubt but your lordship if you <will> either consult your reason or the generous inclinations of your nature will think it fitt *after so long an absence* to send her your blessing & good wishes, which I promise your lordshipp I will with great joy convey to her, if you please to give me commission so to doe; & therein I am sure I shall not onely give her the greatest [*f.*3] consolation she is capable [of but] receave very particular satisfaction myself, if you please to do me the honor to employ me in this occasion. My lord,

*Signed*: your lordshipp's most humble and obedient servant, Thomas Higgons
*NRO: BL/Y/2/83*

---

992 Sir Thomas Higgons (c.1624–1691), envoy to Venice
993 Hatton Berners (d.1713) of Wiggenhall St Mary; he married Bridget Leach, step-daughter of Sir Thomas Higgons by his second wife Bridget Grenville, sister of the 1st earl of Bath, who was previously married to Simon Leach of Cadleigh, Devon (*ODNB*, Blomefield, *Norfolk*, IX, pp 176–183).

# John Fisher to Robert, Viscount Yarmouth

**1678, September 24, Westminster**. My lord, though I am this afternoon much tormented with a fit of the gripes, yet if I be able to write never so little, I must acquaint your lordship that the parliament is to be prorogued again to the 21st of October, which will be acceptable to them that resolve not to set out till next weeke, but some that are upon the road already wilbe very angry at it, as much as Mr Mallet[994] who hath at last found a way into the Tower.

I suppose the Queen is come to town & we expect the King to morrow, & to go to Newmarket next weeke.

We kill parliament men here every day, amongst the rest, Sir John Holland & Mr Crouch are said to be dead, & I could name you the men appointed to succeed them, but they are a pair of old connivers, that write & walk too after they are dead, but Sir Kingsmill Lucy of Andover is past it in earnest.

We hope by the meeting, the mutuall ratifications wilbe exchanged betwixt France & Spain, & the Flanders towns evacuated by the French, & our men in them, whose appearance there hath certainly brought on the peace, & obtayned better termes for Spain, than otherwise they could have got for themselves. What the Northern Kings will get by their holding off, we shall soon hear. The letters now from Hamburgh speak as if the Isle of Rugen is like to be lost, though Coningsmarke hath beaten off the Danes in their first attack, but the Brand[*enburgers*] coming in behind him, pres him to retire to Straelsend, where the letters say they believe they will be overpowered.

I am not able to hold up my head longer, but with the presentment of all our humble services to your lordship & my lady, am forced to break off, & shall be glad to rest.

*Signed*: My lord, your lordship's most faithfull servant, John Fisher

*Postscript*: Sir Thomas Garret will never think himself growing old (though a grandfather) but singles bucks out of the heard at Euston Parke, till he endangers himself by a fall, & gives the occasion (as I imagin) to kill his brother Holland.[995]

*Addressed*: These present to the right honourable the Lord Viscount Yarmouth Lord Lieutenant of the County of Norfolke &c att Oxnead Hall in Norfolk [*franked*, per Norwich post, *postmark*]

*NRO: BL/Y/2/84*

# Robert Paston to Robert, Viscount Yarmouth

**1678, September 26, London**. My lord, being commanded down Munday was sennight to Stamford to view those quarters I took the opportunity of seing some of my freinds which has prevented my paying my duty to your lordship ever since: I was very civilly received by Mr Tryons[996] who kept me with him four or five days in

---

[994] Michael Mallet (c.1632–post 1683), an unstable MP who finally uttered 'mad extravagant words' against the King (Henning, *Commons*, III, pp 7–10)

[995] Sir Thomas Garrard or Garrett's son was married to Sir John Holland's daughter.

[996] Presumably Peter Tryon of Harringworth, Northants, father-in-law of Charles Bertie

which time I waited on my Lord Westmerland and my Lord Brudenall[997] being both
his neighbors. They shew me all the civility possible and at the latter I mett with my
Lord [f.2] and Lady Arundale and my Lord Mountague,[998] and my Lady
Northumberland[999] who came a visiting while I was there. We were very merry and
danced till day light. My cousin Ralph Mountagu stands in my late Lord Obrien's
place *for Northampton* and tho my Lord Treasurer does endeavour to sett up
another it is beleved he will carry it.[1000] Their is one recommend to the town from
above,[1001] his name is not known but spends his mony freely among them to little
purpose. I came to London yesterday where att my arrive I received my mother's
packett, I sent her letter to Mr Brunscall but have not any [f.3] answer of it. To day
I have bin to give my Lord Plymouth joy, who was this day sennight married att
Wimbledon very privately, his settlements are yett to make for thers but £4,000 a
year more yett given him, which is out of the excise, he has his appartment att the
Cockpitt, and lies it out every day till 12 a clock. The parliment is prorouged till the
21 of the next month <??> *till* which time the King intends to pass his time <till>
*att* Newmarkett. Here is no news stirring since the peace is declared. I was last night
at my brother's, they presents their humble duty to your lordship and as soon [f.4]
as my sister is well she will certainly be for Norfolke. I am sorry that I cannott waite
on her that I might have a better opportunity of <of> paying my duty to your lordship and off assuring your lordship with all respect and submission how much I am,

*Signed*: your lordship's most dutyfull and obedient son, Robert Paston
*Postscript*: Pray my lord present my humble duty to my mother and service to my sister
Betty.
*NRO: BL/Y/2/85*

## Sir John Holland to Robert, Viscount Yarmouth

**1678, October 9, Quidenham**. My lord, I presume your lordshipp is now busied
in the execution of what I heare was latly directed by letters from the lords of the
Councell to all the lord leiutenants in England, touching the search & disarming of
the papists upon the detection of a plott[1002] designed to have been executed by some
of that perswasion, against the life of the King, who God in mercy to the nation long
preserve. Our religion, our allegeance aye our interest oblige us to this prayer & may
they perish with the[i]r first thought (whosoever they are) that goeth about but to
imagine the least evill against him.

   997 Francis, lord Brudenell, brother of the countess of Shrewsbury, and their brother-in-law Charles
Fane, earl of Westmorland
   998 Edward, lord Montagu of Boughton, father of Ralph Montagu
   999 She had married Ralph Montagu as her second husband in 1673.
   1000 Montagu's acquisition of a seat in parliament gave him a secure platform from which to launch
his attack on Lord Danby in the following December.
   1001 Danby's candidate was Sir William Temple, but his campaign began too late and he was soundly
defeated.
   1002 The Popish Plot was alleged by Titus Oates to be a Catholic conspiracy to murder the King. He
named Colman in his deposition to Sir Edmund Berry Godfrey, and the fact that Colman had been in
correspondence with France and the subsequent murder of Godfrey was gave credence to the plot and led
to a national crisis. Colman was found guilty of treason and executed on 3 December 1678.

I ame sorry for some of our frends of that perswasion, who are like to bee involved in the ill consequences, though I ame confident they neither were privy nor would bee to any such damnable design.

I heare Mr Coleman, who was at first but secured in a messenger's hand, have been since committed to prison (it is sayd) upon some discoveryes made by some papers found in his closset upon search, which I ame sorry for, yett I know not soe much as his person but somwhat of his reputation I doe, & that hee have been very kind & frendly upon occasion to a neere relation of mine, & therfore cannot but have some concerne for him & heartely wish hee may bee found innocent, but if hee bee guilty lett him goe, I can have noe compassion for him nor for any whosoever they are that are involved in the same guilt with him.

My lord if we heare of noe furthur prorogation very suddainly I shall prepare to sett out from hence towards Westminster upon Munday sevenight wher what noyse & worke the relation of this plott will make wee must expect. But I heare as yett ther is but *one* wittnes in the case which may bee sufficient evidence in parliament, though not at the bar in Westminster Hall. If your lordshipp or my lady (to whom wee all from hence present the humblest of our services) have any commands for mee they shall find a ready observance from

*Signed*: your lordshipp's most humble servant, J Holland
*Addressed*: For the Lord Viscount Yarmouth at Oxnead
*NRO: BL/Y/2/86*

## John Fisher to Robert, Viscount Yarmouth

**1678, October 15, Westminster**. My lord, I hear here of your lordship's having taken order for disarming the popish recusants in your country, but the messenger that was sent from hence to search at Bodney[1003] & Oxborough for a person he had a warrant for, is returned again without him. But here has been much inquiring & searching for Sir Edmund Bury Godfrey[1004] these three daies, & nobody can find him. He went out on Saturday in the forenoon, & said he would come in at dinner, but was never seen since, and his brother & servants were to day at the committee of the Councell, making relation therof there, & complayning, they believed some of the popish party had made away with him, because he was the justice that tooke the first examinations touching this discovery of the plot, upon which they [*sic*] have been so many since accused, but I hear he was observed to be melancholy & much discomposed a day or two before, so that what is become of him, God knowes.

Wee almost thought wee had lost the Dutches[1005] & the rest of the lords & ladyes that went to sea, but now wee hear they got ovr safe the next day after they went

---

[1003] The home of the Tasburgh family who were Roman Catholics (*The Visitation of Norfolk, 1664* (NRS (1934) V, p.215).

[1004] Godfrey's disappearance and murder, after hearing Oates' deposition, produced a hysterical reaction throughout the country as it was thought to confirm the validity of the plot.

[1005] Mary, duchess of York: she and her stepdaughter the Lady Anne were sailing to the Netherlands to visit her older stepdaughter Princess Mary of Orange, later Mary II. They sailed on 1 October and returned on 16 October. (*ODNB*)

aboard, & were ready to return again on Sunday & yesterday, or as soon as the wind will serve.

Now the town begins to fill again, the Dutches of Mazarine[1006] lay on Fryday night at Audlyend in her return from Newmarket, & I saw the Dutches of Portsmouth allight out of her coach this evening & her train, from Wilton,[1007] and wee expect his Majesty & the court here to morrow by noon.

Sevrall foraign packets came togeathr today, & the ratification of the peace not being come from Spain, the French will not evacuate the Flanders towns, & excuse themselves hereby from delivering Maestricht, & take this opportunity to send one army into the country of Juliers for winter quarters, & the other about Treves.

Mr Sackvill[1008] dyed last weeke of the malignant feaver he brought with him out of Flanders.

I saw Ser[gean]t Knight[1009] here two dais since, who presents his service to your lordship, & wish he had had time to have wayted upon your lordship upon your kind invitation.

I perceive Sir John & the alderman[1010] have ventured earnest again for next Monday, & I hear nothing to the contrary, but they will sit, there is some thinke they may adjourn for a few daies. Thus with my humblest service presented, I remayn, my lord,

*Signed*: your lordship's most faithfull servant, J Fisher
*Addressed*: For the right honourable the Lord Viscount Yarmouth Lord Lieutenant of the County of Norfolk &c at Oxnead Hall in Norfolk [*franked, with postmark*]
*NRO: BL/Y/2/87*

## John Fisher to Robert, Viscount Yarmouth

**1678, October 17, Westminster**. My Lord, I cannot but acquaint your lordship (though I doubt not but others will too) that his Majesty got safe hither yesterday by two at afternoon, and the Dutches &c by ten at night.

No Sir Edmund is found yet, some will have him spirited, others say he is marryed to Mrs Offley the lawyer's widow, which the Duke of Norfolk had the fortune to hear from a cabinet maker neer him, & speaking of it *at* court, was sent for up to the Councell, & from thence sent back to the cabinet maker's again to inquire better into it, but the cabinet man could not make it out, not the widow own it.

The ratifications of the peace have not found the way yet from Madrid to Nimeguen, so that the French stick still in their old quarters, but are providing themselves new not farr off, & some into the Duke of Brand[enburg's] country, that may prove as bad for England, Holland, Spain & Germany, as where they now are, as you may please to read in the *Gazette*, by those they have allready possest themselves

[1006] Hortense Mancini, duchesse Mazarin, mistress of Charles II. The King had bought Audley End from the Howard family, earls of Suffolk, in 1668 to use when attending the races at Newmarket.
[1007] Wilton House, Wiltshire, home of her sister Henriette and brother-in-law the 7th earl of Pembroke.
[1008] Captain Edward Sackville (1644–1678), MP for East Grinstead
[1009] John Knight (d.1680), sergeant-surgeon to Charles II
[1010] Sir John Holland and Alderman Briggs, MPs

of, & others they are like to do.

I thinke the Councell have drawn up an abstract of their discoveryes touching the plot, & presented them to his Majesty, that they may be considered of, how to proceed thereon, before & in the parliament, which holds, as is supposed, on Monday, though some thinke, there maybe some short adjournment till the holly-dayes that happen in the end of this & beginning of the next month be over, & that the House be full, to communicate to them the great affairs both at home and abroad.

I hear the Lord Cheif Baron's son has a yo[*unger*] son.

Sir Ch[*arles Harbord*] & all here present our humble services to your lordship & my noble lady. I remayn, my lord,

*Signed*: your lordship's most faithfull servant, John Fisher
*Addressed*: These present to the right honourable the Lord Viscount Yarmouth Lord Lieutenant of the County of Norfolk &c at Oxnead Hall in Norfolk [*franked*, per Norwich post]
*NRO: BL/Y/2/88*

## William Aglionby to William Paston

**1678, November 3, Frankfort**. Honnored sir, I have received heere your most obliging one from London for which I give you my most humble thankes and am verry sorry that the first which you honnored mee with never came to my hands for it might have been of some use to mee at the Hague though I thanke God that neither that calumny nor any other has done mee any injury with my Lord Embassador[1011] and yett the malice of some people has been soe great as to spread a report of my beeing a papist and I found my lord soe pressed uppon the point by his friends that I thought myselfe bound in point of generosity and gratitude for his manny favours, not to oblige him to undertake to protect mee openly till I had cleared myselfe which I will doe by the grace of God verry shortly by a printed apology; and in the meane time I have resolved to see some of the German courts which my lord has consented to and favourd mee with his [*f.2*] letters of recommendation. This is the true cause of my retreate which I acquaint you with my honnord friend: but the account which I give to the world by my lord's order is that hee having told mee that hee had a mind to end his embassy verry shortly I desird of him leave to see some courts in Germany and this is soe farr true that I beleeve hee will within these three months bee in England for a better employment; I suppose you know by this time it is hee who stands at Northhampton against Mr Montaigue; how it will bee I cannot tell but this I am sure that to sett up a man absent for the court against all the interest of my Lord Montague in Northamptonshire is a bold thing and cannot bee thought to succeed for any but for one who has soe cleare a reputation of a lover of his prince and country as Sir W. Temple has. Heere is no newes but that the winter quarters fright the people more then a French army and I scapd verry narrowly beeing taken by a party of Lunebourg horse who know noe friends. If there happens any thing worth your knowing I shall not fayle to acquitt myselfe of that duty and am in the meane time with all respect, sir,

1011  Sir William Temple

*Signed*: your most humble and most obedient servant, Will: Aglionby
*Addressed*: The honnorable William Paston esquire at his house in Swallow Street beyond Picadilly, Londres, *post paié jusqu'a Anvers*[1012]
*NRO: BL/Y/2/89*

## Statement defining rods, canes and cork as unwrought wood, and so part of Lord Yarmouth's grant

**1678, December 7**. *Report by Mr Dawson, Mr Brewer & Mr Dickinson to the commissioners of his Majesty's customs, upon reading John Blake's petition*
*Endorsed*: Copie of Mr Dawson's, Mr Dickinson's & Mr Brewer's certificate to the commissioners
*NRO: BL/Y/2/90*

## Robert, Viscount Yarmouth to Rebecca, Viscountess Yarmouth

**1678, December 13**. My dearest hart, these windy spleenetick vapors have according to their nature alarummed mee soe that I sent for the doctor who is now with mee, who finds my body & temper in an exelent posture, and laughs att the other concernes, and heere was my cousin Ayde who has and is much worse of them then I am who has soe perfectly anatomised all those kinds of sumptomes, that I resolve nott to contribute to them by any feares of my owne butt butt [*sic*] by good diett and the doctor's care endeavor to free my self of them. I have had great fitts of weeping which eases when itt's over, and have putt on one of your spleene stones by the doctor's approbation, besides I take all fitting medecines, and Mrs Cooper I thanke her is most dilegent and tender of mee. I received yesterday this letter from the lord chancelor of which I send you the coppy, pray find a meanes if possibly by my son Robin, att least to speake with Mr Harris, my Lord Chancelor's cheif gentleman, and instruct mee by the next post what I am to doe and accordingly I shall send up Mr Doughty and som other witness to attest I cannot com in person which I think would att the present cost mee my life to performe. I cannott wonder att the implacable malice of Sir John, having had soe many evidences of itt which has ever out runn [*f.*2] the reasons of my jealousy. God forgive him I pray God and graunt mee a Christian charity towards him and noe farther, for the disadvantages wee are under by his meanes, and what wee have suffered from his trechery is nott yett knowne, though I hope itt will appeare.

My Lord Townshend went up on Tuesday in a sad condition beeing an houre before they could gett him into his coach, hee takes little butt spoone meat, and vomitts up whatever hee takes, yett hee was resolved to goe.

I am very glad att what you putt mee in hopes of that 36[1013] will agree matters civily and without 37 [*Sir John Clayton*]: I should allsoe bee glad that the mischeif 37 [*Sir John Clayton*] has don with 34 might bee countermined by 12 14 1 2, and

---

[1012] i.e. Antwerp
[1013] The Yarmouths were using a new cipher. Because so little has survived it has been impossible to decode most of it.

that afterwards a gard may bee sett upon *37* [*him*] never for us to have to doe with him upon any accompt who can bee soe base as to betray the concernes of a family soe nearly related to him and to add God knows what on his owne accompt. I shall say nothing more of all the concernes you write to mee of. God can [*in*] his mercy make some of them effectuall, and I thanke God I am every day endeavoring to fitt my self for a reformation of life and to resist all temptations of sin as much as in mee lies for which I pray his grace to fortifye mee and so in life or death to give me a resignation to his blessed will. Remember mee to Robin, I am pleased hee is soe dutyfull & kind to you & mee, God will reward him for itt, it was well enough don to speake loud to his uncle, butt further is nott well amongst kindred, nor excusably warrantable, att further distances: pray lett him know this from mee.

[*f.*3] Remember me to my daughter Paston and my son, I thanke them for their kindness to you, deare Charles *& B[*e*]ttie* present their dutys, dispose my [*sic*].

I wonder you should discourage a younger brother from advancing himself, they say shee has a very good fortune and the woman made an exelent wife and I am sure I licke her person very well, I doubt of the craft in the catching.[1014]

Pray excuse mee by Lewis to Mr Fisher this post and lett him know Mrs Harbord is finely well and the colonel tooke his leave of mee to goe abroad for his owne business till Christmas.

Honest Sir Nevile Catlyne now heere presents his service to you & to my son, I shall conclude nothing can give mee a greater fellicity then your company in an happy meeting as to this world: and when God calls mee out of itt you are the dearest thing I have to part with,

*Signed*: who am yours, Yarmouth

*Postscript*: I have received all the thinges you sent mee, dispose my service where you see itt convenient. I write to your mother this post, I sent to see the bishop, who presents his service. Pray write a letter to Mrs Cooper & Hurton about Christmas, really I cannot mind those concernes I have other matters in my head.

*NRO: BL/Y/2/91*

## Robert, Viscount Yarmouth to Rebecca, Viscountess Yarmouth

**1678, December 16**. My dearest deare, I humbly thanke you for all your deare letters which are great cures to the spleene, which as I never felt all the varietyes of before, soe I beginn now to have less feares of them, then the nature of the disease and the manner of itts working made mee have att first. Dr Hawse reports mee in such a condition of body as hee has nott seene mee, and chides Mrs Cooper for having beene affected with my complaints. I am glad with all my hart att what you write mee of *22 36*, itt is a very good thing don, when *37* [*Sir John Clayton*] the old *82* [*villain*] was laying his new inventions, I hope whatever ill nature of itt self may doe hee shall *nott* bee the instrument of *3454* to *87* [*you*]: God Almighty preserve

[1014] It appears from subsequent letters that Lord Yarmouth's second son Robert was wooing a widow. He did in fact marry one in 1680, although possibly not this same lady, and his younger brothers Jasper and Thomas also married widows. As Lord Yarmouth pointed out this was an advantageous course for a younger son to take.

and bless you in all thinges and crowne your endeavors with som success, and send us if itt bee his blessed will an happy and joyfull meeting; I shall pray hartily for itt and hope to offer up the sacrifice of praise and thankesgiving heere in the family on Christmas day, that God would bee me[r]cifall unto itt, and preserve itt. I doe suppose 36 will expect to have somwhat to doe in 22 still and if itt bee soe he diserves itt I am contented. My Lord Bishop of Norwich is mightily troubled that hee cannott goe up,[1015] I beeleeve, wee shall agree to morrowe to send one a peece that may vouch for both of us on Thursday after I have received your letters, butt tomorrowe I send Mr Doughty to talke with his lordshipp about itt. His steward was heere with [f.2] mee on Saterday to enquire after you and the rest of my family, pray present my service to my daughter Paston & my son and to Mrs Howard[1016] and little Charlotte. Remember mee kindly to Robin. I am nott in an humor of writing letters, butt returne him thankes for his. Pray if you can send mee som wax candles from the back stairs or elswhere to burne somtimes in the parlor or in my owne chamber, for the nasty candles we have heere infects my spleene and my nose.

I am mighty jealous that any thing in the last letters should make you thinke you had nott the truth in the worst colors, and soe coole you in the persuit of your business, butt lett mee now assure you that though I will as neere as I can by God's help live in a posture to dye, yett I doe hope with his favor to have the happiness of my life protracted in living with you one seven yeares longer[1017] who am with all the kindlness imaginable

*Signed*: yours, Yarmouth

*Postscript*: Betty & Charles presents their dutys. Mrs Cooper who is most oblidgingly kind and carefull of mee writes herself. My duty to your mother. Mr Gough presents his humble service to you and is now sending to bee informed whether the reversion can bee secured from the Crowne (which som seemes to doubt) Mr Bulwer <wri> writes to his man about itt. [f.3] I thanke God I am finely well and drank your health hartily att dinner.

*NRO: BL/Y/2/92*

---

[1015] i.e. to the House of Lords

[1016] Stuarta Howard (1670–1706), daughter of Charlotte Paston by her first marriage to James Howard (d.1669), nephew and heir presumptive, after his father, to the 3rd earl of Suffolk. In the event, both James and his father predeceased the earl. James was buried in Chiswick parish church and his mother-in-law, Lady Shannon, left money for a marble monument to him (TNA: PROB11/365). Stuarta later became a maid in waiting to her cousin Princess Mary of Orange. In the 1690s her name was linked with that of the duke of Portland, whose mistress she may have been, and her half-brother Charles Paston was rumoured to have fought a duel on her behalf. Her grandmother Lady Shannon left Stuarta the lease of her house in Pall Mall, and she was her residuary legatee, but Charles Paston borrowed from her and left her financially embarrassed (British Library: Add. MSS 27448, f.385). She died unmarried in 1706. (Eveline Cruickshanks, Stuart Handley, D.W. Hayton, *The Commons, 1690–1715*, (Cambridge, 2002), V, pp 110–111).

[1017] In the seventeenth century one's life span was counted in 'climacterics' – periods at (usually) seven year intervals when a person was liable to some change in health or fortune. Having survived a life-threatening illness, Lord Yarmouth felt entitled to hope to survive for a further seven years, but he died less than five years later.

# Robert, Viscount Yarmouth to Rebecca, Viscountess Yarmouth

**1678, December 18**. My dearest sowle, your letters come safe to my hands, and I thanke you for them, they are great comforts to mee. I am glad to find your letter soe full of good hopes, and will cheere up my self, in the hopes of enjoying your company, in the meane time pray feare nott my solitude, itt's the least thing I feare. I have consulted my self about wrighting to Sir John, whose proceedings must needes seeme abominable to those that take the advantages of his treacherie butt I deferr itt yett nott beeing resolved which way to methodize my detestation of him, butt thinke to express itt in a letter to Mr Henshaw to shew him butt will respite itt till I receive your answer. I know no great hurt he can doe us, more then what hee has don with *34*: now you say hee is of the *22 19* [*affair*] and *36*: a greater knave never received benifitts from any man to bee soe rewarded, God forgive him as a Christian, and keep mee in my resolutions never to relaps into any negotiation with him: as to my owne health though this cruell spleene has treated mee after a way I never knew, yett you saw all the effects of itt upon mee, and now I hope itt's breaking up with the schoole boyes, for my temper of body never was in soe good a condition as now: and soe the doctor [*f.2*] thinkes, butt though they have formidable appearances they are nott dangerous butt I hope I shall live the rest of my life soe as nott to feare death for I have good resolutions in mee, pray God enable mee to keep them (from whome I find dayly comforts).

Upon consulting the bishop who sends his chaplain and secretary up to morrowe, I send with them Mr Peckover & Mr Doughty,[1018] nott thinking itt fitt to stay for more advice, and am sorrie therefore I putt you to the trouble of speaking either to my Lord Chancelor or Mr Harrise. I have written by Mr Doughty to my Lord Chancelor and sent you the coppie of my letter by him, pray be kind to Doughty he is soe to mee, and find a corner in your lodging for him & Peckover to pigg in. I shall send for the box and open itt as you direct. I suppose *37* [*Sir John Clayton*] has intercepted *1 23 24 19* with *34* butt that's a thing *57* and *86* [*I*] makes noe great count of itt, I doe supose *37* [*Sir John Clayton*] by *65* may have been working at *26 82* [*villainy*] butt if *3:4* once are *53* wee shall have good Sir John thinke to whine of all his villanie to us. I had a letter from *73* this week very civill and allsoe allsoe [*sic*] from *42* and *72*. I find by the stile of the two last som flagging in their stile concerning *45* which makes mee hope *87* [*you/your*] *10* will nott bee *49* in *31*. Sir John Pettus writes mee word that hee hopes *18 19* [*affair*] may doe well in time. My service to my daughter Paston, and my son, and to little Charlotte: to my son Robert, my kindness [*f.3*] and harty blessing, I shall find a time to write to him for his many letters to mee, and for his duty to you, I love him well. Charles and my daughter Betty presents their dutys to you. I received the inclosed from Mr D & L[1019] which I shewed Mr Doughty; itt's an honest letter butt I shall not write to them till I heare from you.

Present my duty to your mother, bee very silent in all matters of *10*: there are som

---

[1018] John Doughty and Matthew Peckover deposed on oath that Lord Yarmouth was so ill of the stone that he was unable to attend the session of the House of Lords (*House of Lords Journal*, volume 13, 23 December 1678). Oddly, none of Yarmouth's letters mention the stone.

[1019] Joseph Dawson and Henry Loades were deputy farmers of the wood farm (British Library: Add. MSS 27448, f.300).

which gratifye themselves with sifting; you must write a letter to Suckling, which you may direct to be left att Alderman Briggs att Norwich for him, itt will doe better then to com from hence, & pray doe this the next post.

If you can propose or find mee out a way to provide for itt, I hope att our next meeting to make you a mother for all the scurvey and spleene.

All heere presents their service, mine where you see cawse.

God preserve and keep you and comfort and support you; by Mr Doughty who goes for Norwich this evening in order for the coach to morrowe, I send you a note for to receive the orange farme if Sir John according to his last letter will pay itt, otherwise wee must process his worship out of the exchequer.

I am licke Sir Martyn Marrall[1020] I can never have don, I am with all imaginable kindness,

*Signed*: yours, Yarmouth
*NRO: BL/Y/2/93*

## William Paston to Robert, Viscount Yarmouth

**1678, December 18**. My lord, this night has produced great matters which though tyred & wear[i]ed as I am I could not omitt the letting your lordship know for we rise not till nere ten aclock this night; just as we were adjourning this day about one we had a message delivered by the chancellor of the exchequer[1021] that his Majesty did order him to acquaint the House that the King had received information that Mr Mountagu when he was embassador in France had *had* private conferences with the Pope's nuntio without any such instructions from his Majesty, & that the King might have a fuller account of that matter had caused his papers to be seized; the House did at first say twas a breach of priviledge & severall other things at length ordered that five or six memembers [*sic*] should attend the King to know whether his Majesty had received the information upon oath & whether [*f.2*] the matter was criminall; they went to the House of Lords to waite on his Majesty who returned them this answer that he had much businesse & desired they would come to him at Whitehall. As soon as this was reported to the House Mr Mountagu stood up & maid a speech, the conclusion was that he had matters of great importance to informe the House & desired they would appoint a day, severall desired it might be immediately and it was ordered that four members should goe & fetch the papers presently who accordingly did for it seems it [*sic*] had had information that his papers would be seized & soe removed these two letters he produced under my Lord Treasurer's own hand to him in France which the House did think fitt to bring in an impeachment against my Lord Treasurer, a previous question was put & it was carried by neare 60 voices, the Noes were 116 & Ays were 179 that were for an impeachment.[1022] This is all at present

[1020] Sir Martin Mar-all, a character in a play of that name by John Dryden which was first performed in 1667. A hidden actor sings and plays the lute while Sir Martin mimes, and he continues to mime after the music ceases.      [1021] Sir John Ernle

[1022] Ralph Montagu had been ambassador to France but had been dismissed from all his posts by Charles II following a letter to the King from Barbara duchess of Cleveland denouncing him for, among other things, his alleged affair with the countess of Sussex, her own and the King's daughter. Montagu blamed Lord Danby and allied himself with Danby's enemies. Danby's attempt to destroy Montagu back-

*Signed*: from your most obedient son, Will: Paston
*Postscript*: My wife presents her duty to your lordship. My service to my sister Betey, Mr Gough, & Mr Peckover
*NRO: BL/Y/2/94*

## Robert, Viscount Yarmouth to Rebecca, Viscountess Yarmouth

**[1678, December 29]**.[1023] I send in the morning to Norwich though the 30 of December, for *38-19*, which I shall open myself, I shall bee glad to heare of any good newse, which your last letters seemed to promise. I should bee glad that what *15* sayes of *3-4* might proove true, I thinke *37* [*Sir John Clayton*] has don his worke there as well as elswhere against *87* & *86* [*us*].

I give you noe accompt of myself because Mrs Cooper writes by the doctor's owne directions and this letter must serve you and my sonn for I am soe vigilant in his matters as I cannot write att the present more. Remember mee most kindly to him, my service to my daughter Paston & little Charlotte.

Betty and Charles presents their dutys, Charles is a brave boy, my duty to your mother pray excuse my nott writing to her upon the hurry you knowe I am now in, which makes mee say in hast God prosper you and keep you and send us a joyfull meeting: which I passionately desire with speed and luck: I am with hart and soule

*Signed:* yours, Yarmouth
*Postscript:* I perceive my daughter Alberti had nott received yours nor mine.
Charles has a great desire to bee a parlament man and has proposed itt to mee to stand att Norwich: I desire the colonel would write to him nott to oppose him, pray make him write the child a letter or [?]mama he longs for itt. I writt to Sawtell you should acknowledge his carefullness, excuse the last letter which I was faine to conclude in hast.
*British Library: Add. MSS 28621, f. 36*

## Robert, Viscount Yarmouth to Rebecca, Viscountess Yarmouth

**1678[/9], January 10**. My dearest sowle, I have received thy letter with the narrative concerning the conclusion with Mr Dickinson, in which if everything bee nott as you would have had itt yett I am glad itt's don att last though as hee would have itt, I doe expect the messenger to morrowe, and shall proceed as you desire in the signing and sealing of them, and shall alter the word advise for direct in the commission of inspection.[1024] I had a most kind letter from Mr Henshaw as ever man had, in which he acquaints mee that hee is marrying his daughter att last to the man she refused,[1025] and that hee doth abhor the horrid action of Sir John in shewing your letter on soe

fired disastrously; he narrowly escaped impeachment and spent several years in the Tower (Browning, *Leeds*, I, pp 301–329).

[1023] Dated from contents, first page missing
[1024] Dickinson was one of the sub-farmers of the wood farm.
[1025] She married Thomas Halsey (1655–1715) of Great Gaddesden, later MP for Hertfordshire (Henning, *Commons*, II, pp 468–9).

unjust a point of revenge where hee had beene soe much oblidged, which hee sayth
Sir John will speedily find will make even those eschew him whome hee thought to
have gained by itt (indeed I cannott butt admire you should in passion or any other
way write anything to him nott fitt for a markett cross). I hope itt's his last shock
though by the inclosed you'l see his impudence in writing to mee and itt's very fitt
counsell should presently bee advised in for the man is bent to mischeif. I am very
glad of what you say as to *1 51 4*: I wish itt may produce the effects *86* [*I*] desires, if
itt bee onely to give *37* [*Sir John Clayton*] an abatement, for hee is a man beyound
all rules of morality or humane society. Dr Hawse came hether to give mee a visitt,
and admires my body and sayth hee could never have thought itt should have beene
in the condition itt is especially my leggs, hee see my pull 1800 strokes sitting, and
200 more standing, and walke sixty turnes att three severall times as fast as I could
walk in the parler. He adviseth mee to goe on with the *aurum potabile*, butt nott [*f*.2]
to neglect the steele water which I find doth mee soe much good and hinders nott att
all the operation of the other medecine, which is very good muskadine, butt whatt
gold is in itt, or how dissolved is best knowne to the artist[1026] himself (who Mr
Henshaw sure mistakes for another kn[*igh*]t doctor of the same name that is famous
for an ague powder) who he sayth was an apothecary's man. However these wind is
all that troubles mee which I hope are much abated in their violence & manner of
proceeding, though somtimes they doe very much affect my head and stomach and
make mee dismally dull and melancholy, butt the doctor chides mee most extreamely
for what I cannott help, however hee desires mee to proceed in my way then which
a better cannott bee proposed, to use my exercise within dores till the weather growes
warmer and the yeare advanceth, and hee perswades mee I may rubb out seven
yeares, nay hee will nott stint mee for hee thinkes mee in a better posture then ever
he knew mee since I was a man. God is the disposer of life and death, to him I resigne
my self, and shall doe the best I can for the meanes of my owne preservation. Deare
Charles, Thom & Betty present their dutys to you, Charles thrives bravely and growes
a stout fellow, Thom I cannot gett of[*f*] till Monday, itt falling this yeare to the advantage of schoole boyes, Bettie is very dutyfull, and very pritty, as to Robin som of his
qualityes are necessary for a younger brother. I shall observe your advice which I well
enough apprehend, butt I most hartily wish hee could perswade the widdowe that a
younger brother with nothing is the properest man for the menagement of too good
joynters, butt I beleeve that less then I feare itt or desire to prevent itt.

　　Charles, Thom and Betty are all going to Mrs Hogan's att Northwalsham this day
to give her a visitt.

　　[*f*.3] You will certainly thinke I ly when I tell you with all the industry I can use
this country affords noe mallard nor teale, scarce foure couple att a time are to bee
procured for love or money, therefore nott to delude Mrs Brumly[1027] any longer I
will make her amends by the next Fridayes carts of the noblest py I can make heere,
of fatt swanns, and such other fowle or thinges as may fitt itt for *39* view, and for the
puddings Mrs Cooper sayth the carts is too long a passage for them to bee good, they
must att the least bee sent up by the coach, which she intends to doe.

[1026] Dr Francis Anthony (1550–1623), alchemist and physician
[1027] Possibly Lady Yarmouth's housekeeper at Suffolk Street

Mrs Harbord is buried on Sunday and my coach attends her to Besthorpe.[1028]

I am glad *31* speaks kindly of *86 87* [us] and doe beleeve that *50* may bee properly now dooing, with *39* in any *19* [affair], I shall bee glad to heare of any progress in any thing.

I showed Doughty your brother's letter, he sayth noe councell would advise a man against paying rent which he may immediately bee arrested for, wee thinke hee att last must have his lease, butt perhapps wee may gett in covenants in the new one for reentry in case he payes itt nott att the time, you must advise what's to bee done.

My duty to your mother, my service to my daughter Paston and my son, and Mrs Charlotte, God Almighty preserve and bless you my deare hart and prosper you,

*Signed*: I am yours most passionately, Yarmouth
*NRO: BL/Y/2/95*

## Robert, Viscount Yarmouth to Rebecca, Viscountess Yarmouth

**1678[/9], January 13**. My dearest deare, on Saterday night I sent an horse and a man for Mr Dickinson's messenger, whome I treated very civilly, next day in the afternoone I perused all the writings, and then with Hurton and himself sealed and wittnessed them. The commission to Mr Dickinson to inspect and advise, butt nott direct, I drew up all with my owne hand, which lookes as if I had don itt for the greater honor of him; the copy of itt I have heere inclosed, which you had best keep by you though perhapps hee will shew you his. I putt up all the wrightings in the same manner I received them, those of Mr Thirsby's chamber in a pacquett by themselves, those I sealed to Mr Dickinson in a pacquett by themselves, both pacquetts inclosed on one of white paper directed to your self, and covered with gray paper directed to your self all sealed by my owne seale and Mr Fisher's direction in every paper as I found them; I am very well pleased the matter is over. Mr Thirsby's letter is a very good one, pray keep itt, butt how will the flaw hee speakes on that *36* made playne bee now secured from *37* [Sir John Clayton's] *82* [villainy]: itt's true itt's now *36* interest to make *22* as firme and as good as he can, for his owne sake, but I see that *37* [Sir John Clayton] is to bee eschewed as a venomous creature that will infect all our friends with the leven of his malice which he has fermented soe desperately with *3 4* that I feare *51 1 15* will nott doe what *86* [I] soe much wishes and desires. I am in a temper that I hope, I have made som conquest of my owne sinns, and I thanke God I sett such a gard on my mouth, as I never lett [f.2] an oath com out of my mouth.[1029] I will sett one on my hart where I will fix all the charitie I can butt where soe long a course of tryall has by soe great a traine of evidences convinced mee of the wickedness of *37* [Sir John Clayton]: and still by my owne good nature relapsed into the error of beleeving his oathes, teares and fals expressions, in the nick of those confidences has hee struck mee every where, soe that till a totall seperation of our interests bee compleated, we must stand upon a strict gard from his malice. You say you beleeve that *3 4* doe nott much regard *37* [Sir John Clayton], I beleeve soe too, but

---

[1028] Anne, wife of Colonel Philip Harbord; she was a daughter of Sir William Drury of Besthorpe.
[1029] Lord Yarmouth renounced swearing during his illness (Hildeyard, *Sermon*, p.31)

yett hee is b\*u\*yed up their with hopes of som great disigne, though I must needes fancie that my ridding him from my employment will not make his creditt the greater with those that he procures to hate mee. For the close of the accompt drawne by Mr Fisher, trouble nott your self; if Sir John had nott beene acquitted what had I beene the better, though itt's true a man would detest to signe any paper to him butt what['s] necessary: and soe about the orange farme, after you have advised with Sir Robert Clayton, what must bee don had best bee don and there's an end of dooing with him; his very acquaintance has beene unfortunate to mee butt itt has beene most sufficiently recompensed with that sister which is the object of his hatred. I am very glad you sent to see how my cosin Coke did & pray send againe from mee & your self as you doe now & then I hope, itt's an ill time of the yeare, and I looke upon all in the small pox to bee in great danger, I wish well to him & his recovery: Mr Dickinson's messenger is gon this morning by four of the clock to the Norwich coach and has promised in person to bee with you on Wedensday in the evening and to deliver you [f.3] them himself, I treated him very civily butt noe monie (I suppose Mr Dickinson payes him), we dranke your health. On Friday shall bee sent away Mrs Brumly's pye of fatt swanns, mallards, and hares beaten and all the things you write are noe ommission of ours: John Woodden and all the world have beene imployed, and att one time wee never could make up above eight mallard, Mrs Feltham has none, the poulterer that bys from the dequoys has soe small parcells as was never heard of; the puddings and linkes shall com then or els the Monday after by the coach & bee there as soone as the pye. What you write mee in the end of your letter of 28 29 would doe very well, if itt might nott interfare with any other pretence, butt that shows that 22 is nott in the hands that sought itt.

My coach went yesterday morning beeing Sunday to accompanie Mrs Harbord's funerall to Besthorpe near Attleborowe, I sent Mr Doughty in itt, and itt coms not home till this night.

Charles, Betty & Thom present their dutys to you, mine to your mother who I desire would persist in 4 19 [affair] for 37 [Sir John Clayton] would abate his triumph in that particular. All heere Mrs Cooper and Mr Gough presents their humble service and Sir Robert Clayton will presently decide the point of the curate on Friday. After I had written came in Sir William Rant, Mr Preston (who brought a young pritty boy his son to play with Charles), Thomas Corie, Mr Burton school-master of Norwich and som others, soe that when I thinke I am to bee alone, I am mistaken. The aurum potabile I received safe and have taken one glass of itt this morning to your health which meethinkes should be enough for mee in one day, butt pray desire Dr [Goodall] [f.4] that I may see Dr Anthonie's booke[1030] which I have nott and I would be glad to goe to work to make itt if I could tell how to doe itt well. I use soe much exercise with walking that I feare I shall have a touch of the gout, my vapors are much better and the nature changed, yett somtimes they will mount to my crowne, butt my experience tells mee itt's nothing butt wind which both rores in my body and somtimes makes a louder noyse to my releif. I can never have don when I begin, I send you the coppy of Dickinson's commission, of my letter to him, & his

---

[1030] *Medicinae Chymicae et Veri Potabilis Auri Assertio* (1610)

letter to mee, a note of the writings sent up, and doe most hartily pray to God for your comfort support success, and the felicity of your sowle and body.

*Signed*: I am yours, Yarmouth

*Postscript*: My service to my son and daughter Paston, I am glad the Norfolk journey has produced kind effects. I had almost forgotten to tell you that pore Sir Edmond Bacon is fallen soe high into his old distemper that hee is remooved to a man that treats mad men where he is under custody att the present as Dr Smyth told mee, who came with Thomas Corie to dinner on Friday.

Lett Lewis Miko get mee too paire of spectacles to fitt in their turnes, to the tortoise shell spectacle case I sent up by Mr Dickinson's man to give him.

Pray gett Don to putt me in the way of making some *aurum potabile*. I have good receipts my selfe and this man can bee noe more a conjurer then other men.

Tell Dr Goodall that <Age> Angelus Sala pretends to sett downe Dr Anthonie's receipt of the *aurum potabile* as well as other receipts of itt.

*NRO: BL/Y/2/96*

## Robert, Viscount Yarmouth to Rebecca, Viscountess Yarmouth

**1678[/9], January 17.** My dearest hart, your letters are my constant refreshments and consolations, and were itt nott for them this separation would be insupportable. I am very glad of what you say of *39* I shall as soone as conveniently may bee send word to *70* how kind *87* [*you*] has been to them. Heere was yesterday with mee L[*ieutenant*] C[*olonel*] Harbord who brought mee a gold ring for his wife,[1031] the biggest I ever saw and the heaviest; hee takes itt mightly kindly I told him you had visited my Lady Kilmurrey[1032] to condole the loss of her sister. His brother Will Harbord has beene with him, and att Gunton, and att Yarmouth endeavoring to have gon beyound sea, soe affraid hee is of beeing taken, and I doe believe hee is now privily att Gunton, hee is an odd blade and nott of his eldest brother's temper.[1033] I much feare I cannott enter upon the orange farme without suing Sir John for hee tooke care nott to insert that clawse of reentry for want of payment, which if I be constrained to make him another lease, I hope I may att least insist to have that inserted butt itt will be much better if I can avoyd him, for his remembrance is to mee an abomination. I am hartily sorry for my pritty Lady Jones[1034] & by the description of my cousin Coke's case, in Mr Fisher's letter to mee, I take itt to bee verie dangerous. My Lady Jones I tooke for graunted was recovered, because she had beene soe long sick of them. I am mightily concerned att your mother's nott beeing well, pray present my duty to her and my

---

[1031]  i.e. a mourning ring

[1032]  Anne Harbord's sister Bridget Drury, who married as her first husband Charles Needham, 4th viscount Kilmorey.

[1033]  William Harbord (1635–1692), second son of Sir Charles Harbord, was an ally of Ralph Montagu in his attempt to ruin Danby by revealing his negotiations with the French. He was chairman of the committee put in charge of Montagu's papers, but he seems to have taken fright at the prorogation of parliament in December 1678. He was subsequently active promoting the investigation of the Popish Plot and measures against Roman Catholics. (*ODNB*)

[1034]  Mary, widow of Sir Samuel Jones, and wife of Yarmouth's cousin, Charles Bertie, died 13 Jan 1679.

thankes for all her favors, which I desire she would continue in *3 4*: for *86* [*I*] cares not for good words, and resolves never to bee *20* [*well?*] anywhere but where *87* [*you*] is *53*: butt itt's most evident that *37* [*Sir John Clayton*] has beene the *82* [*villain*] of the world and has don his all severall times to worke the ruine of my family, butt God Almighty can disappoint his ingratitude to mee and I am loth hee should know how much hee has troubled mee. You may bee sure I shall answer none of his letters, for the matter is above words, and therefore silence and admiration, and great caution with a totall seperation of interests, are the ammunition wee are to deale with him in. *37* [*Sir John Clayton*] is great with *7* son who is much with *34*, now from Sir Will Doyly you may know somthing of *37* [*Sir John Clayton*].

[*f.*2] I had a letter yesterday from Secretary Williamson to desire mee forthwith in his Majesty's name to transmitt by his hands a list of all the militia in Norfolke which shall bee as speedily performed as I can.[1035]

My Lord Cheif Baron and his lady oblidge mee most extraordinarily in their civilitys to you, pray returne them my most particular thankes, and find out a way to make my Lord of Salesbury[1036] a compliment from mee for his favor of enquiring after mee. Though I cannot att all beleeve what you say, I cannott imagine how *39* can proceed in *35 95* butt that the *82 37* [*villainous Sir John Clayton*] has layd a block in the way of all thinges that *87* [*you*] can have any appearance in, what becoms of *65* you say nothing of *10 67*: I should bee very glad to heare any good newse of *18 19* [*affair*] and that *31* would bee kind in itt butt I doe nott heare that the too judges hands are yett procured, and the tearme beginns the next week. I had the inclosed letter from Robin the last night by which I find hee is nott soe suddainely to bee disbanded as was expected. Mrs Brumly's pye coms away this day by the carts post payd att Norwich directed to you, on Monday com the puddings if wee can take them a place in the coach, and then they will arrive both the same day without beeing musty, of which you shall have notice by the Monday's post from hence. I saw the pye just now in my chamber, itt's a brave one and fitt for *39 40* to tast of. I hear nothing of *74 76 77* a great while. I am sorrie I putt you on such a sleeveless[1037] [*errand*], you shall <have> have noe more of them from mee. I hope Mr Dickinson's messenger came to you on Wedensday night, with all the papers as I writt you word. I am sorrie for my Lady Boyer's[1038] death. My fitt of the gout has nott beene severe yett I cannott sett my foot to the ground though I pully as much as ever, itt's the wind that <sho> shootes downe thither and I hope will loose itts way to my stomach and head; I take now butt one glass of *aurum potabile* every morning as soone as I rise, and in the afternoone Dr Hawse's steele drinke. My deare hart pray God preserve and comfort you and send us a speedy meeting. Remember mee to my son & daughter Paston, to little Charlotte and Mrs Howard, Thom is this day gon to schoole, Betty and Charles presents their dutys, and I am

[1035] For this list see *CSPD, 1679–80*, p.32

[1036] The 3rd earl of Salisbury was an ally of Lord Shaftesbury. As Danby was heading towards impeachment, Salisbury was rumoured to be the next lord treasurer, and it seems that Lord Yarmouth was establishing a line of communication with the country party. [1037] i.e. futile

[1038] Probably Margaret, Lady Bowyer, Sir John Clayton's mother in law. Her date of death is given on a memorial in Denman church, Buckinghamshire, as 8 January 1678 but this is presumably Old Style dating.

*Signed*: yours till death, Yarmouth

*Postscript*: [*f.*3] I send you Secretary Williamson's letter to mee, you may shew itt and my answer to my son Paston and returne mee them againe. You may make Mr Fisher enquire of Secretary Coke[1039] if you see nott Sir Joseph himself how they are accepted and for what end sent for. Sir Joseph in his subscription gives mee the compliment of my faithfull servant. I beleeve noe lord leiftenant makes soe quick a returne. On Monday I send to by *71 72*.

*NRO: BL/Y/2/97*

## Robert, Viscount Yarmouth to Rebecca, Viscountess Yarmouth

**1678[/9], January 20**. My dearest deare, I must allwaies begin with my thankes for your most kind letters and for your great sedulity, to drive on those concernes of which you seeme to have to have to have [*sic*] soe good hopes of. Since my last heere has beene Colonell Knyvett & Captaine[1040] and young Bedingfeld, and Goldwell, they dined heere on Friday; on Saterday night came in Mr Ost, and with him Mr Linstead[1041] of Lynn, we had much discourse about the next election in which there will bee noe dispute against the mayor, one Captaine Turner[1042] a very great friend of mine. Hee offers att least in complement his interest to Mr Ost, who absolutely att the present refuseth medling with itt, and the mayor has sent mee a complement that whosoever I will nominate shall have his interest (butt this must nott bee knowne) soe wee have agreed, that if neither the mayor nor Mr Ost stand to make way for Sir Nevile Catlyn, butt I beleeve the feare of the expence will make him avoid itt. I shall have an accompt on Wedensday night from Mr Ost & Mr Linstead, and then I shall be able to say more, butt Taylor[1043] will stand and certainly carrie itt against any butt the mayor or his interest; they are gon away this morning. I have this day sent Doughty (to whome lickwise for my sake Sir Thomas Garrard has given the keeping of his courts) to *69 70 71* and written the historie of *87* [*your*] obligation to the *19* [*affair*] to *39* & *31*: which will certainly bee received with great satisfaction. As to the matter now in dispute with Sir John, concerning the orange farm, I am apt to beeleeve that the first contrivance of itt was Dickinson's, and that hee beares a share in the advantage therefore I wonder how hee should come to draw up the case against him. I am sure hee has formerly pleaded for his nott paying the rent into my hands, therefore his advice is nott wholy in that point to bee relied on. You say that *17* will write mee good newse, concerning *18 19* [*affair*]; itt will com seasonably now in my gout which I thanke God is nott very violent though itt hinders my walking att the present, and I find itt the effects of wind, which has new wayes of venting ittself and is nott soe toublesom to my head as formerly; I hope good weather & the spring with God's blessing will restore mee.

---

[1039] John Cooke, under-secretary, see Aylmer, *The Crown's Servants*, p.71

[1040] Probably Captain John Knyvett

[1041] Probably William Linstead, collector of customs of Lynn

[1042] Captain John Turner (c.1632–1712), mayor of Lynn

[1043] Simon Taylor (c.1633–1689), who had previously opposed Coke in 1675, was elected in 1679 and knighted in 1684.

[*f.2*] I had a most kind letter from Sir Charles Harbord which I have answered this post and inclosed itt to Mr Fisher. I have sent to knowe when my Cousin Coke's body coms downe that I may send my coach to performe my last civilityes to him. Mr Linsted will give mee notice, who had a letter from Mr Ramsey who seemed incertaine whether itt would com downe or noe, and withall did desire Mr Linstead nott to engage his vote, by which they imagine sombody may bee offered them, butt this I know whosoever has itt must give mee his thankes, for I have a greater interest there then *10* has as I am made [*to*] beleeve by such as should know butt Ile make noe bussle openly, but reserve my self for occasions; the mayor is entirely mine and hee is all that can steere which way he pleaseth.

I am sorrie for the fate of my pore cousin Coke, who as you say has had little joy in his match and thinges are now in a distracted posture, every body fearing to loose their money, and Lynn £4,000 behind though £6,000 has beene payd;[1044] my Lady Anne is a fine young widdowe and will presently repaire her loss.[1045]

I should be glad to see *39* once performe somwhat which I suppose *41 50* engage hee shall doe, as for the *19* [*affair*] *35* I wonder that should nott moove that carries on ittself, I doe wish however matters moove that *51 1 15* would doe what they were about, to allay the triumph of ingrateful inhumane *37* [*Sir John Clayton*].

Sir John Holland writt to mee a very kind letter which I have answered.

I am glad you received the writings safe and that Mr Dickinson is pleased; I hope *37* [*Sir John Clayton*] shall nott influence him any more, butt nothing can influence him against his owne interest.

Pray present my service to Dr Goodale, tell him how much I thinke myself oblidged to his civilityes, butt Mrs Wilcock has nott yett found the way to Dr Hawys his [*house*] with the booke; the boy called there last night when hee went to take a place for the puddings in the coach.

My duty to your mother, my service to my daughter Paston & my son who I will wright to when hee is returned, Betty & Charles, who playes an howre [*f.3*] att a time with Nurs Port att cards, presents his duty to you, hee would faine have a pack of cards that should bee all trumps.

All heere pray for your speedy returne which happy day God send and in the meane time give you all his choysest blessings which from my soule I desire

*Signed*: as being from my sowle, yours Yarmouth
*NRO: BL/Y/2/98*

## Sir Joseph Williamson to Robert, Viscount Yarmouth

**1678/9, January 21, Whitehall**. My lord, I have this evening received the favour of your lordshipp's of the 17th inclosing the lists of your militia which I shall not faile

---

[1044] Coke's generous settlement on his wife (whom he had married 'for perfect love'), coupled with his ruinous expenses at the King's Lynn election in 1675, left his estate heavily in debt (Henning, *Commons*, II, 101–2). Lady Anne erected a magnificent monument to her husband at St Mary, Tittleshall, 'as a mark of her entire love and affection' but there are hints in these letters that the marriage was not happy.

[1045] She married Captain Horatio Walpole, uncle of Sir Robert Walpole, 1st earl of Orford, in March 1691 'to the great dissatisfaction of all her relations' (British Library: Add. MSS 34095, f.305).

to represent to his Majestie together with an account of your lordshipp's diligence in that service according to what you are pleased to say to me in your letter. I am with respect & esteeme, my lord,

*Signed*: your lordship's most humble & faithfull servant, J Williamson
*Endorsed*: A true copy examined
*NRO: BL/Y/2/99*

## George Stebbing[1046] to Colonel William Paston

**1678[/9], January 29, Norwich**. Sir, I doubt not but the honest part of our city of Norwich still retaine that high esteeme for your honour, which they formerly signifyed to the world at your honourable election for their representative in parliament, but it's likewise as evident that an other sort of men, who neither wish well to the King's Majestie nor his interest, are still as active as ever to deceive the people by all the lyes & tricks imaginable. There be some already report that your honour will not appeare for another election in Norwich but decline it, how farr such a report may impose upon some men without a signification of your pleasure to the city I know not, but that, & your honour's appearance in person, will confute such reports, & give sufficient testimony of your continued affection to the persons & place you have represented. There are others very loyall men who <wh> would attempt to choose your honour a new second[1047] this tyme, but that cannot be done without great hazard if it [*sic*] all. If I have troubled your honour with a relation of what you have already received, I am ignorant of it, & beg pardon, being moved by a hearty principle of loyalty to the King's Majesty, which I shall alwayes own to be my duty, & for that reason make bold to style my selfe,

*Signed*: your honour's most faithfull servant, Geo: Stebbing
*Addressed*: For the honourable Colonel Paston at house at the further end of Swallow Street <in Westminster> London [*postmark*]
*NRO: BL/Y/2/100*

## Robert, Viscount Yarmouth to Rebecca, Viscountess Yarmouth

**1678[/9], January 29**. My deare sowle, excuse mee now if in a great hurry of business I am butt short, my son's business is soe fixed at Norwich as I beleeve there's none will oppose him, if they should itt will bee in vayne. By last post Mr Doughty gave you som accompt who by Mr Sawtell's prudence had time to gett to Norwich time enough to fix the matter which indeed without speaking to, were resolved on. Mr Gough has beene with the bishop & the deane who are all as one man for my sonn, and the expence this way cannott exceed £100. Dr Hawse now with me tells mee from Dr Collings' owne mouth they will nott one appeare against my son, but itt's nott a point matter. The bishop and I joyne in for Sir Nevile Catlyne and for Sir Christopher Calthorp; Sir John Hobart & Sir John Holland will stand for knights

---

[1046] Later sheriff (Miller, 'Containing Division in Restoration Norwich', p.1038).
[1047] i.e. to replace Briggs who was a moderate royalist.

of the shire, butt they had better lett itt alone, for Catlyne & Calthorp will certainely carrie itt and Sir John expecting to loose itt in the county will have his reserve for Norwich butt all to little purpose, wee shall vigorously oppose him everywhere and doe my best to serve his Majesty to my power and poverty. I have written to Mr Host to make friends att [*Castle*] Rising for Robin, if my Lord Arundell writes to his servant Cuffant itt may bee don and I hope itt will nott displease the Duke; though father and son doe nott sett [*f.*2] their horns together, itt's from neither of their interests to place such a man there. Your owne sence will best discover our strength Monday sevenight in the election for the county, and Sir John Holland's strength depends on my Lord Duke of Norfolke's tennants who ly about him and he engaged for Sir Robert Kemp: butt I have written to Mr Corie on Monday who sayd hee would take of twenty two townes from that engagement. I wish at least my Lord Duke would wright to Mr Corie to engage where I engage all his tennants, hee is sure itt will bee for his interest soe to doe.

Yesterday heere dined my cousin Windham and by my retentiveness hee finds I shall oppose all hee can goe about to promote, I feared he would have asked mee somwhat about himself butt hee had more witt.

Just now I parted with Mr Bulwer who I have sent you a kiss by, I had som discourse with him about Dawson & Loades. I cannot unhinge the maine to heele of the bargaine for the inconstancy of menn, who att this rate I have just reason to feare will bee very troublesom, however discourse the thing fairely with Mr Bulwer, for I shall nott bee such a foole as upon every whedle to throwe my self into more difficultyes. As to their papers, I have nott yett time to read them over, what's just and favorable they need nott doubt mee in butt I have soe much business now on my hands as till I see how thinges workes I can doe nothing els. I am sending to Lynn to Mr Host to Sir [*Christopher*] Calthorp to Sir Nevile Catlyne.

*[Incomplete and unsigned]*
*British Library: Add. MSS 28621, f. 39*

## [Lord Yarmouth] to unnamed

**1678/9, January 31**. Sir, his Majesty haveing thought fitt to dissolve the late parliament and to issue forth writts for new elections, tis expected that the writt for chuseing knights of the sheire in this county will be executed on Monday the tenth day of February next. I hope the electors in this county will make choyce of such persons as are of unquestionable loyallty, and that will be most serviceable to the King, the church, and the country. Now I finde the inclination of this country to be most for Sir Christopher Calthorpe and Sir Nevill Catelyn, which agrees with my judgment and shall have my concurrence, and I hope all my freinds will industriously joyne with me therein. Wherefore I desire you to use your utmost diligence in this juncture of affaires to promote their election for the service both of the King and people, whereby you will engage them and sir, your affectionate friend

*Unsigned copy*
*NRO: BL/Y/2/101*

# John Gough to Rebecca, Viscountess Yarmouth

**1678[/9], January 31, Oxnead**. Right honourable, you must needs thinke that it is a very busy time with *us*; my lord is almost wearied with writing & has enjoyned mee to give your honour an account how squares go here, wherein your honour must pardon mee if I be as breif as well I can seeing this is the fourteenth letter I have writ this day, and my hand is almost weary. On Tuesday from Norwich Sir Nevill Catline was sent for with speed to come to my lord & on Wednesday came hither with Captain Cook, that same morning had my lord dispatched a letter to Sir Christopher Calthorpe to desire his comeing to Oxnead but the messenger not finding him at home & delaying his return put us a little behind hand. Sir Nevill resolves to stand & there is not much doubt but Sir Christopher will do the like who was yesterday sent after into Suffolk & desired to meet the gentlemen of the country at Norwich tomorrow. This morning his lordship has been sending messengers with letters to the militia officers to desire there concurrence with him in the election of the above named persons, I hope the successe will answer our expectations. Sir J Hobart resolves to stand and has sent a letter to his setter[1048] Mr Hirne to acquaint the people with so much. Mr Windham labours for him tooth & naile & has been with severall persons to engage them. They have done so much as to set the fanatick party already a bawling and yesterday at Northwalsham the cry for Hobart was very rife. His agents are very diligent to do all they can for him & no doubt will make some kind of bustle but I do not apprehend much from all they can do with all imaginable tricks & for my own part do not question the election of the partyes my lord thinks of; though in the mean while I hope they will not find us a sleep or secure. The Norwich businesse I think will be safe enough though what is talk't of should really happen, that two of the ejected aldermen should make an opposition. I humbly thank your honour for remembring my affair, which my lord has not as yet had leisure particularly to inform mee of, but only in generall has told mee so much as obliges mee to a gratefull return. I beg my most humble duty & service to the colonel whom I hope shortly to see. I am, right honourable,

*Signed*: your honour's most dutifull chap[lain] & obedient servant, John Gough
*Addressed*: These to the right honourable the Lady Viscountess Yarmouth in Suffolk Street in London humbly present
*NRO: BL/Y/2/102*

# John Doughty to Colonel William Paston

**1678/9, January 31, Oxnead**. Honored sir, in my last I told your honour I thought itt very convenient you should bee att the county election, which now is (I thinke) really necessary, and that you wou'd please to order your buisines soe, as to lay att Thetford on Friday night & to gett out early next morne, soe as to dyne att the clubb att Norwich on Saturday. My lord's coach will attend you att Wyndham, together with the horses, & such things as are necessary for rideing into the citty, itt being absolutely necessary to appeare as great as can bee, both for the incouragement of

---

[1048] i.e. one who places a combatant in position, a term used in cockfighting

freinds & discountenance of opposers, who now are upon their last leggs, & if baffled (which there's all that can possible bee done to effect) will never bee able to appeare above board againe, which they are very sensible of, therefore are extraordinary diligent. Sir, your appearing will seeme in effect my lord's, & all persons of sence will take care how they steere in respect both of the present circumstances of interest from my lord & for the future in you, which all cautious men will have an eye to, & therefore your presence must bee extreamely usefull & considerable in this junctoe [*sic*] both for the effect which <*word deleted*> is desired, as alsoe for the acquainting your selfe with the country gentlemen. [*f.*2] Here's all arts & industry used by the Sir Johns[1049] that is possible, & therefore must bee countermined by all indeavours. As to your owne election, I make noe doubt off, butt the moles are att worke & if things should nott goe well for the county, I feare you would find them putting *upp* amongst the stones in the citty, though nott to effect, yett to a disturbance, which may cause you both trouble & expence. I can say noe [*more*] butt that I doe intend to waite upon you att Wyndham, to pay that respect which I am ingaged too & most heartily am, sir,

*Signed*: your most faithfull servant, Jo. Doughty
*Postscript*: Itt is thought your appearance will bee properer then my lord's (that is publikely) yett if his lordship's health will permitt, I find my lord's inclynations are to itt.
*Addressed*: For the honourable Colonell Paston
*NRO: BL/Y/2/103*

## Robert, Viscount Yarmouth to un-named

**1678/9, February 4, Oxnead**. Sir, I understand that there is great interest makeing <*words deleted*> for setting upp of persons for knights of the shire without acquainting me therewith, which I thinke ought not to bee without my knowledge, bearing that office I doe under his Majestie in this county. Sir Christopher Calthorpe & Sir Neville Catelyn being persons of undoubted loyalty & worth, & haveing declared their intention to stand for this county, I have ingaged my interest to promote their election, which I question not will bee carried by great odds against those who have sett upp themselves without my concurrence, & shall vigorously oppose their designes to the disrepute (I doubt not) of such as shall appeare on their behalfes. You may acquaint any of your or my freinds (as you have opportunity) how ill I resent such proceedings, that I will have itt knowne what office itt is I beare. I am, sir,

*Signed*: your affectionate freind & servant, Yarmouth
*In John Doughty's hand but signed by Yarmouth*[1050]
*NRO: BL/Y/2/104*

---

[1049] Sir John Hobart and Sir John Holland
[1050] Copies of this letter were sent to (among others) John Hildeyard, Edward Britiff, and Henry Scarburgh of North Walsham. A copy was used by Sir John Hobart when he challenged the election of Calthorpe and Catelyn, and was considered proof that Lord Yarmouth had tried to coerce the voters. For a further copy *see* British Library: Add. MSS 36988, f.135.

# Sir Christopher Calthorpe to Robert, Viscount Yarmouth

**1678[/*9*], February 5**. My lord, since it was youre lordship's pleasure to think mee in a capacity of serving the countie in that publique & honourable imployment, now to bee supplied, I have in part jointly with Sir Nevile, in part by myselfe singly applied myselfe for his & my concerns against the day. My lord I found myselfe prevented[1051] by youre lordship in most places, & must ever acknowledge myselfe oblieged in the highest manner for the honour you have done mee, for though privacy was more suiteable to my inclinations & the whole past current of my life, since it is my fortune to have both habit & almost nature altered, I must acknowledge the way is honourable, & the service of my King, the church & country, added to your lordship's, is such an invitation for a change, as has the greatest influence possible on mee. I find every day such necessity of attending this affaire at home as I cannot possibly weight on your lordship this week, yet think it my duty, as to returne my thanks for all youre favoures, so to acquaint your lordship that I meet with such encouragement from my neighboures, & those gentlemen I have returnes from, as I begin to have some confidence I may bee able to serve Sir Nevile, if not obtaine for myselfe also the publique testimony of the country to comply with youre lordship's choise. I have inclosed a coppy of what I received from Sir John Holland this day in answere to Sir Nevile's & mine to him. Cosen Long's is to the same effect. From all the rest I have received anything of answer I find the same civilityes. But I will trouble youre lordship no further at this time then at the begging you will believe I am

*Signed:* your lordship's most obedient & faithfull servant, Chr: Calthorpe
*Postscript:* My lord I have taken care for Marshland men. I humbly desire the tender of my faithfull service to the collonell.
*Addressed:* These for the right honourable Robert *Lord* Viscount Yarmouth at Oxnead
*NRO: BL/Y/2/106*

# Robert, Viscount Yarmouth to Rebecca, Viscountess Yarmouth

**1678[/*9*], February 12**. My dearest deare, I hope just as I am writing to you, you are reading the short newse of our victory, though som hundreds of people that had given their votes for our friends came out of towne in dispaire, of which I presume you found Mr Gough's letter full of, soe great was the impudence of the rabble of the other party, nott countenanced by one gentleman in the country butt Wyndham, Rookwood, and Earle which is none, all the gentry were most unanimous and all the others' surprising tricks & falshoods failed them. Sir Christopher had 2243: Sir Neville 2242: and Sir John 1733 of which many were personns excommunicated, and som others that polled two or three times over as wee suspect. I shall to morrowe have a coppie of the poll from the shreeve; your son who behaved himself mighty well, wee thinke most sure on Monday, butt who will bee the other is yett uncertaine. The bottome of your letter seemed to promise som good hopes, pray God send effects, and comfort & support you under the damned malice of your wicked brother. Wee heare strange newse of Sir

[1051] i.e. forestalled, anticipated

Joseph Williamson beeing out of his place and my Lord of Sunderland in,[1052] I hope what I have written was to a secretary of state that will not make my letters a maygame.[1053] There's noe prospect that gives mee any encouragement yett att Thetford for Robin, itt's soe blocked up with many pretenders, and Robin shall nott venture on weake hopes, that has such strong ones for the widdowe in which I love his confidence, which is a good forerunner of sucess. There's soe many have given you the relation of Monday's adventure that I shall onely say that though Worcester & rebellion rang about the hill, and som little slight rudenesses passed (as will att all those times), yett I beleeve there were as few or fewer as will happen in any other place.

[f.2] Your sonns brought home Thom the last night with them and my son goos to Norwich nott till Friday or Saterday, as shall bee most expedient; his friends are very kind to him. Sir Christopher Calthorpe is just now gon from hence and presents his most humble service & thankes to you, soe doth Sir Neville. I eat well & sleep pretty well butt these vapors doe soe afflect mee that if I had nott a little beene used to them, I should still have my old feares. I hope this spring and the weather comming on to bee better will bee a meanes to perfect my recovery, some seasonable favors to my family would be a powrefull cordiall. Pray present my duty to your mother, and my humble serice to my daughter Paston; Charles, Betty and Thom present their dutys to you. Mr Ost is mighty kind and has promised to goe right, soe has Captaine Turner of Lynn & to make Franke Taylor goe soe too having an hanke[1054] upon him. I am glad Sir Robert Howard tooke any civility kindly from mee, I have nott had one syllable from Mr Fisher this forthgnight, som blewness in time of elections. I have noe more to say att the present butt leave you to the variety of other letters, and from the bottome of my hart pray for your fillicity & that God Almighty will in his mercy vouchsafe us a joyfull & speedy meeting, for with my sowle I am yours,

*Signed:* Yarmouth
*NRO: BL/Y/2/107*

## John Doughty to Rebecca, Viscountess Yarmouth

**1678/9, February.**[1055] Madam, to make good what the tyme would not permit mee the last <tyme> post <in> relateing to the county election I shall now give your honour the trouble of a full relation.

On Monday after Sir Nevill Catelyn & Sir Christopher Calthorpe had brought in the freeholders that came with them being about 1000 a peece, with Colonel Paston's freinds which hee brought into Norwich about the number of 700, betweene ten & eleven a clock, the knights tooke their chaires on the Castle Hill, & noe body appeared against them till after eleven nere halfe an hour, & just as the sheriffe was about to declare them elected (which if hee had done there could not have been any further dispute or question the tyme limitte by the law being past) Mr Herne comes upp the hill as itt seemes itt was agreed off long before that the freeholders that were for Sir John Hobart should take him upp for Sir John, & accordingly they did, &

---

[1052] Williamson was replaced as secretary of state by the earl of Sunderland on 20 February 1679.
[1053] i.e. a laughing stock
[1054] i.e. a power of check or restraint
[1055] There is a hole in the paper at this point.

upon itt they went to the poll presently which Sir Christopher's & Sir Nevill's clarkes being nimble *att*, & makeing what dispatch they could possibly, had almost finished the poll before five a clock, & Sir John Hobart's clarkes fearing they should not hold out soe long as the other, writeing slowly did not end <finish> their polls till almost seven a clock, & by that meanes most people concluded Sir John Hobart had carried the day, till the bookes were cast upp & the difference then appeared beyond all expectation. Never did man act soe like a mountebanke in the world as Herne did on the chaire insomuch as hee has by a generall vogue outdone all the Merry Andrews that ever were seene att Bartholomew Faire & now goes by that name. There <not> *was* not scarce the face of gentleman *appeared* for Hobart, except Mr Wyndham, Mr Ralph Earle, Capt Rookewood, & Mr Spelman, that were active, butt these were very violent <Sir Roger Potts &> (Sir James Johnson brought a great [f.2] number from Yarmouth), Sir Robert Yallopp[1056] voted butt went noe further & there [were][1057] very few other of any note.

That which ma[de the] opposition any thing dangerous, was the letters that were sen[t from] Sir John Holland to my lord, Sir Nevill & Sir Christopher, (the[copi]es whereof my lord sent your ladyshipp upp) by which itt was given [ou]t that noe opposition would bee, & soe that the badnes of the weather (itt being knee deep with snow & very great drifts) with this report above 500 that would have come for Sir Christopher & Sir Nevill stayed att home, & this was endeavoured by their party to bee as much spread abroad as was possible all Weddensday, Thursday, & Fryday, both by letters from Sir John Hobart *aswell as* his adherents, butt on Saturday afternoone private posts were dispatched away to Yarmouth (from whence there came nere 400 for Hobart) & other places to make out their party & by the security wee were in, of noe opposition, to trick us out of the election. This was not knowne to our party till almost noone on Sunday & then butt to a few, butt (thankes bee to God) the election is well over & much for my lord's honour, who has been very vigilant & industrious in carryeing itt on, & soe has the colonel for the tyme hee was here before the choice, & att itt, being one of the gentlemen that stood severall houres att Sir John's poll to see things should bee carried faire. The fanaticks in Norwich now threaten strongly to make opposition on Monday, butt that will bee to lesse purpose then that of the county. Tis thought Mr Wyndham will ride for itt, I wish hee would, because (I am sure) he'le be sufficiently baffled.

As for Thetford, Mr Harbord is thought absolutely sure & soe is Sir Joseph Williamson, butt yett Major De Grey will putt for itt, & venture his fortune, though as hee told Mr Robert Paston hee thinks hee shall loose itt.[1058] Sir Thomas Garrett promised Mr Robert his interest butt (I feare) tis to noe purpose to endeavour att itt, for the other interests are very close fixt, Mr Cory will doe his utmost, if tis thought convenient to stirr in itt, & the report here yesterday of Sir Joseph Williamson's being removed from being secretary, & that my Lord Sunderland was in his place, makes the resolution concerning this matter stand still, till your ladyshipp's letters come tomorrow eyther of confirmation or advice.

---

[1056] Sir Robert Yallopp (1637–1705) of Bowthorpe.        [1057] A small piece is torn out of this page.

[1058] William Harbord and Sir Joseph Williamson were elected; De Grey and Paston did not stand. De Grey was elected for Thetford in 1685.

I most humbly thanke your ladyshipp for your most obligeing letter, & shall ever to the utmost of my power make itt my endeavour *to contribute* all the satisfaction & honour I can possible to my lord, & your honour's noble family, in approveing my selfe,

*Signed:* your honour's most faithfull servant, Jo. Doughty
*Addressed:* These for the right honourable the Lady Viscountesse Yarmouth
*NRO: BL/Y/2/108*

## John Hildeyard to Rebecca, Viscountess Yarmouth

**1678[/9], February 17, Norwich**. May it please your honor, the last Monday's successe, after such stratagemes and artifices to prevent us, gave us a faire promise of our successe on this *day*, and though last night the sheriffes of this city weer allarmed with a note to erect a fourth booth for Sir John Hobart after nine of the clock yet that by a full expresse was contradicted before eleven, and the collonell's interest was soe fixt (and in this city ever will bee soe), that he that was appoynted to poll at the third booth, I meane one Councellour Norris, after two houres tryall of his interest gave it over and in issue numbered 313, Alderman Brigges whose interest was happly twistred [*sic*] with the collonell's brought to his poll 1589, but our darling collonell, who might have carryed whom he pleased along with him reacht in his number to 1900. I did never find that all their trickes prevayled to the collonell's disadvantage farther then to keep some two or three hundred foreigners[1059] which weer for him the last time from appearing; which they weer the more inclined to doe because the weather was bad and their journey long, otherwise he had run thorough all their obstacles and arrived at equall number to that which reported him burgesse to this city the last yeare. Madam, you see by these two elections my deare lord's interest notwithstanding all their craft that oppose increases rather then diminishes and soe it must needs doe while with such zeale he promotes the King's and the Church her interest, whosoever joynes bothe together as his lordship doth taketh right measures to be secure of God's blessing, the King's favour, the love and affections of all good men. It is not credible the phanatickes should ever heerafter find so bold an hero as should dare to head them *in this country* their beeing thus often thus notoriously baffled will surely make them modest, and their abettors ashamed. God in mercy blesse the King, and strengthen the hands of his friends in all other countyes of this nation as well as this that wee *may* see a loyall affectionate and religious parliament that may heale our breaches and maintaine our King in all the rights of his prerogative without which his sacred Majesty can not be safe nor his subjects happy. I know this comes supernumerary to better pens yet because I was willing to shew my ambition to be numbred among the friends of my lord & your honor I presumed to thrust myselfe forward in the crowd, and with all duty to subscribe,

*Signed:* your honor's most obedient & affectionate, Jo Hildeyerd
*Addressed:* This to the right honourable the Lady Viscountesse Yarmouth at her lodgings in Suffolk Street near Charing Crosse with all duty & service humbly present
*NRO: BL/Y/2/109*

[1059] Probably freemen who lived out of town

## Robert, Viscount Yarmouth to Rebecca, Viscountess Yarmouth

**1678[/*9*], February 19**. My dear hart, I onely now borrowe time to write a word having twenty or thirty gentlemen that coms to take their leaves of your son, heere is the Duke of Yorkes officers and Sir Harrie Littleton's brother,[1060] who commands the regiment now quartered in Norwich. You have had soe perticular an accompt of the honor don to your son att Norwich that Ile say noe more of itt, you'l have the relation from himself on Saterday night for hee and Robin goe from hence to morrowe, wee are att the present parting with five fidlers and a great company of our friends. Robin is eager after the widdowe, and hopes strongly to prevaile. Charles told Nurs Port that amongst all her nursery of his grand papa's children, his uncle Robin was the best. The little rouge is now walking on the table butt will nott goe to London. I am very sorie you have gotten a cold butt I hope to morrowe to heare you have *beene* abroad and that your business goes *20 [well]*: you have sayd nothing of that of Mrs N[*ell*] G[*wynn*]: I beleeve itt com to nothing, pray God graunt *95* bee reallie as itt's represented, after to morrowe I shall have leisure to write you longer letters, for till I have the happiness to see you, there's nothing in the world *soe* pleasing to mee as to write to you. I thinke I shall write a letter to my Lord Treasurer by my son to morrowe, which you shall see before itt's delivered. My duty to your mother, my service to my daughter, your sonns remember their dutys to you, soe doth Bettie and Charles, and all heere,

*Signed*: and I with all my sowle am yours, Yarmouth
*Addressed*: For the right honorable the Lady Viscountess Yarmouth att her howse in Suffolke Street, London [*franked Yarmouth*]
*NRO: BL/Y/2/110*

## Robert, Viscount Yarmouth to Rebecca, Viscountess Yarmouth

**1678[/*9*], February 21**. My dearest hart, I doe receive your consolation for your feares of my son's loosing his election the better because I know before this time you understand you were more affraide then hurt, and I thinke England cannott shew the licke circumstances twice together in one place. I wish all countys were licke ours; which I feare they will nott bee, I am sure those I heare of are nott. I am willing to hope the delay of your of your [*sic*] business of *95* is onely the ordinary course of delay and want of dispatch, and not the influences of *37* [*Sir John Clayton*] who I am glad is going to live twelve miles of the towne; I care nott if itt were 12,000 for a wors man to mee never lived. My son comes up with a vigorous intention to sollicitt the affaire of *95* out of which hee builds the hopes of his fortune, pray God itt may answer his expectation, and that wee may nott find som obstacles nott forseene. They both went from hence yesterday morning, and I hope are well with you before this coms to your hands. I presume though Verdon could not com soe soone as you hoped for, hee has seene you before now. I am glad these elections are soe well over, they are the most troublesom thinges in nature and the most vexatious though a man getts the better as I have don in all points, I thanke God. You are much beholding to my Lady

[1060] Sir Charles Littleton (c.1629–1716)

Lindsey if shee setts all right and then *37* [*Sir John Clayton*] will see the ends of his labor in that place. I received my daughter's letter, butt Major Ward beeing heere before itt was resolved thatt I should send over Rawlins with the £5, and that one of the major's sisters should stand, Betty's close[1061] nott beeing fitt to goe abroad in, my Lord Bishop has one stands for him, and the other godfather is Sir William Adams. I have written to your mother, as you desired mee, and I am glad that Don continews his old friendship, which is a well established one. I suppose by this time, my cousin Peregrine Bertie and my cousin Charles are returned from Stamford where I am sorry to heare thinges goes soe cross.[1062] I have told my son that even in the few dayes before the parlament if our business bee nott advanced ten thousand delayes will then protract itt, therefore the push must bee made home, nott to stay on [f.2] long dependances, which is wors then a speedy deniall. My son is a very solid young blade and understands matters with a quick intelligence, butt I hope I may heare to morrowe, that the reference to Sir Charles Harbord is gotten, unless Mr Brent (who is nott to bee offended) for severall reasons, should thinke that any other attendant on that affaire is a diminution of his province.

I thought the business of Sir Robert Howard had beene dead because, till the last, in som letters before you had sayd nothing of itt. Pray speake well of Sir John Holland for hee is very civill to us. How Yarmouth election went yesterday Mr Doughty from thence will write you word. I should bee very well I hope, if I could see thinges goe well, for the doctor despises those vapors which are troublesom to mee, butt now I doe intend to gett into the ayre in a day or too; I eate and sleepe well enough, and every body says I looke well, and I hope God Almighty will free mee from these which change their shapes soe often, and are soe very troublesom somtimes to mee. I have worne my sute you sent mee downe, and licke itt mighty well, itt's prittily fancied according to your good genious, the coate is a little too bigg in the wast, the breches very easy, and the sute very commode.[1063] Pray present my service to my daughter, Ile write to her by the next post, remember mee kindly to my son, who has promised mee now & then to goe to a window and write to mee. Honest Charles who is a man of noe dissimulation, when I told him the colonel was gon, sayd and I am glad hees gon without mee. Robin has great hopes of the widdowe, I told him I would write to you about him, and as our business toke effect wee would bee very kind to him, you knowe better how to say to him then I doe, butt hee is a nimble youth & diserves encouragement, which cannott bee beyound our owne possibilityes. I wish sombody would enquire of Sir Thomas Higgon, for I feare the letters wee sent to Venice are miscarried becuse wee heare nothing of them. Betty presents her duty, I wish you would give Mrs Cooper a line from your owne hand to tell her how infinitely I am sensible of the diligent [f.3] care shee has of mee. I am glad to heare *31* is merry, I wish thinges may goe right for all the hopes the phaniaticks give themselves, which reallie when they com to bee seene in a plaine view are butt a few in comparison of those which are better disposed, if nott thorough paced. Sir William Rant cam in to see my son just as hee was gon who has lost a friend att Blickling and

[1061] i.e. clothes
[1062] The Berties failed to be elected and were not successful until 1685 (Henning, *Commons*, I, p.306).
[1063] i.e. suitable

att Felbrigg for this bout of the election. I thinke it would nott bee amiss for my son to goe make a visitt to the Duke of Norfolke before he goes away, to know how wee may serve him heere in his absence. I should be glad if *17 18 19* [*affair*] would produce anything the next tearme butt then, I doe suppose midsommer tearme will bee sayd to bee the properest time. I confess I cannott bee in love with histories without effects; I am old and, [*sic*] and menn's lives are nott long enough to embarke in affaires whose course is soe tedious, and perhapps frivolous. I wish itt may proove otherwise, for I pray to God every day to crowne your industry with such success as may makes us experience the continuation of his miraculous preservations in many brinkes of approaching ruine & contempt. I have nothing more now to say

*Signed*: butt with my hart & sowle I am yours, Yarmouth
*Postscript*: Sir Neville Catline, Mr Haughton and Alderman Briggs now with mee with som others present their service to you.
*NRO: BL/Y/2/111*

# Robert, Viscount Yarmouth to Rebecca, Viscountess Yarmouth

**1678[/*9*], February 24**. My deare sowle, my letter to your deare son which you will see cutts of[*f*] much of my business to you. I am glad to find you cheereful. The best newse from hence, after what you have had of the elections, is that I mend very much, though I have my spleenetick vapors, which I hope I shall overcom, I sleep & eat pritty well, and people that observes my countinance, thinkes better of mee then I doe of myselfe. My Lord Treasurer putting on the backside[1064] our petition, that itt was given him by the King's owne hand, was I suppose intended as a marke of favor, pray God itt may answer the tenth part of my sonn's expectations either in valew, or in any time to doe us good. I have inclosed Mr Fisher's letter, that part of itt which concernes the matter and nature of the petition with his owne comment upon't, which is a divelish cold pye and I beleive hee speakes as hee thinks. I am sure som effects of the Kinges kindness would cure mee butt the dispensations[1065] I live under, I cannott overcom the trouble of. Coventry & Huntington are chosen att Yarmouth, Sir Joseph & Harbord will bee for Thetford this day as itt's more then presumed. Alderman Briggs dined heere the other day, who is extraordinary civill to mee and has shewne itt to your son, who might have without doubt have [*sic*] carried itt for any other if he had butt proposed itt, for never any man was more a darling of the citty, and som are pleased to say soe of the country too. I am very glad to heare you fancy the King has an eye on the Presbitereans, for I doubt this parlament by the choise wee heare of [*f.2*] in other places, will consist of those from whome the King can expect noe great matters. I long to heare what was concluded of the letter I gave your son for my Lord Treasurer if you approoved itt, for I thought I calculated itt without any low or dispairing stile and sayd enough to touch *37* [*Sir John Clayton*] *87* [*you*] in the right straine. I hope his Majesty will doe my family som right in his long deferred promise[1066] and I could wish my daughter Paston were

---

[1064] i.e. endorsing          [1065] i.e. expenditure, disbursements
[1066] Probably his promise to make Lord Yarmouth an earl, see p.385 below

made sensible of her owne interest even to demand itt of the King, for that which he forgetts to others, itt's hard hee should prolong att soe tedious a rate to those soe neare him. I hinted these thinges to my son, butt I thinke hee did nott much apprehend itt. I shall bee most glad to see you, butt you best [*know*] our circomstances, and doe allso know you are the hinge our affaires hangs upon. I doubt nott butt I may bee able to come up in Easter tearme if thinges should proove effectuall towards my well beeing there, otherwise the whirlepoole of misadventures will hurt me wors there then att home butt if you write mee word you'l undertake for the keeping of itt, Ile lay you £1,000 I gett you with child att our next meeting. Sir Phillip Woodhowse and his lady have sent this day their chaplaine to see how I doe, Major Doughty & Mr Bulwer ly now both very ill, one of an ague, Mr Bulwer of a cold. I hope tomorrowes letters will bring mee mee [*sic*] word your son was with you before the pacquett was sealed. Charles & Betty present their dutys, mine to your mother, I send you blue Fisher's letter to peruse and mine to him which pray lett bee delivered, lett mee have a list of the parlament men as soone as itt coms out.

God keep you & comfort & prosper you. I am yours and very well att the writing heereof I thanke God

*Signed*: Yarmouth

*Postscript*: Remember mee kindly to Robin. All presents their dutys: I hope you'l not forgett to write to Mrs Cooper

*NRO: BL/Y/2/112*

## Eustace Burneby[1067] to Rebecca, Viscountess Yarmouth

**1678[/9], February 26**. Madam, I received your honour's this morning and the latter parte made me amends for the former 1000 fold and indeed it hath been my interior thoughts this three monthes, which I pray with all my soule may come to passe which will give all occasion of true rejoycing, and certainely my beleife is the same as your ladyship's, which is that so good a martyr[1068] for his country at last can never bring forth other then good to his posterity, and surely at last it will be believed that he[1069] is not damned because he was not within the pale of the Romayne. These clouds I hope will be dispersed, and this I dare saye with an humble confidence that at present there is no other waye then the true way, which is his highnesses truely going to church as it is now settled by goverment and to publish himselfe to be of the same religion which his father was of, from which nothing could divert him even death it selfe, but I am to full when I thinke out, and certainely it is the purest & most refined, without swerving either to the right or the left. I pray heartily to God to open his eyes and that it may come to passe according to your ladyship's hopes & my

---

[1067] Eustace Burneby, paper maker and inventor (*The Newes*, 52, 6 July 1665, p.4; *CSPD, 1673–5*, Dec 1674; *A History of the County of Middlesex: Volume 2* (1911), pp 195–197). William Paston had obbtained a patent for the printing of briefs, writs, etc., in 1678 and this may have brought him into contact with Burneby. It is likely that the Pastons were petitioning for a further patent for the making of paper by a company in which the duke of York, who had wide business interests, would have been involved; nothing further is heard of this but the new Whig administration would have been averse to granting anything which might benefit the duke, let alone the Pastons.

[1068] i.e. Charles I                                                    [1069] i.e. the duke of York

beleife and *now* to our buisnes: as to the paper no dispute but it will goe *on* for if any of this last should faile I have others will doe it, though as yet I see no reason to doubt but confidence of agreement, as to the other it will certainly be a greate thing after if the news holds, and will certainly doe the Duke more good next to his change, then any one thing that I can foresee, & establish him in the thoughts & well wishes of the people, which will make his countenance [*f.*2] at once be both beloved & feared, and I dare undertake to bring good substantiall citizens there in for £50,000 stock & the one halfe to give to the pattentee & partners as first undertakers, & yet reserve the Duke's share and enough for us, and therefore a little patience madam was a good word spocke to me by the Duke & in good season, and that very word proceeded reiterated to answer a modest bold word I then spoke which I will tell your ladyship by word of mouth whenever I have the honor to see your ladyship.

Now madam as to the *petit concerne*, I am satisfied of your ladyship's concerns as well as my owne which must suddenly alter & therefore will not inlarge, saving to beg my pardon, and shall onely send a person tomorrow morning aboute eleven a clock to your ladyship with a noate from my selfe to desire your ladyship to pay £30 at the 25 March next, which I pray onely your ladyship to favor me to promise the payment & I doubt not but to serve your ladyship before that tyme in greater matters. I did adventure to promise yesterday so to doe, and in one word your ladyship shall no waye suffer by it upon my word, not else but with a thousand well wishes to your ladyship & most humble thankes for the good news. I begg leave to remayne allwayes in quality of, madam,

*Signed*: your honour's most humble & obedient servant, Eustace Burneby
*Addressed*: These for the right honourable the Lady Yarmouth
*NRO: BL/Y/2/113*

## Robert, Viscount Yarmouth to Rebecca, Viscountess Yarmouth

**1678[/9], February 26**. My deare hart, I am very glad to find by yours that my sons came safe to you on Saterday night, and I am allsoe glad to heare you say that all your *19* [*affair*] is *20* [*well*], which God graunt som speedie evidence of that is effectuall. I am very glad to heare my Lord Cheif Baron coms this circute for my triall with Yarmouth[1070] is to bee att Bury assizes. Now they mooved strongly by Baldock the last tearme to have had a tryall att the barr, which the court denied them upon the assertions of my cownsell that *there* had beene a tryall there before and that the sute had beene vexatiously menaged by the towne against mee, soe itt's to be tried in the country unless the judge of the assizes shall upon any new matter of evidence allow a tryall att the barr, which wee must endeavor to prevent that wee may have a determination now, in which I desire noe favor from the judge butt as the meritts of the cawse shall guide him to, and the saving mee £200 charges. I suppose Mr Warkhowse may have beene with you, or els you may sent to him att Lincolnes In[*n*] to com to you for I doe assure you if I carrie this tryall I shall have itt in my power to be quitts with the Yarmouth favors. Wee all heere have the newse of the Duke's

---

[1070] The trial was over the mooring posts but produced no conclusive results (Gauci, *Great Yarmouth*, p.147).

intentions to goe to the church, which every body will bee very glad to heare confirmed, as I should bee what you say of *3–4*: I long to heare whether you thought itt fitt my letter should bee presented or noe. Heere is now with mee Sir William Adams who lay heere the last night and presents his service to you. I am sorry to heare of such elections as wee doe, therefore I would faine know how the whole list goes, I have nothing of the least newse to write to you this time, Charles and Betty present their dutys to you, and I desire you will present mine to your mother [*f.*2] and to my son and daughter Paston and to little Charlotte. Remember mee to Robin.

All heere present their dutys and service to you butt wee have a sickly family, agues running up & downe generally, pray God preserve you & send us a comfortable & speedy meeting is the prayers of

*Signed*: my deare hart, yours Yarmouth

*Postscript*: I hope *15* pusheth on our affaire before the sitting of the parlament for then little business will bee don, I should bee glad to heare Mr Fisher's <business> objections answered. I heare Dr Ridgely has left London and *is* gon into Yorkshire, pray send mee word how *37* [*Sir John Clayton*] steeres his course. I love you with all my sowle and take my cheif pleasure in reading your letters.

*Addressed:* These for the right honorable the Lady Viscountess Yarmouth att her howse in Suffolke Street, London [*franked Yarmouth*]

*Endorsed*: Letter office February 28 78 at twelve a clock at noone, ES

*NRO: BL/Y/2/114*

## Robert, Viscount Yarmouth to Rebecca, Viscountess Yarmouth

**1678[/*9*], February 28**. My deare sowle, I thanke you for the kindness of your letters which are allwayes most acceptable to mee. I am sorry to find that som of *17 19 95* are nott good for by the same rule the rest may proove soe too, since that search which was firmely insisted upon was made for all, and att the best will render the thing nott soe valewable as my son thought, and pray God itt bee nott inconsiderable. I am glad to heare you say that other *19* [*affair*] are *48*: God putt some good period to them. As for the noyse of the election, & mine & the bishop's letters, trouble nott your head, wee have defeated a strong contrivance against the right interest, and could their harts bee looked into they are ashamed & confounded att itt, and thinke to extenuate their repuls by this way of a pretence upon noe manner of foundation, neither doe I yett beleeve they will petition, for unless itt bee a parlament that is resolved to turne all right out of dores, they will see such apparent evidence as will give the petitioners shame enough. This they knowe as well as wee and therefore unless the devill posseseth them, they will never throwe away money in vaine, and for my letters I care nott if they were on the parlament howse dore, and for Sir [*John*] Hobart there is noe place for him now in Norfolke, for if hee were to stand againe, hee will find us better provided for him, and for Lynn, the mayor is rivited fast enough and their are twenty more would carry itt before him if there were a vacancy, for my Lord Townshend's influence prevailes nott in that place att all. I am glad to heare what you sayd of *3–4 51 12: 1*. I wish it may succeed since you did nott thinke itt fitt that *86* [*my*] letter should be delivered, I hope *15* has made my returne of compliment att least by word of mouth. [*f.*2] You write mee word of *37* [*Sir John Clayton's*] remoovall, I wish you could tell mee hee were gon, for hee is a most pestilent beast. For what you press of Dawson & Loades, itt's a business of soe great concerne to mee as I will nott precipitate my self into itt, I give them all the conveniencys and they when they have gotten the thing upon that very inducement play child's play with mee, soe I must bee lyable to every thing by consequence they will demand or els bee threatned with their throwing up the care of what they have for their owne advantage undertaken. I have made Doughty write a letter to them, which you may either deliver or nott as you shall see cawse.

Honest Sir Will Adams has stayed with mee since Tuesday, he presents his humble service to you. I find the courtiers, Sir John Pettus and his lady, begin to find that London preferments worke soe slow, everie man of parts & lady of beauty nott meeting with advancements sutable to their meritts, soe they are, or att least the lady, first comming to Rackey,[1071] and the widdowe Allington[1072] to bord with them, till Sir Will Adams getts her to Sprowston for good and all which I believe hee has faire hopes of as allsoe for her daughter for his son. Charles was soe fond of his letter that hee would nott lett itt be opened a great while, he presents his duty to you and Betty allsoe. Yesterday I sent them with Mrs Coopers and Hunts to Mr Barspooles[1073] to dinner where they were mightily entertained, and Charles very freely opened his apron to my discretion, though full of very good sweetmeats, itt's a most sweet boy growne & soe strong and healthfull as can bee. As for what you write me word concerning Barney[1074] I thought itt too inconsiderable to write to you, itt's a thing nott ripe for any hope, beside you may bee sure one of that name will marrie for money; if hee coms heere hee shall bee welcom butt if invited, itt's wors, lett God's good [*f.*3] providence take itts effect without any dequoys. However the goodwill of friends I doe much esteeme and cherish.

Pray present my duty to your mother, and tell her I pray for her health, my humble service to my daughter Paston, and to your deare son Billie. Remember mee to Robin, thanke him for his letter, I wish hee may find the widdowe when itt coms to the matter, what I feare hee will nott gett, I know no cawse of dispaire in the thing, pray bee nott pumped by my Lady Baker nor Mrs Chamberlaine[1075] say nothing to them for them to tell againe to my Lady Hobarte, I am very glad that *12* continues your friend I knowe noe reason to the contrary, the great lady you told mee you intended a visitt to I never heard you performed itt. As to what you write to mee of an howse, I doe nott flatter myself with soe much happiness, as to [*be*] able to live in any howse without dunns. For my health I find my self exelent well, this wind & vapor is somtimes very troublesom somtimes nott att all, the rest of my body in very good plight; att the present I have a small remembrance in my foot of the gout which

---

[1071] i.e. Rackheath near Norwich

[1072] Jane, widow of William Alington of Bury, was a half-sister of Mary, Lady Pettus, *see* Margaret Toynbee, 'Some Friends of Sir Thomas Browne' (*Norfolk Archaeology*, XXXI (1957), pp 377–394); Adams married her as his second wife on 25 August 1679.

[1073] Possibly Miles Barspoole who received a commission in Paston's regiment in 1682 (British Library, Add. MSS 27448, f.98), who may have been the same person as Miles Baispoole of Aylsham (NRO: NEV/1/113–125).     [1074] See also p.239, where a match with Mary Paston seems to be discussed.

[1075] Presumably Elizabeth Chamberlaine, mother of William Windham of Felbrigg

amounts nott to paine, and if I may beleeve the doctor hee thinkes my condition good and indeed has a great care to keep itt soe, hee laughs att the wind and sayes that the spring & the ayre will chase them away quite. God keep you, and send us speedily together, is the prayers of

*Signed*: yours, Yarmouth
*NRO: BL/Y/2/115*

## J.H.[1076] to Sir James [Johnson]

**1679 March**. Sir James, I am glad you are soe well pleased at a preparation for a second combate. I wish I had had the courage to have under tooke the first but now I can not face the enemy in the open field yet I have hopes of a faire enconter in a well *chosen* place, equall judges, and no alowance of imbuscadoes and I question not but your towne can furnish good gunners to hitt the marke, which with your helpe, as my cheife engeneer, and the store of amunition I shall provide, I make no doubt, if you and your friends can furnish my quiver with well headed arrows but I shall shoote the enemy wiht [sic] good advantage, and if the starrs favor me beate them from theyr posts, and lodge in theyr trenches, to the satisfaction of all my good friends in your towne, who appeared in the field for me, unto whome I shall endeavor to express all possible gratitude.

*Signed*: Sir, I am yours, J:H:
*NRO: BL/Y/2/116*

## Robert, Viscount Yarmouth to Rebecca, Viscountess Yarmouth

**1678/9, March 24**. My deare hart, wee have scanned Sir John Hobartes petition which must needes take fire in a Howse of Commons as itt's suggested, butt when the notirious [sic] falshoods coms to appeare in every perticular, thoug[h] I know faction has noe bound yett perhapps there may bee noe need of another election. Heere are a great many gentlemen resolved to bee att the hearing of itt and to bee very bold in their testimonyes. My letter, which Mr Britiff[1077] has I doe nott doubt putt into their hands, I send you up heere the coppie of, taken in peeces and answered by Mr Doughty, to bee sheewne to counsell now though the time may bee comming about wherein lord leiftenants are less to bee made of then cheif constables, yett I cannott thinke that my saying after Sir John Hobart had declared hee would nott stand, that I [thought] that none would or ought without making mee acquainted, can butt att the worst bee butt a civility that I was mistaken in when I thought itt due, and this onely in a private letter communicated to one whose father to his dying day owned his rise from this family to whome hee was a meniall servant, and this unworthy fellowe to produce a private letter, as a malitious evidence against mee. Lett them

---

[1076] This letter, supposed to be from Sir John Hobart, appeared as an election broadside with a few minor differences (NRO: WKC 7/6).

[1077] Identified as Edward Britiff in Sir John Hobart's list of witnesses, 1679 (NRO: WKC 7/6); the letter (see p.370 above and Add. MSS 27447, ff 399–401) was sent to a number of freeholders and was construed as a threat.

proove any menace and Ile give up the cawse; that of Hurton is the falsest lye that could have beene suggested, butt hee will bee att the hearing himself & soe will Mr Negus who is a person will speake boldly and well, soe will Mr Ward of Brooke, Captaine Haughton; wee heare Sir Jacob Astley will stay in towne and Sir Will Adams if nott in towne will bee found att his house in Essex where hee may bee sent to. I hope the gentry will have this inspired into them who know the justice of the cawse to bee unanimous [f.2] *and nott bee* foiled heere if <itt> they bee soe in the Howse and therefore in the interim they must unite, in which wee [be] nott unactive and desire my son to mend the [?]kn[igh]ts of itt there to whome pray present my service and this to them and lett them know that I am nott to bee discouraged by any malice from my zeale to my friends and if heat or hast has thrust in any one expression into a letter (they will confess with me) I doubt nott itt is a small fault to bee a ground for the vacating soe just pertentions [sic]. I shall onely once more assist them by all the influences I can cast butt their shall bee noe more Mr Britiffs nor any body els to shew my letters, thee letter allsoe that was written to the officers the coppy I enclose, and when you have these I have sayd all I can for my self.

I cannott beleeve my Lord Treasurer will fly, hee must bee tried by his peers att the last and if I bee one and others of my mind there should bee noe reason for soe hasty a journey, butt violent stormes and fury none can appease, and this must create violence againe.

For my journey on Monday <com sev> this day sevenight neither my health nor any circumstance can concurr itt; I am now on the brink of recoverie of a most desperate disease, as any man has waded through. I am just now taking the [word illegible] of the spring to prepare my self for <itt> the journey which I intend in Easter weeke or the week after and therefore I desire positively to knowe by Saterday night next, whether this may nott excuse my sending up wittnesses by the Monday coach att the time you expected my comming.

I knew when you spoke of Mr Secheverill[1078] what power my Lady Mary Henningham[1079] had with him butt mee thinkes Mr Cheek[1080] for old friendship might represent mee att least to my Lord Russell as one that never disobliged him nor any of his family [f.3] and in that discourse hee may give such a character of Sir John Hobart, as I know hee thinkes of him.

I am extreamely pleased to heare you say Mr Seamour has promised you to bee a friend, pray endeavor to keep him soe, if my Lord Russell could bee butt abated, for conversion there's noe hopes of, itt would bee a great prop taken away.

There must bee som very impudent talking lawyer retained against the day, for I must expect to have all the dirt throwne in my face that the priviledge *of the* Howse can warrant, yett I hope when they consider my letter, itt will bee noe such bugbeare for if one man expects a civility that another will nott pay him, itt's noe treason to hint itt to a private friend nor noe menace for the incivility of the disappointment butt itt may well bee presumed that a man that has any interest of a lowse will creep

[1078] William Sacheverell (1638–1691), a leading member of the country party

[1079] Lady Mary Heveningham, widow of the regicide

[1080] Cheeke had married a cousin of William, Lord Russell, and her sister had married William Harbord, so he was now a supporter of the emerging Whig party.

to oppose one that uses him with neglect, if itt bee butt to demonstrate that hee is nott inconsiderable.

I hope I shall see to morrowe what the sent[*?ence*]s have printed, heere dines with mee to morrowe the high shreeve, and Captaine Haughton and som others, wee shall provide the best ten wee can. Mr Doughty is very active & very ingenious and shall bee there att the hearing. I doubt I must send him up on Monday next according as I heare the force of my summons from you, which I sent to Mr Fisher about too, butt that happens ill for then he can hardly bee at my Yarmouth triall in which wee have great hopes, I would have sayd confidence if I had nott beene under a melancholy dispensation.

I believe *31* will give good words, butt itt [*is*] *86* [*my*] fate to bee ever unfortunate, what I write to you is to my son to who I love next to you, pray God bring us together speedily wherever itt bee or however itt bee

*Signed*: I am from my sowle yours, Yarmouth

*Postscript*: [*f.4*] Pray read this letter to Sir Christopher Calthorp and Sir Neville Catelyn, for I writt in such hast I cannott read itt myself.

This day is for the chusing the clerke of the convocation att Norwich where I have sent Gough to inspire & animate the clergie for the second encounter as Mr Doughty will doe the atturneys who beare the greatest sway in the concernes of the common freeholders, Mr Warkhouse wee are sure will doe his endeavor.

You writt mee word you tooke your leave of my Lord Cheif Baron butt did nott say hee came our circute butt I take itt for granted hee doth, and intend to send Wooden to Thetford with a present of som fish.

Som good newse of surprise would bee very welcom to mee after all this cursed damnd cold pyes.

I[*f*] you could gett Mr Seymour instructed out of Mr Doughty's and what I have written hee may turne the scale, for his testimony and interest is prevalent in that place, and wee must gett one such if possably. Pray give my particular thankes to Sir Charles Harbord tell him I am beholding to him for his endeavors of keeping mee from hanging & starving; Charles & Betty's and everybody's duties, Mrs Cooper has an ague. Remember my duty to your mother & to my son Robert. God preserve you sowle and body.

*NRO: BL/Y/2/117*

## Robert, Viscount Yarmouth to Rebecca, Viscountess Yarmouth

**1678[/*9*], March 26**. My deare hart, the onely good newse I can tell you is that I dayly growe better and better, which I think is a miracle having such considerations as I have upon my spiritts. Heere dined yesterday the high shreeve of Norfolke who happens to bee my very neare kinsman,[1081] an honest gentleman and one that sticks stoutly to us, Negus who is a most honest man and will appeare and tell such a tale as will convince all butt infidells, Captaine Haughton, Golwin, Le Strange, Captaine Guibbon, wee had our caball, and on Saterday at Norwich <wee> *they* all meet, to fix the method of their appearance, in the meane time Godwell is gon to March

---

[1081] Thomas Peirson or Pierson of Wisbech: no relationship has been uncovered.

land[1082] to fix all the gentlemen there; Mr Scarbrogh has used mee soe licke a gentleman as I thought none of that opinion ever could have don, for hee has nott onely never shewne my letter to mortall, butt even denied the sight of itt to his owne friend & mine Mr Negus, assuring him that nott onely to him to whome he could denie nothing els, he would denie this butt to all the world besides, and that was much the worst letter; Hyliard's originall I have, Britiff's is nothing, and Negus and Le Strange are of the opinion hee has nott delivered itt, of which you shall certainly know the truth by Monday's post for Mr Negus will write you a full narrative. I am now in hast going to dinner to my cousin Ayde's with Mr Negus, Le Strange, L Col Woodhowse and Captaine Weld, therefore I shall now say noe more, pray acquaint my [f.2] son with this to whome by the next post I shall write. Surely you did nott thinke what you sayd when you perswaded mee to make myself an Howse of Commons man againe. On my word there will bee stories told and prooved will very nearly touch Mr Windham, who will stand with Sir John att the next election where I beleeve they will meet such an opposition as never was in this county; I am nott concerned one farthing att the petition, which as the bishop sayd has sett forth the matter full-lye, and Mr Hurton will swinge itt away with all the boldness in world. I have soe many sad thoughts that I think they will not lett this progress of my health goe on. Sir Thomas Hare they say intends to com which makes mee nott yett pull downe the bed & hangings, and I am sorrie there's noe other way butt I wish that were the worst. My duty to your mother, Charles and Betty presents their dutys,

*Signed*: I am from my sowle yours, Yarmouth
*Postscript*: Pray informe Mr Fisher that I take itt mighty kindly of Mr Scarburgh.[1083]
*NRO: BL/Y/2/118*

## Robert, Viscount Yarmouth to Charles II

**1679, July 17**. As your Majestyes person is sacred to mee soe is your royall word, and under a less <presumption> warrant this presumption could nott bee authorised, I therefore humbly begg of your Majesty to remember your promise soe long depended upon and renewed when I waighted on you att Whitehall to make mee an earle when you made any and *nott* longer to forgett mee, since this justice of your Majesty will enable mee the better to serve you when the country sees mee borne up as well as others by your Majesty's favor soe long expected. My owne lameness at present <of the gout> hind<ring>*ers* mee from attending your Majesty myself butt I cannott doubt of a gratious answer in the present order for a warrant, which my friend that brings this can receive your Majesty's commands for <mee there is butt one title and by that> which in all humility I beg as well as the title of

*Signed:* Your Majestyes most dutyfully devoted subject, Yarmouth
*Draft in Lord Yarmouth's hand*
*British Library: Add. MSS 27447, f. 412*

1082 i.e. Marshland
1083 Scarburgh was one of John Fisher's 'ancient friends' and is mentioned in his will (TNA: PROB11/391).

The King    ▽

The Queene    ⊓

The Duke    ✳✳

The Dutchess    ♀

my L͟d Trea͞t    #

my Lady Danby    ⊸

Lady Shrewsbury    ꝺ

Dutchess of Ports-    ꝑ
mouth ——

Peregrine Bertie    ♒

S͟r John Clayton    ✳

That conceirne    ♌
of Cours ——

S͟r John Pettus    ♈

Francis Compton    ♉

The B͟p of London    ♌

Brounsekille    ♍

Littersby    ♎

Brounsills affaire    ♏

M͟r Henry Bidingfd    ♐
Elder

my Lady Bidingfd    ♑

M͟r Henry Bidingfd    ♊
younger ——

L͟d Peterborough    ⊸

my Lady Peterborugh    ♌

Earle of Bathe    ⊕

my Lady Bathe    o

my Lady Shannon    o°

Daughter Paston    δ

Son Paston    ⚡

That business    ✕

Strangers    Ⅲ

more Anight    Ⅰ

my Lord Yarmouth — ↗    304

My Lady Yarmouth · ○

Key to the Paston cipher used in 1677–1678

(© The British Library Board)

# APPENDIX 1
# The Ciphers

Ciphers were widely used in the seventeenth century as letters sent by the public post were frequently intercepted and read.[1] They ranged from those where every letter in a word is replaced by a number or another letter,[2] to symbols employed for privacy and speed by diarists unfamiliar with shorthand.[3] Ciphers where symbols, numbers, or capital letters are substituted for names and topics were widely used by diplomats;[4] they are simple but very effective as it is impossible to decipher a single intercepted letter. This was the kind of cipher used by Lord and Lady Yarmouth to keep their intrigues secret, and to allow them to comment frankly on, for example, the likelihood of the King keeping his promises. None of their letters in cipher discuss politics as such: all are concerned with Lady Yarmouth's efforts to win some financial advantage for her family and most of Lord Yarmouth's replies do little more than comment on her progress.

Five different ciphers were used in the letters between Lord Yarmouth (at Oxnead) and Lady Yarmouth (in London) between 1675 and 1682, being changed at the end of each period of separation, but only Lord Yarmouth's half of the correspondence has survived. Each party used a key, but only two of these are extant. The first is for 1677–78, and the second is for 1682: neither is complete as there are extra symbols in the text which do not appear in the keys.[5] The names of individuals and the topics under discussion are represented by symbols or numbers while the rest of the text is *en clair*; the topics were pre-decided and appear in the keys as, for example, 'that concern of ours'.

This volume contains letters using four different ciphers dating from 1675, 1676, 1677–1678, and 1678–1679. That for 1677–1678 has a key so the identifications have been put into the text in brackets in a different font and the symbols or numbers have been deleted. Where there is not a key but a good run of letters has survived it has been possible to make some identifications based on cumulative information and small slips by the writer revealing some character's actions, whereabouts, or gender. The symbols have been left in the text to indicate that these identifications are the work of the editor.

There is only one example of the 1675 cipher, using one symbol and one number, making identifications impossible. The cipher of 1676 however was used in twenty-five letters, often extensively. The first clue to an identification came when Lord Yarmouth referred to '∇' as 'her': 'I hope the letter I writt to ∇ will please her'. The

---

[1]  *See* A. Marshall, *Intelligence and Espionage in the Reign of Charles II, 1660–1685* (Cambridge, 1994), *passim*

[2]  Browning, *Leeds*, II, pp 532, encoded letter from Lord Danby to Lord Sunderland, 12 Aug 1678

[3]  Lady Mary Rich, for example, used symbols in devotional passages in her diaries (Charlotte Fell-Smith, *Mary Rich, Countess of Warwick (1625–1678): her Family and Friends* (London, 1901).

[4]  Browning, *Leeds*, II, pp 563–7, letters to Lord Danby from J. Brisbane

[5]  British Library: Add. MSS 27447, ff 303–304.

most likely person to be referred to was Lady Danby as she is extensively mentioned
*en clair*, so her name was tentatively pasted in every time ▽ appeared in the text which
produced, in the same paragraph, the statement that Lady Anne Coke was faine to
comply with ▽ (Lady Danby was her mother) and, in the next letter, the hope that
'▽ may have noe more pretences to quarrell a while' (Lady Danby was notorious for
her temper). All other references fitted, and also showed that cipher ▽ was frequently
next to cipher ✧. The symbols ▽ and ✧ often share a verb, e.g. ▽ and ✧ 'are kind',
▽ and ✧ 'esteem', ▽ and ✧ 'design'. The most likely person to be bracketed with
Lady Danby was her husband Lord Danby, the lord treasurer, and once again the
substitution of his name in place of ✧ made perfect sense: e.g. 'he tells mee my Lord
✧ is perfectly kind to mee which my Lord Treasurer himself expressed much at
Holkham'. Another couple frequently found together are *600* and *700*. A little exper-
imenting made it clear that *600* was Lord Yarmouth himself, and that *700* was his
wife. Similarly *19* and *24* are linked – but *19* comes to dinner while *24* is in London.
The names of Sir Henry Bedingfeld and his son were substituted and again fitted convincingly. These identifications have been added in brackets but the symbols have
been left.

The topics discussed in 1676 presented more of a problem but it has been possible
to identify one of them as the proposed new lease of the excise of which Lord
Yarmouth hoped to be one of the farmers. This is described in Andrew Browning,
*Thomas Osborne, Earl of Danby and Duke of Leeds* (I, pp 209–11, III, pp 4–6), and referred
to in Robert Brent's letter to Lord Yarmouth.[6] The cipher for the excise is 𝒦 and
identification is confirmed in the following passage by Lord Yarmouth: 'I have sufficiently examined the business of 𝒦 [*the excise*] and shall have customers [i.e.
customs officers] enough if itt falls into my hands'. He then proposes discussing terms
with Christopher Jay of Norwich which is confirmed in a letter from Jay to Lady
Yarmouth.[7] Unfortunately it is impossible to identify most of Yarmouth's proposed
partners in this venture because it was abortive; they certainly included Sir George
Wakeman and Peregrine Bertie but it has not been possible to identify their ciphers.

Even where a key exists, as for the letters for 1677–1678, a few extra individuals
were added, and most cannot be identified because their names only appear once or
twice. However one addition to this cipher has been identified because Lord
Yarmouth comments on a proposed match between *12*'s daughter and ☽ [*Lady
Shrewsbury's*] son. This is mentioned in another contemporary source[8] enabling *12*
to be identified as William Chiffinch, keeper of the King's private closet.

The cipher used in December 1678 to March 1679 consists of numbers rather than
symbols and is not used as extensively as the earlier ciphers. By 1678 Lord
Yarmouth's uneasy relationship with Sir John Clayton, his brother-in-law, had
become nothing short of a feud. He wrote of Clayton's implacable malice and the
need to exclude him from their affairs, so when he also wrote that 'a gard may bee
sett upon *37* never for us to have to doe with him upon any accompt who can bee
soe base as to betray the concernes of a family soe nearly related to him', it was
obvious that *37* was Clayton, and the frequently named objects of his malice, *86* and

---

6 Above p.236          7 Above p.252          8 Above p.313

*87*, were Lord and Lady Yarmouth themselves. It has not been possible to identify other names because there are limited examples of this cipher and most of the numbers simply appear in lists. It is possible that *10* is Lord Townshend, because Lord Yarmouth comments on his interest in King's Lynn, but there are not enough mentions of *10* to confirm this. This cipher introduces the use of adjectives, which are also used in the 1682 cipher: *82* is 'villainous' or 'villainy' (always attached to references to Clayton), *20* appears to mean 'well', while the figure *19* is a topic and has been translated as [*affair*].

The principal subjects discussed in connection with Clayton must be the farms of wood and oranges because Clayton was still involved in both, and in the parts of the letters written *en clair* there is discussion of a new contract with new conditions which was being drawn up. Apart from this, the Pastons appear to have been involved in the setting up of a company for the making of paper, probably by an improved method. There is one letter from the inventor Eustace Burneby who may be represented by a cipher but it has not been possible to identify this. Only a few letters use this cipher as Lord Yarmouth increasingly wrote about his electioneering rather than Lady Yarmouth's affairs in London, and without personal comments and small slips by the writer this kind of code is indecipherable.

# The Family of Sir Robert Paston, 1st earl of Yarmouth

Sir William Paston, *c*.1610–1663, married
(1) Lady Katherine Bertie, daughter of Robert Bertie, 1st earl of Lindsey, and Elizabeth Montagu. She died on 3 January 1637. He married
(2) Margaret Hewitt, daughter of Sir William Hewitt, on 27 July 1640 at St Mary Aldermanbury. She died 23 May 1669, having married George Strode in 1668.

By his first wife, Sir William had one surviving son:

**Sir Robert Paston** was born on 29 May 1631 and died on 8 March 1683. He was created viscount Yarmouth in 1673, and 1st earl of Yarmouth in 1679. He married (15 June 1651) Rebecca Clayton, daughter of Sir Jasper Clayton and Mary Thompson; she was born *c*.1635 and died on 4 February 1694. Their surviving children were:

1. Margaret Paston, born 25 January 1652; married (1673) Girolamo Alberti di Conti of Venice.

2. William Paston, 2nd earl of Yarmouth, born June 1654, died on 25 December 1732 at Epsom. He married
   (1) Charlotte Howard (*c*.1650–1684) on 17 July 1672, illegitimate daughter of Charles II and Elizabeth, viscountess Shannon, and widow of James Howard (d.1669), nephew of 3rd earl of Suffolk; and
   (2) Elizabeth Wiseman (1647–1730), daughter of Dudley, 4th baron North, and widow of Sir Robert Wiseman.

Surviving children of William Paston by his first wife:
   Charles, Lord Paston (1674–1718) married Elizabeth Pitt; d.s.p.
   Charlotte Paston (1675–1735) married
      (1) Thomas Herne of Haveringland, 12 June 1703, and
      (2) Major Thomas Weldon.
   Rebecca Paston (born 1681) married Sir John Holland of Quidenham, 8 May 1699.
   William Paston (1682–1711)

Stepdaughter of William Paston:
   Stuarta Howard (1670–1706)

3. Robert Paston (April 1656–1705) married
   (1) in 1680, Hester Mainwaring, widow of Sir William Grobham Howe; and (2) in 1689, Anne, daughter of Philip Harbord and Anne Drury; and died 1705, d.s.p.m.

4. Jasper Paston (*c*.1660–1685) married (1683) Margery Devereux (d.1694), widow of (1) Mr Mansell, and (2) Sir Palmes Fairborne (1644–1680), governor of Tangier; d.s.p.

5. Thomas Paston (1663–1691), married Dorothy, daughter of Edward Darcy, and widow of Sir William Rokeby. Children: Rebecca Paston married Sir Stafford Fairborne, Robert Paston (d.1711).

6. Mary Paston (?1664–1676)

7. Elizabeth Paston (?1667–1686)

# Index

Abergavenny, 11th baron *see* Nevill, George

Adams, Sir William (1634–1687), 2nd bt, of Sprowston Hall, deputy lieutenant, 107, 174–5, 178, 207, 212–4, 234, 237, 245–6, 253, 262, 266–7, 280, 283, 292, 307, 319, 376, 380–1, 383
letter from, 269

Adcock, John, tailor and fanatic, Norwich, 318n, 321, 330

Admiralty, court of, 301–5

Adrianople, 94

Africa, 58

Aglionby, William (d.1705), FRS and diplomat, 18, 108–18
letters from, 109–18, 120–1, 353–4

Agur Hall, 89

Ainsworth/Aynsworth, Mrs [Elizabeth], Bishop's Stortford, 245

Albemarle, dukes of *see sub* Monck

Alberti de Conti, Girolamo, Venetian resident, 12–13, 348
letter from, 146

Alberti de Conti, Margaret (b.1652), 2, 3, 5, 10, 12–13, 25, 57, 64, 79, 82, 113, 120, 128, 130–2, 135, 138–9, 348, 359

alchemy and chemistry, 2, 9, 25, 27, 39, 42–4, 65, 67, 71, 80, 84–5, 87–90, 93–6, 99–102, 104–5, 107–8, 124–5, 127, 129, 132–3, 135, 137, 140, 221, 362–3

Aldeburgh, Suffolk, 14

alderman, gives present to Paston, 107

Aldrich/Aldridge, Mrs [of Swardeston?], 272

Alington, Jane (d.1727), 381

Allen, John, cook at Oxnead, 334

Allen, Richard, servant of Sir William Paston, 139

Allin, John, Skeyton, 74

Allin, Sir Thomas (c.1612–1685), 1st bt, naval commander, 89, 328

Amboise, France, 152

Andover, Hampshire, 349

Andrews, Anne, widow, 139

Angers, France, 112–13, 116–8, 120, 122, 148–9, 153

Annesley, Arthur (1614–1686), 1st earl of Anglesey, FRS, lord privy seal, 99, 129–30, 293n, 296–7, 302n, 308–9, 312, 314–5

Annyson, Richard, Norwich, 345

Anson, George (1697–1762), baron, admiral, 4

Anthony, Dr Francis (1550–1623), alchemist and physician, 360n, 362–3

Antwerp, Belgium, 354n

archaeology, 80

Aretino, Pietro (1492–1556), 45

Arlington, 1st earl of *see* Bennet, Henry

Armagnac, Louis (1641–1718), comte de, 118n

Armiger, William, of North Creake, 204, 243

Arran, earl of *see* Butler, Richard

Arundel, earl and countess of *see sub* Howard

Arundel House, London, 75n, 327

Ashe, Sir Joseph (1617–1686), 1st bt, of Twickenham, 26n, 82, 295, 298, 309, 311, 319

Ashley, Lord, *see* Cooper, Anthony Ashley

Ashmole, Elias (1617–1692), astrologer and antiquary, 107, 137n

asses' milk, 69

Astley, Barbara, 144n, 330n

Astley, Herbert (d.1681), dean of Norwich, 144n, 184, 200, 209–10, 272, 311, 367

Astley, Isaac (d.1688), 3rd baron, of Reading, 229

Astley, Sir Jacob (1640–1729), 1st bt, of Melton Constable, deputy lieutenant, 122, 184, 198–9, 206, 209–10, 212, 217, 229, 237, 290, 383

Atkins/Atkyns, Sir Robert (c.1621–1710), judge and politician, 118

Atthill, Anthony, Cawston, 228

Attleborough, Norfolk, 172, 198, 200, 245–7, 271, 276, 362

Atwood, a ruined Yarmouth merchant, and wife, 180

Audley End, Suffolk, 105, 352

Avery, Francis, purchases jewels, 41n

aviaries/volleries, 68, 73

Avignon, France, 91

Ayde, Elizabeth, of Horstead, 320

Ayde, John, of Horstead, 200, 266, 292, 319–20, 334, 354, 385

Ayliff, Mr, 59

Aylsham, Norfolk, 20, 74, 296

Ayscue, Sir George (c.1615–1672), naval officer, 66, 71, 140

Backhouse, Flower, Lady *see* Hyde, Flower, viscountess Cornbury

Backhouse, William (1593–1662), alchemist and antiquary, 42n

Backhouse, Sir William (d.1669), of Swallowfield, 42n, 57, 96, 99, 130n

Backwell, Edward (c.1618–1683), banker, 106, 141, 209, 229

Bacon, Sir Edmund (d.1685), 4th bt, of Redgrave, deputy lieutenant, 196, 251, 254, 363

Bacon, Francis (d.1692), steward, then recorder of Norwich, 345–6

Bacon, Sir Henry (d.1686), of Herringfleet, 3rd bt of Mildenhall, 175

Bacon, Sir Nicholas (1510–1579), lord keeper, 11

Bacon, Philemon (d.1666), naval officer, 66

Bacon, Thomas, 322, 345n

Bagshot, Surrey, 94

Bainbrigg, Thomas (1636–1703), Trinity College, Cambridge, 103–4

Baker, Lady Anne, 318, 381

Balderston, a dissenter, Norwich, 345

Baldock, Sir Robert (1625–1691), recorder of Yarmouth, 188, 271, 289, 379

Balmentier, Mr, Paris, 111

Baniers, a dangerous talker, Norwich, 317

Barber, Captain, 167–8

Bark/Back, Mr, 230

Barnard, [?Edward, rector of Diss], letter to, 151–2

Barnardiston, Sir Samuel (1620–1707), 1st bt, 151n, 193

Barnet, Middlesex, 84

Barney see Berney

Barspoole/Baispoole, [? Miles], 381

Bartholomew Fair, London, 373

Barton Mills, Suffolk, 196, 200, 207

Barwick, 105

Batelier/Battilier/Batailhe, Mr, 91, 109, 111–12, 114, 117

Bath, earl and countess of see sub Grenville

Bath, Somerset, 96, 220

Baxter, Colonel, parliamentarian, 138

Beckhall, Norfolk, 144, 162, 176, 178, 181, 206, 210, 217, 239, 286, 288, 292, 295, 297, 311, 334, 342–3

Bedfordshire, 274

Bedingfeld, Lady Anne (d.1682), 342–3

Bedingfeld, Christopher, 243

Bedingfeld, Edward, son of Sir Henry the elder, 334

Bedingfeld, Sir Henry the elder (c.1614–1685), 1st bt, of Oxburgh, 15n, 20, 163, 167, 176, 184, 203–7, 209, 212, 216–7, 219, 223–7, 230–3, 254, 256, 272, 283, 285, 292, 296n-7, 309, 315, 318, 320–1, 327, 329–32, 334, 339, 341, 343, 346–8; see also sub Beckhall

Bedingfeld, Sir Henry the younger (c.1636–1704), 2nd bt, of Oxburgh, 15n, 20–1, 144n, 197, 199–200, 206–7, 210, 215–6, 225–7, 231–2, 252n, 280, 297–8, 311, 329, 334, 342–3

letter from, 194–5

Bedingfeld, John (d.1693), son of Sir Henry the elder, 337

Bedingfeld, Margaret (d.1703), Lady, 16, 20, 110, 217, 223, 231–2, 256, 274, 296n, 311, 343, 346, 348

letters from, 144, 162–3, 183–4, 203–4

Bedingfeld, young, 253, 365

Bedingfield, [Thomas, 1617–1678], priest, 297, 347

Bellefonds, Bernardin Gigault (1630–1694), maréchal de France, 102–3

Bendish, Robert (d.1693), alderman of Norwich, 122, 185, 267, 280, 312, 318, 321–3, 328, 335, 339, 345

letters from, 323, 336–7

Bendish, Sarah, 339

Bennet, Henry (1618–1685), 1st earl of Arlington, 61, 118n, 130, 133, 136, 165n, 212, 215–6, 226, 343; see also Euston

Bergen, Norway, 96

Berkeley, Charles (1599–1668), 1st viscount Fitzhardinge and earl of Falmouth, 52, 54, 59

Berkeley, Christian, Lady, 126

Berkeley, Sir John (c.1607–1678), lord lieutenant of Ireland, 126

Berkeley, Mary (1645–1679), countess of Falmouth, 131

Berkeley, Sir William (1639–1666), naval officer, 66

Berkshire, earl and countess of see sub Howard

Berners, Hatton (d.1713), Wiggenhall St Mary, 348

Berney/Barney [?of Reedham], 5, 239, 272, 381

Berney, Captain John, 266, 290

Bertie, Aunt, 48, 55

Bertie, Charles (c.1641–1711), secretary to the treasury, 68n, 256, 258, 312, 344, 349n, 363n, 376

Bertie, Eleanora, Lady Norris, later countess of Abingdon, 142

Bertie, Elizabeth, countess of Lindsey, 233, 375–6

Bertie, Henry (c.1656–1734), 116, 283

Bertie, James (1653–1699), 5th Lord Norris, later 1st earl of Abingdon, 142

Bertie, Mary (Lady Jones), 363

Bertie, Montagu (1608–1666), 2nd earl of Lindsey, 7, 50–1, 53–4, 56, 59

Bertie, Peregrine (c.1635–1701), 205, 208, 215, 233, 251–3, 283, 286–8, 290, 292, 294, 298,

309, 311–2, 316, 318, 321–2, 327, 329–30, 340, 342, 344, 376

Bertie, Robert (1630–1701), 3rd earl of Lindsey, 93, 208–9, 226, 230, 309

Bertie, Vere (d.1681), 281, 283

Besthorpe, Norfolk, 361–2

bezoar stones, 341, 354

Bickley, Sir Francis (d.1681), 2nd bt, of Attleborough, deputy lieutenant, 198, 200, 246–7

letter from, 276

Bigilsey, Thomas, Skeyton, 74

Bill/Billie *see* Paston, William

Bilboa, Spain, 81

Birmingham, Warwickshire, 104

Birton *see* Burton

Bishop's Stortford, Suffolk, 196, 244, 245n

Blacklowe's executor, 219

Bladwell, Sir John (1616–1680), of Rougham, deputy lieutenant, 230

Blake, John, of London, 354

Blanges/Blakes, lodgings in London, 53–5

Blanquefort *see* Duras

Blenkarne/Blinkhorne, Dr Simon, 330, 334

Blickling, Norfolk, 10, 14, 122–3, 175, 226, 235, 254, 283, 292, 306–7, 310, 334, 376

Blois, France, 152

Blome, Mr, letter to, 155–6

Blomefield, Francis (1705–1752), Norfolk historian, 29–30

Blood, Thomas (1618–1680), adventurer and spy, 119–20, 126, 142

Blount, Anne (d.1669), countess of Newport, 86

Bodney, Norfolk, 351

Bokenham, Hugh (c.1634–1694), alderman of Norwich, 336

Bond, Sir Thomas (d.1685) 1st bt, of Peckham, 110–14

Bonfoy/Bonfois, Susanna, 11, 102, 138

Bonnivert, Gideon, natural philosopher, 213n, 216–8, 223

books and pamphlets, 42n, 44–5, 51, 80, 84, 86, 88, 96, 104, 107–8, 124n, 129, 137–8, 147, 196, 203n, 255n, 296n, 362, 366; *see also* London Gazette

Bouillon, 3rd duc de (1641–1721), 118

Bower, Richard, government agent, Yarmouth, 21–2, 177, 241–3, 245, 249, 252, 256–7, 259–65, 268, 270–1, 326

Bowles, Sir William, master of tents and toils, 44

Bowyer, Margaret, Lady (d.1679), 81, 364

Bowyer, Sir William, 1st bt, 48n, 59n, 73n, 86n

Bowyer, [?William (1639–1722), 2nd bt], 81

Bowyer family, 59, 81, 261n

Boyle, Elizabeth (c.1622–1681), viscountess Shannon, 11, 143n, 282, 290, 295, 297, 347, 356n

Bracon Ash, Norfolk, 240

Bradfer-Lawrence, H.L., antiquary and collector, 30

Bradfield, Edward, Cawston, 228

Bradford, Mr, advises on lighthouses, 91–2

Bradford, Thomas (d.1703), alderman of Yarmouth, 175

letters from, 184, 256–7

Braems, Sir Arnold (1602–1681), of Bridge, Kent, 59n, 109

Bragg, Mr, friend of Sir John Hobart, 223

Brampton, Norfolk, 80

Brandenburg, Frederick William I (1620–1688), elector of, 349, 352

Brandsby, Captain, 237

Bransby, Thomas [? of Caister], letters from, 242–4

Brent, Robert, [? of Lark Stoke], 196, 199, 208, 212–14, 216, 226–7, 229, 235–8, 251, 376

letter from, 236–7

Brentford, Middlesex, 107

Bret, Mr [? Richard Brett (d.1689), commissioner for admiralty droits], 201

Brewer, [John, customs official], 354

Brewster, Colonel, parliamentarian, 242

Brewster, John, steward at Blickling, 317

Brickenden, Richard, 100–2, 253

letter from, 107–8

brick making, 53

Bridgeman, Sir Orlando (1609–1674), lord keeper, 77n, 81

Briggs, Augustine (c.1618–1684), alderman and MP for Norwich, 24, 50, 198, 226, 234, 244, 280, 290, 305, 307–9, 313, 332, 339, 352, 358, 374, 377

Britiff, Edward, 370n, 382–3, 385

Brooke/Broke, Sir Robert (c.1637–1669), 91

Brooke, Norfolk, 383

Broome, Norfolk, 209, 212, 237

Brown, innkeeper at Yarmouth, 185

Browne, Mrs, at cavalcade, 272

Browne, Sir Thomas (1605–1682), physician and author, 2, 62n, 72, 285, 335, 339n

Brudenell, Francis (d.1698), baron, 350

Bruges, Belgium, 279

Brumley, Mrs, 231, 360, 362, 364

Brunskell, Percival, attorney, 22–3, 27, 282, 290, 293–4, 296, 299, 312–5, 317, 319, 326–8, 330–1, 333, 335, 337, 340–1, 344, 350; *see also* greenwax

Brussels, 279–80

Buckhurst, baron *see* Sackville, Charles
Buckingham, duke and duchess of *see sub* Villiers
Bude, Guillaume (1467–1540), scholar, 147
bull baiting, 231
Bullard, Mr, 139
Bulstrode, Sir Richard (1617–1711), diplomat, 280
Bulwer, Anne (c.1631–1704), 168–9, 291–2, 295, 313, 316
Bulwer, Thomas (c.1612–1694), attorney, of Buxton, 48, 63, 74, 155, 168–9, 186, 197–8, 211–12, 216, 219, 235, 238, 253, 285, 289, 291–2, 295, 313, 316, 356, 368, 378
    letter from, 169–70
Bungay, Suffolk, 259
Burges/se, Mr, 86, 89
Burneby, Eustace, paper maker, letter from, 378–9
Burton, Deborah, of the Exchange, 138
Burton/Birton, Daniel (d.1704), clergyman, Skeyton, 74
Burton, Hezekiah (c.1632–1681), clergyman, 77, 79; family of, 82n
Burton, John, schoolmaster, Norwich, 296, 362
Burwell, Nicholas (d.1671), of Grays Inn, 68, 71–3, 90, 252n
Bury St Edmund's, Suffolk, 99, 145, 245–6, 248, 379, 381n
Busby?, servant, 288
Butler, James (1610–1688), 1st duke of Ormond, 119, 212, 215–6
Butler, Richard (1639–1686), 1st earl of Arran, 55
Butler, Thomas (1634–1680), earl of Ossory, 105, 140, 280
Buxton, Norfolk, 48n, 67n, 80n, 169

Caister, Norfolk, 4, 174–5, 178–80, 182–3
Calais, France, 108–9, 112, 146
Call, Andrew (d.1698), clergyman, Mautby, 173–5, 182
Calthorpe, Sir Christopher (c.1645–1718), MP, deputy lieutenant, 24, 214–5, 367–73, 384
    letter from, 371
Calthorpe/Colthorpe, Mr, London, 47
Calthorpe, Mr, in cavalcade, 272
Cambridge, Edgar (1667–1671), duke of, 88
Cambridge, 245
    Stourbridge Fair, 182
    University, 1, 19, 46n, 103–4, 86
Cambridgeshire, 274
Campden, 3rd viscount *see* Noel, Baptist
Candia, Crete, 94, 96–7
candles, 53, 356
Canterbury, Kent, 299

Capel, Arthur (c.1632), 1st earl of Essex, 221n
Carlisle, 1st earl of *see* Howard, Charles
Carnegie, Anna (d.1695), countess of Southesk, 135
carpets, 344
Carr, Sir Robert [1637–1682?], 293
Carrington, 1st viscount *see* Smyth, Charles
Caryll/Carrell, Richard, of Harting, and wife, 339, 342
Cary, Lady Elizabeth, 131
Cary/Carey, Jack, 65
Cary/Carey, Martha (1601–1677), countess of Monmouth, 73
Caseman, Gossling, 139
Castlemaine, countess of *see* Palmer, Barbara
Castle Rising, Norfolk, 6, 12n, 20, 244, 343, 368
Catania, Sicily, 86
Catelyn, Sir Neville (1634–1702), MP, deputy lieutenant, 14, 15, 19, 24, 151, 154, 156–162, 174–5, 185, 210, 212, 237–9, 270, 272, 274, 280, 290, 292, 298, 312–13, 332, 355, 365, 367–73, 377, 384
    letter from, 274–5
Catherine (1638–1705), Queen, 10, 48, ?50, 63, 65, 84, 86, 99, 102, 105–6, 133, 136, 196n, 349
Catton, Norfolk, 173, 199, 201–2
Caulier/Collier, John, Yarmouth, 211
cavalcades, 14–16, 20, 172–82, 197–203, 246–7, 271–2, 280–1, 310–11, 329, 369
Cavendish, William, Lord (1641–1707), later 1st duke of Devonshire, 91, 213, 218
caves, Gloucestershire, 97
Cawston, Norfolk, 19, 167n, 227–8, 276, 342
Cecil, James (d.1683), 3rd earl of Salisbury, 364n
Chamberlaine, Mrs Elizabeth (d.1679), 381
Charenton, Paris, protestant graveyard, 99
charity, 178, 309
Charleroi, Belgium, 279–80
Charles I (1600–1649), 51, 154, 378
Charles II (1630–1685), 13, 63, 66, 77–8, 81, 86, 89, 91–4, 97–9, 102–3, 106, 118–20, 126–7, 129, 133–4, 138–40, 142, 149, 165, 168, 171, 190, 192–3, 196n, 198, 202–3, 205–6, 222–6, 230–3, 235–6, 242, 248–9, 251, 254, 259–63, 265, 268–70, 275–6, 279–80, 284, 286–7, 289–90, 293–4, 296–8, 301–6, 308–10, 312–33, 337, 339–43, 346–7, 349–50, 352, 358, 367–8, 371, 374, 377–8
    and the Pastons, 3, 6, 8, 10–12, 16–18, 21–2, 24–5, 27, 44, 46–61, 63–6, 69n, 72, 75–7, 133–4, 136, 143, 145–6, 183, 185, 210–16, 235, 239, 297, 341, 343, 378, 385
    visits Norfolk, 10, 27, 123n, 124, 126, 133–4, 136

Charles II (1661–1700) of Spain, 80–1

Charles XI (1655–1697) of Sweden, 129

Charlton, Mr, a creditor, 78

Charost, Louis Armand (1640–1717), duc de, governor of Calais, 146

Chaucer, Geoffrey (c.1340–1400), 96

Cheeke, Dorothy, 90n

Cheeke, Letitia, 90n, 235, 315

Cheeke, Thomas (d.1688), of Pirgo, 44, 66–9, 79, 81–2, 90, 103, 148–9, 153, 235, 315, 319, 383

cheese, 95, 138, 324–5, 348

Chelsea, Middlesex, 146, 255n

chemistry see alchemy

cherries, 226, 231, 233 & n

Cheshire, 27

chess, 125, 342

Chiffinch/Chiffins, William (d.1691), royal official, 139, 253, 312–5, 320, 322, 330, 341–2

Child, Madam, 244

Church, Henery, Skeyton, 74

cider, 44, 172

ciphers, 18, 32, 177n, 205n, 229n, 256, 282n, 293n, 297, 312, 354n, 387–9

Clarendon, 1st earl of see Hyde, Edward

Clark, Paul, 226

Clarke, Sir William (c.1624–1666), 66

Clayton, Alice, 86, 90

Clayton, Alice (d.1718), Lady, 48n, 50, 53n, 54, 57, 73, 78, 82, 113, 116, 121, 255

Clayton, George, 59n, 62, 78, 82n, 163–4, 207, 233, 281, 283, 289, 295, 307, 314, 316

Clayton, Hester, 59n, 82n

Clayton, Sir Jasper (d.1660), 1–2, 62n, 78n

Clayton, Sir John, 2, 8–11, 16, 43–6, 48, 50, 53–5, 57, 59, 73, 78–9, 81–2, 95, 104, 111, 113, 116, 121, 124–5, 127–34, 137, 142, 152, 176, 208, 213, 216–7, 219, 221, 231, 255, 261, 283, 286, 288–90, 292, 294, 312, 322, 327, 329, 340, 342, 344, 347, 354–5, 357, 359–66, 371, 375–7, 380–1
    letters from, 39–40, 45–6, 85–6, 89–93
    letter to, 130–2

Clayton, Mary (d.1693), Lady, 2n, 8, 10–11, 47–50, 54, 65, 78, 82–4, 113, 116, 121, 123, 139, 199, 208, 213, 218–9, 239, 245, 255, 285, 287, 289–90, 293–4, 296, 298, 308–9, 311–2, 315–6, 318, 322, 327–30, 333, 335, 339, 341–2, 347, 355–7, 359, 361–3, 366, 372, 375–6, 378, 380–1, 384–5

Clayton, Prudence (d.1711), 65n

Clayton, Sir Robert (1629–1707), MP and banker, 9–13, 16–17, 22, 212–3, 287n, 291, 320, 322, 326, 362

Clayton, Thomas, Norwich, letter from, 310

Clayton, William (b.1669), 81

clergy, 19, 22, 156–8, 173–4, 179, 188–9, 201, 231, 264, 272–4, 276–7, 293–4, 296, 384

Cleveland, duchess of see Palmer, Barbara

Cleveland, earl of see Wentworth, Thomas

Clifford, Sir Thomas (1630–1673), 134

clothes, clothing, fabrics, 48–9, 78, 85–6, 89, 91, 105–6, 110, 131, 138–9, 153, 190, 196, 199, 203, 214, 220, 227, 233–4, 266, 288, 295, 297, 308, 314, 316, 327, 330–1, 346, 348, 376

coach and linings, purchase of, 85, 90, 290, 292

coal, 7, 60

Cobb, Mr, nephew of Sir Henry Bedingfeld, 318, 321

Cock, Mr, takes letter to Sir Robert Clayton, 291

Cockey, Mark, alderman of Norwich, 324–5, 336–7

coffee and coffee houses, 21–2, 177, 221n, 241–3, 252, 257, 264–5, 268

Coke, Lady Anne (1657–1722), 199, 204, 207, 209–10, 213, 215, 219, 223, 227, 231–3, 243, 245, 289, 298, 366

Coke/Cooke, cousin, 148

Coke, Sir Edward (1552–1634), lord chief justice, 83, 126n, 151n, 243n

Coke, John (1635–1671), of Holkham, MP, 126, 209n

Coke, Robert (c.1651–1679), of Holkham, MP, deputy lieutenant, 14, 126n, 154, 157, 195–6, 198–9, 207, 209–10, 212–6, 219, 223, 225, 227, 237, 239, 245–6, 247n, 251, 254, 281, 293, 297–8, 321–3, 362–3, 365n, 366
    letters from, 243, 322–3

Colbert, Jean-Baptiste (1619–1683), French minister, 138

Collinges, Dr John (c.1624–1691), clergyman, 162n, 314–15, 321, 325n, 345–6, 367

Colman, Edward (1636–1678), 252, 350n

Cologne/Köln, Germany, 126, 137

Colston, Sir Joseph, of Pudding Norton, 163

Colthorpe see Calthorpe

Coltishall, Norfolk, 173, 178, 266

Combachius, L.H., 137

Compton Census, 191n

Condé, Louis (1621–1686), prince de, 111n, 137–8, 146

Conisford, Norwich, 247

Constantinople, 94

conventicles, 249, 325

Cook, Sir William (c.1630–1708), 2nd bt, of Broome, deputy lieutenant, 174n, 196, 200, 209, 212, 214–5, 237, 270, 274, 323, 369
    letter from, 274

Cooke, John (d.1691), undersecretary, 365
Cooper, Anthony Ashley (1621–1683), 1st earl of
    Shaftesbury, 13, 15, 23, 57, 93, 99, 133,
    192–3, 224, 364n
Cooper, Susan, housekeeper at Oxnead, 20, 163,
    197–9, 205, 212–13, 227, 230, 236, 283,
    286, 316, 320, 338–9, 354–6, 359–60, 362,
    376, 378, 381, 384
    letters from, 181–2, 203
Copenhagen, Denmark, 208n, 220
Copthall, [?Essex], 253
Corie, Francis (c.1596–1678), MP and recorder
    for Norwich, 230n, 266, 272n, 307n, 332
Corie, Thomas (1613–1687), town clerk of
    Norwich, 50n, 230n, 248, 295, 305, 328,
    331–2, 337, 341, 347, 362–3, 368, 373
    letter from, 345–6
Cornbury, viscount and viscountess see sub Hyde
Cornwallis, Charles, 10–11
Cornwallis, Mrs [?Penelope], 88
Corrance, John (c.1616–1694), London, 238–9
Courtais see Curtis
Coventry, Henry (c.1618–1686), 129
Coventry, Sir William (1627–1686), MP for
    Yarmouth, lord of the treasury, etc., 77–8,
    81, 145, 377
Cradock, Anne, 62n
Cradock, Elizabeth, 339
Cramond, barons see sub Richardson
Crane, Mr, of Castle Rising, 244
Crequi, François (1625–1687), maréchal de
    France, 165, 280
cricket, 66
Cringleford, Norfolk, 200
Crisp, Sir Nicholas (d.1666), 64, 96n
Crofts, Dorothy, baroness (d.1663), 162
Cromer, Norfolk, 301–5
Cromleholme, Samuel (1618–1672), school-
    master, 78
Cromwell, Oliver (1599–1658), 14, 81n, 314n,
    318
Crook, John (c.1613–1669), bookseller, London, 81
Cropley, Captain William (d.1720), 271
Cross, Mr, cleans picture frame, 213
Crostwick/Crostwich, Norfolk, 68n, 96n, 138
Crouch, Thomas (1607–1679), MP for
    Cambridge University, 46, 59, 349
crown jewels, 119
Croxton Park, Norfolk, 342
Crumwell, John, Norwich, 345
Cuffant, Mr, Castle Rising, 368
Cullier, Robert, Tasburgh, 345
Curtis/Courtais, Francis (d.1680), clergyman,
    Brampton, & wife, 158, 168

customs, 242, see also glassware, oranges, wood,
    and Great Yarmouth, proposed development
    & customhouse

Dalmahoy, Thomas (d.1682), Guildford, 127
Dalmatia, 134
Danby, earl and countess of see sub Osborne
Dartmouth, Devon, 81
Darvoe, Francis, 139
Dashwood, George (d.1682), revenue farmer,
    207n, 229
Davy, Jehosophat (d.1689), alderman of Norwich,
    337, 343n, 345–6
Davys, Sir John, of Berkshire, 142
Dawson, John (d.1678), collector of customs for
    Yarmouth, 89, 211, 217, 225, 234, 251–2,
    254, 256, 301
    letter from, 259, letter to, 286
Dawson, Joseph, 354, 357n, 368, 381
Daynes, Henry, Raydon, 290
deafness, 183
Deane, Thomas, Skeyton, 74
Dee, Rowland, merchant, London, 68, 71
De Grey/De Gray, Captain, 234
De Grey, Major Edmund, 234
De Grey, William (1652–1687), of Merton,
    deputy lieutenant, 373
    letter from, 155–6
Delahaye/De La Haye, Peter (d.1684),
    confectioner, 139
Denham, Sir John (1615–1669), 51n, 80
Denham, Middlesex, 73, 86, 89, 90, 104
Denmark, 96, 142, 208n, 220
Derbyshire, 27
De Paris see Parisiensis
Dereham, [Frances], 225
Dereham, East, Norfolk, 62, 144n
Devon, 98
Dewing, John, William, senior & junior, Cawston,
    228
De Witt, Johan (1625–1672), grand pensionary of
    Holland, 141, 280
Desbrough/Disbrowe, John (c.1608–1680), par-
    liamentarian, 142
Dick, servant at Oxnead, 59, 71
Dickinson, William, surveyor general of the
    customs, 57–8, 64, 95, 106, 145, 176, 225,
    292, 295, 354, 359, 361–6
Digby, Lady Ann see Spencer, Ann
Digby, John, Lord (1634–1698), later 3rd earl of
    Bristol, 224, 227
Digby, Mr, naval officer, 140
'Don', see Henshaw, Thomas
Dornay, Frank (d.1678), 326

Dorset, 5th earl of *see* Sackville, Richard

Dorset, 69n, 95, 224

Doughty, John, Lord Yarmouth's secretary, 20 &n, 205–6, 213, 223n, 229–30, 232, 244, 245–6, 253–4, 289, 292, 298, 300, 307, 312–4, 316–8, 325, 328, 332–3, 335, 343, 346, 354, 356–8, 361–2, 365, 367, 370, 376, 381–2, 384
  letters from, 266–7, 269–71, 280–1, 301–2, 305–6, 345, 369–70, 372–4

Doughty, Major Robert (d.1679), of Aylsham, 20–2, 74n, 164, 186, ?199, 200–2, 204–5n, 216, 219, 223, 227, 230, 240, 250–1, 255, 266–7, 270–1, 279, 285, 289, 295, 299, 301, 314, 320, 322, 334, 378
  letter from, 192–3, letter to, 241

Doughty, Robert, younger, 192, ?199, 200
  letters from, 258–9, 261–3

Doughty, William (d.1678), of Aylsham, letter from, 74

Dover, Kent, 108

Downing, Sir George (1623–1684), 89, 98, 106, 138, 142

Doyly, Sir William (c.1614–1677), 1st bt, of Shotesham, MP for Yarmouth, deputy lieutenant, 15n, 20–2, 58, 65, 82–3, 155, 187, 189, 196–8, 200–2, 204, 206, 210, 212–13, 217–8, 227, 233, 237, 244–6, 249, 272, 280, 282, 291, 296, 317n
  letters from, 201–2, 224; *see also* Shotesham

Doyly, Sir William (d.c.1680), 2nd bt, of Shotesham, deputy lieutenant, 15n, 83n, 196, 198, 212, 247, 280, 290–1, 320, 364

drainage, 8, 266, 281

drunkenness and sobriety, 63–4, 90, 103n, 143, 168, 177, 179, 211, 214–5, 254, 283, 288, 298, 309

Dublin, 119, 124

Duckett, William (1624–1686), 100

duelling, 72, 82, 88, 91, 105n, 356n

Dunblane, Viscount *see* Osborne, Peregrine

Duncombe, Sir John (1622–1687), 99, 211, 221, 223–5

Dunkirk, 109

Dunster, Giles, surveyor-general of customs, 251–2, 254, 256, 259, 262
  letter from, 258

Duras, Louis (1641–1709), marquis de Blanquefort, 2nd earl of Feversham, 96

Dutch: ambassador *see* Van Beuningen
  cartoon, 51, 138
  fleet and wars, 6, 13, 58–9, 66, 68, 70–1, 74, 94n, 96, 129, 135, 138, 140–4, 187, 226
  murderous servant, 60
  tiles, 65, 67

Dysart, countess of *see* Maitland, Elizabeth

Earle, Erasmus (1590–1667), 47n, 66, 69–70, 72

Earle, John (1622–1697), 47, 65, 70–2, 74, 251

Earle, Ralph, 251, 371, 373

East, [?Edward (c.1602–1696)], watchmaker, 138

East Dereham, Norfolk, 62, 144n

Eaton, Mr, merchant, 48, 78, 139

Eaton, Katherine, 139

Eaton, Norfolk, 200, 247

Edinburgh, 102

education of the Paston children, 1, 64, 78, 86, 94–5, 103–4, 112–3, 116–7, 120–2, 138–9, 149–50, 157, 213, 216–8, 223, 273, 296, 339, 360, 364,

Eldred, [Joseph (d.1676), of North Walsham], 231

elections *see sub* Norfolk, Norwich, Great Yarmouth, King's Lynn, Thetford

Eliott, Mr, young, 326

Elmham, Norfolk, 297–8

Elveden, Norfolk, 271

Elwes, Sir John (1635–1702), 47n

Empson, Henry, Skeyton, 74

England, Benjamin (d.1711), alderman of Yarmouth, 289
  letters from, 261, 275–7, 286, 347

England, Sir George (d.1677), Yarmouth, 174, 271

England, George (1643–1702), MP for Yarmouth, 154–5
  letters from, 241–3, 257, 259–61, 263–6, 268–9

England, Thomas (d.1693), alderman of Yarmouth, 169, 176, 180, 211, 230, 237, 239
  letters from, 147, 154, 241–3, 263–6, 268–9

England, young, captain, 239

Ent, Sir George (1604–1689), physician, 120

Erasmus, Desiderius (1466–1536), 147

Ernle/Earnly, Sir John (c.1620–1697), chancellor of the exchequer, 221, 224, 232, 234, 358n

Erpingham, North, hundred of, 122

Essex, 44n, 105n, 171n, 307, 383

Etna, Mount, Sicily, 86

Euston, Suffolk, 118n, 136n, 281, 349

Evelyn, John (1620–1706), 2, 18n, 44, 120n, 134n

Everard, Charles (d.1665), London, 68, 71

Everard, Sir Richard (c.1625–1694), 47

excise, farm of, 17, 20, 22, 27, 66n, 196n, 207, 212–13, 215–18, 223, 225–7, 229–30, 232, 235, 237–8, 241, 252–3, 293n, 314n, 350

Fairchild, John, Cawston, 228

fairs, 105, 175, 182, 373

Falmouth, Mary, countess of *see* Berkeley, Mary

fanatics, 76, 119, 147, 156, 162, 188–90, 192–4,
    197, 285, 310, 312, 315–6, 318, 321, 324–5,
    336, 369, 373–4, 376
Fane, Charles (d.1691), 3rd earl of Westmorland,
    350
Fanshaw, Mr [?Henry], 220
Faucet/Fawcett, [?Robert, clergyman, Aylsham],
    158
Felbrigg, Norfolk, 26, 69n, 82n, 164, 377
Feltham, Mrs, has no mallards, 362
Fenn, Sir John, 29
Filmer, Sir Edward (d.1669), of East Sutton, 99
Finch, Elizabeth (d. c.1696), viscountess
    Maidstone, 272
Finch, Heneage (1628–1689), 3rd earl of
    Winchilsea, diplomat, 86
Finch, Heneage (1621–1682), lord chancellor
    1675, later earl of Nottingham, 243n, 293–4,
    297, 326, 354, 357
Finch, Mr, a lawyer, 283
fire-eating, 178
fish and fishing, 16, 97, 104n, 145, 172, 183,
    225–6, 229, 230–1, 260, 280–1, 335, 339,
    347, 384
Fisher, John (d. c.1688), auditor, 60, 72, 165, 171,
    175–9, 195–6, 206, 213, 215–6, 253, 270,
    283, 289, 308, 313, 316, 321, 343, 355,
    361–3, 365–6, 372, 377–8, 380, 384–5
    letters from, 106–7, 171–5, 177–8, 202, 281–2,
    349, 351–3
Fitch, Sir Thomas (c.1637–1688), building con-
    tractor, 176n-8
Fitzcharles, Bridget (1661–1718), countess of
    Plymouth, 17n, 204, 210, 243, 346n
Fitzcharles, Charles (1657–1680), earl of
    Plymouth, 17, 146–9, 153, 233, 279, 346n,
    350
Fitzhardinge, viscount  see Berkeley, Charles
Fitzroy, Charles (1662–1730), earl of
    Southampton, 102
Fitzroy, Henry (1663–1690), 1st duke of Grafton,
    102n, 343
Flamborough Head, Yorks, 8n, 89n
Flanders, 349, 352
Fleet, Mrs Jane, housekeeper at Holkham,
    209–10, 215, 223
Flegg, Norfolk, 173
Fletcher, Mrs, ?midwife, 60
Florence, Italy, 39
Floyd, Dr, 57, see also Lloyd
Flynt, Roger (d.1686), clergyman, 185–6, 210,
    218, 230, 334
    letters from, 147–8, 182–3
food and drink, 46, 57, 66, 73, 87, 95, 128,

138–9, 152, 171–4, 177–8, 196, 211, 252,
    281, 310, 335, 338, 347–8, 360, 362, 364,
    366; see also cider, coffee, fish, fruit, oysters,
    potatoes, poultry and game, nog, turtles,
    wine
Fowell, Sir John (1623–1677), 2nd bt, 80
fowling, 278–9
foxes, tame, 86
Fraizer, Sir Alexander (?1607–1681), physician,
    63, 65, 70n
Fraizer/Frayser, Bettie, 63
Fraizer/Frayser, Mary (d.1695), Lady, 63
France, 11, 18, 39, 48n, 70, 80–2, 88, 91, 96, 99,
    102, 105, 108–118, 120–3, 126, 134, 141–2,
    146–7, 149, 152–3, 279, 334, 350n, 358
    French army and wars, 39, 70, 74, 81, 94, 109,
    111n, 126, 134, 137–8, 141–4, 146–8, 165,
    279–80, 334, 349, 352–3
Francis, Mr, 155
Franck, a servant at Oxnead, 53, 59
Frankfurt, Germany, 353
Fraser, James (1645–1731), 255n
Fraser/Frayser see also Fraizer
Frayser, Mr, brings song, 66
Frayser, Mrs, 73
Frederick III (1609–1670) of Denmark, 96n
Freeman, Robert, alderman of Norwich, 312
Frescheville, John (1606–1682), baron Frescheville
    of Staveley, 208n
Froud, Mr [?Philip], 297
fruit, 7, 10, 78, 89, 100, 111, 134–5, 152, 226,
    231, 233, 245, 321
Fulham, Middlesex, 78; see also Parson's Green
furniture and furnishings, 56, 67, 72–3; see also
    Oxnead, furnishings

Gamble, Harold, Cawston, 227–8
gambling and card games, 3, 88, 210, 244, 366
Gammon, John, servant at Oxnead, 233, 291
gardening see Oxnead, gardens and park
Gardiner, Francis, alderman of Norwich, 336
Garnet, Mr, pays Henshaw £100, 81
Garrard/Garrett, Sarah, Lady, 271
Garrard/Garrett, Sir Thomas (d.c.1690), 2nd bt,
    of Langford, deputy lieutenant, 197,
    199–200, 280, 349, 365, 373
Garret's grove, Norfolk, 79
Garwood, William, Cawston, 228
Gascoigne, Sir Bernard (1614–1687), army officer
    and diplomat, 105–6
Gayer/Geare, Sir Robert, of Stoke, Bucks, 71
Gazette see London Gazette
Gerard, Charles (c.1659–1701), 2nd earl of
    Macclesfield, 146–7

Germany, 134, 352–3

Ghent, Belgium, 279

Giles, Richard, Cawston, 228

Gill, Alexander (1565–1635), schoolmaster and author, 124

glassware, 7, 9, 13, 16, 54, 85, 89–90, 146, 283

Gleane, Sir Peter (1617–1696), MP, 21, 207, 209, 212, 214–5, 230, 251, 287
  letters from, 277–9, 284–5

Gloucestershire, 97

Goddard, Jonathan (c.1617–1675), physician and chemist, 43n, 125, 313

Godfrey, Sir Edmund Berry (1621–1678), magistrate, 350–2

Godfrey, Richard (Dick), customer of King's Lynn, 298

Godfrey, Thomas, Cawston, 228

Goding, Mr, a creditor, 78

Godolphin, Sir John (d.c.1679), 13

Godolphin, Sidney (1645–1712), 1st earl of Godolphin, 81

Godwel/Godwell/Goldwell, 365, 384

Godwick, Norfolk, 243, 297–8

Goldsmiths' Hall, London, 52

Golwin, Mr, 284

Gooch, Thomas, mayor of Thetford, 246

Gooch, Thomas (d.1688), alderman of Yarmouth, letters from, 147, 154

Goodall, Dr Charles (c.1642–1712), physician, 320, 327, 362–3, 366

Gorg, Mr, tutor, 139

Gough, John (d.1684), clergyman, Oxnead, 14, 19, 20, 107, 139, 154, 158, 163, 170–1, 197, 216–7, 219, 227–8, 230, 236, 240, 254–5, 270, 283, 299, 314, 316, 333, 335, 338–9, 343, 356, 359, 367, 371, 384
  letters from, 149–50, 156–7, 163–9, 179–80, 184–7, 191–4, 199–201, 240, 247–8, 299–300, 303–5, 324, 362, 369

Goulston/Gulston, Sir William (c.1641–1687), 22, 287

gout, 2, 16, 80, 93, 113, 118, 136, 142, 181, 184, 214, 226, 229, 231, 235, 263, 290–1, 293, 325, 362, 364–5, 381, 385

Grafton, duke of see Fitzroy, Henry

grampus, 97

grand tour, 10, 11, 18, 108–18, 120–2, 146–9, 152–3

Great Yarmouth, Norfolk, 67, 171, 185–7, 193, 197, 210–11, 237–8, 266, 285, 289, 295, 347, 363, 373, 379, 384; et passim
  acts of parliament, 6, 46–7, 49–53, 55–9, 276
  bailiffs' letters, 77, 147, 154, 184, 241–3, 256–7, 259–61, 263–6, 268–9, 275–7, 286

coffee house, 242, 252, 257, 264–5, 269

curate, 264

elections, 314, 317, 376–7

fishing, 145, 183, 260, 347

high steward, 17, 147, 154–5, 173–84

nonconformists, 22, 249

plague, 62

proposed custom house and development, 17, 27, 60, 100, 145, 169, 176–8, 183, 185, 211, 214, 216–8, 225–6, 230, 232, 234–8, 251, 254, 256, 258–9, 267, 269–71, 275–6

shipping, 145, 174, 176–8, 225

Southtown, 5–6, 10, 11, 13, 71, 100n

survey, 60, 237, 288

see also Bower; Norfolk, militia

Greene, Mr & Mrs, 346

Greensmith, [John], excise officer, 241

greenwax [Brunskell's affair], 22–3, 27, 282n, 286–7, 289–90, 293–4, 296–7, 299, 307, 311–16, 319, 321, 326–333, 335, 337, 340–2, 344

Greenwich, Kent, 97

Grenville/Granville, Bernard (1631–1701), groom of the bedchamber, 282n, 317, 326, 341

Grenville, Jane, countess of Bath, 48

Grenville, John (1628–1701), 1st earl of Bath, 48, 344, 348n

Gressenhall, Norfolk, 278

Grevys, Richard, of Moseley, 88, 104n

Griffenfeld, Peder (1635–1699), count, 220

Griffin, John, servant, 219

Grimston, Sir Samuel (1644–1700), 88n

Guildford, Surrey, 127

Guise, Louis Joseph (1650–1671), duc de, 125

guitar, lessons, 122

Gunfleet, Essex, 66

guns and gunnery, 97–8, 103, 129, 135, 174–6, 179–80, 182, 184, 221, 278, 334, 382

Gunton, Norfolk, 173n, 363

Guybon, Sir Francis (c.1639–1705), 243, 384

Gwynne, Nell (c.1651–1687), 375

Gyldenløve, Ulrik Frederik (1638–1704), Danish ambassador, 96

Hague, The, Netherlands, 129, 353

Hales, Sir Edward (1645–1695), 95

Hall, John (d.1684), alderman of Yarmouth, 289

Halsey, Thomas (1655–1715), of Great Gaddesden, 359n

Hamburg, Germany, 349

Hamilton/Hambleton, Sir George, 82

Hampden, Elizabeth (d.1665), 54

Hampden, John (1595–1643), 14, 54n, 131n

Hampton Court, Surrey, 99
Harbord, Anne, wife of Philip, (1640–1679), 355, 361–3
Harbord, Catherine, wife of John, 271, 320
Harbord, Sir Charles (1596–1679), of Stanninghall, 59, 60n, 107, 172n, 200, 202, 204, 213, 215, 218, 266, 280–2, 295, 308, 339, 353, 366, 376, 384
Harbord, Sir Charles (1642–1672), 107
Harbord, Captain John (1637–1711), 173, 175, 178, 200, 231, 271, 320, 341
Harbord, Colonel Philip (d.1687), deputy lieutenant, 237, 262, 266, 272, 280, 286n, 308, 320, 341, 355, 363
Harbord, William (1635–1692), MP for Thetford, 363, 373, 377, 383n
Hare, Sir Thomas (c.1658–1693), 2nd bt, of Stow Bardolph, 385
Harly/Harley, [?William (d.1707)], clergyman, 179
Harman, Sir John (d.1673), naval officer, 142
Harris, Mr, the lord chancellor's gentleman, 326, 354, 356
Harvey, Sir Daniel (1631–1672), 66, 333n
Harvey, Elizabeth, Lady, 233
Harwich, Essex, 66, 105, 129, 145n, 333, 336
Hatton, Charles, 12
Haughton see Houghton
Haveringland, Norfolk, 194n, 322
Hawes, Robert, alderman of Norwich, 336
Hawys/Hawse, John, physician, 229, 230, 232, 235, 238, 313, 327, 354–5, 357, 359–60, 364, 366, 376; see also sub Hughes, Dr Owen
Haylett, William, clergyman, Hevingham and Stratton Strawless, 296
hearth money, 98
Helwis, Nicholas, alderman of Norwich, 336
Henrietta Maria (1609–1669), queen, 48, 81
Henriette Anne (1644–1670), duchess of Orleans, 97, 102
Henshaw, Anne (d.1671), 78, 97, 120, 130, 132, 135, 140
Henshaw, Anne, daughter of Thomas, 79, 97, 120, 221, 227, 231n, 234, 236, 240, 244, 246, 253, 255, 359
Henshaw, Benjamin, 57n, 141
Henshaw, Nathaniel (c.1628–1673), physician, 57n, 123–4, 126, 130
Henshaw, Thomas (1618–1700), alchemist and writer, 2, 8–10, 30–1, 39n, 51–2, 57, 68n, 73, 78–9, 82, 85, 90, 100n, 108n, 111, 120, 142n, 176, 208, 210, 227, 231, 292, 297, 314–6, 357, 359–60, 363, 376
  letters from, 42–4, 69–70, 79–85, 87–9,

93–106, 118–20, 123–135, 137–8, 140–2, 220–1, 315
Henshaw, Major Thomas (d.1670), 68n, 105
Herbert, Margaret, Lady, 78
Herbert, William (c.1621–1669), 5th earl of Pembroke, 99
Herbert, William (1653–1683), 7th earl of Pembroke, 299, 352n
Herne/Hyrne/Hirn, Clement (d.1694), of Haveringland, 194, 227–8, 231, 250–1, 301, 303, 322, 326, 369, 372–3
Hesilrige, Sir Arthur (1601–1661), army officer, 138
Hethersett, Wormley, mayor of Thetford, 171
Hethersett, Norfolk, 272
Heveningham, Lady Mary (d. c.1696), of Ketteringham, 11n, 232n, 272, 383
Heveningham, William, regicide, 158n, 232n
Heveningham, Sir William (d.1678), of Ketteringham, 232n, 235, 272
Hewitt/Hewytt, Robin, brother of Lady Paston, 69
Hewitt/Hewytt, [Ursula,] Lady, 69n
Hewitt, Sir William (d.1637), 1, 2n
Hewitt family, 47n
Hickling, Norfolk, 279
Hicks, Mrs, 105
highwaymen, 14, 119, 135, 163–6, 169–70
Higgons, Sir Thomas (c.1624–1691), envoy to Venice, 376
  letter from, 348
Hildesly, Stephen, sub-commissioner of excise, 293
Hildeyard, Elizabeth, 273, 277
Hildeyard, Jack, 273
Hildeyard/Hyliard, Dr John (d. c.1703), clergyman, Cawston, 3, 19, 25, 27n, 168–9, 185, 199, 217, 227–8, 231, 250–1, 282, 288, 293, 296, 308, 315, 326, 334, 343, 361n, 370n, 385
  letters from, 167, 273–4, 276–7, 308, 310, 374
Hingham, Norfolk, 156
Hobart, John 'Old Commonwealth', & wife, 185n, 316–7, 324, 330
Hobart, Sir John (1628–1683), 3rd bt, of Blickling, MP, 10, 14–15, 18, 20–1, 24–5, 136, 160–2, 175, 181, 184, 186–90, 192–5, 206, 209, 212, 214–6, 223–4, 226, 229–33, 235, 247, 251, 283n, 293, 301–5, 314, 316–7, 322, 326, 330, 347, 367–74, 376, 380, 382–3, 385
  letters from, 122–3; see also Blickling
Hobart, Mary, Lady, 54n, 131, 216, 235, 254, 314, 316, 318, 321, 381

Hobart, Mary (d.1865), wife of Old
    Commonwealth Hobart, 330
Hoddesdon, Herts, 195, 244
Hodges, Mr, Lincolns Inn Fields, 74
Hodges, Dr [?Nathaniel (1629–1688), physician],
    141
Hoet, [Peter], merchant, 205, 225n, 227n, 245
Hogan, [Mary (d.c.1698)], North Walsham, 58n,
    225, 360
Hoggan, Lady Yarmouth's cousin, 58, 225n
Holden's medicine, 125
Holkham, Norfolk, 14, 126n, 199, 204–10, 213,
    216, 231–2, 253, 292
Holland, Alathea (d.1679), Lady, 73, 172
Holland, Bryan, 271
Holland, Sir John (1603–1701), MP, 1st bt, of
    Quidenham, 14, 17n, 21, 46, 52, 72–3, 155,
    158, 160–2, 171–2, 175, 184, 186, 192, 195,
    197–8, 200, 206, 223–4, 229, 234, 238,
    244n, 251, 255–6, 271, 277, 314, 316, 320,
    334, 340, 344, 349, 352, 366–8, 370–1, 373,
    376
    letters from, 151–2, 165, 204, 248, 350–1
Holland, ?Tom, 284
Holland, countess of see Rich, Elizabeth
Holland, Netherlands, 105, 129, 138, 141–2,
    280n, 299, 324–5, 352
Holland House, Kensington, 129, 135
Holmes, Sir Robert (c.1622–1692), naval officer,
    140
Hooker, Mr, London, 49
Horner, Mr, formerly Paston's tenant, 339
Horning, Norfolk, 266
horses, 12, 14, 26, 94, 106, 109, 118, 122, 126,
    141, 148, 153, 178, see also Paston, Robert,
    horses
Horsham St Faith, Norfolk, fair at, 175
Hoste, James (1633–1699), of Sandringham, 343,
    365–6, 368, 372,
Houghton/Haughton, Captain John, 383–4
Houghton/Haughton, Robert, of Ranworth,
    174–5, 266, 295, 377
House of Commons and House of Lords, see
    Parliament
Housman, Mr, who saw us on board, 109
Howard, Charles (c.1615–1679), 2nd earl of
    Berkshire, 242n, 252, 255, 315–6, 343
Howard, Charles (1628–1685), 1st earl of Carlisle,
    88
Howard, Dorothy, countess of Berkshire, 315,
    343
Howard, Lady Frances, 244
Howard, Henry (1628–1684), earl marshal, 6th
    duke of Norfolk, 7, 10, 12n, 15, 16, 20, 25,

75n, 126n, 144, 146, 171–3n, 210, 212, 214–
    5, 223, 225, 229, 233, 237, 244, 246–8, 250–
    2, 258, 264, 309, 311, 315–6, 318–21,
    326–9, 331–3, 339, 341, 343, 347, 352, 368,
    377
    letter from, 136
Howard, Henry (1655–1701), earl of Arundel,
    later 7th duke of Norfolk, 220, 244, 250,
    341, 343, 350, 368
Howard, James (1619–1689), 3rd earl of Suffolk,
    60, 196, 352n, 356n
Howard, James (d.1669), 11, 356n
Howard, Jane (d.1693), duchess of Norfolk, 341,
    343
Howard, Mary (1659–1705), countess of Arundel,
    later duchess of Norfolk, 220n, 343n, 350
Howard, P., lieutenant colonel, 143–4
Howard, Philip (1629–1694), cardinal, 136
Howard, Sir Robert (1626–1698), 23n, 291–3,
    372, 376
    letter to, 290–1
Howard, Stuarta (1670–1706), 356, 364
Howard, Lord Thomas (d.1689), 331
Howse, 65, 326
Huby, [?John], one of the duke of Norfolk's gentle-
    men, 173, 175, 178, 226, 266, 316, 329
Hughes, Dr Owen, commissary, 19, 21, 193,
    212–13, 217, 227, 229n, 247, 250, 253–4,
    287, 301, 303–4, 367, see also sub Hawys, Dr
    John
    letters from, 187–91, 228–9, 302–3
Hunstanton, Norfolk, 195n
Hunt, [James, surveyor], 60
Hunt, Mrs, servant, 338, 346, 381
hunting, 94, 99, 127, 134, 199, 215, 254, 349
Huntington, Richard (d.1690), alderman and MP
    for Yarmouth, 237, 257, 267, 269, 271, 314,
    347, 377
    letters from, 77, 241–3, 259–61, 263–6, 268–9,
    275–7, 286
Huntington, Robert, major, 314
Hurton, John, steward at Oxnead, 22, 26, 47–50,
    63, 66, 185, 230, 236, 238, 254, 288, 309,
    328–30, 344, 355, 361, 383, 385
    letters from, 154–5, 158–9, 180–1, 197–8
Hyde, Edward (1609–1674), 1st earl of
    Clarendon, 6, 13, 15, 46, 49, 51n, 64, 78n,
    84–5n, 90n, 147
Hyde, Edward (1645–1665), 51
Hyde, Flower (d.1700), viscountess Cornbury,
    42n, 130
Hyde, Henry (1638–1709), viscount Cornbury,
    42n, 49, 90
Hyliard see Hildeyard

Hyrne *see* Herne

Ingilby, Sir Henry, Ripley Castle, Yorks, 30
Ireland, 63n, 119, 124, 126, 193, 220–1, 227
Isleham, Cambridgeshire, 307
Italy, 4, 39, 45, 96n, 115, 134, 348
Ives, John (1751–1776), herald and antiquary, 30
Izzard, Mr (d.1671), attorney, 135

Jamaica, 97
James, servant, 79, 90
Jay, Christopher (c.1605–1677), alderman and
    MP for Norwich, 184–5, 187, 252–3, 266,
    280–2
Jefferys, Francis, vintner, 139
Jegon, Robin, 67, 73
Jermyn, Henry (1605–1684), earl of St Albans,
    103, 119
Jermyn, Henry (c.1636–1708), 3rd baron Jermyn,
    141
jewellery and plate, 54, 81, 83, 119; *see also*
    Paston, Robert, jewellery and plate
John, Don, (1629–1679), of Austria, 81
Johnson, Sir James (b.1615), of Yarmouth, 77,
    174, 215, 237, 239, 289, 373, 382
Jolly, David, shoemaker, 139
Jones, Sir Harry (d.1673), lieutenant colonel, 134
Jones, Mary, Lady *see* Bertie, Mary
Jones, Richard (1641–1712), earl of Ranelagh,
    314
Jones, Sir William (c.1630–1682), attorney-
    general, 286n, 287, 289–90
Jonson, cook, 138
Juliers/Jülich, Germany, 352

Keeling, Sir John (1607–1671), judge, 119
Kelsey, Thomas (d. post 1676), parliamentarian,
    142
Kemp, Sir Robert (1628–1710), 2nd bt, of
    Gissing, MP, 14–15, 19, 21, 151, 154–162,
    186, 194–5, 206, 211, 247, 251, 334, 368
    letters from, 144–5, 344
Kensington, 14, 68, 100, 104n, 135n, 165
    Holland House, 130, 135
    Pondhouse, 104, 221n
Kerouaille, Louise de (1649–1734), duchess of
    Portsmouth, 127, 199n, 219, 283, 287, 290,
    341, 346, 352, as 'the sick lady', 199, 206
Kevitt, Messrs, Yarmouth, 175
Kilby, a servant at Oxnead, 171, 226
Killigrew, Harry, 80
Killigrew, Mary, 11n
Killigrew, Peter (c.1634–1705), of Arwennack, 47n
Killigrew, Sir Robert, 11n

Killigrew/Killegrew, Sir William, 49
Kilmorey, Bridget, viscountess *see* Needham,
    Bridget
King, Mr, jeweller, 138–9
King, Thomas (d.1688), London, letter from, 145
King's drops, 313–6, 320,
King's Lynn, Norfolk, 14–15, 254, 256, 298n, 368
    elections, 154, 156, 365–6, 372, 380
Kirle/Kyrle, Captain, 213
Knight, Davy, brewer, 139
Knight, John (c.1622–1680), serjeant-surgeon to
    Charles II, 352
Knight, Mary (c.1631–c.1698), singer, 283, 287,
    290, 295, 312, 315, 317, 319–20, 322,
    326–7, 329–30, 332–3, 335, 337, 340–2, 346
Knyvett, Captain John, 220, 253, 316, 365
Knyvett, Sir John (d.1673), of Ashwellthorpe, 140
Knyvett, Thomas (1596–1658), 4n
Knyvett, Colonel Thomas (1656–1693), of
    Ashwellthorpe, deputy lieutenant, 238, 253,
    280, 316, 322n, 365
Konigsmark, Count [?Karl Johann, 1659–1686],
    349
Kuffler, Johannes Sibertus (1595–1677), chemist
    and inventor, 85

Lably, Mr, 138
Lake, Dr [Arthur (c.1567–1626), bishop of Bath
    and Wells], 196
Lambert, John (c.1619–c.1684), army officer and
    parliamentarian, 142
land tax, 106
Lancaster, duchy of, 301, 304
Lane, Mr, of Watlington, Northants, 196, 200
Langley Abbey, Norfolk, 214
Langly, Mr, pewterer, 138
Lant, Mr, will carry book, 186
Larissa, Macedonia, 94
Larling, Norfolk, 197, 200, 248, 271
Latimer, viscount and viscountess *see sub* Osborne
Lauderdale, duke and duchess of *see sub* Maitland
Layer, Christopher, high sheriff, 275n
Leaman, John, servant, 46
Le Febre, Nicaise (d.1669), King's chemist, 80
Lee, Eleanora *see* Bertie, Eleanora
Lee, Mrs, London, friend or foe?, 316
Lee & Hoet, 225n, 227n, 245
Leech, Sir Robert, [of Chesterfield], 135
Le Gros, Bridget (d.1663), 62n
Le Gros, Frances, 68n
Le Gros, Thomas, of Crostwick, 2, 96, 138n
Leigh, Mr, unkind to Sir Peter Gleane, 277–9
Lennard, Anne (1661–1722), countess of Sussex,
    295n, 358n

Leonard, servant, 288

Le Roy alias King, John, jeweller, 138

L'estrange, Edward (1640–1715), clerk to the militia, 20n, 195, 200, 250, 253, 266n, 290, 384–5
  letters from, 243–4, 267, 278

Levar, Mr, 139

Lichfield, Staffordshire, 97

lighthouses, 8–9, 17, 89n, 91–3, 261n, 262n, 286n

Lilly, William (1602–1681), astrologer, 118

Lindsey, earl and countess of  see sub Bertie

Ling, Norfolk, 48

Linstead, [William, collector, of Lynn], 365–6

Linsted, Mr, Norwich, 158

Lionne, Paula de, 125

Litcham, Norfolk, 188

Littlebury, Essex, 171, 195, 244, 256

Littleton, [Adam (1627–1694), schoolmaster and philologist], 86

Littleton, Sir Charles (c.1629–1716), 375n

Littleton, Sir Henry (c.1624–1693), 375

Littleton, Sir Thomas (c.1621–1681), 2nd bt, joint commissioner of the navy, 92

Livingston, Anne (d.1692), countess of Newburgh, 233

Lloyd, Mr James, ?alchemist, 132

Lloyd, Dr [?James], 107

Loades, Henry, 357n, 368, 381

Loftus, Adam, [?viscount Lisburne], 118

Loire, river 152–3

Lomb, John, churchwarden of Cawston, 227–8

London and Westminster
  Arundel House, 75, 327
  Bartholomew Fair, 373
  Broad Sanctuary, 60
  Chancery Lane, 326
  Charing Cross, 147, 242–3, 374
  Clerkenwell, bawdy houses at, 119
  Cockpit, 350
  Coldharbour, fire at, 135
  Durham Yard, 82
  Exchange, 54, 75n, 139, 258
  Fire of London, 7, 62n, 73n, 75n, 76, 146
  Gatehouse prison, 78
  Goldsmiths' Hall, 52
  Hyde Park, 103
  Gresham's College, 43n, 75n
  Lincoln's Inn & Fields, 55, 74–5, 77, 135, 379
  lodgings, 53, 55–6, 60, 67, 73
  Lombard Street, 5, 62, 208
  Old Southampton Bldgs, 322
  Pall Mall, 28, 213, 356n
  Portugal Row, 55
  Quaker inn, 56–7

Queen Street, 3, 67, 74–5

Rich's shop, 295

silk weavers, 165

St James Street, 176

Somerset House, 48, 104

Suffolk Street, 17–18, 27, 109n

Sun inn, 54–5

Swallow Street, 354, 367

Thames Street, 258

Tower, 25, 44n, 77–8, 81, 119, 129, 135, 142, 349

Trinity House, 9, 90n, 91

Wallingford House, 225, 258

Westminster Hall, 351

Westminster School, 1

Whitehall, 44, 48, 99, 103, 118n, 126, 165, 192, 299, 331, 358, 366, 385

Worcester House, 46, 137

see also Chelsea, Fulham, Kensington, Parson's Green; et passim

London Gazette, 94, 96, 119, 125, 134, 142, 165, 352

Long, cousin of Sir Christopher Calthorpe, 371

Longueville, Charles (1649–1672), duc de, 118

Lorraine, Charles (1643–1690), duc de, 280

Lorraine, army of, 137

Loughrie, Thomas, Skeyton, 74

Louis XIV (1638–1715), king of France, 81, 91, 94, 102, 126, 134, 140–1

Louis (1661–1711), dauphin of France, 81

Love, Mr, 44

Lovelace, John (c.1642–1693), 3rd baron, 94

Lucas, John (1606–1671), 1st baron Lucas of Shenfield, 56

Lucy, Sir Kingsmill (d.1678), 2nd bt, 349

Lucy/Lacy, Mr, earl of Suffolk's steward, 196

Ludham, Norfolk, 147, 173, 182, 266, 286

Lully, Raymond (d.1315), 104

Lulman, Captain Robert (d.1709), postmaster, Norwich, 289

Lumbert, Mr, attorney, 219

Luneburg, Germany, 353

Luxembourg, François Henri de Montmorency-Bouteville (1628–1695), duc de, 279

Lynn  see King's Lynn, Norfolk

Lyons, France, 148

Lyttleton  see Littleton


Maastricht/Maestricht, Netherlands, 352

Macedonia, 94

Madathanus, Henry, 137

Madrid, Spain, 81, 352

Maidstone, Elizabeth, viscountess  see Finch, Elizabeth

Maine, river, 153

Maitland, Elizabeth (c.1626–1698), duchess of Lauderdale, 142, 225–6, 230, 233

Maitland, John (1616–1682), duke of Lauderdale, 99, 102, 142

Mallet, Michael (c.1632–post 1683), 349

Manchester, 2nd earl of see Montagu, Edward

Mancini, Hortense (1646–1699), duchesse Mazarin, 352

Man[n], [Esther] Mrs Alderman, 272

Manners, John (1604–1679), 8th earl of Rutland, 99

Manners, John (1638–1711), baron de Roos, later duke of Rutland, 72

Mannock, Sir Francis (d.1686), 2nd bt, of Gifford's Hall, 253

Manock, Mr & Mrs, 272

Manser, John (d.1694), alderman of Norwich, 198n, 201

Margatson, Gilbert, Cawston, 228

Marillac, M. de, 118

Marlingford, Norfolk, 63

Marsham, Norfolk, 73

Marshland, Norfolk, 371, 384–5

Martill, John, Skeyton, 75

Martin, 'Honest Tom' (1679–1771), antiquary, 29

Mason, Sir William, 266

Mautby, Norfolk, 49, 61, 173–5, 182, 281–2

Maynard, Katherine, Lady, 307

Mazarin see Mancini

Mazey, Henry (d.1677), clergyman and school-master, 273

medicine and illnesses, 57, 62, 69, 72, 82, 88, 94, 105, 116, 130, 132, 137, 141, 224, 334–5, 354, 363; see also gout, plague, scurvy, small-pox, and Robert Paston, health

Medowe, Sir Thomas (1624–1688), MP for Great Yarmouth, 21, 174, 211, 237, 239, 314
letter from, 221

melon seed, 111

Merton, Norfolk, 156

Mesnard, Mr, Paris, 147

Metcalfe, Richard, Skeyton, 75

Mexico, 97

Michell, Mrs, 162

Mico/Micqueau, Lewis, gentleman servant, 50, 208, 210, 219, 234–5, 238, 253, 283, 287–8, 290–1, 295, 320, 327, 341, 355, 363

Middleton, John (c.1608–1674), 1st earl of Middleton, governor of Tangier, 130

Middleton, Martha (1636–1706), countess of Middleton, 10n, 130

Middleton see also Myddelton

Milbourne, Luke (1649–1720), clergyman and poet, 264n

militia see Norfolk, militia

mining, 8, 25, 27, 97, 101

Mingay, John, 266

Monck, Christopher (1653–1688), 2nd duke of Albemarle, 78

Monck, George (1608–1670), 1st duke of Albemarle, 66n, 68, 70, 78, 99, 133, 141

Monmouth, duke of see Scott, James

Monmouth, countess of see Carey/Cary, Martha

Montagu, Edward (1602–1671), 2nd earl of Manchester, 4, 7, 44, 56, 58, 82, 105n, 118

Montagu, Edward (1625–1672), 1st earl of Sandwich, 7, 140

Montagu, Edward (d.1683), 2nd baron Montagu of Boughton, 350, 353

Montagu, Ralph (1638–1709), ambassador to France, later 1st duke of Montagu, 7, 110–14, 350, 353, 358

Montagu, William (c.1618–1706), chief baron of the exchequer, 244–8, 250–1, 253–4, 292, 294, 316, 353, 364, 379, 384

Montpellier, France, 85n, 109

Mordaunt, Elizabeth (1633–1679), viscountess Mordaunt of Avalon, 44n, 45, 78, 84, 105, 130–1, 134
letter from, 45

Mordaunt, Henry (c.1623–1697), 2nd earl of Peterborough, 78, 282n, 299n, 321, 330, 343

Mordaunt, John (1626–1675), 1st viscount Mordaunt of Avalon, 7, 44n, 78, 84, 90, 105, 112, 131, 135
letter from, 44–6

Mordaunt, Penelope (c.1622–1702), countess of Peterborough, 141, 328, 343

Morgan, Sir Henry (c.1635–1688), privateer, 97–8

Morris, John, financier, 9–10, 12, 16, 22, 287n

Moutham, Isaac, clerk of the peace, 205, 266, 295, 334n

Mundesley, Norfolk, 228

music, musicians, songs, 54, 59, 66, 122, 135, 146, 171, 178, 198, 200, 210, 245, 309, 311, 375

Musports ?school at Fulham, 78

Myddelton, Sir Richard (1655–1716), 117

Myddelton, Sir Thomas (1651–1684), of Chirk, 117

Mylius, Johann Daniel (c.1583–1642), alchemist, 87

Myngs, Sir Christopher (c.1625–1666), naval officer, 71

navy and naval actions, 9, 51n, 58, 66, 68, 70, 89n, 106, 129, 135, 140–4, 186–7, 333, 335–6, 341

Needham, Bridget (d.1696), viscountess Kilmorey, 363

Negus, Henry (d.1682), of Hoveton, 266, 279, 383–5

Neile, Sir Paul, patron of science, 44

Neve/Neave/s, [?Oliver], 230

Nevill, George (d.1666), 11th baron Abergavenny, 67

Newburgh, countess of see Livingston, Anne

New Forest, Hampshire, 99

Newmarket, Suffolk, 99n, 105n, 141, 171, 196, 199–200, 203, 205–6, 208–10, 217, 244, 275, 289–90, 292–3, 349–50, 352

Newport, countess of see Blount, Anne

Newton, Mr, delivers letter, 206

Nimeguen/Nijmegen, Netherlands, 352

Nockolls, Mr, Norwich, 345

Noel, Baptist (c.1611–1682), 3rd viscount Campden, 225, 254

Noell, Edward, wrote poem on chemistry, 42, 104

nog, 46, 65, 86, 201, 205, 214, 283, 288

Norfolk, duke and duchess of see sub Howard

Norfolk, 192; et passim
    elections, 14–15, 24, 151–2, 154–162, 186, 367–73, 380, 385
    justices of the peace, 151, 159–60, 178, 180, 189, 190, 192, 203–6, 237, 241, 243–4, 248–9, 262, 269, 281, 334, 345
    lord lieutenancy, 15–24, 27–8, 343
    militia, 16, 20–1, 159–162, 190, 192, 195, 204, 206, 209, 212, 215–6, 219, 221, 231–2, 234, 237–45, 249, 256–9, 262–3, 266–7, 269–70, 273–4, 290, 364, 366–7, 369
    subscription for shrievalty, 15, 190, 258, 261–3, 270, 275, 297–8, 316, 325
    tax collection, 122, 318, 322–3, 334
    vice-admiralty, 201, 226–9, 301–5, 335–6
    see also cavalcades

Norris, James, 5th baron see Bertie, James

Norris, Counsellor [John], 374

North, Sir Francis (1637–1685), lord chief Justice, MP for King's Lynn, 281n, 283

North, [?Roger (1653–1734)], 283

Northampton, 350, 353

Northamptonshire, 72, 353

North Creake, Norfolk, 204n, 243

North Erpingham hundred, Norfolk, 122

Northumberland, countess of see Percy, Elizabeth

North Walsham, Norfolk, 58n, 214, 225, 292–3, 360, 369
    school, 234, 270

Norway, 96

Norwich, 14, 20, 23, 25, 136, 156, 159–162, 184–5, 192–3, 203, 206, 226, 250, 266, 294; et passim
    bishops see Reynolds and Sparrow
    castle, 243, 246, 290, 372
    cathedral (Christchurch), 25, 230, 237, 281, 283n
    cavalcades, 172–3, 197–203, 246–7, 271–2, 280–1, 310–11, 329, 369
    Chapelfield, 226, 266, 322
    Conisford house, 247
    corporation, 31, 316, 326–9, 331, 333, 336–7, 369
    dean see Astley, Herbert
    Duke's Palace, 246, 248
    elections, 23–4, 280–3, 285, 294, 305–318, 321–6, 330, 332, 339, 367, 369–70,
    fanatics, 194, 285, 310, 312, 315–6, 318, 321, 324–5, 336, 345–6, 373–4
    freemen, 23, 313, 318, 326, 374n
    guildhall, 198, 247, 343
    hackney coach, 85–6, 91, 312, 316, 362
    King's Head, 159, 281
    Maid's Head, 334
    market and market cross, 159, 198, 201, 246, 272, 305, 311, 324
    Maudlin/Magdalen gates, 201
    post, 305–6
    school, 235, 273, 296, 339, 360, 362, 364
    St Giles, 246–7
    St Peter Mancroft, 272
    St Stephen's gate, 172, 201, 246–7
    White Swan, 159, 266

Norwood, Colonel Henry (c.1614–1689), 130

Nourse, Mary, 2, 48n, 255

Oakes, James, gets a pension, 206, 266

Oblivion, Act of, 249

O'Brien, Lady Catherine (d.1702), Lady Ibracken, 330, 346n

O'Brien, Henry (c.1642–1678), Lord Ibracken, 350

O'Brien, Mr, youngest, 102

Offly, [?Robert], 91

Offley, Mrs, lawyer's widow, 352

Okey, John (c.1606–1662), regicide, 138

Oliver, Harry, ?gardener at Oxnead, 69

Oliver, little, pension for, 266

Orange, Mary (1662–1694), princess of, later Queen, 25, 292, 295, 356n

Orange, William (1650–1702), prince of, later William III, 25, 105, 107, 279–80, 290n, 292n, 294, 297, 299 oranges and orange farm, 7, 16, 78, 85, 89, 139, 320, 358, 362–3, 365

Orleans, duchesse d' *see* Henriette Anne

Orleans, France, 112–13, 152

Ormond, 1st duke of *see* Butler, James

Osborne, Lady Anne *see* Coke, Lady Anne

Osborne, Bridget (c.1629–1704), countess of Danby, later duchess of Leeds, 9, 17–18, 21, 55n, 118n, 191–2, 196, 205–7, 209–10, 212–13, 215–9, 223–7, 229, 231–5, 238–9, 244, 252–5, 282–3, 285–7, 289–90, 294, 298, 312, 314, 316, 319, 321, 323, 325, 329–30, 340, 342, 344, 347

Osborne, Lady Bridget *see* Fitzcharles, Bridget, countess of Plymouth

Osborne, Edward (1654–1689), viscount Latimer, 116–7, 209–10, 219, 346

Osborne, Elizabeth (d.1680), viscountess Latimer, 346

Osborne, Leonard, alderman of Norwich, 336

Osborne, Peregrine (1659–1729), viscount Dunblane, 12n, 116–7, 204, 210

Osborne, Lady Sophia (d.1746), 346

Osborne, Sir Thomas (1632–1712), earl of Danby, later 1st duke of Leeds, 8–9, 12–15, 17–19, 21, 23n, 24, 27, 42n, 55, 79, 89, 91–3, 102, 145, 195–6, 199, 204–11, 213, 215–21, 223–7, 229, 231–9, 244–5, 250–3, 259–261, 283, 286–7, 289–92, 294, 297–9, 307–9, 312, 314, 316, 319, 321–30, 332–4, 342, 345–7, 350, 358, 364n, 375, 377, 383
  letters to, 258, 324–5

Ossory, earl of *see* Butler, Thomas, earl of Ossory

Ost *see* Hoste

Ostend, Netherlands, 279, privateers, 277

otter hunting, 199, 215

Oughtred, William (c.1575–1660), mathematician, 100n

Overton, Robert (1609–1679), army officer and parliamentarian, 142

Oxburgh/Oxborough, Norfolk, 144n, 194, 286, 351

Oxford, 19, 94, 107, 135

Oxnead/Oxnett, Norfolk, 4–5, 22, 42, 45, 162, 173, 190, 212, 224, 226, 231, 239, 253–4; *et passim*
  alterations, 8, 65, 67, 71, 219, 226, 233, 235, 239
  chapel, 8, 19n, 65, 67–9, 71, 73, 85, 90, 168, 197, 220, 286, 294, 331
  church and churchyard, 53, 168, 220, 286, 340
  demolition, 29
  furnishings, 4, 8, 56, 65, 67–8, 139, 162, 199, 208, 219, 233, 235, 239, 254, 344, 385

gardens and park, 44, 54, 59–60, 68–9, 71, 73, 155, 162, 187, 205, 217, 226, 230–1, 233, 251
  painting, 4, 73
  'portaloo', 123
  royal visit, 10, 27, 123n, 124, 126, 133–4, 136, 138–9
  servants, 57, 66, 68–9, 71, 73, 196, 203, 288, 337–9
  *see also* Paston, Robert, love for Oxnead

oysters, 184, 207

Page, John, 266

Paine, Adrian (d.1686), alderman of Norwich, 185, 336

Paine, has a seal or two of Lord Yarmouth's, 226

painting and painters, 4, 16n, 71, 73, 85, 162, 210n, 213–4, 219, 240, 271n

Palgrave, Sir Augustine (c.1629–1711), 2nd bt, of Norwood Barningham, 198, 215

Palmer, Barbara (c.1640–1709), countess of Castlemaine, duchess of Cleveland, 52n, 59, 63, 67, 70n, 76n, 102, 358n

Palmer, C.J., Yarmouth historian, 30

Palmer, Sir Geoffrey (1598–1670), 1st bt, attorney general, 64n

Palmer, [Herbert], 82, Palmer family, 59n

Pank, Christophar, Skeyton, 74

paper making, 27, 378n

Pargeter, John, goldsmith, 99

Paris, 26n, 39–40, 60, 91, 99n, 108–18, 146–9, 153, 334

Parisiensis, Christopher, Benedictine monk, 80, 84, 120, 124

parliament, 6–8, 13–14, 22–4, 46, 48–59, 91, 106, 145, 185–6, 215, 223, 236, 257, 282, 300, 306, 312, 314–9, 330, 340, 344, 349–53, 356–8, 374, 377, 380, 382–3: *see also* elections *sub* Great Yarmouth, King's Lynn, Norfolk and Norwich

Parmenter, William, alderman of Norwich, 336

Parris, Thomas, master gunner, 221

Parson's Green, Middlesex, 5, 10, 40, 44n, 45, 61, 63, 65, 82, 105, 348
  Villa Cary, 44, 78

Paston, Agnes/Ann (d.1676), of Appleton, 220, 334

Paston, Charles (1673–1718), 163, 177, 180, 183, 199, 205–6, 214, 231–2, 235, 239–40, 246, 253, 255, 286, 289, 295, 299, 310–11, 320, 327, 329, 340–1, 343–4, 347, 355–7, 359–60, 362, 364, 366, 372, 375–6, 378, 380–1, 384–5

Paston, Charlotte (c.1650–1685), later countess of
  Yarmouth, 11–12, 139, 143n, 145, 147, 150,
  154, 157, 176–7, 180, 183, 186, 192, 196,
  199, 201, 205–6, 214, 227, 231, 240, 246,
  253, 255, 282–3, 287, 289, 292, 295, 297,
  299, 307–8, 310–11, 316, 319–20, 327, 329,
  330, 333, 335, 339, 341, 344, 347, 350,
  355–7, 359, 361, 363–4, 366, 372, 375–8,
  380–1
Paston, Charlotte (1676–1735), 199n, 205–6, 214,
  231, 240, 246, 253, 255, 295, 299, 310–11,
  320, 327, 329, 344, 347, 356–7, 359, 361,
  364, 380
Paston, Sir Clement (d.1598), admiral, 4
Paston, Clement, of Barningham, 285
Paston, Elizabeth 'Betty' (c.1667–1686), 86, 157,
  164, 171, 173, 177, 180–1, 187, 194, 199,
  203, 212, 214, 217–8, 223n, 252, 254,
  287–8, 299, 308–9, 316, 318, 320, 338–9,
  341–2, 344, 346, 350, 355–7, 359–60, 362,
  364, 366, 372, 375–6, 380–1, 384–5
Paston, Frances (d.1675), 5, 11n, 88n
Paston, Jasper (c.1660–1685), 78, 150, 157, 164,
  173, 180–1, 187, 194, 203, 212, 282, 299,
  309, 311, 328, 338–9, 341
Paston, Katherine (d.1629), Lady, 5, 29
Paston, Lady Katherine (d.1637), 1, 7, 26n, 118n
Paston, Margaret (d.1669), Lady, 1–3, 5, 47n, 50,
  54, 68n, 69, 72, 82, 84–5n
Paston, Margaret 'Peg' see Alberti, Margaret
Paston, Mary 'Mal' (c.1664–1676), 17, 22, 154,
  157, 171, 173, 181, 186, 191–2, 196, 206,
  213, 218, 227, 234, 236, 239–40, 244, 246,
  253, 255
  death of, and burial of heart, 271–3
Paston, Mr, chaplain, 220
Paston, Rebecca (c.1635–1694), countess of
  Yarmouth
  books, 52
  character, 18
  dowry, 2
  examines Hurton's accounts, 197, 288,
    328–30
  illnesses, 96, 215, 217–8, 282, 296, 312, 317,
    375
  letters from, 77–9, letters to, passim
  portrait, 320
  pregnancy & childbirth, 52, 55n, 60, 62, 67,
    69, 73
  religion, 19, 114–16, 165–6, 168, 276–7, 310
  works for family advancement, 299, 321
Paston, Robert (1631–1683), 1st earl of Yarmouth
  alchemy, 9, 87, 124–5, 362–3
  angry letter, 337–40

burns wife's letters, 19, 176, 235
character, 14–16, 125, 184, 209, 217, 344
cipher, 256, 297
clothes, 78, 85–6, 89, 91, 214, 220, 227, 233–4,
  295, 297, 314, 327, 376
death, 25
debts, 1–28, 58, 71, 78, 82–4, 138–9, 180, 217,
  235, 289, 291–2, 335
depression, 55, 75, 79, 199, 229, 252, 254, 315,
  355, 360, 377–8, 384–5
descendants, 26n, 390–1
diet, 57, 214–5, 255, 288, 309, 320
ennoblement, 8, 12, 16, 24, 28, 53, 60–1, 66,
  143–4, 246, 377–8, 385
entail, 3
exercise machine, 320, 360, 364
goes fishing, 225
health, 2–3, 16, 24–5, 51, 56, 141, 163–70,
  181, 202, 214, 226, 229–31, 233, 235, 239,
  254, 263, 290–2, 294, 300, 309, 311, 313–6,
  319–20, 325, 327, 329, 331–2, 335, 340–3,
  347, 354–8, 360, 362, 364–5, 370, 372,
  376–8, 381–5
high steward of Great Yarmouth, 17, 147,
  154–5, 173–84
horses, 48–9, 56, 58–60, 69, 71, 73, 154,
  196–7, 280, 283, 287–8, 307, 309, 314,
  337–8, 340–1
jewellery and plate, 4, 8, 40–2, 51–2, 55, 58,
  60, 83, 138–9, 174, 176, 183, 329, 363
lawsuits, 8, 25, 53, 83, 219, 238–9, 354, 379,
  382–4
lord lieutenancy, 15–28, 191–5, 217; et passim
love for Oxnead, 5, 56, 172, 199, 206, 212,
  226, 231, 239, 251, 253–4
love for wife, 2, 227, 253, 287, 309; et passim
petitions king, 75–7, 146, 385
portrait, 51, 213–4, 220
praises wife, 18, 217, 226, 287, 289, 314, 320,
  333, 377–8
quarrels with Sir John Clayton, 11, 44, 152,
  208, 213, 217, 219, 221, 231, 255, 354–5,
  357, 359–62, 364, 366, 371, 375, 381
religion, 19, 199n, 202, 204, 231–3, 272–3,
  276–7, 296, 310, 354–7, 360
renounces swearing, 19, 361
sends money to King, 3
shot by highwaymen, 14, 19, 163–70, 172
spectacles, 326–7, 363
vice admiral, 201, 213, 216, 226–9, 301–5,
  308, 335–6
wedding anniversaries, 2n, 66, 71, 73, 87, 226,
  339–40, 343
see also Norfolk, militia

Paston, Robert 'Robin' (1656–1705), 17, 48–9, 78, 177, 219, 290–2, 295, 297–300, 308–9, 311, 313, 316, 318–9, 327, 329–32, 335, 337–8, 343, 347, 354–7, 360, 364, 368, 373, 375–6, 378, 380, 384
letters from, 146–9, 152–4, 279–80, 349–50
Paston, Thomas (1614–c.1654), 5, 88n
Paston, Thomas (1663–1691), 78, 150, 157, 162, 164, 173, 180–1, 187, 194, 203, 212, 273, 282, 296, 298, 308–9, 311, 330, 338–9, 342, 360, 362, 364, 372
Paston, Sir William (1528–1610), 4, 234n
Paston, Sir William (c.1610–1663), 1st bt., 1–4, 10, 20, 26n, 27, 40n, 41n, 47n, 49n, 68n, 96n, 128n, 131, 138–9, 158n, 232n, 338
Paston, William, of Appleton, 144n, 220n, 285
Paston, William 'Billie' (1654–1732), later 2nd earl of Yarmouth, 1, 5, 22–3, 25–6, 29, 46, 48–50, 58, 60–1, 66, 69, 71, 78, 94, 138–9, 145, 149–50, 154, 157, 176–7, 180, 183, 186, 192, 196, 199, 205, 213–14, 216, 227, 229, 231, 235, 240, 246, 251, 253, 255, 280–3, 286, 289–90, 292, 294–5, 300, 305–19, 323–4, 327–8, 330–3, 335, 337–8, 341, 344, 347, 350, 355–7, 359, 361, 363–7, 371–8, 380–1, 383–4
character, 109, 112–3, 344
education, 64, 78, 86, 94–95, 103–4, 138
grand tour, 10–11, 18, 108–18, 120–2
illnesses, 116, 120, 139, 295
letters from, 108–18, 285, 299, 358–9
letters to, 146–7, 240, 305–6, 308, 353–4, 367, 369–70
marriage, 11–12, 139, 143
militia, 267, 270, 282–3
MP for Norwich, 358
Paston, Wolstan, 252
Paston, Norfolk, 228
Paulet, Charles (1631–1699), viscount St John, later 1st duke of Bolton, 93, 99
peas, 232–3
Peck, Mr [?Thomas], 200
Peckover, Matthew, gentleman servant, 196, 199, 206, 208, 212, 216, 219, 230, 235–6, 239, 283, 288, 308–9, 314, 334, 336, 357, 359
letter from, 271–2
Peirson/Pierson, Thomas, of Wisbeach, 298, 371, 384
Pell, John (d.1686), of Dersingham, 15, 190, 246–7
Pembroke, earls of see sub Herbert
Pennant, Mrs, ?midwife, 60
Pen Park Hole, Bristol, 97
Pepper, Dr Robert (d.1700), chancellor of Norwich, 188, 198, 217, 293–4

Percy, Elizabeth (c.1646–1690), countess of Northumberland, 137, 343, 350
Percy, Lady Elizabeth (1667–1722), later duchess of Somerset, 343n
Peterborough, earl and countess of see sub Mordaunt
Pettus, Captain, 281, 327
Pettus, Sir John (d.1698), 3rd bt, of Rackheath, deputy lieutenant, 68n, 200, 202, 208, 212, 215, 218, 232, 252–3, 266, 280, 282, 290, 293, 307–8, 311, 317, 347, 357, 381
Pettus, Mary (d.1728), Lady, 68n, 218, 252, 347, 381n
Pettus, Mr, 218
Peyton, [?Thomas, of Rougham], 253
phanatics see fanatics
Philippo, Elisha, high sheriff in 1675, 160
Phillipps, Samuel, servant of Lord Townshend, 226, 306
philosopher's stone see alchemy
plague, 62, 68n, 73n, 74
plate see jewellery and plate
Plymouth, earl and countess of see sub Fitzcharles
Plymouth, Devon, 93, 99
poll tax, 335
Pondhouse see sub Kensington
Pontoise, France, 60
Popish Plot, 23, 350–3, 363n
Port, Nurse, servant at Oxnead, 58, 220, 286, 366, 375
'portaloo' 123n
Porter, Sir Charles (1631–1696), 63–5, 72
Porter, James (b.1638), 130
Porter, Sarah, 65
Portsmouth, duchess of see Keroualle, Louise de
postal services, 48, 58, 64–5, 74, 92, 107, 114–5, 145–6, 154, 164, 173, 179, 185, 197, 208–11, 213, 218, 230, 245, 252, 259, 282, 289–90, 305–6, 342, 345, 364, 373, 387
potatoes, 93
Potts, Sir John (d.1678), 2nd bt, of Mannington, 158, 247
Potts, Mary, Lady, 347
Potts, Sir Roger (d.1711), 3rd bt, of Mannington, 247, 347, 373
poultry and game, 53, 147, 172, 181, 253, 261, 281, 297–8, 310, 360, 362
Powle, Sir Richard (1628–1678), 96
Prattant, Humphrey, gentleman servant to Sir William Paston, 47
prayer, permitted form of, 168, 220, 296
Pregnani, Abbé, 99n
Presbyterians, 19, 53, 119, 154, 173, 189, 195, 230, 307n, 377

pressing of seamen, 333, 335–6, 341
Preston, Jacob, and family, of Beeston, 234, 266, 362
Prideaux, Humphrey (1648–1724), dean of Norwich, 7n, 326n
privateers, 277
processions  see cavalcades
Puckle, Martin, & brother, Norwich, 318, 321–3
Pursly, Robert, servant to Thomas Henshaw, 89
Pysar, Robin, porter at Oxnead, 196, 203, 213

Quakers, 19, 154, 227, 327
Quidenham, Norfolk, 151, 172–3, 200, 204, 223, 248, 350

Rackheath/Rackey, Norfolk, 208, 381
Radford, William (1623–1673), schoolmaster, 64
Rafaell's drops, 320
Ramsey, Mr, works for lord treasurer, 294, 297–8, 366
Ramsey, Mrs, 254
Ranelagh, earl of  see Jones, Richard
Ransome, Mr [?clergyman], 158
Rant, Sir Thomas (c.1604–1671), MP, 68n, 122
Rant, Captain William, 272
Rant, Sir William (d.1711) of Thorpe Market, 234, 272, 290, 301–5, 362, 376
Rawlins, Francis, gentleman servant to Lord Yarmouth, 48, 50, 139, 181n, 184, 203–4, 212, 226, 288, 307, 334, 337–8, 347, 376
Raymond, Sir Thomas (1627–1683), sergeant at law, 326
Raynham, Norfolk, 6, 10, 15n, 62, 126n, 143, 176, 181, 212, 215–6, 226, 284, 306–7
recusants  see Roman Catholics
Reeve, Thomas, and daughter, 233, 326, 329, 338
Repton, John Adey (1775–1860), 4
Reynolds, Edward (1599–1676), bishop of Norwich, 19, 172n, 190–1, 198, 200, 206–7, 234, 253
Reynolds, Mary (d.1683), 207
Rhone, river, 91
Rhumel, Johann Conrad, 84, 87, 141
Rich, Sir Charles (c.1619–1677), 1st bt, of London and Mulbarton, 198, 295
Rich, Sir Edwin (1594–1675), 11–12
Rich, Elizabeth, countess of Holland, 105n, 118
Rich, Sir Robert (d.1699), of Roos Hall, 198n
Richardson, Henry (1650–1701), 3rd baron Cramond, 181
Richardson, Thomas (c.1627–1674), 2nd baron Cramond, MP for Norfolk, 66, 74, 151
Riche [?], Sir Thomas, 200

Richelieu, Cardinal (1585–1642), 116–7
Richer, John (d.1683), mayor of Norwich, 280n, 306, 309, 312, 315–8, 324–5, 327–8, 331–3
Richmond, duke and duchess of  see sub Stuart
Richmond, Surrey, 64n, 66–7, 69, 71, 103
Ridgely, Dr, 380
Ripley, George (d. c.1490), alchemist, 88, 107, 137
Rising  see Castle Rising
Robin  see Paston, Robert 'Robin'
Rochester, 2nd earl of  see Wilmot, John
Rochester, Kent, 110
Rock, Mrs, creditor, 58
Roman Catholics, 10, 13, 16, 19–21, 23, 25, 60, 95n, 98–9, 114n-15, 118, 126n, 136n, 144, 153, 162, 173n, 195–6n, 203, 350–1, 353, 363n, 378
Rome, Italy, 39, 148, 158
Rookwood, Captain Nicholas, 230, 371, 373
Roper, [Christopher, page of honour to the Queen], 106
Rosan, comte de (d.1669), 96
Rosse, Thomas (c.1620–1675), courtier, 129
Rous/Rowse, Sir John (c.1656–1730), 2nd bt, of Henham, 220, 253, 280, 319–20
Rous/Rowse, Philippa (d.1685), Lady, 319–20
Rowe, John, alderman of Yarmouth, 174
Royal Society, 8, 26, 43–4, 75, 108n
Rugen, Isle of, Germany, 349
Rumbold, Henry (d.1688), 10, 12, 128–31, 135
Rumelius  see Rhumel
Runton, Norfolk, 147n, 288
Rupert (1619–1682), prince, 66, 68, 70, 120, 134
Rushwood, Sir James, 109
Russell, Mr, messenger, 287, 291
Russell, Lady Rachel (d.1723), 99n
Russell, William (1639–1683), Lord, 99, 383
Rutherford, Andrew (d.1664), earl of Teviot, governor of Tangier, 130
Rutland, 8th earl of  see Manners, John
Ruttland, Mr, semster, 139
Rutty/Ruttie, Thomas (d.1699), merchant, London, 50, 233, 294, 320
Rutty, Mr, Norwich, 295

Sacheverell, William (c.1638–1691), 383
Sackville, Charles (1643–1706), baron Buckhurst, later 6th earl of Dorset, 102
Sackville, Edward (1644–1678), 352
Sackville, Richard (1622–1677), 5th earl of Dorset, 56
sacrament, taking of, 71, 199n, 202, 204, 232–3, 299, 340
Sadler, Mrs [Susannah, of Lammas], 214
St Albans, earl of  see Jermyn, Henry

St John, viscount  see Paulet, Charles
St Kitts, West Indies, 74
Sala, Angelus (d.1637), physician and scientist, 84n, 363
Salisbury, 3rd earl of  see Cecil, James
Sanderson, Bridget (1593–1682), Lady, 48
Sandford, Francis (1630–1694), herald, 7n, 16
Sandwich, 1st earl of  see Montagu, Edward
Sandys, Sir George, 95
Saumur, France, 112, 118, 148–9, 152–3
Savile, Harry (c.1642–1687), courtier, 24, 77–8, 81, 239
Sawtell, [Edmond], of the Letter Office, 359, 367
Sawyer, Sir Robert (c.1633–1692), 334
Saxony, Julius Francis (d.1689), duke of, 97
Sayer[s], John, the King's cook, 196
scandalum magnatum, 19, 188–9, 224, 227
Scarburgh/Scarborrowe, Henry, North Walsham, 214, 370n, 385
Schomburg, Frederick Herman de (1615–1690), 1st duke of Schomburg, general, 143, 280
schools and schoolmasters, 64, 70, 86, 150, 157, 174, 234–5, 265, 296; see also education of Paston children, and Norwich, school
Scotland, 102, 120, 134–5
Scott, James (1649–1685), duke of Monmouth, 17, 60, 96, 142, 215, 233n
scurvy and scurvy grass, 16, 235, 239, 254, 311, 320, 325, 332, 335, 343, 358
sedan chairs, 111–12
Sendivogius, Michel (1566–1636), Polish alchemist, 80, 100–2, 108, 127, 129, 132, 135
Sedley, Sir Charles (1639–1701), 54, 102, 130
Severn, river, 97
sewers, commission of, 266, 281, 286, 292, 295
Seymour, Sir Edward (1633–1708), 4th bt, 162, 334
Seymour, Francis (c.1590–1664), baron Seymour of Trowbridge, 137
Seymour, John (d.1675), 4th duke of Somerset, 137
Seymour, Mr, 383–4
Seymour, William (d.1671), 3rd duke of Somerset, 137
Shaftesbury, earls of  see sub Cooper
Shannon, Elizabeth, viscountess  see Boyle, Elizabeth
Sharinge, John, Skeyton, 74–5
Sheerness, Kent, 94
Sheldon, Gilbert (1598–1677), archbishop of Canterbury, 191
Sheldrake, William, alderman of Norwich, 336
Sherrad, Madam, 138

Shotesham, Norfolk, 58, 175, 282–3
Shrewsbury, countess of  see Talbot, Anna Maria
Shrewsbury, Shropshire, 104
Sidney, Lady Diana (d.1670), 103
silk and silk weavers, 153, 165, 288
Skeyton, presentation to living of, 74–5
Skowldinge, [?Robert], Norwich, 345
slate quarries, 153
smallpox, 11, 22, 26n, 48n, 78, 125, 137, 139, 271n, 362–3
Smallwood, Mr, 323
Smyth/Smith, Alice (d.1678), Lady, of Irmingland, 167, 310
Smyth, Charles (c.1598–1665), 1st viscount Carrington, 60
Smith/Smyth, Dr [?George of Lowestoft, d.1702], 230, 363
Smyth, Giles, Skeyton, 74
Smith, Mr, Broad Sanctuary, Westminster, 60
Smith, Mr, 181, 310
Smith, Mrs, linendraper, 139
Smyth, Robert, Skeyton, 74
Smyth, Thomas, Waxham, 277–9, 285
Snelling, Matthew (1621–1678), courtier and miniature painter, 210, 213, 215, 244–5, 251–2, 254
Somerset, dukes of  see sub Seymour
Somerset House  see sub London,
Sourceau, Claude, tailor, Covent Garden, 86
Southampton, 4th earl of  see Wriothesley, Thomas
Southampton, earl, later duke, of  see Fitzroy, Charles
Southampton, Hampshire, 99
Southesk, Anna, countess of  see Carnegie, Anna
Southtown  see sub Great Yarmouth
Southwell, Sir Robert (1635–1702), 291
Spain, 146, 349, 352
Spanish army, 280
Sparow, Willyam, Skeyton, 75
Sparrow, Anthony (1612–1685), bishop of Norwich, and family, 19, 24, 253, 262, 270, 280–1, 286, 292–4, 296, 311, 321, 325, 339, 345, 355–7, 367, 376, 380, 385
spectacles, 326–7, 363
Speering, a Norfolk brickmaker, 53
Spelman, Mr, 204, 373
Spencer, Anne, countess of Sunderland, 54
Spencer, Robert (1641–1702), 2nd earl of Sunderland, 54, 372–3
Spendlove, John, Skeyton, 74–5
Sperin, William, Skeyton, 75
Spragge, Sir Edward (c.1629–1673), naval officer, 140

Sprowston, Norfolk, 107n, 269, 381
Stafford, Sir Edmund/Dr Edward, 120
Stafford, Staffordshire, 97
Stamford, Lincolnshire, 349, 376
Stanninghall, Norfolk, 59n, 286
Stebbing, George, Norwich, letter from, 367
Sterling, painter, 240
Stevenson, Matthew (d.1684), poet, 203
Stockholm, 88
stockings and stocking makers, 100, 198n, 295, 297
Stone, Nicholas (1586/87–1647), architect, 4
Stop of the Exchequer, 14n, 140, 207n, 229n
Stralsund/Straelsend, Germany, 349
Strode, Sir George (1626–1701), 69n, 82n
Stuart, Charles (1639–1672), 3rd duke of
      Richmond, 54, 59, 91, 142n, 208
Stuart, Frances (1647–1702), duchess of
      Richmond, 105–6
subsidy, 106n, 122
Suckling, Robert (1602–1690), of Woodton and
      Barsham, deputy lieutenant, 198, 236, 272,
      326, 358
Suffolk, 3rd earl of  see Howard, James
Suffolk, 6, 68n, 118n, 151n, 219–20, 239, 251,
      259, 274, 297–8, 369
sugar, 95, 135, 320, 347
suicide, 65, 88
Sunderland, earl and countess of  see sub Spencer
Sussex, Anne, countess of  see Lennard, Anne
Swallowfield, Berkshire, 42, 130n
Swanton, Norfolk, 187
swearing, 19, 222, 361
Sweden, 88, 129

Talbot, Anna Maria (1642–1702), countess of
      Shrewsbury, 105, 130, 283, 287, 290, 296,
      308, 313, 315, 322, 340–2, 346
Tangiers, Morocco, 130
Tasburgh, Captain Jack, of Bodney, 20, 173, 175,
      177–8, 205, 351n
Tasburgh, Mrs, 271
Tasburgh, Norfolk, 345
taxation, 13, 106, 122, 318, 322–3, 334
Taylor, Frank, King's Lynn, 372
Taylor, Simon (c.1633–1689), MP, of King's
      Lynn, 365
Tempest, [?Robert, goldsmith, London], 52
Temple, Sir William (1628–1699), 350n, 353
tennis, 110, 113, 116
Terne, Henry (d.1666), naval officer, 66
Teviot, earl of  see Rutherford, Andrew
Thacker, Thomas, alderman of Norwich, 336
Thaxter, Edmund (d.1690), alderman of
      Yarmouth, 174–5, 182, 239

letters from, 77, 184, 241–3, 256–7, 259–61,
      263–6, 268–9
theatre and plays, 9n, 50, 57, 78n, 89n, 91, 95n,
      98n, 138, 358
Thetford, Norfolk, 6, 171, 177n, 193, 196–200,
      215, 244–8, 256, 271, 276, 369, 372–3, 377,
      384
Thexton, Robert (d.1709), clergyman, 225
Thompson, Norfolk, 155
Thrigby, Norfolk, 222
Thursby/Thirsby, William, counsellor at law, 361
      letter from, 249–50
Thurston, Hamon (d.1694), 262–3, 267
      letter from, 241
Tidy, Mrs, ? midwife, 60
tobacco and smoking, 235, 344
Todd, John, alderman of Norwich, 336
Tomlinson, Robin, servant, 330–1
toothache, 248
Torrington, earl of  see Monck, Christopher
Tottington, Norfolk, 155
tortoises, 208
Tours, France, 111–17, 120–1, 153
Townshend, Horatio (1630–1687), baron, later
      1st viscount, 6–7, 9n, 10, 14–16, 19–21,
      24–6, 28, 51–2, 56–7, 60, 62, 65–6, 82n,
      136, 151, 155–6, 159–162, 181, 184,
      188–91, 193–6, 206, 212, 214–5, 223,
      226–7, 229–30, 237, 245, 250, 254, 284–5,
      293, 306, 335, 354, 380
      letters from, 75, 143; see also Raynham
Townshend, Mary, viscountess, 82n, 176n, 212,
      254, 319
Townshend, Thomas, of Horstead and Norwich,
      62n, 230
      letters from, 62, 300–1
Trevor, Sir John (1624–1672), 117–8
Trevor, Mr [?John], 118, 121
Trevor, Ruth (d.1687), Lady, 54n, 131, 220, 223,
      233, 318
Trier/Treves, Germany, 165, 352
Trinity House, 9, 90n, 91
Tryon, Peter, of Harringworth, 349
Tubbing, Captain W., 298
Turenne, Henri (1611–1675), vicomte de, 147,
      165
Turkington, John, clergyman, 188–9, 250, 254
Turner, Dawson (1775–1858), banker and anti-
      quary, 30
Turner, Captain John (c.1632–1712), mayor of
      King's Lynn, MP, 365, 372, 380
Turnor/Turner, Sir Edmond (d.1707), a farmer
      of the customs, 64
Turnor, Sir Edward (c.1617–1676) speaker, 52n

turtles, 73
Tuthill, Robert, Crostwick, 138
Tuttington, Norfolk, 192, 258–9, 261–2
Tyndall, craftsman working at Oxnead, 71
Tysy?, William, hatter, 139

Ubbeston, Suffolk, 145
Umphrie/Umphrye, Edward, Raphe, and
    Thomas, Skeyton, 74
Uxbridge, Middlesex, 86

Valensy, Mr, Paris, 111
Van Beuningen, Conrad (1622–1693), Dutch
    ambassador, 142
Van Ghent, Willem Joseph (1626–1672), Dutch
    admiral, 129
Vaudemont, Charles Henri (1649–1723), prince
    de, 280
Vaughan, Francis (1638–1667), 2nd baron
    Vaughan, 99
Vaughan, Roger (c.1641–1672), 81
Vaughan, Thomas (1621–1666), alchemist, 39n
Venice, Italy, 13, 85, 348, 376; see also Alberti di
    Conti
Verdon, Samuel, under sheriff, 298, 316, 332,
    375
Vienna, Austria, 39
Villa Cary see sub Parson's Green
Villahermosa, Carlos de Gurrea (1634–1692),
    duque de, 279
Villars, Pierre (1623–1698), marquis de, 81
Villiers, Colonel Edward (c.1620–1689), 92
Villiers, Lady Frances (1630–1677), 292
Villiers, George (1628–1687), 2nd duke of
    Buckingham, 7, 8, 56, 72, 77, 78n, 81n, 86,
    92, 102, 105n, 129–30, 133, 138
Villiers, Mary (1638–1704), duchess of
    Buckingham, 105–6
Vine/Vynn/Winn, Jeremy, alderman of Norwich,
    313, 326, 336
Vyner, Sir Robert (1631–1688), goldsmith and
    banker, 11
Voulger, Guillaume de, merchant banker, Paris,
    149

Wade/Wayed, Mr, of Hampshire, 79
Wake, Mr, at the Exchange, 139
Wakeman, Sir George (1627–post 1685), physi-
    cian, 196, 206, 213–4, 218, 235, 252, 297,
    316
Waldegrave/Waldgrave, Major, 173, 175, 178,
    205, 230–1
Walker, Obadiah (1616–1699), 94–5, 100
Waller, Edmund (1606–1687), poet, 8, 86, 103

Walpole, Captain Horatio, 366n
Walpole, Robert (1650–1700), deputy lieutenant,
    68n, 246
Ward, Captain, 272
Ward, Sir Edward (d.1686), 2nd bt, of Bixley, 272
Ward, Major Edward, deputy lieutenant, 266,
    376
Ward, George, of Brooke, 266, 383
Ward, Mr, servant, 110–12
Ward family, 295
Warkhouse, John (d.1706), attorney, Aylsham,
    139, 193, 218, 223, 269, 379, 384
Warnes, Edward (d.1700), clergyman, letters
    from, 222, 272–3
Watts, [William, surveyor of Yarmouth], 234
Waxham, Norfolk, 278
weather, 50, 54, 59–60, 87, 97, 103, 208, 216,
    225, 227, 247, 313, 319, 373
Webster, Nicolas, Skeyton, 75
Weld, Gascoigne, of Bracon Ash, 298
Weld, Captain Thomas, 385
Weldon, Major Thomas, 29
Wells, Norfolk, 243, 254
Wenman, Richard, alderman of Norwich, 336
Wentworth, [Philadelphia (d.1696)], Lady, 233
Wentworth, Thomas (1591–1667), earl of
    Cleveland, 60
Wentworth, Thomas (c.1613–1665), 5th baron,
    60
Westminster see London and Westminster
Westmorland, 3rd earl of see Fane, Charles
Wharton, Edmund (d.1717), clergyman, Sloley
    and Worstead, 154, 168–9, 186, 300
    letter from, 170
White or Messenger, Richard, seized lands at
    Thrigby, 222
Whitehall see sub London and Westminster
Whitley, Colonel Roger (1618–1697), deputy
    postmaster, 289–90
Whittie/Whitty, John (d.1666), naval officer, 66
Wickes, goldsmith, 196
Wigett, John (d.1692), alderman of Norwich, 336
Wilcock, Mrs, has not delivered book, 366
Wilkins, John (1614–1672), bishop of Chester, 81
William, laboratory assistant at Oxnead, 65, 67
Williams, Sir Thomas (c.1621–1712), 1st bt, of
    Elham, 80
Williamson, Sir Joseph (1633–1701), secretary of
    state, 11, 22, 24, 177, 241, 249, 256, 260,
    318, 321–2, 326, 330–2, 345–6, 364–5,
    371–3, 377
    letter from, 331, 366–7
Wilmot, George (1647–1680), 2nd earl of
    Rochester, 80, 91

Wilton, Wiltshire, 352

Wimbledon, Surrey, 350

Winchester, Hampshire, 99

Winchilsea, 3rd earl of *see* Finch, Heneage

Windebank, Frances, later Lady Hales, 95

Windham, Lady Frances (d.1704), 301–5

Windham, Katherine (1652–1729), 82n, 176, 226, 232, 235, 254, 295, 319

Windham, William (1647–1689), of Felbrigg, deputy lieutenant, 5, 26, 69n, 82, 176, 205–6, 212, 215, 217–8, 226, 231–2, 235, 237, 239, 246, 254, 272, 294–5, 298, 309, 311, 318–20, 368–9, 371, 373, 376, 381n, 385
   letter from, 164

Windsor, Berkshire, 43, 102, 127, 134, 219, 230

wine, 46, 85, 89, 91, 93, 123, 128, 152, 168, 173–4, 178, 180, 197, 210, 212, 214, 332, 335n, 344

wine duty, 316

Winnington, Sir Francis (1634–1700), solicitor-general, 315, 326–9, 332, 337

Winterton, Norfolk, 4, 92

Wiseman, John, 68n

Wiseman, Mrs [Margaret], 68–9, 72, 78, 88n, 113, 120

Witton, a Paston tenant and employee, 46–7, 49

Wodehouse, Lucy (d.1684), Lady, 378

Wodehouse, Sir Philip (c.1608–1681), 3rd bt, of Kimberley, deputy lieutenant, 184, 198, 200, 206, 217, 229, 237, 378, 385

women's letters, 45, 77–9, 81–2, 144, 162–3, 181–4, 203–4

Wood, Thomas (1626–1699), of Bracon Ash, and

his son Thomas Wood the younger, 210, 240, 253, 272

wood farm, 7–8, 11–12, 16–17, 22, 25, 27, 57n, 60n, 62–4n, 66, 71–2, 75–7, 82n, 89, 106, 146, 255, 294, 335, 354, 357n, 359n, 361–2

Woodden/Waden, John (d.1693), servant at Oxnead, 54, 78, 154, 362, 384

Worcester, [battle of], 372

Worcester House *see* London, Worcester House

Worcestershire, 94, 97, 104

wreck, 228–9, 301–5

Wren, Sir Christopher (1632–1723), 8, 80, 86

Wren, Matthew (1629–1672), 90

Wrench, John (d.1697), alderman of Norwich, 336

Wriothesley, Thomas (1608–1667), 4th earl of Southampton, 48n

Wymondham, Norfolk, 172, 197, 200–2, 245, 247, 271, 280, 369–70

Yallopp, Dorothy (d.1720), Lady, 272

Yallopp, Sir Robert (1637–1705), of Bowthorpe, 181, 373

Yarmouth, earl and countess of *see sub* Paston

York, Anne (1637–1671), duchess of, 67, 96, 99

York, James (1633–1701), duke of, later James II, 13, 23, 25, 27n, 47, 66, 81, 88n, 90n, 97, 102, 126–7, 129, 134–5n, 140, 142, 146, 171, 199n, 231, 292n, 297n, 319, 321, 330, 333, 343, 346, 348, 375, 378–80

York, Mary Beatrice (1658–1718), duchess of, later queen, 351–2

York, Yorkshire, 119

Yorkshire, 57, 265, 380